Plays for the Theatre

A Drama Anthology

TENTH EDITION

Plays for the Theatre

A Drama Anthology

TENTH EDITION

Oscar G. Brockett
University of Texas at Austin

Robert J. Ball
University of the Incarnate Word

WADSWORTH
CENGAGE Learning™

Australia • Brazil • Japan • Korea • Mexico • Singapore • Spain • United Kingdom • United States

WADSWORTH
CENGAGE Learning™

Plays for the Theatre: A Drama Anthology, Tenth Edition
Oscar G. Brockett and Robert J. Ball

Senior Publisher: Lyn Uhl

Publisher: Michael Rosenberg

Development Editor:
Stephanie Carpenter

Assistant Editor: Jillian D'Urso

Editorial Assistant: Erin Pass

Media Editor: Jessica Badiner

Marketing Manager:
Bryant Chrzan

Marketing Coordinator:
Darlene Macanan

Marketing Communications
Manager:
Christine Dobberpuhl

Content Project Manager:
Georgia Young

Art Director: Linda Helcher

Print Buyer: Justin Palmeiro

Permissions Editor, Text:
Margaret Chamberlain-Gaston

Production Service:
Lachina Publishing Services

Cover and Text Designer:
Red Hanger Design

Photo Manager: John Hill

Cover Image:
Robbie Jack/©Corbis

Compositor:
Lachina Publishing Services

For product information and
technology assistance, contact us at **Cengage Learning
Customer & Sales Support, 1-800-354-9706**

For permission to use material from this text or product,
submit all requests online at **cengage.com/permissions**
Further permissions questions can be emailed to
permissionrequest@cengage.com

Library of Congress Control Number: 2009936339

ISBN-13: 978-1-4390-8268-3

ISBN-10: 1-4390-8268-5

Wadsworth
20 Channel Center Street
Boston, MA 02210
USA

Cengage Learning is a leading provider of customized learning solutions with office locations around the globe, including Singapore, the United Kingdom, Australia, Mexico, Brazil, and Japan. Locate your local office at **international.cengage.com/region**

Cengage Learning products are represented in Canada by Nelson Education, Ltd.

For your course and learning solutions, visit
www.cengage.com

Purchase any of our products at your local college store or at our preferred online store **www.ichapters.com**

Printed in the U.S.A.
2 3 4 5 6 7 14 13 12 11 10

Contents

Preface

he tenth edition of *Plays for the Theatre* contains fourteen plays. Two of these plays are new to this collection: Octavio Solis' gripping contemporary drama, *Lydia*, and Steven Dietz's midlife crisis comedy, *Becky's New Car*. Both of these plays were nominee finalists for the prestigious 2009 American Theatre Critics Association award for the best new play that debuted in regional theatre.

Selecting plays for an anthology is always risky business. For each play chosen, many others, perhaps equally worthy, must be rejected as we seek to provide a broad selection of representative, exciting, and culturally diverse plays from the past and present.

The works included in this anthology come from many periods, representing the drama of ancient Greece, the Middle Ages, seventeenth-century England and France, late nineteenth-century Norway and England, and a wide range of twentieth- and twenty-first century American drama. As such, they provide a broad cultural perspective.

The collection includes plays by Sophocles, Shakespeare, Molière, Ibsen, Wilde, O'Neill, and Williams, as well as an anonymous author of a medieval mystery play. This edition also includes a Noh drama attributed to the Japanese master playwright Zeami, and an African drama by Nobel Prize–winner Wole Soyinka. As in previous editions, the anthology contains recent American plays chosen for their dramatic power as well as their cultural diversity and artistic excellence. These include plays by Pulitzer Prize–winning African American dramatist August Wilson, and a Pulitzer Prize–winning play by Paula Vogel. Each of these plays is discussed at some length in a companion book, *The Essential Theatre*, Tenth Edition, also published by Wadsworth Cengage. This companion volume places each of the plays included in *Plays for the Theatre* within its historical and cultural context. Although each of these books can stand alone, together they provide a greater understanding of the plays than when used separately.

We would like to thank Melissa Gaspar and Amanda Ireta for their valuable assistance, as well as the reviewers who took time to provide insight and guidance on this project:

Pamela Fields, *Scottsdale Community College*
J. Omar Hansen, *Brigham Young University*
James R. Hartman, *Schoolcraft College*
Cliff Langford, *Northwest Arkansas Community College*
Sandie Melton, *Arkansas State University—Mountain Home*
Maureen Connolly McFeely, *Hofstra University*
Jeffrey Milet, *Lehigh University*
Eric Thibodeaux-Thompson, *University of Illinois—Springfield*

Finally, we thank the staff at Wadsworth Cengage Learning: Michael Rosenberg, Stephanie P. Carpenter, Erin Mitchell, Jill D'Urso, Erin Pass, and Georgia Young.

Oscar G. Brockett
Robert J. Ball

Oedipus Rex
(C. 430 B.C.)

O
EDIPUS REX was first performed in Athens at the City Dionysia (a major religious and civic festival held annually in honor of Dionysus, the god of wine and fertility) in competition with works by two other playwrights. Each dramatist presented three tragedies and one satyr play each time he competed before the audience of approximately fifteen thousand spectators. Sophocles was awarded first prize for the group of plays that included *Oedipus Rex*.

The most striking feature of Greek tragedy is the alternation of dramatic episodes with choral passages. In Sophocles' day, the tragic chorus included fifteen performers who sang (or recited) and danced the choral passages to musical accompaniment. Other typical features of Greek tragedy are the small number of individualized characters, the restriction of the action to a single place, the tightly unified plot, the serious and philosophic tone, and the poetic language.

The action of *Oedipus Rex* is extremely concentrated: A complete reversal of the protagonist's fortune takes place in a single day. The story follows Oedipus, king of Thebes, as he attempts to discover the murderer of Laïos, the former king, after an oracle declares that the plague now destroying the city will not be lifted until the guilty one is cast out. Oedipus' search gradually uncovers terrible truths about the past and his own origins. The initial suspicion that Oedipus himself may be the slayer of Laïos is rapidly followed by other electrifying moments (among them Iocastê's recognition that she is not only Oedipus' wife but also his mother), and the ultimate outcome: blindness, exile, and anguish for the once powerful king.

The Greek philosopher Aristotle thought that *Oedipus Rex* was an ideal example of the tragic form because Sophocles combined "recognition" (a sudden change from ignorance to knowledge) and reversal of fortune at the same moment. Oedipus recognizes the truth of who he is and what he has done, and in that moment his stature changes from king to pariah. Aristotle believed that this combination of recognition and reversal of fortune increased a tragedy's power to evoke a strong emotional reaction.

Sophocles is admired particularly for his skillful management of extensive plot materials: He accomplishes the gradual unveiling of mystery after mystery and a steady increase in dramatic tension with the utmost economy of means. Although, like most great plays, *Oedipus Rex* is open to many interpretations, most critics have agreed that a central concern is the uncertainty of fate and humanity's helplessness in the face of destiny.

Sophocles

Oedipus Rex

English Version by Dudley Fitts and Robert Fitzgerald

Persons Represented

OEDIPUS
A PRIEST
CREON
TEIRESIAS
IOCASTÊ [JOCASTA]
MESSENGER
SHEPHERD OF LAÏOS
SECOND MESSENGER
CHORUS OF THEBAN ELDERS

THE SCENE———Before the palace of OEDIPUS, *King of Thebes. A central door and two lateral doors open onto a platform which runs the length of the façade. On the platform, right and left, are altars; and three steps lead down into the "orchestra," or chorus-ground. At the beginning of the action these steps are crowded by suppliants who have brought branches and chaplets of olive leaves and who lie in various attitudes of despair.* OEDIPUS *enters.*

PROLOGUE

OEDIPUS: My children, generations of the living
    In the line of Kadmos, nursed at his ancient hearth:
    Why have you strewn yourselves before these altars
    In supplication, with your boughs and garlands?
    The breath of incense rises from the city   5
    With a sound of prayer and lamentation.
                             Children,
    I would not have you speak through messengers,
    And therefore I have come myself to hear you—
    I, Oedipus, who bear the famous name.   10

    [*To a* PRIEST.]

    You, there, since you are eldest in the company,
    Speak for them all, tell me what preys upon you,
    Whether you come in dread, or crave some blessing:

Tell me, and never doubt that I will help you
In every way I can; I should be heartless   15
Were I not moved to find you suppliant here.
PRIEST: Great Oedipus, O powerful King of Thebes!
    You see how all the ages of our people
Cling to your altar steps: here are boys
Who can barely stand alone, and here are priests   20
By weight of age, as I am a priest of God,
And young men chosen from those yet unmarried;
As for the others, all that multitude,
They wait with olive chaplets in the squares,
At the two shrines of Pallas, and where Apollo   25
Speaks in the glowing embers.
                          Your own eyes,
Must tell you: Thebes is tossed on a murdering sea
And can not lift her head from the death surge.
A rust consumes the buds and fruits of the earth;   30
The herds are sick; children die unborn,
And labor is vain. The god of plague and pyre
Raids like detestable lightning through the city,
And all the house of Kadmos is laid waste,
All emptied, and all darkened; Death alone   35
Battens upon the misery of Thebes.

You are not one of the immortal gods, we know;
Yet we have come to you to make our prayer
As to the man surest in mortal ways
And wisest in the ways of God. You saved us   40
From the Sphinx, that flinty singer, and the tribute
We paid to her so long; yet you were never
Better informed than we, nor could we teach you:
It was some god breathed in you to set us free.

Therefore, O mighty King, we turn to you: 45
Find us our safety, find us a remedy,
Whether by counsel of the gods or men.
A king of wisdom tested in the past
Can act in a time of troubles, and act well.
Noblest of men, restore   50
Life to your city! Think how all men call you
Liberator for your triumph long ago;
Ah, when your years of kingship are remembered,
Let them not say We rose, but later fell—
Keep the State from going down in the storm!   55
Once, years ago, with a happy augury,
You brought us fortune; be the same again!
No man questions your power to rule the land:
But rule over men, not over a dead city!
Ships are only hulls, citadels are nothing,   60
When no life moves in the empty passageways.

OEDIPUS: Poor children! You may be sure I know
  All that you longed for in your coming here.
  I know that you are deathly sick; and yet,
  Sick as you are, not one is as sick as I. 65
  Each of you suffers in himself alone
  His anguish, not another's; but my spirit
  Groans for the city, for myself, for you.
  I was not sleeping, you are not waking me.
  No, I have been in tears for a long while 70
  And in my restless thought walked many ways.
  In all my search, I found one helpful course,
  And that I have taken: I have sent Creon,
  Son of Menoikeus, brother of the Queen,
  To Delphi, Apollo's place of revelation, 75
  To learn there, if he can,
  What act or pledge of mine may save the city.
  I have counted the days, and now, this very day,
  I am troubled, for he has overstayed his time.
  What is he doing? He has been gone too long. 80
  Yet whenever he comes back, I should do ill
  To scant whatever duty God reveals.
PRIEST: It is a timely promise. At this instant
  They tell me Creon is here.
OEDIPUS: O Lord Apollo! 85
  May his news be fair as his face is radiant!
PRIEST: It could not be otherwise: he is crowned with bay,
  The chaplet is thick with berries.
OEDIPUS: We shall soon know;
  He is near enough to hear us now. 90

    [*Enter* CREON.]

                    O Prince:
  Brother: son of Menoikeus:
  What answer do you bring us from the god?
CREON: A strong one. I can tell you, great afflictions
  Will turn out well, if they are taken well. 95
OEDIPUS: What was the oracle? These vague words
  Leave me still hanging between hope and fear.
CREON: Is it your pleasure to hear me with all these
  Gathered around us? I am prepared to speak,
  But should we not go in? 100
OEDIPUS: Let them all hear it.
  It is for them I suffer, more than for myself.
CREON: Then I will tell you what I heard at Delphi.
  In plain words
  The god commands us to expel from the land of Thebes 105
  An old defilement we are sheltering.
  It is a deathly thing, beyond cure;
  We must not let it feed upon us longer.

OEDIPUS: What defilement? How shall we rid ourselves of it?

CREON: By exile or death, blood for blood. It was   110
    Murder that brought the plague-wind on the city.

OEDIPUS: Murder of whom? Surely the god has named him?

CREON: My lord: long ago Laïos was our king,
    Before you came to govern us.

OEDIPUS: I know;   115
    I learned of him from others; I never saw him.

CREON: He was murdered; and Apollo commands us now
    To take revenge upon whoever killed him.

OEDIPUS: Upon whom? Where are they? Where shall we find a clue
    To solve that crime, after so many years?   120

CREON: Here in this land, he said.
                       If we make enquiry,
    We may touch things that otherwise escape us.

OEDIPUS: Tell me: Was Laïos murdered in his house,
    Or in the fields, or in some foreign country?   125

CREON: He said he planned to make a pilgrimage.
    He did not come home again.

OEDIPUS: And was there no one,
    No witness, no companion, to tell what happened?

CREON: They were all killed but one, and he got away   130
    So frightened that he could remember one thing only.

OEDIPUS: What was that one thing? One may be the key
    To everything, if we resolve to use it.

CREON: He said that a band of highwaymen attacked them,
    Outnumbered them, and overwhelmed the King.   135

OEDIPUS: Strange, that a highwayman should be so daring—
    Unless some faction here bribed him to do it.

CREON: We thought of that. But after Laïos' death
    New troubles arose and he had no avenger.

OEDIPUS: What troubles could prevent your hunting down the killers?   140

CREON: The riddling Sphinx's song
    Made us deaf to all mysteries but her own.

OEDIPUS: Then once more I must bring what is dark to light.
    It is most fitting that Apollo shows,
    As you do, this compunction for the dead.   145
    You shall see how I stand by you, as I should,
    To avenge the city and the city's god,
    And not as though it were for some distant friend,
    But for my own sake, to be rid of evil.
    Whoever killed King Laïos might—who knows?—   150
    Decide at any moment to kill me as well.
    By avenging the murdered king I protect myself.
    Come, then, my children: leave the altar steps,
    Lift up your olive boughs!
                  One of you go   155
    And summon the people of Kadmos to gather here.
    I will do all that I can; you may tell them that.

[*Exit a* PAGE.]

So, with the help of God,
We shall be saved—or else indeed we are lost.
PRIEST: Let us rise, children. It was for this we came,   160
And now the King has promised it himself.
Phoibos has sent us an oracle; may he descend
Himself to save us and drive out the plague.

[*Exeunt* OEDIPUS *and* CREON *into the palace by the central door. The* PRIEST *and the*
SUPPLIANTS *disperse R and L. After a short pause the* CHORUS *enters the orchestra.*]

PARODOS

CHORUS: What is God singing in his profound   [STROPHE 1]
Delphi of gold and shadow?   165
What oracle for Thebes, the sunwhipped city?

Fear unjoints me, the roots of my heart tremble.

Now I remember, O Healer, your power, and wonder:
Will you send doom like a sudden cloud, or weave it
Like nightfall of the past?   170

Speak, speak to us, issue a holy sound:
Dearest to our expectancy: be tender!

Let me pray to Athenê, the immortal daughter of Zeus,

    [ANTISTROPHE 1]

And to Artemis her sister
Who keeps her famous throne in the market ring,   175
And to Apollo, bowman at the far butts of heaven-

O gods, descend! Like three streams leap against
The fires of our grief, the fires of darkness;
Be swift to bring us rest!

As in the old time from the brilliant house   180
Of air you stepped to save us, come again!

Now our afflictions have no end,   [STROPHE 2]
Now all our stricken host lies down
And no man fights off death with his mind;
The noble plowland bears no grain,   185
And groaning mothers can not bear—

See, how our lives like birds take wing,
Like sparks that fly when a fire soars,
To the shore of the god of evening.

The plague burns on; it is pitiless,   [ANTISTROPHE 2]   190
Though pallid children laden with death
Lie unwept in the stony ways,

And old gray women by every path
Flock to the strand about the altars

There to strike their breasts and cry   195
Worship of Phoibos in wailing prayers:
Be kind, God's golden child!

There are no swords in this attack by fire,   [STROPHE 3]
No shields, but we are ringed with cries.
Send the besieger plunging from our homes   200
Into the vast sea-room of the Atlantic
Or into the waves that foam eastward of Thrace—

For the day ravages what the night spares—

Destroy our enemy, lord of the thunder!
Let him be riven by lightning from heaven!   205

Phoibos Apollo, stretch the sun's bowstring,   [ANTISTROPHE 3]
That golden cord, until it sings for us,
Flashing arrows in heaven!
                    Artemis, Huntress,
Race with flaring lights upon our mountains!   210

O scarlet god, O golden-banded brow,
O Theban Bacchos in a storm of Maenads,

    [*Enter* OEDIPUS, *C.*]

Whirl upon Death, that all the Undying hate.
Come with blinding torches, come in joy!

SCENE I

OEDIPUS: Is this your prayer? It may be answered. Come,
    Listen to me, act as the crisis demands,
    And you shall have relief from all these evils.
    Until now I was a stranger to this tale,
    As I had been a stranger to the crime.   5
    Could I track down the murderer without a clue?

But now, friends,
    As one who became a citizen after the murder,
    I make this proclamation to all Thebans:
    If any man knows by whose hand Laïos, son of Labdakos,   10

Met his death, I direct that man to tell me everything,
No matter what he fears for having so long withheld it.
Let it stand as promised that no further trouble
Will come to him, but he may leave the land in safety.

Moreover: If anyone knows the murderer to be foreign,   15
Let him not keep silent: he shall have his reward from me.
However, if he does conceal it; if any man
Fearing for his friend or for himself disobeys this edict,
Hear what I propose to do:

I solemnly forbid the people of this country,   20
Where power and throne are mine, ever to receive that man
Or speak to him, no matter who he is, or let him
Join in sacrifice, lustration, or in prayer.
I decree that he be driven from every house,
Being, as he is, corruption itself to us: the Delphic   25
Voice of Zeus has pronounced this revelation.
Thus I associate myself with the oracle
And take the side of the murdered king.

As for the criminal, I pray to God—
Whether it be a lurking thief, or one of a number—   30
I pray that that man's life be consumed in evil and wretchedness.
And as for me, this curse applies no less
If it should turn out that the culprit is my guest here,
Sharing my hearth.
                        You have heard the penalty.   35
I lay it on you now to attend to this
For my sake, for Apollo's, for the sick
Sterile city that heaven has abandoned.
Suppose the oracle had given you no command:
Should this defilement go uncleansed for ever?   40
You should have found the murderer: your king,
A noble king, had been destroyed!
                        Now I,
Having the power that he held for me,
Having his bed, begetting children there   45
Upon his wife, as he would have, had he lived—
Their son would have been my children's brother,
If Laïos had had luck in fatherhood!
(But surely ill luck rushed upon his reign)—
I say I take the son's part, just as though   50
I were his son, to press the fight for him
And see it won! I'll find the hand that brought
Death to Labdakos' and Polydoros' child,
Heir to Kadmos' and Agenor's line.
And as for those who fail me,   55
May the gods deny them the fruit of the earth,
Fruit of the womb, and may they rot utterly!
Let them be wretched as we are wretched, and worse!

For you, for loyal Thebans, and for all
who find my actions right, I pray the favor 60
Of justice, and of all the immortal gods.
CHORAGOS: Since I am under oath, my lord, I swear
I did not do the murder, I can not name
The murderer. Might not the oracle
That has ordained the search tell where to find him? 65
OEDIPUS: An honest question. But no man in the world
Can make the gods do more than the gods will.
CHORAGOS: There is one last expedient—
OEDIPUS: Tell me what it is.
Though it seem slight, you must not hold it back. 70
CHORAGOS: A lord clairvoyant to the lord Apollo,
As we all know, is the skilled Teiresias.
One might learn much about this from him, Oedipus.
OEDIPUS: I am not wasting time:
Creon spoke of this, and I have sent for him— 75
Twice, in fact; it is strange that he is not here.
CHORAGOS: The other matter—that old report—seems useless.
OEDIPUS: Tell me. I am interested in all reports.
CHORAGOS: The King was said to have been killed by highwaymen.
OEDIPUS: I know. But we have no witnesses to that. 80
CHORAGOS: If the killer can feel a particle of dread,
Your curse will bring him out of hiding!
OEDIPUS: No.
The man who dared that act will fear no curse.

[*Enter the blind seer* TEIRESIAS, *led by a* PAGE.]

CHORAGOS: But there is one man who may detect the criminal. 85
This is Teiresias, this is the holy prophet
In whom, alone of all men, truth was born.
OEDIPUS: Teiresias: seer: student of mysteries,
Of all that's taught and all that no man tells,
Secrets of Heaven and secrets of the earth: 90
Blind though you are, you know the city lies
Slick with plague; and from this plague, my lord,
We find that you alone can guard or save us.

Possibly you did not hear the messengers?
Apollo, when we sent to him, 95
Sent us back word that this great pestilence
Would lift, but only if we established clearly
The identity of those who murdered Laïos.
They must be killed or exiled.
                                             Can you use 100
Birdflight or any art of divination
To purify yourself, and Thebes, and me
From this contagion? We are in your hands.
There is no fairer duty
Than that of helping others in distress. 105
TEIRESIAS: How dreadful knowledge of the truth can be

When there's no help in truth! I knew this well,
But made myself forget. I should not have come.

OEDIPUS: What is troubling you? Why are your eyes so cold?

TEIRESIAS: Let me go home. Bear your own fate, and I'll   110
Bear mine. It is better so: trust what I say.

OEDIPUS: What you say is ungracious and unhelpful
To your native country. Do not refuse to speak.

TEIRESIAS: When it comes to speech, your own is neither temperate
Nor opportune. I wish to be more prudent.   115

OEDIPUS: In God's name, we all beg you—

TEIRESIAS: You are all ignorant.
No; I will never tell you what I know.
Now it is my misery; then, it would be yours.

OEDIPUS: What! You do know something, and will not tell us?   120
You would betray us all and wreck the State?

TEIRESIAS: I do not intend to torture myself, or you.
Why persist in asking? You will not persuade me.

OEDIPUS: What a wicked old man you are! You'd try a stone's
Patience! Out with it! Have you no feeling at all?   125

TEIRESIAS: You call me unfeeling. If you could only see
The nature of your own feelings. . .

OEDIPUS: Why,
Who would not feel as I do? Who could endure
Your arrogance toward the city?   130

TEIRESIAS: What does it matter!
Whether I speak or not, it is bound to come.

OEDIPUS: Then, if "it" is bound to come, you are bound to tell me.

TEIRESIAS: No, I will not go on. Rage as you please.

OEDIPUS: Rage? Why not!   135
And I'll tell you what I think:
You planned it, you had it done, you all but
Killed him with your own hands: if you had eyes,
I'd say the crime was yours, and yours alone.

TEIRESIAS: So? I charge you, then,   140
Abide by the proclamation you have made:
From this day forth
Never speak again to these men or to me;
You yourself are the pollution of this country.

OEDIPUS: You dare say that! Can you possibly think you have   145
Some way of going free, after such insolence?

TEIRESIAS: I have gone free. It is the truth sustains me.

OEDIPUS: Who taught you shamelessness? It was not your craft.

TEIRESIAS: You did. You made me speak. I did not want to.

OEDIPUS: Speak what? Let me hear it again more clearly.   150

TEIRESIAS: Was it not clear before? Are you tempting me?

OEDIPUS: I did not understand it. Say it again.

TEIRESIAS: I say that you are the murderer whom you seek.

OEDIPUS: Now twice you have spat out infamy. You'll pay for it!

TEIRESIAS: Would you care for more? Do you wish to be really angry?   155

OEDIPUS: Say what you will. Whatever you say is worthless.

TEIRESIAS: I say you live in hideous shame with those
  Most dear to you. You can not see the evil.
OEDIPUS: It seems you can go on mouthing like this for ever.
TEIRESIAS: I can, if there is power in truth.   160
OEDIPUS: There is:
  But not for you, not for you,
  You sightless, witless, senseless, mad old man!
TEIRESIAS: You are the madman. There is no one here
  who will not curse you soon, as you curse me.   165
OEDIPUS: You child of endless night! You can not hurt me
  Or any other man who sees the sun.
TEIRESIAS: True: it is not from me your fate will come.
  That lies within Apollo's competence.
  As it is his concern.   170
OEDIPUS: Tell me.
  Are you speaking for Creon, or for yourself?
TEIRESIAS: Creon is no threat. You weave your own doom.
OEDIPUS: Wealth, power, craft of statesmanship!
  Kingly position, everywhere admired!   175
  What savage envy is stored up against these,
  If Creon, whom I trusted, Creon my friend,
  For this great office which the city once
  Put in my hands unsought-if for this power
  Creon desires in secret to destroy me!   180

  He has bought this decrepit fortune-teller, this
  Collector of dirty pennies, this prophet fraud—
  Why, he is no more clairvoyant than I am!
             Tell us.
  Has your mystic mummery ever approached the truth?   185
  When that hellcat the Sphinx was performing here,
  What help were you to these people?
  Her magic was not for the first man who came along:
  It demanded a real exorcist. Your birds—
  What good were they? or the gods, for the matter of that? 190
  But I came by,
  Oedipus, the simple man, who knows nothing—
  I thought it out for myself, no birds helped me!
  And this is the man you think you can destroy,
  That you may be close to Creon when he's king!   195
  Well, you and your friend Creon, it seems to me,
  Will suffer most. If you were not an old man,
  You would have paid already for your plot.
CHORAGOS: We can not see that his words or yours
  Have been spoken except in anger, Oedipus,   200
  And of anger we have no need. How can God's will
  Be accomplished best? That is what most concerns us.
TEIRESIAS: You are a king. But where argument's concerned
  I am your man, as much a king as you.
  I am not your servant, but Apollo's.   205

I have no need of Creon to speak for me.

Listen to me. You mock my blindness, do you?
But I say that you, with both your eyes, are blind:
You can not see the wretchedness of your life,
Nor in whose house you live, no, nor with whom.   210
Who are your father and mother? Can you tell me?
You do not even know the blind wrongs
That you have done them, on earth and in the world below.
But the double lash of your parents' curse will whip you
Out of this land some day, with only night   215
Upon your precious eyes.
Your cries then—where will they not be heard?
What fastness of Kithairon will not echo them?
And that bridal-descant of yours—you'll know it then,
The song they sang when you came here to Thebes   220
And found your misguided berthing.
All this, and more, that you can not guess at now,
Will bring you to yourself among your children.
Be angry, then. Curse Creon. Curse my words.
I tell you, no man that walks upon the earth   225
Shall be rooted out more horribly than you.
OEDIPUS: Am I to bear this from him?—Damnation
     Take you! Out of this place! Out of my sight!
TEIRESIAS: I would not have come at all if you had not asked me.
OEDIPUS: Could I have told that you'd talk nonsense, that   230
     You'd come here to make a fool of yourself, and of me?
TEIRESIAS: A fool? Your parents thought me sane enough.
OEDIPUS: My parents again!—Wait: who were my parents?
TEIRESIAS: This day will give you a father, and break your heart.
OEDIPUS: Your infantile riddles! Your damned abracadabra!   235
TEIRESIAS: You were a great man once at solving riddles.
OEDIPUS: Mock me with that if you like; you will find it true.
TEIRESIAS: It was true enough. It brought about your ruin.
OEDIPUS: But if it saved this town?
TEIRESIAS: [to the PAGE] Boy, give me your hand.   240
OEDIPUS: Yes, boy; lead him away.
     —While you are here
     We can do nothing. Go; leave us in peace.
TEIRESIAS: I will go when I have said what I have to say.
     How can you hurt me? And I tell you again: 245
     The man you have been looking for all this time,
     The damned man, the murderer of Laïos,
     That man is in Thebes. To your mind he is foreign-born,
     But it will soon be shown that he is Theban,
     A revelation that will fail to please.   250
                         A blind man,
     Who has his eyes now; a penniless man, who is rich now;
     And he will go tapping the strange earth with his staff

To the children with whom he lives now he will be
Brother and father—the very same; to her 255
Who bore him, son and husband—the very same
Who came to his father's bed, wet with his father's blood.
Enough. Go think that over.
If later you find error in what I have said,
You may say that I have no skill in prophecy. 260

[*Exit* TEIRESIAS, *led by his* PAGE. OEDIPUS *goes into the palace.*]

ODE I

CHORUS: The Delphic stone of prophecies   [STROPHE I]
    Remembers ancient regicide
    And a still bloody hand.
    That killer's hour of flight has come.
    He must be stronger than riderless   265
    Coursers of untiring wind,
    For the son of Zeus armed with his father's thunder
    Leaps in lightning after him;
    And the Furies follow him, the sad Furies.
    Holy Parnassos' peak of snow   [ANTISTROPHE I] 270
    Flashes and blinds that secret man,
    That all shall hunt him down:
    Though he may roam the forest shade
    Like a bull wild from pasture
    To rage through glooms of stone.   275
    Doom comes down on him; flight will not avail him;
    For the world's heart calls him desolate,
    And the immortal Furies follow, forever follow.

    But now a wilder thing is heard   [STROPHE 2]
    From the old man skilled at hearing Fate in the wingbeat of a bird. 280
    Bewildered as a blown bird, my soul hovers and can not find
    Foothold in this debate, or any reason or rest of mind.
    But no man ever brought—none can bring
    Proof of strife between Thebes' royal house,
    Labdakos' line, and the son of Polybos;   285
    And never until now has any man brought word
    Of Laïos' dark death staining Oedipus the King.

    Divine Zeus and Apollo hold   [ANTISTROPHE 2]
    Perfect intelligence alone of all tales ever told;
    And well though this diviner works, he works in his own night; 290
    No man can judge that rough unknown or trust in second sight,
    For wisdom changes hands among the wise.
    Shall I believe my great lord criminal
    At a raging word that a blind old man let fall?

I saw him, when the carrion woman faced him of old,   295
Prove his heroic mind! These evil words are lies.

SCENE II

CREON: Men of Thebes:
    I am told that heavy accusations
    Have been brought against me by King Oedipus.

    I am not the kind of man to bear this tamely.

    If in these present difficulties   5
    He holds me accountable for any harm to him
    Through anything I have said or done—why, then,
    I do not value life in this dishonor.
    It is not as though this rumor touched upon
    Some private indiscretion. The matter is grave.   10
    The fact is that I am being called disloyal
    To the State, to my fellow citizens, to my friends.
CHORAGOS: He may have spoken in anger, not from his mind.
CREON: But did you not hear him say I was the one
    Who seduced the old prophet into lying?   15
CHORAGOS: The thing was said; I do not know how seriously.
CREON: But you were watching him! Were his eyes steady?
    Did he look like a man in his right mind?
CHORAGOS: I do not know.
    I can not judge the behavior of great men.   20
    But here is the King himself.

      [*Enter* OEDIPUS.]

OEDIPUS: So you dared come back.
    Why? How brazen of you to come to my house,
    You murderer!
                Do you think I do not know   25
    That you plotted to kill me, plotted to steal my throne?
    Tell me, in God's name: am I coward, a fool,
    That you should dream you could accomplish this?
    A fool who could not see your slippery game?
    A coward, not to fight back when I saw it?   30
    You are the fool, Creon, are you not? hoping
    Without support or friends to get a throne?
    Thrones may be won or bought: you could do neither.
CREON: Now listen to me. You have talked; let me talk, too.
    You can not judge unless you know the facts.   35
OEDIPUS: You speak well: there is one fact; but I find it hard
    To learn from the deadliest enemy I have.
CREON: That above all I must dispute with you.
OEDIPUS: That above all I will not hear you deny.

CREON: If you think there is anything good in being stubborn   40
    Against all reason, then I say you are wrong.
OEDIPUS: If you think a man can sin against his own kind
    And not be punished for it, I say you are mad.
CREON: I agree. But tell me: what have I done to you?
OEDIPUS: You advised me to send for that wizard, did you not?   45
CREON: I did. I should do it again.
OEDIPUS: Very well. Now tell me:
    How long has it been since Laïos—
CREON: What of Laïos?
OEDIPUS: Since he vanished in that onset by the road?   50
CREON: It was long ago, a long time.
OEDIPUS: And this prophet,
    Was he practicing here then?
CREON: He was; and with honor, as now.
OEDIPUS: Did he speak of me at that time?   55
CREON: He never did:
    At least, not when I was present.
OEDIPUS: But . . . the enquiry?
    I suppose you held one?
CREON: We did, but we learned nothing.   60
OEDIPUS: Why did the prophet not speak against me then?
CREON: I do not know; and I am the kind of man
    Who holds his tongue when he has no facts to go on.
OEDIPUS: There's one fact that you know, and you could tell it.
CREON: What fact is that? If I know it, you shall have it.   65
OEDIPUS: If he were not involved with you, he could not say
    That it was I who murdered Laïos.
CREON: If he says that, you are the one that knows it!—
    But now it is my turn to question you.
OEDIPUS: Put your questions. I am no murderer.   70
CREON: First, then: You married my sister?
OEDIPUS: I married your sister.
CREON: And you rule the kingdom equally with her?
OEDIPUS: Everything that she wants she has from me.
CREON: And I am the third, equal to both of you?   75
OEDIPUS: That is why I call you a bad friend.
CREON: No. Reason it out, as I have done.
    Think of this first: Would any sane man prefer
    Power, with all a king's anxieties,
    To that same power and the grace of sleep?   80
    Certainly not I.
    I have never longed for the king's power—only his rights.
    Would any wise man differ from me in this?
    As matters stand, I have my way in everything
    With your consent, and no responsibilities.   85
    If I were king, I should be a slave to policy.

    How could I desire a scepter more
    Than what is now mine—untroubled influence?

No, I have not gone mad; I need no honors,
Except those with the perquisites I have now.   90
I am welcome everywhere; every man salutes me,
And those who want your favor seek my ear,
Since I know how to manage what they ask.
Should I exchange this case for that anxiety?
Besides, no sober mind is treasonable.   95
I hate anarchy
And never would deal with any man who likes it.

Test what I have said. Go to the priestess
At Delphi; ask if I quoted her correctly.
And as for this other thing: if I am found   100
Guilty of treason with Teiresias,
Then sentence me to death! You have my word
It is a sentence I should cast my vote for—
But not without evidence!
               You do wrong   105
When you take good men for bad, bad men for good.
A true friend thrown aside—why, life itself
Is not more precious!
              In time you will know this well:
For time, and time alone, will show the just man,   110
Though scoundrels are discovered in a day.
CHORAGOS: This is well said, and a prudent man would ponder it.
    Judgments too quickly formed are dangerous.
OEDIPUS: But is he not quick in his duplicity?
    And shall I not be quick to parry him?   115
    Would you have me stand still, hold my peace, and let
    This man win everything, through my inaction?
CREON: And you want—what is it, then? To banish me?
OEDIPUS: No, not exile. It is your death I want,
    So that all the world may see what treason means.   120
CREON: You will persist, then? You will not believe me?
OEDIPUS: How can I believe you?
CREON: Then you are a fool.
OEDIPUS: To save myself?
CREON: In justice, think of me.   125
OEDIPUS: You are evil incarnate.
CREON: But suppose that you are wrong?
OEDIPUS: Still I must rule.
CREON: But not if you rule badly.
OEDIPUS: O city, city!   130
CREON: It is my city, too!
CHORAGOS: Now, my lords, be still, I see the Queen,
    Iocastê, coming from her palace chambers;
    And it is time she came, for the sake of you both.
    This dreadful quarrel can be resolved through her.   135

    [*Enter* IOCASTÊ.]

IOCASTÊ: Poor foolish men, what wicked din is this?
    With Thebes sick to death, is it not shameful

That you should rake some private quarrel up?

[*To* OEDIPUS:]

Come into the house.

—And you, Creon, go now: 140
  Let us have no more of this tumult over nothing.
CREON: Nothing? No, sister: what your husband plans for me
  Is one of two great evils: exile or death.
OEDIPUS: He is right.
                        Why, woman, I have caught him squarely   145
  Plotting against my life.
CREON: No! let me die
  Accurst if ever I have wished you harm!
IOCASTÊ: Ah, believe it, Oedipus!
  In the name of the gods, respect this oath of his   150
  For my sake, for the sake of these people here!   [STROPHE I]

CHORAGOS: Open your mind to her, my lord, Be ruled by her, I beg you!
OEDIPUS: What would you have me do?
CHORAGOS: Respect Creon's word. He has never spoken like a fool,
  And now he has sworn an oath.   155
OEDIPUS: You know what you ask?
CHORAGOS: I do.
OEDIPUS: Speak on, then.
CHORAGOS: A friend so sworn should not be baited so,
  In blind malice, and without final proof.   160
OEDIPUS: You are aware, I hope, that what you say
  Means death for me, or exile at the least.
CHORAGOS: No, I swear by Helios, first in Heaven!
  May I die friendless and accurst,
  The worst of deaths, if ever I meant that!   165
  It is the withering fields
  That hurt my sick heart:
  Must we bear all these ills,
  And now your bad blood as well?
OEDIPUS: Then let him go. And let me die, if I must,   170
  Or be driven by him in shame from the land of Thebes.
  It is your unhappiness, and not his talk,
  That touches me.
                As for him—
  Wherever he goes, hatred will follow him.   175
CREON: Ugly in yielding, as you were ugly in rage!
  Natures like yours chiefly torment themselves.
OEDIPUS: Can you not go? Can you not leave me?
CREON: I can.
  You do not know me; but the city knows me,   180
  And in its eyes, I am just, if not in yours.

[*Exit* CREON.]

                                              [ANTISTROPHE I]
CHORAGOS: Lady Iocastê, did you not ask the King to go to his chambers?

IOCASTÊ: First tell me what has happened.

CHORAGOS: There was suspicion without evidence: yet it rankled
As even false charges will. 185

IOCASTÊ: On both sides?

CHORAGOS: On both.

IOCASTÊ: But what was said?

CHORAGOS: Oh let it rest, let it be done with!
Have we not suffered enough? 190

OEDIPUS: You see to what your decency has brought you:
You have made difficulties where my heart saw none.

CHORAGOS: Oedipus, it is not once only I have told you— [ANTISTROPHE 2]
You must know I should count myself unwise
To the point of madness, should I now forsake you— 195
You, under whose hand,
In the storm of another time,
Our dear land sailed out free.
But now stand fast at the helm!

IOCASTÊ: In God's name, Oedipus, inform your wife as well: 200
Why are you so set in this hard anger?

OEDIPUS: I will tell you, for none of these men deserves
My confidence as you do. It is Creon's work,
His treachery, his plotting against me.

IOCASTÊ: Go on, if you can make this clear to me. 205

OEDIPUS: He charges me with the murder of Laïos.

IOCASTÊ: Has he some knowledge? Or does he speak from hearsay?

OEDIPUS: He would not commit himself to such a charge,
But he has brought in that damnable soothsayer
To tell his story. 210

IOCASTÊ: Set your mind at rest.
If it is a question of soothsayers, I tell you
That you will find no man whose craft gives knowledge
Of the unknowable.
Here is my proof. 215
An oracle was reported to Laïos once
(I will not say from Phoibos himself, but from
His appointed ministers, at any rate)
That his doom would be death at the hands of his own son—
His son, born of his flesh and of mine! 220

Now, you remember the story: Laïos was killed
By marauding strangers where three highways meet.
But his child had not been three days in this world
Before the King had pierced the baby's ankles
And left him to die on a lonely mountainside. 225

Thus, Apollo never caused that child
To kill his father, and it was not Laïos' fate
To die at the hands of his son, as he had feared.
This is what prophets and prophecies are worth!
Have no dread of them. 230

It is God himself
Who can show us what he wills, in his own way.
OEDIPUS: How strange a shadowy memory crossed my mind,
Just now while you were speaking; it chilled my heart.
IOCASTÊ: What do you mean? What memory do you speak of?   235
OEDIPUS: If I understand you, Laïos was killed
At a place where three roads meet.
IOCASTÊ: So it was said;
We have no later story.
OEDIPUS: Where did it happen?   240
IOCASTÊ: Phokis, it is called: at a place where the Theban Way
Divides into the roads toward Delphi and Daulia.
OEDIPUS: When?
IOCASTÊ: We had the news not long before you came
And proved the right to your succession here.   245
OEDIPUS: Ah, what net has God been weaving for me?
IOCASTÊ: Oedipus! Why does this trouble you?
OEDIPUS: Do not ask me yet.
First, tell me how Laïos looked, and tell me
How old he was.   250
IOCASTÊ: He was tall, his hair just touched
With white; his form was not unlike your own.
OEDIPUS: I think that I myself may be accurst
By my own ignorant edict.
IOCASTÊ: You speak strangely.   255
It makes me tremble to look at you, my King.
OEDIPUS: I am not sure that the blind man can not see.
But I should know better if you were to tell me—
IOCASTÊ: Anything—though I dread to hear you ask it.
OEDIPUS: Was the King lightly escorted, or did he ride   260
With a large company, as a ruler should?
IOCASTÊ: There were five men with him in all: one was a herald,
And a single chariot, which he was driving.
OEDIPUS: Alas, that makes it plain enough!
But who—   265
Who told you how it happened?
IOCASTÊ: A household servant,
The only one to escape.
OEDIPUS: And is he still
A servant of ours?   270
IOCASTÊ: No; for when he came back at last
And found you enthroned in the place of the dead king,
He came to me, touched my hand with his, and begged
That I would send him away to the frontier district
Where only the shepherds go—   275
As far away from the city as I could send him.
I granted his prayer; for although the man was a slave,
He had earned more than this favor at my hands.
OEDIPUS: Can he be called back quickly?
IOCASTÊ: Easily.   280

But why?
OEDIPUS: I have taken too much upon myself
     Without enquiry; therefore I wish to consult him.
IOCASTÊ: Then he shall come.
                    But am I not one also   285
     To whom you might confide these fears of yours?
OEDIPUS: That is your right; it will not be denied you,
     Now least of all; for I have reached a pitch
     Of wild foreboding. Is there anyone
     To whom I should sooner speak?   290

     Polybos of Corinth is my father.
     My mother is a Dorian: Meropê.
     I grew up chief among the men of Corinth
     Until a strange thing happened—
     Not worth my passion, it may be, but strange.   295

     At a feast, a drunken man maundering in his cups
     Cries out that I am not my father's son!

     I contained myself that night, though I felt anger
     And a sinking heart. The next day I visited
     My father and mother, and questioned them. They stormed,   300
     Calling it all the slanderous rant of a fool;
     And this relieved me. Yet the suspicion
     Remained always aching in my mind;
     I know there was talk; I could not rest;
     And finally, saying nothing to my parents,   305
     I went to the shrine at Delphi.
     The god dismissed my question without reply;
     He spoke of other things.
                    Some were clear,
     Full of wretchedness, dreadful, unbearable: 310
     As, that I should lie with my own mother, breed
     Children from whom all men would turn their eyes;
     And that I should be my father's murderer.

     I heard all this, and fled. And from that day
     Corinth to me was only in the stars   315
     Descending in that quarter of the sky,
     As I wandered farther and farther on my way
     To a land where I should never see the evil
     Sung by the oracle. And I came to this country
     Where, so you say, King Laïos was killed.   320

     I will tell you all that happened there, my lady.
     There were three highways
     Coming together at a place I passed;
     And there a herald came towards me, and a chariot
     Drawn by horses, with a man such as you describe   325

Seated in it. The groom leading the horses
Forced me off the road at his lord's command;
But as this charioteer lurched over towards me
I struck him in my rage. The old man saw me
And brought his double goad down upon my head   330
As I came abreast.

            He was paid back, and more!
Swinging my club in this right hand I knocked him
Out of his car, and he rolled on the ground.

                       I killed him.   335
I killed them all.
Now if that stranger and Laïos were—kin,
Where is a man more miserable than I?
More hated by the gods? Citizen and alien alike
Must never shelter me or speak to me—   340
I must be shunned by all.

            And I myself
Pronounced this malediction upon myself!
Think of it: I have touched you with these hands,
These hands that killed your husband. What defilement!   345

Am I all evil, then? It must be so,
Since I must flee from Thebes, yet never again
See my own countrymen, my own country,
For fear of joining my mother in marriage
And killing Polybos, my father.   350

                Ah,
If I was created so, born to this fate,
Who could deny the savagery of God?
O holy majesty of heavenly powers!
May I never see that day! Never!   355
Rather let me vanish from the race of men
Than know the abomination destined me!
CHORAGOS: We, too, my lord, have felt dismay at this.
    But there is hope: you have yet to hear the shepherd.
OEDIPUS: Indeed, I fear no other hope is left me.   360
IOCASTÊ: What do you hope from him when he comes?
OEDIPUS: This much:
    If his account of the murder tallies with yours,
    Then I am cleared.
IOCASTÊ: What was it that I said   365
    Of such importance?
OEDIPUS: Why, "marauders," you said,
    Killed the King, according to this man's story.
    If he maintains that still, if there were several,
    Clearly the guilt is not mine: I was alone.   370
    But if he says one man, singlehanded, did it,
    Then the evidence all points to me.
IOCASTÊ: You may be sure that he said there were several;
    And can he call back that story now? He can not.

The whole city heard it as plainly as I. 375
But suppose he alters some detail of it:
He can not ever show that Laïos' death
Fulfilled the oracle: for Apollo said
My child was doomed to kill him; and my child—
Poor baby!—it was my child that died first. 380
No. From now on, where oracles are concerned,
I would not waste a second thought on any.
OEDIPUS: You might be right.
                 But come: let someone go
For the shepherd at once. This matter must be settled. 385
IOCASTÊ: I will send for him.
I would not wish to cross you in anything,
And surely not in this.—Let us go in.

      [*Exeunt into the palace.*]

ODE II

CHORUS: Let me be reverent in the ways of right,   [STROPHE I]
Lowly the paths I journey on; 390
Let all my words and actions keep
The laws of the pure universe
From highest Heaven handed down.
For Heaven is their bright nurse,
Those generations of the realms of light; 395
Ah, never of mortal kind were they begot,
Nor are they slaves of memory, lost in sleep;
Their Father is greater than Time, and ages not.

The tyrant is a child of Pride   [ANTISTROPHE I]
Who drinks from his great sickening cup 400
Recklessness and vanity,
Until from his high crest headlong
He plummets to the dust of hope.
That strong man is not strong.
But let no fair ambition be denied; 405
May God protect the wrestler for the State
In government, in comely policy,
Who will fear God, and on His ordinance wait.

Haughtiness and the high hand of disdain   [STROPHE 2]
Tempt and outrage God's holy law; 410
And any mortal who dares hold
No immortal Power in awe
Will be caught up in a net of pain;
The price for which his levity is sold.
Let each man take due earnings, then, 415
And keep his hands from holy things,

And from blasphemy stand apart—
Else the crackling blast of heaven
Blows on his head, and on his desperate heart;
Though fools will honor impious men,   420
In their cities no tragic poet sings.

Shall we lose faith in Delphi's obscurities,   [ANTISTROPHE 2]
We who have heard the world's core
Discredited, and the sacred wood
Of Zeus at Elis praised no more?   425
The deeds and the strange prophecies
Must make a pattern yet to be understood.
Zeus, if indeed you are lord of all,
Throned in light over night and day,
Mirror this in your endless mind: 430
Our masters call the oracle
Words on the wind, and the Delphic vision blind!
Their hearts no longer know Apollo,
And reverence for the gods has died away.

SCENE III

[*Enter* IOCASTÊ.]

IOCASTÊ: Princes of Thebes, it has occurred to me
　　　To visit the altars of the gods, bearing
　　　These branches as a suppliant, and this incense.
　　　Our King is not himself: his noble soul
　　　Is overwrought with fantasies of dread,   5
　　　Else he would consider
　　　The new prophecies in the light of the old.
　　　He will listen to any voice that speaks disaster,
　　　And my advice goes for nothing.

　　　　　　　　　　To you, then, Apollo,   10
　　　Lycean lord, since you are nearest, I turn in prayer.
　　　Receive these offerings, and grant us deliverance
　　　From defilement. Our hearts are heavy with fear
　　　When we see our leader distracted, as helpless sailors
　　　Are terrified by the confusion of their helmsman.   15

　　　[*Enter* MESSENGER.]

MESSENGER: Friends, no doubt you can direct me:
　　　Where shall I find the house of Oedipus,
　　　Or, better still, where is the King himself?
CHORAGOS: It is this very place, stranger; he is inside.
　　　This is his wife and mother of his children.   20
MESSENGER: I wish her happiness in a happy house,
　　　Blest in all the fulfillment of her marriage.

IOCASTÊ: I wish as much for you: your courtesy
    Deserves a like good fortune. But now, tell me:
    Why have you come? What have you to say to us? 25
MESSENGER: Good news, my lady, for your house and your husband.
IOCASTÊ: What news? Who sent you here?
MESSENGER: I am from Corinth.
    The news I bring ought to mean joy for you,
    Though it may be you will find some grief in it. 30
IOCASTÊ: What is it? How can it touch us in both ways?
MESSENGER: The word is that the people of the Isthmus
    Intend to call Oedipus to be their king.
IOCASTÊ: But old King Polybos—is he not reigning still?
MESSENGER: No. Death holds him in his sepulchre. 35
IOCASTÊ: What are you saying? Polybos is dead?
MESSENGER: If I am not telling the truth, may I die myself.
IOCASTÊ: [to a **MAIDSERVANT**] Go in, go quickly; tell this to your master.
    O riddlers of God's will, where are you now!
    This was the man whom Oedipus, long ago, 40
    Feared so, fled so, in dread of destroying him—
    But it was another fate by which he died.

    [*Enter* OEDIPUS.]

OEDIPUS: Dearest Iocastê, why have you sent for me?
IOCASTÊ: Listen to what this man says, and then tell me
    What has become of the solemn prophecies. 45
OEDIPUS: Who is this man? What is his news for me?
IOCASTÊ: He has come from Corinth to announce your father's death!
OEDIPUS: Is it true, stranger? Tell me in your own words.
MESSENGER: I can not say it more clearly: the King is dead.
OEDIPUS: Was it by treason? Or by an attack of illness? 50
MESSENGER: A little thing brings old men to their rest.
OEDIPUS: It was sickness, then?
MESSENGER: Yes, and his many years.
OEDIPUS: Ah!
    Why should a man respect the Pythian hearth, or 55
    Give heed to the birds that jangle above his head?
    They prophesied that I should kill Polybos,
    Kill my own father; but he is dead and buried,
    And I am here—I never touched him, never,
    Unless he died of grief for my departure, 60
    And thus, in a sense, through me. No. Polybos
    Has packed the oracles off with him underground.
    They are empty words.
IOCASTÊ: Had I not told you so?
OEDIPUS: You had; it was my faint heart that betrayed me. 65
IOCASTÊ: From now on never think of those things again.
OEDIPUS: And yet—must I not fear my mother's bed?
IOCASTÊ: Why should anyone in this world be afraid,
    Since Fate rules us and nothing can be foreseen?
    A man should live only for the present day. 70

     Have no more fear of sleeping with your mother:
     How many men, in dreams, have lain with their mothers!
     No reasonable man is troubled by such things.
OEDIPUS: That is true; only—
     If only my mother were not still alive!   75
     But she is alive. I can not help my dread.
IOCASTÊ: Yet this news of your father's death is wonderful.
OEDIPUS: Wonderful. But I fear the living woman.
MESSENGER: Tell me, who is this woman that you fear?
OEDIPUS: It is Meropê, man; the wife of King Polybos.   80
MESSENGER: Meropê? Why should you be afraid of her?
OEDIPUS: An oracle of the gods, a dreadful saying.
MESSENGER: Can you tell me about it or are you sworn to silence?
OEDIPUS: I can tell you, and I will.
     Apollo said through his prophet that I was the man   85
     Who should marry his own mother, shed his father's blood
     With his own hands. And so, for all these years
     I have kept clear of Corinth, and no harm has come—
     Though it would have been sweet to see my parents again.
MESSENGER: And is this the fear that drove you out of Corinth?   90
OEDIPUS: Would you have me kill my father?
MESSENGER: As for that
     You must be reassured by the news I gave you.
OEDIPUS: If you could reassure me, I would reward you.
MESSENGER: I had that in mind, I will confess: I thought   95
     I could count on you when you returned to Corinth.
OEDIPUS: No: I will never go near my parents again.
MESSENGER: Ah, son, you still do not know what you are doing—
OEDIPUS: What do you mean? In the name of God tell me!
MESSENGER:—If these are your reasons for not going home.   100
OEDIPUS: I tell you, I fear the oracle may come true.
MESSENGER: And guilt may come upon you through your parents?
OEDIPUS: That is the dread that is always in my heart.
MESSENGER: Can you not see that all your fears are groundless?
OEDIPUS: How can you say that? They are my parents, surely?   105
MESSENGER: Polybos was not your father.
OEDIPUS: Not my father?
MESSENGER: No more your father than the man speaking to you.
OEDIPUS: But you are nothing to me!
MESSENGER: Neither was he.   110
OEDIPUS: Then why did he call me son?
MESSENGER: I will tell you:
     Long ago he had you from my hands, as a gift.
OEDIPUS: Then how could he love me so, if I was not his?
MESSENGER: He had no children, and his heart turned to you.   115
OEDIPUS: What of you? Did you buy me? Did you find me by chance?
MESSENGER: I came upon you in the crooked pass of Kithairon.
OEDIPUS: And what were you doing there?
MESSENGER: Tending my flocks.
OEDIPUS: A wandering shepherd?   120
MESSENGER: But your savior, son, that day.

OEDIPUS: From what did you save me?

MESSENGER: Your ankles should tell you that.

OEDIPUS: Ah, stranger, why do you speak of that childhood pain?

MESSENGER: I cut the bonds that tied your ankles together. 125

OEDIPUS: I have had the mark as long as I can remember.

MESSENGER: That was why you were given the name you bear.

OEDIPUS: God! Was it my father or my mother who did it?
    Tell me!

MESSENGER: I do not know. The man who gave you to me 130
    Can tell you better than I.

OEDIPUS: It was not you that found me, but another?

MESSENGER: It was another shepherd gave you to me.

OEDIPUS: Who was he? Can you tell me who he was?

MESSENGER: I think he was said to be one of Laïos' people. 135

OEDIPUS: You mean the Laïos who was king here years ago?

MESSENGER: Yes; King Laïos; and the man was one of his herdsmen.

OEDIPUS: Is he still alive? Can I see him?

MESSENGER: These men here
    Know best about such things. 140

OEDIPUS: Does anyone here
    Know this shepherd that he is talking about?
    Have you seen him in the fields, or in the town?
    If you have, tell me. It is time things were made plain.

CHORAGOS: I think the man he means is that same shepherd 145
    You have already asked to see. Iocastê perhaps
    Could tell you something.

OEDIPUS: Do you know anything
    About him, Lady? Is he the man we have summoned?
    Is that the man this shepherd means? 150

IOCASTÊ: Why think of him?
    Forget this herdsman. Forget it all.
    This talk is a waste of time.

OEDIPUS: How can you say that?
    When the clues to my true birth are in my hands? 155

IOCASTÊ: For God's love, let us have no more questioning!
    Is your life nothing to you?
    My own is pain enough for me to bear.

OEDIPUS: You need not worry. Suppose my mother a slave,
    And born of slaves: no baseness can touch you. 160

IOCASTÊ: Listen to me, I beg you: do not do this thing!

OEDIPUS: I will not listen; the truth must be made known.

IOCASTÊ: Everything that I say is for your own good!

OEDIPUS: My own good
    Snaps my patience, then; I want none of it. 165

IOCASTÊ: You are fatally wrong! May you never learn who you are!

OEDIPUS: Go, one of you, and bring the shepherd here.
    Let us leave this woman to brag of her royal name.

IOCASTÊ: Ah, miserable!
    That is the only word I have for you now. 170
    That is the only word I can ever have.

[*Exit into the palace.*]

CHORAGOS: Why has she left us, Oedipus? Why has she gone
    In such a passion of sorrow? I fear this silence:
    Something dreadful may come of it.
OEDIPUS: Let it come!   175
    However base my birth, I must know about it.
    The Queen, like a woman, is perhaps ashamed
    To think of my low origin. But I
    Am a child of Luck; I can not be dishonored.
    Luck is my mother; the passing months, my brothers,   180
    Have seen me rich and poor.
                       If this is so,
    How could I wish that I were someone else?
    How could I not be glad to know my birth?

ODE III

CHORUS: If ever the coming time were known   [STROPHE 1]   185
    To my heart's pondering,
    Kithairon, now by Heaven I see the torches
    At the festival of the next full moon,
    And see the dance, and hear the choir sing
    A grace to your gentle shade: 190
    Mountain where Oedipus was found,
    O mountain guard of a noble race!
    May the god who heals us lend his aid,
    And let that glory come to pass   195
    For our king's cradling-ground.

    Of the nymphs that flower beyond the years,   [ANTISTROPHE 1]
    Who bore you, royal child,
    To Pan of the hills or the timberline, Apollo,
    Cold in delight where the upland clears,
    Or Hermês for whom Kyllenê's heights are piled?   200
    Or flushed as evening cloud,
    Great Dionysos, roamer of mountains,
    He—was it he who found you there,
    And caught you up in his own proud
    Arms from the sweet god-ravisher   205
    Who laughed by the Muses' fountains?

SCENE IV

OEDIPUS: Sirs: though I do not know the man,
    I think I see him coming, this shepherd we want:
    He is old, like our friend here, and the men

Bringing him seem to be servants of my house.
But you can tell, if you have ever seen him. 5

[*Enter* SHEPHERD *escorted by servants.*]

CHORAGOS: I know him, he was Laïos' man. You can trust him.
OEDIPUS: Tell me first, you from Corinth: is this the shepherd
    We were discussing?
MESSENGER: This is the very man.
OEDIPUS: [*to* SHEPHERD] Come here. No, look at me. You must answer 10
    Everything I ask.—You belonged to Laïos?
SHEPHERD: Yes: born his slave, brought up in his house.
OEDIPUS: Tell me: what kind of work did you do for him?
SHEPHERD: I was a shepherd of his, most of my life.
OEDIPUS: Where mainly did you go for pasturage? 15
SHEPHERD: Sometimes Kithairon, sometimes the hills nearby.
OEDIPUS: Do you remember ever seeing this man out there?
SHEPHERD: What would he be doing there? This man?
OEDIPUS: This man standing here. Have you ever seen him before?
SHEPHERD: No. At least, not to my recollection. 20
MESSENGER: And that is not strange, my lord. But I'll refresh
    His memory: he must remember when we two
    Spent three whole seasons together, March to September,
    On Kithairon or thereabouts. He had two flocks;
    I had one. Each autumn I'd drive mine home 25
    And he would go back with his to Laïos' sheepfold.—
    Is this not true, just as I have described it?
SHEPHERD: True, yes; but it was all so long ago.
MESSENGER: Well, then: do you remember, back in those days,
    That you gave me a baby boy to bring up as my own? 30
SHEPHERD: What if I did? What are you trying to say?
MESSENGER: King Oedipus was once that little child.
SHEPHERD: Damn you, hold your tongue!
OEDIPUS: No more of that!
    It is your tongue needs watching, not this man's. 35
SHEPHERD: My King, my Master, what is it I have done wrong?
OEDIPUS: You have not answered his question about the boy.
SHEPHERD: He does not know. . .He is only making trouble. . .
OEDIPUS: Come, speak plainly, or it will go hard with you.
SHEPHERD: In God's name, do not torture an old man! 40
OEDIPUS: Come here, one of you; bind his arms behind him.
SHEPHERD: Unhappy king! What more do you wish to learn?
OEDIPUS: Did you give this man the child he speaks of?
SHEPHERD: I did.
    And I would to God I had died that very day. 45
OEDIPUS: You will die now unless you speak the truth.
SHEPHERD: Yet if I speak the truth, I am worse than dead.
OEDIPUS: Very well; since you insist upon delaying—
SHEPHERD: No! I have told you already that I gave him the boy.
OEDIPUS: Where did you get him? From your house? From somewhere else? 50

SHEPHERD: Not from mine, no. A man gave him to me.
OEDIPUS: Is that man here? Do you know whose slave he was?
SHEPHERD: For God's love, my King, do not ask me any more!
OEDIPUS: You are a dead man if I have to ask you again.
SHEPHERD: Then. . . Then the child was from the palace of Laïos. 55
OEDIPUS: A slave child? or a child of his own line?
SHEPHERD: Ah, I am on the brink of dreadful speech!
OEDIPUS: And I of dreadful hearing. Yet I must hear.
SHEPHERD: If you must be told, then. . .

                 They said it was Laïos' child; 60
    But it is your wife who can tell you about that.
OEDIPUS: My wife!—Did she give it to you?
SHEPHERD: My lord, she did.
OEDIPUS: Do you know why?
SHEPHERD: I was told to get rid of it. 65
OEDIPUS: An unspeakable mother!
SHEPHERD: There had been prophecies. . .
OEDIPUS: Tell me.
SHEPHERD: It was said that the boy would kill his own father.
OEDIPUS: Then why did you give him over to this old man? 70
SHEPHERD: I pitied the baby, my King.
    And I thought that this man would take him far away
    To his own country.
              He saved him—but for what a fate!
    For if you are what this man says you are, 75
    No man living is more wretched than Oedipus.
OEDIPUS: Ah God!
    It was true!
        All the prophecies!
              —Now, 80
    O, Light, may I look on you for the last time!
    I, Oedipus,
    Oedipus, damned in his birth, in his marriage damned,
    Damned in the blood he shed with his own hand!

    [*He rushes into the palace.*]

ODE IV

CHORUS: Alas for the seed of men.   [STROPHE 1] 85
    What measure shall I give these generations
    That breathe on the void and are void
    And exist and do not exist?

    Who bears more weight of joy
    Than mass of sunlight shifting in images, 90
    Or who shall make his thought stay on
    That down time drifts away?

Your splendor is all fallen.

O naked brow of wrath and tears,
O change of Oedipus!   95
I who saw your days call no man blest—
Your great days like ghosts gone.
That mind was a strong bow.   [ANTISTROPHE I]

Deep, how deep you drew it then, hard archer,
At a dim fearful range,   100
And brought dear glory down!

You overcame the stranger—
The virgin with her hooking lion claws—
And though death sang, stood like a tower
To make pale Thebes take heart.   105

Fortress against our sorrow!

True king, giver of laws,
Majestic Oedipus!
No prince in Thebes had ever such renown,
No prince won such grace of power.   110

And now of all men ever known   [STROPHE 2]
Most pitiful is this man's story:
His fortunes are most changed, his state
Fallen to a low slave's
Ground under bitter fate.   115

O Oedipus, most royal one!
The great door that expelled you to the light
Gave at night—ah, gave night to your glory:
As to the father, to the fathering son.

All understood too late.   120

How could that queen whom Laïos won,
The garden that he harrowed at his height,
Be silent when that act was done?

But all eyes fail before time's eye,   [ANTISTROPHE 2]
All actions come to justice there.   125
Though never willed, though far down the deep past,
Your bed, your dread sirings,
Are brought to book at last.
Child by Laïos doomed to die,
Then doomed to lose that fortunate little death,   130
Would God you never took breath in this air
That with my wailing lips I take to cry:
For I weep the world's outcast.

I was blind, and now I can tell why:
Asleep, for you had given ease of breath   135
To Thebes, while the false years went by.

ÈXODUS

SECOND MESSENGER: Elders of Thebes, most honored in this land,
What horrors are yours to see and hear, what weight
Of sorrow to be endured, if, true to your birth,
You venerate the line of Labdakos!   140
I think neither Istros nor Phasis, those great rivers,
Could purify this place of the corruption
It shelters now, or soon must bring to light—
Evil not done unconsciously, but willed.

The greatest griefs are those we cause ourselves.   145
CHORAGOS: Surely, friend, we have grief enough already;
What new sorrow do you mean?
SECOND MESSENGER: The Queen is dead.
CHORAGOS: Iocastê? Dead? But at whose hand?
SECOND MESSENGER: Her own.   150
The full horror of what happened you can not know,
For you did not see it; but I, who did, will tell you
As clearly as I can how she met her death.

When she had left us,
In passionate silence, passing through the court,   155
She ran to her apartment in the house,
Her hair clutched by the fingers of both hands.
She closed the doors behind her; then, by that bed
Where long ago the fatal son was conceived—
That son who should bring about his father's death—   160
We hear her call upon Laïos, dead so many years,
And heard her wail for the double fruit of her marriage,
A husband by her husband, children by her child.

Exactly how she died I do not know:
For Oedipus burst in moaning and would not let us   165
Keep vigil to the end: it was by him
As he stormed about the room that our eyes were caught.
From one to another of us he went, begging a sword,
Cursing the wife who was not his wife, the mother
Whose womb had carried his own children and himself.   170
I do not know: it was none of us aided him,
But surely one of the gods was in control!
For with a dreadful cry
He hurled his weight, as though wrenched out of himself,
At the twin doors: the bolts gave, and he rushed in.   175
And there we saw her hanging, her body swaying

From the cruel cord she had noosed about her neck.
A great sob broke from him, heartbreaking to hear,
As he loosed the rope and lowered her to the ground.

I would blot out from my mind what happened next! 180
For the King ripped from her gown the golden brooches
That were her ornament, and raised them, and lunged them down
Straight into his own eyeballs, crying, "No more,
No more shall you look on the misery about me,
The horrors of my own doing! Too long you have known 185
The faces of those whom I should never have seen,
Too long been blind to those for whom I was searching!
From this hour, go in darkness!" And as he spoke,
He struck at his eyes—not once, but many times;
And the blood spattered his beard, 190
Bursting from his ruined sockets like red hail.

So from the unhappiness of two this evil has sprung,
A curse on the man and woman alike. The old
Happiness of the house of Labdakos
Was happiness enough: where is it today? 195
It is all wailing and ruin, disgrace, death—all
The misery of mankind that has a name—
And it is wholly and for ever theirs.
CHORAGOS: Is he in agony still? Is there no rest for him?
SECOND MESSENGER: He is calling for someone to lead him to the gates 200
So that all the children of Kadmos may look upon
His father's murderer, his mother's—no,
I can not say it!
                    And then he will leave Thebes,
Self-exiled, in order that the curse 205
Which he himself pronounced may depart from the house.
He is weak, and there is none to lead him,
So terrible is his suffering.
                    But you will see:
Look, the doors are opening; in a moment 210
You will see a thing that would crush a heart of stone.

[*The central door is opened;* OEDIPUS, *blinded, is led in.*]

CHORAGOS: Dreadful indeed for men to see.
Never have my own eyes
Looked on a sight so full of fear.

Oedipus! 215
What madness came upon you, what daemon
Leaped on your life with heavier
Punishment than a mortal man can bear?
No: I can not even
Look at you, poor ruined one. 220
And I would speak, question, ponder,

If I were able. No.
You make me shudder.
OEDIPUS: God. God.
    Is there a sorrow greater? 225
    Where shall I find harbor in this world?
    My voice is hurled far on a dark wind.
    What has God done to me?
CHORAGOS: Too terrible to think of, or to see.
OEDIPUS: O cloud of night,   [STROPHE 1] 230
    Never to be turned away: night coming on,
    I can not tell how: night like a shroud!
    My fair winds brought me here.
                    O God. Again
    The pain of the spikes where I had sight, 235
    The flooding pain
    Of memory, never to be gouged out.
CHORAGOS: This is not strange.
    You suffer it all twice over, remorse in pain,
    Pain in remorse. 240
OEDIPUS: Ah dear friend   [ANTISTROPHE 1]
    Are you faithful even yet, you alone?
    Are you still standing near me, will you stay here,
    Patient, to care for the blind?
                 The blind man! 245
    Yet even blind I know who it is attends me,
    By the voice's tone—
    Though my new darkness hide the comforter.
CHORAGOS: Oh fearful act!
    What god was it drove you to rake black 250
    Night across your eyes?
OEDIPUS: Apollo. Apollo. Dear   [STROPHE 2]
    Children, the god was Apollo.
    He brought my sick, sick fate upon me.
    But the blinding hand was my own! 255
    How could I bear to see
    When all my sight was horror everywhere?
CHORAGOS: Everywhere; that is true.
OEDIPUS: And now what is left?
    Images? Love? A greeting even, 260
    Sweet to the senses? Is there anything?
    Ah, no, friends: lead me away.
    Lead me away from Thebes.
                 Lead the great wreck
    And hell of Oedipus, whom the gods hate. 265
CHORAGOS: Your fate is clear, you are not blind to that.
    Would God you had never found it out!
OEDIPUS: Death take the man who unbound   [ANTISTROPHE 2]
    My feet on that hillside
    And delivered me from death to life! What life? 270
    If only I had died,

This weight of monstrous doom
Could not have dragged me and my darlings down.
CHORAGOS: I would have wished the same.
OEDIPUS: Oh never to have come here   275
    With my father's blood upon me! Never
    To have been the man they call his mother's husband!
    Oh accurst! Oh child of evil,
    To have entered that wretched bed—
                      the selfsame one!   280
    More primal than sin itself, this fell to me.
CHORAGOS: I do not know how I can answer you.
    You were better dead than alive and blind.
OEDIPUS: Do not counsel me any more. This punishment
    That I have laid upon myself is just.   285
    If I had eyes,
    I do not know how I could bear the sight
    Of my father, when I came to the house of Death,
    Or my mother: for I have sinned against them both
    So vilely that I could not make my peace   290
    By strangling my own life.
                  Or do you think my children,
    Born as they were born, would be sweet to my eyes?
    Ah never, never! Nor this town with its high walls,
    Nor the holy images of the gods.   295
            For I,
    Thrice miserable!—Oedipus, noblest of all the line
    Of Kadmos, have condemned myself to enjoy
    These things no more, by my own malediction
    Expelling that man whom the gods declared   300
    To be a defilement in the house of Laïos.
    After exposing the rankness of my own guilt,
    How could I look men frankly in the eyes?
    No, I swear it,
    If I could have stifled my hearing at its source,   305
    I would have done it and made all this body
    A tight cell of misery, blank to light and sound:
    So I should have been safe in a dark agony
    Beyond all recollection.
                Ah Kithairon!   310
    Why did you shelter me? When I was cast upon you,
    Why did I not die? Then I should never
    Have shown the world my execrable birth.

    Ah Polybos! Corinth, city that I believed
    The ancient seat of my ancestors: how fair   315
    I seemed, your child! And all the while this evil
    Was cancerous within me!
              For I am sick
    In my daily life, sick in my origin.

    O three roads, dark ravine, woodland and way   320

Where three roads met: you, drinking my father's blood,
My own blood, spilled by my own hand: can you remember
The unspeakable things I did there, and the things
I went on from there to do?

O marriage, marriage! 325
The act that engendered me, and again the act
Performed by the son in the same bed—

Ah, the net
Of incest, mingling fathers, brothers, sons,
With brides, wives, mothers: the last evil 330
That can be known by men: no tongue can say
How evil!

No. For the love of God, conceal me
Somewhere far from Thebes; or kill me; or hurl me
Into the sea, away from men's eyes for ever. 335

Come, lead me. You need not fear to touch me.
Of all men, I alone can bear this guilt.

[*Enter* CREON.]

CHORAGOS: We are not the ones to decide; but Creon here
May fitly judge of what you ask. He only
Is left to protect the city in your place. 340
OEDIPUS: Alas, how can I speak to him? What right have I
To beg his courtesy whom I have deeply wronged?
CREON: I have not come to mock you, Oedipus,
Or to reproach you either.

[*To* ATTENDANTS:]—You, standing there: 345
If you have lost all respect for man's dignity,
At least respect the flame of Lord Helios:
Do not allow this pollution to show itself
Openly here, an affront to the earth
And Heaven's rain and the light of day. No, take him 350
Into the house as quickly as you can.
For it is proper
That only the close kindred see his grief.
OEDIPUS: I pray you in God's name, since your courtesy
Ignores my dark expectation, visiting 355
With mercy this man of all men most execrable:
Give me what I ask—for your good, not for mine.
CREON: And what is it that you would have me do?
OEDIPUS: Drive me out of this country as quickly as may be
To a place where no human voice can ever greet me. 360
CREON: I should have done that before now—only,
God's will had not been wholly revealed to me.
OEDIPUS: But his command is plain: the parricide
Must be destroyed. I am that evil man.
CREON: That is the sense of it, yes; but as things are, 365
We had best discover clearly what is to be done.
OEDIPUS: You would learn more about a man like me?
CREON: You are ready now to listen to the god.

OEDIPUS: I will listen. But it is to you 370
    That I must turn for help. I beg you, hear me.
    The woman in there—
    Give her whatever funeral you think proper:
    She is your sister.
              —But let me go, Creon!
    Let me purge my father's Thebes of the pollution 375
    Of my living here, and go out to the wild hills,
    To Kithairon, that has won such fame with me,
    The tomb my mother and father appointed for me,
    And let me die there, as they willed I should.
    And yet I know 380
    Death will not ever come to me through sickness
    Or in any natural way: I have been preserved
    For some unthinkable fate. But let that be.

    As for my sons, you need not care for them.
    They are men, they will find some way to live. 385
    But my poor daughters, who have shared my table,
    Who never before have been parted from their father—
    Take care of them. Creon; do this for me.
    And will you let me touch them with my hands
    A last time, and let us weep together? 390
    Be kind, my lord.
    Great prince, be kind!
              Could I but touch them,
    They would be mine again, as when I had my eyes.

    [*Enter* ANTIGONE *and* ISMENE, *attended.*]

    Ah, God! 395
    Is it my dearest children I hear weeping?
    Has Creon pitied me and sent my daughters?
CREON: Yes, Oedipus: I knew that they were dear to you
    In the old days, and know you must love them still.
OEDIPUS: May God bless you for this—and be a friendlier 400
    Guardian to you than he has been to me!
    Children, where are you?
    Come quickly to my hands: they are your brother's—
    Hands that have brought your father's once clear eyes
    To this way of seeing— 405
              Ah dearest ones,
    I had neither sight nor knowledge then, your father
    By the woman who was the source of his own life!
    And I weep for you—having no strength to see you—
    I weep for you when I think of the bitterness 410
    That men will visit upon you all your lives.
    What homes, what festivals can you attend
    Without being forced to depart again in tears?
    And when you come to marriageable age,
    Where is the man, my daughters, who would dare 415

Risk the bane that lies on all my children?
Is there any evil wanting? Your father killed
His father; sowed the womb of her who bore him;
Engendered you at the fount of his own existence!
That is what they will say of you   420
                                        Then, whom
Can you ever marry? There are no bridegrooms for you,
And your lives must wither away in sterile dreaming.

O Creon, son of Menoikeus!
You are the only father my daughters have,   425
Since we, their parents, are both of us gone for ever.
They are your own blood: you will not let them
Fall into beggary and loneliness;
You will keep them from the miseries that are mine!
Take pity on them; see, they are only children,   430
Friendless except for you. Promise me this,
Great Prince, and give me your hand in token of it.

    [**CREON** *clasps his right hand.*]

    Children:
I could say much, if you could understand me,
But as it is, I have only this prayer for you: 435
Live where you can, be as happy as you can—
Happier, please God, than God has made your father!
CREON: Enough. You have wept enough. Now go within.
OEDIPUS: I must; but it is hard.
CREON: Time eases all things.   440
OEDIPUS: But you must promise—
CREON: Say what you desire.
OEDIPUS: Send me from Thebes!
CREON: God grant that I may!
OEDIPUS: But since God hates me. . .   445
CREON: No, he will grant your wish.
OEDIPUS: You promise?
CREON: I can not speak beyond my knowledge.
OEDIPUS: Then lead me in.
CREON: Come now, and leave your children.   450
OEDIPUS: No! Do not take them from me!
CREON: Think no longer
That you are in command here, but rather think
How, when you were, you served your own destruction.

    [*Exeunt into the house all but the* **CHORUS**; *the* **CHORAGOS** *chants directly to the audience:*]

CHORAGOS: Men of Thebes: look upon Oedipus.   455

This is the king who solved the famous riddle
And towered up, most powerful of men.

No mortal eyes but looked on him with envy,
Yet in the end ruin swept over him.

Let every man in mankind's frailty   460
Consider his last day; and let none
Presume on his good fortune until he find
Life, at his death, a memory without pain.

The Shrine in the Fields
(15th Century)

THE SHRINE IN THE FIELDS represents one of the five basic types of Noh plays. A "woman play," it is based on episodes from a famous Japanese novel, *The Tale of Genji*, in which Lord Genji is the lover of Lady Rokujo (the protagonist of *The Shrine in the Fields*) but after a time neglects her. At a festival, attendants on Lord Genji's wife publicly humiliate Lady Rokujo by pushing her carriage out of the procession and disabling it. Lady Rokujo then leaves the capital and goes to Nonomiya, where her daughter is being prepared to become priestess of Ise (the Sun Goddess). While at Nonomiya, Lady Rokujo is visited by Lord Genji, who begs her to return to him. Although she refuses, her love and humiliation keep drawing her back to Nonomiya even after her death.

The major influence on Noh is Zen Buddhism, which teaches that ultimate peace comes from overcoming individual desire in order to achieve union with all being. The protagonists of Noh are ghosts, demons, or obsessed humans whose souls cannot find rest because in life they became too devoted to love, honor, or other goals that pull them back into the physical world.

In Noh, each play occurs in a specific season of the year, and the mood throughout must be in keeping with that season. In this play, the season is autumn. The introductory scene drastically compresses time and place: the itinerant priest (the *waki*) travels almost instantaneously from the capital to Nonomiya. The ghost of Lady Rokujo (in the guise of a village girl) appears and, as the priest questions her, it becomes apparent that she is protecting some secret. Later she returns as herself, the Miyasudokoro (Lady Rokujo) of long ago. As she tells her story, the emotion builds until, as in all Noh plays, it finds expression in a dance. In the final scene, the pull between this and the next world are fully symbolized by passing back and forth through the gate of the shrine. At the end, the freeing of the soul is indicated by rushing out of the "burning house," an image for the world, which, in Buddhist teaching, enlightened persons are counseled to flee as willingly as they would a burning building. Thus, at the end, we are asked to believe that Miyasudokoro has broken her attachment to the world. Overall, *The Shrine in the Fields* does not seek to tell a story or to develop a character so much as to capture a particular mood, to distill a powerful emotion, and to express an attitude about the physical world and human existence.

The Shrine in the Fields (Nonomiya), from *Twenty Plays for the Nō Theatre*, edited by Donald Keene and translated by Paul Varley, © 1970. Reprinted by permission of Columbia University Press.

The Shrine in the Fields (15th Century)

TRANSLATED BY H. PAUL VARLEY

Persons

A TRAVELING PRIEST
A VILLAGE GIRL
MIYASUDOKORO

PLACE————*Sagano in Yamashiro Province*

TIME————*Late autumn, the seventh day of the ninth month*

> [*The stage assistant places a* torii *at the front of the stage. To either upright of the* torii *are attached short sections of fence made of brushwood twigs. The* PRIEST *enters. He carries a rosary in his hand. He stands at the naming-place.*]

PRIEST

I am an itinerant priest. Recently I have been staying in the Capital, where I have visited all the famous sites and relics of the past. Autumn is nearing its close and Sagano will be lovely now. I think I shall go there for a visit. [*He turns towards the* torii, *indicating that he has already arrived in Sagano.*] When I asked people about this wood they told me it is the ancient site of the Shrine in the Fields. I would like   5 to visit the place, though I am no more than a passing stranger.

> [*He advances to stage center, still facing the* torii.]

I enter the wood and I see
A rustic log *torii*
And a fence of brushwood twigs.
Surely nothing has changed from the past!   10
But why should time have spared this place?
Be that as it may, how lucky I am
To have come at this lovely time of year
And be able to worship at such a place.

> [*He kneels and presses his palms together.*]

The Great Shrine at Ise   15
Makes no distinction
Between gods and Buddhas:
The teachings of the Buddhist Law
Have guided me straight along the path,
And I have arrived at the Shrine.   20
My heart is pure in the evening light,
Pure in the clear evening light!

> [*The* GIRL *enters. She wears the* fukai *mask and carries a branch of* sakaki. *She stands at the* shite-*position and faces the musicians.*]

GIRL

Shrine in the Fields
Where I have lived with flowers;
Shrine in the Fields   25
Where I have lived with flowers—
What will be left when autumn has passed?

> [*She faces front.*]

Now lonely autumn ends,
But still my sleeves
Wilt in a dew of tears;   30
The dusk racks my body,
And my heart of itself
Takes on the fading colors
Of the thousand flowers;
It withers, as all things, with neglect.   35
Each year on this day,
Unknown to anyone else,
I return to the old remains.
In the wood at the Shrine in the Fields
Autumn has drawn to a close   40
And the harsh winds blow;
Colors so brilliant
They pierced the senses
Have faded and vanished;
What remains now to recal   45
The memories of the past
What use was it to come here?

> [*She takes a few steps to her right, then faces front.*]

Ahh—how I loathe the attachment
That makes me go back and forth,
Again and again on my journey   50
To this meaningless, fugitive world.

> [*The* PRIEST *rises and faces her.*]

PRIEST

As I was resting in the shade of the trees, thinking about the past and refreshing my mind, a charming young lady has suddenly appeared. Please tell me who you are.

GIRL

It would be appropriate if I had asked who you are. This is Nonomiya, the Shrine
in the Fields, where in ancient days the virgin designated as the Priestess of Ise was   55
temporarily lodged. The custom has fallen into disuse, but today, the seventh day of
the ninth month, is still a time for recalling the past. Each year, unknown to anyone
else, I come to sweep the shrine and to perform a service. I do not know where you
have come from, but your presence here is an intrusion. Please leave at once.

[*She takes two steps towards the* PRIEST.]

PRIEST

No, no. There can be no objection to my being here. I am only a wandering priest   60
who has renounced the uncertain world. But tell me, why should you return here,
to these old ruins, on this particular day each year in search of the past?

GIRL

This is the day when Genji the Shining One visited this place, the seventh day of
the ninth month. He brought with him a twig of *sakaki* and pushed it through the
sacred
fence. Miyasudokoro at once composed this poem: 65
"This sacred enclosure
Has no cypress to mark the spot;[1]
By some error you have picked
A twig of *sakaki* wood."
It happened on this day!   70

PRIEST

That was truly a worthy poem.[2]
—And the *sakaki* branch
You hold in your hand
Is the same color it was in the past.

GIRL

The same color as in the past?   75
How clever to put it that way!
Only the *sakaki* stays green forever,
And in its unvarying shade

PRIEST

On the pathways through the wood,
The autumn deepens   80

GIRL

And leaves turn crimson only to scatter.

PRIEST

In the weed-grown fields

[*She goes to the* torii *and places the* sakaki *branch there. The* PRIEST *kneels.*]

CHORUS

The stalks and leaf tips wither;
Nonomiya, the Shrine in the Fields,
Stands amidst the desolation   85

---

[1] Evergreen is associated with enduring love and devotion.
[2] The poem quoted is from *The Tale of Genji*, where it seems to mean that the visitor has come without invitation, pretending to have been invited.

Of withered stalks and leaves
The seventh day of the ninth month
Has returned again today
To this place of memories.

[*She moves to center stage.*]

How fragile it seemed at the time,   90
This little fence of brushwood twigs.

[*She gazes at the fence.*]

And the house that looked so temporary
Has now become the guardian's hut.

[*She turns towards the gazing-pillar.*]

A dim glow shines from inside:
I wonder if the longing within me   95
Reveals itself outwardly?
How lonely a place is this shrine,
How lonely a place is this palace!

PRIEST
    Please tell me more of the story of Miyasudokoro.

[*The* GIRL *kneels at center stage.*]

CHORUS
    The lady known as Miyasudokoro   100
    Became the wife of the former Crown Prince,
    The brother of Kiritsubo's Emperor,[3]
    A man at the height of his glory;
    They were like the color and perfume
    Of the same flower, indissolubly bound.   105
GIRL
    They knew, of course, the truth
    That those who must meet part—
CHORUS
    Why should it have surprised them?
    But it came so soon—like a nightmare—
    His death that left her alone.   110
GIRL
    She could not remain in that state,
    Helpless and given to tears;
CHORUS
    Soon Genji the Shining One
    Imposed his love and began
    Their clandestine meetings.   115
GIRL
    How did their love affair end?

---

[3] Kiritsubo was Genji's mother.

CHORUS

> And why, after they separated,
> Did his love never turn to hate?
> With customary tenderness
> He made his way through the fields 120
> To distant Nonomiya.
> The autumn flowers had all withered,
> The voices of insects were sparse.
> Oh, the loneliness of that journey!
> Even the wind echoing in the pines 125
> Reminded him there is no end
> To the sadness of autumn.
> So the Prince visited her,
> And with the deepest affection
> Spoke his love in many ways; 130
> How noble and sensitive a man!

GIRL

> Later, by the Katsura River,
> She performs cleansing rite,

CHORUS

> Setting the white-wrapped branches[4]
> Adrift on the river waves; 135
> Herself like a drifting weed,
> No roots or destination,
> She moved at the water's will.
> "Through the waves of the eighty rapids
> Of Suzuki River to Ise, 140
> Who will worry if the waves wet me or no?"
> She wrote this poem to describe her journey.
> Never before had a mother
> Escorted her daughter, the Virgin,
> All the way to the Také Palace.[5] 145
> Mother and daughter on the way
> Felt only the bitterness of regret.

> [*for* PRIEST]

> Now that I have heard your tale,
> I am sure that you are no ordinary woman.
> Please tell me your name. 150

GIRL

> Revealing my name
> Would serve no purpose;
> In my helplessness
> I am ashamed of myself.
> Sooner or later 155
> My name will be known,

---

[4] Streamers of paper or mulberry bark were inscribed with prayers and attached to *sakaki* branches, then tossed into the stream.
[5] The Virgin resided at Ise in the Také Palace.

It can't be helped;
But now say a prayer for one nameless,
And not of this world.

CHORUS

[*for* PRIEST] Not of this world?   160
What strange words to hear!
Then, have you died and departed

GIRL

This world, long ago,
A name my only monument:

CHORUS

Miyasudokoro   165

GIRL

Is myself.

CHORUS

Autumn winds rise at dusk;

[*She stands.*]

Through the forest branches
The evening moonlight shines

[*She goes to the* shite-*position.*]

Dimly illuminating,   170
Under the trees,

[*She looks at the* torii.]

The rustic logs of the *torii*.
She passes between the two pillars
And vanishes without a trace;
She has vanished without a trace.   175

[*She slowly exits. A Villager then enters and performs the* kyōgen *interlude, a lengthy recapitulation of* MIYASUDOKORO'*s story. The* PRIEST *asks the Villager to tell what he knows, and then the two men agree that the* PRIEST *has just seen the ghost of* MIYASUDOKORO. *The* PRIEST *decides to stay and read the sutras and prayers for her. The Villager withdraws.*]

PRIEST

Alone I lie on the forest moss,
A sleeve of my robe spread beneath me—
Under forest trees, a mossy robe:
My mat is grass of the same color.[6]
Unfolding my memories   180
I shall offer prayers all night long;
I shall pray for her repose.

[*The* GIRL, *now revealed as* MIYASUDOKORO, *enters and stands at the* shite-*position.*]

---

[6] A priest's robe was frequently called *kokegoromo*, literally meaning "moss robe." Here it also refers to moss and autumn grass that is faded like the priest's robe.

MIYASUDOKORO

> In this carriage,
> Lovely as the autumn followers
> At Nonomiya,   185
> I too have returned to the past,
> To long ago.

PRIEST

> How strange!
> In the faint moonlight
> The soft sounds   190
> Of an approaching carriage,
> A courtly carriage
> With reed blinds hanging—
> A sight of unimagined beauty!
> It must be you, Miyasudokoro!   195
> But what is the carriage you ride in?

MIYASUDOKORO

> You ask me about my carriage?
> I remember now
> That scene of long ago—
> The Kamo Festival,   200
> The jostling carriages,
> No one could tell
> Who their owners were,
> But thick as dewdrops

PRIEST

> The splendid ranks crowded the place.   205

MIYASUDOKORO

> Pleasure carriages of every description,
> And one among them of special magnificence,
> The Princess Aoi's.

PRIEST

> "Make way for Her Highness's carriage!"
> The servants cried, clearing the crowd,   210
> And in the confusion

MIYASUDOKORO

> I answered, "My carriage is small,
> I have nowhere else to put it."
> I stood my ground,

PRIEST

> But around the carriage   215

MIYASUDOKORO

> Men suddenly swarmed.

> [*Her gestures suggest the actions described.*]

CHORUS

> Grasping the shafts,
> They pushed my carriage back
> Into the ranks of servants.
> My carriage had come for no purpose,   220

My pleasure gone,
And I knew my helplessness.
I realized now
That all that happened
Was surely retribution   225
For the sins of former lives.
Even now I am in agony:
Like the wheels of my carriage
I return again and again—
How long must I still keep returning?   230
I beg you, dispel this delusion!
I beg you, dispel this suffering!

[*She presses her palms together in supplication.*]

MIYASUDOKORO
Remembering the vanished days
I dance, waving at the moon
My flowerlike sleeves,   235
CHORUS
As if begging it to restore the past.

[*She goes to the* shite-*position and begins to dance. As her dance ends, the text resumes.*]

MIYASUDOKORO
Even the moon
At the Shrine in the Fields
Must remember the past;
CHORUS
Its light forlornly trickles   240
Through the leaves to the forest dew.
Through the leaves to the forest dew.
MIYASUDOKORO
This place, once my refuge,
This garden, still lingers
CHORUS
Unchanged from long ago,   245
MIYASUDOKORO
A beauty nowhere else,
CHORUS
Though transient, insubstantial
MIYASUDOKORO
As this little wooden fence
CHORUS
From which he used to brush the dew.

[*She brushes the fence with her fan.*]

I, whom he visited,   250
And he, my lover too,
The whole world turned to dreams,
To aging ruins;

Whom shall I pine for now?
The voices of the pine-crickets   255
Trill *rin, rin,*
The wind howls:

> [*She advances to stage front. She gazes at the* torii.]

How I remember
Nights at the Shrine in the Fields!

> [*Weeping, she withdraws to the area before the musicians and starts to dance. The text resumes when her dance has ended.*]

CHORUS

At this shrine we have always worshiped   260
The divine wind that blows from Ise,

> [*She goes before the* torii.]

The Inner and Outer Shrines.
As I pass to and fro through this *torii*
I seem to wander on the path of delusion:
I waver between life and death.   265

> [*She passes back and forth through the* torii.]

The gods will surely reject me!
Again she climbs in her carriage and rides out
The gate of the Burning House,
The gate of the Burning House.[7]

---

[7] The Burning House is an image for this world, which an enlightened person should flee as eagerly as from a burning house.

Noah and His Sons
(A.D. 1425–1450)

NOAH AND HIS SONS was presented at Wakefield (England), the third of the thirty-two short plays that together dramatized the biblical account of human existence from Creation to the Last Judgment. The entire cycle was presented outdoors during the Corpus Christi festival, a religious celebration of the sacrament of bread and wine (the body and blood of Christ), the union of the human and divine in the person of Christ, and the promise of redemption through His sacrifice.

The central feature of the Corpus Christi festival was a procession (which included representatives from every rank and profession) through the town with the consecrated bread and wine. This procession may have been the inspiration for the staging of the cycle: mounting plays on wagons and performing them at various stops along a processional route. Each play was assigned to a different trade guild that was then responsible for mounting and financing its play. The overall cycle was under the supervision of the town council, and the scripts had to be approved by the church.

Noah and His Sons is one of five plays identified as the work of the "Wakefield Master," works considered far superior to the other plays in the same cycle. *Noah* is noted in part for the variety achieved through the comic bickering of the title character and his wife. Unlike Latin liturgical drama (drama performed within the structure of a church service or liturgy), the Wakefield cycle was written in common English. The playwright, who may have remained anonymous rather than accept individual credit for a work written to promote the greater glory of God, invented scenes between Noah and his wife not present in the Bible. The play humanizes these biblical figures; we witness their arguments and hear each complain about the lot their sex is subjected to in married life. Noah's wife engages in everyday activities (she is busy spinning thread during their first scene together) and does not accept her husband's orders as unquestionable laws. Thus both the language of the play and the relationship between Noah and his wife make the play readily accessible to an English medieval audience.

The play is short (558 lines), made up of sixty-two stanzas of nine lines each. The structure of the stanzas suggests a formalized delivery by the performers. The play is divided into three parts of approximately equal length: the opening expository scene with God and Noah establishing justification for the flood; two scenes of bickering between Noah and his wife; and the scenes showing first the building of the ark and then the time on board. It is clear, entertaining, and didactic.

Noah and His Sons

EDITED BY OSCAR G. BROCKETT

Characters

NOAH
GOD
NOAH'S WIFE
FIRST SON
SECOND SON
THIRD SON
FIRST WIFE
SECOND WIFE
THIRD WIFE

Note: Many obsolete words have been retained so as not to alter unduly the rhyme scheme. The first four lines of each nine-line stanza use both end and midline rhymes; the fifth and ninth lines rhyme, as do lines six through eight. To clarify obsolete words, modern equivalents have been placed in brackets immediately following the words they clarify.

NOAH: Mightful god veray [truly], Maker of all that is,
 Three persons, none say nay, one god in endless bliss,
 Thou made both night and day, beast, fowl, and fish,
 All creatures that live may, wrought thou at thy wish,
  As thou well might;   5
 The sun, the moon, verament [truly],
 Thou made; the firmament,
 The stars also, full fervent,
  To shine thou made full bright.

 Angels thou made full even, all orders that is,   10
 To have the bliss in heaven. This did thou more and less,
 Full marvelous to neven [tell]; yet was there unkindness,
 More by folds seven than I can well express;
  For why?
 Of all angels in brightness   15
 God gave Lucifer most lightness,
 Yet proudly he fled his dais,
  And set him even Him by.
 He thought himself as worthy as Him that him made;
 In brightness, in beauty, therefore God did him degrade; 20

Put him in a low degree soon after, in a brade [minute],
Him and all his menye [minions], where he may be unglad
  For ever.
Shall they never win away,
Hence unto doomsday,
But burn in hell for aye,
  Shall they depart never.

Soon after, that gracious lord in His likeness made man,
That place to be restored, even as he began,
Of the Trinity by accord, Adam and Eve, that woman,
To multiply without discord, in paradise put He them,
  And sayeth to both
Gave in commandment,
On the tree of life to lay no hand;
But yet the false fiend
  Made Him with man wroth,

Enticed man to gluttony, stirred him to sin in pride;
But in paradise securely might no sin abide,
And therefore man full hastily was put out, in that tide [time],
In woe and wretchedness for to be, in pains full cried,
  To know,
First on earth, and then in hell
With fiends for to dwell,
But He his mercy mell [dispenses]
  To those that will Him trow [swear allegiance].

Oil of mercy He has hight [promised], as I have heard said,
To every living wight that would love Him and dread;
But now before His sight every living leyde [person],
Most party day and night, sin in word and deed
  Full bold;
Some in pride, ire, and envy,
Some in covetousness and gluttony,
Some in sloth and lechery,
  And otherwise manifold.

Therefore I dread lest God on us will take vengeance
For sin is now allowed without any repentance;
Six hundred years and odd have I, without distance [dispute],
On earth, as any sod, lived with great grievance
  Always;
And now I wax old,
Sick, sorry, and cold,
As muck upon mold
  I wither away;

But yet will I cry for mercy and call;
Noah thy servant, am I, Lord over all!
Lest me and my fry shall also fall;

25

30

35

40

45

50

55

60

65

Save from villainy and bring to Thy hall
  In heaven;
And keep me from sin,
This world within;   70
Comely king of mankind,
  I pray Thee, hear my stevyn [voice]!

    [GOD *appears above.*]

GOD: Since I have made all thing that is liffand [living],
Duke, emperor, and king, with mine own hand,
For to have their liking by sea and by sand,   75
Every man to my bidding should be bound
  Full fervent;
That made man such a creature,
Fairest of favor,
Man must love me par-amour,   80
  By reason, and repent.

Methought I showed man love when I made him to be
All angels above, like to the Trinity;
And now in great reproof full low lies he,
On earth himself to stuff with sin that displeases me   85
  Most of all;
Vengeance will I take,
In earth for sin's sake,
My anger thus will I wake,
  Both of great and small.   90

I repent full sore that ever I made man,
By me he sets no store, and I am his sovereign;
I will destroy, therefore, both beast, man and woman,
All shall perish, less and more; that bargain may they ban [regret],
  That ill has done.   95
In earth I see right naught
But sin that is unsought [unrepented];
Of those that well has wrought
  Find I almost none.

Therefore shall I undo [destroy] all this middle erd [earth]   100
With floods that shall flow and run with hideous rerd [noise];
I have good cause thereto: of me no man is afeard,
As I say, shall I do: of vengeance draw my sword,
  And make end
Of all that bears life,   105
Save Noah and his wife,
For they would never strive
  With me nor me offend.

To him to great win [joy] hastily will I go,
To Noah my servant, ere I blyn [stop] to warn him of his woe.   110
In earth I see but sin running to and fro,

Among both more and min [less], each the other's foe;
  With all their intent;
They shall I forego [destroy]
With floods that shall flow,   115
I shall work them woe,
  That will not repent.

    [GOD *descends and comes to* NOAH.]

GOD: Noah, my friend, I thee command, from cares thee dispel,
  A ship I do demand of nail and board full well.
  Thou was e'er a trusty man, to me true as steel,   120
  To my bidding obedient; friendship shall thou feel
    To mede [in reward].
  Of length thy ship be
  Three hundred cubits, warn I thee,
  Of height even thirty,   125
    Of fifty also in brede [breadth].

Anoint thy ship with pitch and tar without and also within,
The water out to spar [keep] this is a helpful gyn [means];
Look no man thee mar. Three tiers of chambers begin,
Thou must spend many a spar, this work ere thou win   130
  To end fully.
Make in thy ship also,
Parlors one or two,
And other houses mo [more],
  For beasts that there must be.   135

One cubit in height a window shall thou make;
On the side a doore with slyght [skill] beneath shall thou take;
With thee shall no man fight, nor do thee any kind of hate.
When all is done thus right, thy wife, that is thy mate,
  Take in to thee;   140
Thy sons of good fame,
Shem, Japhet, and Ham,
Take in also them,
  Their wives also three.

For all shall be undone [destroyed] that live on land but ye,   145
With floods that from above shall fall, and that plentily;
It shall begin full soon to rain incessantly,
After seven days' twill come, and endure days forty,
  Without fail.
Take to thy ship also   150
Of each kind, beasts two,
Male and female, but no more,
  Ere thou pull up thy sail.

For they may thee avail when all this thing is wrought;
Stuff thy ship with victual, for hunger that ye perish nought;   155
Of beasts, fowl, and cattle, for them have thou in thought,

For them in my counsel, that some succor be sought,
   In haste;
They must have corn and hay,
And other meat alway;   160
Do now as I thee say,
   In the name of the Holy Ghost.

NOAH: Ah! Benedicite! What art thou that thus
   Tells afore that shall be? Thou art full marvelous!
   Tell me, for charity, thy name so gracious.   165
GOD: My name is of dignity and also full glorious
      To know.
   I am God most mighty,
   One God in Trinity,
   Made thee and each man to be;   170
      To love me well thou owe.

NOAH: I thank thee, lord so dear, that would vouch safe
   Thus low to appear to a simple knave;
   Bless us, lord, here, for charity I it crave,
   The better may we steer the ship that we shall have,   175
      Certain.
GOD: Noah, to thee and thy fry
   My blessing grant I;
   Ye shall wax and multiply,
      And fill the earth again,   180

When all these floods are past and fully gone away.
NOAH: Lord, homeward will I haste as fast as that I may;
   My wife will I frast [ask] what she will say, [*Exit* GOD.]
   And I am aghast that we get some fray
      Betwixt us both;   185
   For she is full testy,
   For little oft angry,
   If anything wrong be,
      Soon is she wroth. [*He goes to his wife.*]

God speed, dear wife, how fare ye?   190
WIFE: Now, as ever I might thrive, the worst is I see thee;
   Do tell me belife [quickly] where has thou thus long be?
   To death may we drive, or live for thee [for all you care],
      For want indeed.
   When we sweat or swink [labor],   195
   Thou does what thou think,
   Yet of meat and of drink
      Have we great need.

NOAH: Wife, we are hard stead with tidings new.
WIFE: But thou were worthy be clad in Stafford blue [*be beaten blue*];   200
   For thou art always afraid, be it false or true;
   But God knows I am led, and that may I rue,

        For ill;
        For I dare be thy borrow [pledge],
        From even unto morrow,   205
        Thou speaks ever of sorrow;
            God send thee once thy fill!

    We women may wary [curse] all ill husbands;
    I have one, by Mary, that loosed me of my bands;
    If he be troubled I must tarry, how so ever it stands,   210
    With semblance full sorry, wringing both my hands
        For dread.
    But yet other while,
    With pleasure and with guile,
    I shall smite and smile,   215
        And quit him his mede [give him what he deserves].

NOAH: Well! hold thy tongue ram-skyt, or I shall thee still!
WIFE: By my thrift, if thou smite, I shall turn thee until!
NOAH: We shall assay as tight! Have at thee, Gill!
        Upon the bone shall it bite!   220
WIFE: Ah, so, marry! thou smitest ill!
        But I suppose
    I shall not in thy debt,
    Flee from this flett [floor]!
    Take thee there a langett [thong]   225
        To tie up thy hose!

NOAH: A! wilt thou so? Marry, that is mine.
WIFE: Thou shall three for two, I swear by God's pain!
NOAH: And I shall return them though, in faith, ere syne [long].
WIFE: Out upon thee, ho!   230
NOAH: Thou can both bite and whine,
        with a rerd [noise];
    For all if she strike,
    Yet fast will she shriek,
    In faith I hold none like   235
        In all middle-earth;

    But I will keep charity, for I have work to do.
WIFE: Here shall no man tarry thee. I pray thee go to!
    Full well may we miss thee as ever have I ro [peace];
        To spin will I dress me.   240
NOAH: Well, farewell, lo!
        But wife,
    Pray for me busily,
    Till again I come unto thee.
WIFE: Even as thou prays for me,   245
        As ever might I thrive. [*Exit* WIFE.]

NOAH: I tarry full long from my work, I trow;
    Now my gear will I fang [take] and thitherward draw;

I may full ill gang [go], the truth for to know,
But if God help not among, I may sit down daw [melancholy]   250
  To ken;
Now assay will I
How I can of wrightry [workmanship],
In nomine patris et filii, et spiritus sancti,
  Amen.   255

To begin of this tree, my bones will I bend,
I trust from the Trinity succor will be sent;
It fares full fair, think me, this work to my hand;
Now blessed be he that this can amend.
  Lo, here the length,   260
Three hundred cubits evenly,
Of breadth, lo, is it fifty,
The height is even thirty
  Cubits full strength.

Now my gown will I cast, and work in my coat,   265
Make will I the mast ere I shift one foot,
A! my back, I trow, will burst! This is a sorry note!
It is wonder that I last, such an old dote
  All dulled,
To begin such a work!   270
My bones are so stark [stiff],
No wonder if they wark [ache],
  For I am full old.

The top and the sail both will I make,
The helm and the castle also will I take;   275
To drive each single nail will I not forsake;
This gear may never fail, that dare I undertake
  At once.
This is a noble gin [device]
These nails so they run,   280
Through more and min [less],
  These boards each one;

Window and door, even as he said,
Three chief chambers, they are well made;
Pitch and tar full sure thereupon laid,   285
This will ever endure, thereof am I paid;
  for why?
It is better wrought
Than I could have thought;
Him that made all of nought   290
  I thank only.

Now will I hie me and nothing be lither [slow],
My wife and my meneye [family], to bring even hither.
Attend hither tidily wife, and consider,
Hence must us flee, all of us together,   295

In haste.
WIFE: Why, sir, what ails you?
    Who is't that assails you?
    To flee it avails you,
      And ye be aghast [afraid].   300

NOAH: [*seeing his wife spinning*] There is yarn on the reel other, my dame.
WIFE: Tell me that each deal, else get ye blame.
NOAH: He that cares may keill [cool] blessed be his name!
    He has for our seyll [happiness] to shield us from shame,
      And said,   305
    All this world about
    With floods so stout,
    That shall run on a route,
      Shall be overlaid.

He said all shall be slain but only we,   310
Our sons that are bayn [obedient] and their wives three;
A ship he bade me ordain, to save us and our fee [property],
Therefore with all our main, thank we that free
    Healer of bayll [sorrow];
Hie us fast, go we thither.   315
WIFE: I know never whither,
    I am dazed and I dither
      For fear of that tale.

NOAH: Be not afeard, have done. Pack up our gear,
    That we be there ere noon without more dere [hindrance].   320
FIRST SON: It shall be done full soon. Brothers, help to bear.
SECOND SON: Full long shall I not hoyne [delay] to do my share,
    Brother Shem.
THIRD SON: Without any yelp,
    With my might shall I help.   325
WIFE: Yet for dread of a skelp [blow]
    Help well thy dam.

NOAH: Now are we there as we should be;
    To get in our gear, our cattle and fee,
    In this vessel here, my children free.   330
WIFE: I was never shut up ere, as now might I be,
    In such an hostel as this,
    In faith I can not find
    Which is before, which is behind.
    But shall we here be confined,   335
      Noah, as have thou bliss?

NOAH: Dame, as it is skill [reason], here must us abide grace;
    Therefore, wife, with good will come into this place.
WIFE: Sir, for Jack nor for Jill will I turn my face
    Till I have on this hill spun a space   340
      on my rok [distaff];
    Well were he, might get me,

Now will I down set me,
Yet reede [warn] I no man let me [stop me],
    For dread of a knock.   345

NOAH: Behold from the heaven the cararacts all,
    That are open full even, great and small,
    And the planets seven gone from their stall,
    These thunders and levyn [lightning] down make fall
        Full stout,   350
    Both halls and bowers,
    Castles and towers;
    Full sharp are these showers,
        That rain about;

Therefore, wife, have done. Come into ship fast.   355
WIFE: Yea, Noah, go patch thy shone [shoes] the better will they last.
FIRST WIFE: Good mother, come in soon, for all is overcast,
    Both the sun and the moon.
SECOND WIFE: And many winds blast
        Full sharp.   360
    These floods so thay run,
    Therefore, mother, come in.
WIFE: In faith, yet will I spin;
    All in vain ye carp.

THIRD WIFE: If ye like ye may spin, Mother, in the ship.   365
NOAH: Now is this twice. Come in, dame, on my friendship.
WIFE: Whether I lose or I win, in faith, for thy fellowship
    Care I not a pin. This spindle will I slip
        Upon this hill,
    Ere I stir one foot.   370
NOAH: Peter! I trow we dote;
    Without any more note
        Come in if ye will.

WIFE: Yea, water nighs so near that I sit not dry;
    Into the ship with a byr [rush] therefore will I hie   375
    For dread that I drown here.
NOAH: Dame, securely,
    It be bought full dear, ye abode so long by
        Out of the ship.
WIFE: I will not, for thy bidding,   380
    Go from door to midding [dunghill; do whatever you demand].
NOAH: In faith, and for your long tarrying
        Ye shall taste of the whip.

WIFE: Spare me not, I pray thee, but even as thou think,
    These great words shall not flay me.   385
NOAH: Abide, dame, and drink,
    For beaten shall thou be, with this staff till thou stink;
    Are the strokes good? say me.
WIFE: What say ye, Wat Wynk?

NOAH: Speak! 390
    Cry me mercy, I say!
WIFE: Thereto say I nay.
NOAH: Unless thou do, by this day,
    Thy head shall I break.

    [*to women in the audience*]

WIFE: Lord, I were at rest and heartily full whole, 395
    Might I once have a mess of widow's coyll [fare];
    For thy soul, without jest, should I deal penny doyll [alms],
    So would more, no frese [fear], that I see in this sole [place]
      Of wives that are here
    For the life they have led 400
    Would their husbands were dead
    For, as ever ate I bread,
      So would I our sire were.

    [*to men in the audience*]

NOAH: Ye men who have wives whilst they are young,
    If you love your lives, chastise their tongue: 405
    Methinks my heart rives, both liver and lung,
    To see such strifes, wedmen among;
      But I,
    As have I bliss,
    Shall chastise this. 410
WIFE: Yet may you miss,
      Nicholl Neddy!

NOAH: I shall make thee still as stone, beginner of blunder!
    I shall beat thee back and bone and break all asunder.

    [*They fight.*]

WIFE: Oh, alas, I am gone! Out upon thee, man's wonder! 415
NOAH: See how she can groan, and I lie under!
      But, wife,
    In this haste let us ho [stop],
    For my back is near in two.
WIFE: And I am beat so blue 420
    That I may not thrive.

    [*They enter the ark.*]

FIRST SON: Ah! why fare ye thus? Father and mother both!
SECOND SON: Ye should not be so spitus [spiteful] standing in such a
    woth [danger].
THIRD SON: These weathers are so hidus [hideous] with many a cold 425
    coth [disease].
NOAH: We will do as ye bid us. We will no more be wroth,
      Dear bairns!
    Now to the helm will I hent [go],
    And to my ship tend. 430
WIFE: I see on the firmament,

Methinks, the seven stars.

NOAH: This is a great flood, wife, take heed.
WIFE: So me thought, as I stood. We are in great dread;
    These waves are so wode [wild].   435
NOAH: Help, God, in this need!
    As thou art steerman good and best, as I rede [counsel],
      Of all;
    Thou rule us in this race,
    As thou me promised has.   440
WIFE: This is a perilous case:
    Help, God, when we call!

NOAH: Wife, attend the steer-tree, and I shall assay
    The deepness of the sea that we bear, if I may.
WIFE: That shall I do full wisely. Now go thy way,   445
    For upon this flood have we floated many a day,
      With pain.
NOAH: Now the water will I sound
    Ah! it is far to the ground;
    This travail I expound   450
      Had I to tyne [lose].

    Above all hills bedeyn [completely] the water is risen late
    Cubits fifteen, but in a higher state
    It may not be, I ween, for this well I wate [know],
    This forty days has rain been. It will therefore abate   455
      Full lele [loyal].
    This water in haste,
    Eft will I test;
    Now am I aghast,
      It is waned a great deal.   460

    Now are the weathers ceased and cataracts quit,
    Both the most and the least.
WIFE: Methink, by my wit,
    The sun shines in the east. Lo, is not yond it?
    We should have a good feast were these floods flit   465
      So spytus [malicious].
NOAH: We have been here, all we,
    Three hundred days and fifty.
WIFE: Yea, now wanes the sea;
    Lord, well is us!   470

NOAH: The third time will I prove [test] what deepness we bear.
WIFE: How long shall thou heave. Lay in thy line there.
NOAH: I may touch with my lufe [hand] the ground even here.
WIFE: Then begins to grufe [grow] to us merry cheer;
    But, husband,   475
           What ground may this be?
NOAH: The hills of Armenia.
WIFE: Now blessed be he

That thus for us ordained!

NOAH: I see tops of hills he [high] many at a sight,   480
    Nothing to hinder me, the weather is so bright.
WIFE: These are of mercy, tokens full right.
NOAH: Dame, thou counsel me what fowl best might
      And cowth [could],
      With flight of wing   485
    Bring, without tarrying,
    Of mercy some tokening
      Either by north or south.

    For this is the first day of the tenth moon.
WIFE: The raven, dare I lay, will come again soon;   490
    As fast as thou may cast him forth, have done,
    He may happen to day come again ere noon
      Without delay.
NOAH: I will cast out also
      Doves one or two: 495
    Go your way, go,
      God send you some prey!

    Now are these fowls flown into separate country;
    Pray we fast each one, kneeling on our knee,
    To him that is alone worthiest of degree,   500
    That he would send anon our fowls some fee
      To glad us.
WIFE: They may not fail of land,
    The water is so wanand [waning].
NOAH: Thank we God all weldand [wielding],   505
    That lord that made us.

    It is a wondrous thing, me thinks soothly,
    They are so long tarrying, the fowls that we
    Cast out in the morning.
WIFE: Sir, it may be   510
    They tarry till they bring.
NOAH: The raven is a-hungry
      Alway;
    He is without any reason,
    If he find any carrion,   515
    As peradventure may befon [befall],
      He will not away;

    The dove is more gentle, her trust I unto,
    Like unto the turtle, for she is ay true.
WIFE: Hence but a little. She comes, lew, lew!   520
    She brings in her bill some novels [signs] new;
      Behold!
    It is of an olive tree
    A branch, thinkest me.
NOAH: It is so, perde [par dieu; by our God],   525

Right so is it called.

Dove, bird full blest, fair might thee befall!
Thou art true for to trust as stone in the wall;
Full well I it wist [knew] thou would come to thy hall.
WIFE: A true token is't we shall be saved all;   530
   For why?
The water, since she come,
Of deepness plumb,
Is fallen a fathom,
   And more hardily [certainly].   535

FIRST SON: These floods are gone. Father, behold!
SECOND SON: There is left right none, and that be ye bold.
THIRD SON: As still as a stone, our ship is stalled.
NOAH: Upon land here anon that we were, fain I would;
   My childer dear,   540
Shem, Japhet, and Ham,
With glee and with gam [sport],
Come we all sam [together],
   We will no longer abide here.

WIFE: Here have we been, Noah, long enough,   545
   With trouble and with teyn [grief], and endured much woe.
NOAH: Behold on this green neither cart nor plough
   Is left, as I ween, neither tree nor bough,
    Nor other thing,
But all is away;   550
Many castles, I say,
Great towns of array,
   Flit [destroyed] has this flowyng [flood].

WIFE: These floods, not afright, all this world so wide
   Has moved with might, on sea and by side.   555
NOAH: To death are they dyght [gone], proudest of pride,
   Every wight that ever was spied,
    With sin,
All are they slain,
And put unto pain.   560
WIFE: From thence again
   May they never win.

NOAH: Win? no, I-wis, but He that might has
   Would remember their mys [misery] and admit them to
    grace;   565
As He in misfortune is bliss, I pray Him in this space,
In heaven high with His, to secure us a place,
   That we,
With His saints in sight,
And His angels bright,   570
May come to His light:
   Amen, for charity.

WILLIAM SHAKESPEARE (1564–1616)

Hamlet, Prince of Denmark
(c. 1600)

uring the sixteenth century, after religious drama was forbidden, the groups that had financed and staged the cycle plays ceased their support of theatre, disapproving of the professional and commercial role that theatre had been forced to adopt in order to survive. The necessity of attracting a paying audience motivated acting companies to offer a different play each day (though the same play might be repeated at intervals during a season), and thus they created an ongoing demand for new plays. Partially for this reason, the years between 1585 and 1610 produced an exceptional number of outstanding English playwrights. Of these, William Shakespeare is universally acknowledged the greatest, and possibly the greatest playwright the world has known.

In addition to being a playwright, Shakespeare was an actor and a shareholder (part owner) both in his acting company and in the theatre in which the company performed. As the company's principal playwright, he wrote an average of two plays each season. Among his thirty-eight surviving plays, *Hamlet* is one of the most admired.

Hamlet, like *Oedipus Rex*, has as its protagonist a man who is charged with punishing the murderer of a king. But Shakespeare uses a much broader canvas than Sophocles does and includes within his drama more facets of his story, more characters, and a wider sweep of time and place. Shakespeare's play develops chronologically and places all important incidents on stage. The only important events that precede the play's opening (Claudius' seduction of his brother's wife and his murder of his brother) are replicated in the play-within-the-play. The rapid shifts in time and place are made possible by theatrical conventions that establish locale and other significant conditions through spoken passages ("spoken decor") that localize as needed the fixed facade against which the action occurred.

Hamlet is thematically rich: the pervasiveness of betrayal (brother of brother, wife of husband, parent of child, friend of friend); the opposing demands made on Hamlet (that he revenge his father's murder and that he adhere to Christian doctrine against murder); the nature of kingship and the need to rule oneself before ruling others; and several other themes. Shakespeare's dramatic poetry is generally conceded to be the finest in the English language. The basic medium is blank verse, which allows the flexibility of ordinary speech while elevating it through imagery and rhythm.

Because of its compelling story, powerful characters, and great poetry, *Hamlet* is one of the world's finest achievements in drama. Although it embodies many ideas typical of its time, it transcends the limitations of a particular era. It continues to move spectators in the theatre as it has since its first presentation around 1600.

Hamlet, Prince of Denmark

Dramatis Personae

CLAUDIUS, *King of Denmark*
HAMLET, *son to the former and nephew to the present king*
POLONIUS, *Lord Chamberlain*
HORATIO, *friend to Hamlet*
LAERTES, *son to Polonius*
VOLTEMAND
CORNELIUS
ROSENCRANTZ
GUILDENSTERN } *courtiers*
OSRIC
A GENTLEMAN
A PRIEST
MARCELLUS
BERNARDO } *officers*
FRANCISCO, *a soldier*
REYNALDO, *servant to Polonius*
PLAYERS
TWO CLOWNS, *grave diggers*
FORTINBRAS, *prince of Norway*
A NORWEGIAN CAPTAIN
ENGLISH AMBASSADORS
GERTRUDE, *queen of Denmark, and mother of Hamlet*
OPHELIA, *daughter to Polonius*
GHOST *of Hamlet's father*
LORDS, LADIES, OFFICERS, SOLDIERS, **SAILORS, MESSENGERS,**
  AND ATTENDANTS

SCENE———*Denmark.*

ACT I

SCENE I———*Elsinore. The guard-platform of the Castle.*

[FRANCISCO *at his post. Enter to him* BERNARDO.]

---

*indicates a note identified by line number. The textual reference is given in bold type, its clarification in roman type.

BERNARDO: Who's there?

FRANCISCO: Nay, answer me. Stand and unfold* yourself.

BERNARDO: Long live the king!

FRANCISCO: Bernardo?

BERNARDO: He.   5

FRANCISCO: You come most carefully upon your hour.

BERNARDO: 'Tis now struck twelve; get thee to bed, Francisco.

FRANCISCO: For this relief much thanks. 'tis bitter cold,
　　　And I am sick at heart.

BERNARDO: Have you had quiet guard?   10

FRANCISCO: Not a mouse stirring.

BERNARDO: Well; good night.
　　　If you do meet Horatio and Marcellus,
　　　The rivals* of my watch, bid them make haste.

　　　　[*Enter* HORATIO *and* MARCELLUS.]

FRANCISCO: I think I hear them. Stand, ho! Who is there?   15

HORATIO: Friends to this ground.

MARCELLUS: And liegemen to the Dane.*

FRANCISCO: Give you good night.

MARCELLUS: O, farewell, honest soldier!
　　　Who hath reliev'd you?   20

FRANCISCO: Bernardo hath my place.
　　　Give you good night.   [*Exit.*]

MARCELLUS: Holla, Bernardo!

BERNARDO: Say—
　　　What, is Horatio there?   25

HORATIO: A piece of him.

BERNARDO: Welcome, Horatio; welcome, good Marcellus.

HORATIO: What, has this thing appear'd again to-night?

BERNARDO: I have seen nothing.

MARCELLUS: Horatio says 'tis but our fantasy,   30
　　　And will not let belief take hold of him
　　　Touching this dreaded sight, twice seen of us;
　　　Therefore I have entreated him along
　　　With us to watch the minutes of this night,
　　　That, if again this apparition come,   35
　　　He may approve* our eyes and speak to it.

HORATIO: Tush, tush, 'twill not appear.

BERNARDO: Sit down awhile,
　　　And let us once again assail your ears,
　　　That are so fortified against our story,   40
　　　What we have two nights seen.

---

^{1, i, 2} **unfold** identify
¹⁴ **rivals** companions
¹⁷ **liegemen to the Dane** loyal subjects to the king of Denmark
³⁶ **approve** confirm

HORATIO: Well, sit we down,
    And let us hear Bernardo speak of this.
BERNARDO: Last night of all,
    When yond same star that's westward from the pole   45
    Had made his course t' illume that part of heaven
    Where now it burns, Marcellus and myself,
    The bell then beating one—

    [*Enter* GHOST.]

MARCELLUS: Peace, break thee off; look where it comes again.
BERNARDO: In the same figure, like the King that's dead.   50
MARCELLUS: Thou art a scholar; speak to it, Horatio.
BERNARDO: Looks 'a not like the King? Mark it, Horatio.
HORATIO: Most like. It harrows me with fear and wonder.
BERNARDO: It would be spoke to.
MARCELLUS: Question it, Horatio.   55
HORATIO: What art thou that usurp'st this time of night
    Together with that fair and warlike form
    In which the majesty of buried Denmark*
    Did sometimes march? By heaven I charge thee, speak!
MARCELLUS: It is offended.   60
BERNARDO: See, it stalks away.
HORATIO: Stay! speak, speak! I charge thee, speak!

    [*Exit* GHOST.]

MARCELLUS: 'Tis gone, and will not answer.
BERNARDO: How now, Horatio! You tremble and look pale.
    Is not this something more than fantasy?   65
    What think you on't?
HORATIO: Before my God, I might not this believe
    Without the sensible and true avouch*
    Of mine own eyes.
MARCELLUS: Is it not like the King?   70
HORATIO: As thou art to thyself:
    Such was the very armour he had on
    When he the ambitious Norway* combated;
    So frown'd he once when, in an angry parle,*
    He smote the sledded Polacks* on the ice.   75
    'Tis strange.
MARCELLUS: Thus twice before, and jump* at this dead hour,
    With martial stalk hath he gone by our watch.

---

[58] **buried Denmark** buried king of Denmark
[68] **avouch** proof
[73] **Norway** king of Norway
[74] **parle** parley
[75] **sledded Polacks** Poles on sleds
[77] **jump** just

HORATIO: In what particular thought to work I know not;
    But, in the gross and scope* of mine opinion,   80
    This bodes some strange eruption to our state.
MARCELLUS: Good now, sit down, and tell me, he that knows,
    Why this same strict and most observant watch
    So nightly toils the subject* of the land;
    And why such daily cast of brazen cannon,   85
    And foreign mart* for implements of war;
    Why such impress* of shipwrights, whose sore task
    Does not divide the Sunday from the week;
    What might be toward,* that this sweaty haste
    Doth make the night joint-labourer with the day: 90
    Who is't that can inform me?
HORATIO: That can I;
    At least, the whisper goes so. Our last King,
    Whose image even but now appear'd to us,
    Was, as you know, by Fortinbras of Norway,   95
    Thereto prick'd on by a most emulate pride,
    Dar'd to the combat; in which our valiant Hamlet—
    For so this side of our known world esteem'd him—
    Did slay this Fortinbras; who, by a seal'd compact,
    Well ratified by law and heraldry,*   100
    Did forfeit, with his life, all those his lands
    Which he stood seiz'd of,* to the conqueror;
    Against the which a moiety competent*
    Was gaged* by our King; which had return'd
    To the inheritance of Fortinbras,   105
    Had he been vanquisher; as, by the same comart*
    And carriage of the article design'd,*
    His fell to Hamlet. Now, sir, young Fortinbras,
    Of unimproved* mettle hot and full,
    Hath in the skirts* of Norway, here and there,   110
    Shark'd up a list of lawless resolutes,*
    For food and diet, to some enterprise
    That hath a stomach in't,* which is no other,
    As it doth well appear unto our state,

---

[80] **gross and scope** general drift
[84] **nightly toils the subject** citizens work by night (as well as by day)
[86] **mart** trade
[87] **impress** forced service
[89] **toward** in preparation
[100] **law and heraldry** heraldic law
[102] **seiz'd of** in possession of
[103] **moiety competent** like portion
[104] **gaged** pledged
[106] **comart** agreement
[107] **carriage of the article design'd** provisions of the pact
[109] **unimproved** unproved
[110] **skirts** borders, outskirts
[111] **Shark'd up a list of lawless resolutes** enlisted a force of desperate men
[113] **hath a stomach in't** requires courage

But to recover of us, by strong hand   115
And terms compulsatory, those foresaid lands
So by his father lost; and this, I take it,
Is the main motive of our preparations,
The source of this our watch, and the chief head*
Of this post-haste and romage* in the land.   120
BERNARDO: I think it be no other but e'en so.
    Well may it sort,* that this portentous figure
Comes armed through our watch; so like the King
That was and is the question of these wars.
HORATIO: A mote it is to trouble the mind's eye.   125
    In the most high and palmy state of Rome,
A little ere the mightiest Julius fell,
The graves stood tenantless, and the sheeted dead
Did squeak and gibber in the Roman streets;
As, stars with trains of fire, and dews of blood,   130
Disasters* in the sun; and the moist star*
Upon whose influence Neptune's empire* stands
Was sick almost to doomsday with eclipse;
And even the like precurse* of fear'd events,
As harbingers preceding still the fates   135
And prologue to the omen coming on,
Have heaven and earth together demonstrated
Unto our climatures* and countrymen.

    [*Reenter* GHOST.]

But, soft, behold! Lo, where it comes again!
I'll cross it,* though it blast me. Stay, illusion.   140

    [GHOST *spreads its arms.*]

If thou hast any sound or use of voice,
Speak to me.
If there be any good thing to be done,
That may to thee do ease and grace to me,
Speak to me.   145
If thou art privy to thy country's fate,
Which happily* foreknowing may avoid,
O, speak!
Or if thou hast uphoarded in thy life

---

[119] **chief head** principal reason
[120] **romage** bustling activity
[122] **sort** turn out
[131] **Disasters** threatening signs
[131] **moist star** the moon
[132] **Neptune's empire** the ocean (the Roman god Neptune's domain)
[134] **precurse** foreshadowing
[138] **climatures** regions
[140] **cross it** cross its path
[147] **happily** haply, perhaps

Extorted treasure in the womb of earth, 150
For which, they say, you spirits oft walk in death,

[*The cock crows.*]

Speak of it. Stay, and speak. Stop it, Marcellus.
MARCELLUS: Shall I strike at it with my partisan?*
HORATIO: Do, if it will not stand.
BERNARDO: 'Tis here! 155
HORATIO: 'Tis here!
MARCELLUS: 'Tis gone!   [*Exit* GHOST.]
We do it wrong, being so majestical,
To offer it the show of violence;
For it is, as the air, invulnerable, 160
And our vain blows malicious mockery.
BERNARDO: It was about to speak, when the cock crew.
HORATIO: And then it started like a guilty thing
Upon a fearful summons. I have heard
The cock, that is the trumpet to the morn, 165
Doth with his lofty and shrill-sounding throat
Awake the god of day; and at his warning,
Whether in sea or fire, in earth or air,
Th' extravagant and erring* spirit hies
To his confine; and of the truth herein 170
This present object made probation.*
MARCELLUS: It faded on the crowing of the cock.
Some say that ever 'gainst* that season comes
Wherein our Saviour's birth is celebrated,
This bird of dawning singeth all night long; 175
And then, they say, no spirit dare stir abroad,
The nights are wholesome, then no planets strike,*
No fairy takes, nor witch hath power to charm,
So hallowed and so gracious is that time.
HORATIO: So have I heard, and do in part believe it. 180
But look, the morn, in russet mantle clad,
Walks o'er the dew of yon high eastward hill.
Break we our watch up; and, by my advice,
Let us impart what we have seen to-night
Unto young Hamlet; for, upon my life, 185
This spirit, dumb to us, will speak to him.
Do you consent we shall acquaint him with it,
As needful in our loves, fitting our duty?
MARCELLUS: Let's do't, I pray; and I this morning know
Where we shall find him most convenient. 190

[*Exeunt.*]

---

[153] **partisan** (weapon)
[169] **extravagant and erring** wandering outside its proper realm
[171] **made probation** gives proof
[173] **ever 'gainst** just before
[177] **strike** exert evil influence

SCENE II————*Elsinore. The Castle.*

[*Flourish.* * *Enter* CLAUDIUS KING OF DENMARK, GERTRUDE THE QUEEN, *and* COUNCILLORS, *including* POLONIUS, *his son* LAERTES, VOLTEMAND, CORNE- LIUS, *and* HAMLET.]

KING: Though yet of Hamlet our dear brother's death
    The memory be green; and that it us befitted
    To bear our hearts in grief, and our whole kingdom
    To be contracted in one brow of woe;
    Yet so far hath discretion fought with nature   5
    That we with wisest sorrow think on him,
    Together with remembrance of ourselves.
    Therefore our sometime sister,* now our queen,
    Th' imperial jointress* to this warlike state,
    Have we, as 'twere with a defeated joy,   10
    With an auspicious and a dropping eye,
    With mirth in funeral, and with dirge in marriage,
    In equal scale weighing delight and dole,
    Taken to wife; nor have we herein barr'd
    Your better wisdoms, which have freely gone   15
    With this affair along. For all, our thanks.
    Now follows that you know: young Fortinbras,
    Holding a weak supposal of our worth,
    Or thinking by our late dear brother's death
    Our state to be disjoint and out of frame,*   20
    Co-leagued with this dream of his advantage*—
    He hath not fail'd to pester us with message
    Importing the surrender of those lands
    Lost by his father, with all bands of law,
    To our most valiant brother. So much for him.   25
    Now for ourself, and for this time of meeting,
    Thus much the business is: we have here writ
    To Norway, uncle of young Fortinbras—
    Who, impotent and bed-rid, scarcely hears
    Of this his nephew's purpose—to suppress   30
    His further gait* herein, in that the levies,
    The lists, and full proportions,* are all made
    Out of his subject;* and we here dispatch
    You, good Cornelius, and you, Voltemand,
    For bearers of this greeting to old Norway;   35
    Giving to you no further personal power

I,ii (stage direction) **Flourish** trumpet fanfare
8   **our sometime sister** my former sister-in-law
9   **jointress** joint ruler
20 **frame** order
21 **advantage** superior power
31 **gait** proceeding
32 **proportions** war supplies
33 **Out of his subject** out of the Norwegian king's subjects

To business with the King more than the scope
Of these dilated articles* allow.
Farewell; and let your haste commend your duty.
CORNELIUS: } In that and in all things we will show our duty.   40
VOLTEMAND: }
KING: We doubt it nothing; heartily farewell.

        [*Exeunt* VOLTEMAND *and* CORNELIUS.]

And now, Laertes, what's the news with you?
You told us of some suit; what is't, Laertes?
You cannot speak of reason to the Dane
And lose your voice.* What wouldst thou beg, Laertes,   45
That shall not be my offer, not thy asking?
The head is not more native* to the heart,
The hand more instrumental to the mouth,
Than is the throne of Denmark to thy father.
What wouldst thou have, Laertes?   50
LAERTES: My dread lord,
     Your leave and favour to return to France;
     From whence though willingly I came to Denmark
     To show my duty in your coronation,
     Yet now, I must confess, that duty done,   55
     My thoughts and wishes bend again toward France,
     And bow them to your gracious leave and pardon.
KING: Have you your father's leave? What says Polonius?
POLONIUS: 'A hath, my lord, wrung from me my slow leave
     By laboursome petition; and at last   60
     Upon his will I seal'd my hard consent.*
     I do beseech you, give him leave to go.
KING: Take thy fair hour, Laertes; time be thine,
     And thy best graces spend it at thy will!
     But now, my cousin* Hamlet, and my son—   65
HAMLET: [*aside*] A little more than kin, and less than kind.
KING: How is it that the clouds* still hang on you?
HAMLET: Not so, my Lord; I am too much in the sun.
QUEEN: Good Hamlet, cast thy nighted colour off,
     And let thine eye look like a friend on Denmark.   70
     Do not for ever with thy vailed lids*
     Seek for thy noble father in the dust.
     Thou know'st 'tis common—all that lives must die,
     Passing through nature to eternity.
HAMLET: Ay, madam, it is common.   75

QUEEN: If it be,
    Why seems it so particular with thee?
HAMLET: Seems, madam! Nay, it is; I know not seems.
    'Tis not alone my inky cloak, good mother,
    Nor customary suits of solemn black,   80
    Nor windy suspiration* of forc'd breath,
    No, nor the fruitful river in the eye,
    Nor the dejected haviour of the visage,
    Together with all forms, moods, shapes of grief,
    That can denote me truly. These, indeed, seem;   85
    For they are actions that a man might play;
    But I have that within which passes show—
    These but the trappings and the suits of woe.
KING: 'Tis sweet and commendable in your nature, Hamlet,
    To give these mourning duties to your father;   90
    But you must know your father lost a father;
    That father lost, lost his; and the survivor bound,
    In filial obligation, for some term
    To do obsequious* sorrow. But to persever
    In obstinate condolement* is a course   95
    Of impious stubbornness; 'tis unmanly grief;
    It shows a will most incorrect to heaven,
    A heart unfortified, a mind impatient,
    An understanding simple and unschool'd;
    For what we know must be, and is as common   100
    As any the most vulgar thing to sense,
    Why should we in our peevish opposition
    Take it to heart? Fie! 'tis a fault to heaven,
    A fault against the dead, a fault to nature,
    To reason most absurd; whose common theme   105
    Is death of fathers, and who still hath cried,
    From the first corse* till he that died to-day,
    'This must be so.' We pray you throw to earth
    This unprevailing* woe, and think of us
    As of a father; for let the world take note   110
    You are the most immediate to our throne;
    And with no less nobility of love
    Than that which dearest father bears his son
    Do I impart toward you. For your intent
    In going back to school in Wittenberg,   115
    It is most retrograde* to our desire;
    And we beseech you bend you* to remain
    Here, in the cheer and comfort of our eye,

---

81 **windy suspiration** heavy sighs
94 **obsequious** funereal
95 **condolement** mourning
107 **corse** corpse
109 **unprevailing** unavailing
116 **retrograde** contrary
117 **bend you** agree

Our chiefest courtier, cousin, and our son.
QUEEN: Let not thy mother lose her prayers, Hamlet: 120
    I pray thee stay with us; go not to Wittenberg.
HAMLET: I shall in all my best obey you, madam.
KING: Why, 'tis a loving and a fair reply.
    Be as ourself in Denmark. Madam, come;
    This gentle and unforc'd accord of Hamlet   125
    Sits smiling to my heart; in grace whereof,
    No jocund health that Denmark drinks to-day
    But the great cannon to the clouds shall tell
    And the King's rouse* the heaven shall bruit* again,
    Re-speaking earthly thunder. Come away.   130

       [Flourish. Exeunt all but HAMLET.]

HAMLET: O, that this too too solid flesh would melt,
    Thaw, and resolve itself into a dew!
    Or that the Everlasting had not fix'd
    His canon* 'gainst self-slaughter! O God! God!
    How weary, stale, flat, and unprofitable,   135
    Seem to me all the uses of this world!
    Fie on't! Ah, fie! 'tis an unweeded garden,
    That grows to seed; things rank and gross in nature
    Possess it merely.* That it should come to this!
    But two months dead! Nay, not so much, not two.   140
    So excellent a king that was to this
    Hyperion* to a satyr, so loving to my mother,
    That he might not beteem* the winds of heaven
    Visit her face too roughly. Heaven and earth!
    Must I remember? Why, she would hang on him   145
    As if increase of appetite had grown
    By what it fed on; and yet, within a month—
    Let me not think on't. Frailty, thy name is woman!—
    A little month, or ere those shoes were old
    With which she followed my poor father's body,   150
    Like Niobe,* all tears—why she, even she—
    O God! a beast that wants discourse of reason*
    Would have mourn'd longer—married with my uncle,
    My father's brother; but no more like my father
    Than I to Hercules. Within a month,   155
    Ere yet the salt of most unrighteous tears
    Had left the flushing in her galled eyes,
    She married. O, most wicked speed, to post*

---

[129] **rouse** drinking, carousing
[129] **bruit** noisily announce
[134] **canon** law
[139] **merely** completely
[142] **Hyperion** the sun god noted for beauty
[143] **beteem** permit
[151] **Niobe** mother in Greek mythology who wept without stopping for the death of her children
[152] **wants discourse of reason** lacks reasoning power
[158] **post** hasten

With such dexterity to incestuous* sheets!
It is not, nor it cannot come to good. 160
But break, my heart, for I must hold my tongue.

[*Enter* HORATIO, MARCELLUS, *and* BERNARDO.]

HORATIO: Hail to your lordship!
HAMLET: I am glad to see you well.
    Horatio—or I do forget myself.
HORATIO: The same, my lord, and your poor servant ever. 165
HAMLET: Sir, my good friend. I'll change* that name with you.
    And what make you from Wittenberg, Horatio?
    Marcellus?
MARCELLUS: My good lord!
HAMLET: I am very glad to see you. [*to* BERNARDO] Good even, sir.— 170
    But what, in faith, make you from Wittenberg?
HORATIO: A truant disposition, good my lord.
HAMLET: I would not hear your enemy say so;
    Nor shall you do my ear that violence,
    To make it truster* of your own report. 175
    Against yourself. I know you are no truant.
    But what is your affair in Elsinore?
    We'll teach you to drink deep ere you depart.
HORATIO: My lord, I came to see your father's funeral.
HAMLET: I prithee do not mock me, fellow-student; 180
    I think it was to see my mother's wedding.
HORATIO: Indeed, my lord, it followed hard upon.
HAMLET: Thrift, thrift, Horatio! The funeral bak'd-meats
    Did coldly furnish forth the marriage tables.
    Would I had met my dearest* foe in heaven 185
    Or ever I had seen that day, Horatio!
    My father—methinks I see my father.
HORATIO: Where, my lord?
HAMLET: In my mind's eye, Horatio.
HORATIO: I saw him once; 'a was a goodly king. 190
HAMLET: 'A* was a man, take him for all in all,
    I shall not look upon his like again.
HORATIO: My lord, I think I saw him yesternight.
HAMLET: Saw who?
HORATIO: My lord, the King your father. 195
HAMLET: The King my father!
HORATIO: Season your admiration* for a while
    With an attent ear, till I may deliver,
    Upon the witness of these gentlemen,
    This marvel to you. 200

---

[159] **incestuous** incestuous because the church considered a sister-in-law equivalent to being a sister
[166] **change** exchange
[175] **truster** believer
[185] **dearest** most hated
[191] **'A** he
[197] **Season your admiration** control your wonder

HAMLET: For God's love, let me hear.

HORATIO: Two nights together had these gentlemen,
 Marcellus and Bernardo, on their watch,
 In the dead waste and middle of the night,
 Been thus encount'red. A figure like your father,   205
 Armed at point exactly, cap-a-pe,*
 Appears before them, and with solemn march
 Goes slow and stately by them; thrice he walk'd
 By their oppress'd and fear-surprised eyes,
 Within his truncheon's length,* whilst they, distill'd*   210
 Almost to jelly with the act of fear,
 Stand dumb and speak not to him. This to me
 In dreadful* secrecy impart they did;
 And I with them the third night kept the watch;
 Where, as they had delivered, both in time,   215
 Form of the thing, each word made true and good,
 The apparition comes. I knew your father;
 These hands are not more like.

HAMLET: But where was this?

MARCELLUS: My lord, upon the platform where we watch.   220

HAMLET: Did you not speak to it?

HORATIO: My lord, I did;
 But answer made it none; yet once methought
 It lifted up its head and did address
 Itself to motion, like as it would speak;   225
 But even then the morning cock crew loud,
 And at the sound it shrunk in haste away
 And vanish'd from our sight.

HAMLET: 'Tis very strange.

HORATIO: As I do live, my honour'd lord, 'tis true;   230
 And we did think it writ down in our duty
 To let you know of it.

HAMLET: Indeed, indeed, sirs, but this troubles me.
 Hold you the watch to-night?

ALL: We do, my lord.   235

HAMLET: Arm'd, say you?

ALL: Arm'd, my lord.

HAMLET: From top to toe?

ALL: My lord, from head to foot.

HAMLET: Then saw you not his face?   240

HORATIO: O yes, my lord; he wore his beaver* up.

HAMLET: What, look'd he frowningly?

HORATIO: A countenance more in sorrow than in anger.

HAMLET: Pale or red?

HORATIO: Nay, very pale.   245

---

[206] **cap-a-pe** head to foot
[210] **truncheon's length** space of a short club
[210] **distill'd** reduced
[213] **dreadful** terrified
[241] **beaver** visor, face guard

HAMLET: And fix'd his eyes upon you?
HORATIO: Most constantly.
HAMLET: I would I had been there.
HORATIO: It would have much amaz'd you.
HAMLET: Very like, very like. Stay'd it long?   250
HORATIO: While one with moderate haste might tell* a hundred.
BOTH: Longer, longer.
HORATIO: Not when I saw't.
HAMLET: His beard was grizzl'd*—no?
HORATIO: It was, as I have seen it in his life,   255
    A sable silver'd.*
HAMLET: I will watch to-night;
    Perchance 'twill walk again.
HORATIO: I warr'nt it will.
HAMLET: If it assume my noble father's person.   260
    I'll speak to it, though hell itself should gape
    And bid me hold my peace, I pray you all,
    If you have hitherto conceal'd this sight,
    Let it be tenable* in your silence still;
    And whatsoever else shall hap to-night,   265
    Give it an understanding, but no tongue;
    I will requite your loves. So, fare you well—
    Upon the platform, 'twixt eleven and twelve,
    I'll visit you.
ALL: Our duty to your honour.   270
HAMLET: Your loves, as mine to you; farewell.

    [*Exeunt all but* HAMLET.]

My father's spirit in arms! All is not well.
I doubt* some foul play. Would the night were come!
Till then sit still, my soul. Foul deeds will rise,
Though all the earth o'erwhelm them, to men's eyes.   [*Exit.*]   275

SCENE III———*Elsinore. The house of* POLONIUS.

    [*Enter* LAERTES *and* OPHELIA *his sister.*]

LAERTES: My necessaries are embark'd. Farewell.
    And, sister, as the winds give benefit
    And convoy* is assistant, do not sleep,
    But let me hear from you.
OPHELIA: Do you doubt that?   5
LAERTES: For Hamlet, and the trifling of his favour,

---

251 **tell** count
254 **grizzl'd** gray
256 **sable silver'd** black mixed with gray
264 **tenable** held
273 **doubt** suspect
I,iii,3 **convoy** conveyance

Hold it a fashion and a toy* in blood,
A violet in the youth of primy* nature,
Forward* not permanent, sweet not lasting,
The perfume and suppliance* of a minute; 10
No more.

OPHELIA: No more but so?

LAERTES: Think it no more;
For nature crescent* does not grow alone
In thews* and bulk, but as this temple* waxes, 15
The inward service of the mind and soul
Grows wide withal. Perhaps he loves you now,
And now no soil nor cautel* doth besmirch
The virtue of his will; but you must fear,
His greatness weigh'd,* his will is not his own; 20
For he himself is subject to his birth:
He may not, as unvalued* persons do,
Carve for himself; for on his choice depends
The sanity and health of this whole state;
And therefore must his choice be circumscrib'd 25
Unto the voice and yielding of that body
Whereof he is the head. Then if he says he loves you,
It fits your wisdom so far to believe it
As he in his particular act and place
May give his saying deed; which is no further 30
Than the main voice of Denmark goes withal.
Then weigh what loss your honour may sustain,
If with too credent* ear you list his songs,
Or lose your heart, or your chaste treasure open
To his unmast'red importunity. 35
Fear it, Ophelia, fear it, my dear sister;
And keep you in the rear of your affection,
Out of the shot and danger of desire.
The chariest maid is prodigal enough
If she unmask her beauty to the moon. 40
Virtue itself scapes not calumnious strokes;
The canker* galls the infants of the spring
Too oft before their buttons* be disclos'd;
And in the morn and liquid dew of youth

---

7   **toy** idle fancy
8   **primy** youthful, springlike
9   **Forward** premature
10   **suppliance** diversion
14   **crescent** increasing
15   **thews** sinews
15   **temple** the body
18   **cautel** deceit
20   **greatness weigh'd** high rank considered
22   **unvalued** of low rank
33   **credent** credulous
42   **canker** worm
43   **buttons** buds

Contagious blastments are most imminent. 45
Be wary, then; best safety lies in fear:
Youth to itself rebels, though none else near.
OPHELIA: I shall the effect of this good lesson keep
As watchman to my heart. But, good my brother,
Do not, as some ungracious* pastors do, 50
Show me the steep and thorny way to heaven,
Whiles, like a puff'd and reckless libertine,
Himself the primrose path of dalliance treads
And recks not his own rede.*
LAERTES: O, fear me not! 55

[*Enter* POLONIUS.]

I stay too long. But here my father comes.
A double blessing is a double grace;
Occasion smiles upon a second leave.
POLONIUS: Yet here, Laertes! Aboard, aboard, for shame!
The wind sits in the shoulder of your sail, 60
And you are stay'd for. There—my blessing with thee!
And these few precepts in thy memory
Look thou character.* Give thy thoughts no tongue,
Nor any unproportion'd* thought his act.
Be thou familiar, but by no means vulgar. 65
Those friends thou hast, and their adoption tried,
Grapple them to thy soul with hoops of steel;
But do not dull thy palm with entertainment
Of each new-hatch'd, unfledg'd comrade. Beware
Of entrance to a quarrel; but, being in, 70
Bear't that th' opposed may beware of thee.
Give every man thy ear, but few thy voice;
Take each man's censure, but reserve thy judgment.
Costly thy habit as thy purse can buy,
But not express'd in fancy; rich, not gaudy; 75
For the apparel oft proclaims the man;
And they in France of the best rank and station
Are of a most select and generous choice in that.
Neither a borrower nor a lender be;
For loan oft loses both itself and friend, 80
And borrowing dulls the edge of husbandry.*
This above all—to thine own self be true,
And it must follow, as the night the day,
Thou canst not then be false to any man.
Farewell; my blessing season* this in thee! 85

---

50 **ungracious** without themselves being in God's grace
54 **recks not his own rede** doesn't heed his own advice
63 **character** inscribe
64 **unproportion'd** unconsidered
81 **husbandry** thrift
85 **season** make fruitful

LAERTES: Most humbly do I take my leave, my lord.

POLONIUS: The time invites you; go, your servants tend.*

LAERTES: Farewell, Ophelia; and remember well
    What I have said to you.

OPHELIA: 'Tis in my memory lock'd,   90
    And you yourself shall keep the key of it.

LAERTES: Farewell.

POLONIUS: What is't, Ophelia, he hath said to you?

OPHELIA: So please you, something touching the Lord Hamlet.

POLONIUS: Marry,* well bethought!   95
    'Tis told me he hath very oft of late
    Given private time to you; and you yourself
    Have of your audience been most free and bounteous.
    If it be so—as so 'tis put on me,
    And that in way of caution—I must tell you   100
    You do not understand yourself so clearly
    As it behooves my daughter and your honour.
    What is between you? Give me up the truth.

OPHELIA: He hath, my lord, of late made many tenders
    Of his affection to me.   105

POLONIUS: Affection! Pooh! You speak like a green girl,
    Unsifted* in such perilous circumstance.
    Do you believe his tenders, as you call them?

OPHELIA: I do not know, my lord, what I should think.

POLONIUS: Marry, I will teach you: think yourself a baby   110
    That you have ta'en these tenders for true pay
    Which are not sterling. Tender yourself more dearly;
    Or—not to crack the wind of the poor phrase,
    Running it thus—you'll tender me a fool.*

OPHELIA: My lord, he hath importun'd me with love   115
    In honourable fashion.

POLONIUS: Ay, fashion you may call it; go to, go to.

OPHELIA: And hath given countenance to his speech, my lord,
    With almost all the holy vows of heaven.

POLONIUS: Ay, springes to catch woodcocks!* I do know,   120
    When the blood burns, how prodigal the soul
    Lends the tongue vows. These blazes, daughter,
    Giving more light than heat—extinct in both,
    Even in their promise, as it is a-making—
    You must not take for fire. From this time   125
    Be something scanter of your maiden presence;
    Set your entreatments* at a higher rate
    Than a command to parle. For Lord Hamlet,

---

⁸⁷ **tend** await

⁹⁵ **Marry** By the Virgin Mary

¹⁰⁷ **Unsifted** untried

¹¹⁴ **tender me a fool** present me with a baby

¹²⁰ **springes to catch woodcocks** snares to catch unwary birds

¹²⁷ **entreatments** conversations

Believe so much in him, that he is young,
And with a larger tether may he walk   130
Than may be given you. In few, Ophelia,
Do not believe his vows; for they are brokers,*
Not of that dye* which their investments* show,
But mere implorators* of unholy suits,
Breathing like sanctified and pious bonds,*   135
The better to beguile. This is for all—
I would not, in plain terms, from this time forth
Have you so slander* any moment leisure
As to give words or walk with the Lord Hamlet.
Look to't, I charge you. Come your ways.   140
OPHELIA: I shall obey, my lord.   [*Exeunt.*]

SCENE IV———*Elsinore. The guard-platform of the Castle.*

[*Enter* HAMLET, HORATIO, *and* MARCELLUS.]

HAMLET: The air bites shrewdly;* it is very cold.
HORATIO: It is a nipping and an eager* air.
HAMLET: What hour now?
HORATIO: I think it lacks of twelve.
MARCELLUS: No, it is struck.   5
HORATIO: Indeed? I heard it not. It then draws near the season
     Wherein the spirit held his wont to walk.

     [*A flourish of trumpets, and two pieces go off.*]

     What does this mean, my lord?
HAMLET: The King doth wake* to-night and takes his rouse,*
     Keeps wassail, and the swagg'ring up-spring* reels,   10
     And, as he drains his draughts of Rhenish* down,
     The kettledrum and trumpet thus bray out
     The triumph of his pledge.*
HORATIO: Is it a custom?
HAMLET: Ay, marry, is't;   15
     But to my mind, though I am native here
     And to the manner born, it is a custom

---

132 **brokers** procurers
133 **dye** kind
133 **investments** outer garments
134 **implorators** solicitors
135 **bonds** pledges
138 **slander** disgrace
I,iv,1 **shrewdly** bitterly
2   **eager** sharp
9   **wake** revel
9   **rouse** carouses
10 **up-spring** dance
11 **Rhenish** Rhine wine
13 **The triumph of his pledge** drinking a glass of wine in one draught

More honour'd in the breach than the observance.
This heavy-headed revel east and west
Makes us traduc'd and tax'd of* other nations; 20
They clepe* us drunkards, and with swinish phrase
Soil our addition,* and, indeed, it takes
From our achievements, though perform'd at height,
The pith and marrow of our attribute.*
So, oft it chances in particular men 25
That, for some vicious mole* of nature in them,
As in their birth, wherein they are not guilty,
Since nature cannot choose his origin;
By the o'ergrowth of some complexion,*
Oft breaking down the pales* and forts of reason; 30
Or by some habit that too much o'er-leavens*
The form of plausive* manners—that these men,
Carrying, I say, the stamp of one defect,
Being nature's livery or fortune's star,*
His virtues else, be they as pure as grace, 35
As infinite as man may undergo,
Shall in the general censure* take corruption
From that particular fault. The dram of eale
Doth all the noble substance of a doubt
To his own scandal. 40

[*Enter* GHOST.]

HORATIO: Look, my lord, it comes.
HAMLET: Angels and ministers of grace defend us!
Be thou a spirit of health* or goblin damn'd,
Bring with thee airs from heaven or blasts from hell,
Be thy intents wicked or charitable, 45
Thou com'st in such a questionable* shape
That I will speak to thee. I'll call thee Hamlet,
King, father, royal Dane. O, answer me!
Let me not burst in ignorance, but tell
Why thy canoniz'd* bones, hearsed in death, 50
Have burst their cerements;* why the sepulchre

---

[20] **tax'd of** accused by
[21] **clepe** call
[22] **addition** honor
[24] **attribute** reputation
[26] **mole** blemish
[29] **complexion** natural disposition
[30] **pales** walls
[31] **o'er-leavens** overdoes, corrupts
[32] **plausive** pleasing
[34] **nature's livery or fortune's star** determined by nature or by the stars
[37] **general censure** popular judgment
[43] **spirit of health** good spirit
[46] **questionable** of dubious identity
[50] **canoniz'd** buried according to church rules
[51] **cerements** burial garments

Wherein we saw thee quietly enurn'd
Have op'd his ponderous and marble jaws
To cast thee up again. What may this mean
That thou, dead corse, again in complete steel   55
Revisits thus the glimpses of the moon,
Making night hideous, and we fools of nature
So horridly to shake our disposition*
With thoughts beyond the reaches of our souls?
Say, why is this? wherefore? What should we do?   60

      [**GHOST** *beckons* HAMLET.]

HORATIO: It beckons you to go away with it,
    As if some impartment* did desire
    To you alone.
MARCELLUS: Look with what courteous action
    It waves you to a more removed ground.   65
    But do not go with it.
HORATIO: No, by no means.
HAMLET: It will not speak; then I will follow it.
HORATIO: Do not, my lord.
HAMLET: Why, what should be the fear?   70
    I do not set my life at a pin's fee;
    And for my soul, what can it do to that,
    Being a thing immortal as itself?
    It waves me forth again; I'll follow it.
HORATIO: What if it tempt you toward the flood, my lord,   75
    Or to the dreadful summit of the cliff
    That beetles* o'er his base into the sea,
    And there assume some other horrible form,
    Which might deprive your sovereignty of reason
    And draw you into madness? Think of it: 80
    The very place puts toys* of desperation,
    Without more motive, into every brain
    That looks so many fathoms to the sea
    And hears it roar beneath.
HAMLET: It waves me still.   85
    Go on; I'll follow thee.
MARCELLUS: You shall not go, my lord.
HAMLET: Hold off your hands.
HORATIO: Be rul'd; you shall not go.
HAMLET: My fate cries out,   90
    And makes each petty arture* in this body
    As hardy as the Nemean lion's nerve.* [**GHOST** *beckons.*]

---

58 **shake our disposition** unsettle our minds
62 **impartment** message to impart
77 **beetles** juts out
81 **toys** notions
91 **arture** artery
92 **Nemean lion's nerve** sinews of the mythical lion slain by Heracles

Still am I call'd. Unhand me, gentlemen.
By heaven, I'll make a ghost of him that lets* me.
I say, away! Go on; I'll follow thee.   95

    [*Exeunt* GHOST *and* HAMLET.]

HORATIO: He waxes desperate with imagination.
MARCELLUS: Let's follow; 'tis not fit thus to obey him.
HORATIO: Have after. To what issue will this come?
MARCELLUS: Something is rotten in the state of Denmark.
HORATIO: Heaven will direct it.   100
MARCELLUS: Nay, let's follow him.   [*Exeunt.*]

      SCENE V————*Elsinore. The Battlements of the Castle.*

    [*Enter* GHOST *and* HAMLET.]

HAMLET: Whither wilt thou lead me? Speak. I'll go no further.
GHOST: Mark me.
HAMLET: I will.
GHOST: My hour is almost come,
    When I to sulph'rous and tormenting flames   5
    Must render up myself.
HAMLET: Alas, poor ghost!
GHOST: Pity me not, but lend thy serious hearing
    To what I shall unfold.
HAMLET: Speak; I am bound to hear.   10
GHOST: So art thou to revenge, when thou shalt hear.
HAMLET: What?
GHOST: I am thy father's spirit,
    Doom'd for a certain term to walk the night,
    And for the day confin'd to fast in fires,   15
    Till the foul crimes done in my days of nature
    Are burnt and purg'd away. But that I am forbid
    To tell the secrets of my prison-house,
    I could a tale unfold whose lightest word
    Would harrow up thy soul, freeze thy young blood,   20
    Make thy two eyes, like stars, start from their spheres,
    Thy knotted and combined locks to part,
    And each particular hair to stand an end,
    Like quills upon the fretful porpentine.*
    But this eternal blazon* must not be   25
    To ears of flesh and blood. List, list, O, list!
    If thou didst ever thy dear father love—
HAMLET: O God!
GHOST: Revenge his foul and most unnatural murder.
HAMLET: Murder!   30

---

⁹⁴ **lets** hinders
^{I.v.24} **fretful porpentine** fearful porcupine
²⁵ **eternal blazon** revelation about eternity

GHOST: Murder most foul, as in the best it is;
But this most foul, strange, and unnatural.
HAMLET: Haste me to know't, that I, with wings as swift
As meditation or the thoughts of love,
May sweep to my revenge.   35
GHOST: I find thee apt;
And duller shouldst thou be than the fat weed
That roots itself in ease on Lethe wharf,*
Wouldst thou not stir in this. Now, Hamlet, hear:
'Tis given out that, sleeping in my orchard,   40
A serpent stung me; so the whole ear of Denmark
Is by a forged process* of my death
Rankly abus'd; but know, thou noble youth,
The serpent that did sting thy father's life
Now wears his crown.   45
HAMLET: O my prophetic soul!
My uncle!
GHOST: Ay, that incestuous, that adulterate* beast,
With witchcraft of his wits, with traitorous gifts—
O wicked wit and gifts that have the power   50
So to seduce—won to his shameful lust
The will of my most seeming virtuous queen.
O Hamlet, what a falling off was there,
From me, whose love was of that dignity
That it went hand in hand even with the vow   55
I made to her in marriage; and to decline
Upon a wretch whose natural gifts were poor
To those of mine!
But virtue, as it never will be moved,
Though lewdness court it in a shape of heaven,   60
So lust, though to a radiant angel link'd,
Will sate itself in a celestial bed
And prey on garbage.
But soft! methinks I scent the morning air.
Brief let me be. Sleeping within my orchard,   65
My custom always of the afternoon,
Upon my secure* hour thy uncle stole,
With juice of cursed hebona* in a vial,
And in the porches of my ears did pour
The leperous distilment; whose effect   70
Holds such an enmity with blood of man
That swift as quicksilver it courses through
The natural gates and alleys of the body;
And with a sudden vigour it doth posset*

---

38 **Lethe wharf** bank of the river of forgetfulness in Hades
42 **forged process** false account
48 **adulterate** adulterous
67 **secure** unsuspecting
68 **hebona** poisonous plant
74 **posset** curdle

And curd, like eager* droppings into milk,   75
The thin and wholesome blood. So did it mine;
And a most instant tetter* bark'd about,
Most lazar-like,* with vile and loathsome crust,
All my smooth body.
    Thus was I, sleeping, by a brother's hand   80
Of life, of crown, of queen, at once dispatch'd;
Cut off even in the blossoms of my sin,
Unhous'led, disappointed, unanel'd;*
No reck'ning made, but sent to my account
With all my imperfections on my head   85
O, horrible! O, horrible! most horrible!
If thou hast nature in thee, bear it not;
Let not the royal bed of Denmark be
A couch for luxury* and damned incest.
But howsoever thou pursuest this act,   90
Taint not thy mind, nor let thy soul contrive
Against thy mother aught; leave her to heaven,
And to those thorns that in her bosom lodge
To prick and sting her. Fare thee well at once.
The glowworm shows the matin* to be near,   95
And gins to pale his uneffectual fire.
Adieu, adieu, adieu! Remember me.   [*Exit.*]
HAMLET: O all you host of heaven! O earth! What else?
And shall I couple hell? O, fie! Hold, hold, my heart;
And you, my sinews, grow not instant old,   100
But bear me stiffly up. Remember thee!
Ay, thou poor ghost, whiles memory holds a seat
In this distracted globe.* Remember thee!
Yea, from the table* of my memory
I'll wipe away all trivial fond* records,   105
All saws* of books, all forms, all pressures* past,
That youth and observation copied there,
And thy commandment all alone shall live
Within the book and volume of my brain,
Unmix'd with baser matter. Yes, by heaven!   110
O most pernicious woman!
O villain, villain, smiling, damned villain!
My tables—meet it is I set it down

---

75 **eager** acid
77 **tetter** inflammation of the skin
78 **lazar-like** leperlike
83 **Unhous'led, disappointed, unanel'd** without the sacrament of communion, unabsolved of sin, without extreme unction
89 **luxury** lust
95 **matin** morning
103 **globe** head
104 **table** tablet
105 **fond** foolish
106 **saws** maxims
106 **pressures** impressions

That one may smile, and smile, and be a villain;
At least I am sure it may be so in Denmark. [*writing*]   115
So, uncle, there you are. Now to my word:
It is 'Adieu, adieu! Remember me.'
I have sworn't.
HORATIO: [*within*] My lord, my lord!

[*Enter* HORATIO *and* MARCELLUS.]

MARCELLUS: Lord Hamlet!   120
HORATIO: Heavens secure him!
HAMLET: So be it!
MARCELLUS: Illo, ho, ho,* my lord!
HAMLET: Hillo, ho, ho, boy! Come, bird, come.
MARCELLUS: How is't, my noble lord?   125
HORATIO: What news, my lord?
HAMLET: O, wonderful!
HORATIO: Good my lord, tell it.
HAMLET: No; you will reveal it.
HORATIO: Not I, my lord, by heaven!   130
MARCELLUS: Nor I, my lord.
HAMLET: How say you, then; would heart of man once think it?
    But you'll be secret?
BOTH: Ay, by heaven, my lord!
HAMLET: There's never a villain dwelling in all Denmark   135
    But he's an arrant knave.
HORATIO: There needs no ghost, my lord, come from the grave
    To tell us this.
HAMLET: Why, right; you are in the right;
    And so, without more circumstance* at all,   140
    I hold it fit that we shake hands and part;
    You, as your business and desire shall point you—
    For every man hath business and desire,
    Such as it is; and for my own poor part,
    Look you, I will go pray.   145
HORATIO: These are but wild and whirling words, my lord.
HAMLET: I am sorry they offend you, heartily;
    Yes, faith, heartily.
HORATIO: There's no offence, my lord.
HAMLET: Yes, by Saint Patrick, but there is, Horatio,   150
    And much offence, too. Touching this vision here—
    It is an honest ghost,* that let me tell you.
    For your desire to know what is between us,
    O'ermaster't as you may. And now, good friends,
    As you are friends, scholars, and soldiers,   155
    Give me one poor request.
HORATIO: What is't, my lord? We will.
HAMLET: Never make known what you have seen to-night.

---

123 **Illo, ho, ho** falconer's call to his hawk
140 **circumstance** details
152 **honest ghost** true ghost of his father rather than a demon

BOTH: My lord, we will not.

HAMLET: Nay, but swear't. 160

HORATIO: In faith,
    My lord, not I.

MARCELLUS: Nor I, my lord, in faith.

HAMLET: Upon my sword.

MARCELLUS: We have sworn, my lord, already. 165

HAMLET: Indeed, upon my sword, indeed.

GHOST: [*cries under the stage*] Swear.

HAMLET: Ha, ha, boy! say'st thou so? Art thou there, true-penny?*
    Come on. You hear this fellow in the cellarage:
    Consent to swear. 170

HORATIO: Propose the oath, my lord.

HAMLET: Never to speak of this that you have seen,
    Swear by my sword.

GHOST: [*beneath*] Swear.

HAMLET: Hic et ubique?* Then we'll shift our ground. 175
    Come hither, gentlemen,
    And lay your hands again upon my sword.
    Swear by my sword
    Never to speak of this that you have heard.

GHOST: [*beneath*] Swear, by his sword. 180

HAMLET: Well said, old mole! Canst work i' th' earth so fast?
    A worthy pioneer!* Once more remove, good friends.

HORATIO: O day and night, but this is wondrous strange!

HAMLET: And therefore as a stranger give it welcome.
    There are more things in heaven and earth, Horatio, 185
    Than are dreamt of in your philosophy.
    But come.
    Here, as before, never, so help you mercy,
    How strange or odd soe'er I bear myself—
    As I perchance hereafter shall think meet 190
    To put an antic disposition* on—
    That you, at such times, seeing me, never shall,
    With arms encumb'red* thus, or this head-shake,
    Or by pronouncing of some doubtful phrase,
    As 'Well, well, we know' or 'We could, an if we would' 195
    Or, 'If we list to speak' or 'There be, an if they might'
    Or such ambiguous giving out, to note
    That you know aught of me—this do swear,
    So grace and mercy at your most need help you.

GHOST: [*beneath*] Swear. 200

HAMLET: Rest, rest, perturbed spirit! So, gentlemen,
    With all my love I do commend me* to you;

---

[168] **true-penny** honest fellow
[175] **Hic et ubique** here and everywhere
[182] **pioneer** miner
[191] **antic disposition** strange behavior
[193] **encumb'red** folded
[202] **commend me** entrust myself

And what so poor a man as Hamlet is
May do t'express his love and friending to you,
God willing, shall not lack. Let us go in together;   205
And still your fingers on your lips, I pray.
The time is out of joint. O cursed spite,
That ever I was born to set it right!
Nay, come, let's go together.   [*Exeunt.*]

ACT II

SCENE I———*Elsinore. The house of* POLONIUS.

[*Enter* POLONIUS *and* REYNALDO.]

POLONIUS: Give him this money and these notes, Reynaldo.
REYNALDO: I will, my lord.
POLONIUS: You shall do marvellous wisely, good Reynaldo,
    Before you visit him, to make inquire
    Of his behaviour.   5
REYNALDO: My lord, I did intend it.
POLONIUS: Marry, well said; very well said. Look you, sir,
    Enquire me first what Danskers* are in Paris;
    And how, and who, what means, and where they keep,*
    What company, at what expense; and finding   10
    By this encompassment and drift of question
    That they do know my son, come you more nearer
    Than your particular demands will touch it.
    Take you, as 'twere, some distant knowledge of him;
    As thus: 'I know his father and his friends,   15
    And in part him.' Do you mark this, Reynaldo?
REYNALDO: Ay, very well, my lord.
POLONIUS: 'And in part him—but' you may say 'not well;
    But if't be he I mean, he's very wild;
    Addicted so and so'; and there put on him   20
    What forgeries you please; marry, none so rank
    As may dishonour him; take heed of that;
    But, sir, such wanton, wild, and usual slips
    As are companions noted and most known
    To youth and liberty.   25
REYNALDO: As gaming, my lord.
POLONIUS: Ay, or drinking, fencing, swearing, quarrelling.
    Drabbing*—you may go so far.

II,i,8 **Danskers** Danes
9   **keep** dwell
28 **Drabbing** womanizing

REYNALDO: My lord, that would dishonour him.

POLONIUS: Faith, no; as you may season it in the charge.　　　　　30
　　　You must not put another scandal on him,
　　　That he is open to incontinency;
　　　That's not my meaning. But breathe his faults so quaintly*
　　　That they may seem the taints of liberty;
　　　The flash and outbreak of a fiery mind,　　　　　35
　　　A savageness in unreclaimed blood,
　　　Of general assault.*

REYNALDO: But, my good lord—

POLONIUS: Wherefore should you do this?

REYNALDO: Ay, my lord,　　　　　40
　　　I would know that.

POLONIUS: Marry, sir, here's my drift,
　　　And I believe it is a fetch of warrant:*
　　　You laying these slight sullies on my son,
　　　As 'twere a thing a little soil'd wi' th' working,　　　　　45
　　　Mark you,
　　　Your party in converse, him you would sound,
　　　Having ever seen in the prenominate crimes*
　　　The youth you breathe of guilty, be assur'd
　　　He closes with you in this consequence—*　　　　　50
　　　'Good sir' or so, or 'friend' or 'gentleman'
　　　According to the phrase or the addition*
　　　Of man and country.

REYNALDO: Very good, my lord.

POLONIUS: And then, sir, does 'a* this—'a does—What was　　　　　55
　　　I about to say? By the mass, I was about to say something;
　　　Where did I leave?

REYNALDO: At 'closes in the consequence,' at 'friend or so' and 'gentleman.'

POLONIUS: At 'closes in the consequence'—ay, marry,
　　　He closes thus: 'I know the gentleman;　　　　　60
　　　I saw him yesterday, or t'other day,
　　　Or then, or then; with such, or such; and, as you say,
　　　There was 'a gaming; there o'ertook in's rouse;
　　　There falling out at tennis'; or perchance
　　　'I saw him enter such a house of sale,'　　　　　65
　　　Videlicet,* a brothel, or so forth. See you now
　　　Your bait of falsehood take this carp of truth;
　　　And thus do we of wisdom and of reach,
　　　With windlasses and with assays of bias,*

---

³³ **quaintly** ingeniously
³⁷ **Of general assault** common to all men
⁴³ **fetch of warrant** justifiable device
⁴⁸ **Having . . . crimes** if he has ever seen the aforementioned crimes
⁵⁰ **He closes . . . this consequence** agrees with you
⁵² **addition** title
⁵⁵ **'a** he
⁶⁶ **Videlicet** namely
⁶⁹ **windlasses . . . bias** indirect means

By indirections find directions out;   70
So, by my former lecture and advice,
Shall you my son. You have me, have you not?
REYNALDO: My lord, I have.
POLONIUS: God buy ye; fare ye well.
REYNALDO: Good my lord!   75
POLONIUS: Observe his inclination in yourself.*
REYNALDO: I shall, my lord.
POLONIUS: And let him ply his music.
REYNALDO: Well, my lord.
POLONIUS: Farewell!   [*Exit* REYNALDO.]   80

        [*Enter* OPHELIA.]

    How now, Ophelia! What's the matter?
OPHELIA: O my lord, my lord, I have been so affrighted!
POLONIUS: With what, i' th' name of God?
OPHELIA: My lord, as I was sewing in my closet,*
    Lord Hamlet, with his doublet all unbrac'd,*   85
    No hat upon his head, his stockings fouled,
    Ungart'red and down-gyved* to his ankle;
    Pale as his shirt, his knees knocking each other,
    And with a look so piteous in purport
    As if he had been loosed out of hell   90
    To speak of horrors—he comes before me.
POLONIUS: Mad for thy love?
OPHELIA: My lord, I do not know,
    But truly I do fear it.
POLONIUS: What said he?   95
OPHELIA: He took me by the wrist, and held me hard;
    Then goes he to the length of all his arm,
    And, with his other hand thus o'er his brow,
    He falls to such a perusal of my face
    As 'a would draw it. Long stay'd he so.   100
    At last, a little shaking of mine arm,
    And thrice his head thus waving up and down,
    He rais'd a sigh so piteous and profound
    As it did seem to shatter all his bulk
    And end his being. That done, he lets me go,   105
    And, with his head over his shoulder turn'd,
    He seem'd to find his way without his eyes;
    For out adoors he went without their help
    And to the last bended their light on me.
POLONIUS: Come, go with me. I will go seek the King.   110
    This is the very ecstasy* of love,
    Whose violent property fordoes* itself,

---

76 **in yourself** for yourself
84 **closet** private room
85 **doublet all unbrac'd** jacket entirely unlaced/open
87 **down-gyved** hanging down
111 **ecstasy** madness

And leads the will to desperate undertakings
As oft as any passion under heaven
That does afflict our natures. I am sorry—
What, have you given him any hard words of late?   115
OPHELIA: No, my good lord; but, as you did command,
    I did repel his letters, and denied
    His access to me.
POLONIUS: That hath made him mad.   120
    I am sorry that with better heed and judgment
    I had not quoted* him. I fear'd he did but trifle,
    And meant to wreck thee; but beshrew my jealousy!*
    By heaven, it is as proper to our age
    To cast beyond ourselves in our opinions   125
    As it is common for the younger sort
    To lack discretion. Come, go we to the King.
    This must be known; which, being kept close, might move
    More grief to hide than hate to utter love.*
    Come.   [*Exeunt.*]   130

SCENE II———*Elsinore. The Castle.*

[*Flourish. Enter* KING, QUEEN, ROSENCRANTZ, GUILDENSTERN, *and attendants.*]

KING: Welcome, dear Rosencrantz and Guildenstern!
    Moreover that we much did long to see you,
    The need we have to use you did provoke
    Our hasty sending. Something have you heard
    Of Hamlet's transformation; so I call it,   5
    Sith* nor th' exterior nor the inward man
    Resembles that it was. What it should be,
    More than his father's death, that thus hath put him
    So much from th' understanding of himself,
    I cannot deem of. I entreat you both   10
    That, being of so* young days brought up with him,
    And sith so neighboured to his youth and haviour,
    That you vouchsafe your rest* here in our court
    Some little time; so by your companies
    To draw him on to pleasures, and to gather,   15
    So much as from occasion you may glean,
    Whether aught to us unknown afflicts him thus
    That, open'd,* lies within our remedy.
QUEEN: Good gentlemen, he hath much talk'd of you;

---

[112] **property fordoes** quality destroys
[122] **quoted** noted
[123] **beshrew my jealousy** curse on my suspicions
[127–129] **Come, go . . . utter love** telling the king may anger him, but not telling him might anger him more
[II,i,6] **Sith** since
[11] **of so** from such
[13] **vouchsafe your rest** consent to remain
[18] **open'd** revealed

And sure I am two men there is not living   20
    To whom he more adheres. If it will please you
    To show us so much gentry* and good will
    As to expend your time with us awhile
    For the supply and profit of our hope,
    Your visitation shall receive such thanks   25
    As fits a king's remembrance.
ROSENCRANTZ: Both your Majesties
    Might, by the sovereign power you have of us,
    Put your dread pleasures more into command
    Than to entreaty.   30
GUILDENSTERN: But we both obey,
    And here give up ourselves, in the full bent,*
    To lay our service freely at your feet,
    To be commanded.
KING: Thanks, Rosencrantz and gentle Guildenstern.   35
QUEEN: Thanks, Guildenstern and gentle Rosencrantz.
    And I beseech you instantly to visit
    My too much changed son. Go, some of you,
    And bring these gentlemen where Hamlet is.
GUILDENSTERN: Heavens make our presence and our practices   40
    Pleasant and helpful to him!
QUEEN: Aye amen! [*Exeunt* ROSENCRANTZ, GUILDENSTERN, *and some attendants.*]

      [*Enter* POLONIUS.]

POLONIUS: Th' ambassadors from Norway, my good lord,
    Are joyfully return'd.
KING: Thou still hast been the father of good news.   45
POLONIUS: Have I, my lord? I assure you, my good liege,
    I hold my duty, as I hold my soul,
    Both to my God and to my gracious King;
    And I do think—or else this brain of mine
    Hunts not the trail of policy so sure   50
    As it hath us'd to do—that I have found
    The very cause of Hamlet's lunacy.
KING: O, speak of that; that do I long to hear.
POLONIUS: Give first admittance to th' ambassadors;
    My news shall be the fruit to that great feast.   55
KING: Thyself do grace to them, and bring them in.

      [*Exit* POLONIUS.]

He tells me, my dear Gertrude, he hath found
    The head and source of all your son's distemper.
QUEEN: I doubt it is no other but the main,
    His father's death and our o'erhasty marriage.   60
KING: Well, we shall sift him.

---

22 **gentry** courtesy
32 **in the full bent** entirely

[*Reenter* POLONIUS, *with* VOLTEMAND *and* CORNELIUS.]

Welcome, my good friends!
Say, Voltemand, what from our brother Norway?
VOLTEMAND: Most fair return of greetings and desires.
Upon our first,* he sent out to suppress   65
His nephew's levies; which to him appear'd
To be a preparation 'gainst the Polack;
But, better look'd into, he truly found
It was against your Highness. Whereat griev'd,
That so his sickness, age, and impotence,   70
Was falsely borne in hand,* sends out arrests
On Fortinbras; which he, in brief, obeys;
Receives rebuke from Norway; and, in fine,
Makes vow before his uncle never more
To give th' assay of arms against your Majesty.   75
Whereon old Norway, overcome with joy,
Gives him threescore thousand crowns in annual fee,
And his commission to employ those soldiers,
So levied as before, against the Polack;
With an entreaty, herein further shown, [*gives a paper*]   80
That it might please you to give quiet pass
Through your dominions for this enterprise,
On such regards of safety and allowance
As therein are set down.
KING: It likes us well;   85
And at our more considered time we'll read,
Answer, and think upon this business.
Meantime we thank you for your well-took labour.
Go to your rest; at night we'll feast together.
Most welcome home!   [*Exeunt* AMBASSADORS *and attendants.*]   90
POLONIUS: This business is well ended.
My liege, and madam, to expostulate
What majesty should be, what duty is,
Why day is day, night night, and time is time,
Were nothing, but to waste night, day, and time.   95
Therefore, since brevity is the soul of wit,
And tediousness the limbs and outward flourishes,
I will be brief. Your noble son is mad.
Mad call I it; for, to define true madness,
What is't but to be nothing else but mad?   100
But let that go.
QUEEN: More matter with less art.
POLONIUS: Madam, I swear I use no art at all.
That he's mad, 'tis true: 'Tis true 'is pity;
And pity 'is 'tis true. A foolish figure!   105
But farewell it, for I will use no art.
Mad let us grant him, then; and now remains

---

65 **first** first meeting
71 **falsely borne in hand** deceived

That we find out the cause of this effect;
Or rather say the cause of this defect,
For this effect defective comes by cause.   110
Thus it remains, and the remainder thus.
Perpend.*
I have a daughter—have while she is mine—
Who in her duty and obedience, mark,
Hath given me this. Now gather, and surmise. [*reads*]   115

'*To the celestial, and my soul's idol, the most beautified Ophelia.*' That's an ill
phrase, a vile phrase; 'beautified' is a vile phrase. But you shall hear.
Thus: [*reads*]
'*In her excellent white bosom, these, &c.*'

QUEEN: Came this from Hamlet to her?   120
POLONIUS: Good madam, stay awhile; I will be faithful. [*reads*]
     '*Doubt thou the stars are fire;*
          Doubt that the sun doth move;
     Doubt* truth to be a liar;
          But never doubt I love.   125
'*O dear Ophelia, I am ill at these numbers.* I have not art to reckon my groans;*
     but that I love thee best, O most best, believe it. Adieu.
                         '*Thine evermore, most dear lady, whilst*
                              this machine is to him,
                                   Hamlet.'   130

This, in obedience, hath my daughter shown me;
And more above,* hath his solicitings,
As they fell out by time, by means, and place,
All given to mine ear.
KING: But how hath she   135
     Receiv'd his love?
POLONIUS: What do you think of me?
KING: As of a man faithful and honourable.
POLONIUS: I would fain prove so. But what might you think,
     When I had seen this hot love on the wing,   140
     As I perceiv'd it, I must tell you that,
     Before my daughter told me—what might you,
     Or my dear Majesty your Queen here think,
     If I had play'd the desk or table-book;*
     Or given my heart a winking,* mute and dumb;   145
     Or look'd upon this love with idle sight—
     What might you think? No, I went round to work,
     And my young mistress thus I did bespeak:
     'Lord Hamlet is a prince out of thy star;
     This must not be.' And then I prescripts gave her,   150

---

112 **Perpend** consider carefully
124 **Doubt** suspect
126 **ill at these numbers** unskilled at versifying
132 **above** besides
144 **play'd the desk or table-book** been a passive receiver of secrets
145 **winking** closed my eyes

That she should lock herself from his resort,
Admit no messengers, receive no tokens.
Which done, she took the fruits of my advice;
And he repelled, a short tale to make,
Fell into a sadness, then into a fast,   155
Thence to a watch,* thence into a weakness,
Thence to a lightness,* and, by this declension,
Into the madness wherein now he raves
And all we mourn for.
KING: Do you think 'tis this?   160
QUEEN: It may be, very like.
POLONIUS: Hath there been such a time—I would fain know that—
   ·That I have positively said ''tis so,'
   When it prov'd otherwise?
KING: Not that I know.   165
POLONIUS: Take this from this,* if this be otherwise.
   If circumstances lead me, I will find
   Where truth is hid, though it were hid indeed
   Within the centre.*
KING: How may we try it further?   170
POLONIUS: You may know sometimes he walks four hours together,
   Here in the lobby.
QUEEN: So he does, indeed.
POLONIUS: At such a time I'll loose my daughter to him.
   Be you and I behind an arras* then;   175
   Mark the encounter: if he love her not,
   And be not from his reason fall'n thereon,
   Let me be no assistant for a state,
   But keep a farm and carters.
KING: We will try it.   180

   [*Enter* HAMLET, *reading on a book.*]

QUEEN: But look where sadly the poor wretch comes reading.
POLONIUS: Away, I do beseech you, both away:
   I'll board him presently.* O, give me leave.

   [*Exeunt* KING *and* QUEEN.]

   How does my good Lord Hamlet?
HAMLET: Well, God-a-mercy.   185
POLONIUS: Do you know me, my lord?
HAMLET: Excellent well; you are a fishmonger.*
POLONIUS: Not I, my lord.
HAMLET: Then I would you were so honest a man.

---

156 **watch** wakefulness
157 **lightness** mental derangement
166 **this from this** (indicating by pointing) head from body
169 **centre** center of the earth
175 **arras** tapestry
183 **board him presently** accost him at once
187 **fishmonger** dealer in fish (slang for procurer)

POLONIUS: Honest, my lord! 190

HAMLET: Ay, sir; to be honest, as this world goes, is to be one man pick'd out of ten thousand.

POLONIUS: That's very true, my lord.

HAMLET: For if the sun breed maggots in a dead dog, being a good kissing carrion—Have you a daughter? 195

POLONIUS: I have, my lord.

HAMLET: Let her not walk i' th' sun. Conception* is a blessing. But as your daughter may conceive—friend, look to't.

POLONIUS: How say you by that? [*aside*] Still harping on my daughter. Yet he knew me not at first; 'a said I was a fishmonger. 'A is far gone, far gone. And truly in 200 my youth I suff'red much extremity for love. Very near this. I'll speak to him again.—What do you read, my lord?

HAMLET: Words, words, words.

POLONIUS: What is the matter, my lord?

HAMLET: Between who? 205

POLONIUS: I mean, the matter that you read, my lord.

HAMLET: Slanders, sir; for the satirical rogue says here that old men have grey beards; that their faces are wrinkled; their eyes purging thick amber and plum-tree gum; and that they have a plentiful lack of wit, together with most weak hams—all which, sir, though I most powerfully and potently be- 210 lieve, yet I hold it not honesty to have it thus set down; for you yourself, sir, shall grow old as I am, if, like a crab, you could go backward.

POLONIUS: [*aside*] Though this be madness, yet there is method in't.—Will you walk out of the air, my lord?

HAMLET: Into my grave? 215

POLONIUS: Indeed, that's out of the air. [*aside*] How pregnant sometimes his replies are! a happiness that often madness hits on, which reason and sanity could not so prosperously be delivered of. I will leave him, and suddenly contrive the means of meeting between him and my daughter.—My lord. I will take my leave of you. 220

HAMLET: You cannot, sir, take from me anything that I will more willingly part withal—except my life, except my life, except my life.

[*Enter* ROSENCRANTZ *and* GUILDENSTERN.]

POLONIUS: Fare you well, my lord.

HAMLET: These tedious old fools!

POLONIUS: You go to seek the Lord Hamlet; there he is. 225

ROSENCRANTZ: [*to* POLONIUS] God save you, sir!

[*Exit* POLONIUS.]

GUILDENSTERN: My honour'd lord!

ROSENCRANTZ: My most dear lord!

HAMLET: My excellent good friends! How dost thou, Guildenstern? Ah, Rosencrantz! Good lads, how do you both? 230

ROSENCRANTZ: As the indifferent* children of the earth.

---

¹⁹⁷ **Conception** understanding; becoming pregnant
²³¹ **indifferent** ordinary

GUILDENSTERN: Happy in that we are not over-happy;
    On fortune's cap we are not the very button.
HAMLET: Nor the soles of her shoe?
ROSENCRANTZ: Neither, my lord. 235
HAMLET: Then you live about her waist, or in the middle of her favours?
GUILDENSTERN: Faith, her privates we.
HAMLET: In the secret parts of Fortune? O, most true; she is a strumpet. What
    news?
ROSENCRANTZ: None, my lord, but that the world's grown honest. 240
HAMLET: Then is doomsday near. But your news is not true. Let me question more
    in particular. What have you, my good friends, deserved at the hands of
    Fortune, that she sends you to prison hither?
GUILDENSTERN: Prison, my lord!
HAMLET: Denmark's a prison. 245
ROSENCRANTZ: Then is the world one.
HAMLET: A goodly one; in which there are many confines, wards, and dungeons,
    Denmark being one o' th' worst.
ROSENCRANTZ: We think not so, my lord.
HAMLET: Why, then, 'tis none to you; for there is nothing either good or bad, but 250
    thinking makes it so. To me it is a prison.
ROSENCRANTZ: Why, then your ambition makes it one; 'tis too narrow for your
    mind.
HAMLET: O God, I could be bounded in a nutshell and count myself a king of
    infinite space, were it not that I have bad dreams. 255
GUILDENSTERN: Which dreams indeed are ambition; for the very substance of the
    ambitious is merely the shadow of a dream.
HAMLET: A dream itself is but a shadow.
ROSENCRANTZ: Truly, and I hold ambition of so airy and light a quality that it is
    but a shadow's shadow. 260
HAMLET: Then are our beggars bodies, and our monarchs and oustretch'd heroes
    the beggars' shadows. Shall we to th' court? for, by my fay,* I cannot reason.
BOTH: We'll wait upon you.
HAMLET: No such matter. I will not sort you with the rest of my servants; for, to
    speak to you like an honest man, I am most dreadfully attended. But, in the 265
    beaten way of friendship, what make you at Elsinore?
ROSENCRANTZ: To visit you, my lord; no other occasion.
HAMLET: Beggar that I am, I am even poor in thanks; but I thank you; and sure,
    dear friends, my thanks are too dear a half-penny.* Were you not sent for?
    Is it your own inclining? It is a free visitation? Come, come, deal justly with 270
    me. Come, come; nay, speak.
GUILDENSTERN: What should we say, my lord?
HAMLET: Why, any thing. But to th' purpose: you were sent for; and there is a
    kind of confession in your looks, which your modesties have not craft
    enough to colour; I know the good King and Queen have sent for you. 275
ROSENCRANTZ: To what end, my lord?
HAMLET: That you must teach me. But let me conjure you by the rights of our

---

[262] **fay** faith
[269] **too dear a half-penny** not worth a half-penny

fellowship, by the consonancy of our youth, by the obligation of our ever-
preserved love, and by what more dear a better proposer can charge you
withal, be even and direct with me, whether you were sent for or no?   280

ROSENCRANTZ: [*aside to* GUILDENSTERN] What say you?

HAMLET: [*aside*] Nay, then, I have an eye of you.—If you love me, hold not off.

GUILDENSTERN: My lord, we were sent for.

HAMLET: I will tell you why; so shall my anticipation prevent your discovery,*
and your secrecy to the King and Queen moult no feather. I have of late—   285
but wherefore I know not—lost all my mirth, forgone all custom of exer-
cises; and indeed it goes so heavily with my disposition that this goodly
frame, the earth, seems to me a sterile promontory; this most excellent
canopy the air, look you, this brave o'er-hanging firmament, this majestical
roof fretted* with golden fire—why, it appeareth no other thing to me than   290
a foul and pestilent congregation of vapours. What a piece of work is man!
How noble in reason! how infinite in faculties! in form and moving, how
express* and admirable! in action, how like an angel! in apprehension, how
like a god! the beauty of the world! the paragon of animals! And yet, to me,
what is this quintessence of dust? Man delights not me—no, nor woman   295
neither, though by your smiling you seem to say so.

ROSENCRANTZ: My lord, there was no such stuff in my thoughts.

HAMLET: Why did ye laugh, then, when I said 'Man delights not me'?

ROSENCRANTZ: To think, my lord, if you delight not in man, what lenten entertainment the players shall receive from you. We coted* them on the way;   300
and hither are they coming to offer you service.

HAMLET: He that plays the king shall be welcome—his Majesty shall have tribute on me; the adventurous knight shall use his foil and target;* the lover
shall not sigh gratis; the humorous man shall end his part in peace; the
clown shall make those laugh whose lungs are tickle o' th' sere;* and the lady   305
shall say her mind freely, or the blank verse shall halt* for't. What players
are they?

ROSENCRANTZ: Even those you were wont to take such delight in—the tragedians
of the city.

HAMLET: How chances it they travel? Their residence, both in reputation and profit,   310
was better both ways.

ROSENCRANTZ: I think their inhibition* comes by the means of the late innovation.*

HAMLET: Do they hold the same estimation they did when I was in the city? Are
they so followed?

ROSENCRANTZ: No, indeed, are they not.   315

HAMLET: How comes it? Do they grow rusty?

ROSENCRANTZ: Nay, their endeavour keeps in the wonted pace; but there is, sir,

---

[284] **prevent your discovery** forestall your disclosure

[290] **fretted** adorned

[293] **express** exact

[300] **coted** overtook

[303] **target** shield

[305] **tickle o' th' sere** on a hair trigger

[306] **halt** limp

[312] **inhibition** hindrance

[312] **innovation** probably a reference to the boys' theatre companies that were at this time offering serious competition to the adult companies

an eyrie* of children, little eyases that cry out on the top of question,* and
are most tyrannically clapp'd* for't. These are now the fashion, and so berattle the common stages*—so they call them—that many wearing rapiers   320
are afraid of goose quills* and dare scarce come thither.

HAMLET: What, are they children? Who maintains 'em? How are they escoted?*
Will they pursue the quality* no longer than they can sing? Will they not
say afterwards, if they should grow themselves to common players—as it is
most like, if their means are no better—their writers do them wrong to make   325
them exclaim against their own succession?*

ROSENCRANTZ: Faith, there has been much to-do on both sides; and the nation
holds it no sin to tarre* them to controversy. There was for a while no
money bid for argument,* unless the poet and the player went to cuffs in
the question.   330

HAMLET: Is't possible?

GUILDENSTERN: O, there has been much throwing about of brains.

HAMLET: Do the boys carry it away?

ROSENCRANTZ: Ay, that they do, my lord—Hercules and his load,* too.

HAMLET: It is not very strange; for my uncle is King of Denmark, and those that 335
would make mows at him while my father lived give twenty, forty, fifty, a
hundred ducats apiece for his picture in little. 'Sblood, there is something in
this more than natural, if philosophy could find it out.

[*a flourish*]

GUILDENSTERN: There are the players.

HAMLET: Gentlemen, you are welcome to Elsinore. Your hands, come then; th'   340
appurtenance of welcome is fashion and ceremony. Let me comply* with
you in this garb;* lest my extent* to the players, which, I tell you, must show
fairly outwards, should more appear like entertainments than yours. You are
welcome. But my uncle-father and aunt-mother are deceived.

GUILDENSTERN: In what, my dear lord?   345

HAMLET: I am but mad north-north-west; when the wind is southerly I know a
hawk from a handsaw.

[*Reenter* POLONIUS.]

POLONIUS: Well be with you, gentlemen!

HAMLET: Hark you, Guildenstern, and you, too—at each ear a hearer: that great
baby you see there is not yet out of his swaddling clouts.

---

[318] **eyrie** nest
[318] **little eyases . . . question** young hawks that cry shrilly above others in a debate
[319] **tyrannically clapp'd** violently applauded
[319–20] **berattle the common stages** put down the public theatres
[321] **goose quills** pens (of those who satirize the public theatres and their audiences)
[322] **escoted** financially supported
[323] **quality** profession of acting
[326] **succession** future profession
[328] **tarre** incite
[329] **argument** for a playscript
[334] **Hercules and his load** reference to the Globe Theatre, whose sign showed Hercules carrying the globe on his shoulders
[341] **comply** be courteous
[342] **garb** outward show
[342] **extent** behavior

ROSENCRANTZ: Happily* he is the second time come to them; for they say an old   350
    man is twice a child.

HAMLET: I will prophesy he comes to tell me of the players; mark it. You say
    right, sir: a Monday morning; 'twas then indeed.

POLONIUS: My lord, I have news to tell you.   355

HAMLET: My lord, I have news to tell you. When Roscius was an actor in
    Rome—

POLONIUS: The actors are come hither, my lord.

HAMLET: Buzz, buzz!

POLONIUS: Upon my honour—   360

HAMLET: They came each actor on his ass—

POLONIUS: The best actors in the world, either for tragedy, comedy, history,
    pastoral, pastoral-comical, historical-pastoral, tragical-historical, tragical-
    comical-historical-pastoral, scene individable, or poem unlimited. Seneca
    cannot be too heavy nor Plautus too light. For the law of writ and the lib-   365
    erty,* these are the only men.

HAMLET: O Jephthah, judge of Israel, what a treasure hadst thou!

POLONIUS: What a treasure had he, my lord?

HAMLET: Why—

                      'One fair daughter, and no more,   370
                      The which he loved passing well.'

POLONIUS: [aside] Still on my daughter.

HAMLET: Am I not i' th' right, old Jephthah?

POLONIUS: If you call me Jephthah, my lord, I have a daughter that I love pass-
    ing well.   375

HAMLET: Nay, that follows not.

POLONIUS: What follows then, my lord?

HAMLET: Why—

                      'As by lot, God wot'

and then, you know,   380

                  'It came to pass, as most like it was.'

The first row of the pious chanson* will show you more; for look where my
abridgement* comes.

    [*Enter the* PLAYERS.]

You are welcome, masters; welcome all.—I am glad to see thee well.—
Welcome, good friends.—O, my old friend! Why thy face is valanc'd* since   385
I saw thee last; com'st thou to beard me in Denmark?—What, my young
lady* and mistress! By'r lady, your ladyship is nearer to heaven than when I
saw you last by the altitude of a chopine.* Pray God, your voice, like a piece
of uncurrent gold, be not crack'd within the ring.*—Masters, you are all

---

³⁵⁰ **Happily** perhaps
^{365–66} **law of writ and the liberty** sticking to the text and improvising
³⁸² **first row of the pious chanson** first stanza of a religious song
³⁸³ **abridgement** interruption
³⁸⁵ **valanc'd** furnished with a beard
^{386–87} **young lady** boy who played female roles
³⁸⁸ **chopine** thick-soled shoe
³⁸⁹ **crack'd within the ring** comparing a boy's breaking voice with a cracked coin (which it was illegal to use)

welcome. We'll e'en to't like French falconers, fly at anything we see. We'll   390
have a speech straight. Come, give us a taste of your quality; come, a passionate speech.

FIRST PLAYER: What speech, my good lord?

HAMLET: I heard thee speak me a speech once, but it was never acted; or, if it was,
not above once; for the play, I remember, pleas'd not the million; 'twas   395
caviary to the general.* But it was—as I received it, and others whose judgments in such matters cried in the top of mine*—an excellent play, well di-
gested in the scenes, set down with as much modesty as cunning.* I remember one said there were no sallets* in the lines to make the matter
savoury, nor no matter in the phrase that might indict the author of affec-   400
tation; but call'd it an honest method, as wholesome as sweet, and by very
much more handsome than fine.* One speech in it I chiefly lov'd; 'twas
Aeneas' tale to Dido; and thereabout of it especially where he speaks of
Priam's slaughter. If it live in your memory, begin at this line—let me see:
   'The rugged Pyrrhus, like th' Hyrcanian beast,'*   405
'Tis not so; it begins with Pyrrhus.
   'The rugged Pyrrhus, he whose sable* arms,
   Black as his purpose, did the night resemble
   When he lay couched in the ominous horse,*
   Hath now this dread and black complexion smear'd   410
   With heraldry more dismal; head to foot
   Now is he total gules, horridly trick'd*
   With blood of fathers, mothers, daughters, sons,
   Bak'd and impasted* with the parching streets,
   That lend a tyrannous and damned light   415
   To their lord's murder. Roasted in wrath and fire,
   And thus o'er-sized* with coagulate gore,
   With eyes like carbuncles, the hellish Pyrrhus
   Old grandsire Priam seeks.'
So proceed you.   420

POLONIUS: Fore God, my lord, well spoken, with good accent and good discretion.

FIRST PLAYER: *'Anon he finds him*
   Striking too short at Greeks; his antique sword,
   Rebellious to his arm, lies where it falls,
   Repugnant to command. Unequal match'd,   425
   Pyrrhus at Priam drives, in rage strikes wide;
   But with the whiff and wind of his fell sword

---

[396] **caviary to the general** too rich for the common audience
[397] **top of mine** agreed with or exceeded mine
[398] **modesty as cunning** restraint as cleverness
[399] **sallets** salads (spicy jests)
[402] **more handsome than fine** well proportioned rather than ornamented
[405] **Hyrcanian beast** tiger
[407] **sable** black
[409] **ominous horse** the wooden horse used in taking Troy
[412] **total gules, horridly trick'd** entirely red, horridly adorned
[414] **impasted** encrusted
[417] **o'er-sized** smeared over

> Th' unnerved father falls. Then senseless Ilium,*
> Seeming to feel this blow, with flaming top
> Stoops to his base,* and with a hideous crash   430
> Takes prisoner Pyrrhus' ear. For, lo! his sword,
> Which was declining on the milky head
> Of reverend Priam, seem'd i' th' air to stick.
> So, as a painted tyrant, Pyrrhus stood
> And, like a neutral to his will and matter,   435
> Did nothing.
> But as we often see, against* some storm,
> A silence in the heavens, the rack* stand still,
> The bold winds speechless, and the orb below
> As hush as death, anon the dreadful thunder   440
> Doth rend the region; so, after Pyrrhus' pause,
> A roused vengeance sets him new a-work;
> And never did the Cyclops' hammers fall
> On Mars' armour, forg'd for proof eterne,*
> With less remorse than Pyrrhus' bleeding sword   445
> Now falls on Priam.
> Out, out, thou strumpet, Fortune! All you gods,
> In general synod,* take away her power;
> Break all the spokes and fellies* from her wheel,
> And bowl the round nave* down the hill of heaven,   450
> As low as to the fiends.'

POLONIUS: This is too long.

HAMLET: It shall to the barber's, with your beard. Prithee say on. He's for a jig,
  or a tale of bawdry, or he sleeps. Say on; come to Hecuba.

FIRST PLAYER: 'But who, ah, who had seen the mobled* queen—'   455

HAMLET: 'The mobled queen'?

POLONIUS: That's good; 'mobled queen' is good.

FIRST PLAYER: 'Run barefoot up and down, threat'ning the flames
> With bisson rheum,* a clout* upon that head
> Where late the diadem stood, and for a robe,   460
> About her lank and all o'er-teemed loins,*
> A blanket, in the alarm of fear caught up—
> Who this had seen, with tongue in venom steep'd,
> 'Gainst Fortune's state would treason have pronounc'd.
> But if the gods themselves did see her then,   465

---

428 **Ilium** Troy
430 **Stoops to his base** collapses
437 **against** before
438 **rack** clouds
444 **proof eterne** to last forever
448 **synod** council
449 **fellies** rims
450 **nave** hub
455 **mobled** muffled
459 **bisson rheum** blinding tears
459 **clout** rag
461 **o'er-teemed loins** exhausted with childbearing

> *When she saw Pyrrhus make malicious sport*
> *In mincing with his sword her husband's limbs,*
> *The instant burst of clamour that she made—*
> *Unless things mortal move them not at all—*
> *Would have made milch* the burning eyes of heaven,*   470
> *And passion in the gods.'*

POLONIUS: Look whe'er* he has not turn'd his colour, and has tears in 's eyes. Prithee no more.

HAMLET: 'Tis well; I'll have thee speak out the rest of this soon.—Good my lord, will you see the players well bestowed? Do you hear: let them be well used;   475 for they are the abstract and brief chronicles of the time; after your death you were better have a bad epitaph than their ill report while you live.

POLONIUS: My lord, I will use them according to their desert.

HAMLET: God's bodkins, man, much better. Use every man after his desert, and who shall 'scape whipping? Use them after your own honour and dignity;   480 the less they deserve, the more merit is in your bounty. Take them in.

POLONIUS: Come, sirs.

HAMLET: Follow him, friends. We'll hear a play to-morrow. Dost thou hear me, old friend; can you play 'The Murder of Gonzago'?

FIRST PLAYER: Ay, my lord.   485

HAMLET: We'll ha't to-morrow night. You could, for a need, study a speech of some dozen or sixteen lines which I would set down and insert in't, could you not?

FIRST PLAYER: Ay, my lord.

HAMLET: Very well. Follow that lord; and look you mock him not. [*Exeunt*   490 POLONIUS *and* PLAYERS.] My good friends, I'll leave you till night. You are welcome to Elsinore.

ROSENCRANTZ: Good my lord!

         [*Exeunt* ROSENCRANTZ *and* GUILDENSTERN.]

HAMLET: Ay, so God buy to you! Now I am alone.
> O, what a rogue and peasant slave am I!   495
> Is it not monstrous that this player here,
> But in a fiction, in a dream of passion,
> Could force his soul so to his own conceit*
> That from her working all his visage wann'd;
> Tears in his eyes, distraction in's aspect,   500
> A broken voice, and his whole function* suiting
> With forms* to his conceit? And all for nothing!
> For Hecuba!
> What's Hecuba to him or he to Hecuba,
> That he should weep for her? What would he do,   505
> Had he the motive and the cue for passion
> That I have? He would drown the stage with tears,
> And cleave the general ear with horrid speech;

---

470 **milch** moist
472 **whe'er** whether
498 **conceit** imagination
501 **function** action
502 **forms** bodily expressions

Make mad the guilty, and appal the free,*
Confound the ignorant, and amaze indeed   510
The very faculties of eyes and ears.
Yet I,
A dull and muddy-mettl'd* rascal, peak,
Like John-a-dreams,* unpregnant of* my cause,
And can say nothing; no, not for a king   515
Upon whose property and most dear life
A damn'd defeat was made. Am I a coward?
Who calls me villain, breaks my pate across,
Plucks off my beard and blows it in my face,
Tweaks me by the nose, gives me the lie i' th' throat   520
As deep as to the lungs? Who does me this?
Ha!
'Swounds, I should take it; for it cannot be
But I am pigeon-liver'd* and lack gall
To make oppression bitter, or ere this   525
I should 'a fatted all the region kites*
With this slave's offal. Bloody, bawdy villain!
Remorseless, treacherous, lecherous, kindless* villain!
O, vengeance!
Why, what an ass am I! This is most brave,   530
That I, the son of a dear father murder'd,
Prompted to my revenge by heaven and hell,
Must, like a whore, unpack my heart with words,
And fall a-cursing like a very drab,*
A scullion!* Fie upon't! foh!   535
About,* my brains. Hum—I have heard
That guilty creatures, sitting at a play,
Have by the very cunning of the scene
Been struck so to the soul that presently*
They have proclaim'd their malefactions;   540
For murder, though it have no tongue, will speak
With most miraculous organ. I'll have these players
Play something like the murder of my father
Before mine uncle. I'll observe his looks;
I'll tent* him to the quick. If 'a do blench,*   545
I know my course. The spirit that I have seen

---

509 **appal the free** terrify the guiltless
513 **muddy-mettl'd** weak spirited
513–14 **peak, Like John-a-dreams** mope like a dreamer
514 **unpregnant of** unmoved by
524 **pigeon-liver'd** a coward
526 **kites** scavenger birds
528 **kindless** unnatural
534 **drab** prostitute
535 **scullion** kitchen servant
536 **About** to work
539 **presently** immediately
545 **tent** probe
545 **blench** blanch

May be a devil; and the devil hath power
T'assume a pleasing shape; yea and perhaps
Out of my weakness and my melancholy,
As he is very potent with such spirits,   550
Abuses me to damn me. I'll have grounds
More relative* than this. The play's the thing
Wherein I'll catch the conscience of the King.   [*Exit.*]

ACT III

SCENE I———*Elsinore. The Castle.*

[*Enter* KING, QUEEN, POLONIUS, OPHELIA, ROSENCRANTZ, *and* GUILDENSTERN.]

KING: And can you by no drift of conference*
  Get from him why he puts on this confusion,
  Grating so harshly all his days of quiet
  With turbulent and dangerous lunacy?
ROSENCRANTZ: He does confess he feels himself distracted,   5
  But from what cause 'a will by no means speak.
GUILDENSTERN: Nor do we find him forward to be sounded;*
  But, with a crafty madness, keeps aloof
  When we would bring him on to some confession
  Of his true state.   10
QUEEN: Did he receive you well?
ROSENCRANTZ: Most like a gentleman.
GUILDENSTERN: But with much forcing of his disposition.*
ROSENCRANTZ: Niggard of question; but of our demands
  Most free in his reply.   15
QUEEN: Did you assay* him
  To any pastime?
ROSENCRANTZ: Madam, it so fell out that certain players
  We o'er-raught* on the way. Of these we told him;
  And there did seem in him a kind of joy   20
  To hear of it. They are here about the court,
  And, as I think, they have already order
  This night to play before him.
POLONIUS: 'Tis most true;

---

552 **relative** certain
III,i,1 **conference** conversation
7 **forward to be sounded** willing to be questioned
13 **forcing of his disposition** effort
16 **assay** tempt
19 **o'er-raught** overtook

And he beseech'd me to entreat your Majesties 25
To hear and see the matter.
KING: With all my heart; and it doth much content me
To hear him so inclin'd.
Good gentlemen, give him a further edge,
And drive his purpose into these delights. 30
ROSENCRANTZ: We shall, my lord.

[*Exeunt* ROSENCRANTZ *and* GUILDENSTERN.]

KING: Sweet Gertrude, leave us, too;
For we have closely* sent for Hamlet hither,
That he, as 'twere by accident, may here
Affront* Ophelia. 35
Her father and myself—lawful espials*—
Will so bestow ourselves that, seeing unseen,
We may of their encounter frankly judge,
And gather by him, as he is behav'd,
If't be th' affliction of his love or no 40
That thus he suffers for.
QUEEN: I shall obey you;
And for your part, Ophelia, I do wish
That your good beauties be the happy cause
Of Hamlet's wildness; so shall I hope your virtues 45
Will bring him to his wonted way again,
To both your honours.
OPHELIA: Madam, I wish it may.   [*Exit* QUEEN.]
POLONIUS: Ophelia, walk you here.—Gracious, so please you,
We will bestow ourselves.—Read on this book; 50
That show of such an exercise may colour*
Your loneliness.—We are oft to blame in this:
'Tis too much prov'd, that with devotion's visage
And pious action we do sugar o'er
The devil himself. 55
KING: [aside] O, 'tis too true!
How smart a lash that speech doth give my conscience!
The harlot's cheek, beautied with plast'ring art,
Is not more ugly to the thing that helps it
Than is my deed to my most painted word. 60
O heavy burden!
POLONIUS: I hear him coming; let's withdraw, my lord.

[*Exeunt* KING *and* POLONIUS.]

[*Enter* HAMLET.]

---

33 **closely** secretly
35 **Affront** meet face to face
36 **espials** observers
51 **colour** give an excuse for

HAMLET: To be, or not to be—that is the question;
       Whether 'tis nobler in the mind to suffer
       The slings and arrows of outrageous fortune,   65
       Or to take arms against a sea of troubles,
       And by opposing end them? To die, to sleep—
       No more; and by a sleep to say we end
       The heart-ache and the thousand natural shocks
       That flesh is heir to. 'tis a consummation   70
       Devoutly to be wish'd. To die, to sleep;
       To sleep, perchance to dream. Ay, there's the rub;*
       For in that sleep of death what dreams may come,
       When we have shuffled off this mortal coil,*
       Must give us pause. There's the respect*   75
       That makes calamity of so long life;
       For who would bear the whips and scorns of time,
       Th' oppressor's wrong, the proud man's contumely,
       The pangs of despis'd love, the law's delay,
       The insolence of office, and the spurns   80
       That patient merit of th' unworthy takes,
       When he himself might his quietus* make
       With a bare bodkin?* Who would these fardels* bear,
       To grunt and sweat under a weary life,
       But that the dread of something after death—   85
       The undiscover'd country, from whose bourn*
       No traveller returns—puzzles the will,
       And makes us rather bear those ills we have
       Than fly to others that we know not of?
       Thus conscience does make cowards of us all;   90
       And thus the native hue of resolution
       Is sicklied o'er with the pale cast* of thought,
       And enterprises of great pitch and moment,
       With this regard, their currents turn awry
       And lose the name of action.—Soft you now!   95
       The fair Ophelia.—Nymph, in thy orisons*
       Be all my sins rememb'red.
OPHELIA: Good my lord,
       How does your honour for this many a day?
HAMLET: I humbly thank you; well, well, well.   100
OPHELIA: My lord, I have remembrance of yours
       That I have longed to re-deliver.
       I pray you now receive them.

---

[72] **rub** impediment
[74] **shuffled off this mortal coil** separated body from soul
[75] **respect** consideration
[82] **quietus** end
[83] **bodkin** dagger
[83] **fardels** burdens
[86] **bourn** region
[92] **cast** color
[96] **orisons** prayers

HAMLET: No, not I;
    I never gave you aught.   105
OPHELIA: My honour'd lord, you know right well you did,
    And with them words of so sweet breath compos'd
    As made the things more rich; their perfume lost,
    Take these again; for to the noble mind
    Rich gifts wax poor when givers prove unkind.   110
    There, my lord.
HAMLET: Ha, Ha! Are you honest?*
OPHELIA: My lord?
HAMLET: Are you fair?
OPHELIA: What means your lordship?   115
HAMLET: That if you be honest and fair, your honesty should admit no discourse
    to your beauty.
OPHELIA: Could beauty, my lord, have better commerce than with honesty?
HAMLET: Ay, truly; for the power of beauty will sooner transform honesty from
    what it is to a bawd* than the force of honesty can translate beauty into his   120
    likeness. This was sometime a paradox, but now the time gives it proof. I
    did love you once.
OPHELIA: Indeed, my lord, you made me believe so.
HAMLET: You should not have believ'd me; for virtue cannot so inoculate our old
    stock but we shall relish of it.* I loved you not.   125
OPHELIA: I was the more deceived.
HAMLET: Get thee to a nunnery. Why wouldst thou be a breeder of sinners? I am
    myself indifferent honest,* but yet I could accuse me of such things that it
    were better my mother had not borne me: I am very proud, revengeful, am-
    bitious; with more offences at my beck than I have thoughts to put them in,   130
    imagination to give them shape, or time to act them in. What should such
    fellows as I do crawling between earth and heaven? We are arrant knaves, all;
    believe none of us. Go thy ways to a nunnery. Where's your father?
OPHELIA: At home, my lord.
HAMLET: Let the doors be shut upon him, that he may play the fool nowhere but   135
    in's own house. Farewell.
OPHELIA: O, help him, you sweet heavens!
HAMLET: If thou dost marry, I'll give thee this plague for thy dowry: be thou as
    chaste as ice, as pure as snow, thou shalt not escape calumny. Get thee to a
    nunnery, go, farewell. Or, if thou wilt needs marry, marry a fool; for wise   140
    men know well enough what monsters* you make of them. To a nunnery
    go; and quickly, too. Farewell.
OPHELIA: O heavenly powers, restore him!
HAMLET: I have heard of your paintings, too, well enough; God hath given you
    one face, and you make yourselves another. You jig and amble, and you lisp,   145
    and nickname God's creatures, and make your wantonness your ignorance.*
    Go to, I'll no more on't; it hath made me mad. I say we will have no more

---

[112] **Are you honest?** are you modest; chaste; truthful
[120] **bawd** procurer
[124–25] **virtue cannot . . . relish of it** virtue cannot shield us from still desiring sinful pleasures
[128] **indifferent honest** modestly virtuous
[141] **monsters** cuckolds
[146] **make your wantonness your ignorance** excuse your wantonness by pretending ignorance

marriage: those that are married already, all but one, shall live; the rest shall keep as they are. To a nunnery, go.

> [*Exit.*]

OPHELIA: O, what a noble mind is here o'erthrown!　　　　　　　　150
　　The courtier's, soldier's, scholar's, eye, tongue, sword;
　　Th' expectancy and rose* of the fair state,
　　The glass of fashion and the mould of form,*
　　Th' observ'd of all observers—quite, quite down!
　　And I, of ladies most deject and wretched,　　　　　　　155
　　That suck'd the honey of his music vows,
　　Now see that noble and most sovereign reason,
　　Like sweet bells jangled, out of time and harsh;
　　That unmatch'd form and feature of blown* youth
　　Blasted with ecstasy.* O, woe is me　　　　　　　160
　　T' have seen what I have seen, see what I see!

> [*Reenter* KING *and* POLONIUS.]

KING: Love! His affections do not that way tend;
　　Nor what he spake, though it lack'd form a little,
　　Was not like madness. There's something in his soul
　　O'er which his melancholy sits on brood;　　　　　　165
　　And I do doubt* the hatch and the disclose
　　Will be some danger; which to prevent
　　I have in quick determination
　　Thus set it down: he shall with speed to England
　　For the demand of our neglected tribute.　　　　　　170
　　Haply the seas and countries different,
　　With variable objects, shall expel
　　This something-settled matter in his heart
　　Whereon his brains still beating puts him thus
　　From fashion of himself. What think you on't?　　　　　175
POLONIUS: It shall do well. But yet do I believe
　　The origin and commencement of his grief
　　Sprung from neglected love. How now, Ophelia!
　　You need not tell us what Lord Hamlet said;
　　We heard it all. My lord, do as you please;　　　　　180
　　But if you hold it fit, after the play
　　Let his queen mother all alone entreat him
　　To show his grief. Let her be round* with him;
　　And I'll be placed, so please you, in the ear
　　Of all their conference. If she find him not,*　　　　　185
　　To England send him; or confine him where

---

152 **expectancy and rose** hope
153 **mould of form** pattern of excellent behavior
159 **blown** blooming
160 **ecstasy** madness
166 **doubt** fear
183 **round** blunt
185 **find him not** doesn't find out what is bothering him

Your wisdom best shall think.

KING: It shall be so:

Madness in great ones must not unwatch'd go.

[*Exeunt.*]

SCENE II————*Elsinore. The Castle.*

[*Enter* HAMLET *and three of the* PLAYERS.]

HAMLET: Speak the speech, I pray you, as I pronounc'd it to you, trippingly on
the tongue; but if you mouth it, as many of our players do, I had as lief the
towncrier spoke my lines. Nor do not saw the air too much with your hand,
thus, but use all gently; for in the very torrent, tempest, and, as I may say,
whirlwind of your passion, you must acquire and beget a temperance that   5
may give it smoothness. O, it offends me to the soul to hear a robustious
periwig-pated* fellow tear a passion to tatters, to very rags, to split the ears
of the groundlings,* who, for the most part, are capable of nothing* but
inexplicable dumb shows* and noise. I would have such a fellow whipp'd for
o'erdoing Termagant; it out-herods Herod.* Pray you avoid it.   10

FIRST PLAYER: I warrant your honour.

HAMLET: Be not too tame neither, but let your own discretion be your tutor. Suit
the action to the word, the word to the action; with this special observance,
that you o'erstep not the modesty of nature; for anything so o'erdone is
from* the purpose of playing, whose end, both at the first and now, was and   15
is to hold, as 'twere, the mirror up to nature; to show virtue her own feature,
scorn her own image, and the very age and body of the time his form and
pressure.* Now, this overdone or come tardy off, though it makes the un-
skilful laugh, cannot but make the judicious grieve; the censure of the which
one must, in your allowance, o'erweigh a whole theatre of others. O, there   20
be players that I have seen play—and heard others praise, and that highly—
not to speak it profanely, that, neither having th' accent of Christians,
nor the gait of Christian, pagan, nor man, have so strutted and bellowed that I
have thought some of Nature's journeymen* had made men, and not made
them well, they imitated humanity so abominably.   25

FIRST PLAYER: I hope we have reform'd that indifferently* with us, sir.

HAMLET: O, reform it altogether. And let those that play your clowns speak no
more than is set down for them; for there be of them that will themselves
laugh, to set on some quantity of barren spectators to laugh, too, though in
the meantime some necessary question of the play be then to be considered.   30

III,ii,7 **periwig-pated** wig-wearing
8   **groundlings** spectators who stood in the space surrounding the stage; presumably the poorest and least-
educated spectators
8   **are capable of nothing** understand nothing
9   **dumb shows** silent miming (used, as later in this scene, as prologues to plays)
10   **Termagant . . . Herod** exaggeratedly overacted roles in medieval mystery plays
15   **from** contrary to
18   **pressure** image
24   **journeymen** workers not yet masters of their craft
26   **indifferently** mostly

That's villainous, and shows a most pitiful ambition in the fool that uses it.
Go, make you ready.

[*Exeunt* PLAYERS.]

[*Enter* POLONIUS, ROSENCRANTZ, *and* GUILDENSTERN.]

How now, my lord! Will the King hear this piece of work?
POLONIUS: And the Queen, too, and that presently.
HAMLET: Bid the players make haste.   [*Exit* POLONIUS.]   35
    Will you two help to hasten them?
ROSENCRANTZ: Ay, my lord.   [*Exeunt they two.*]
HAMLET: What, ho, Horatio!

    [*Enter* HORATIO.]

HORATIO: Here, sweet lord, at your service.
HAMLET: Horatio, thou art e'en as just a man   40
    As e'er my conversation cop'd withal.*
HORATIO: O my dear lord!
HAMLET: Nay, do not think I flatter;
    For what advancement may I hope from thee,
    That no revenue hast but thy good spirits   45
    To feed and clothe thee? Why should the poor be flatter'd?
    No, let the candied* tongue lick absurd pomp,
    And crook the pregnant hinges of the knee*
    Where thrift* may follow fawning. Dost thou hear?
    Since my dear soul was mistress of her choice   50
    And could of men distinguish her election,
    S'hath seal'd thee* for herself; for thou hast been
    As one, in suff'ring all, that suffers nothing;
    A man that Fortune's buffets and rewards
    Hast ta'en with equal thanks; and blest are those   55
    Whose blood* and judgment are so well commingled
    That they are not a pipe for Fortune's finger
    To sound what stop she please. Give me that man
    That is not passion's slave, and I will wear him
    In my heart's core, ay, in my heart of heart,   60
    As I do thee. Something too much of this.
    There is a play to-night before the King;
    One scene of it comes near the circumstance
    Which I have told thee of my father's death.
    I prithee, when thou seest that act afoot,   65
    Even with the very comment* of thy soul

---

[41] **cop'd withal** met with
[47] **candied** sugared, flattering
[48] **pregnant hinges of the knee** quick to curtsy and kneel
[49] **thrift** profit
[52] **S'hath seal'd thee** my soul has chosen you
[56] **blood** feelings
[66] **very comment** deepest wisdom

Observe my uncle. If his occulted* guilt
Do not itself unkennel in one speech,
It is a damned ghost that we have seen,
And my imaginations are as foul   70
As Vulcan's stithy.* Give him heedful note;
For I mine eyes will rivet to his face;
And, after, we will both our judgments join
In censure of his seeming.*

HORATIO: Well, my lord.   75
    If 'a steal aught the whilst this play is playing,
    And 'scape detecting, I will pay the theft.

> [*Enter trumpets and kettledrums. Danish march. Sound a flourish. Enter* KING,
> QUEEN, POLONIUS, OPHELIA, ROSENCRANTZ, GUILDENSTERN, *and other*
> LORDS *attendant, with the guard carrying torches.*]

HAMLET: They are coming to the play; I must be idle.*
    Get you a place.
KING: How fares our cousin Hamlet?   80
HAMLET: Excellent, i' faith; of the chameleon's dish.* I eat the air promise-
    cramm'd; you cannot feed capons so.
KING: I have nothing with this answer, Hamlet; these words are not mine.
HAMLET: No, nor mine now. [*to* POLONIUS] My lord, you play'd once in th' uni-
    versity, you say?   85
POLONIUS: That did I, my lord, and was accounted a good actor.
HAMLET: What did you enact?
POLONIUS: I did enact Julius Caesar; I was kill'd i' th' Capitol; Brutus kill'd me.
HAMLET: It was a brute part of him to kill so capital a calf there. Be the players
    ready?   90
ROSENCRANTZ: Ay, my lord; they stay upon your patience.
QUEEN: Come hither, my dear Hamlet, sit by me.
HAMLET: No, good mother; here's metal more attractive.*
POLONIUS: [*to the* KING] O, ho! do you mark that?
HAMLET: Lady, shall I lie in your lap? [*lying down at* OPHELIA's *feet*]   95
OPHELIA: No, my lord.
HAMLET: I mean, my head upon your lap?
OPHELIA: Ay, my lord.
HAMLET: Do you think I meant country matters?*
OPHELIA: I think nothing, my lord.   100
HAMLET: That's a fair thought to lie between maids' legs.
OPHELIA: What is, my lord?
HAMLET: Nothing.
OPHELIA: You are merry, my lord.
HAMLET: Who, I?   105

---

67 **occulted** hidden
71 **Vulcan's stithy** forge of the Greek god
74 **censure of his seeming** judgment on his response
78 **be idle** play the fool
81 **chameleon's dish** air on which chameleons were thought to live
93 **attractive** magnetic
99 **country matters** a sexual innuendo

OPHELIA: Ay, my lord.

HAMLET: O God, your only jig-maker!* What should a man do but be merry? For look you how cheerfully my mother looks, and my father died within's two hours.

OPHELIA: Nay, 'tis twice two months, my lord. 110

HAMLET: So long? Nay then, let the devil wear black, for I'll have a suit of sables. O heavens! die two months ago, and not forgotten yet? Then there's hope a great man's memory may outlive his life half a year; but, by'r lady, 'a must build churches, then; or else shall 'a suffer not thinking on, with the hobby-horse,* whose epitaph is 'For O, for O, the hobby-horse is forgot!' 115

[*The trumpet sounds. Hautboys play. The Dumb Show enters.*]

[*Enter a* KING *and a* QUEEN, *very lovingly; the* QUEEN *embracing him and he her. She kneels, and makes a show of protestation unto him. He takes her up, and declines his head upon her neck. He lies him down upon a bank of flowers; she, seeing him asleep, leaves him. Anon comes in a* FELLOW, *takes off his crown, kisses it, pours poison in the sleeper's ears, and leaves him. The* QUEEN *returns; finds the* KING *dead, and makes passionate action. The* POISONER, *with some two or three* MUTES, *comes in again, seeming to condole with her. The dead body is carried away. The* POISONER *woos the* QUEEN *with gifts: she seems harsh awhile, but in the end accepts his love. Exeunt.*]

OPHELIA: What means this, my lord?

HAMLET: Marry, this is miching mallecho;* it means mischief.

OPHELIA: Belike this show imports the argument* of the play.

[*Enter* PROLOGUE.]

HAMLET: We shall know by this fellow: the players cannot keep counsel; they'll tell all. 120

OPHELIA: Will 'a tell us what this show meant?

HAMLET: Ay, or any show that you show him. Be not you asham'd to show, he'll not shame to tell you what it means.

OPHELIA: You are naught, you are naught.* I'll mark the play.

PROLOGUE: *For us, and for our tragedy,* 125
  Here stooping to your clemency,
  We beg your hearing patiently.

[*Exit.*]

HAMLET: Is this a prologue, or the posy of a ring?*

OPHELIA: 'Tis brief, my lord.

HAMLET: As woman's love. 130

[*Enter the* PLAYER KING *and* QUEEN.]

---

[107] **jig-maker** composer of songs and dances (jigs were often performed as afterpieces in the theatre, and often by the fool)
[114] **hobby-horse** mock horse worn by a performer in mummers' plays
[117] **miching mallecho** sneaky mischief
[118] **argument** plot
[124] **naught** naughty
[128] **posy of a ring** sentiment inscribed in a ring

PLAYER KING: *Full thirty times hath Phoebus' cart* gone round*
    Neptune's salt wash* and Tellus's* orbed ground,
    And thirty dozen moons with borrowed sheen
    About the world have times twelve thirties been,
    Since love our hearts and Hymen* did our hands   135
    Unite comutual in most sacred bands.
PLAYER QUEEN: *So many journeys may the sun and moon*
    Make us again count o'er ere love be done!
    But, woe is me, you are so sick of late,
    So far from cheer and from your former state,   140
    That I distrust* you. Yet, though I distrust,
    Discomfort you, my lord, it nothing must;
    For women fear too much even as they love,
    And women's fear and love hold quantity,
    In neither aught, or in extremity.   145
    Now, what my love is, proof hath made you know;
    And as my love is siz'd, my fear is so.
    Where love is great, the littlest doubts are fear;
    Where little fears grow great, great love grows there.
PLAYER KING: *Faith, I must leave thee, love, and shortly, too:*   150
    My operant* powers their functions leave to do;
    And thou shalt live in this fair world behind,
    Honour'd, belov'd; and haply one as kind
    For husband shalt thou—
PLAYER QUEEN: *O, confound the rest!*   155
    Such love must needs be treason in my breast.
    In second husband let me be accurst!
    None wed the second but who kill'd the first.
HAMLET: That's wormwood, wormwood.*
PLAYER QUEEN: *The instances* that second marriage move**   160
    Are base respects of thrift,* but none of love.
    A second time I kill my husband dead,
    When second husband kisses me in bed.
PLAYER KING: *I do believe you think what now you speak;*
    But what we do determine oft we break.   165
    Purpose is but the slave to memory,
    Of violent birth, but poor validity;*
    Which now, the fruit unripe, sticks on the tree;
    But fall unshaken when they mellow be.
    Most necessary 'tis that we forget   170

---

[131] **Phoebus' cart** the sun god's chariot
[132] **Neptune's salt wash** the sea
[132] **Tellus** Roman goddess of the Earth
[135] **Hymen** god of marriage
[141] **distrust** am anxious about
[151] **operant** active
[159] **wormwood** a bitter herb
[160] **instances** motives
[160] **move** induce
[161] **base respects of thrift** considerations of profit
[167] **validity** strength

To pay ourselves what to ourselves is debt.
What to ourselves in passion we propose,
The passion ending, doth the purpose lose,
The violence of either grief or joy
Their own enactures* with themselves destroy.   175
Where joy most revels grief doth most lament;
Grief joys, joy grieves, on slender accident.
This world is not for aye; nor 'tis not strange
That even our loves should with our fortunes change;
For 'tis a question left us yet to prove,   180
Whether love lead fortune or else fortune love.
The great man down, you mark his favourite flies;
The poor advanc'd makes friends of enemies.
And hitherto doth love on fortune tend;
For who not needs shall never lack a friend,   185
And who in want a hollow friend doth try,
Directly seasons* him his enemy.
But, orderly to end where I begun,
Our wills and fates do so contrary run
That our devices still are overthrown;   190
Our thoughts are ours, their ends none of our own.
So think thou wilt no second husband wed;
But die thy thoughts when thy first lord is dead.
PLAYER QUEEN: *Nor earth to me give food, nor heaven light,*
Sport and repose lock from me day and night,   195
To desperation turn my trust and hope,
An anchor's* cheer in prison be my scope,
Each opposite that blanks* the face of joy
Meet what I would have well, and it destroy,
Both here and hence pursue my lasting strife,   200
If, once a widow, ever I be wife!
HAMLET: If she should break it now!
PLAYER KING: *'Tis deeply sworn. Sweet, leave me here awhile;*
My spirits grow dull, and fain I would beguile
The tedious day with sleep.   [*Sleeps.*] 205
PLAYER QUEEN: *Sleep rock thy brain,*
And never come mischance between us twain!
HAMLET: Madam, how like you this play?
QUEEN: The lady doth protest too much, methinks.
HAMLET: O, but she'll keep her word.   210
KING: Have you heard the argument?* Is there no offence in't?
HAMLET: No, no; they do but jest, poison in jest; no offence i' th' world.
KING: What do you call the play?
HAMLET: 'The Mouse-trap.' Marry, how? Tropically.* This play is the image of a

---

175 **enactures** acts
187 **seasons** ripens him into
197 **anchor's** anchorite, hermit
198 **opposite that blanks** adverse thing that makes the face blanch
211 **argument** plot
214 **Tropically** figuratively

murder done in Vienna: Gonzago is the duke's name; his wife, Baptista. You   215
shall see anon. 'Tis a knavish piece of work; but what of that? Your Majesty,
and we that have free* souls, it touches us not. Let the galled jade* wince,
our withers are unwrung.

> [*Enter* LUCIANUS.]

This is one Lucianus, nephew to the King.
OPHELIA: You are as good as a chorus, my lord.   220
HAMLET: I could interpret* between you and your love, if I could see the puppets
    dallying.
OPHELIA: You are keen, my lord, you are keen.
HAMLET: It would cost you a groaning to take off mine edge.*
OPHELIA: Still better, and worse.   225
HAMLET: So you mis-take* your husbands.—Begin, murderer; pox, leave thy
    damnable faces and begin. Come; the croaking raven doth bellow for
    revenge.
LUCIANUS: *Thoughts black, hands apt, drugs fit, and time agreeing;*
    Confederate season, else no creature seeing;*   230
    Thou mixture rank, of midnight weeds collected,
    With Hecate's ban thrice blasted, thrice infected.*
    *Thy natural magic and dire property***
    On wholesome life usurps immediately.
    [*Pours the poison in his ears.*]
HAMLET: 'A poisons him i' th' garden for his estate. His name's Gonzago. The   235
    story is extant, and written in very choice Italian. You shall see anon how
    the murderer gets the love of Gonzago's wife.
OPHELIA: The King rises.
HAMLET: What, frighted with false fire!*
QUEEN: How fares my lord?   240
POLONIUS: Give o'er the play.
KING: Give me some light. Away!
POLONIUS: Lights, lights, lights!

> [*Exeunt all but* HAMLET *and* HORATIO.]

HAMLET: Why, let the strucken deer go weep,
    The hart ungalled play;   245
    For some must watch, while some must sleep;
    Thus runs the world away.
    Would not this, sir, and a forest of feathers*—if the rest of my fortunes turn

---

217 **free** souls free of guilt
217 **galled jade** chafed horse
221 **interpret** explain like a puppet master if he could see the puppets playing wantonly
224 **cost . . . edge** a sexual reference
226 **mis-take** err in taking
230 **Confederate season** the opportunity offered me
232 **Hecate's ban** the goddess of sorcery's curse
233 **property** nature
239 **false fire** blank firing of a gun
248 **forest of feathers** costume with feathers

Turk* with me—with two Provincial roses on my raz'd shoes,* get me a fellowship in a cry of players,* sir? 250

HORATIO: Half a share.

HAMLET: A whole one, I.
For thou dost know, O Damon dear,
This realm dismantled was
Of Jove himself; and now reigns here 255
A very, very—peacock.

HORATIO: You might have rhym'd.

HAMLET: O good Horatio, I'll take the ghost's word for a thousand pound. Didst
perceive?

HORATIO: Very well, my lord. 260

HAMLET: Upon the talk of the poisoning.

HORATIO: I did very well note him.

HAMLET: Ah, ha! Come, some music. Come, the recorders.
For if the King like not the comedy,
Why, then, belike he likes it not, perdy.* 265

Come, some music.

[*Reenter* ROSENCRANTZ *and* GUILDENSTERN.]

GUILDENSTERN: Good my lord, vouchsafe me a word with you.

HAMLET: Sir, a whole history.

GUILDENSTERN: The King, sir—

HAMLET: Ay, sir, what of him? 270

GUILDENSTERN: Is, in his retirement, marvellous distemp'red.

HAMLET: With drink, sir?

GUILDENSTERN: No, my lord, rather with choler.*

HAMLET: Your wisdom should show itself more richer to signify this to his doctor; for for me to put him to his purgation would perhaps plunge him into 275
far more choler.

GUILDENSTERN: Good my lord, put your discourse into some frame,* and start
not so wildly from my affair.

HAMLET: I am tame, sir. Pronounce.

GUILDENSTERN: The Queen, your mother, in most great affliction of spirit, hath 280
sent me to you.

HAMLET: You are welcome.

GUILDENSTERN: Nay, good my lord, this courtesy is not of the right breed. If it
shall please you to make me a wholesome answer, I will do your mother's
commandment; if not, your pardon and my return shall be the end of my 285
business.

248–49 **turn Turk** go badly
249 **raz'd shoes** shoes ornamented with slashes
250 **cry of players** company of actors
265 **perdy** by God (par dieu)
273 **choler** anger
277 **frame** order, control

HAMLET: Sir, I cannot.

ROSENCRANTZ: What, my lord?

HAMLET: Make you a wholesome* answer, my wit's diseas'd. But, sir, such answer as I can make, you shall command: or rather, as you say, my mother. There-fore no more, but to the matter: my mother, you say— 290

ROSENCRANTZ: Then thus she says: your behaviour hath struck her into amazement and admiration.*

HAMLET: O wonderful son, that can so stonish a mother! But is there no sequel at the heels of this mother's admiration? Impart. 295

ROSENCRANTZ: She desires to speak with you in her closet ere you go to bed.

HAMLET: We shall obey, were she ten times our mother. Have you any further trade with us?

ROSENCRANTZ: My lord, you once did love me.

HAMLET: And do still, by these pickers and stealers.* 300

ROSENCRANTZ: Good my lord, what is your cause of distemper? You do surely bar the door upon your own liberty, if you deny your griefs to your friend.

HAMLET: Sir, I lack advancement.*

ROSENCRANTZ: How can that be, when you have the voice of the King himself for your succession in Denmark? 305

HAMLET: Ay, sir, but 'While the grass grows'—the proverb* is something musty.

[*Reenter the* PLAYERS, *with recorders.*]

O, the recorders! Let me see one. To withdraw* with you—why do you go about to recover the wind of me,* as if you would drive me into a toil?*

GUILDENSTERN: O my lord, if my duty be too bold, my love is too unmannerly.*

HAMLET: I do not well understand that. Will you play upon this pipe? 310

GUILDENSTERN: My lord, I cannot.

HAMLET: I pray you.

GUILDENSTERN: Believe me, I cannot.

HAMLET: I do beseech you.

GUILDENSTERN: I know no touch of it, my lord. 315

HAMLET: It is as easy as lying: govern these ventages* with your fingers and thumb, give it breath with your mouth, and it will discourse most eloquent music. Look you, these are the stops.

GUILDENSTERN: But these cannot I command to any utterance of harmony; I have not the skill. 320

HAMLET: Why, look you now, how unworthy a thing you make of me! You would play upon me; you would seem to know my stops; you would pluck out the heart of my mystery; you would sound me from my lowest note to the top of

---

[289] **wholesome** sane
[293] **admiration** wonder
[300] **pickers and stealers** hands
[303] **advancement** promotion
[306] **proverb** (the rest of the proverb is "the horse starveth")
[307] **withdraw** speak privately
[308] **recover the wind of me** get on the windward side of me
[308] **toil** snare
[309] **duty . . . unmannerly** if I have seemed rude it is because my love for you leads me beyond good manners
[316] **ventages** vents, stops on a musical instrument

my compass;* and there is much music, excellent voice, in this little organ,*   325
yet cannot you make it speak. 'Sblood, do you think I am easier to be play'd
on than a pipe? Call me what instrument you will, though you can fret me,
yet you cannot play upon me.

    [*Reenter* POLONIUS.]

    God bless you, sir!
POLONIUS: My lord, the Queen would speak with you, and presently.
HAMLET: Do you see yonder cloud that's almost in shape of a camel?   330
POLONIUS: By th' mass, and 'tis like a camel indeed.
HAMLET: Methinks it is like a weasel.
POLONIUS: It is back'd like a weasel.
HAMLET: Or like a whale?
POLONIUS: Very like a whale.   335
HAMLET: Then I will come to my mother by and by. [*aside*] They fool me to the
    top of my bent.*—I will come by and by.
POLONIUS: I will say so.   [*Exit* POLONIUS.]
HAMLET: 'By and by' is easily said. Leave me, friends.

    [*Exeunt all but* HAMLET.]

'Tis now the very witching time of night,   340
When churchyards yawn, and hell itself breathes out
Contagion to this world. Now could I drink hot blood,
And do such bitter business as the day
Would quake to look on. Soft! now to my mother.
O heart, lose not thy nature; let not ever   345
The soul of Nero* enter this firm bosom.
Let me be cruel, not unnatural:
I will speak daggers to her, but use none.
My tongue and soul in this be hypocrites—
How in my words somever she be shent,*   350
To give them seals* never, my soul, consent!

    [*Exit.*]

               SCENE III————*Elsinore. The Castle.*

    [*Enter* KING, ROSENCRANTZ, *and* GUILDENSTERN.]

KING: I like him not; nor stands it safe with us
    To let his madness range. Therefore prepare you;
    I your commission will forthwith dispatch,

---

[324] **compass** range
[324] **organ** the recorder
[336-37] **fool me . . . my bent** they force me to play the fool to the fullest
[346] **Nero** Roman emperor who killed his mother
[350] **shent** rebuked
[351] **give them seals** confirm them with deeds

And he to England shall along with you.
The terms* of our estate may not endure   5
Hazard so near's as doth hourly grow
Out of his brows.
GUILDENSTERN: We will ourselves provide.
　　　Most holy and religious fear it is
　　　To keep those many many bodies safe   10
　　　That live and feed upon your Majesty.
ROSENCRANTZ: The single and peculiar* life is bound
　　　With all the strength and armour of the mind
　　　To keep itself from noyance;* but much more
　　　That spirit upon whose weal depends and rests   15
　　　The lives of many. The cease of majesty
　　　Dies not alone, but like a gulf* doth draw
　　　What's near it with it. It is a massy wheel,
　　　Fix'd on the summit of the highest mount,
　　　To whose huge spokes ten thousand lesser things   20
　　　Are mortis'd and adjoin'd; which when it falls,
　　　Each small annexment, petty consequence,
　　　Attends the boist'rous ruin. Never alone
　　　Did the king sigh, but with a general groan.
KING: Arm* you, I pray you, to this speedy voyage;   25
　　　For we will fetters put about this fear,
　　　Which now goes too free-footed.
ROSENCRANTZ: We will haste us.

　　　　　[*Exeunt* ROSENCRANTZ *and* GUILDENSTERN.]

　　　　　[*Enter* POLONIUS.]

POLONIUS: My lord, he's going to his mother's closet.
　　　Behind the arras I'll convey myself   30
　　　To hear the process.* I'll warrant she'll tax him home;*
　　　And, as you said, and wisely was it said,
　　　'Tis meet that some more audience than a mother,
　　　Since nature makes them partial, should o'erhear
　　　The speech, of vantage.* Fare you well, my liege.   35
　　　I'll call upon you ere you go to bed,
　　　And tell you what I know.
KING: Thanks, dear my lord.　　　　　　　　　　[*Exit* POLONIUS.]
　　　O, my offence is rank, it smells to heaven;

III,iii,5 **terms** conditions
¹² **peculiar** private
¹⁴ **noyance** injury
¹⁷ **gulf** whirlpool
²⁵ **Arm** prepare
³¹ **process** proceedings
³¹ **tax him home** rebuke him sharply
³⁵ **of vantage** from some advantageous place

It hath the primal eldest curse* upon't— 40
A brother's murder! Pray can I not,
Though inclination be as sharp as will.
My stronger guilt defeats my strong intent,
And, like a man to double business bound,
I stand in pause where I shall first begin, 45
And both neglect. What if this cursed hand
Were thicker than itself with brother's blood,
Is there not rain enough in the sweet heavens
To wash it white as snow? Whereto serves mercy
But to confront the visage of offence? 50
And what's in prayer but this twofold force,
To be forestalled ere we come to fall,
Or pardon'd being down? Then I'll look up;
My fault is past. But, O, what form of prayer
Can serve my turn? 'Forgive me my foul murder'! 55
That cannot be; since I am still possess'd
Of those effects* for which I did the murder—
My crown, mine own ambition, and my queen.
May one be pardon'd and retain th' offence?
In the corrupted currents of this world 60
Offence's gilded hand may shove by justice;
And oft 'tis seen the wicked prize itself
Buys out the law. But 'tis not so above:
There is no shuffling;* there the action lies
In his true nature; and we ourselves compell'd, 65
Even to the teeth and forehead of our faults,
To give in evidence. What then? What rests?*
Try what repentance can. What can it not?
Yet what can it when one cannot repent?
O wretched state! O bosom black as death! 70
O limed* soul, that, struggling to be free,
Art more engag'd!* Help, angels. Make assay:
Bow, stubborn knees; and, heart, with strings of steel,
Be soft as sinews of the new-born babe.
All may be well. *[He kneels.]* 75

    [*Enter* HAMLET.]

HAMLET: Now might I do it pat, now 'a is a-praying;
    And now I'll do't—and so 'a goes to heaven,
    And so am I reveng'd. That would be scann'd.*

---

40 **primal eldest curse** oldest curse (Cain's murder of his brother Abel)
57 **effects** things gained
64 **shuffling** trickery
67 **rests** remains
71 **limed** trapped (birds were caught by liming tree limbs with a sticky substance)
72 **engag'd** entrapped
78 **would be scann'd** needs to be thought about

A villain kills my father; and for that,
I, his sole son, do this same villain send   80
To heaven.
Why, this is hire and salary, not revenge.
'A took my father grossly, full of bread,*
With all his crimes broad blown, as flush* as May;
And how his audit* stands who knows save heaven?   85
But in our circumstance and course of thought
'Tis heavy with him; and am I then reveng'd
To take him in the purging of his soul,
When he is fit and season'd for his passage?
No.   90
Up, sword, and know thou a more horrid hent.
When he is drunk asleep, or in his rage;
Or in th' incestuous pleasure of his bed;
At game, a-swearing, or about some act
That has no relish of salvation in't—   95
Then trip him, that his heels my kick at heaven,
And that his soul may be as damn'd and black
As hell, whereto it goes. My mother stays.
This physic* but prolongs thy sickly days.   [*Exit.*]
KING: [*rising*] My words fly up, my thoughts remain below.   100
Words without thoughts never to heaven go.   [*Exit.*]

SCENE IV———*The* QUEEN'*s closet.*

[*Enter* QUEEN *and* POLONIUS.]

POLONIUS: 'A will come straight. Look you lay home* to him;
        Tell him his pranks have been too broad* to bear with,
        And that your Grace hath screen'd and stood between
        Much heat and him. I'll silence me even here.
        Pray you be round with him.   5
HAMLET: [*within*] Mother, mother, mother!
QUEEN: I'll warrant you. Fear me not.
        Withdraw, I hear him coming.

[POLONIUS *goes behind the arras.*]

    [*Enter* HAMLET.]

HAMLET: Now, mother, what's the matter?
QUEEN: Hamlet, thou hast thy father much offended.   10
HAMLET: Mother, you have my father much offended.

---

83 **full of bread** worldly gratifications
84 **crimes . . . flush** sins in full bloom as flowers in May
85 **audit** account
99 **physic** (to Claudius) this medicine (prayer)
III,iv,1 **lay home** rebuke him sharply
2 **broad** unrestrained

QUEEN: Come, come, you answer with an idle* tongue.

HAMLET: Go, go, you question with a wicked tongue.

QUEEN: Why, how now, Hamlet!

HAMLET: What's the matter now? 15

QUEEN: Have you forgot me?

HAMLET: No, by the rood,* not so:
>You are the Queen, your husband's brother's wife;
>And—would it were not so!—you are my mother.

QUEEN: Nay then, I'll set those to you that can speak. 20

HAMLET: Come, come, and sit you down; you shall not budge.
>You go not till I set you up a glass*
>Where you may see the inmost part of you.

QUEEN: What wilt thou do? Thou wilt not murder me?
>Help, help, ho! 25

POLONIUS: [*behind*] What, ho! help, help, help!

HAMLET: [*draws*] How now! a rat?
>Dead, for a ducat, dead!

[*kills* POLONIUS *with a pass through the arras*]

POLONIUS: [*behind*] O, I am slain!

QUEEN: O me, what hast thou done? 30

HAMLET: Nay, I know not:
>Is it the King?

QUEEN: O, what a rash and bloody deed is this!

HAMLET: A bloody deed!—almost as bad, good mother,
>As kill a king and marry with his brother. 35

QUEEN: As kill a king!

HAMLET: Ay, lady, it was my word. [*parting the arras*]
>Thou wretched, rash, intruding fool, farewell!
>I took thee for thy better. Take thy fortune;
>Thou find'st to be too busy is some danger. 40
>Leave wringing of your hands. Peace; sit you down,
>And let me wring your heart; for so I shall,
>If it be made of penetrable stuff;
>If damned custom have not braz'd* it so
>That it be proof and bulwark against sense.* 45

QUEEN: What have I done that thou dar'st wag thy tongue
>In noise so rude against me?

HAMLET: Such an act
>That blurs the grace and blush of modesty;
>Calls virtue hypocrite; takes off the rose 50
>From the fair forehead of an innocent love,
>And sets a blister there,* makes marriage-vows

---

12 **idle** foolish
17 **rood** cross
22 **glass** mirror
44 **braz'd** hardened
45 **proof . . . sense** armored against feeling
52 **sets a blister** brands (as a harlot)

As false as dicers' oaths. O, such a deed
As from the body of contraction* plucks
The very soul, and sweet religion makes   55
A rhapsody* of words. Heaven's face does glow
O'er this solidity and compound mass
With heated visage, as against the doom—
Is thought-sick at the act.
QUEEN: Ay me, what act,   60
    That roars so loud and thunders in the index?*
HAMLET: Look here upon this picture and on this,
    The counterfeit presentment* of two brothers.
    See what a grace was seated on this brow;
    Hyperion's curls; the front* of Jove himself;   65
    An eye like Mars, to threaten and command;
    A station* like the herald Mercury
    New lighted on a heaven-kissing hill—
    A combination and a form indeed
    Where every god did seem to set his seal,   70
    To give the world assurance of a man.
    This was your husband. Look you now what follows:
    Here is your husband, like a mildew'd ear
    Blasting his wholesome brother. Have you eyes?
    Could you on this fair mountain leave to feed,   75
    And batten* on this moor? Ha! have you eyes?
    You cannot call it love; for at your age
    The heyday in the blood is tame, it's humble,
    And waits upon the judgment; and what judgment
    Would step from this to this? Sense, sure, you have,   80
    Else could you not have motion; but sure that sense
    Is apoplex'd;* for madness would not err,
    Nor sense to ecstasy* was ne'er so thrall'd
    But it reserv'd some quantity of choice
    To serve in such a difference. What devil was't   85
    That thus hath cozen'd you at hoodman-blind?*
    Eyes without feeling, feeling without sight.
    Ears without hands or eyes, smelling sans* all,
    Or but a sickly part of one true sense
    Could not so mope.* O shame! where is thy blush?   90
    Rebellious hell,

---

54 **contraction** marriage contract
56 **rhapsody** senseless string
61 **index** prologue
63 **counterfeit presentment** represented image
65 **front** forehead
67 **station** bearing
76 **batten** feed gluttonously
82 **apoplex'd** paralyzed
83 **ecstasy** madness
86 **hoodman-blind** cheated you at blindman's buff
88 **sans** without
90 **so mope** be so stupid

If thou canst mutine in a matron's bones,
To flaming youth let virtue be as wax
And melt in her own fire; proclaim no shame
When the compulsive ardour gives the charge,   95
Since frost itself as actively doth burn,
And reason panders will.*
QUEEN: O Hamlet, speak no more!
Thou turn'st my eyes into my very soul;
And there I see such black and grained spots   100
As will not leave their tinct.*
HAMLET: Nay, but to live
In the rank sweat of an enseamed* bed,
Stew'd in corruption, honeying and making love
Over the nasty sty!   105
QUEEN: O, speak to me no more!
These words like daggers enter in my ears;
No more, sweet Hamlet.
HAMLET: A murderer and a villain!
A slave that is not twentieth part the tithe*   110
Of your precedent lord; a vice* of kings;
A cutpurse of the empire and the rule,
That from a shelf the precious diadem stole
And put it in his pocket!
QUEEN: No more!   115

      [*Enter* GHOST.]

HAMLET: A king of shreds and patches—
Save me, and hover o'er me with your wings,
You heavenly guards! What would your gracious figure?
QUEEN: Alas, he's mad!
HAMLET: Do you not come your tardy son to chide,   120
That, laps'd in time and passion, lets go by
Th' important acting of your dread command?
O, say!
GHOST: Do not forget; this visitation
Is but to whet thy almost blunted purpose.   125
But look, amazement on thy mother sits.
O, step between her and her fighting soul!
Conceit* in weakest bodies strongest works.
Speak to her, Hamlet.
HAMLET: How is it with you, lady?   130
QUEEN: Alas, how is't with you,
That you do bend your eye on vacancy,

---

⁹⁷ **reason panders will** reason acts as a panderer for desire
¹⁰¹ **tinct** color
¹⁰³ **enseamed** rumpled
¹¹⁰ **tithe** tenth part
¹¹¹ **vice** wicked character in medieval plays
¹²⁸ **Conceit** imagination

And with th' incorporal* air do hold discourse?
Forth at your eyes and spirits wildly peep;
And, as the sleeping soldiers in th' alarm,   135
Your bedded* hairs like life in excrements*
Start up and stand an end. O gentle son,
Upon the heat and flame of thy distemper
Sprinkle cool patience! Whereon do you look?
HAMLET: On him, on him! Look you how pale he glares.   140
His form and cause conjoin'd, preaching to stones,
Would make them capable.*—Do not look upon me,
Lest with this piteous action you convert
My stern effects;* then what I have to do
Will want true colour—tears perchance for blood.   145
QUEEN: To whom do you speak this?
HAMLET: Do you see nothing there?
QUEEN: Nothing at all; yet all that is I see.
HAMLET: Nor did you nothing hear?
QUEEN: No, nothing but ourselves.   150
HAMLET: Why, look you there. Look how it steals away.
My father, in his habit* as he liv'd!
Look where he goes even now out at the portal.

       [*Exit* GHOST.]

QUEEN: This is the very coinage of your brain.
This bodiless creation ecstasy   155
Is very cunning in.
HAMLET: Ecstasy!
My pulse as yours doth temperately keep time.
And makes as healthful music. It is not madness
That I have utt'red. Bring me to the test,   160
And I the matter will re-word which madness
Would gambol* from. Mother, for love of grace,
Lay not that flattering unction* to your soul,
That not your trespass but my madness speaks:
It will but skin and film the ulcerous place,   165
Whiles rank corruption, mining* all within,
Infects unseen. Confess yourself to heaven;
Repent what's past; avoid what is to come;
And do not spread the compost on the weeds,
To make them ranker. Forgive me this my virtue;   170
For in the fatness of these pursy* times

---

133 **incorporal** empty, bodiless
136 **bedded** flat-lying
136 **excrements** outgrowths
142 **capable** receptive
143–44 **convert my stern effects** divert my serious purpose
152 **habit** garment
162 **gambol** start away
163 **unction** ointment
166 **mining** undermining
171 **pursy** bloated

Virtue itself of vice must pardon beg,
Yea, curb* and woo for leave to do him good.
QUEEN: O Hamlet, thou hast cleft my heart in twain.
HAMLET: O, throw away the worser part of it,   175
  And live the purer with the other half.
  Good night—but go not to my uncle's bed;
  Assume a virtue, if you have it not.
  That monster custom, who all sense doth eat,
  Of habits devil, is angel yet in this,   180
  That to the use* of actions fair and good
  He likewise gives a frock or livery
  That aptly is put on. Refrain to-night;
  And that shall lend a kind of easiness
  To the next abstinence; the next more easy;   185
  For use almost can change the stamp of nature,
  And either curb the devil, or throw him out,
  With wondrous potency. Once more, good night;
  And when you are desirous to be blest,
  I'll blessing beg of you. For this same lord   190
  I do repent; but Heaven hath pleas'd it so,
  To punish me with this, and this with me,
  That I must be their scourge and minister.
  I will bestow him, and will answer well
  The death I gave him. So, again, good night.   195
  I must be cruel only to be kind;
  Thus bad begins and worse remains behind.
  One word more, good lady.
QUEEN: What shall I do?
HAMLET: Not this, by no means, that I bid you do: 200
  Let the bloat King tempt you again to bed;
  Pinch wanton on your cheek; call you his mouse;
  And let him, for a pair of reechy* kisses,
  Or paddling in your neck with his damn'd fingers,
  Make you to ravel all this matter out,   205
  That I essentially am not in madness,
  But mad in craft. 'Twere good you let him know;
  For who that's but a queen, fair, sober, wise,
  Would from a paddock,* from a bat, a gib,*
  Such dear concernings hide? Who would do so?   210
  No, in despite of sense and secrecy,
  Unpeg the basket on the house's top,
  Let the birds fly, and, like the famous ape,
  To try conclusions,* in the basket creep
  And break your own neck down.   215

---

173 **curb** bow low
181 **use** practice
203 **reechy** foul
209 **paddock** toad
209 **gib** tomcat
214 **try conclusions** make experiments

QUEEN: Be thou assur'd, if words be made of breath
    And breath of life, I have no life to breathe
    What thou hast said to me.
HAMLET: I must to England; you know that?
QUEEN: Alack,   220
    I had forgot. 'Tis so concluded on.
HAMLET: There's letters seal'd; and my two school-fellows,
    Whom I will trust as I will adders fang'd—
    They bear the mandate;* they must sweep my way
    And marshal me to knavery. Let it work;   225
    For 'tis the sport to have the engineer
    Hoist with his own petar;* and't shall go hard
    But I will delve one yard below their mines
    And blow them at the moon, O, 'tis most sweet
    When in one line two crafts* directly meet.   230
    This man shall set me packing.
    I'll lug the guts into the neighbour room.
    Mother, good night. Indeed, this counsellor
    Is now most still, most secret, and most grave,
    Who was in life a foolish prating knave.   235
    Come, sir, to draw toward an end with you.
    Good night, mother.

    [*Exeunt severally;* HAMLET *tugging in* POLONIUS.]

ACT IV

SCENE I————*Elsinore. The Castle.*

[*Enter* KING, QUEEN, ROSENCRANTZ, *and* GUILDENSTERN.]

KING: There's matter in these sighs, these profound heaves,
    You must translate; 'tis fit we understand them.
    Where is your son?
QUEEN: Bestow this place on us a little while.

    [*Exeunt* ROSENCRANTZ *and* GUILDENSTERN.]

    Ah, mine own lord, what have I seen to-night!   5
KING: What, Gertrude? How does Hamlet?
QUEEN: Mad as the sea and wind, when both contend
    Which is the mightier. In his lawless fit,

---

224 **mandate** command
227 **petar** bomb
230 **crafts** intrigues

Behind the arras hearing something stir,
Whips out his rapier, cries 'A rat, a rat!'   10
And in this brainish apprehension* kills
The unseen good old man.

KING: O heavy deed!
It had been so with us had we been there.
His liberty is full of threats to all—   15
To you yourself, to us, to every one.
Alas, how shall this bloody deed be answer'd?
It will be laid to us, whose providence*
Should have kept short, restrain'd, and out of haunt,*
This mad young man. But so much was our love,   20
We would not understand what was most fit;
But, like the owner of a foul disease,
To keep it from divulging, let it feed
Even on the pith of life. Where is he gone?

QUEEN: To draw apart the body he hath kill'd;   25
O'er whom his very madness, like some ore
Among a mineral of metals base,*
Shows itself pure: 'a weeps for what is done.

KING: O Gertrude, come away!
The sun no sooner shall the mountains touch   30
But we will ship him hence; and this vile deed
We must with all our majesty and skill
Both countenance and excuse. Ho Guildenstern!

[*Reenter* ROSENCRANTZ *and* GUILDENSTERN.]

Friends, both go join you with some further aid:
Hamlet in madness hath Polonius slain,   35
And from his mother's closet hath he dragg'd him;
Go seek him out; speak fair, and bring the body
Into the chapel. I pray you haste in this.

[*Exeunt* ROSENCRANTZ *and* GUILDENSTERN.]

Come, Gertrude, we'll call up our wisest friends
And let them know both what we mean to do   40
And what's untimely done; so haply slander—
Whose whisper o'er the world's diameter,
As level as the cannon to his blank,*
Transports his pois'ned shot—may miss our name,
And hit the woundless* air. O, come away!   45
My soul is full of discord and dismay.   [*Exeunt.*]

IV,i,11 **brainish apprehension** mad imagination
18 **providence** foresight
19 **out of haunt** away from association with others
26–27 **ore . . . base** like gold among baser metals
43 **blank** white center of a target
45 **woundless** invulnerable

SCENE II———Elsinore. The Castle.

[*Enter* HAMLET.]

HAMLET: Safely stow'd.

GENTLEMEN: [*within*] Hamlet! Lord Hamlet!

HAMLET: But soft! What noise? Who calls on Hamlet? O, here they come!

[*Enter* ROSENCRANTZ *and* GUILDENSTERN.]

ROSENCRANTZ: What have you done, my lord, with the dead body?

HAMLET: Compounded it with dust, whereto 'tis kin.   5

ROSENCRANTZ: Tell us where 'tis, that we may take it thence. And bear it to the chapel.

HAMLET: Do not believe it.

ROSENCRANTZ: Believe what?

HAMLET: That I can keep your counsel, and not mine own. Besides, to be de-   10
manded of* a sponge—what replication* should be made by the son of a king?

ROSENCRANTZ: Take you me for a sponge, my lord?

HAMLET: Ay, sir; that soaks up the King's countenance,* his rewards, his author-
ities. But such officers do the King best service in the end: he keeps them like an   15
ape an apple in the corner of his jaw; first mouth'd to be last swallowed;
when he needs what you have glean'd, it is but squeezing you and, sponge,
you shall be dry again.

ROSENCRANTZ: I understand you not, my lord.

HAMLET: I am glad of it; a knavish speech sleeps in a foolish ear.   20

ROSENCRANTZ: My lord, you must tell us where the body is, and go with us to the King.

HAMLET: The body is with the King, but the King is not with the body. The King is a thing—

GUILDENSTERN: A thing, my lord!   25

HAMLET: Of nothing. Bring me to him. Hide fox, and all after.*   [*Exeunt.*]

SCENE III———Elsinore. The Castle.

[*Enter* KING, *attended.*]

KING: I have sent to seek him, and to find the body.
How dangerous is it that this man goes loose!
Yet must not we put the strong law on him:
He's lov'd of the distracted* multitude,
Who like not in their judgment but their eyes;   5

IV,ii,10–11 **demanded of** questioned by
¹¹ **replication** reply
¹⁴ **countenance** favor
²⁶ **Hide fox, and all after** call in game (as in hide-and-seek)
IV,iii,4 **distracted** confused

And where 'tis so, th' offender's scourge is weigh'd,
But never the offence. To bear* all smooth and even,
This sudden sending him away must seem
Deliberate pause.* Diseases desperate grown
By desperate appliance are reliev'd,   10
Or not at all.

> [*Enter* ROSENCRANTZ.]

How now! what hath befall'n?
ROSENCRANTZ: Where the dead body is bestow'd, my lord,
   We cannot get from him.
KING: But where is he?   15
ROSENCRANTZ: Without, my lord; guarded, to know your pleasure.
KING: Bring him before us.
ROSENCRANTZ: Ho, Guildenstern! bring in the lord.

> [*Enter* HAMLET *and* GUILDENSTERN.]

KING: Now, Hamlet, where's Polonius?
HAMLET: At supper.
KING: At supper! Where?   20
HAMLET: Not where he eats, but where 'a is eaten; a certain convocation of
   politic* worms are e'en at him. Your worm is your only emperor for diet: we
   fat all creatures else to fat us, and we fat ourselves for maggots; your fat king
   and your lean beggar is but variable service*—two dishes, but to one table.   25
   That's the end.
KING: Alas, alas!
HAMLET: A man may fish with the worm that hath eat of a king, and eat of the fish
   that hath fed of that worm.
KING: What dost thou mean by this?   30
HAMLET: Nothing but to show you how a king may go a progress through the
   guts of a beggar.
KING: Where is Polonius?
HAMLET: In heaven; send thither to see; if your messenger find him not there,
   seek him i' th' other place yourself. But if, indeed, you find him not within   35
   this month, you shall nose him as you go up the stairs into the lobby.
KING: [*to attendants*] Go seek him there.
HAMLET: 'A will stay till you come.   [*Exeunt attendants.*]
KING: Hamlet, this deed, for thine especial safety—
   Which we do tender,* as we dearly grieve   40
   For that which thou hast done—must send thee hence
   With fiery quickness. Therefore prepare thyself;
   The bark is ready, and the wind at help,
   Th' associates tend,* and everything is bent
   For England.   45

---

[7]   **bear** carry out
[9]   **pause** planning
[23]   **politic** statesmanlike
[25]   **variable service** different courses
[40]   **tender** hold dear
[44]   **tend** wait

HAMLET: For England!

KING: Ay, Hamlet.

HAMLET: Good!

KING: So is it, if thou knew'st our purposes.

HAMLET: I see a cherub that sees them. But, come; for England! Farewell, dear   50
    mother.

KING: Thy loving father, Hamlet.

HAMLET: My mother: father and mother is man and wife; man and wife is one flesh;
    and so, my mother. Come, for England.   [*Exit.*]

KING: Follow him at foot;* tempt him with speed aboard;   55
    Delay it not; I'll have him hence to-night.
    Away! for everything is seal'd and done
    That else leans* on th' affair. Pray you make haste.

      [*Exeunt all but the* KING.]

    And, England, if my love thou hold'st at aught—
    As my great power thereof may give thee sense,   60
    Since yet thy cicatrice* looks raw and red
    After the Danish sword, and thy free awe*
    Pays homage to us—thou mayst not coldly set
    Our sovereign process;* which imports at full,
    By letters congruing to that effect,   65
    The present* death of Hamlet. Do it, England:
    For like the hectic* in my blood he rages,
    And thou must cure me. Till I know 'tis done,
    Howe'er my haps,* my joys were ne'er begun.   [*Exit.*]

        SCENE IV———*A plain in Denmark.*

      [*Enter* FORTINBRAS *with his army over the stage.*]

FORTINBRAS: Go, Captain, from me greet the Danish king.
    Tell him that by his license Fortinbras
    Craves the conveyance of a promis'd march
    Over his kingdom. You know the rendezvous.
    If that his Majesty would aught with us,   5
    We shall express our duty in his eye;*
    And let him know so.

CAPTAIN: I will do't, my lord.

---

55 **at foot** closely
58 **leans** depends
61 **cicatrice** scar
62 **free awe** uncompelled submission
63–64 **coldly set our sovereign process** disregard our royal command
66 **present** immediate
67 **hectic** fever
69 **haps** fortunes
IV,iv,6 **in his eye** in his presence

FORTINBRAS: Go softly* on.   [*Exeunt all but the* CAPTAIN.]
   [*Enter* HAMLET, ROSENCRANTZ, GUILDENSTERN, *and others.*]
HAMLET: Good sir, whose powers are these?   10
CAPTAIN: They are of Norway, sir.
HAMLET: How purpos'd, sir, I pray you?
CAPTAIN: Against some part of Poland.
HAMLET: Who commands them, sir?
CAPTAIN: The nephew to old Norway, Fortinbras.   15
HAMLET: Goes it against the main* of Poland, sir,
    Or for some frontier?
CAPTAIN: Truly to speak, and with no addition,
    We go to gain a little patch of ground
    That hath in it no profit but the name.   20
    To pay five ducats, five, I would not farm it;
    Nor will it yield to Norway or the Pole
    A ranker* rate should it be sold in fee.*
HAMLET: Why, then the Polack never will defend it.
CAPTAIN: Yes, it is already garrison'd.   25
HAMLET: Two thousand souls and twenty thousand ducats
    Will not debate* the question of this straw.
    This is th' imposthume* of much wealth and peace,
    That inward breaks, and shows no cause without
    Why the man dies. I humbly thank you, sir.   30
CAPTAIN: God buy you, sir.
ROSENCRANTZ: Will't please you go, my lord?
HAMLET: I'll be with you straight. Go a little before.

     [*Exeunt all but* HAMLET.]

    How all occasions do inform against me,
    And spur my dull revenge! What is a man,   35
    If his chief good and market* of his time
    Be but to sleep and feed? A beast, no more!
    Sure he that made us with such large discourse,*
    Looking before and after, gave us not
    That capability and godlike reason   40
    To fust* in us unus'd. Now, whether it be
    Bestial oblivion, or some craven scruple
    Of thinking too precisely on th' event—
    A thought which, quarter'd, hath but one part wisdom
    And ever three parts coward—I do not know   45
    Why yet I live to say 'This thing's to do,'

---

9 **softly** slowly
16 **main** main part
23 **ranker** higher
23 **in fee** outright
27 **debate** settle
28 **imposthume** ulcer
36 **market** profit
38 **discourse** understanding
41 **fust** grow moldy

Sith I have cause, and will, and strength, and means,
To do't. Examples gross* as earth exhort me:
Witness this army, of such mass and charge,*
Led by a delicate and tender prince, 50
Whose spirit, with divine ambition puff'd,
Makes mouths at the invisible event,*
Exposing what is mortal and unsure
To all that fortune, death, and danger dare,
Even for an egg-shell. Rightly to be great 55
Is not to stir without great argument,*
But greatly* to find quarrel in a straw,
When honour's at the stake. How stand I, then,
That have a father kill'd, a mother stain'd,
Excitements* of my reason and my blood, 60
And let all sleep, while to my shame I see
The imminent death of twenty thousand men
That, for a fantasy and trick of fame,
Go to their graves like beds, fight for a plot
Whereon the numbers cannot try the cause, 65
Which is not tomb enough and continent*
To hide the slain? O, from this time forth,
My thoughts be bloody, or be nothing worth!   [*Exit.*]

SCENE V———*Elsinore. The Castle.*

[*Enter* QUEEN, HORATIO, *and a* GENTLEMAN.]

QUEEN: I will not speak with her.
GENTLEMAN: She is importunate, indeed distract.
    Her mood will needs be pitied.
QUEEN: What would she have?
GENTLEMAN: She speaks much of her father; says she hears 5
    There's tricks i' th' world, and hems, and beats her heart;
    Spurns enviously at straws;* speaks things in doubt,*
    That carry but half sense. Her speech is nothing,
    Yet the unshaped use of it doth move
    The hearers to collection;* they yawn* at it, 10
    And botch the words up fit to their own thoughts;
    Which, as her winks and nods and gestures yield them,

---

48 **gross** large
49 **charge** expense
52 **Makes mouths . . . event** scorns the outcome
56 **argument** reason
57 **greatly** nobly
60 **Excitements** incentives
66 **continent** container
IV,v,7 **Spurns . . . straws** objects to insignificant matters
7 **in doubt** uncertainly
10 **collection** gather and listen
10 **yawn** gape

Indeed would make one think there might be thought,
Though nothing sure, yet much unhappily.
HORATIO: 'Twere good she were spoken with; for she may strew   15
Dangerous conjectures in ill-breeding minds.
QUEEN: Let her come in.   [*Exit* GENTLEMAN.]

    [*aside*] To my sick soul, as sin's true nature is,

Each toy seems prologue to some great amiss.*
So full of artless jealousy* is guilt,   20
It spills* itself in fearing to be spilt.

    [*Enter* OPHELIA *distracted.*]

OPHELIA: Where is the beauteous Majesty of Denmark?
QUEEN: How now, Ophelia!
OPHELIA: [*sings*]
                How should I your true love know
                    From another one?   25
                  By his cockle hat and staff,
                    *And his sandal shoon.**
QUEEN: Alas, sweet lady, what imports this song?
OPHELIA: Say you? Nay, pray you, mark.   [*sings*]
                He is dead and gone, lady,   30
                He is dead and gone;
              At his head a grass-green turf,
                At his heels a stone.
    O, ho!
QUEEN: Nay, but, Ophelia—   35
OPHELIA: Pray you, mark.   [*sings*]
    White his shroud as the mountain snow—

    [*Enter* KING.]

QUEEN: Alas, look here, my lord.
OPHELIA: *Larded* with sweet flowers;*
              Which bewept to the grave did not go   40
                With true-love showers.
KING: How do you, pretty lady?
OPHELIA: Well, God dild* you! They say the owl was a baker's daughter. Lord,
    we know that we are, but know not what we may be. God be at your table!
KING: Conceit* upon her father.   45
OPHELIA: Pray let's have no words of this; but when they ask you what it means,
    say you this: [*sings*]
              To-morrow is Saint Valentine's day,
              All in the morning betime,

---

[19] **amiss** misfortune
[20] **artless jealousy** crude suspicion
[21] **spills** destroys
[27] **shoon** shoes
[39] **Larded** decorated
[43] **dild** reward
[45] **Conceit** brooding

> *And I a maid at your window,*   50
> *To be your Valentine.*
> *Then up he rose, and donn'd his clothes,*
> *And dupp'd* the chamber-door;*
> *Let in the maid, that out a maid*
> *Never departed more.*   55

KING: Pretty Ophelia!

OPHELIA: Indeed, la, without an oath, I'll make an end on't.   [*sings*]

> *By Gis* and by Saint Charity,*
> *Alack, and fie for shame!*
> *Young men will do't, if they come to't;*   60
> *By Cock, they are to blame.*
> *Quoth she 'Before you tumbled me,*
> *You promis'd me to wed.'*

He answers:

> *'So would I 'a done, by yonder sun,*   65
> *An thou hadst not come to my bed.'*

KING: How long hath she been thus?

OPHELIA: I hope all will be well. We must be patient; but I cannot choose but
weep to think they would lay him i' th' cold ground. My brother shall know
of it; and so I thank you for your good counsel. Come, my coach! Good   70
night, ladies; good night, sweet ladies, good night, good night.

    [*Exit.*]

KING: Follow her close; give her good watch, I pray you.

    [*Exit* HORATIO.]

O, this is the poison of deep grief; it springs
All from her father's death. And now behold—
O Gertrude, Gertrude!   75
When sorrows come, they come not single spies,
But in battalions! First, her father slain;
Next, your son gone, and he most violent author
Of his own just remove; the people muddied,*
Thick and unwholesome in their thoughts and whispers   80
For good Polonius' death; and we have done but greenly*
In hugger-mugger* to inter him; poor Ophelia
Divided from herself and her fair judgment,
Without the which we are pictures, or mere beasts;
Last, and as much containing as all these,   85
Her brother is in secret come from France;
Feeds on his wonder,* keeps himself in clouds,

---

⁵³ **dupp'd** opened
⁵⁸ **Gis** Jesus
⁷⁹ **muddied** confused
⁸¹ **greenly** foolishly
⁸² **hugger-mugger** secret haste
⁸⁷ **wonder** suspicion

And wants not buzzers* to infect his ear
With pestilent speeches of his father's death;
Wherein necessity, of matter beggar'd,*   90
Will nothing stick* our person to arraign
In ear and ear. O my dear Gertrude, this,
Like to a murd'ring piece,* in many places
Gives me superfluous death.   *[a noise within]*

QUEEN: Alack, what noise is this?   95
KING: Attend!

      [*Enter a* GENTLEMAN.]

Where are my Switzers!* Let them guard the door.
What is the matter?
GENTLEMAN: Save yourself, my lord:
    The ocean, overpeering of his list,*   100
    Eats not the flats with more impetuous haste
    Than young Laertes, in a riotous head,*
    O'erbears your officers. The rabble call him lord;
    And, as the world were now but to begin,
    Antiquity forgot, custom not known,   105
    The ratifiers and props of every word,
    They cry 'Choose we; Laertes shall be king.'
    Caps, hands, and tongues, applaud it to the clouds,
    'Laertes shall be king, Laertes king.'
QUEEN: How cheerfully on the false trail they cry!   110
      [*noise within*]
    O, this is counter, you false Danish dogs!
KING: The doors are broke. [*Enter* LAERTES, *with others, in arms.*]
LAERTES: Where is this king?—Sirs, stand you all without.
ALL: No, let's come in.
LAERTES: I pray you give me leave.   115
ALL: We will, we will.
      [*Exeunt.*]
LAERTES: I thank you. Keep the door.—O thou vile king,
    Give me my father!
QUEEN: Calmly, good Laertes.
LAERTES: That drop of blood that's calm proclaims me bastard;   120
    Cries cuckold to my father; brands the harlot
    Even here, between the chaste unsmirched brow
    Of my true mother.
KING: What is the cause, Laertes,
    That thy rebellion looks so giant-like?   125

---

[88] **buzzers** tale bearers
[90] **beggar'd** lacking facts
[91] **Will nothing stick** will not hesitate
[93] **murd'ring piece** cannon
[97] **Switzers** Swiss guards
[100] **list** shore
[102] **in a riotous head** with a rebellious mob

Let him go, Gertrude; do not fear our person:
There's such divinity doth hedge a king
That treason can but peep to what it would,
Acts little of his will. Tell me, Laertes,
Why thou art thus incens'd. Let him go, Gertrude.   130
Speak, man.

LAERTES: Where is my father?

KING: Dead.

QUEEN: But not by him.

KING: Let him demand his fill.   135

LAERTES: How came he dead? I'll not be juggled with.
To hell, allegiance! Vows, to the blackest devil!
Conscience and grace, to the profoundest pit!
I dare damnation. To this point I stand,
That both the worlds I give to negligence,*   140
Let come what comes; only I'll be reveng'd
Most thoroughly for my father.

KING: Who shall stay you?

LAERTES: My will, not all the world's.
And for my means, I'll husband them* so well   145
They shall go far with little.

KING: Good Laertes,
If you desire to know the certainty
Of your dear father, is't writ in your revenge
That, swoopstake,* you will draw both friend and foe,   150
Winner and loser?

LAERTES: None but his enemies.

KING: Will you know them, then?

LAERTES: To his good friends thus wide I'll ope my arms
And, like the kind life-rend'ring pelican,   155
Repast* them with my blood.

KING: Why, now you speak
Like a good child and a true gentleman.
That I am guiltless of your father's death,
And am most sensibly in grief for it,   160
It shall as level to your judgment 'pear'
As day does to your eye.   [*A noise within:* 'Let her come in.']

LAERTES: How now! What noise is that?
[*Reenter* OPHELIA.]
O, heat dry up my brains! tears seven times salt
Burn out the sense and virtue* of mine eye!   165
By heaven, thy madness shall be paid with weight
Till our scale turn the beam.* O rose of May!

---

[140] **both the worlds . . . negligence** I care not what may happen to me in this world or the next
[145] **husband them** use them economically
[150] **swoopstake** in a full sweep
[155-56] **pelican, repast** (pelicans were thought to use their own blood to feed their young)
[165] **virtue** power
[167] **scale turn the beam** weigh down the balance of a scale

Dear maid, kind sister, sweet Ophelia!
O heavens! is't possible a young maid's wits
Should be as mortal as an old man's life?
Nature is fine* in love; and where 'tis fine   170
It sends some precious instance* of itself
After the thing it loves.

OPHELIA: [*sings*]

> They bore him barefac'd on the bier;
> Hey non nonny, nonny, hey nonny;   175
> And in his grave rain'd many a tear—
> Fare you well, my dove!

LAERTES: Hadst thou thy wits, and didst persuade revenge,
    It could not move thus.
OPHELIA: You must sing 'A-down, a-down,' an you call him a-down-a. O, how the   180
    wheel becomes it! It is the false steward, that stole his master's daughter.
LAERTES: This nothing's more than matter.*
OPHELIA: There's rosemary, that's for remembrance; pray you, love, remember.
    And there is pansies, that's for thoughts.
LAERTES: A document* in madness—thoughts and remembrance fitted.   185
OPHELIA: There's fennel for you, and columbines. There's rue for you; and here's
    some for me. We may call it herb of grace a Sundays. O, you must wear your
    rue with a difference. There's a daisy. I would give you some violets, but they
    wither'd all when my father died. They say 'a made a good end.
    [*sings*] For bonny sweet Robin is all my joy.   190
LAERTES: Thought and affliction, passion, hell itself,
    She turns to favour* and to prettiness.
OPHELIA: [*sings*]

> And will 'a not come again
> And will 'a not come again?
> No, no, he is dead,   195
> Go to thy death-bed,
> He never will come again.
> His beard was as white as snow,
> All flaxen was his poll;*
> He is gone, he is gone,   200
> And we cast away moan:
> God-a-mercy on his soul!

And of all Christian souls, I pray God. God buy you.

    [*Exit.*]

LAERTES: Do you see this, O God?
KING: Laertes, I must commune with your grief,   205

---

171 **fine** refined
172 **instance** sample
182 **nothing's . . . matter** this nonsense contains more meaning than does a statement of great matter
185 **document** lesson
192 **favour** to beauty
199 **flaxen was his poll** his hair was white

Or you deny me right. Go but apart,
Make choice of whom your wisest friends you will,
And they shall hear and judge 'twixt you and me.
If by direct or by collateral* hand
They find us touch'd,* we will our kingdom give,   210
Our crown, our life, and all that we call ours,
To you in satisfaction; but if not,
Be you content to lend your patience to us,
And we shall jointly labour with your soul
To give it due content.   215
LAERTES: Let this be so.
His means of death, his obscure funeral—
No trophy, sword, nor hatchment,* o'er his bones,
No noble rite nor formal ostentation*—
Cry to be heard, as 'twere from heaven to earth,   220
That I must call't in question.
KING: So you shall;
And where th' offence is, let the great axe fall.
I pray you go with me.   [*Exeunt.*]

SCENE VI———*Elsinore. The Castle.*

[*Enter* HORATIO *with an* ATTENDANT.]

HORATIO: What are they that would speak with me?
ATTENDANT: Sea-faring men, sir; they say they have letters for you.
HORATIO: Let them come in.   [*Exit* ATTENDANT.]
     I do not know from what part of the world
     I should be greeted, if not from Lord Hamlet.   5

[*Enter* SAILORS.]

SAILOR: God bless you, sir.
HORATIO: Let Him bless thee, too.
SAILOR: 'A shall, sir, an't please Him. There's a letter for you, sir; it came from
     th'ambassador that was bound for England—if your name be Horatio, as I
     am let to know it is.   10
HORATIO: [*reads*] 'Horatio, when thou shalt have overlook'd* this, give these
     fellows some means to the King: they have letters for him. Ere we were two
     days old at sea, a pirate of very warlike appointment gave us chase. Finding
     ourselves too slow of sail, we put on a compelled valour; and in the grapple
     I boarded them. On the instant they got clear of our ship; so I alone became   15
     their prisoner. They have dealt with me like thieves of mercy; but they knew
     what they did; I am to do a good turn for them. Let the King have the letters
     I have sent; and repair thou to me with as much speed as thou wouldest fly

---

209 **collateral** indirect
210 **touch'd** implicated
218 **hatchment** stone bearing coat of arms
219 **ostentation** ceremony
IV,vi,11 **overlook'd** read

death. I have words to speak in thine ear will make thee dumb; yet are they
much too light for the bore of the matter. These good fellows will bring thee   20
where I am. Rosencrantz and Guildenstern hold their course for England; of
them I have much to tell thee. Farewell.

He that thou knowest thine, Hamlet.'

Come, I will give you way for these your letters,
And do't the speedier that you may direct me   25
To him from whom you brought them.   [*Exeunt.*]

SCENE VII———*Elsinore. The Castle.*

[*Enter* KING *and* LAERTES.]

KING: Now must your conscience my acquittance seal,
  And you must put me in your heart for friend,
  Sith you have heard, and with a knowing ear,
  That he which hath your noble father slain
  Pursu'd my life.   5
LAERTES: It well appears. But tell me
  Why you proceeded not against these feats,
  So crimeful and so capital* in nature,
  As by your safety, wisdom, all things else,
  You mainly were stirr'd up.   10
KING: O, for two special reasons,
  Which may to you, perhaps, seem much unsinew'd,*
  But yet to me th' are strong. The Queen his mother
  Lives almost by his looks; and for myself,
  My virtue or my plague, be it either which—   15
  She is so conjunctive* to my life and soul
  That, as the star moves not but in his sphere,
  I could not but by her. The other motive,
  Why to a public count I might not go,
  Is the great love the general gender* bear him;   20
  Who, dipping all his faults in their affection,
  Work like the spring that turneth wood to stone,
  Convert his gyves* to graces; so that my arrows,
  Too slightly timber'd* for so loud a wind,
  Would have reverted to my bow again,   25
  But not where I have aim'd them.
LAERTES: And so have I a noble father lost;
  A sister driven into desp'rate terms,
  Whose worth, if praises may go back again,
  Stood challenger on mount of all the age   30
  For her perfections. But my revenge will come.

IV,vii,8 **capital** deserving death
12 **unsinew'd** weak
16 **conjunctive** closely united
20 **general gender** common people
23 **gyves** fetters
24 **timber'd** shafted

KING: Break not your sleeps for that. You must not think
    That we are made of stuff so flat and dull
    That we can let our beard be shook with danger,
    And think it pastime. You shortly shall hear more   35
    I lov'd your father, and we love our self;
    And that, I hope, will teach you to imagine—

    [*Enter a* MESSENGER *with letters.*]

    How now! What news?
MESSENGER: Letters, my lord, from Hamlet:
    These to your Majesty; this to the Queen.   40
KING: From Hamlet! Who brought them?
MESSENGER: Sailors, my lord, they say; I saw them not.
    They were given me by Claudio; he receiv'd them
    Of him that brought them.
KING: Laertes, you shall hear them.   45
    Leave us   [*Exit* MESSENGER.]
    [*reads*] 'High and Mighty. You shall know I am set naked* on your kingdom.
    To-morrow shall I beg leave to see your kingly eyes; when I shall, first asking
    your pardon thereunto, recount the occasion of my sudden and more
    strange return.   50
                        Hamlet.'

    What should this mean? Are all the rest come back?
    Or is it some abuse,* and no such thing?
LAERTES: Know you the hand?
KING: 'Tis Hamlet's character. 'Naked'!   55
    And in a postscript here, he says 'alone.'
    Can you devise* me?
LAERTES: I am lost in it, my lord. But let him come;
    It warms the very sickness in my heart
    That I shall live and tell him to his teeth   60
    'Thus didest thou.'
KING: If it be so, Laertes—
    As how should it be so, how otherwise?—
    Will you be rul'd by me?
LAERTES: Ay, my lord;   65
    So you will not o'errule me to a peace.
KING: To thine own peace. If he be now return'd,
    As checking at* his voyage, and that he means
    No more to undertake it, I will work him
    To an exploit now ripe in my device,   70
    Under the which he shall not choose but fall;
    And for his death, no wind of blame shall breathe;
    But even his mother shall uncharge the practice
    And call it accident.

---

[47] **naked** destitute
[53] **abuse** deception
[57] **devise** advise
[68] **checking at** abandoning

LAERTES: My lord, I will be rul'd   75
    The rather, if you could devise it so
    That I might be the organ.
KING: It falls right.
    You have been talk'd of since your travel much,
    And that in Hamlet's hearing, for a quality   80
    Wherein they say you shine. Your sum of parts
    Did not together pluck such envy from him
    As did that one; and that, in my regard,
    Of the unworthiest siege.*
LAERTES: What part is that, my lord?   85
KING: A very riband in the cap of youth,
    Yet needful, too; for youth no less becomes
    The light and careless livery that it wears
    Than settled age his sables and his weeds,*
    Importing health and graveness. Two months since   90
    Here was a gentleman of Normandy—
    I have seen myself, and serv'd against, the French,
    And they can well on horseback; but this gallant
    Had witchcraft in't; he grew into his seat,
    And to such wondrous doing brought his horse,   95
    As had he been incorps'd and demi-natur'd
    With the brave beast. So far he topp'd my thought,
    That I, in forgery* of shapes and tricks,
    Come short of what he did.
LAERTES: A Norman was't?   100
KING: A Norman.
LAERTES: Upon my life, Lamord.
KING: The very same.
LAERTES: I know him well. He is the brooch* indeed
    And gem of all the nation.   105
KING: He made confession* of you;
    And gave you such a masterly report
    For art and exercise in your defence,
    And for your rapier most especial,
    That he cried out 'twould be a sight indeed   110
    If one could match you. The scrimers* of their nation
    He swore had neither motion, guard, nor eye,
    If you oppos'd them. Sir, this report of his
    Did Hamlet so envenom with his envy
    That he could nothing do but wish and beg   115
    Your sudden coming o'er, to play with you.
    Now out of this—

---

84 **siege** rank
89 **weeds** sober attire
98 **forgery** invention
104 **brooch** ornament
106 **confession** report
111 **scrimers** fencers

LAERTES: What out of this, my lord?

KING: Laertes, was your father dear to you?
    Or are you like the painting of a sorrow,   120
    A face without a heart?

LAERTES: Why ask you this?

KING: Not that I think you did not love your father;
    But that I know love is begun by time,
    And that I see, in passages of proof,*   125
    Time qualifies* the spark and fire of it.
    There lives within the very flame of love
    A kind of wick or snuff that will abate it;
    And nothing is at a like goodness still;
    For goodness, growing to a pleurisy,*   130
    Dies in his own too much. That we would do,
    We should do when we would; for this 'would' changes,
    And hath abatements and delays as many
    As there are tongues, are hands, are accidents;
    And then this 'should' is like a spendthrift's sigh   135
    That hurts by easing. But to the quick* of th' ulcer:
    Hamlet comes back; what would you undertake
    To show yourself in deed your father's son
    More than in words?

LAERTES: To cut his throat i' th' church.   140

KING: No place, indeed, should murder sanctuarize;*
    Revenge should have no bounds. But, good Laertes,
    Will you do this? Keep close within your chamber.
    Hamlet return'd shall know you are come home.
    We'll put on those shall praise your excellence,   145
    And set a double varnish on the fame
    The Frenchman gave you; bring you, in fine,* together,
    And wager on your heads. He, being remiss,
    Most generous, and free from all contriving,
    Will not peruse the foils; so that with ease   150
    Or with a little shuffling, you may choose
    A sword unbated,* and, in a pass of practice,*
    Requite him for your father.

LAERTES: I will do't;
    And for that purpose I'll anoint my sword.   155
    I bought an unction of a mountebank,
    So mortal that but dip a knife in it,
    Where it draws blood no cataplasm* so rare,

---

[125] **passages of proof** proved cases
[126] **qualifies** diminishes
[130] **pleurisy** excess
[136] **quick** sensitive part
[141] **sanctuarize** protect
[147] **in fine** finally
[152] **unbated** not blunted
[152] **pass of practice** treacherous thrust
[158] **cataplasm** poultice

Collected from all simples* that have virtue
Under the moon, can save the thing from death   160
That is but scratch'd withal. I'll touch my point
With this contagion, that, if I gall him slightly,
It may be death.
KING: Let's further think of this;
Weigh what convenience both of time and means   165
May fit us to our shape.* If this should fail,
And that our drift look through* our bad performance,
'Twere better not assay'd, therefore this project
Should have a back or second, that might hold
If this did blast in proof.* Soft! let me see.   170
We'll make a solemn wager on your cunnings—
I ha't.
When in your motion you are hot and dry—
As make your bouts more violent to that end—
And that he calls for drink, I'll have preferr'd him   175
A chalice for the nonce,* whereon but sipping,
If he by chance escape your venom'd stuck,*
Our purpose may hold there. But stay; what noise?

[*Enter* QUEEN.]

QUEEN: One woe doth tread upon another's heel,
So fast they follow. Your sister's drown'd, Laertes.   180
LAERTES: Drown'd? O, where?
QUEEN: There is a willow grows aslant the brook
That shows his hoar* leaves in the glassy stream;
Therewith fantastic garlands did she make
Of crowflowers, nettles, daisies, and long purples   185
That liberal* shepherds give a grosser name,
But our cold maids do dead men's fingers call them.
There, on the pendent boughs her coronet weeds
Clamb'ring to hang, an envious sliver broke;
When down her weedy trophies and herself   190
Feel in the weeping brook. Her clothes spread wide
And, mermaid-like, awhile they bore her up;
Which time she chanted snatches of old lauds,*
As one incapable* of her own distress,
Or like a creature native and indued*   195

---

159 **simples** medicinal herbs
166 **shape** role
167 **drift look through** purpose show through
170 **blast in proof** fail in performance
176 **nonce** occasion
177 **stuck** thrust
183 **hoar** silver gray
186 **liberal** coarse-mouthed
193 **lauds** hymns
194 **incapable** unaware
195 **indued** in harmony with

> Unto that element; but long it could not be
> Till that her garments, heavy with their drink,
> Pull'd the poor wretch from her melodious lay
> To muddy death.

LAERTES: Alas, then she is drown'd!   200
QUEEN: Drown'd, drown'd.
LAERTES: Too much of water hast thou, poor Ophelia,
> And therefore I forbid my tears; but yet
> It is our trick,* nature her custom holds,
> Let shame say what it will. When these are gone,   205
> The woman* will be out. Adieu, my lord.
> I have a speech o' fire that fain would blaze
> But that this folly douts it.   [*Exit.*]
KING: Let's follow, Gertrude.
> How much I had to do to calm his rage!   210
> Now fear I this will give it start again;
> Therefore let's follow.   [*Exeunt.*]

ACT V

SCENE I———*Elsinore. A churchyard.*

[*Enter two* CLOWNS *with spades and picks.*]

FIRST CLOWN: Is she to be buried in Christian burial when she wilfully seeks her
> own salvation?
SECOND CLOWN: I tell thee she is; therefore make her grave straight.* The
> crowner* hath sat on her, and finds it Christian burial.
FIRST CLOWN: How can that be, unless she drown'd herself in her own defence?   5
SECOND CLOWN: Why, 'tis found so.
FIRST CLOWN: It must be 'se offendendo';* it cannot be else. For here lies the
> point: if I drown myself wittingly, it argues an act; and an act hath three
> branches—it is to act, to do, to perform; argal,* she drown'd herself
> wittingly.   10
SECOND CLOWN: Nay, but hear you, Goodman Delver.
FIRST CLOWN: Give me leave. Here lies the water; good. Here stands the man;
> good. If the man go to this water and drown himself, it is, will he, nill he,
> he goes—mark you that; but if the water come to him and drown him, he
> drowns not himself. Argal, he that is not guilty of his own death shortens   15
> not his own life.

---

²⁰⁴ **trick** way
²⁰⁶ **woman** womanly part
^{V,i,3} **straight** straight way
⁴   **crowner** coroner
⁷   **se offendendo** false latin, instead of "se defendendo" meaning "in self-defense"
⁹   **argal** false Latin for "ergo" ("therefore")

SECOND CLOWN: But is this law?

FIRST CLOWN: Ay, marry is't; crowner's quest* law.

SECOND CLOWN: Will you ha' the truth an't? If this had not been a gentlewoman, she should have been buried out a Christian burial. 20

FIRST CLOWN: Why, there thou say'st; and the more pity that great folk should have count'nance* in this world to drown or hang themselves more than their even Christen.* Come, my spade. There is no ancient gentlemen but gard'ners, ditchers, and grave-makers; they hold up* Adam's profession.

SECOND CLOWN: Was he a gentleman? 25

FIRST CLOWN: 'A was the first that ever bore arms.*

SECOND CLOWN: Why, he had none.

FIRST CLOWN: What, art a heathen? How dost thou understand the Scripture? The Scripture says Adam digg'd. Could he dig without arms? I'll put another question to thee. If thou answerest me not to the purpose, confess thyself— 30

SECOND CLOWN: Go to.

FIRST CLOWN: What is he that builds stronger than either the mason, the shipwright, or the carpenter?

SECOND CLOWN: The gallows-maker; for that frame outlives a thousand tenants. 35

FIRST CLOWN: I like thy wit well; in good faith the gallows does well; but how does it well? It does well to those that do ill. Now thou dost ill to say the gallows is built stronger than the church; argal, the gallows may do well to thee. To't again, come.

SECOND CLOWN: Who builds stronger than a mason, a shipwright, or a carpenter? 40

FIRST CLOWN: Ay, tell me that, and unyoke.*

SECOND CLOWN: Marry, now I can tell.

FIRST CLOWN: To't.

SECOND CLOWN: Mass, I cannot tell.

[*Enter* HAMLET *and* HORATIO, *afar off.*]

FIRST CLOWN: Cudgel thy brains no more about it, for your dull ass will not mend his pace with beating, and when you are ask'd this question next, say 'a grave-maker': the house he makes lasts till doomsday. Go, get thee to Yaughan; fetch me a stoup* of liquor. [*Exit* SECOND CLOWN.] 45

[*digs and sings*]

> *In youth, when I did love, did love*
> *Methought it was very sweet,* 50
> *To contract-o-the time for-a my behove,**
> *O, methought there-a-was nothing-a meet.*

HAMLET: Has this fellow no feeling of his business, that 'a sings in grave-making?

---

18 **crowner's quest** coroner's inquest
22 **count'nance** privilege
23 **even Christen** fellow Christian
24 **hold up** keep up
26 **bore arms** had a coat of arms
41 **unyoke** quit work for the day
48 **stoup** tankard
51 **behove** advantage

HORATIO: Custom hath made it in him a property of easiness.*
HAMLET: 'Tis e'en so; the hand of little employment hath the daintier sense. 55
FIRST CLOWN: [*sings*]

> *But age, with his stealing steps,*
> *Hath clawed me in his clutch,*
> *And hath shipped me intil the land,*
> *As if I had never been such.*

[*throws up a skull*]

HAMLET: That skull had a tongue in it, and could sing once. How the knave jowls* 60
it to the ground, as if 'twere Cain's jawbone, that did the first murder! This
might be the pate of a politician, which this ass now o'erreaches; one that
would circumvent God, might it not?
HORATIO: It might, my lord.
HAMLET: Or of a courtier; which could say 'Good morrow, sweet lord! How dost 65
thou, sweet lord?' This might be my Lord Such-a-one, that praised my Lord
Such-a-one's horse, when 'a meant to beg it—might it not?
HORATIO: Ay, my lord.
HAMLET: Why, e'en so; and now my Lady Worm's, chapless,* and knock'd about
the mazard* with a sexton's spade. Here's fine revolution, an we had the 70
trick to see't. Did these bones cost no more the breeding but to play at loggats*
with them? Mine ache to think on't.
FIRST CLOWN: [*sings*]

> *A pick-axe and a spade, a spade*
> *For and a shrouding sheet:*
> *O, a pit of clay for to be made* 75
> *For such a guest is meet.*

[*throws up another skull*]

HAMLET: There's another. Why may not that be the skull of a lawyer? Where be
his quiddities* now, his quillets,* his cases, his tenures,* and his tricks? Why
does he suffer this rude knave now to knock him about the sconce* with a
dirty shovel, and will not tell him of his action of battery? Hum! This fellow 80
might be in's time a great buyer of land, with his statutes, his recognizances,
his fines,* his double vouchers, his recoveries. Is this the fine* of his fines,
and the recovery of his recoveries, to have his fine pate full of fine dirt? Will
his vouchers vouch him no more of his purchases, and double ones, too, than
the length and breadth of a pair of indentures?* The very conveyances of his 85
lands will scarcely lie in this box; and must th' inheritor himself have no
more, ha?

---

54 **Custom . . . easiness** constant practice has made it easy
60 **jowls** hurls
69 **chapless** missing the lower jaw
70 **mazard** head
71 **loggats** a game involving throwing at objects
78 **quiddities, quillets, tenures** legal terms
79 **sconce** head
82–83 **fines, fine** play on words for documents, death, and so on
85 **indentures** contracts

HORATIO: Not a jot more, my lord.

HAMLET: Is not parchment made of sheep-skins?

HORATIO: Ay, my lord, and of calves' skins, too. 90

HAMLET: They are sheep and calves which seek out assurance in that. I will speak
 to this fellow. Whose grave's this, sirrah?

FIRST CLOWN: Mine, sir. [*sings*]

O, a pit of clay for to be made
For such a guest is meet. 95

HAMLET: I think it be thine indeed, for thou liest in't.

FIRST CLOWN: You lie out on't, sir, and therefore 'tis not yours. For my part, I do
 not lie in't, yet it is mine.

HAMLET: Thou dost lie in't, to be in't and say it is thine; 'tis for the dead, not for
 the quick; therefore thou liest. 100

FIRST CLOWN: 'Tis a quick lie, sir; 'twill away again from me to you.

HAMLET: What man dost thou dig it for?

FIRST CLOWN: For no man, sir.

HAMLET: What woman, then?

FIRST CLOWN: For none neither. 105

HAMLET: Who is to be buried in't?

FIRST CLOWN: One that was a woman, sir; but, rest her soul, she's dead.

HAMLET: How absolute* the knave is! We must speak by the card,* or equivoca-
 tion will undo us. By the Lord, Horatio, this three years I have took note of
 it: the age is grown so picked* that the toe of the peasant comes so near the 110
 heel of the courtier, he galls his kibe.* How long hast thou been a gravemaker?

FIRST CLOWN: Of all the days i' th' year, I came to't that day that our last King
 Hamlet overcame Fortinbras.

HAMLET: How long is that since?

FIRST CLOWN: Cannot you tell that? Every fool can tell that: it was that very day 115
 that young Hamlet was born—he that is mad, and sent into England.

HAMLET: Ay, marry, why was he sent into England?

FIRST CLOWN: Why, because 'a was mad: 'a shall recover his wits there; or, if 'a do
 not, 'tis no great matter there.

HAMLET: Why? 120

FIRST CLOWN: 'Twill not be seen in him there: there the men are as mad as he.

HAMLET: How came he mad?

FIRST CLOWN: Very strangely, they say.

HAMLET: How strangely?

FIRST CLOWN: Faith, e'en with losing his wits. 125

HAMLET: Upon what ground?

FIRST CLOWN: Why, here in Denmark. I have been sexton here, man and boy,
 thirty years.

HAMLET: How long will a man lie i' th' earth ere he rot?

---

[108] **absolute** positive, certain
[108] **card** exactly
[110] **picked** refined
[111] **kibe** sore on the heel

FIRST CLOWN: Faith, if 'a be not rotten before 'a die—as we have many pocky   130
    corses* now-a-days that will scarce hold the laying in—'a will last you some
    eight year or nine year. A tanner will last you nine year.

HAMLET: Why he more than another?

FIRST CLOWN: Why, sir, his hide is so tann'd with his trade that 'a will keep out
    water a great while; and your water is a sore decayer of your whoreson dead   135
    body. Here's a skull now; this skull has lien you i' th' earth three and twenty
    years.

HAMLET: Whose was it?

FIRST CLOWN: A whoreson mad fellow's it was. Whose do you think it was?

HAMLET: Nay, I know not.   140

FIRST CLOWN: A pestilence on him for a mad rogue! 'A poured a flagon of Rhen-
    ish on my head once. This same skull, sir, was, sir, Yorick's skull, the King's
    jester.

HAMLET: This?

FIRST CLOWN: E'en that.   145

HAMLET: Let me see. [*takes the skull*] Alas, poor Yorick! I knew him, Horatio: a
    fellow of infinite jest, of most excellent fancy; he hath borne me on his back
    a thousand times. And now how abhorred in my imagination it is! My gorge
    rises at it. Here hung those lips that I have kiss'd I know not how oft. Where
    be your gibes now, your gambols, your songs, your flashes of merriment   150
    that were wont to set the table on a roar? Not one now to mock your own
    grinning—quite chap-fall'n?* Now get you to my lady's chamber, and tell
    her, let her paint an inch thick, to this favour* she must come; make her
    laugh at that. Prithee, Horatio, tell me one thing.

HORATIO: What's that, my lord?   155

HAMLET: Dost thou think Alexander look'd o' this fashion i' th' earth?

HORATIO: E'en so.

HAMLET: And smelt so? Pah   [*throws down the skull*]

HORATIO: E'en so, my lord.

HAMLET: To what base uses we may return, Horatio! Why may not imagination   160
    trace the noble dust of Alexander till 'a find it stopping a bung-hole?

HORATIO: 'Twere to consider too curiously* to consider so.

HAMLET: No, faith, not a jot; but to follow him thither with modesty enough, and
    likelihood to lead it, as thus: Alexander died, Alexander was buried, Alexan-
    der returneth to dust; the dust is earth; of earth we make loam, and why of   165
    that loam whereto he was converted might they not stop a beer-barrel?
           Imperious Caesar, dead and turn'd to clay,
           Might stop a hole to keep the wind away.
           O, that that earth which kept the world in awe
           *Should patch a wall t' expel the winter's flaw!**   170
    But soft! but soft! awhile. Here comes the King.

    [*Enter the* KING, QUEEN, LAERTES, *in funeral procession after the coffin, with*
    PRIEST *and* LORDS *attendant.*]

---

130 **pocky corses** corpses of those with syphilis
152 **chap-fall'n** jawless (down in the mouth)
153 **favour** appearance, condition
162 **curiously** minutely
170 **flaw** gust

The Queen, the courtiers. Who is this they follow?
And with such maimed* rites? This doth betoken
The corse they follow did with desperate hand
Fordo it own life. 'Twas of some estate.*   175
Couch* we awhile and mark.   [*retiring with* **HORATIO**]
LAERTES: What ceremony else?
HAMLET: That is Laertes, a very noble youth. Mark.
LAERTES: What ceremony else?
PRIEST: Her obsequies have been so far enlarg'd   180
  As we have warrantise. Her death was doubtful;
  And, but that great command o'ersways the order,
  She should in ground unsanctified have lodg'd
  Till the last trumpet; for charitable prayers,
  Shards, flints, and pebbles, should be thrown on her;   185
  Yet here she is allow'd her virgin crants,*
  Her maiden strewments, and the bringing home
  Of bell and burial.
LAERTES: Must there no more be done?
PRIEST: No more be done.   190
  We should profane the service of the dead
  To sing sage requiem and such rest to her
  As to peace-parted souls.
LAERTES: Lay her i' th' earth;
  And from her fair and unpolluted flesh   195
  May violets spring! I tell thee, churlish priest,
  A minist'ring angel shall my sister be
  When thou liest howling.
HAMLET: What, the fair Ophelia!
QUEEN: Sweets to the sweet; farewell! [*scattering flowers*]   200
  I hop'd thou shouldst have been my Hamlet's wife;
  I thought thy bride-bed to have deck'd, sweet maid,
  And not have strew'd thy grave.
LAERTES: O, treble woe
  Fall ten times treble on that cursed head   205
  Whose wicked deed thy most ingenious sense*
  Depriv'd thee of! Hold off the earth awhile,
  Till I have caught her once more in mine arms.

      [*leaps into the grave*]

  Now pile your dust upon the quick and dead,
  Till of this flat a mountain you have made   210
  T' o'er-top old Pelion or the skyish head
  Of blue Olympus.

---

173 **maimed** curtailed
175 **estate** high rank
176 **Couch** hide
186 **crants** garlands
206 **ingenious sense** finely endowed mind

HAMLET: [*advancing*] What is he whose grief
    Bears such an emphasis, whose phrase of sorrow
    Conjures the wand'ring stars, and makes them stand   215
    Like wonder-wounded hearers? This is I,
    Hamlet, the Dane.   [*leaps into the grave*]
LAERTES: The devil take thy soul! [*grappling with him*]
HAMLET: Thou pray'st not well.
    I prithee take thy fingers from my throat;   220
    For, though I am not splenitive* and rash,
    Yet have I in me something dangerous,
    Which let thy wiseness fear. Hold off thy hand.
KING: Pluck them asunder.
QUEEN: Hamlet! Hamlet!   225
ALL: Gentlemen!
HORATIO: Good my lord, be quiet.

     [*The attendants part them, and they come out of the grave.*]

HAMLET: Why, I will fight with him upon this theme
    Until my eyelids will no longer wag.
QUEEN: O my son, what theme?   230
HAMLET: I lov'd Ophelia: forty thousand brothers
    Could not, with all their quantity of love
    Make up my sum. What wilt thou do for her?
KING: O, he is mad, Laertes.
QUEEN: For love of God, forbear him.   235
HAMLET: 'Swounds, show me what th'owt do:
    Woo't weep, woo't fight, woo't fast, woo't tear thyself,
    Woo't drink up eisel,* eat a crocodile?
    I'll do't. Dost come here to whine?
    To outface me with leaping in her grave?   240
    Be buried quick with her, and so will I;
    And, if thou prate of mountains, let them throw
    Millions of acres on us, till our ground,
    Singeing his pate against the burning zone,*
    Make Ossa like a wart! Nay, an thou'lt mouth,   245
    I'll rant as well as thou.
QUEEN: This is mere madness;
    And thus awhile the fit will work on him;
    Anon, as patient as the female dove
    When that her golden couplets are disclos'd*   250
    His silence will sit drooping.
HAMLET: Hear you, sir:
    What is the reason that you use me thus?

---

[221] **splenitive** fiery spirited
[238] **eisel** vinegar
[244] **burning zone** the sun
[250] **golden couplets are disclos'd** doves were thought to lay only two eggs; here the reference is to young, just-hatched doves

I lov'd you ever. But it is no matter.
Let Hercules himself do what he may, 255
The cat will mew, and dog will have his day. [*Exit.*]
KING: I pray thee, good Horatio, wait upon him.

[*Exit* HORATIO.]

[*to* LAERTES] Strengthen your patience in our last night's speech;
We'll put the matter to the present push.*—
Good Gertrude, set some watch over your son.— 260
This grave shall have a living* monument.
An hour of quiet shortly shall we see;
Till then in patience our proceeding be. [*Exeunt.*]

SCENE II———*Elsinore. The Castle.*

[*Enter* HAMLET *and* HORATIO.]

HAMLET: So much for this, sir; now shall you see the other.
You do remember all the circumstance?
HORATIO: Remember it, my lord!
HAMLET: Sir, in my heart there was a kind of fighting
That would not let me sleep. Methought I lay 5
Worse than the mutines in the bilboes.* Rashly,
And prais'd be rashness for it—let us know,
Our indiscretion sometime serves us well,
When our deep plots do pall,* and that should learn us
There's a divinity that shapes our ends, 10
Rough-hew them how we will.
HORATIO: That is most certain.
HAMLET: Up from my cabin,
My sea-gown scarf'd about me, in the dark
Grop'd to find out them; had my desire; 15
Finger'd* their packet, and in fine withdrew
To mine own room again, making so bold,
My fears forgetting manners, to unseal
Their grand commission; where I found, Horatio,
Ah, royal knavery! an exact command, 20
Larded* with many several sorts of reasons,
Importing Denmark's health and England's, too,
With, ho! such bugs and goblins in my life*—

---

²⁵⁹ **present push** immediate test
²⁶¹ **living** lasting
ⱽ·ⁱⁱ·⁶ **mutines in the bilboes** mutineers in chains
⁹ **pall** fail
¹⁶ **Finger'd** stole
²¹ **Larded** enriched
²³ **bugs . . . my life** imagined terrors if were allowed to live

That, on the supervise,* no leisure bated,*
No, not to stay the grinding of the axe,   25
My head should be struck off.
HORATIO: Is't possible?
HAMLET: Here's the commission; read it at more leisure.
But wilt thou hear now how I did proceed?
HORATIO: I beseech you.   30
HAMLET: Being thus benetted round with villainies—
Ere I could make a prologue to my brains,
They had begun the play—I sat me down;
Devis'd a new commission; wrote it fair.
I once did hold it, as our statists* do,   35
A baseness to write fair,* and labour'd much
How to forget that learning; but sir, now
It did me yeoman's service. Wilt thou know
Th' effect* of what I wrote?
HORATIO: Ay, good my lord.   40
HAMLET: An earnest conjuration from the King,
As England was his faithful tributary,
As love between them like the palm might flourish,
As peace should still her wheaten garland wear
And stand a comma* tween their amities,   45
And many such like as's of great charge,
That, on the view and knowing of these contents,
Without debatement further more or less,
He should those bearers put to sudden death,
Not shriving-time* allow'd.   50
HORATIO: How was this seal'd?
HAMLET: Why, even in that was heaven ordinant.*
I had my father's signet in my purse,
Which was the model of that Danish seal;
Folded the writ up in the form of th' other;   55
Subscrib'd it, gave't th' impression, plac'd it safely,
The changeling never known. Now, the next day
Was our sea-fight; and what to this was sequent
Thou knowest already.
HORATIO: So Guildenstern and Rosencrantz go to't.   60
HAMLET: Why, man, they did make love to this employment;
They are not near my conscience; their defeat
Does by their own insinuation* grow:
'tis dangerous when the baser nature comes

---

24 **supervise** reading
24 **leisure bated** delay allowed
35 **statists** statesmen
36 **fair** clearly
39 **effect** purport
45 **comma** link
50 **shriving-time** time to be absolved of sin
52 **ordinant** on my side
63 **insinuation** meddling

Between the pass and fell* incensed points   65
  Of mighty opposites.
HORATIO: Why, what a king is this!
HAMLET: Does it not, think thee, stand me now upon*—
  He that hath kill'd my king and whor'd my mother,
  Popp'd in between th' election* and my hopes;   70
  Thrown out his angle for my proper life,*
  And with such coz'nage*—is't not perfect conscience
  To quit* him with this arm? And is't not to be damn'd
  To let this canker of our nature come
  In further evil?   75
HORATIO: It must be shortly known to him from England
  What is the issue of the business there.
HAMLET: It will be short; the interim is mine.
  And a man's life's no more than to say 'one.'
  But I am very sorry, good Horatio,   80
  That to Laertes I forgot myself;
  For by the image of my cause I see
  The portraiture of his. I'll court his favours.
  But sure the bravery of his grief did put me
  Into a tow'ring passion.   85
HORATIO: Peace; who comes here?

  [*Enter young* OSRIC.]

OSRIC: Your lordship is right welcome back to Denmark.
HAMLET: I humbly thank you, sir. [*aside to* HORATIO] Dost know this water-fly?
HORATIO: [*aside to* HAMLET] No, my good lord.
HAMLET: [*aside to* HORATIO] Thy state is the more gracious; for 'tis a vice to   90
  know him. He hath much land, and fertile. Let a beast be lord of beasts, and
  his crib shall stand at the king's mess!* 'Tis a chough,* but, as I say,
  spacious* in the possession of dirt.
OSRIC: Sweet lord, if your lordship were at leisure, I should impart a thing to you
  from his Majesty.   95
HAMLET: I will receive it, sir, with all diligence of spirit. Put your bonnet to his
  right use, 'tis for the head.
OSRIC: I thank your lordship; it is very hot.
HAMLET: No, believe me, 'tis very cold; the wind is northerly.
OSRIC: It is indifferent cold, my lord, indeed.   100
HAMLET: But yet methinks it is very sultry and hot for my complexion.*
OSRIC: Exceedingly, my lord; it is very sultry, as 'twere—I cannot tell how. But,

---

65 **pass and fell** thrust and cruel
68 **stand me now upon** became incumbent on me
70 **election** selection to be king
71 **angle for my proper life** tried to end my own life
72 **coz'nage** trickery
73 **quit** pay back
92 **mess** table
92 **chough** chatterer
93 **spacious** well off
101 **complexion** temperament

my lord, his Majesty bade me signify to you that 'a has laid a great wager on your head. Sir, this is the matter—

HAMLET: I beseech you, remember.   105

[HAMLET *moves him to put on his hat.*]

OSRIC: Nay, good my lord; for my ease, in good faith. Sir, here is newly come to court Laertes; believe me, an absolute gentleman, full of most excellent differences,* of very soft society and great showing. Indeed, to speak feelingly of him, he is the card* or calendar of gentry, for you shall find in him the continent* of what part a gentleman would see.   110

HAMLET: Sir, his definement* suffers no perdition* in you; though, I know, to divide him inventorially would dozy* th' arithmetic of memory, and yet but yaw neither in respect of his quick sail. But, in the verity of extolment, I take him to be a soul of great article, and his infusion of such dearth and rareness, as to make true diction of him, his semblable is his mirror, and who else   115
would trace him, his umbrage, nothing more.

OSRIC: Your lordship speaks most infallibly of him.

HAMLET: The concernancy,* sir? Why do we wrap the gentleman in our more rawer breath?

OSRIC: Sir?   120

HORATIO: [*aside to* HAMLET] Is't not possible to understand in another tongue? You will to't, sir, really.

HAMLET: What imports the nomination of this gentleman?

OSRIC: Of Laertes?

HORATIO: [*aside*] His purse is empty already; all's golden words are spent.   125

HAMLET: Of him, sir.

OSRIC: I know you are not ignorant—

HAMLET: I would you did, sir; yet, in faith, if you did, it would not much approve* me. Well, sir.

OSRIC: You are not ignorant of what excellence Laertes is—   130

HAMLET: I dare not confess that, lest I should compare with him in excellence; but to know a man well were to know himself.

OSRIC: I mean, sir, for his weapon; but in the imputation* laid on him by them, in his meed* he's unfellowed.

HAMLET: What's his weapon?   135

OSRIC: Rapier and dagger.

HAMLET: That's two of his weapons—but well.

OSRIC: The King, sir, hath wager'd him with six Barbary horses; against the which he has impon'd,* as I take it, six French rapiers and poniards, with

---

[107] **differences** distinguishing characteristics
[109] **card** model
[110] **continent** summary
[111] **definement** description
[111] **perdition** loss (this entire speech mocks Osric's use of overblown language)
[112] **dozy** dizzy
[118] **concernancy** meaning
[128] **approve** commend
[133] **imputation** reputation
[134] **meed** merit
[139] **impon'd** wagered

their assigns,* as girdle, hangers, and so—three of the carriages, in faith, are   140
very dear to fancy, very responsive to the hilts, most delicate carriages, and
of very liberal conceit.

HAMLET: What call you the carriages?

HORATIO: [*aside to* HAMLET] I knew you must be edified by the margent* ere you
had done.   145

OSRIC: The carriages, sir, are the hangers.

HAMLET: The phrase would be more germane to the matter if we could carry a
cannon by our sides. I would it might be hangers till then. But on: six Barbary horses against six French swords, their assigns, and three liberal conceited carriages; that's the French bet against the Danish. Why is this all   150
impon'd, as you call it?

OSRIC: The King, sir, hath laid, sir, that in a dozen passes between yourself and
him he shall not exceed you three hits; he hath laid on twelve for nine, and it
would come to immediate trial if your lordship would vouchsafe the answer.

HAMLET: How if I answer no?   155

OSRIC: I mean, my lord, the opposition of your person in trial.

HAMLET: Sir, I will walk here in the hall. If it please his Majesty, it is the breathing time of day* with me; let the foils be brought, the gentlemen willing, and
the King hold his purpose, I will win for him an I can; if not, I will gain nothing but my shame and the odd hits.   160

OSRIC: Shall I redeliver you e'en so?

HAMLET: To this effect, sir, after what flourish your nature will.

OSRIC: I commend my duty to your lordship.

HAMLET: Yours, yours. [*Exit* OSRIC.] He does well to commend it himself; there
are no tongues else for 's turn.   165

HORATIO: This lapwing runs away with the shell on his head.

HAMLET: 'A did comply, sir, with his dug before 'a suck'd it.* Thus has he, and
many more of the same bevy, that I know the drossy age dotes on, only got
the tune of the time and outward habit of encounter*—a kind of yesty* collection, which carries them through and through the most fann'd and win-   170
nowed opinions; and do but blow them to their trial, the bubbles are out.*

[*Enter a* LORD.]

LORD: My lord, his Majesty commended him to you by young Osric, who brings
back to him that you attend him in the hall. He sends to know if your pleasure hold to play with Laertes, or that you will take longer time.

HAMLET: I am constant to my purposes; they follow the king's pleasure: if his fit-   175
ness speaks, mine is ready now—or whensoever, provided I be so able as
now.

LORD: The King and Queen and all are coming down.

HAMLET: In happy time.

---

[140] **assigns** accompaniments
[144] **margent** exaggerated terminology
[157-58] **breathing time of day** time when I do my exercises
[167] **'A did comply . . . suck'd it** He was ceremoniously polite to his mother's breast before he sucked it
[169] **habit of encounter** superficial way of talking to people
[169] **yesty** frothy
[171] **blow them . . . bubbles are out** question them and they are at a loss

LORD: The Queen desires you to use some gentle entertainment* to Laertes be-   180
    fore you fall to play.
HAMLET: She well instructs me.   [*Exit* LORD.]
HORATIO: You will lose this wager, my lord.
HAMLET: I do not think so; since he went into France I have been in continual
    practice. I shall win at the odds. But thou wouldst not think how ill all's   185
    here about my heart; but it is no matter.
HORATIO: Nay, good my lord—
HAMLET: It is but foolery; but it is such a kind of gaingiving* as would perhaps
    trouble a woman.
HORATIO: If your mind dislike anything, obey it. I will forestall their repair hither,   190
    and say you are not fit.
HAMLET: Not a whit, we defy augury: there is a special providence in the fall of
    a sparrow. If it be now, 'tis not to come; if it be not to come, it will be now;
    if it be not now, yet it will come—the readiness is all. Since no man owes of
    aught he leaves, what is't to leave betimes?* Let be.   195

    [*A table prepared. Trumpets, drums, and officers with cushions, foils, and daggers.*
    Enter KING, QUEEN, LAERTES, *and all the state.*]

KING: Come, Hamlet, come, and take this hand from me.

    [*The* KING *puts* LAERTES' *hand into* HAMLET'S.]

HAMLET: Give me your pardon, sir. I have done you wrong;
    But pardon't, as you are a gentleman.
    This presence* knows,
    And you must needs have heard how I am punish'd   200
    With a sore distraction. What I have done
    That might your nature, honour, and exception,*
    Roughly awake, I here proclaim was madness.
    Was't Hamlet wrong'd Laertes? Never Hamlet.
    If Hamlet from himself be ta'en away,   205
    And when he's not himself does wrong Laertes,
    Then Hamlet does it not, Hamlet denies it.
    Who does it, then? His madness. If't be so,
    Hamlet is of the faction* that is wrong'd;
    His madness is poor Hamlet's enemy.   210
    Sir, in this audience,
    Let my disclaiming from a purpos'd evil
    Free me so far in your most generous thoughts
    That I have shot my arrow o'er the house
    And hurt my brother.   215

---

[180] **gentle entertainment** be courteous
[188] **gaingiving** misgiving
[195] **betimes** early
[199] **presence** assembly
[202] **exception** disapproval
[209] **faction** group

LAERTES: I am satisfied in nature,
   Whose motive in this case should stir me most
   To my revenge; but in my terms of honour
   I stand aloof, and will no reconcilement
   Till by some elder masters of known honour   220
   I have a voice and precedent of peace
   To keep my name ungor'd—but till that time
   I do receive your offer'd love like love,
   And will not wrong it.
HAMLET: I embrace it freely;   225
   And will this brother's wager frankly play.
   Give us the foils. Come on.
LAERTES: Come, one for me.
HAMLET: I'll be your foil, Laertes; in mine ignorance
   Your skill shall, like a star i' th' darkest night,   230
   Stick fiery off* indeed.
LAERTES: You mock me, sir.
HAMLET: No, by this hand.
KING: Give them the foils, young Osric. Cousin Hamlet,
   You know the wager?   235
HAMLET: Very well, my lord;
   Your Grace has laid the odds a' th' weaker side.
KING: I do not fear it: I have seen you both;
   But since he's better'd,* we have therefore odds.
LAERTES: This is too heavy; let me see another.   240
HAMLET: This likes me well. These foils have all a length?

    [They prepare to play.]

OSRIC: Ay, my good lord.
KING: Set me the stoups of wine upon that table.
   If Hamlet give the first or second hit,
   Or quit in answer of the third exchange,   245
   Let all the battlements their ordnance fire;
   The King shall drink to Hamlet's better breath,
   And in the cup an union* shall he throw,
   Richer than that which four successive kings
   In Denmark's crown have worn. Give me the cups;   250
   And let the kettle* to the trumpet speak,
   The trumpet to the cannoneer without,
   The cannons to the heavens, the heaven to earth,
   'Now the King drinks to Hamlet.' Come, begin—
   And you, the judges, bear a wary eye.   255
HAMLET: Come on, sir.

---

[231] **stick fiery off** stand out brilliantly
[239] **better'd** improved
[248] **union** pearl
[251] **kettle** kettledrum

LAERTES: Come, my lord.   [*They play.*]
HAMLET: One.
LAERTES: No.
HAMLET: Judgment?   260
OSRIC: A hit, a very palpable hit.
LAERTES: Well, again.
KING: Stay, give me drink. Hamlet, this pearl is thine;
    Here's to thy health. [*drum, trumpets, and shot*] Give him the cup.
HAMLET: I'll play this bout first; set it by awhile.   265
    Come. [*They play.*] Another hit; what say you?
LAERTES: A touch, a touch, I do confess't.
KING: Our son shall win.
QUEEN: He's fat,* and scant of breath.
    Here, Hamlet, take my napkin, rub thy brows.   270
    The Queen carouses to thy fortune, Hamlet.
HAMLET: Good madam!
KING: Gertrude, do not drink.
QUEEN: I will, my lord; I pray you pardon me.
KING: [*aside*] It is the poison'd cup; it is too late.   275
HAMLET: I dare not drink yet, madam; by and by.
QUEEN: Come, let me wipe thy face.
LAERTES: My lord, I'll hit him now.
KING: I do not think't.
LAERTES: [*aside*] And yet it is almost against my conscience.   280
HAMLET: Come, for the third. Laertes, you do but dally;
    I pray you pass with your best violence;
    I am afeard you make a wanton* of me.
LAERTES: Say you so? Come on.   [*They play.*]
OSRIC: Nothing, neither way.   285
LAERTES: Have at you now!

    [LAERTES *wounds* HAMLET; *then, in scuffling, they change rapiers, and* HAMLET
    wounds LAERTES.]

KING: Part them; they are incens'd.
HAMLET: Nay, come again.   [*The* QUEEN *falls.*]
OSRIC: Look to the Queen there, ho!
HORATIO: They bleed on both sides. How is it, my lord?   290
OSRIC: How is't, Laertes?
LAERTES: Why, as a woodcock, to mine own springe,* Osric;
    I am justly kill'd with mine own treachery.
HAMLET: How does the Queen?
KING: She swoons to see them bleed.   295
QUEEN: No, no, the drink, the drink! O my dear Hamlet!
    The drink, the drink! I am poison'd.   [*dies*]
HAMLET: O, villainy! Ho! let the door be lock'd.
    Treachery! Seek it out.   [LAERTES *falls.*]

------

269 **fat** sweaty
283 **wanton** spoiled child
292 **springe** snare

LAERTES: It is here, Hamlet. Hamlet, thou art slain; 300
    No med'cine in the world can do thee good;
    In thee there is not half an hour's life;
    The treacherous instrument is in thy hand,
    Unbated and envenom'd. The foul practice*
    Hath turn'd itself on me; lo, here I lie, 305
    Never to rise again. Thy mother's poison'd.
    I can no more. The King, the King's to blame.
HAMLET: The point envenom'd, too!
    Then, venom, to thy work.   [*stabs the* KING]
ALL: Treason! treason! 310
KING: O, yet defend me, friends; I am but hurt.
HAMLET: Here, thou incestuous, murd'rous, damned Dane,
    Drink off this potion. Is thy union here?
    Follow my mother.   [KING *dies.*]
LAERTES: He is justly serv'd: 315
    It is a poison temper'd* by himself.
    Exchange forgiveness with me, noble Hamlet.
    Mine and my father's death come not upon thee,
    Nor thine on me!   [*dies*]
HAMLET: Heaven make thee free of it! I follow thee. 320
    I am dead, Horatio. Wretched Queen, adieu!
    You that look pale and tremble at this chance,
    That are but mutes or audience to this act,
    Had I but time, as this fell sergeant Death
    Is strict in his arrest, O, I could tell you— 325
    But let it be. Horatio, I am dead:
    Thou livest; report me and my cause aright
    To the unsatisfied.
HORATIO: Never believe it.
    I am more an antique Roman* than a Dane; 330
    Here's yet some liquor left.
HAMLET: As th'art a man,
    Give me the cup. Let go. By heaven, I'll ha't.
    O good Horatio, what a wounded name,
    Things standing thus unknown, shall live behind me! 335
    If thou didst ever hold me in thy heart,
    Absent thee from felicity awhile,
    And in this harsh world draw thy breath in pain,
    To tell my story. [*march afar off, and shot within*] What warlike noise
        is this? 340
OSRIC: Young Fortinbras, with conquest come from Poland,
    To th'ambassadors of England gives
    This warlike volley.
HAMLET: O, I die, Horatio!

---

³⁰⁴ **foul practice** deception
³¹⁶ **temper'd** mixed
³³⁰ **antique Roman** given to suicide

The potent poison quite o'er-crows* my spirit.   345
I cannot live to hear the news from England,
But I do prophesy th' election lights
On Fortinbras; he has my dying voice.
So tell him, with th' occurrents,* more and less,
Which have solicited*—the rest is silence.   [*dies*]   350
HORATIO: Now cracks a noble heart. Good night, sweet prince,
And flights of angels sing thee to thy rest!   [*march within*]
Why does the drum come hither?

> [*Enter* FORTINBRAS *and* ENGLISH AMBASSADORS, *with drum, colours, and*
> *attendants.*]

FORTINBRAS: Where is this sight?
HORATIO: What is it you would see?   355
If aught of woe or wonder, cease your search.
FORTINBRAS: This quarry* cries on havoc.* O proud death,
What feast is toward* in thine eternal cell
That thou so many princes at a shot
So bloodily hast struck?   360
FIRST AMBASSADOR: The sight is dismal;
And our affairs from England come too late:
The ears are senseless that should give us hearing
To tell him his commandment is fulfill'd
That Rosencrantz and Guildenstern are dead.   365
Where should we have our thanks?
HORATIO: Not from his* mouth,
Had it th' ability of life to thank you:
He never gave commandment for their death.
But since, so jump* upon this bloody question,   370
You from the Polack wars, and you from England,
And here arrived, give order that these bodies
High on a stage* be placed to the view;
And let me speak to th' yet unknowing world
How these things came about. So shall you hear   375
Of carnal, bloody, and unnatural acts;
Of accidental judgments, casual* slaughters;
Of deaths put on by cunning and forc'd cause;
And, in this upshot, purposes mistook
Fall'n on th' inventors' heads—all this can I   380
Truly deliver.

---

³⁴⁵ **o'er-crows** overpowers
³⁴⁹ **occurrents** occurrences
³⁵⁰ **solicited** incited
³⁵⁷ **quarry** heap of slain bodies
³⁵⁷ **cries on havoc** proclaims general slaughter
³⁵⁸ **toward** in preparation
³⁶⁷ **his** Claudius'
³⁷⁰ **jump** precisely
³⁷³ **stage** platform
³⁷⁷ **casual** unplanned

FORTINBRAS: Let us haste to hear it,
  And call the noblest to the audience.
  For me, with sorrow I embrace my fortune;
  I have some rights of memory* in this kingdom,   385
  Which now to claim my vantage doth invite me.
HORATIO: Of that I shall have also cause to speak,
  And from his mouth whose voice will draw on more.*
  But let this same be presently perform'd,
  Even while men's minds are wild, lest more mischance 390
  On* plots and errors happen.
FORTINBRAS: Let four captains
  Bear Hamlet like a soldier to the stage;
  For he was likely, had he been put on,
  To have prov'd most royal; and for his passage*   395
  The soldier's music and the rite of war
  Speak loudly for him.
  Take up the bodies. Such a sight as this
  Becomes the field, but here shows much amiss.
  Go, bid the soldiers shoot.   400

   [*Exeunt marching. A peal of ordnance shot off.*]

---

[385] **rights of memory** past claims
[388] **voice will draw on more** vote will influence others
[391] **On** on top of earlier
[395] **passage** death

MOLIÈRE (JEAN-BAPTISTE POQUELIN, 1622–1673)

Tartuffe
(1664, 1667, 1669)

hile English drama of Shakespeare's time owed much to medieval conventions, French dramatists after the 1630s looked back to Greece and Rome for their standards. This conscious imitation of the classics gave rise to a set of literary standards summed up in the term *neoclassicism*. These included the unities of time, place, and action; strict distinction between tragedy and comedy, with no intermingling of the two; the use of universalized character types; and the demand that drama teach moral lessons. Many of the plays written in compliance with these demands now seem lifeless, but the tragedies of Racine and the comedies of Molière, written in France during the last half of the seventeenth century, reached a peak of artistry in the neoclassical mode. Unlike plays of earlier eras, these were written for the proscenium arch stage and for perspective settings composed of wings, drops, and borders.

Molière is one of the most skillful and inventive comic dramatists of all time, and *Tartuffe* is one of his most admired plays. Within the restricted frame of one room, one day, and one main story, using a limited number of characters and little physical action, Molière creates an excellent comedy of character. The action of *Tartuffe*, divided into five acts, develops through five stages: the demonstration of Tartuffe's complete hold over Orgon; the unmasking of Tartuffe; Tartuffe's attempted revenge; the foiling of Tartuffe's plan; and the happy resolution. Molière has been criticized for delaying Tartuffe's first appearance until the third act, but he makes skillful use of this delay by having all the other characters establish his hypocrisy and Orgon's gullibility in trusting Tartuffe. The resolution, in which Tartuffe is suddenly discovered to be a notorious criminal, has also been criticized as overly contrived, but it is emotionally satisfying because it punishes Tartuffe and reestablishes the norm.

In *Tartuffe* Molière uses the verse form that by that time had become standard in French tragedy—the alexandrine (twelve-syllable lines, with each pair of adjacent lines rhyming). Richard Wilbur's translation, used here, is generally considered one of the finest now available both for its accuracy and for its rendition of Molière's verse.

When *Tartuffe* was written in 1664, it was immediately denounced as an attack on religious piety. The controversy was so intense that Louis XIV forbade the play's production. Molière rewrote it in 1667, only to have it banned once more. Finally, in 1669 he was able to gain permission for its production. It has remained in the repertory continuously since that time. It is still performed more often than any other play by Molière.

MOLIÈRE

Tartuffe

TRANSLATED INTO ENGLISH VERSE BY RICHARD WILBUR

Characters

MME. PERNELLE, *Orgon's mother*
ORGON, *Elmire's husband*
ELMIRE, *Orgon's wife*
DAMIS, *Orgon's son, Elmire's stepson*
MARIANE, *Orgon's daughter, Elmire's stepdaughter, in love with Valère*
VALÈRE, *in love with Mariane*
CLÉANTE, *Orgon's brother-in-law*
TARTUFFE, *a hypocrite*
DORINE, *Mariane's lady's-maid*
M. LOYAL, *a bailiff*
A POLICE OFFICER
FLIPOTE, *Mme. Pernelle's maid*

The scene throughout: ORGON'S *house in Paris*

ACT I

SCENE I

MADAME PERNELLE: Come, come, Flipote; it's time I left this place.
ELMIRE: I can't keep up, you walk at such a pace.
MADAME PERNELLE: Don't trouble, child; no need to show me out.
    It's not your manners I'm concerned about.

(*continued from page 165*) amateur, motion picture, recitation, lecturing, public reading, radio broadcasting, and television are strictly reserved. Particular emphasis is laid on the question of readings, permission for which must be secured from the author's agent in writing. Inquiries on professional rights (except for amateur rights) should be addressed to Mr. Gilbert Parker, Curtis Brown, Ltd., 10 Astor Place, New York, NY 10003; inquiries on translation rights should be addressed to Harcourt Brace & Company, Publishers, Orlando, FL 32887. The amateur rights of *Tartuffe* are controlled exclusively by the Dramatists Play Service, Inc., 440 Park Avenue South, New York, New York. No amateur performance of the play may be given without obtaining in advance the written permission of the Dramatists Play Service, Inc., and paying the requisite fee.

ELMIRE: We merely pay you the respect we owe. 5
    But, Mother, why this hurry? Must you go?
MADAME PERNELLE: I must. This house appals me. No one in it
    Will pay attention for a single minute.
    Children, I take my leave much vexed in spirit.
    I offer good advice, but you won't hear it. 10
    You all break in and chatter on and on.
    It's like a madhouse with the keeper gone.
DORINE: If . . .
MADAME PERNELLE: Girl, you talk too much, and I'm afraid
    You're far too saucy for a lady's-maid. 15
    You push in everywhere and have your say.
DAMIS: But . . .
MADAME PERNELLE: You, boy, grow more foolish every day.
    To think my grandson should be such a dunce!
    I've said a hundred times, if I've said it once, 20
    That if you keep the course on which you've started,
    You'll leave your worthy father broken-hearted.
MARIANE: I think . . .
MADAME PERNELLE: And you, his sister, seem so pure,
    So shy, so innocent, and so demure. 25
    But you know what they say about still waters.
    I pity parents with secretive daughters.
ELMIRE: Now, Mother . . .
MADAME PERNELLE: And as for you, child, let me add
    That your behavior is extremely bad, 30
    And a poor example for these children, too.
    Their dear, dead mother did far better than you.
    You're much too free with money, and I'm distressed
    To see you so elaborately dressed.
    When it's one's husband that one aims to please, 35
    One has no need of costly fripperies.
CLÉANTE: Oh, Madam, really . . .
MADAME PERNELLE: You are her brother, Sir,
    And I respect and love you; yet if I were
    My son, this lady's good and pious spouse, 40
    I wouldn't make you welcome in my house.
    You're full of worldly counsels which, I fear,
    Aren't suitable for decent folk to hear.
    I've spoken bluntly, Sir; but it behooves us
    Not to mince words when righteous fervor moves us. 45
DAMIS: Your man Tartuffe is full of holy speeches . . .
MADAME PERNELLE: And practices precisely what he preaches.
    He's a fine man, and should be listened to.
    I will not hear him mocked by fools like you.
DAMIS: Good God! Do you expect me to submit 50
    To the tyranny of that carping hypocrite?
    Must we forgo all joys and satisfactions
    Because that bigot censures all our actions?
DORINE: To hear him talk—and he talks all the time—
    There's nothing one can do that's not a crime. 55
    He rails at everything, your dear Tartuffe.

MADAME PERNELLE: Whatever he reproves deserves reproof.
    He's out to save your souls, and all of you
    Must love him, as my son would have you do.
DAMIS: Ah no, Grandmother, I could never take   60
    To such a rascal, even for my father's sake.
    That's how I feel, and I shall not dissemble.
    His every action makes me seethe and tremble
    With helpless anger, and I have no doubt
    That he and I will shortly have it out.   65
DORINE: Surely it is a shame and a disgrace
    To see this man usurp the master's place—
    To see this beggar who, when first he came,
    Had not a shoe or shoestring to his name
    So far forget himself that he behaves   70
    As if the house were his, and we his slaves.
MADAME PERNELLE: Well, mark my words, your souls would fare far better
    If you obeyed his precepts to the letter.
DORINE: You see him as a saint. I'm far less awed;
    In fact, I see right through him. He's a fraud.   75
MADAME PERNELLE: Nonsense!
DORINE: His man Laurent's the same, or worse;
    I'd not trust either with a penny purse.
MADAME PERNELLE: I can't say what his servant's morals may be;
    His own great goodness I can guarantee.   80
    You all regard him with distaste and fear
    Because he tells you what you're loath to hear,
    Condemns your sins, points out your moral flaws,
    And humbly strives to further Heaven's cause.
DORINE: If sin is all that bothers him, why is it   85
    He's so upset when folk drop in to visit?
    Is Heaven so outraged by a social call
    That he must prophesy against us all?
    I'll tell you what I think: if you ask me,
    He's jealous of my mistress' company.   90
MADAME PERNELLE: Rubbish! [*to* ELMIRE] He's not alone, child, in complaining
    Of all of your promiscuous entertaining.
    Why, the whole neighborhood's upset, I know,
    By all these carriages that come and go,
    With crowds of guests parading in and out   95
    And noisy servants loitering about.
    In all of this, I'm sure there's nothing vicious;
    But why give people cause to be suspicious?
CLÉANTE: They need no cause, they'll talk in any case.
    Madam, this world would be a joyless place   100
    If, fearing what malicious tongues might say,
    We locked our doors and turned our friends away.
    And even if one did so dreary a thing,
    D'you think those tongues would cease their chattering?
    One can't fight slander; it's a losing battle;   105
    Let us instead ignore their tittle-tattle.

Let's strive to live by conscience's clear decrees,
And let the gossips gossip as they please.
DORINE: If there is talk against us, I know the source:
    It's Daphne and her little husband, of course. 110
    Those who have greatest cause for guilt and shame
    Are quickest to besmirch a neighbor's name.
    When there's a chance for libel, they never miss it;
    When something can be made to seem illicit
    They're off at once to spread the joyous news, 115
    Adding to fact what fantasies they choose.
    By talking up their neighbor's indiscretions
    They seek to camouflage their own transgressions,
    Hoping that others' innocent affairs
    Will lend a hue of innocence to theirs, 120
    Or that their own black guilt will come to seem
    Part of a general shady color-scheme.
MADAME PERNELLE: All that is quite irrelevant. I doubt
    That anyone's more virtuous and devout
    Than dear Orante; and I'm informed that she 125
    Condemns your mode of life most vehemently.
DORINE: Oh, yes, she's strict, devout, and has no taint
    Of worldliness; in short, she seems a saint.
    But it was time which taught her that disguise;
    She's thus because she can't be otherwise. 130
    So long as her attractions could enthrall,
    She flounced and flirted and enjoyed it all,
    But now that they're no longer what they were
    She quits a world which fast is quitting her,
    And wears a veil of virtue to conceal 135
    Her bankrupt beauty and her lost appeal.
    That's what becomes of old coquettes today:
    Distressed when all their lovers fall away,
    They see no recourse but to play the prude,
    And so confer a style on solitude. 140
    Thereafter, they're severe with everyone,
    Condemning all our actions, pardoning none,
    And claiming to be pure, austere, and zealous
    When, if the truth were known, they're merely jealous,
    And cannot bear to see another know 145
    The pleasures time has forced them to forgo.
MADAME PERNELLE: [*initially to* ELMIRE] That sort of talk is what you like to hear;
    Therefore you'd have us all keep still, my dear,
    While Madam rattles on the livelong day.
    Nevertheless, I mean to have my say. 150
    I tell you that you're blest to have Tartuffe
    Dwelling, as my son's guest, beneath this roof;
    That Heaven has sent him to forestall its wrath
    By leading you, once more, to the true path;
    That all he reprehends is reprehensible, 155
    And that you'd better heed him, and be sensible.

These visits, balls, and parties in which you revel
Are nothing but inventions of the Devil.
One never hears a word that's edifying:
Nothing but chaff and foolishness and lying,   160
As well as vicious gossip in which one's neighbor
Is cut to bits with épée, foil, and saber.
People of sense are driven half-insane
At such affairs, where noise and folly reign
And reputations perish thick and fast.   165
As a wise preacher said on Sunday last,
Parties are Towers of Babylon, because
The guests all babble on with never a pause;
And then he told a story which, I think . . .
[*to* CLÉANTE] I heard that laugh, Sir, and I saw that wink!   170
Go find your silly friends and laugh some more!
Enough; I'm going; don't show me to the door.
I leave this household much dismayed and vexed;
I cannot say when I shall see you next.
[*slapping* FLIPOTE] Wake up, don't stand there gaping into space! 175
I'll slap some sense into that stupid face.
Move, move, you slut.
[*All except* CLÉANTE *and* DORINE *exit.*]

SCENE II

CLÉANTE: I think I'll stay behind;
    I want no further pieces of her mind.
    How that old lady . . .   180
DORINE: Oh, what wouldn't she say
    If she could hear you speak of her that way!
    She'd thank you for the *lady,* but I'm sure
    She'd find the *old* a little premature.
CLÉANTE: My, what a scene she made, and what a din!   185
    And how this man Tartuffe has taken her in!
DORINE: Yes, but her son is even worse deceived;
    His folly must be seen to be believed.
    In the late troubles, he played an able part
    And served his king with wise and loyal heart,   190
    But he's quite lost his senses since he fell
    Beneath Tartuffe's infatuating spell.
    He calls him brother, and loves him as his life,
    Preferring him to mother, child, or wife.
    In him and him alone will he confide;   195
    He's made him his confessor and his guide;
    He pets and pampers him with love more tender
    Than any pretty mistress could engender,
    Gives him the place of honor when they dine,
    Delights to see him gorging like a swine,   200
    Stuffs him with dainties till his guts distend,
    And when he belches, cries "God bless you, friend!"
    In short, he's mad; he worships him; he dotes;

His deeds he marvels at, his words he quotes;
Thinking each act a miracle, each word   205
Oracular as those that Moses heard.
Tartuffe, much pleased to find so easy a victim,
Has in a hundred ways beguiled and tricked him,
Milked him of money, and with his permission
Established here a sort of Inquisition.   210
Even Laurent, his lackey, dares to give
Us arrogant advice on how to live;
He sermonizes us in thundering tones
And confiscates our ribbons and colognes.
Last week he tore a kerchief into pieces   215
Because he found it pressed in a *Life of Jesus:*
He said it was a sin to juxtapose
Unholy vanities and holy prose.

SCENE III

ELMIRE: [*to* CLÉANTE] You did well not to follow; she stood in the door
    And said *verbatim* all she'd said before.   220
    I saw my husband coming. I think I'd best
    Go upstairs now, and take a little rest.
CLÉANTE: I'll wait and greet him here; then I must go.
    I've really only time to say hello.
DAMIS: Sound him about my sister's wedding, please.   225
    I think Tartuffe's against it, and that he's
    Been urging Father to withdraw his blessing.
    As you well know, I'd find that most distressing.
    Unless my sister and Valère can marry,
    My hopes to wed *his* sister will miscarry,   230
    And I'm determined . . .
DORINE: He's coming.

SCENE IV

ORGON: Ah, Brother, good-day.
CLÉANTE: Well, welcome back. I'm sorry I can't stay.
    How was the country? Blooming, I trust, and green?   235
ORGON: Excuse me, Brother; just one moment.
    [*to* DORINE] Dorine . . .
    [*to* CLÉANTE] To put my mind at rest, I always learn
    The household news the moment I return.
    [*to* DORINE] Has all been well, these two days I've been gone? 240
    How are the family? What's been going on?
DORINE: Your wife, two days ago, had a bad fever,
    And a fierce headache which refused to leave her.
ORGON: Ah. And Tartuffe?
DORINE: Tartuffe? Why, he's round and red,   245
    Bursting with health, and excellently fed.
ORGON: Poor fellow!

DORINE: That night, the mistress was unable
    To take a single bite at the dinner-table.
    Her headache-pains, she said, were simply hellish.   250
ORGON: Ah. And Tartuffe?
DORINE: He ate his meal with relish,
    And zealously devoured in her presence
    A leg of mutton and a brace of pheasants.
ORGON: Poor fellow!   255
DORINE: Well, the pains continued strong,
    And so she tossed and tossed the whole night long,
    Now icy-cold, now burning like a flame.
    We sat beside her bed till morning came.
ORGON: Ah. And Tartuffe?   260
DORINE: Why, having eaten, he rose
    And sought his room, already in a doze,
    Got into his warm bed, and snored away
    In perfect peace until the break of day.
ORGON: Poor fellow!   265
DORINE: After much ado, we talked her
    Into dispatching someone for the doctor.
    He bled her, and the fever quickly fell.
ORGON: Ah. And Tartuffe?
DORINE: He bore it very well.   270
    To keep his cheerfulness at any cost,
    And make up for the blood *Madame* had lost,
    He drank, at lunch, four beakers full of port.
ORGON: Poor fellow!
DORINE: Both are doing well, in short.   275
    I'll go and tell *Madame* that you've expressed
    Keen sympathy and anxious interest.

SCENE V

CLÉANTE: That girl was laughing in your face, and though
    I've no wish to offend you, even so
    I'm bound to say that she had some excuse.   280
    How can you possibly be such a goose?
    Are you so dazed by this man's hocus-pocus
    That all the world, save him, is out of focus?
    You've given him clothing, shelter, food, and care;
    Why must you also . . .   285
ORGON: Brother, stop right there.
    You do not know the man of whom you speak.
CLÉANTE: I grant you that. But my judgment's not so weak
    That I can't tell, by his effect on others . . .
ORGON: Ah, when you meet him, you two will be like brothers!   290
    There's been no loftier soul since time began.
    He is a man who . . . a man who . . . an excellent man.
    To keep his precepts is to be reborn,
    And view this dunghill of a world with scorn.

Yes, thanks to him I'm a changed man indeed. 295
Under his tutelage my soul's been freed
From earthly loves, and every human tie:
My mother, children, brother, and wife could die,
And I'd not feel a single moment's pain.
CLÉANTE: That's a fine sentiment, Brother; most humane. 300
ORGON: Oh, had you seen Tartuffe as I first knew him,
Your heart, like mine, would have surrendered to him.
He used to come into our church each day
And humbly kneel nearby, and start to pray.
He'd draw the eyes of everybody there 305
By the deep fervor of his heartfelt prayer;
He'd sigh and weep, and sometimes with a sound
Of rapture he would bend and kiss the ground;
And when I rose to go, he'd run before
To offer me holy-water at the door. 310
His serving-man, no less devout than he,
Informed me of his master's poverty;
I gave him gifts, but in his humbleness
He'd beg me every time to give him less.
"Oh, that's too much," he'd cry, "too much by twice! 315
I don't deserve it. The half, Sir, would suffice."
And when I wouldn't take it back, he'd share
Half of it with the poor, right then and there.
At length, Heaven prompted me to take him in
To dwell with us, and free our souls from sin. 320
He guides our lives, and to protect my honor
Stays by my wife, and keeps an eye upon her;
He tells me whom she sees, and all she does,
And seems more jealous than I ever was!
And how austere he is! Why, he can detect 325
A mortal sin where you would least suspect;
In smallest trifles, he's extremely strict.
Last week, his conscience was severely pricked
Because, while praying, he had caught a flea
And killed it, so he felt, too wrathfully. 330
CLÉANTE: Good God, man! Have you lost your common sense—
Or is this all some joke at my expense?
How can you stand there and in all sobriety . . .
ORGON: Brother, your language savors of impiety.
Too much free-thinking's made your faith unsteady, 335
And as I've warned you many times already,
'Twill get you into trouble before you're through.
CLÉANTE: So I've been told before by dupes like you:
Being blind, you'd have all others blind as well;
The clear-eyed man you call an infidel, 340
And he who sees through humbug and pretense
Is charged, by you, with want of reverence.
Spare me your warnings, Brother; I have no fear
Of speaking out, for you and Heaven to hear,

Against affected zeal and pious knavery.   345
There's true and false in piety, as in bravery,
And just as those whose courage shines the most
In battle, are the least inclined to boast,
So those whose hearts are truly pure and lowly
Don't make a flashy show of being holy.   350
There's a vast difference, so it seems to me,x
Between true piety and hypocrisy:
How do you fail to see it, may I ask?
Is not a face quite different from a mask?
Cannot sincerity and cunning art,   355
Reality and semblance, be told apart?
Are scarecrows just like men, and do you hold
That a false coin is just as good as gold?
Ah, Brother, man's a strangely fashioned creature
Who seldom is content to follow Nature,   360
But recklessly pursues his inclination
Beyond the narrow bounds of moderation,
And often, by transgressing Reason's laws,
Perverts a lofty aim or noble cause.
A passing observation, but it applies.   365
ORGON: I see, dear Brother, that you're profoundly wise;
You harbor all the insight of the age.
You are our one clear mind, our only sage,
The era's oracle, its Cato, too,
And all mankind are fools compared to you.   370
CLÉANTE: Brother, I don't pretend to be a sage,
Nor have I all the wisdom of the age.
There's just one insight I would dare to claim:
I know that true and false are not the same;
And just as there is nothing I more revere   375
Than a soul whose faith is steadfast and sincere,
Nothing that I more cherish and admire
Than honest zeal and true religious fire,
So there is nothing that I find more base
Than specious piety's dishonest face   380
Than these bold mountebanks, these histrios
Whose impious mummeries and hollow shows
Exploit our love of Heaven, and make a jest
Of all that men think holiest and best;
These calculating souls who offer prayers   385
Not to their Maker, but as public wares,
And seek to buy respect and reputation
With lifted eyes and sighs of exaltation;
These charlatans, I say, whose pilgrim souls
Proceed, by way of Heaven, toward earthly goals,   390
Who weep and pray and swindle and extort,
Who preach the monkish life, but haunt the court,
Who make their zeal the partner of their vice—
Such men are vengeful, sly, and cold as ice,

And when there is an enemy to defame 395
They cloak their spite in fair religion's name,
Their private spleen and malice being made
To seem a high and virtuous crusade,
Until, to mankind's reverent applause,
They crucify their foe in Heaven's cause. 400
Such knaves are all too common; yet, for the wise,
True piety isn't hard to recognize,
And happily, these present times provide us
With bright examples to instruct and guide us.
Consider Ariston and Périandre; 405
Look at Oronte, Alcidamas, Clitandre;
Their virtue is acknowledged; who could doubt it?
But you won't hear them beat the drum about it.
They're never ostentatious, never vain,
And their religion's moderate and humane; 410
It's not their way to criticize and chide:
They think censoriousness a mark of pride,
And therefore, letting others preach and rave,
They show, by deeds, how Christians should behave.
They think no evil of their fellow man, 415
But judge of him kindly as they can.
They don't intrigue and wangle and conspire;
To lead a good life is their one desire;
The sinner wakes no rancorous hate in them;
It is the sin alone which they condemn; 420
Nor do they try to show a fiercer zeal
For Heaven's cause than Heaven itself could feel.
These men I honor, these men I advocate
As models for us all to emulate.
Your man is not their sort at all, I fear: 425
And, while your praise of him is quite sincere,
I think that you've been dreadfully deluded.
ORGON: Now then, dear Brother, is your speech concluded?
CLÉANTE: Why, yes.
ORGON: Your servant, Sir. [*He turns to go.*] 430
CLÉANTE: No, Brother; wait.
There's one more matter. You agreed of late
That young Valère might have your daughter's hand.
ORGON: I did.
CLÉANTE: And set the date, I understand. 435
ORGON: Quite so.
CLÉANTE: You've now postponed it; is that true?
ORGON: No doubt.
CLÉANTE: The match no longer pleases you?
ORGON: Who knows? 440
CLÉANTE: D'you mean to go back on your word?
ORGON: I won't say that.
CLÉANTE: Has anything occurred
Which might entitle you to break your pledge?

ORGON: Perhaps.   445
CLÉANTE: Why must you hem and haw, and hedge?
    The boy asked me to sound you in this affair . . .
ORGON: It's been a pleasure.
CLÉANTE: But what shall I tell Valère?
ORGON: Whatever you like.   450
CLÉANTE: But what have you decided?
    What are your plans?
ORGON: I plan, Sir, to be guided
    By Heaven's will.
CLÉANTE: Come, Brother, don't talk rot.   455
    You've given Valère your word; will you keep it, or not?
ORGON: Good day.
CLÉANTE: This looks like poor Valère's undoing;
    I'll go and warn him that there's trouble brewing.

ACT II

SCENE I

ORGON: Mariane.
MARIANE: Yes, Father?
ORGON: A word with you; come here.
MARIANE: What are you looking for?
ORGON: [*peering into a small closet*] Eavesdroppers, dear.   5
    I'm making sure we shan't be overheard.
    Someone in there could catch our every word.
    Ah, good, we're safe. Now, Mariane, my child,
    You're a sweet girl who's tractable and mild,
    Whom I hold dear, and think most highly of.   10
MARIANE: I'm deeply grateful, Father, for your love.
ORGON: That's well said, Daughter; and you can repay me
    If, in all things, you'll cheerfully obey me.
MARIANE: To please you, Sir, is what delights me best.
ORGON: Good, good. Now, what d'you think of Tartuffe, our guest?   15
MARIANE: I, Sir?
ORGON: Yes. Weigh your answer; think it through.
MARIANE: Oh, dear. I'll say whatever you wish me to.
ORGON: That's wisely said, my Daughter. Say of him, then,
    That he's the very worthiest of men,
    And that you're fond of him, and would rejoice   20
    In being his wife, if that should be my choice.
    Well?
MARIANE: What?
ORGON: What's that?   25
MARIANE: I . . .
ORGON: Well?

MARIANE: Forgive me, pray.
ORGON: Did you not hear me?
MARIANE: Of *whom,* Sir, must I say   30
    That I am fond of him, and would rejoice
    In being his wife, if that should be your choice?
ORGON: Why, of Tartuffe.
MARIANE: But, Father, that's false, you know.
    Why would you have me say what isn't so?   35
ORGON: Because I am resolved it shall be true.
    That it's my wish should be enough for you.
MARIANE: You can't mean, Father . . .
ORGON: Yes, Tartuffe shall be
    Allied by marriage to this family,   40
    And he's to be your husband, is that clear?
    It's a father's privilege . . .

SCENE II

ORGON: [*to* DORINE] What are you doing in here?
    Is curiosity so fierce a passion
    With you, that you must eavesdrop in this fashion?   45
DORINE: There's lately been a rumor going about—
    Based on some hunch or chance remark, no doubt—
    That you mean Mariane to wed Tartuffe.
    I've laughed it off, of course, as just a spoof.
ORGON: You find it so incredible?   50
DORINE: Yes, I do.
    I won't accept that story, even from you.
ORGON: Well, you'll believe it when the thing is done.
DORINE: Yes, yes, of course. Go on and have your fun.
ORGON: I've never been more serious in my life.   55
DORINE: Ha!
ORGON: Daughter, I mean it; you're to be his wife.
DORINE: No, don't believe your father; it's all a hoax.
ORGON: See here, young woman . . .
DORINE: Come, Sir, no more jokes;   60
    You can't fool us.
ORGON: How dare you talk that way?
DORINE: All right, then: we believe you, sad to say.
    But how a man like you, who looks so wise
    And wears a moustache of such splendid size,   65
    Can be so foolish as to . . .
ORGON: Silence, please!
    My girl, you take too many liberties.
    I'm master here, as you must not forget.
DORINE: Do let's discuss this calmly; don't be upset.   70
    You can't be serious, Sir, about this plan.
    What should that bigot want with Mariane?
    Praying and fasting ought to keep him busy.
    And then, in terms of wealth and rank, what is he?

Why should a man of property like you   75
Pick out a beggar son-in-law?
ORGON: That will do.
  Speak of his poverty with reverence.
  His is pure and saintly indigence
  Which far transcends all worldly pride and pelf.   80
  He lost his fortune, as he says himself,
  Because he cared for Heaven alone, and so
  Was careless of his interests here below.
  I mean to get him out of his present straits
  And help him to recover his estates—   85
  Which, in his part of the world, have no small fame.
  Poor though he is, he's a gentleman just the same.
DORINE: Yes, so he tells us; and, Sir, it seems to me
  Such pride goes very ill with piety.
  A man whose spirit spurns this dungy earth   90
  Ought not to brag of lands and noble birth;
  Such worldly arrogance will hardly square
  With meek devotion and the life of prayer.
  . . . But this approach, I see, has drawn a blank;
  Let's speak, then, of his person, not his rank.   95
  Doesn't it seem to you a trifle grim
  To give a girl like her to a man like him?
  When two are so ill-suited, can't you see
  What the sad consequence is bound to be?
  A young girl's virtue is imperilled, Sir,   100
  When such a marriage is imposed on her;
  For if one's bridegroom isn't to one's taste,
  It's hardly an inducement to be chaste,
  And many a man with horns upon his brow
  Has made his wife the thing that she is now.   105
  It's hard to be a faithful wife, in short,
  To certain husbands of a certain sort,
  And he who gives his daughter to a man she hates
  Must answer for her sins at Heaven's gates.
  Think, Sir, before you play so risky a role.   110
ORGON: This servant-girl presumes to save my soul!
DORINE: You would do well to ponder what I've said.
ORGON: Daughter, we'll disregard this dunderhead.
  Just trust your father's judgment. Oh, I'm aware
  That I once promised you to young Valère;   115
  But now I hear he gambles, which greatly shocks me;
  What's more, I've doubts about his orthodoxy.
  His visits to church, I note, are very few.
DORINE: Would you have him go at the same hours as you,
  And kneel nearby, to be sure of being seen?   120
ORGON: I can dispense with such remarks, Dorine.

    [*to* MARIANE]

  Tartuffe, however, is sure of Heaven's blessing,

And that's the only treasure worth possessing.
This match will bring you joys beyond all measure;
Your cup will overflow with every pleasure;   125
You two will interchange your faithful loves
Like two sweet cherubs, or two turtle-doves.
No harsh word shall be heard, no frown be seen,
And he shall make you happy as a queen.
DORINE: And she'll make him a cuckold, just wait and see.   130
ORGON: What language!
DORINE: Oh, he's a man of destiny;
    He's *made* for horns, and what the stars demand
    Your daughter's virtue surely can't withstand.
ORGON: Don't interrupt me further. Why can't you learn   135
    That certain things are none of your concern?
DORINE: It's for your own sake that I interfere.

      [*She repeatedly interrupts* ORGON *just as he is turning to speak to his daughter.*]

ORGON: Most kind of you. Now, hold your tongue, d'you hear?
DORINE: If I didn't love you . . .
ORGON: Spare me your affection.   140
DORINE: I'll love you, Sir, in spite of your objection.
ORGON: Blast!
DORINE: I can't bear, Sir, for your honor's sake,
    To let you make this ludicrous mistake.
ORGON: You mean to go on talking?   145
DORINE: If I didn't protest
    This sinful marriage, my conscience couldn't rest.
ORGON: If you don't hold your tongue, you little shrew . . .
DORINE: What, lost your temper? A pious man like you?
ORGON: Yes! Yes! You talk and talk. I'm maddened by it.   150
    Once and for all, I tell you to be quiet.
DORINE: Well, I'll be quiet. But I'll be thinking hard.
ORGON: Think all you like, but you had better guard
    That saucy tongue of yours, or I'll . . . [*turning back to* MARIANE] Now, child,
    I've weighed this matter fully.   155
DORINE: [*aside*] It drives me wild
    That I can't speak.

      [ORGON *turns his head, and she is silent.*]

ORGON: Tartuffe is no young dandy,
    But, still, his person . . .
DORINE: [*aside*] Is as sweet as candy.   160
ORGON: Is such that, even if you shouldn't care
    For his other merits . . .

      [*He turns and stands facing* DORINE, *arms crossed.*]

DORINE: [*aside*] They'll make a lovely pair.
    If I were she, no man would marry me
    Against my inclination, and go scot-free.   165
    He'd learn, before the wedding-day was over,

How readily a wife can find a lover.
ORGON: [*to* DORINE] It seems you treat my orders as a joke.
DORINE: Why, what's the matter? 'Twas not to you I spoke.
ORGON: What *were* you doing? 170
DORINE: Talking to myself, that's all.
ORGON: Ah! [*aside*] One more bit of impudence and gall,
    And I shall give her a good slap in the face.

> [*He puts himself in position to slap her;* DORINE, *whenever he glances at her,*
> *stands immobile and silent.*]

    Daughter, you shall accept, and with good grace,
    The husband I've selected . . . Your wedding-day . . . 175
    [*to* DORINE] Why don't you talk to yourself?
DORINE: I've nothing to say.
ORGON: Come, just one word.
DORINE: No thank you, Sir. I pass.
ORGON: Come, speak; I'm waiting. 180
DORINE: I'd not be such an ass.
ORGON: [*turning to* MARIANE] In short, dear Daughter, I mean to be obeyed,
    And you must bow to the sound choice I've made.
DORINE: [*moving away*] I'd not wed such a monster, even in jest.

> [ORGON *attempts to slap her, but misses.*]

ORGON: Daughter, that maid of yours is a thorough pest; 185
    She makes me sinfully annoyed and nettled.
    I can't speak further; my nerves are too unsettled.
    She's so upset me by her insolent talk,
    I'll calm myself by going for a walk.

SCENE III

DORINE: [*returning*] Well, have you lost your tongue, girl? Must I play 190
    Your part, and say the lines you ought to say?
    Faced with a fate so hideous and absurd,
    Can you not utter one dissenting word?
MARIANE: What good would it do? A father's power is great.
DORINE: Resist him now, or it will be too late. 195
MARIANE: But . . .
DORINE: Tell him one cannot love at a father's whim;
    That you shall marry for yourself, not him;
    That since it's you who are to be the bride,
    It's you, not he, who must be satisfied; 200
    And that if his Tartuffe is so sublime,
    He's free to marry him at any time.
MARIANE: I've bowed so long to Father's strict control,
    I couldn't oppose him now, to save my soul.
DORINE: Come, come, Mariane. Do listen to reason, won't you? 205
    Valère has asked your hand. Do you love him, or don't you?
MARIANE: Oh, how unjust of you! What can you mean
    By asking such a question, dear Dorine?

You know the depth of my affection for him;
I've told you a hundred times how I adore him. 210
DORINE: I don't believe in everything I hear;
Who knows if your professions were sincere?
MARIANE: They were, Dorine, and you do me wrong to doubt it;
Heaven knows that I've been all too frank about it.
DORINE: You love him, then? 215
MARIANE: Oh, more than I can express.
DORINE: And he, I take it, cares for you no less?
MARIANE: I think so.
DORINE: And you both, with equal fire,
Burn to be married? 220
MARIANE: That is our one desire.
DORINE: What of Tartuffe, then? What of your father's plan?
MARIANE: I'll kill myself, if I'm forced to wed that man.
DORINE: I hadn't thought of that recourse. How splendid!
Just die, and all your troubles will be ended! 225
A fine solution. Oh, it maddens me
To hear you talk in that self-pitying key.
MARIANE: Dorine, how harsh you are! It's most unfair.
You have no sympathy for my despair.
DORINE: I've none at all for people who talk drivel 230
And, faced with difficulties, whine and snivel.
MARIANE: No doubt I'm timid, but it would be wrong . . .
DORINE: True love requires a heart that's firm and strong.
MARIANE: I'm strong in my affection for Valère,
But coping with my father is his affair. 235
DORINE: But if your father's brain has grown so cracked
Over his dear Tartuffe that he can retract
His blessing, though your wedding-day was named,
It's surely not Valère who's to be blamed.
MARIANE: If I defied my father, as you suggest, 240
Would it not seem unmaidenly, at best?
Shall I defend my love at the expense
Of brazenness and disobedience?
Shall I parade my heart's desires, and flaunt . . .
DORINE: No, I ask nothing of you. Clearly you want 245
To be Madame Tartuffe, and I feel bound
Not to oppose a wish so very sound.
What right have I to criticize the match?
Indeed, my dear, the man's a brilliant catch.
Monsieur Tartuffe! Now, there's a man of weight! 250
Yes, yes, Monsieur Tartuffe, I'm bound to state,
Is quite a person; that's not to be denied;
'Twill be no little thing to be his bride.
The world already rings with his renown;
He's a great noble—in his native town; 255
His ears are red, he has a pink complexion,
And all in all, he'll suit you to perfection.
MARIANE: Dear God!

DORINE: Oh, how triumphant you will feel
    At having caught a husband so ideal! 260

MARIANE: Oh, do stop teasing, and use your cleverness
    To get me out of this appalling mess.
    Advise me, and I'll do whatever you say.

DORINE: Ah no, a dutiful daughter must obey
    Her father, even if he weds her to an ape. 265
    You've a bright future; why struggle to escape?
    Tartuffe will take you back where his family lives,
    To a small town aswarm with relatives—
    Uncles and cousins whom you'll be charmed to meet.
    You'll be received at once by the elite, 270
    Calling upon the bailiff's wife, no less—
    Even, perhaps, upon the mayoress,
    Who'll sit you down in the *best* kitchen chair.
    Then, once a year, you'll dance at the village fair
    To the drone of bagpipes—two of them, in fact— 275
    And see a puppet-show, or an animal act.
    Your husband . . .

MARIANE: Oh, you turn my blood to ice!
    Stop torturing me, and give me your advice.

DORINE: [*threatening to go*] Your servant, Madam. 280

MARIANE: Dorine, I beg of you . . .

DORINE: No, you deserve it; this marriage must go through.

MARIANE: Dorine!

DORINE: No.

MARIANE: Not Tartuffe! You know I think him . . . 285

DORINE: Tartuffe's your cup of tea, and you shall drink him.

MARIANE: I've always told you everything, and relied . . .

DORINE: No. You deserve to be tartuffified.

MARIANE: Well, since you mock me and refuse to care,
    I'll henceforth seek my solace in despair: 290
    Despair shall be my counsellor and friend,
    And help me bring my sorrows to an end.

       [*She starts to leave.*]

DORINE: There now, come back; my anger has subsided.
    You do deserve some pity, I've decided.

MARIANE: Dorine, if Father makes me undergo 295
    This dreadful martyrdom, I'll die, I know.

DORINE: Don't fret; it won't be difficult to discover
    Some plan of action . . . But here's Valère, your lover.

SCENE IV

VALÈRE: Madam, I've just received some wondrous news
    Regarding which I'd like to hear your views. 300

MARIANE: What news?

VALÈRE: You're marrying Tartuffe.

MARIANE: I find

That Father does have such a match in mind.
VALÈRE: Your father, Madam . . .   305
MARIANE: . . . has just this minute said
     That it's Tartuffe he wishes me to wed.
VALÈRE: Can he be serious?
MARIANE: Oh, indeed he can;
     He's clearly set his heart upon the plan.   310
VALÈRE: And what position do you propose to take,
     Madam?
MARIANE: Why—I don't know.
VALÈRE: For heaven's sake—
     You don't know?   315
MARIANE: No.
VALÈRE: Well, well!
MARIANE: Advise me, do.
VALÈRE: Marry the man. That's my advice to you.
MARIANE: That's your advice?   320
VALÈRE: Yes.
MARIANE: Truly?
VALÈRE: Oh, absolutely.
     You couldn't choose more wisely, more astutely.
MARIANE: Thanks for this counsel; I'll follow it, of course.   325
VALÈRE: Do, do; I'm sure 'twill cost you no remorse.
MARIANE: To give it didn't cause your heart to break.
VALÈRE: I gave it, Madam, only for your sake.
MARIANE: And it's for your sake that I take it, Sir.
DORINE: [*withdrawing to the rear of the stage*]   330
     Let's see which fool will prove the stubborner.
VALÈRE: So! I am nothing to you, and it was flat
     Deception when you . . .
MARIANE: Please, enough of that.
     You've told me plainly that I should agree   335
     To wed the man my father's chosen for me,
     And since you've deigned to counsel me so wisely,
     I promise, Sir, to do as you advise me.
VALÈRE: Ah, no 'twas not by me that you were swayed.
     No, your decision was already made;   340
     Though now, to save appearances, you protest
     That you're betraying me at my behest.
MARIANE: Just as you say.
VALÈRE: Quite so. And I now see
     That you were never truly in love with me.   345
MARIANE: Alas, you're free to think so if you choose.
VALÈRE: I choose to think so, and here's a bit of news:
     You've spurned my hand, but I know where to turn
     For kinder treatment, as you shall quickly learn.
MARIANE: I'm sure you do. Your noble qualities   350
     Inspire affection . . .
VALÈRE: Forget my qualities, please.
     They don't inspire you overmuch, I find.

But there's another lady I have in mind
Whose sweet and generous nature will not scorn   355
To compensate me for the loss I've borne.
MARIANE: I'm no great loss, and I'm sure that you'll transfer
    Your heart quite painlessly from me to her.
VALÈRE: I'll do my best to take it in my stride.
    The pain I feel at being cast aside   360
    Time and forgetfulness may put an end to.
    Or if I can't forget, I shall pretend to.
    No self-respecting person is expected
    To go on loving once he's been rejected.
MARIANE: Now, that's fine, high-minded sentiment.   365
VALÈRE: One to which any sane man would assent.
    Would you prefer it if I pined away
    In hopeless passion till my dying day?
    Am I to yield you to a rival's arms
    And not console myself with other charms?   370
MARIANE: Go then: console yourself; don't hesitate.
    I wish you to; indeed, I cannot wait.
VALÈRE: You wish me to?
MARIANE: Yes.
VALÈRE: That's the final straw.   375
    Madam, farewell. Your wish shall be my law.

[*He starts to leave, and then returns: this repeatedly.*]

MARIANE: Splendid.
VALÈRE: [*coming back again*] This breach, remember, is of your making;
    It's you who've driven me to the step I'm taking.
MARIANE: Of course.   380
VALÈRE: [*coming back again*] Remember, too, that I am merely
    Following your example.
MARIANE: I see that clearly.
VALÈRE: Enough. I'll go and do your bidding, then.
MARIANE: Good.   385
VALÈRE: [*coming back again*] You shall never see my face again.
MARIANE: Excellent.
VALÈRE: [*walking to the door, then turning about*] Yes?
MARIANE: What?
VALÈRE: What's that? What did you say?   390
MARIANE: Nothing. You're dreaming.
VALÈRE: Ah. Well, I'm on my way.
    Farewell, *Madame.*

[*He moves slowly away.*]

MARIANE: Farewell.
DORINE: [*to* MARIANE] If you ask me,   395
    Both of you are as mad as mad can be.
    Do stop this nonsense, now. I've only let you
    Squabble so long to see where it would get you.
    Whoa there, Monsieur Valère!

[*She goes and seizes* VALÈRE *by the arm; he makes a great show of resistance.*]

VALÈRE: What's this, Dorine?   400
DORINE: Come here.
VALÈRE: No, no, my heart's too full of spleen.
    Don't hold me back; her wish must be obeyed.
DORINE: Stop!
VALÈRE: It's too late now; my decision's made.   405
DORINE: Oh, pooh!
MARIANE: [*aside*] He hates the sight of me, that's plain.
    I'll go, and so deliver him from pain.
DORINE: [*leaving* VALÈRE, *running after* MARIANE] And now *you* run away!
    Come back.   410
MARIANE: No, no.
    Nothing you say will keep me here. Let go!
VALÈRE: [*aside*] She cannot bear my presence, I perceive.
    To spare her further torment, I shall leave.
DORINE: [*leaving* MARIANE, *running after* VALÈRE] Again! You'll not escape, Sir; don't you   415
    try it.
    Come here, you two. Stop fussing, and be quiet.

[*She takes* VALÈRE *by the hand, then* MARIANE, *and draws them together.*]

VALÈRE: [*to* DORINE] What do you want of me?
MARIANE: [*to* DORINE] What is the point of this?
DORINE: We're going to have a little armistice.   420
    [*to* VALÈRE] Now, weren't you silly to get so overheated?
VALÈRE: Didn't you see how badly I was treated?
DORINE: [*to* MARIANE] Aren't you a simpleton, to have lost your head?
MARIANE: Didn't you hear the hateful things he said?
DORINE: [*to* VALÈRE] You're both great fools. Her sole desire, Valère,   425
    Is to be yours in marriage. To that I'll swear.
    [*to* MARIANE] He loves you only, and he wants no wife
    But you, Mariane. On that I'll stake my life.
MARIANE: [*to* VALÈRE] Then why you advised me so, I cannot see.
VALÈRE: [*to* MARIANE] On such a question, why ask advice of *me*?   430
DORINE: Oh, you're impossible. Give me your hands, you two.

    [*to* VALÈRE] Yours first.

VALÈRE: [*giving* DORINE *his hand*] But why?
DORINE: [*to* MARIANE] And now a hand from you.
MARIANE: [*also giving* DORINE *her hand*] What are you doing?
DORINE: There: a perfect fit.   435
    You suit each other better than you'll admit.

[VALÈRE *and* MARIANE *hold hands for some time without looking at each other.*]

VALÈRE: [*turning toward* MARIANE] Ah, come, don't be so haughty. Give a man
    A look of kindness, won't you, Mariane?

[MARIANE *turns toward* VALÈRE *and smiles.*]

DORINE: I'll tell you, lovers are completely mad!

VALÈRE: [*to* MARIANE] Now come, confess that you were very bad   440
    To hurt my feelings as you did just now.
    I have a just complaint, you must allow.
MARIANE: You must allow that you were most unpleasant . . .
DORINE: Let's table that discussion for the present;
    Your father has a plan which must be stopped.   445
MARIANE: Advise us, then; what means must we adopt?
DORINE: We'll use all manner of means, and all at once.
    [*to* MARIANE] Your father's addled; he's acting like a dunce.
    Therefore you'd better humor the old fossil.
    Pretend to yield to him, be sweet and docile,   450
    And then postpone, as often as necessary,
    The day on which you have agreed to marry.
    You'll thus gain time, and time will turn the trick.
    Sometimes, for instance, you'll be taken sick,
    And that will seem good reason for delay;   455
    Or some bad omen will make you change the day—
    You'll dream of muddy water, or you'll pass
    A dead man's hearse, or break a looking-glass
    If all else fails, no man can marry you
    Unless you take his ring and say "I do."   460
    But now, let's separate. If they should find
    Us talking here, our plot might be divined.
    [*to* VALÈRE] Go to your friends, and tell them what's occurred,
    And have them urge her father to keep his word.
    Meanwhile, we'll stir her brother into action,   465
    And get Elmire, as well, to join our faction.
    Good-bye.
VALÈRE: [*to* MARIANE] Though each of us will do his best,
    It's your true heart on which my hopes shall rest.
MARIANE: [*to* VALÈRE] Regardless of what Father may decide,   470
    None but Valère shall claim me as his bride.
VALÈRE: Oh, how those words content me! Come what will . . .
DORINE: Oh, lovers, lovers! Their tongues are never still.
    Be off, now.
VALÈRE: [*turning to go, then turning back*] One last word . . .   475
DORINE: No time to chat:
    You leave by this door; and *you* leave by that.

    [DORINE *pushes them, by the shoulders, toward opposing doors.*]

ACT III

SCENE I

DAMIS: May lightning strike me even as I speak,
    May all men call me cowardly and weak,
    If any fear or scruple holds me back

From settling things, at once, with that great quack!

DORINE: Now, don't give way to violent emotion.   5
    Your father's merely talked about this notion,
    And words and deeds are far from being one.
    Much that is talked about is left undone.

DAMIS: No, I must stop that scoundrel's machinations;
    I'll go and tell him off; I'm out of patience.   10

DORINE: Do calm down and be practical. I had rather
    My mistress dealt with him—and with your father.
    She has some influence with Tartuffe, I've noted.
    He hangs upon her words, seems most devoted,
    And may, indeed, be smitten by her charm.   15
    Pray Heaven it's true! 'Twould do our cause no harm.
    She sent for him, just now, to sound him out
    On this affair you're so incensed about;
    She'll find out where he stands, and tell him, too
    What dreadful strife and trouble will ensue   20
    If he lends countenance to your father's plan.
    I couldn't get in to see him, but his man
    Says that he's almost finished with his prayers.
    Go, now. I'll catch him when he comes downstairs.

DAMIS: I want to hear this conference, and I will.   25

DORINE: No, they must be alone.

DAMIS: Oh, I'll keep still.

DORINE: Not you. I know your temper. You'd start a brawl,
    And shout and stamp your foot and spoil it all.
    Go on.   30

DAMIS: I won't; I have a perfect right . . .

DORINE: Lord, you're a nuisance! He's coming; get out of sight.

    [DAMIS *conceals himself in a closet at the rear of the stage.*]

SCENE II

TARTUFFE: [*observing* DORINE, *and calling to his manservant offstage*] Hang up my hair-
    shirt, put my scourge in place,
    And pray, Laurent, for Heaven's perpetual grace.   35
    I'm going to the prison now, to share
    My last few coins with the poor wretches there.

DORINE: [*aside*] Dear God, what affectation! What a fake!

TARTUFFE: You wished to see me?

DORINE: Yes . . .   40

TARTUFFE: [*taking a handkerchief from his pocket*] For mercy's sake,
    Please take this handkerchief, before you speak.

DORINE: What?

TARTUFFE: Cover that bosom, girl. The flesh is weak,
    And unclean thoughts are difficult to control.   45
    Such sights as that can undermine the soul.

DORINE: Your soul, it seems, has very poor defenses,
    And flesh makes quite an impact on your senses.

It's strange that you're so easily excited;
My own desires are not so soon ignited,   50
And if I saw you naked as a beast,
Not all your hide would tempt me in the least.
TARTUFFE: Girl, speak more modestly; unless you do,
I shall be forced to take my leave of you.
DORINE: Oh, no, it's I who must be on my way;   55
I've just one little message to convey.
Madame is coming down, and begs you, Sir,
To wait and have a word or two with her.
TARTUFFE: Gladly.
DORINE: [*aside*] *That* had a softening effect!   60
I think my guess about him was correct.
TARTUFFE: Will she be long?
DORINE: No: that's her step I hear.
Ah, here she is, and I shall disappear.

SCENE III

TARTUFFE: May heaven, whose infinite goodness we adore,   65
Preserve your body and soul forevermore,
And bless your days, and answer thus the plea
Of one who is its humblest votary.
ELMIRE: I thank you for that pious wish. But please,
Do take a chair and let's be more at ease.   70

     [*They sit down.*]

TARTUFFE: I trust that you are once more well and strong?
ELMIRE: Oh, yes: the fever didn't last for long.
TARTUFFE: My prayers are too unworthy, I am sure,
To have gained from Heaven this most gracious cure;
But lately, Madam, my every supplication   75
Has had for object your recuperation.
ELMIRE: You shouldn't have troubled so. I don't deserve it.
TARTUFFE: Your health is priceless, Madam, and to preserve it
I'd gladly give my own, in all sincerity.
ELMIRE: Sir, you outdo us all in Christian charity.   80
You've been most kind. I count myself your debtor.
TARTUFFE: 'Twas nothing, Madam. I long to serve you better.
ELMIRE: There's a private matter I'm anxious to discuss.
I'm glad there's no one here to hinder us.
TARTUFFE: I, too, am glad; it floods my heart with bliss   85
To find myself alone with you like this.
For just this chance I've prayed with all my power—
But prayed in vain, until this happy hour.
ELMIRE: This won't take long, Sir, and I hope you'll be
Entirely frank and unconstrained with me.   90
TARTUFFE: Indeed, there's nothing I had rather do
Than bare my inmost heart and soul to you.
First, let me say that what remarks I've made

About the constant visits you are paid
Were prompted not by any mean emotion, 95
But rather by a pure and deep devotion,
A fervent zeal . . .
ELMIRE: No need for explanation.
Your sole concern, I'm sure, was my salvation.
TARTUFFE: [*taking* ELMIRE'S *hand and pressing her fingertips*] Quite so; and such great fer- 100
vor do I feel . . .
ELMIRE: Ooh! Please! You're pinching!
TARTUFFE: 'Twas from excess of zeal.
I never meant to cause you pain, I swear.
I'd rather . . . [*He places his hand on* ELMIRE'S *knee.*] 105
ELMIRE: What can your hand be doing there?
TARTUFFE: Feeling your gown; what soft, fine-woven stuff!
ELMIRE: Please, I'm extremely ticklish. That's enough.

[*She draws her chair away;* TARTUFFE *pulls his after her.*]

TARTUFFE: [*fondling the lace collar of her gown*] My, my, what lovely lacework on your
dress! 110
The workmanship's miraculous, no less.
I've not seen anything to equal it.
ELMIRE: Yes, quite. But let's talk business for a bit.
They say my husband means to break his word
And give his daughter to you, Sir. Had you heard? 115
TARTUFFE: He did once mention it. But I confess
I dream of quite a different happiness.
It's elsewhere, Madam, that my eyes discern
The promise of that bliss for which I yearn.
ELMIRE: I see: you care for nothing here below. 120
TARTUFFE: Ah, well—my heart's not made of stone, you know.
ELMIRE: All your desires mount heavenward, I'm sure,
In scorn of all that's earthly and impure.
TARTUFFE: A love of heavenly beauty does not preclude
A proper love for earthly pulchritude; 125
Our senses are quite rightly captivated
By perfect works our Maker has created.
Some glory clings to all that Heaven has made;
In you, all Heaven's marvels are displayed.
On that fair face, such beauties have been lavished, 130
The eyes are dazzled and the heart is ravished;
How could I look on you, O flawless creature,
And not adore the Author of all Nature,
Feeling a love both passionate and pure
For you, this triumph of self-portraiture? 135
At first, I trembled lest that love should be
A subtle snare that Hell had laid for me;
I vowed to flee the sight of you, eschewing
A rapture that might prove my soul's undoing;
But soon, fair being, I became aware 140
That my deep passion could be made to square

With rectitude, and with my bounden duty.
I thereupon surrendered to your beauty.
It is, I know, presumptuous on my part
To bring you this poor offering of my heart,   145
And it is not my merit, Heaven knows,
But your compassion on which my hopes repose.
You are my peace, my solace, my salvation;
On you depends my bliss—or desolation;
I bide your judgment and, as you think best,   150
I shall be either miserable or blest.
ELMIRE: Your declaration is most gallant, Sir,
But don't you think it's out of character?
You'd have done better to restrain your passion
And think before you spoke in such a fashion.   155
It ill becomes a pious man like you . . .
TARTUFFE: I may be pious, but I'm human, too:
With your celestial charms before his eyes,
A man has not the power to be wise.
I know such words sound strangely, coming from me,   160
But I'm no angel, nor was meant to be,
And if you blame my passion, you must needs
Reproach as well the charms on which it feeds.
Your loveliness I had no sooner seen
Than you became my soul's unrivalled queen;   165
Before your seraph glance, divinely sweet,
My heart's defenses crumbled in defeat,
And nothing fasting, prayer, or tears might do
Could stay my spirit from adoring you.
My eyes, my sighs have told you in the past   170
What now my lips make bold to say at last,
And if, in your great goodness, you will deign
To look upon your slave, and ease his pain—
If, in compassion for my soul's distress,
You'll stoop to comfort my unworthiness,   175
I'll raise to you, in thanks for that sweet manna,
An endless hymn, an infinite hosanna.
With me, of course, there need be no anxiety,
No fear of scandal or of notoriety.
These young court gallants, whom all the ladies fancy,   180
Are vain in speech, in action rash and chancy;
When they succeed in love, the world soon knows it;
No favor's granted them but they disclose it
And by the looseness of their tongues profane
The very altar where their hearts have lain.   185
Men of my sort, however, love discreetly,
And one may trust our reticence completely.
My keen concern for my good name insures
The absolute security of yours;
In short, I offer you, my dear Elmire,   190
Love without scandal, pleasure without fear.

ELMIRE: I've heard your well-turned speeches to the end,
     And what you urge I clearly apprehend.
     Aren't you afraid that I may take a notion
     To tell my husband of your warm devotion,   195
     And that, supposing he were duly told,
     His feelings toward you might grow rather cold?
TARTUFFE: I know, dear lady, that your exceeding charity
     Will lead your heart to pardon my temerity;
     That you'll excuse my violent affection   200
     As human weakness, human imperfection;
     And that—O fairest!—you will bear in mind
     That I'm but flesh and blood, and am not blind.
ELMIRE: Some women might do otherwise, perhaps,
     But I shall be discreet about your lapse;   205
     I'll tell my husband nothing of what's occurred
     If, in return, you'll give your solemn word
     To advocate as forcefully as you can
     The marriage of Valère and Mariane,
     Renouncing all desire to dispossess   210
     Another of his rightful happiness,
     And . . .

SCENE IV

DAMIS: [*emerging from the closet where he has been hiding*] No! We'll not hush up this
     vile affair;
     I heard it all inside that closet there,   215
     Where Heaven, in order to confound the pride
     Of this great rascal, prompted me to hide.
     Ah, now I have my long-awaited chance
     To punish his deceit and arrogance,
     And give my father clear and shocking proof   220
     Of the black character of his dear Tartuffe.
ELMIRE: Ah no, Damis; I'll be content if he
     Will study to deserve my leniency.
     I've promised silence—don't make me break my word;
     To make a scandal would be too absurd.   225
     Good wives laugh off such trifles, and forget them;
     Why should they tell their husbands, and upset them?
DAMIS: You have your reasons for taking such a course,
     And I have reasons, too, of equal force.
     To spare him now would be insanely wrong.   230
     I've swallowed my just wrath for far too long
     And watched this insolent bigot bringing strife
     And bitterness into our family life.
     Too long he's meddled in my father's affairs,
     Thwarting my marriage-hopes, and poor Valère's.   235
     It's high time that my father was undeceived,
     And now I've proof that can't be disbelieved—
     Proof that was furnished me by Heaven above.

It's too good not to take advantage of.
This is my chance, and I deserve to lose it   240
If, for one moment, I hesitate to use it.
ELMIRE: Damis . . .
DAMIS: No, I must do what I think right.
Madam, my heart is bursting with delight,
And, say whatever you will, I'll not consent   245
To lose the sweet revenge on which I'm bent.
I'll settle matters without more ado;
And here, most opportunely, is my cue.

SCENE V

DAMIS: Father, I'm glad you've joined us. Let us advise you
Of some fresh news which doubtless will surprise you.   250
You've just now been repaid with interest
For all your loving-kindness to our guest.
He's proved his warm and grateful feelings toward you;
It's with a pair of horns he would reward you.
Yes, I surprised him with your wife, and heard   255
His whole adulterous offer, every word.
She, with her all-too-gentle disposition,
Would not have told you of his proposition;
But I shall not make terms with brazen lechery,
And feel that not to tell you would be treachery.   260
ELMIRE: And I hold that one's husband's peace of mind
Should not be spoilt by tattle of this kind.
One's honor doesn't require it: to be proficient
In keeping men at bay is quite sufficient.
These are my sentiments, and I wish, Damis,   265
That you had heeded me and held your peace. [*Exit.*]

SCENE VI

ORGON: Can it be true, this dreadful thing I hear?
TARTUFFE: Yes, Brother, I'm a wicked man, I fear:
A wretched sinner, all depraved and twisted,
The greatest villain that has ever existed.   270
My life's one heap of crimes, which grows each minute;
There's naught but foulness and corruption in it;
And I perceive that Heaven, outraged by me,
Has chosen this occasion to mortify me.
Charge me with any deed you wish to name;   275
I'll not defend myself, but take the blame.
Believe what you are told, and drive Tartuffe
Like some base criminal from beneath your roof;
Yes, drive me hence, and with a parting curse:
I shan't protest, for I deserve far worse.   280
ORGON: [*to* DAMIS] Ah, you deceitful boy, how dare you try
To stain his purity with so foul a lie?

DAMIS: What! are you taken in by such a bluff?
    Did you not hear . . . ?

ORGON: Enough, you rogue, enough!   285

TARTUFFE: Ah. Brother, let him speak: you're being unjust.
    Believe his story; the boy deserves your trust.
    Why, after all, should you have faith in me?
    How can you know what I might do, or be?
    Is it on my good actions that you base   290
    Your favor? Do you trust my pious face?
    Ah, no, don't be deceived by hollow shows;
    I'm far, alas, from being what men suppose;
    Though the world takes me for a man of worth,
    I'm truly the most worthless man on Earth.   295
    [*to* DAMIS] Yes, my dear son, speak out now: call me the chief
    Of sinners, a wretch, a murderer, a thief;
    Load me with all the names men most abhor;
    I'll not complain; I've earned them all, and more;
    I'll kneel here while you pour them on my head   300
    As a just punishment for the life I've led.

ORGON: [*to* TARTUFFE] This is too much, dear Brother. [*to* DAMIS] Have you no heart?

DAMIS: Are you so hoodwinked by this rascal's art . . . ?

ORGON: Be still, you monster. [*to* TARTUFFE] Brother, I pray you, rise.
    [*to* DAMIS] Villain!   305

DAMIS: But . . .

ORGON: Silence!

DAMIS: Can't you realize . . . ?

ORGON: Just one word more, and I'll tear you limb from limb.

TARTUFFE: In God's name, Brother, don't be harsh with him.   310
    I'd rather far be tortured at the stake
    Than see him bear one scratch for my poor sake.

ORGON: [*to* DAMIS] Ingrate!

TARTUFFE: If I must beg you, on bended knee,
    To pardon him . . .   315

ORGON: [*falling to his knees, addressing* TARTUFFE] Such goodness cannot be!
    [*to* DAMIS] Now, *there's* true charity!

DAMIS: What, you . . . ?

ORGON: Villain, be still!
    I know your motives; I know you wish him ill: 320
    Yes, all of you—wife, children, servants, all—
    Conspire against him and desire his fall,
    Employing every shameful trick you can
    To alienate me from this saintly man.
    Ah, but the more you seek to drive him away,   325
    The more I'll do to keep him. Without delay,
    I'll spite this household and confound its pride
    By giving him my daughter as his bride.

DAMIS: You're going to force her to accept his hand?

ORGON: Yes, and this very night, d'you understand?   330
    I shall defy you all, and make it clear
    That I'm the one who gives the orders here.

Come, wretch, kneel down and clasp his blessed feet,
And ask his pardon for your black deceit.
DAMIS: I ask that swindler's pardon? Why, I'd rather . . .   335
ORGON: So! You insult him, and defy your father!
A stick! A stick! [*to* TARTUFFE] No, no—release me, do.
[*to* DAMIS] Out of my house this minute! Be off with you,
And never dare set foot in it again.
DAMIS: Well, I shall go, but . . .   340
ORGON: Well, go quickly, then.
I disinherit you; an empty purse
Is all you'll get from me—except my curse!

SCENE VII

ORGON: How he blasphemed your goodness! What a son!
TARTUFFE: Forgive him, Lord, as I've already done.   345
[*to* ORGON] You can't know how it hurts when someone tries
To blacken me in my dear Brother's eyes.
ORGON: Ahh!
TARTUFFE: The mere thought of such ingratitude
Plunges my soul into so dark a mood . . .   350
Such horror grips my heart . . . I gasp for breath,
And cannot speak, and feel myself near death.
ORGON: [*He runs, in tears, to the door through which he has just driven his son.*]
You blackguard! Why did I spare you? Why did I not
Break you in little pieces on the spot?   355
Compose yourself, and don't be hurt, dear friend.
TARTUFFE: These scenes, these dreadful quarrels, have got to end.
I've much upset your household, and I perceive
That the best thing will be for me to leave.
ORGON: What are you saying!   360
TARTUFFE: They're all against me here;
They'd have you think me false and insincere.
ORGON: Ah, what of that? Have I ceased believing in you?
TARTUFFE: Their adverse talk will certainly continue,
And charges which you now repudiate   365
You may find credible at a later date.
ORGON: No, Brother, never.
TARTUFFE: Brother, a wife can sway
Her husband's mind in many a subtle way.
ORGON: No, no.   370
TARTUFFE: To leave at once is the solution;
Thus only can I end their persecution.
ORGON: No, no, I'll not allow it; you shall remain.
TARTUFFE: Ah, well; 'twill mean much martyrdom and pain,
But if you wish it . . .   375
ORGON: Ah!
TARTUFFE: Enough; so be it.
But one thing must be settled, as I see it.
For your dear honor, and for our friendship's sake,

There's one precaution I feel bound to take. 380
I shall avoid your wife, and keep away . . .
ORGON: No, you shall not, whatever they may say.
It pleases me to vex them, and for spite
I'd have them see you with her day and night.
What's more, I'm going to drive them to despair 385
By making you my only son and heir;
This very day, I'll give to you alone
Clear deed and title to everything I own.
A dear, good friend and son-in-law-to-be
Is more than wife, or child, or kin to me. 390
Will you accept my offer, dearest son?
TARTUFFE: In all things, let the will of Heaven be done.
ORGON: Poor fellow! Come, we'll go draw up the deed.
Then let them burst with disappointed greed!

ACT IV

SCENE I

CLÉANTE: Yes, all the town's discussing it, and truly,
Their comments do not flatter you unduly.
I'm glad we've met, Sir, and I'll give my view
Of this sad matter in a word or two.
As for who's guilty, that I shan't discuss; 5
Let's say it was Damis who caused the fuss;
Assuming, then, that you have been ill-used
By young Damis, and groundlessly accused,
Ought not a Christian to forgive, and ought
He not to stifle every vengeful thought? 10
Should you stand by and watch a father make
His only son an exile for your sake?
Again I tell you frankly, be advised:
The whole town, high and low, is scandalized;
This quarrel must be mended, and my advice is 15
Not to push matters to a further crisis.
No, sacrifice your wrath to God above,
And help Damis regain his father's love.
TARTUFFE: Alas, for my part I should take great joy
In doing so. I've nothing against the boy. 20
I pardon all, I harbor no resentment;
To serve him would afford me much contentment.
But Heaven's interest will not have it so:
If he comes back, then I shall have to go.
After his conduct—so extreme, so vicious— 25
Our further intercourse would look suspicious.
God knows what people would think! Why, they'd describe

My goodness to him as a sort of bribe;
They'd say that out of guilt I made pretense
Of loving-kindness and benevolence—   30
That, fearing my accuser's tongue, I strove
To buy his silence with a show of love.

CLÉANTE: Your reasoning is badly warped and stretched,
And these excuses, Sir, are most farfetched.
Why put yourself in charge of Heaven's cause?   35
Does Heaven need our help to enforce its laws?
Leave vengeance to the Lord, Sir; while we live,
Our duty's not to punish, but forgive;
And what the Lord commands, we should obey
Without regard to what the world may say.   40
What! Shall the fear of being misunderstood
Prevent our doing what is right and good?
No, no; let's simply do what Heaven ordains,
And let no other thoughts perplex our brains.

TARTUFFE: Again, Sir, let me say that I've forgiven   45
Damis, and thus obeyed the laws of Heaven;
But I am not commanded by the Bible
To live with one who smears my name with libel.

CLÉANTE: Were you commanded, Sir, to indulge the whim
Of poor Orgon, and to encourage him   50
In suddenly transferring to your name
A large estate to which you have no claim?

TARTUFFE: 'Twould never occur to those who know me best
To think I acted from self-interest.
The treasures of this world I quite despise;   55
Their specious glitter does not charm my eyes;
And if I have resigned myself to taking
The gift which my dear Brother insists on making,
I do so only, as he well understands,
Lest so much wealth fall into wicked hands,   60
Lest those to whom it might descend in time
Turn it to purposes of sin and crime,
And not, as I shall do, make use of it
For Heaven's glory and mankind's benefit.

CLÉANTE: Forget these trumped-up fears. Your argument   65
Is one the rightful heir might well resent;
It *is* a moral burden to inherit
Such wealth, but give Damis a chance to bear it.
And would it not be worse to be accused
Of swindling, than to see that wealth misused?   70
I'm shocked that you allowed Orgon to broach
This matter, and that you feel no self-reproach;
Does true religion teach that lawful heirs
May freely be deprived of what is theirs?
And if the Lord has told you in your heart   75
That you and young Damis must dwell apart,
Would it not be the decent thing to beat

    A generous and honorable retreat,
    Rather than let the son of the house be sent,
    For your convenience, into banishment?   80
    Sir, if you wish to prove the honesty
    Of your intentions . . .
TARTUFFE: Sir, it is half-past three.
    I've certain pious duties to attend to,
    And hope my prompt departure won't offend you.   85
CLÉANTE: [*alone*] Damn.

SCENE II

DORINE: Stay, Sir, and help Mariane, for Heaven's sake!
    She's suffering so, I fear her heart will break.
    Her father's plan to marry her off tonight
    Has put the poor child in a desperate plight.   90
    I hear him coming. Let's stand together, now,
    And see if we can't change his mind, somehow,
    About this match we all deplore and fear.

SCENE III

ORGON: Hah! Glad to find you all assembled here.
    [*to* MARIANE] This contract, child, contains your happiness,   95
    And what it says I think your heart can guess.
MARIANE: [*falling to her knees*] Sir, by that Heaven which sees me here distressed,
    And by whatever else can move your breast,
    Do not employ a father's power, I pray you,
    To crush my heart and force it to obey you,   100
    Nor by your harsh commands oppress me so
    That I'll begrudge the duty which I owe—
    And do not so embitter and enslave me
    That I shall hate the very life you gave me.
    If my sweet hopes must perish, if you refuse   105
    To give me to the one I've dared to choose,
    Spare me at least—I beg you, I implore—
    The pain of wedding one whom I abhor;
    And do not, by a heartless use of force,
    Drive me to contemplate some desperate course.   110
ORGON: [*feeling himself touched by her*] Be firm, my soul. No human weakness, now.
MARIANE: I don't resent your love for him. Allow
    Your heart free rein, Sir; give him your property,
    And if that's not enough, take mine from me;
    He's welcome to my money; take it, do,   115
    But don't, I pray, include my person, too.
    Spare me, I beg you; and let me end the tale
    Of my sad days behind a convent veil.
ORGON: A convent! Hah! When crossed in their amours,
    All lovesick girls have the same thought as yours.   120
    Get up! The more you loathe the man, and dread him,

The more ennobling it will be to wed him.
Marry Tartuffe, and mortify your flesh!
Enough; don't start that whimpering afresh.
DORINE: But why . . . ? 125
ORGON: Be still, there. Speak when you're spoken to.
Not one more bit of impudence out of you.
CLÉANTE: If I may offer a word of counsel here . . .
ORGON: Brother, in counseling you have no peer;
All your advice is forceful, sound, and clever; 130
I don't propose to follow it, however.
ELMIRE: [to ORGON] I am amazed, and don't know what to say;
Your blindness simply takes my breath away.
You are indeed bewitched, to take no warning
From our account of what occurred this morning. 135
ORGON: Madam, I know a few plain facts and one
Is that you're partial to my rascal son;
Hence, when he sought to make Tartuffe the victim
Of a base lie, you dared not contradict him.
Ah, but you underplayed your part, my pet; 140
You should have looked more angry, more upset.
ELMIRE: When men make overtures, must we reply
With righteous anger and a battle-cry?
Must we turn back their amorous advances
With sharp reproaches and with fiery glances? 145
Myself, I find such offers merely amusing,
And make no scenes and fusses in refusing;
My taste is for good-natured rectitude,
And I dislike the savage sort of prude
Who guards her virtue with her teeth and claws, 150
And tears men's eyes out for the slightest cause:
The Lord preserve me from such honor as that,
Which bites and scratches like an alley-cat!
I've found that a polite and cool rebuff
Discourages a lover quite enough. 155
ORGON: I know the facts, and I shall not be shaken.
ELMIRE: I marvel at your power to be mistaken.
Would it, I wonder, carry weight with you
If I could *show* you that our tale was true?
ORGON: Show me? 160
ELMIRE: Yes.
ORGON: Rot.
ELMIRE: Come, what if I found a way
To make you see the facts as plain as day?
ORGON: Nonsense. 165
ELMIRE: Do answer me; don't be absurd.
I'm not now asking you to trust our word.
Suppose that from some hiding-place in here
You learned the whole sad truth by eye and ear—
What would you say of your good friend, after that? 170

ORGON: Why, I'd say . . . nothing, by Jehoshaphat!
    It can't be true.
ELMIRE: You've been too long deceived,
    And I'm quite tired of being disbelieved.
    Come now: let's put my statements to the test,   175
    And you shall see the truth made manifest.
ORGON: I'll take that challenge. Now do your uttermost.
    We'll see how you make good your empty boast.
ELMIRE: [*to* DORINE] Send him to me.
DORINE: He's crafty; it may be hard   180
    To catch the cunning scoundrel off his guard.
ELMIRE: No, amorous men are gullible. Their conceit
    So blinds them that they're never hard to cheat.
    Have him come down. [*to* CLÉANTE *and* MARIANE] Please leave us, for a bit.

    [DORINE, CLÉANTE, *and* MARIANE *exit.*]

SCENE IV

ELMIRE: Pull up this table, and get under it.   185
ORGON: What?
ELMIRE: It's essential that you be well-hidden.
ORGON: Why there?
ELMIRE: Oh, Heavens! Just do as you are bidden.
    I have my plans; we'll soon see how they fare.   190
    Under the table, now; and once you're there,
    Take care that you are neither seen nor heard.
ORGON: Well, I'll indulge you, since I gave my word
    To see you through this infantile charade.
ELMIRE: Once it is over, you'll be glad we played.   195

    [*to her husband, who is now under the table*]

    I'm going to act quite strangely, now, and you
    Must not be shocked at anything I do.
    Whatever I may say, you must excuse
    As part of that deceit I'm forced to use.
    I shall employ sweet speeches in the task   200
    Of making that impostor drop his mask;
    I'll give encouragement to his bold desires,
    And furnish fuel to his amorous fires.
    Since it's for your sake, and for his destruction,
    That I shall seem to yield to his seduction,   205
    I'll gladly stop whenever you decide
    That all your doubts are fully satisfied.
    I'll count on you, as soon as you have seen
    What sort of man he is, to intervene,
    And not expose me to his odious lust   210
    One moment longer than you feel you must.
    Remember: you're to save me from my plight
    Whenever . . . He's coming! Hush! Keep out of sight!

SCENE V

TARTUFFE: You wish to have a word with me, I'm told.
ELMIRE: Yes. I've a little secret to unfold.   215
    Before I speak, however, it would be wise
    To close that door, and look for spies.

     [TARTUFFE *goes to the door, closes it, and returns.*]

    The very last thing that must happen now
    Is a repetition of this morning's row.
    I've never been so badly caught off guard.   220
    Oh, how I feared for you! You saw how hard
    I tried to make that troublesome Damis
    Control his dreadful temper, and hold his peace.
    In my confusion, I didn't have the sense
    Simply to contradict his evidence;   225
    But as it happened, that was for the best,
    And all has worked out in our interest.
    This storm has only bettered your position;
    My husband doesn't have the least suspicion,
    And now, in mockery of those who do,   230
    He bids me be continually with you.
    And that is why, quite fearless of reproof,
    I now can be alone with my Tartuffe,
    And why my heart—perhaps too quick to yield—
    Feels free to let its passion be revealed.   235
TARTUFFE: Madam, your words confuse me. Not long ago,
    You spoke in quite a different style, you know.
ELMIRE: Ah, Sir, if that refusal made you smart,
    It's little that you know of woman's heart,
    Or what that heart is trying to convey   240
    When it resists in such a feeble way!
    Always, at first, our modesty prevents
    The frank avowal of tender sentiments;
    However high the passion which inflames us,
    Still, to confess its power somehow shames us.   245
    Thus we reluct, at first, yet in a tone
    Which tells you that our heart is overthrown,
    That what our lips deny, our pulse confesses,
    And that, in time, all noes will turn to yesses.
    I fear my words are all too frank and free,   250
    And a poor proof of woman's modesty;
    But since I'm started, tell me, if you will—
    Would I have tried to make Damis be still,
    Would I have listened, calm and unoffended,
    Until your lengthy offer of love was ended,   255
    And be so very mild in my reaction,
    Had your sweet words not given me satisfaction?
    And when I tried to force you to undo
    The marriage-plans my husband has in view,
    What did my urgent pleading signify   260

If not that I admired you, and that I
Deplored the thought that someone else might own
Part of a heart I wished for mine alone?
TARTUFFE: Madam, no happiness is so complete
As when, from lips we love, come words so sweet; 265
Their nectar floods my every sense, and drains
In honeyed rivulets through all my veins.
To please you is my joy, my only goal;
Your love is the restorer of my soul;
And yet I must beg leave, now, to confess 270
Some lingering doubts as to my happiness.
Might this not be a trick? Might not the catch
Be that you wish me to break off the match
With Mariane, and so have feigned to love me?
I shan't quite trust your fond opinion of me 275
Until the feelings you've expressed so sweetly
Are demonstrated somewhat more concretely,
And you have shown, by certain kind concessions,
That I may put my faith in your professions.
ELMIRE: [*She coughs, to warn her husband.*] Why be in such a hurry? Must my heart 280
Exhaust its bounty at the very start?
To make that sweet admission cost me dear,
But you'll not be content, it would appear,
Unless my store of favors is disbursed
To the last farthing, and at the very first. 285
TARTUFFE: The less we merit, the less we dare to hope,
And with our doubts, mere words can never cope.
We trust no promised bliss till we receive it;
Not till a joy is ours can we believe it.
I, who so little merit your esteem, 290
Can't credit this fulfillment of my dream,
And shan't believe it, Madam, until I savor
Some palpable assurance of your favor.
ELMIRE: My, how tyrannical your love can be,
And how it flusters and perplexes me! 295
How furiously you take one's heart in hand,
And make your every wish a fierce command!
Come, must you hound and harry me to death?
Will you not give me time to catch my breath?
Can it be right to press me with such force, 300
Give me no quarter, show me no remorse,
And take advantage, by your stern insistence,
Of the fond feelings which weaken my resistance?
TARTUFFE: Well, if you look with favor upon my love,
Why, then, begrudge me some clear proof thereof? 305
ELMIRE: But how can I consent without offense
To Heaven, toward which you feel such reverence?
TARTUFFE: If Heaven is all that holds you back, don't worry.
I can remove that hindrance in a hurry.
Nothing of that sort need obstruct our path. 310
ELMIRE: Must one not be afraid of Heaven's wrath?

TARTUFFE: Madam, forget such fears, and be my pupil,
 And I shall teach you how to conquer scruple.
 Some joys, it's true, are wrong in Heaven's eyes;
 Yet Heaven is not averse to compromise;   315
 There is a science, lately formulated,
 Whereby one's conscience may be liberated,
 And any wrongful act you care to mention
 May be redeemed by purity of intention.
 I'll teach you, Madam, the secrets of that science;   320
 Meanwhile, just place on me your full reliance.
 Assuage my keen desires, and feel no dread:
 The sin, if any, shall be on my head.

  [ELMIRE *coughs, this time more loudly.*]

 You've a bad cough.
ELMIRE: Yes, yes. It's bad indeed.   325
TARTUFFE: [*producing a little paper bag*] A bit of licorice may be what you need.
ELMIRE: No, I've a stubborn cold, it seems. I'm sure it
 Will take much more than licorice to cure it.
TARTUFFE: How aggravating.
ELMIRE: Oh, more than I can say.   330
TARTUFFE: If you're still troubled, think of things this way:
 No one shall know our joys, save us alone,
 And there's no evil till the act is known;
 It's scandal, Madam, which makes it an offense,
 And it's no sin to sin in confidence.   335
ELMIRE: [*having coughed once more*] Well, clearly I must do as you require,
 And yield to your importunate desire.
 It is apparent, now, that nothing less
 Will satisfy you, and so I acquiesce.
 To go so far is much against my will;   340
 I'm vexed that it should come to this; but still,
 Since you are so determined on it, since you
 Will not allow mere language to convince you,
 And since you ask for concrete evidence, I
 See nothing for it, now, but to comply.   345
 If this is sinful, if I'm wrong to do it,
 So much the worse for him who drove me to it.
 The fault can surely not be charged to me.
TARTUFFE: Madam, the fault is mine, if fault there be,
 And . . .   350
ELMIRE: Open the door a little, and peek out;
 I wouldn't want my husband poking about.
TARTUFFE: Why worry about the man? Each day he grows
 More gullible; one can lead him by the nose.
 To find us here would fill him with delight,   355
 And if he saw the worst, he'd doubt his sight.
ELMIRE: Nevertheless, do step out for a minute

Into the hall, and see that no one's in it.

    [TARTUFFE *exits.*]

SCENE VI

ORGON: [*coming out from under the table*] That man's a perfect monster, I must admit!
    I'm simply stunned. I can't get over it.   360
ELMIRE: What, coming out so soon? How premature!
    Get back in hiding, and wait until you're sure.
    Stay till the end, and be convinced completely;
    We mustn't stop till things are proved concretely.
ORGON: Hell never harbored anything so vicious!   365
ELMIRE: Tut, don't be hasty. Try to be judicious.
    Wait, and be certain that there's no mistake.
    No jumping to conclusions, for Heaven's sake!

    [*She places* ORGON *behind her, as* TARTUFFE *reenters.*]

SCENE VII

TARTUFFE: [*not seeing* ORGON] Madam, all things have worked out to perfection;
    I've given the neighboring rooms a full inspection;   370
    No one's about; and now I may at last . . .
ORGON: [*intercepting him*] Hold on, my passionate fellow, not so fast!
    I should advise a little more restraint.
    Well, so you thought you'd fool me, my dear saint!
    How soon you wearied of the saintly life—   375
    Wedding my daughter, and coveting my wife!
    I've long suspected you, and had a feeling
    That soon I'd catch you at your double-dealing.
    Just now, you've given me evidence galore;
    It's quite enough; I have no wish for more.   380
ELMIRE: [*to* TARTUFFE] I'm sorry to have treated you so slyly,
    But circumstances forced me to be wily.
TARTUFFE: Brother, you can't think . . .
ORGON: No more talk from you;
    Just leave this household, without more ado.   385
TARTUFFE: What I intended . . .
ORGON: That seems fairly clear.
    Spare me your falsehoods and get out of here.
TARTUFFE: No, I'm the master, and you're the one to go!
    This house belongs to me, I'll have you know,   390
    And I shall show you that you can't hurt *me*
    By this contemptible conspiracy,
    That those who cross me know not what they do,
    And that I've means to expose and punish you,
    Avenge offended Heaven, and make you grieve   395
    That ever you dared order me to leave.

    [TARTUFFE *exits.*]

SCENE VIII

ELMIRE: What was the point of all that angry chatter?
ORGON: Dear God, I'm worried. This is no laughing matter.
ELMIRE: How so?
ORGON: I fear I understood his drift.   400
    I'm much disturbed about that deed of gift.
ELMIRE: You gave him . . . ?
ORGON: Yes, it's all been drawn and signed.
    But one thing more is weighing on my mind.
ELMIRE: What's that?   405
ORGON: I'll tell you; but first let's see if there's
    A certain strong-box in his room upstairs.

──────────── **ACT V** ────────────

SCENE I

CLÉANTE: Where are you going so fast?
ORGON: God knows!
CLÉANTE: Then wait;
    Let's have a conference, and deliberate
    On how this situation's to be met.   5
ORGON: That strong-box has me utterly upset;
    This is the worst of many, many shocks.
CLÉANTE: Is there some fearful mystery in that box?
ORGON: My poor friend Argas brought that box to me
    With his own hands, in utmost secrecy;   10
    'Twas on the very morning of his flight.
    It's full of papers which, if they came to light,
    Would ruin him—or such is my impression.
CLÉANTE: Then why did you let it out of your possession?
ORGON: Those papers vexed my conscience, and it seemed best   15
    To ask the counsel of my pious guest.
    The cunning scoundrel got me to agree
    To leave the strong-box in his custody,
    So that, in case of an investigation,
    I could employ a slight equivocation   20
    And swear I didn't have it, and thereby,
    At no expense to conscience, tell a lie.
CLÉANTE: It looks to me as if you're out on a limb.
    Trusting him with that box, and offering him
    That deed of gift, were actions of a kind   25
    Which scarcely indicate a prudent mind.
    With two such weapons, he has the upper hand,
    And since you're vulnerable, as matters stand,
    You erred once more in bringing him to bay.
    You should have acted in some subtler way.   30

ORGON: Just think of it: behind that fervent face,
    A heart so wicked, and a soul so base!
    I took him in, a hungry beggar, and then . . .
    Enough, by God! I'm through with pious men:
    Henceforth I'll hate the whole false brotherhood,   35
    And persecute them worse than Satan could.
CLÉANTE: Ah, there you go—extravagant as ever!
    Why can you not be rational? You never
    Manage to take the middle course, it seems,
    But jump, instead, between absurd extremes.   40
    You've recognized your recent grave mistake
    In falling victim to a pious fake;
    Now, to correct that error, must you embrace
    An even greater error in its place,
    And judge our worthy neighbors as a whole   45
    By what you've learned of one corrupted soul?
    Come, just because one rascal made you swallow
    A show of zeal which turned out to be hollow,
    Shall you conclude that all men are deceivers,
    And that, today, there are no true believers?   50
    Let atheists make that foolish inference;
    Learn to distinguish virtue from pretense,
    Be cautious in bestowing admiration,
    And cultivate a sober moderation.
    Don't humor fraud, but also don't asperse   55
    True piety; the latter fault is worse,
    And it is best to err, if err one must,
    As you have done, upon the side of trust.

SCENE II

DAMIS: Father, I hear that scoundrel's uttered threats
    Against you; that he pridefully forgets   60
    How, in his need, he was befriended by you,
    And means to use your gifts to crucify you.
ORGON: It's true, my boy. I'm too distressed for tears.
DAMIS: Leave it to me, Sir; let me trim his ears.
    Faced with such insolence, we must not waver.   65
    I shall rejoice in doing you the favor
    Of cutting short his life, and your distress.
CLÉANTE: What a display of young hotheadedness!
    Do learn to moderate your fits of rage.
    In this just kingdom, this enlightened age,   70
    One does not settle things by violence.

SCENE III

MADAME PERNELLE: [*entering with* ELMIRE *and* MARIANE]
    I hear strange tales of very strange events.
ORGON: Yes, strange events which these two eyes beheld.
    The man's ingratitude is unparalleled.   75

I save a wretched pauper from starvation,
House him, and treat him like a blood relation,
Shower him every day with my largesse,
Give him my daughter, and all that I possess;
And meanwhile the unconscionable knave   80
Tries to induce my wife to misbehave;
And not content with such extreme rascality,
Now threatens me with my own liberality,
And aims, by taking base advantage of
The gifts I gave him out of Christian love,   85
To drive me from my house, a ruined man,
And make me end a pauper, as he began.

DORINE: Poor fellow!

MADAME PERNELLE: No, my son, I'll never bring
    Myself to think him guilty of such thing.   90

ORGON: How's that?

MADAME PERNELLE: The righteous always were maligned.

ORGON: Speak clearly, Mother. Say what's on your mind.

MADAME PERNELLE: I mean that I can smell a rat, my dear.
    You know how everybody hates him, here.   95

ORGON: That has no bearing on the case at all.

MADAME PERNELLE: I told you a hundred times, when you were small,
    That virtue in this world is hated ever;
    Malicious men may die, but malice never.

ORGON: No doubt that's true, but how does it apply?   100

MADAME PERNELLE: They've turned you against him by a clever lie.

ORGON: I've told you, I was there and saw it done.

MADAME PERNELLE: Ah, slanderers will stop at nothing, Son.

ORGON: Mother, I'll lose my temper . . . For the last time,
    I tell you I was witness to the crime.   105

MADAME PERNELLE: The tongues of spite are busy night and noon,
    And to their venom no man is immune.

ORGON: You're talking nonsense. Can't you realize
    I saw it; saw it; saw it with my eyes?
    Saw, do you understand me? Must I shout it   110
    Into your ears before you'll cease to doubt it?

MADAME PERNELLE: Appearances can deceive, my son. Dear me,
    We cannot always judge by what we see.

ORGON: Drat! Drat!

MADAME PERNELLE: One often interprets things awry;   115
    Good can seem evil to a suspicious eye.

ORGON: Was I to see his pawing at Elmire
    As an act of charity?

MADAME PERNELLE: Till his guilt is clear
    A man deserves the benefit of the doubt.   120
    You should have waited, to see how things turned out.

ORGON: Great God in Heaven, what more proof did I need?
    Was I to sit there, watching, until he'd . . .
    You drive me to the brink of impropriety.

MADAME PERNELLE: No, no, a man of such surpassing piety   125

Could not do such a thing. You cannot shake me.
 I don't believe it, and you shall not make me.
ORGON: You vex me so that, if you weren't my mother,
 I'd say to you . . . some dreadful thing or other.
DORINE: It's your turn now, Sir, not to be listened to;   130
 You'd not trust us, and now she won't trust you.
CLÉANTE: My friends, we're wasting time which should be spent
 In facing up to our predicament.
 I fear that scoundrel's threats weren't made in sport.
DAMIS: Do you think he'd have the nerve to go to court?   135
ELMIRE: I'm sure he won't: they'd find it all too crude
 A case of swindling and ingratitude.
CLÉANTE: Don't be too sure. He won't be at a loss
 To give his claims a high and righteous gloss;
 And clever rogues with far less valid cause   140
 Have trapped their victims in a web of laws.
 I say again that to antagonize
 A man so strongly armed was most unwise.
ORGON: I know it; but the man's appalling cheek
 Outraged me so, I couldn't control my pique.   145
CLÉANTE: I wish to Heaven that we could devise
 Some truce between you, or some compromise.
ELMIRE: If I had known what cards he held, I'd not
 Have roused his anger by my little plot.
ORGON: [*to* DORINE, *as* M. LOYAL *enters*] What is that fellow looking for? Who is he? 150
 Go talk to him—and tell him that I'm busy.

SCENE IV

MONSIEUR LOYAL: Good day, dear sister. Kindly let me see
 Your master.
DORINE: He's involved with company,
 And cannot be disturbed just now, I fear.   155
MONSIEUR LOYAL: I hate to intrude; but what has brought me here
 Will not disturb your master, in any event.
 Indeed, my news will make him most content.
DORINE: Your name?
MONSIEUR LOYAL: Just say that I bring greetings from   160
 Monsieur Tartuffe, on whose behalf I've come.
DORINE: [*to* ORGON] Sir, he's a very gracious man, and bears
 A message from Tartuffe, which, he declares,
 Will make you most content.
CLÉANTE: Upon my word,   165
 I think this man had best be seen, and heard.
ORGON: Perhaps he has some settlement to suggest.
 How shall I treat him? What manner would be best?
CLÉANTE: Control your anger, and if he should mention
 Some fair adjustment, give him your full attention.   170
MONSIEUR LOYAL: Good health to you, good Sir. May Heaven confound
 Your enemies, and may your joys abound.

ORGON: [*aside, to* CLÉANTE] A gentle salutation: it confirms
    My guess that he is here to offer terms.
MONSIEUR LOYAL: I've always held your family most dear;   175
    I served your father, Sir, for many a year.
ORGON: Sir, I must ask your pardon; to my shame,
    I cannot now recall your face or name.
MONSIEUR LOYAL: Loyal's my name; I come from Normandy,
    And I'm a bailiff, in all modesty.   180
    For forty years, praise God, it's been my boast
    To serve with honor in that vital post,
    And I am here, Sir, if you will permit
    The liberty, to serve you with this writ . . .
ORGON: To—*what?*   185
MONSIEUR LOYAL: Now, please, Sir, let us have no friction:
    It's nothing but an order of eviction.
    You are to move your goods and family out
    And make way for new occupants, without
    Deferment or delay, and give the keys . . .   190
ORGON: I? Leave this house?
MONSIEUR LOYAL: Why yes, Sir, if you please.
    This house, Sir, from the cellar to the roof,
    Belongs now to the good Monsieur Tartuffe,
    And he is lord and master of your estate   195
    By virtue of a deed of present date,
    Drawn in due form, with clearest legal phrasing . . .
DAMIS: Your insolence is utterly amazing!
MONSIEUR LOYAL: Young man, my business here is not with you,
    But with your wise and temperate father, who,   200
    Like every worthy citizen, stands in awe
    Of justice, and would never obstruct the law.
ORGON: But . . .
MONSIEUR LOYAL: Not for a million, Sir, would you rebel
    Against authority; I know that well.   205
    You'll not make trouble, Sir, or interfere
    With the execution of my duties here.
DAMIS: Someone may execute a smart tattoo
    On that black jacket of yours, before you're through.
MONSIEUR LOYAL: Sir, bid your son be silent. I'd much regret   210
    Having to mention such a nasty threat
    Of violence, in writing my report.
DORINE: [*aside*] This man Loyal's a most disloyal sort!
MONSIEUR LOYAL: I love all men of upright character,
    And when I agreed to serve these papers, Sir,   215
    It was your feelings that I had in mind.
    I couldn't bear to see the case assigned
    To someone else, who might esteem you less
    And so subject you to unpleasantness.
ORGON: What's more unpleasant than telling a man to leave   220
    His house and home?
MONSIEUR LOYAL: You'd like a short reprieve?

If you desire it, Sir, I shall not press you,
But wait until tomorrow to dispossess you.
Splendid. I'll come and spend the night here, then,   225
Most quietly, with half a score of men.
For form's sake, you might bring me, just before
You go to bed, the keys to the front door.
My men, I promise, will be on their best
Behavior, and will not disturb your rest.   230
But bright and early, Sir, you must be quick
And move out all your furniture, every stick:
The men I've chosen are both young and strong,
And with their help it shouldn't take you long.
In short, I'll make things pleasant and convenient,   235
And since I'm being so extremely lenient,
Please show me, Sir, a like consideration,
And give me your entire cooperation.
ORGON: [*aside*] I may be all but bankrupt, but I vow
I'd give a hundred louis, here and now,   240
Just for the pleasure of landing one good clout
Right on the end of that complacent snout.
CLÉANTE: Careful; don't make things worse.
DAMIS: My bootsole itches
To give that beggar a good kick in the breeches.   245
DORINE: Monsieur Loyal, I'd love to hear the whack
Of a stout stick across your fine broad back.
MONSIEUR LOYAL: Take care: a woman, too, may go to jail if
She uses threatening language to a bailiff.
CLÉANTE: Enough, enough, Sir. This must not go on.   250
Give me that paper, please, and then begone.
MONSIEUR LOYAL: Well, *au revoir*. God give you all good cheer!
ORGON: May God confound you, and him who sent you here!

SCENE V

ORGON: Now, Mother, was I right or not? This writ
Should change your notion of Tartuffe a bit.   255
Do you perceive his villainy at last?
MADAME PERNELLE: I'm thunderstruck. I'm utterly aghast.
DORINE: Oh, come, be fair. You mustn't take offense
At this new proof of his benevolence.
He's acting out of selfless love, I know.   260
Material things enslave the soul, and so
He kindly has arranged your liberation
From all that might endanger your salvation.
ORGON: Will you not ever hold your tongue, you dunce?
CLÉANTE: Come, you must take some action, and at once.   265
ELMIRE: Go tell the world of the low trick he's tried.
The deed of gift is surely nullified
By such behavior, and public rage will not
Permit the wretch to carry out his plot.

SCENE VI

VALÈRE: Sir, though I hate to bring you more bad news,   270
    Such is the danger that I cannot choose.
    A friend who is extremely close to me
    And knows my interest in your family
    Has, for my sake, presumed to violate
    The secrecy that's due to things of state,   275
    And sends me word that you are in a plight
    From which your salvation lies in flight.
    That scoundrel who's imposed upon you so
    Denounced you to the King an hour ago
    And, as supporting evidence, displayed   280
    The strong-box of a certain renegade
    Whose secret papers, so he testified,
    You had disloyally agreed to hide.
    I don't know just what charges may be pressed,
    But there's a warrant out for your arrest;   285
    Tartuffe has been instructed, furthermore,
    To guide the arresting officer to your door.
CLÉANTE: He's clearly done this to facilitate
    His seizure of your house and your estate.
ORGON: That man, I must say, is a vicious beast!   290
VALÈRE: Quick, Sir; you mustn't tarry in the least.
    My carriage is outside, to take you hence;
    This thousand louis should cover all expense.
    Let's lose no time, or you shall be undone;
    The sole defense, in this case, is to run.   295
    I shall go with you all the way, and place you
    In a safe refuge to which they'll never trace you.
ORGON: Alas, dear boy, I wish that I could show you
    My gratitude for everything I owe you.
    But now is not the time; I pray the Lord   300
    That I may live to give you your reward.
    Farewell, my dears; be careful . . .
CLÉANTE: Brother, hurry.
    We shall take care of things; you needn't worry.

SCENE VII

TARTUFFE: Gently, Sir, gently; stay right where you are.   305
    No need for haste; your lodging isn't far.
    You're off to prison, by order of the Prince.
ORGON: This is the crowning blow, you wretch; and since
    It means my total ruin and defeat,
    Your villainy is now at last complete.   310
TARTUFFE: You needn't try to provoke me; it's no use.
    Those who serve Heaven must expect abuse.
CLÉANTE: You are indeed most patient, sweet, and blameless.
DORINE: How he exploits the name of Heaven! It's shameless.

TARTUFFE: Your taunts and mockeries are all for naught;   315
    To do my duty is my only thought.
MARIANE: Your love of duty is most meritorious,
    And what you've done is little short of glorious.
TARTUFFE: All deeds are glorious, Madam, which obey
    The sovereign Prince who sent me here today.   320
ORGON: I rescued you when you were destitute;
    Have you forgotten that, you thankless brute?
TARTUFFE: No, no, I well remember everything;
    But my first duty is to serve my King.
    That obligation is so paramount   325
    That other claims, beside it, do not count;
    And for it I would sacrifice my wife,
    My family, my friend, or my life.
ELMIRE: Hypocrite!
DORINE: All that we most revere, he uses   330
    To cloak his plots and camouflage his ruses.
CLÉANTE: If it is true that you are animated
    By pure and loyal zeal, as you have stated,
    Why was this zeal not roused until you'd sought
    To make Orgon a cuckold, and been caught?   335
    Why weren't you moved to give your evidence
    Until your outraged host had driven you hence?
    I shan't say that the gift of all his treasure
    Ought to have damped your zeal in any measure;
    But if he is a traitor, as you declare,   340
    How could you condescend to be his heir?
TARTUFFE: [*to the* OFFICER] Sir, spare me all this clamor; it's growing shrill.
    Please carry out your orders, if you will.
OFFICER: Yes, I've delayed too long, Sir. Thank you kindly.
    You're just the proper person to remind me.   345
    Come, you are off to join the other boarders
    In the King's prison, according to his orders.
TARTUFFE: Who? I, Sir?
OFFICER: Yes.
TARTUFFE: To prison? This can't be true!   350
OFFICER: I owe an explanation, but not to you.
    [*to* ORGON] Sir, all is well; rest easy, and be grateful.
    We serve a Prince to whom all sham is hateful,
    A Prince who sees into our inmost hearts,
    And can't be fooled by any trickster's arts.   355
    His royal soul, though generous and human,
    Views all things with discernment and acumen;
    His sovereign reason is not lightly swayed,
    And all his judgments are discreetly weighed.
    He honors righteous men of every kind,   360
    And yet his zeal for virtue is not blind,
    Nor does his love of piety numb his wits
    And make him tolerant of hypocrites.
    'Twas hardly likely that this man could cozen

A King who's foiled such liars by the dozen.   365
With one keen glance, the King perceived the whole
Perverseness and corruption of his soul,
And thus high Heaven's justice was displayed:
Betraying you, the rogue stood self-betrayed.
The King soon recognized Tartuffe as one   370
Notorious by another name, who'd done
So many vicious crimes that one could fill
Ten volumes with them, and be writing still.
But to be brief: our sovereign was appalled
By this man's treachery toward you, which he called   375
The last, worst villainy of a vile career,
And bade me follow the impostor here
To see how gross his impudence could be,
And force him to restore your property.
Your private papers, by the King's command,   380
I hereby seize and give into your hand.
The King, by royal order, invalidates
The deed which gave this rascal your estates,
And pardons, furthermore, your grave offense
In harboring an exile's documents.   385
By these decrees, our Prince rewards you for
Your loyal deeds in the late civil war,
And shows how heartfelt is his satisfaction
In recompensing any worthy action,
How much he prizes merit, and how he makes   390
More of men's virtues than of their mistakes.
DORINE: Heaven be praised!
MADAME PERNELLE: I breathe again, at last.
ELMIRE: We're safe.
MARIANE: I can't believe the danger's past.   395
ORGON: [*to* TARTUFFE] Well, traitor, now you see . . .
CLÉANTE: Ah, Brother, please,
    Let's not descend to such indignities.
    Leave the poor wretch to his unhappy fate,
    And don't say anything to aggravate   400
    His present woes; but rather hope that he
    Will soon embrace an honest piety,
    And mend his ways, and by a true repentance
    Move our just King to moderate his sentence.
    Meanwhile, go kneel before your sovereign's throne   405
    And thank him for the mercies he has shown.
ORGON: Well said: let's go at once and, gladly kneeling,
    Express the gratitude which all are feeling.
    Then, when that first great duty has been done,
    We'll turn with pleasure to a second one,   410
    And give Valère, whose love has proven so true,
    The wedded happiness which is his due.

A Doll's House
(1879)

bsen's early plays (beginning in 1850) were poetic dramas about Norwegian legend or history. In the 1870s, Ibsen deliberately abandoned his earlier approach to write prose plays about contemporary life. *A Doll's House* and *Ghosts* made Ibsen the most controversial playwright in Europe, for the former was thought to attack the institution of marriage and the family, and the latter brought the taboo subject of venereal disease to the stage. Ibsen's prose plays were thought to epitomize realism, a new movement then under way. Subsequently, his prose works were said to have initiated the modern drama.

Undergirding *A Doll's House* is the basic assumption that hereditary and environmental forces determine character and action. What each character is and does is explained by information about background, upbringing, and experience. During the course of the action, we learn enough about all the characters to understand how they have arrived at where they are. Ibsen could have made his play melodramatic by depicting Krogstad as villain and Nora as persecuted heroine. Instead, all of the characters strive for what they consider right. Thus instead of a type, each character appears to be a complex, fallible human being.

A Doll's House is usually read today as a play about the status of women in the late nineteenth century. It pleases Torvald to think of Nora as incapable of making decisions, even about what she should wear to a party. The play also shows that women were legally reduced to the state of childhood (or doll) because a wife was required to have her husband's consent in almost all matters, whereas her husband could act wholly independently, even disposing of property originally hers without her consent or knowledge. The ending of the play shocked audiences and critics not because the play's potential villain relents and saves Nora and Torvald from public disgrace—that type of sentimental resolution was all too common—but because Nora insists on discussing what has happened with her husband and their roles as husband and wife. At the end of the play, Nora's alienation is not only from her husband but also from society in general. She chooses to leave her husband and children because, finding herself in disagreement with both law and public opinion and not yet certain of her own convictions, she does not believe herself ready to meet her responsibilities as a wife and mother. It was this ending that made the play so controversial, for it challenged the status quo.

A Doll's House could serve as a model of cause-to-effect dramatic structure. The first act sets up masterfully and with seeming naturalness all of the conditions out of which the subsequent action grows logically and seemingly inevitably.

Henrik Ibsen

A Doll's House

Translated by William Archer
(with emendations by Oscar G. Brockett)

Characters

TORVALD HELMER
NORA, *his wife*
DOCTOR RANK
MRS. LINDE
NILS KROGSTAD
THE HELMERS' THREE YOUNG CHILDREN
ANNE, *their nurse*
A HOUSEMAID
A PORTER

The action of the play takes place in the Helmers' house.

ACT I

SCENE———*A room furnished comfortably and tastefully but not extravagantly. At the back, a door to the right leads to the entrance-hall, another to the left leads to* HELMER'*s study. Between the doors stands a piano. In the middle of the left-hand wall is a door, and beyond it a window. Near the window are a round table, armchairs, and a small sofa. In the right-hand wall, at the farther end, another door; and on the same side, nearer the footlights, a stove, two easy chairs, and a rocking chair; between the stove and the door, a small table. Engravings on the walls; a cabinet with china and other small objects; a small book-case with well-bound books. The floors are carpeted, and a fire burns in the stove. It is winter.*

A bell rings in the hall; shortly afterwards the door is heard to open. Enter NORA, *humming a tune and in high spirits. She is in out-door dress and carries a number of parcels; these she lays on the table to the right. She leaves the outer door open after her, and through it is seen a* PORTER *who is carrying a Christmas tree and a basket, which he gives to the* MAID, *who has opened the door.*

NORA: Hide the Christmas tree carefully, Helen. Be sure the children don't see it till this evening, when it is trimmed. [*to the* PORTER *taking out her purse*] How much?

PORTER: A half-crown.

NORA: There's a crown. No, keep the change. [*The* PORTER *thanks her, and goes out.* NORA *the door. She is laughing to herself, as she takes off her hat and coat. She takes a packet of macaroons from her pocket and eats one or two; then goes cautiously to her husband's door and listens.*] Yes, he is in. [*Still humming, she goes to the table on the right.*]

HELMER: [*calls out from his room*] Is that my little lark twittering out there?

NORA: [*busy opening some of the parcels*] Yes, it is!

HELMER: Is it my little squirrel bustling about?

NORA: Yes!

HELMER: When did my squirrel come home?

NORA: Just now. [*puts the bag of macaroons into her pocket and wipes her mouth*] Come in here, Torvald, and see what I have bought.

HELMER: Don't disturb me. [*A little later he opens the door and looks into the room, pen in hand.*] Bought, did you say? All these things? Has my little spendthrift been wasting money again?

NORA: Yes, but, Torvald, this year we really can let ourselves go a little. This is the first Christmas that we have not needed to economize.

HELMER: Still, you know, we can't spend money recklessly.

NORA: Yes, Torvald, we may be a wee bit more reckless now, mayn't we? Just a tiny wee bit! You are going to have a big salary and earn lots and lots of money.

HELMER: Yes, after the New Year; but then it will be a whole quarter before the salary is due.

NORA: Pooh! We can borrow till then.

HELMER: Nora! [*goes up to her and takes her playfully by the ear*] The same little featherhead! Suppose, now, that I borrowed one thousand crowns to-day, and you spent it all in the Christmas week, and then on New Year's Eve a roof tile fell on my head and killed me, and—

NORA: [*putting her hands over his mouth*] Oh! don't say such horrid things.

HELMER: Still, suppose that happened—what then?

NORA: If that were to happen, I don't suppose I should care whether I owed money or not.

HELMER: Yes, but what about the people who had lent it?

NORA: They? Who would care about them? I wouldn't know who they were.

HELMER: How like a woman! But seriously, Nora, you know what I think about that. No debt, no borrowing. There can be no freedom or beauty about a home that depends on borrowing and debt. We two have kept bravely on the straight road so far, and we will go on the same way for the short time left.

NORA: [*moving towards the stove*] As you please, Torvald.

HELMER: [*following her*] Come, come, my little skylark must not droop her wings. What is this! Is my little squirrel sulking? [*taking out his purse*] Nora, what do you think I've got here?

NORA: [*turning round quickly*] Money!

HELMER: There you are. [*gives her some money*] Do you think I don't know what a lot is needed for housekeeping at Christmas-time?

NORA: [*counting*] One-two-three! Thank you, thank you, Torvald; that will keep me going for a long time.

HELMER: Indeed it must.

NORA: Yes, yes, it will. But come here and let me show you what I have bought. And all so cheap! Look, here is a new suit for Ivar, and a sword; and a horse and trumpet for Bob; and a doll and a doll's bed for Emmy—they are very plain, but anyway she'll soon break them. And here are dress materials and handkerchiefs for the maids; old Anne ought really to have something better.

HELMER: And what is in this parcel?   55

NORA: [*crying out*] No, no! You mustn't see that till this evening.

HELMER: Very well. But now tell me, you extravagant little person, what would you like for yourself?

NORA: For myself? Oh, I'm sure I don't want anything.

HELMER: Yes, but you must. Tell me something reasonable that you would particularly like   60 to have.

NORA: No, I really can't think of anything—unless, Torvald—

HELMER: Well?

NORA: [*playing with his coat buttons, and without raising her eyes to his*] if you really want to give me something, you might—you might—   65

HELMER: Well, out with it!

NORA: [*speaking quickly*] You might give me money, Torvald. Only just as much as you can afford; and then one of these days I will buy something with it.

HELMER: But, Nora—

NORA: Oh, do! dear Torvald; please, please do! Then I will wrap it up in beautiful gold   70 paper and hang it on the Christmas tree. Wouldn't that be fun?

HELMER: What are little people called that are always wasting money?

NORA: Spendthrifts—I know. Let's do what you suggest, Torvald, and then I shall have time to think what I need most. That is a very sensible plan, isn't it?

HELMER: [*smiling*] Indeed it is—that is to say, if you were really to save out of the money   75 I give you, and then really buy something for yourself. But if you spend it all on the housekeeping and any number of unnecessary things, then I merely have to pay up again.

NORA: Oh but, Torvald—

HELMER: You can't deny it, my dear little Nora. [*puts his arm around her waist*] It's a sweet   80 little spendthrift, but she uses up a lot of money. One would hardly believe how expensive such little persons are!

NORA: It's a shame to say that. I do really save all I can.

HELMER: [*laughing*] That's very true—all you can. But you can't save anything!

NORA: [*smiling quietly and happily*] You haven't any idea how many expenses we skylarks   85 and squirrels have, Torvald.

HELMER: You are an odd little soul. Very like your father. You always find some new way of wheedling money out of me, and, as soon as you have got it, it seems to melt in your hands. You never know where it has gone. Still, one must take you as you are. It is in the blood; for indeed it is true that you can inherit these things, Nora.   90

NORA: Ah, I wish I had inherited many of papa's qualities.

HELMER: And I would not wish you to be anything but just what you are, my sweet little skylark. But, do you know, it strikes me that you are looking rather—what shall I say—rather guilty to-day?

NORA: Do I?   95

HELMER: You do, really. Look straight at me.

NORA: [*looks at him*] Well?

HELMER: [*wagging his finger at her*] Hasn't Miss Sweet-Tooth been breaking rules in town to-day?

NORA: No; what makes you think that?   100

HELMER: Hasn't she paid a visit to the pastry shop?

NORA: No, I assure you, Torvald—

HELMER: Not been nibbling sweets?

NORA: No, certainly not.

HELMER: Not even taken a bite at a macaroon or two?   105

NORA: No, Torvald, I assure you really—

HELMER: There, there, of course I was only joking.

NORA: [*going to the table on the right*] I wouldn't think of going against your wishes.

HELMER: No, I am sure of that; besides, you gave me your word—[*going up to her*] Keep your little Christmas secrets to yourself, my darling. They will all be revealed tonight   110
when the Christmas tree is lit, no doubt.

NORA: Did you remember to invite Doctor Rank?

HELMER: No. But there is no need; he will come to dinner with us as he always does. However, I will ask him when he comes in this morning. I have ordered some good wine. Nora, you can't think how I am looking forward to this evening.   115

NORA: So am I! And how the children will enjoy themselves, Torvald!

HELMER: It is splendid to feel that one has a secure job and a big enough income. It's delightful to think of, isn't it?

NORA: It's wonderful.

HELMER: Do you remember last Christmas? For a full three weeks beforehand you shut   120
yourself up every evening till long after midnight, making ornaments for the Christmas tree and all the other fine things that were to be a surprise to us. It was the dullest three weeks I ever spent!

NORA: I didn't find it dull.

HELMER: [*smiling*] But there was precious little to show for it, Nora.   125

NORA: Oh, you shouldn't tease me about that again. How could I help the cat's getting in and tearing everything to pieces?

HELMER: Of course you couldn't, poor little girl. You had the best of intentions to please us all, and that's the main thing. But it is a good thing that our hard times are over.

NORA: Yes, it is really wonderful.   130

HELMER: This time I needn't be all alone and bored and you needn't ruin your dear eyes and your pretty little hands—

NORA: [*clapping her hands*] No, Torvald, I don't have to any longer, do I! It's wonderful to hear you say so! [*taking his arm*] Now I will tell you how I have been thinking we ought to arrange things, Torvald. As soon as Christmas is over—[*A bell rings in the*   135
hall.] There's the doorbell. [*She tidies the room a little.*] There's someone at the door. What a nuisance!

HELMER: If it is a caller, remember I am not at home.

MAID: [*in the doorway*] A lady to see you, ma'am—a stranger.

NORA: Ask her to come in.   140

MAID: [*to* HELMER] The doctor came at the same time, sir.

HELMER: Did he go straight into my study?

MAID: Yes, sir.

[HELMER *goes into his room. The* MAID *ushers in* MRS. LINDE, *who is in travelling clothes and shuts the door.*]

MRS. LINDE: [*in a dejected and timid voice*] How do you do, Nora?

NORA: [*doubtfully*] How do you do—   145

MRS. LINDE: You don't recognise me, I suppose.

NORA: No, I'm afraid—yes, to be sure, I seem to—[*suddenly*] Yes! Christine! Is it really you?

MRS. LINDE: Yes, it is I.

NORA: Christine! To think of my not recognising you! And yet how could I—[*in a gentle voice*] How you've changed, Christine! 150

MRS. LINDE: Yes, I have indeed. In nine, ten long years—

NORA: Is it so long since we met? I suppose it is. The last eight years have been a happy time for me, I can tell you. And so now you have come into town, and have taken this long journey in winter—that was brave of you.

MRS. LINDE: I arrived by boat this morning. 155

NORA: To have some fun at Christmas-time, of course. How delightful! We will have such fun together! But take off your things. You are not cold, I hope. [*helps her*] Now we will sit down by the stove, and be comfortable. No, take this armchair; I will sit here in the rocking chair. [*takes her hands*] Now you look like your old self again; it was only the first moment—You are a little paler, Christine, and perhaps a little thinner. 160

MRS. LINDE: And much, much older, Nora.

NORA: Perhaps a little older; very, very little; certainly not much. [*stops suddenly and speaks seriously*] What a thoughtless creature I am, chattering away like this. My poor, dear Christine, do forgive me.

MRS. LINDE: What do you mean, Nora? 165

NORA: [*gently*] Poor Christine, you are a widow.

MRS. LINDE: Yes; it is three years ago now.

NORA: Yes, I know; I saw it in the papers. I assure you, Christine, I meant to write to you at the time, but I always put it off and something always prevented me.

MRS. LINDE: I quite understand, dear. 170

NORA: It was very bad of me, Christine. Poor thing, how you must have suffered. And he left you nothing?

MRS. LINDE: No.

NORA: And no children?

MRS. LINDE: No. 175

NORA: Nothing at all, then?

MRS. LINDE: Not even sorrow or grief to live upon.

NORA: [*looking incredulously at her*] But, Christine, is that possible?

MRS. LINDE: [*smiles sadly and strokes her hair*] It sometimes happens, Nora.

NORA: So you are quite alone. How dreadfully sad that must be. I have three lovely children. You can't see them just now, for they are out with their nurse. But now you must tell me everything. 180

MRS. LINDE: No, no; I want to hear about you.

NORA: No, you must begin. I mustn't be selfish to-day; to-day I must only think of your affairs. But there is one thing I must tell you. Have you heard about our great piece of good luck? 185

MRS. LINDE: No, what is it?

NORA: Just imagine, my husband has been made manager of the Bank!

MRS. LINDE: Your husband? What good luck!

NORA: Yes, tremendous! A lawyer's profession is such an uncertain thing, especially if he won't undertake unsavoury cases; and naturally Torvald has never been willing to do that, and I quite agree with him. You may imagine how pleased we are! He'll begin his job in the Bank at the New Year, and then he'll have a big salary and lots of commissions. For the future we can live quite differently—we can do just as we like. I feel so relieved and so happy, Christine! It will be splendid to have heaps of money and not need to have any anxiety, won't it? 190 195

MRS. LINDE: Yes, anyhow I think it would be delightful to have what one needs.

NORA: No, not only what one needs, but heaps and heaps of money.

MRS. LINDE: [*smiling*] Nora, Nora, haven't you learnt sense yet? In our schooldays you were a great spendthrift.

NORA: [*laughing*] Yes, that is what Torvald says now. [*wags her finger at her*] But "Nora, Nora" isn't so silly as you think. We have not been in a position for me to waste money. We have both had to work.

MRS. LINDE: You, too!

NORA: Yes; odds and ends, needlework, crochetings, embroidery, and that kind of thing. [*dropping her voice*] And other things as well. You know Torvald left his office when we were married? There was no prospect of promotion there, and he had to try and earn more than before. But during the first year he overworked himself dreadfully. You see, he had to make money every way he could, and he worked early and late; but he couldn't stand it, and fell dreadfully ill, and the doctors said it was necessary for him to go south.

MRS. LINDE: You spent a whole year in Italy, didn't you?

NORA: Yes. It was no easy matter to get away, I can tell you. It was just after Ivar was born; but naturally we had to go. It was a wonderfully beautiful trip and it saved Torvald's life. But it cost a tremendous lot of money, Christine.

MRS. LINDE: So I should think.

NORA: It cost about forty-eight hundred crowns. That's a lot, isn't it?

MRS. LINDE: Yes, and in emergencies like that it is lucky to have the money.

NORA: We got the money from papa.

MRS. LINDE: Oh, I see. It was just about that time that he died, wasn't it?

NORA: Yes; and just think of it, I couldn't go and nurse him. I was expecting little Ivar's birth every day and I had my poor sick Torvald to look after. My dear, kind father—I never saw him again, Christine. That was the saddest time I have known since our marriage.

MRS. LINDE: I know how fond you were of him. And then you went off to Italy?

NORA: Yes; you see, we had money then, and the doctors insisted on our going, so we started a month later.

MRS. LINDE: And your husband came back quite well?

NORA: As sound as a bell!

MRS. LINDE: But—the doctor?

NORA: What doctor?

MRS. LINDE: I thought your maid said the gentleman who arrived here just as I did, was the doctor?

NORA: Yes, that was Doctor Rank, but he doesn't come here professionally. He is our closest friend, and comes in at least once every day. No, Torvald has not had an hour's illness since then, and our children are strong and healthy and so am I. [*jumps up and claps her hands*] Christine! Christine! it's good to be alive and happy! But how horrid of me; I am talking of nothing but my own affairs. [*sits on a stool near her, and rests her arms on her knees*] You mustn't be angry with me. Tell me, is it really true that you did not love your husband? Why did you marry him?

MRS. LINDE: My mother was alive then, and was bedridden and helpless, and I had to provide for my two younger brothers; so I didn't think I was justified in refusing his offer.

NORA: No, perhaps you were quite right. He was rich at that time, then?

MRS. LINDE: I believe he was quite well off. But his business was a precarious one; and, when he died, it all went to pieces and there was nothing left.

NORA: And then?——

MRS. LINDE: Well, I had to turn my hand to anything I could find—first a small shop, then a small school, and so on. The last three years have seemed like one long working-day, with no rest. Now it is at an end, Nora. My poor mother needs me no more, for she is gone; and the boys don't need me either; they have got jobs and can shift for themselves. 250

NORA: What a relief you must feel—

MRS. LINDE: No, indeed; I only feel my life unspeakably empty. No one to live for any more. [*gets up restlessly*] That was why I could not stand the life in my little backwater any longer. I hope it may be easier here to find something which will busy me and occupy my thoughts. If only I could have the good luck to get some regular work— office work of some kind— 255

NORA: But, Christine, that is so frightfully tiring, and you look tired out now. You had far better go away to some watering-place.

MRS. LINDE: [*walking to the window*] I have no father to give me money for a journey, Nora. 260

NORA: [*rising*] Oh, don't be angry with me.

MRS. LINDE: [*going up to her*] It is you that mustn't be angry with me, dear. The worst of a position like mine is that it makes one so bitter. No one to work for, and yet obliged to be always on the look-out for chances. One must live, and so one becomes selfish. When you told me of the happy turn your fortunes have taken—you will hardly believe it—I was delighted not so much on your account as on my own. 265

NORA: How do you mean?—Oh, I understand. You mean that perhaps Torvald could get you something to do.

MRS. LINDE: Yes, that was what I was thinking of. 270

NORA: He must, Christine. Just leave it to me; I will broach the subject very cleverly—I will think of something that will please him very much. It will make me so happy to be of some use to you.

MRS. LINDE: How kind you are, Nora, to be so anxious to help me! It is doubly kind in you, for you know so little of the burdens and troubles of life. 275

NORA: I—? I know so little of them?

MRS. LINDE: [*smiling*] My dear! Small household cares and that sort of thing! You are a child, Nora.

NORA: [*tosses her head and crosses the stage*] You ought not to be so superior.

MRS. LINDE: No! 280

NORA: You are just like the others. They all think that I am incapable of anything really serious—

MRS. LINDE: Come, come—

NORA: —that I have gone through nothing in this world of cares.

MRS. LINDE: But, my dear Nora, you have just told me all your troubles. 285

NORA: Pooh!—Those were trifles. [*lowering her voice*] I have not told you the important thing.

MRS. LINDE: The important thing! What do you mean?

NORA: You look down on me, Christine—but you shouldn't. You are proud, aren't you, of having worked so hard and so long for your mother? 290

MRS. LINDE: Indeed, I don't look down on any one. But it is true that I am proud and glad to think that I was privileged to make the end of my mother's life almost free from care.

NORA: And you are proud to think of what you have done for your brothers.

MRS. LINDE: I think I have the right to be. 295

NORA: I think so, too. But now, listen to this; I, too, have something to be proud and glad of.

MRS. LINDE: I have no doubt you have. But what do you refer to?

NORA: Speak low. Suppose Torvald were to hear! He mustn't on any account—no one in the world must know, Christine, except you.

MRS. LINDE: But what is it?

NORA: Come here. [*pulls her down on the sofa beside her*] Now I'll show you that I also have something to be proud and glad of. It was I who saved Torvald's life.

MRS. LINDE: "Saved"? How?

NORA: I told you about our trip to Italy. Torvald would never have recovered if he had not gone there—

MRS. LINDE: Yes, but your father gave you the necessary funds.

NORA: [*smiling*] Yes, that is what Torvald and all the others think, but—

MRS. LINDE: But—

NORA: Papa didn't give us a crown. It was I who procured the money.

MRS. LINDE: You? All that large sum?

NORA: Forty-eight hundred crowns. What do you think of that?

MRS. LINDE: But, Nora, how could you possibly do it? Did you win a prize in the Lottery?

NORA: [*contemptuously*] In the Lottery? There would have been no credit in that.

MRS. LINDE: But where did you get it then?

NORA: [*humming and smiling with an air of mystery*] Hm, hm! Aha!

MRS. LINDE: Because you couldn't have borrowed it.

NORA: Couldn't I? Why not?

MRS. LINDE: No, a wife cannot borrow without her husband's consent.

NORA: [*tossing her head*] Oh, if it's a wife who has any head for business—a wife who has the wit to be a little bit clever—

MRS. LINDE: I don't understand it at all, Nora.

NORA: There is no need you should. I never said I had borrowed the money. I may have got it some other way. [*lies back on the sofa*] Perhaps I got it from some admirer. When you're as attractive as I am—

MRS. LINDE: You're mad.

NORA: Now, you know you're full of curiosity, Christine.

MRS. LINDE: Listen to me, Nora dear. Haven't you been a little bit foolish?

NORA: [*sits up straight*] Is it foolish to save your husband's life?

MRS. LINDE: It seems to me foolish without his knowledge, to—

NORA: But it was absolutely necessary that he not know! My goodness, can't you understand that? It was necessary he should have no idea what a dangerous condition he was in. It was to me that the doctors came and said that his life was in danger, and that the only thing to save him was to live in the south. Do you suppose I didn't try, first of all, to get what I wanted as if it were for myself? I told him how much I should love to travel abroad like other young wives; I tried tears and entreaties with him; I told him that he ought to remember the condition I was in, and that he ought to be kind and indulgent to me; I even hinted that he might raise a loan. That nearly made him angry, Christine. He said I was thoughtless, and that it was his duty as my husband not to indulge me in my whims and caprices—as I believe he called them. Very well, I thought, you must be saved—and that was how I came to devise a way out of the difficulty—

MRS. LINDE: And did your husband never find out from your father that the money hadn't come from him?

NORA: No, never. Papa died just at that time. I had meant to let him into the secret and beg him never to reveal it. But he was so ill then—unfortunately there was no need to tell him.

MRS. LINDE: And since then have you never told your secret to your husband?

NORA: Good Heavens, no! How could you think that? A man who has such strong opin- 350 ions about these things! And besides, how painful and humiliating it would be for Torvald, with his male pride, to know that he owed me anything! It would upset our relationship altogether; our beautiful happy home would no longer be the same.

MRS. LINDE: Do you mean never to tell him about it?

NORA: [*meditatively, and with a half smile*] Yes—some day, perhaps, after many years, when 355 I'm no longer as attractive as I am now. Don't laugh at me! I mean, of course, when Torvald is no longer as devoted to me as he is now; when my dancing and dressing-up and reciting have palled on him; then it may be a good thing to have something in reserve—[*breaking off*] What nonsense! That time will never come. Now, what do you think of my great secret, Christine? Do you still think I am of no use? I can 360 tell you, too, that this affair has caused me a lot of worry. It has been by no means easy for me to meet my payments punctually. I may tell you that there is something that is called, in business, quarterly interest, and another thing called payment in installments, and it is always so dreadfully difficult to manage them. I have had to save a little here and there, where I could, you understand. I have not been able to 365 put aside much from my housekeeping money, for Torvald must have a good table. I couldn't let my children be shabbily dressed; I have felt obliged to use up all he gave me for them, the sweet little darlings!

MRS. LINDE: So it has all had to come out of your own expenses, poor Nora?

NORA: Of course. Besides, I was the one responsible for it. Whenever Torvald has given 370 me money for new dresses and such things, I have never spent more than half of it; I have always bought the simplest and cheapest things. Thank Heaven, any clothes look good on me, and so Torvald has never noticed it. But it was often very hard on me, Christine—because it is delightful to be really well dressed, isn't it?

MRS. LINDE: Quite so. 375

NORA: Well, then I have found other ways of earning money. Last winter I was lucky enough to get a lot of copying to do; so I locked myself up and sat writing every evening until quite late at night. Many a time I was desperately tired; but all the same it was a tremendous pleasure to sit there working and earning money. It was like being a man. 380

MRS. LINDE: How much have you been able to pay off in that way?

NORA: I can't tell you exactly. You see, it is very difficult to keep an account of a business matter of that kind. I only know that I have paid every penny that I could scrape together. Many a time I was at my wits' end. [*smiles*] Then I used to sit here and imagine that a rich old gentleman had fallen in love with me— 385

MRS. LINDE: What! Who was it?

NORA: —that he had died; and that when his will was opened it contained, written in big letters, the instruction: "The lovely Mrs. Nora Helmer is to have all I possess paid over to her at once in cash."

MRS. LINDE: But, my dear Nora—who could the man be! 390

NORA: Good gracious, can't you understand? There was no old gentleman at all; it was only something that I used to sit here and imagine, when I couldn't think of any way of getting money. But it's all the same now; the tiresome old person can stay where he is, as far as I am concerned; I don't care about him or his will, either, for I am free from care now. [*jumps up*] My goodness, it's delightful to think of, Christine! Free 395 from care! To be able to be free from care, quite free from care; to be able to play and romp with the children; to be able to keep the house beautifully and have everything just as Torvald likes it! And, think of it, soon the spring will come and the big blue

sky! Perhaps we shall be able to take a little trip—perhaps I shall see the sea again!
    Oh, it's a wonderful thing to be alive and be happy. [*a bell is heard in the hall*]   400
MRS. LINDE: [*rising*] There's the doorbell; perhaps I had better go.
NORA: No, don't go; no one will come in here; it is sure to be for Torvald.
SERVANT: [*at the hall door*] Excuse me, ma'am—there is a gentleman to see the master,
    and as the doctor is with him—
NORA: Who is it?   405
KROGSTAD: [*at the door*] It is I, Mrs. Helmer. [MRS. LINDE *starts, trembles, and turns to*
    the window.]
NORA: [*takes a step towards him, and speaks in a strained, low voice*] You? What is it? What
    do you want to see my husband about?
KROGSTAD: Bank business—in a way. I have a small post in the Bank, and I hear your   410
    husband is to be our chief now—
NORA: Then it is—
KROGSTAD: Nothing but dry business matters, Mrs. Helmer; absolutely nothing else.
NORA: Be so good as to go into the study, then. [*She bows indifferently to him and shuts the*
    door into the hall; then comes back and makes up the fire in the stove.]   415
MRS. LINDE: Nora—who was that man?
NORA: A lawyer named Krogstad.
MRS. LINDE: Then it really was he.
NORA: Do you know the man?
MRS. LINDE: I used to—many years ago. At one time he was a solicitor's clerk in our town.   420
NORA: Yes, he was.
MRS. LINDE: He is greatly altered.
NORA: He made a very unhappy marriage.
MRS. LINDE: He is a widower now isn't he?
NORA: With several children. There now, it's burning. [*shuts the door of the stove and moves*   425
    the rocking chair aside]
MRS. LINDE: They say he carried on various kinds of business.
NORA: Really! Perhaps he does; I don't know anything about it. But don't let's think of
    business: it is so boring.
DOCTOR RANK: [*comes out of* HELMER's *study. Before he shuts the door he calls to him.*] No,   430
    my dear fellow, I won't disturb you; I would rather go in to your wife for a little
    while. [*shuts the door and sees* MRS. LINDE] I beg your pardon; I'm afraid I'm disturb-
    ing you, too.
NORA: No, not at all. [*introducing him*] Doctor Rank, Mrs. Linde.
RANK: I have often heard Mrs. Linde's name mentioned here. I think I passed you on the   435
    stairs when I arrived, Mrs. Linde?
MRS. LINDE: Yes, I go up very slowly; I can't manage stairs well.
RANK: Ah! Some slight internal weakness?
MRS. LINDE: No, the fact is I have been overworking myself.
RANK: Nothing more than that? Then I suppose you have come to town to amuse yourself   440
    with our entertainments?
MRS. LINDE: I have come to look for work.
RANK: Is that a good cure for overwork?
MRS. LINDE: One must live, Doctor Rank.
RANK: Yes, the general opinion seems to be that it's necessary.   445
NORA: Look here, Doctor Rank—you know you want to live.
RANK: Certainly. However wretched I may feel, I want to prolong the agony as long as
    possible. All my patients are like that. And so are those who are morally sick—one
    of them, and a bad case, too, is at this very moment with Helmer—
MRS. LINDE: [*sadly*] Ah!   450
NORA: Whom do you mean?

RANK: A lawyer, Krogstad, a fellow you don't know at all. He suffers from a diseased moral character, Mrs. Helmer; but even he began talking about it being highly important that he should live.

NORA: Did he? What did he want to speak to Torvald about?   455

RANK: I have no idea; I only heard that it was something about the Bank.

NORA: I didn't know this—what's his name—Krogstad had anything to do with the Bank.

RANK: Yes, he has some sort of appointment there. [*to* MRS. LINDE] I don't know whether you find also in your part of the world that there are certain people who go zealously   460
sniffing about to smell out moral corruption, and, as soon as they have found some, put the person concerned into some lucrative position where they can keep their eye on him. Healthy natures are left out in the cold.

MRS. LINDE: Still I think the sick are those who most need taking care of.

RANK: [*shrugging his shoulders*] Yes, there you are. That is the sentiment that is turning   465
Society into a hospital.

> [NORA, *who has been absorbed in her thoughts, breaks out into smothered laughter and claps her hands.*]

RANK: Why do you laugh at that? Have you any notion what Society really is?

NORA: What do I care about tiresome Society? I am laughing at something quite different, something extremely amusing. Tell me, Doctor Rank, are all the people who are employed in the Bank dependent on Torvald now?   470

RANK: Is that what you find so extremely amusing?

NORA: [*smiling and humming*] That's my affair! [*walking about the room*] It's perfectly glorious to think that we have—that Torvald has so much power over so many people. [*takes the packet from her pocket*] Doctor Rank, what do you say to a macaroon?

RANK: What, macaroons? I thought they were forbidden here.   475

NORA: Yes, but these are some Christine gave me.

MRS. LINDE: What! I?

NORA: Oh, well, don't be alarmed! You couldn't know that Torvald had forbidden them. I must tell you that he's afraid they will spoil my teeth. But—once in a while—That's so, isn't it, Doctor Rank? Here [*puts a macaroon into his mouth*] you must have one,   480
too, Christine. And I shall have one, just a little one—or at most two. [*walking about*] I am tremendously happy. There is just one thing in the world now that I should dearly love to do.

RANK: Well, what is that?

NORA: It's something I should dearly love to say so Torvald could hear me.   485

RANK: Well, why can't you say it?

NORA: No, I daren't; it's so shocking.

MRS. LINDE: Shocking?

RANK: Well, I should not advise you to say it. Still, with us you might. What is it you would so much like to say so Torvald could hear?   490

NORA: I should just love to say—Well, I'm damned!

RANK: Are you mad?

MRS. LINDE: Nora, dear—!

RANK: Say it, here he is!

NORA: [*hiding the packet*] Hush! Hush! Hush! [HELMER *comes out of his room, with his coat*   495
over his arm and his hat in his hand.]

NORA: Well, Torvald dear, have you got rid of him?

HELMER: Yes, he's gone.

NORA: Let me introduce you—this is Christine, who has come to town.

HELMER: Christine—? Excuse me, but I don't know—   500

NORA: Mrs. Linde, dear; Christine Linde.

HELMER: Of course. A school friend of my wife, I presume?

MRS. LINDE: Yes, we've known each other since then.

NORA: And just think, she's taken a long journey in order to see you.

HELMER: What do you mean?   505

MRS. LINDE: No, really I—

NORA: Christine is tremendously clever at office work and she's frightfully anxious to work under some clever man, so as to improve—

HELMER: Very sensible, Mrs. Linde.

NORA: And when she heard you had been appointed manager of the Bank—the news was   510
telegraphed, you know—she travelled here as quick as she could, Torvald, I'm sure
you will be able to do something for Christine, for my sake, won't you?

HELMER: Well, it is not altogether impossible. I presume you are a widow, Mrs. Linde?

MRS. LINDE: Yes.

HELMER: And have had some experience of office work?   515

MRS. LINDE: Yes, a fair amount.

HELMER: Ah! well, it's very likely I may be able to find something for you.

NORA: [*clapping her hands*] What did I tell you? What did I tell you?

HELMER: You have just come at a fortunate moment, Mrs. Linde.

MRS. LINDE: How am I to thank you?   520

HELMER: There's no need. [*puts on his coat*] But to-day you must excuse me—

RANK: Wait a minute, I'll come with you. [*brings his fur coat from the hall and warms it at
the fire*]

NORA: Don't be long away, Torvald dear.

HELMER: About an hour, not more.   525

NORA: Are you going, too, Christine?

MRS. LINDE: [*putting on her cloak*] Yes, I must go and look for a room.

HELMER: Oh, well then, we can walk together.

NORA: [*helping her*] What a pity it is we are so short of space here; I am afraid it is impossible
for us—   530

MRS. LINDE: Please don't think of it! Good-bye, Nora dear, and many thanks.

NORA: Good-bye for the present. Of course you will come back this evening. And you,
too, Doctor Rank. What do you say? If you are well enough? Oh, you must be! Wrap
yourself up well. [*They go to the door all talking together. Children's voices are heard on
the staircase.*]   535

NORA: There they are. There they are! [*She runs to open the door. The* NURSE *comes in with
the children.*] Come in! Come in! [*stoops and kisses them*] Oh, you sweet blessings!
Look at them, Christine! Aren't they darlings?

RANK: Don't let's stand here in the draught.

HELMER: Come along, Mrs. Linde; the place will only be bearable for a mother now!   540
[RANK, HELMER, *and* MRS. LINDE *go downstairs. The* NURSE *comes forward with
the children;* NORA *shuts the hall door.*]

NORA: How fresh and well you look! Such red cheeks!—like apples and roses. [*The children
all talk at once while she speaks to them.*] Have you had great fun? That's splendid!
What, you pulled both Emmy and Bob along on the sled?—both at once?—that *was*   545
good. You are a clever boy, Ivar. Let me take her for a little, Anne. My sweet little
baby doll! [*takes the baby from the* MAID *and dances it up and down*] Yes, yes, mother
will dance with Bob, too. What! Have you been snowballing? I wish I had been

there, too! No, no, I will take their things off, Anne; please let me do it, it's such fun. Go in now, you look half frozen. There's some hot coffee for you on the stove.   550

[*The* NURSE *goes into the room on the left.* NORA *takes off the children's things and throws them about, while they all talk to her at once.*]

NORA: Really! Did a big dog run after you? But it didn't bite you? No, dogs don't bite nice little dolly children. You mustn't look at the parcels, Ivar. What are they? Ah, I daresay you would like to know. No, no—it's something nasty! Come, let us have a game! What shall we play? Hide-and-Seek? Yes, we'll play Hide-and-Seek. Bob shall hide first. Must I hide? Very well, I'll hide first. [*She and the children laugh and shout, and*   555 *romp in and out of the room; at last* NORA *hides under the table, the children rush in and look for her, but do not see her; they hear her smothered laughter, run to the table, lift up the cloth and find her. Shouts of laughter. She crawls forward and pretends to frighten them. Fresh laughter. Meanwhile there has been a knock at the hall door, but none of them has noticed it. The door is half opened, and* KROGSTAD *appears. He waits*   560 *a little; the game goes on.*]

KROGSTAD: Excuse me, Mrs. Helmer.

NORA: [*with a stifled cry, turns round and gets up on to her knees*] Ah! What do you want?

KROGSTAD: Excuse me, the outer door was ajar; I suppose someone forgot to shut it.

NORA: [*rising*] My husband is out, Mr. Krogstad.   565

KROGSTAD: I know that.

NORA: What do you want here, then?

KROGSTAD: A word with you.

NORA: With me?—[*to the children, gently*] Go in to nurse. What? No, the strange man won't do mother any harm. When he's gone we will have another game. [*She takes*   570 *the children into the room on the left, and shuts the door after them.*] You want to speak to me?

KROGSTAD: Yes, I do.

NORA: To-day? It is not the first of the month yet.

KROGSTAD: No, it is Christmas Eve, and it will depend on yourself what sort of a Christmas   575 you will spend.

NORA: What do you want? To-day it is absolutely impossible for me—

KROGSTAD: We won't talk about that till later on. This is something different. I presume you can give me a moment?

NORA: Yes—yes, I can—although—   580

KROGSTAD: Good. I was in Olsen's Restaurant and saw your husband going down the street—

NORA: Yes?

KROGSTAD: With a lady.

NORA: What then?   585

KROGSTAD: May I make so bold as to ask if it was a Mrs. Linde?

NORA: It was.

KROGSTAD: Just arrived in town?

NORA: Yes, to-day.

KROGSTAD: She's a great friend of yours, isn't she?   590

NORA: She is. But I don't see—

KROGSTAD: I knew her, too, once upon a time.

NORA: I'm aware of that.

KROGSTAD: Are you? So you know all about it; I thought as much. Then I can ask you, without beating about the bush—is Mrs. Linde to have an appointment in the Bank?   595

NORA: What right have you to question me, Mr. Krogstad?—You, one of my husband's subordinates! But since you ask, you shall know. Yes, Mrs. Linde *is* to have an appointment. And it was I who pleaded her cause, Mr. Krogstad, let me tell you that.

KROGSTAD: I was right in what I thought, then.

NORA: [*walking up and down*] Sometimes one has a tiny little bit of influence, I should 600 hope. Because one is a woman, it doesn't necessarily follow that—. When anyone is in a subordinate position, Mr. Krogstad, they should really be careful to avoid offending anyone who—who—

KROGSTAD: Who has influence?

NORA: Exactly. 605

KROGSTAD: [*changing his tone*] Mrs. Helmer, you will be so good as to use your influence on my behalf.

NORA: What? What do you mean?

KROGSTAD: You will be so kind as to see that I am allowed to keep my subordinate position in the Bank. 610

NORA: What do you mean by that? Who proposes to take your post away from you?

KROGSTAD: Oh, there is no necessity to keep up the pretence of ignorance. I can quite understand that your friend is not very anxious to expose herself to the chance of rubbing shoulders with me; and I quite understand, too, whom I have to thank for being discharged. 615

NORA: But I assure you—

KROGSTAD: Very likely; but, to come to the point, the time has come when I should advise you to use your influence to prevent that.

NORA: But, Mr. Krogstad, I *have* no influence.

KROGSTAD: Haven't you? I thought you said yourself just now— 620

NORA: Naturally I didn't mean you to put that construction on it. I! What should make you think I have any influence of that kind with my husband?

KROGSTAD: Oh, I have known your husband from our student days. I don't suppose he's any more unassailable than other husbands.

NORA: If you speak slightingly of my husband, I shall turn you out of the house. 625

KROGSTAD: You are bold, Mrs. Helmer.

NORA: I'm not afraid of you any longer. As soon as the New Year comes, I shall in a very short time be free of the whole thing.

KROGSTAD: [*controlling himself*] Listen to me, Mrs. Helmer. If necessary, I am prepared to fight for my small post in the Bank as if I were fighting for my life. 630

NORA: So it seems.

KROGSTAD: It's not only for the sake of the money; indeed, that weighs least with me in the matter. There's another reason—well, I may as well tell you. My position is this. I daresay you know, like everybody else, that once, many years ago, I was guilty of an indiscretion. 635

NORA: I think I've heard something of the kind.

KROGSTAD: The matter never came into court; but every way seemed to be closed to me after that. So I took to the business that you know of. I had to do something; and, honestly, I don't think I've been one of the worst. But now I must cut myself free from all that. My sons are growing up; for their sake I must try and win back as much 640 respect as I can in the town. This post in the Bank was like the first step up for me— and now your husband is going to kick me downstairs again into the mud.

NORA: But you must believe me, Mr. Krogstad; it's not in my power to help you at all.

KROGSTAD: Then it's because you haven't the will; but I have means to compel you.

NORA: You don't mean that you will tell my husband that I owe you money? 645

KROGSTAD: Hm!—Suppose I were to tell him?

NORA: It would be shameful of you. [*sobbing*] To think of his learning my secret, which has been my joy and pride, in such an ugly, clumsy way—that he should learn it from you! And it would put me in a horribly disagreeable position—

KROGSTAD: Only disagreeable? 650

NORA: [*impetuously*] Well, do it, then!—and it will be the worse for you. My husband will see for himself what a blackguard you are, and you certainly won't keep your post then.

KROGSTAD: I asked you if it was only a disagreeable scene at home that you were afraid of?

NORA: If my husband does get to know of it, of course he will at once pay you what is still owing, and we shall have nothing more to do with you. 655

KROGSTAD: [*coming a step nearer*] Listen to me, Mrs. Helmer. Either you have a very bad memory or you know very little of business. I shall be obliged to remind you of a few details.

NORA: What do you mean?

KROGSTAD: When your husband was ill, you came to me to borrow forty-eight hundred 660 crowns.

NORA: I didn't know any one else to go to.

KROGSTAD: I promised to get you that amount—

NORA: Yes, and you did so.

KROGSTAD: I promised to get you that amount, on certain conditions. Your mind was so 665 taken up with your husband's illness, and were so anxious to get the money for your journey, that you seem to have paid no attention to the conditions of our bargain. Therefore it will not be amiss if I remind you of them. Now, I promised to get the money on the security of a bond which I drew up.

NORA: Yes, and which I signed. 670

KROGSTAD: Good. But below your signature there were a few lines constituting your father a surety for the money; those lines your father should have signed.

NORA: Should? He did sign them.

KROGSTAD: I had left the date blank; that is to say your father should himself have inserted the date on which he signed the paper. Do you remember that? 675

NORA: Yes, I think I remember—

KROGSTAD: Then I gave you the bond to send by post to your father. Is that not so?

NORA: Yes.

KROGSTAD: And you naturally did so at once, because five or six days afterwards you brought me the bond with your father's signature. And then I gave you the money. 680

NORA: Well, haven't I been paying it off regularly?

KROGSTAD: Fairly so, yes. But—to come back to the matter in hand—that must have been a very trying time for you, Mrs. Helmer?

NORA: It was, indeed.

KROGSTAD: Your father was very ill, wasn't he? 685

NORA: He was very near his end.

KROGSTAD: And died soon afterwards?

NORA: Yes.

KROGSTAD: Tell me, Mrs. Helmer, can you by any chance remember what day your father died?—on what day of the month, I mean. 690

NORA: Papa died on the 29th of September.

KROGSTAD: That is correct; I have ascertained it for myself. And, as that is so, there is a discrepancy [*taking a paper from his pocket*] which I cannot account for.

NORA: What discrepancy? I don't know—

KROGSTAD: The discrepancy consists, Mrs. Helmer, in the fact that your father signed this 695 bond three days after his death.

NORA: What do you mean? I don't understand—

KROGSTAD: Your father died on the 29th of September. But, look here; your father has
dated his signature the 2nd of October. It is a discrepancy, isn't it? [NORA *is silent.*]
Can you explain it to me? [NORA *is still silent.*] It is a remarkable thing, too, that the   700
words "2nd of October," as well as the year, are not written in your father's handwriting but in one that I think I know. Well, of course it can be explained; your father
may have forgotten to date his signature, and someone else may have dated it before
they knew of his death. There is no harm in that. It all depends on the signature of the
name; and *that* is genuine, I suppose, Mrs. Helmer? It was your father himself who   705
signed his name here?

NORA: [*after a short pause, throws her head up and looks defiantly at him*] No, it was not. It
was I that wrote papa's name.

KROGSTAD: Are you aware that is a dangerous confession?

NORA: In what way? You'll have your money soon.   710

KROGSTAD: Let me ask you a question; why did you not send the paper to your father?

NORA: It was impossible; papa was so ill. If I'd asked him for his signature, I should have
had to tell him what the money was to be used for; and when he was so ill himself I
couldn't tell him that my husband's life was in danger—it was impossible.

KROGSTAD: It would have been better for you if you had given up your trip abroad.   715

NORA: No, that was impossible. That trip was to save my husband's life; I couldn't give
that up.

KROGSTAD: But did it never occur to you that you were committing a fraud on me?

NORA: I couldn't take that into account; I didn't trouble myself about you at all. I couldn't
bear you, because you put so many heartless difficulties in my way, although you   720
knew what a dangerous condition my husband was in.

KROGSTAD: Mrs. Helmer, you evidently do not realize clearly what it is that you have been
guilty of. But I can assure you that my one false step, which lost me all my reputation, was nothing more or nothing worse than what you have done.

NORA: You? Do you ask me to believe that you were brave enough to run a risk to save   725
your wife's life?

KROGSTAD: The law cares nothing about motives.

NORA: Then it must be a very foolish law.

KROGSTAD: Foolish or not, it is the law by which you will be judged, if I produce this
paper in court.   730

NORA: I don't believe it. Is a daughter not to be allowed to spare her dying father anxiety
and care? Is a wife not to be allowed to save her husband's life? I don't know much
about law; but I am certain that there must be laws permitting such things as that.
Have you no knowledge of such laws—you who are a lawyer? You must be a very
poor lawyer, Mr. Krogstad.   735

KROGSTAD: Maybe. But matters of business—such business as you and I have had
together—do you think I don't understand that? Very well. Do as you please. But let
me tell you this—if I lose my position a second time, you shall lose yours with me.
[*He bows, and goes out through the hall.*]

NORA: [*appears buried in thought for a short time, then tosses her head*] Nonsense! Trying to   740
frighten me like that!—I am not so silly as he thinks. [*begins to busy herself putting the
children's things in order*] And yet—? No, it's impossible! I did it for love's sake.

THE CHILDREN: [*in the doorway on the left*] Mother, the stranger has gone out through
the gate.

NORA: Yes, dears, I know. But, don't tell anyone about the stranger. Do you hear? Not even   745
papa.

CHILDREN: No, mother; but will you come and play again?

NORA: No, no—not now.

CHILDREN: But, mother, you promised.

NORA: Yes, but I can't now. Go in; I have such a lot to do. Go in, my sweet little darlings. 750
[*She gets them into the room by degrees and shuts the door on them; then sits down on the sofa, takes up a piece of needlework and sews a few stitches, but soon stops.*] No! [*throws down the work, gets up, goes to the hall door and calls out*] Helen! bring the tree in. [*goes to the table on the left, opens a drawer, and stops again*] No, no! it is quite impossible! 755

MAID: [*coming in with the tree*] Where shall I put it, ma'am?

NORA: Here, in the middle of the floor.

MAID: Shall I get you anything else?

NORA: No, thank you. I have all I want.

[Exit MAID.]

NORA: [*begins dressing the tree*] A candle here—and flowers here—. The horrible man! It's 760
all nonsense—there's nothing wrong. The tree shall be splendid! I'll do everything I can think of to please you, Torvald!—I'll sing for you, dance for you—[HELMER *comes in with some papers under his arm.*] Oh! are you back already?

HELMER: Yes. Has anyone been here?

NORA: Here? No. 765

HELMER: That's strange. I saw Krogstad going out of the gate.

NORA: Did you? Oh yes, I forgot, Krogstad was here for a moment.

HELMER: Nora, I can see from your manner that he has been here begging you to say a good word for him.

NORA: Yes. 770

HELMER: And you were to appear to do it of your own accord; you were to conceal from me the fact of his having been here; didn't he beg that of you, too?

NORA: Yes, Torvald, but—

HELMER: Nora, Nora, and you would be a party to that sort of thing? To have any talk with a man like that, and give him any sort of promise? And to tell me a lie into the 775
bargain?

NORA: A lie—?

HELMER: Didn't you tell me no one had been here? [*shakes his finger at her*] My little song-bird must never do that again. A song-bird must have a clean beak to chirp with—no false notes! [*puts his arm round her waist*] That's so, isn't it? Yes, I'm sure it is. [*lets her* 780
go] We will say no more about it. [*sits down by the stove*] How warm and snug it is here! [*turns over his papers*]

NORA: [*after a short pause, during which she busies herself with the Christmas tree*] Torvald!

HELMER: Yes.

NORA: I am looking forward tremendously to the fancy dress ball at the Stenborgs' the day 785
after to-morrow.

HELMER: And I'm tremendously curious to see what you're going to surprise me with.

NORA: It was very silly of me to want to do that.

HELMER: What do you mean?

NORA: I can't hit upon anything that will do; everything I think of seems so silly and 790
insignificant.

HELMER: Does my little Nora acknowledge that at last?

NORA: [*standing behind his chair with her arms on the back of it*] Are you very busy, Torvald?

HELMER: Well—

NORA: What are all those papers? 795

HELMER: Bank business.

NORA: Already?

HELMER: I have got authority from the retiring manager to undertake the necessary changes in the staff and in the reorganization of the work; and I must make use of the Christmas week for that, so as to have everything in order for the new year. 800

NORA: Then that was why this poor Krogstad—

HELMER: Hm!

NORA: [*leans against the back of his chair and strokes his hair*] If you hadn't been so busy I should have asked you a tremendously big favour, Torvald.

HELMER: What's that? Tell me. 805

NORA: There is no one has such good taste as you. And I do so want to look nice at the costume ball. Torvald, couldn't you take me in hand and decide what I shall go as, and what sort of a dress I shall wear?

HELMER: Aha! So my obstinate little woman is obliged to get someone to come to her rescue? 810

NORA: Yes, Torvald, I can't get along at all without your help.

HELMER: Very well, I'll think it over, we shall manage to hit on something.

NORA: That is nice of you. [*goes to the Christmas tree. A short pause.*] How pretty the red flowers look—. But, tell me, was it really something very bad that this Krogstad was guilty of? 815

HELMER: He forged someone's name. Have you any idea what that means?

NORA: Isn't it possible that he was driven to do it by necessity?

HELMER: Yes; or, as in so many cases, by imprudence. I am not so heartless as to condemn a man altogether because of a single false step of that kind.

NORA: No, you wouldn't, would you, Torvald? 820

HELMER: Many a man has been able to retrieve his character, if he has openly confessed his fault and taken his punishment.

NORA: Punishment—?

HELMER: But Krogstad did nothing of that sort; he got himself out of it by a cunning trick, and that is why he has gone under altogether. 825

NORA: But do you think it would—?

HELMER: Just think how a guilty man like that has to lie and play the hypocrite with everyone, how he has to wear a mask in the presence of those near and dear to him, even before his own wife and children. And about the children—that's the most terrible part of it all, Nora.

NORA: How? 830

HELMER: Because such an atmosphere of lies infects and poisons the whole life of a home. Each breath the children take in such a house is full of the germs of evil.

NORA: [*coming nearer him*] Are you sure of that?

HELMER: My dear, I have often seen it in the course of my life as a lawyer. Almost everyone who has gone to the bad early in life has had a deceitful mother. 835

NORA: Why do you only say—mother?

HELMER: It seems most commonly to be the mother's influence, though naturally a bad father's would have the same result. Every lawyer is familiar with the fact. This Krogstad, now, has been persistently poisoning his own children with lies and dissimulation; that's why I say he has lost all moral character. [*holds out his hands to her*] That's why 840 my sweet little Nora must promise me not to plead his cause. Give me your hand on it. Come, come, what's this? Give me your hand. There now, that's settled. I assure you it would be quite impossible for me to work with him; I literally feel physically ill when I am in the company of such people.

NORA: [*takes her hand out of his and goes to the opposite side of the Christmas tree*] How hot 845 it is in here; and I have such a lot to do.

HELMER: [*getting up and putting his papers in order*] Yes, and I must try and read through some of these before dinner; and I must think about your costume, too. And it's just possible I may have something ready in gold paper to hang up on the tree. [*puts his hand on her head*] My precious little singing-bird! [*He goes into his room and shuts the* 850 *door after him.*]

NORA: [*after a pause, whispers*] No, no—it isn't true. It's impossible; it must be impossible.

[*The* NURSE *opens the door on the left.*]

NURSE: The little ones are begging so hard to be allowed to come in to mamma.

NORA: No, no, no! Don't let them come in to me! You stay with them, Anne.

NURSE: Very well, ma'am. [*shuts the door*] 855

NORA: [*pale with terror*] Deprave my little children? Poison my home? [*A short pause. Then she tosses her head.*] It's not true. It can't possibly be true.

ACT II

THE SAME SCENE———*The Christmas tree is in the corner by the piano, stripped of its ornaments and with burnt-down candle-ends on its disheveled branches.* NORA's *cloak and hat are lying on the sofa. She is alone in the room, walking about uneasily. She stops by the sofa and takes up her cloak.*

NORA: [*drops the cloak*] Someone is coming now! [*goes to the door and listens*] No—it's no one. Of course, no one will come to-day, Christmas Day—nor to-morrow, either. But, perhaps—[*opens the door and looks out*] No, nothing in the mail box; it's quite empty. [*comes forward*] What rubbish! Of course he can't be in earnest about it. Such a thing couldn't happen; it's impossible—I have three little children. 5

[*Enter the* NURSE *from the room on the left, carrying a big cardboard box.*]

NURSE: At last I've found the box with the fancy dress.

NORA: Thanks; put it on the table.

NURSE: [*doing so*] But it's very much in want of mending.

NORA: I should like to tear it into a hundred thousand pieces.

NURSE: What an idea! It can easily be put in order—just a little patience. 10

NORA: Yes, I'll go and get Mrs. Linde to come and help me with it.

NURSE: What, out again? In this horrible weather? You'll catch cold, ma'am, and make yourself ill.

NORA: Well, worse than that might happen. How are the children?

NURSE: The poor little souls are playing with their Christmas presents, but— 15

NORA: Do they ask much for me?

NURSE: You see, they're so accustomed to have their mamma with them.

NORA: Yes, but nurse, I shan't be able to be so much with them now as I was before.

NURSE: Oh well, young children easily get accustomed to anything.

NORA: Do you think so? Do you think they would forget their mother if she went away 20 altogether?

NURSE: Good heavens!—went away altogether?

NORA: Nurse, I want you to tell me something I have often wondered about—how could you have the heart to put your own child out among strangers?

NURSE: I was obliged to, if I wanted to be little Nora's nurse.   25
NORA: Yes, but how could you be willing to do it?
NURSE: What, when I was going to get such a good place by it? A poor girl who has got into
    trouble should be glad to. Besides, that wicked man didn't do a single thing for me.
NORA: But I suppose your daughter has quite forgotten you.
NURSE: No, indeed she hasn't. She wrote to me when she was confirmed, and when she   30
    was married.
NORA: [*putting her arms around her neck*] Dear old Anne, you were a good mother to me
    when I was little.
NURSE: Little Nora, poor dear, had no other mother but me.
NORA: And if my little ones had no other mother, I'm sure you would—. What nonsense   35
    I'm talking! [*opens the box*] Go in to them. Now I must—. You will see to-morrow
    how charming I'll look.
NURSE: I'm sure there will be no one at the ball so charming as you, ma'am. [*goes into the
    room on the left*]
NORA: [*begins to unpack the box, but soon pushes it away from her*] If only I dared go out. If   40
    only no one would come. If only I could be sure nothing would happen here in the
    meantime. Stuff and nonsense! No one will come. Only I mustn't think about it. I'll
    brush my muff. What lovely, lovely gloves! Out of my thoughts, out of my thoughts!
    One, two, three, four, five, six—[*screams*] Ah! there is someone coming—. [*makes a
    movement towards the door, but stands irresolute*]   45

[*Enter* MRS. LINDE *from the hall, where she has taken off her cloak and hat.*]

NORA: Oh, it's you, Christine. There is no one else out there, is there? How good of you
    to come!
MRS. LINDE: I heard you were up asking for me.
NORA: Yes, I was passing by. As a matter of fact, it's something you could help me with. Let
    us sit down here on the sofa. Look here. To-morrow evening there is to be a costume   50
    ball at the Stenborgs', who live above us; and Torvald wants me to go as a Neapolitan
    fisher-girl, and dance the Tarantella that I learned on Capri.
MRS. LINDE: I see; you're going to perform a character.
NORA: Yes, Torvald wants me to. Look, here's the dress; Torvald had it made for me there,
    but now it's all so torn, and I haven't any idea—.   55
MRS. LINDE: We'll easily put that right. It's only some of the trimming come unsewn here
    and there. Needle and thread? Now then, that's all we need.
NORA: It *is* nice of you.
MRS. LINDE: [*sewing*] So you're going to be dressed up to-morrow, Nora. I'll tell you
    what—I'll come in for a moment and see you in your fine feathers. But I have com-   60
    pletely forgotten to thank you for a delightful evening yesterday.
NORA: [*gets up, and crosses the stage*] Well, I don't think yesterday was as pleasant as usual.
    You ought to have come to town a little earlier, Christine. Certainly Torvald does
    understand how to make a house attractive.
MRS. LINDE: And so do you, it seems to me; you are not your father's daughter for nothing.   65
    But tell me, is Doctor Rank always as depressed as he was yesterday?
NORA: No; yesterday it was very noticeable. I must tell you that he suffers from a very
    dangerous disease. He has tuberculosis of the spine, poor creature. His father was a
    horrible man who committed all sorts of excesses; and that's why his son was sickly
    from childhood, do you understand?   70
MRS. LINDE: [*dropping her sewing*] But my dearest Nora, how do you know anything about
    such things?
NORA: [*walking about*] Pooh! When you have three children, you get visits now and then

from—from married women, who know something of medical matters, and they talk about one thing and another. 75

MRS. LINDE: [*goes on sewing. A short silence*] Does Doctor Rank come here every day?

NORA: Every day regularly. He's Torvald's best friend, and a great friend of mine, too. He's just like one of the family.

MRS. LINDE: But tell me this—is he perfectly sincere? I mean, isn't he the kind of man that is very anxious to make himself agreeable? 80

NORA: Not in the least. What makes you think that?

MRS. LINDE: When you introduced him to me yesterday, he declared he had often heard my name mentioned in this house; but afterwards I noticed that your husband hadn't the slightest idea who I was. So how could Doctor Rank—?

NORA: That's quite right, Christine. Torvald is so absurdly fond of me that he wants me 85 absolutely to himself, as he says. At first he used to seem almost jealous if I mentioned any of my friends back home, so naturally I gave up doing so. But I often talk about such things with Doctor Rank, because he likes hearing about them.

MRS. LINDE: Listen to me, Nora. You are still very like a child in many things, and I'm older than you in many ways and have a little more experience. Let me tell you this— 90 you ought to make an end of it with Doctor Rank.

NORA: What ought I to make an end of?

MRS. LINDE: Of two things, I think. Yesterday you talked some nonsense about a rich admirer who was to leave you money—

NORA: An admirer who doesn't exist, unfortunately! But what then? 95

MRS. LINDE: Is Doctor Rank well off?

NORA: Yes, he is.

MRS. LINDE: And has no one to provide for?

NORA: No, no one; but—

MRS. LINDE: And comes here every day? 100

NORA: Yes, I told you so.

MRS. LINDE: But how can this well-bred man be so tactless?

NORA: I don't understand you at all.

MRS. LINDE: Don't pretend, Nora. Do you suppose I don't guess who lent you the forty-eight hundred crowns? 105

NORA: Are you out of your senses? How can you think of such a thing! A friend of ours, who comes here every day! Do you realize what a horribly painful position that would be?

MRS. LINDE: Then it really isn't he?

NORA: No certainly not. It would never have entered my head for a moment. Besides, he had no money to lend then; he came into his money afterwards. 110

MRS. LINDE: Well, I think that was lucky for you, my dear Nora.

NORA: No, it would never have come into my head to ask Doctor Rank. Although I am quite sure that if I had asked him—

MRS. LINDE: But of course you won't.

NORA: Of course not. I have no reason to think it could possibly be necessary. But I'm 115 quite sure that if I told Doctor Rank—

MRS. LINDE: Behind your husband's back?

NORA: I must make an end of it with the other one, and that will be behind his back, too. I must make an end of it with him.

MRS. LINDE: Yes, that's what I told you yesterday, but— 120

NORA: [*walking up and down*] A man can put a thing like that straight much easier than a woman—

MRS. LINDE: One's husband, yes.

NORA: Nonsense! [*standing still*] When you pay off a debt you get your bond back, don't
you? 125

MRS. LINDE: Yes, as a matter of course.

NORA: And can tear it into a hundred thousand pieces, and burn it—the nasty dirty paper!

MRS. LINDE: [*looks hard at her, lays down her sewing and gets up slowly*] Nora, you are keeping something from me.

NORA: Do I look as if I were? 130

MRS. LINDE: Something has happened to you since yesterday morning. Nora, what is it?

NORA: [*going nearer to her*] Christine! [*listens*] Hush! There's Torvald come home. Do you
mind going in to the children for the present? Torvald can't bear to see dressmaking
going on. Let Anne help you.

MRS. LINDE: [*gathering some of the things together*] Certainly—but I'm not leaving till we've 135
had it out with one another. [*She goes into the room on the left, as* HELMER *comes in
from the hall.*]

NORA: [*going up to* HELMER] I have wanted you so much, Torvald dear.

HELMER: Was that the dressmaker?

NORA: No, it was Christine; she is helping me to put my costume in order. You will see I 140
shall look quite smart.

HELMER: Wasn't that a happy thought of mine, now?

NORA: Splendid! But don't you think it's nice of me, too, to do as you wish?

HELMER: Nice?—because you do as your husband wishes? Well, well, you little rogue, I'm
sure you did not mean it in that way. But I'm not going to disturb you; you will want 145
to be trying on your costume, I expect.

NORA: I suppose you're going to work.

HELMER: Yes. [*shows her a bundle of papers*] Look at that. I have just been to the Bank.
[*turns to go into his room*]

NORA: Torvald. 150

HELMER: Yes.

NORA: If your little squirrel were to ask you something very, very prettily—?

HELMER: What then?

NORA: Would you do it?

HELMER: I should like to hear what it is, first. 155

NORA: Your squirrel would run about and do all her tricks if you would be nice, and do
what she wants.

HELMER: Speak plainly.

NORA: Your skylark would chirp about in every room, with her song rising and falling—

HELMER: Well, my skylark does that anyhow. 160

NORA: I'd be a fairy and dance for you in the moonlight, Torvald.

HELMER: Nora—you surely don't mean that request you made of me this morning?

NORA: [*going near him*] Yes, Torvald, I beg you so earnestly—

HELMER: Have you really the nerve to bring up that question again?

NORA: Yes, dear, you *must* do as I ask; you *must* let Krogstad keep his post in the Bank. 165

HELMER: My dear Nora, it is his post that I have arranged for Mrs. Linde to have.

NORA: Yes, you've been awfully kind about that; but you could just as well dismiss some
other clerk instead of Krogstad.

HELMER: This is simply incredible obstinacy! Because you chose to give him a thoughtless
promise that you would speak for him, I am expected to— 170

NORA: That isn't the reason, Torvald. It is for your own sake. This fellow writes in the most
scurrilous newspapers; you've told me so yourself. He can do you an unspeakable
amount of harm. I am frightened to death of him—

HELMER: Ah, I understand; it is recollections of the past that scare you.

NORA: What do you mean? 175

HELMER: Naturally you are thinking of your father.

NORA: Yes—yes, of course. Just recall in your mind what these malicious creatures wrote in the papers about papa, and how horribly they slandered him. I believe they would have procured his dismissal if the Department had not sent you over to inquire into it, and if you had not been so kindly disposed and helpful to him. 180

HELMER: My little Nora, there is an important difference between your father and me. Your father's reputation as a public official was not above suspicion. Mine is, and I hope it will continue to be so, as long as I hold my office.

NORA: You never can tell what mischief these men may contrive. We ought to be so well off, so snug and happy here in our peaceful home, and have no cares—you and I and 185 the children, Torvald! That's why I beg you so earnestly—

HELMER: And it's just by interceding for him that you make it impossible for me to keep him. It's already known at the Bank that I mean to dismiss Krogstad. Is it to get about now that the new manager has changed his mind at his wife's bidding—

NORA: And what if it did? 190

HELMER: Of course!—if only this obstinate little person can get her way! Do you suppose I'm going to make myself ridiculous before my entire staff, to let people think that I am a man to be swayed by all sorts of outside influence? I should very soon feel the consequences of that, I can tell you! And besides, there is something that makes it quite impossible for me to have Krogstad in the Bank as long as I am manager. 195

NORA: Whatever is that?

HELMER: His moral failings I might perhaps have overlooked, if necessary—

NORA: Yes, you could—couldn't you?

HELMER: And I hear he is a good worker, too. But I knew him when we were boys. It was one of those rash friendships that so often prove an embarrassment later in life. I may 200 as well tell you plainly, we were once on first-name terms with one another. But this tactless fellow lays no restraint on himself when other people are present. On the contrary, he thinks it gives him the right to adopt a familiar tone with me, and every minute it is "I say, Helmer, old fellow!" and that sort of thing. It's extremely painful for me. He would make my position in the Bank intolerable. 205

NORA: Torvald, I don't believe you mean that.

HELMER: Don't you? Why not?

NORA: Because it is such a petty way of looking at things.

HELMER: What are you saying? Petty? Do you think I'm petty?

NORA: No, just the opposite, dear—it's exactly for that reason. 210

HELMER: It's the same thing. You say my point of view is petty, so I must be so, too. Petty. Very well—I must put an end to this. [*goes to the hall door and calls*] Helen!

NORA: What are you going to do?

HELMER: [*looking among his papers*] Settle it. [*Enter* MAID.] Look here; take this letter and go downstairs with it at once. Find a messenger and tell him to deliver it, and be 215 quick. The address is on it, and here is the money.

MAID: Very well, sir. [*exit with the letter*]

HELMER: [*putting his papers together*] Now then, little Miss Obstinate.

NORA: [*breathless*] Torvald—what was that letter?

HELMER: Krogstad's dismissal. 220

NORA: Call her back, Torvald! There is still time. Oh Torvald, call her back! Do it for my sake—for your own sake—for the children's sake! Do you hear me, Torvald? Call her back! You don't know what that letter can bring upon us.

HELMER: It's too late.

NORA: Yes, it's too late. 225

HELMER: My dear Nora, I can forgive the anxiety you are in, although really it is an insult to me. It is, indeed. Isn't it an insult to think that I should be afraid of a starving journalist's vengeance? But I forgive you nevertheless, because it's such eloquent witness to your great love for me. [*takes her in his arms*] And that's as it should be, my own darling Nora. Come what will, you may be sure I'll have both courage and strength if they be 230 needed. You'll see I am man enough to take everything upon myself.

NORA: [*in a horror-stricken voice*] What do you mean by that?

HELMER: Everything, I say

NORA: [*recovering herself*] You'll never have to do that.

HELMER: That's right. Well, we'll share it, Nora, as man and wife should. That's how it 235 should be. [*caressing her*] Are you happy now? There, there!—not these frightened dove's eyes! The whole thing is only the wildest fantasy—Now, you must go and play through the Tarantella and practice with your tambourine. I'll go into the inner office and shut the door, and I'll hear nothing, you can make as much noise as you please. [*turns back at the door*] And when Rank comes, tell him where he can find me. 240 [*nods to her, takes his papers and goes into his room and shuts the door after him*]

NORA: [*bewildered with anxiety, stands as if rooted to the spot, and whispers*] He was capable of doing it. He will do it. He will do it in spite of everything—No, not that! Never, never! Anything rather than that! Oh, for some help, some way out of it! [*the doorbell rings*] Doctor Rank! Anything rather than that—anything, whatever it is! [*She puts 245 her hands over her face, pulls herself together, goes to the door and opens it. RANK is standing without, hanging up his coat. During the following dialogue it begins to grow dark.*]

NORA: Good-day, Doctor Rank. I knew your ring. But you mustn't go into Torvald now; I think he is busy with something. 250

RANK: And you?

NORA: [*brings him in and shuts the door after him*] Oh, you know very well I always have time for you.

RANK: Thank you. I shall make use of as much of it as I can.

NORA: What do you mean by that? As much of it as you can? 255

RANK: Well, does that alarm you?

NORA: It was such a strange way of putting it. Is anything likely to happen?

RANK: Nothing but what I've long been prepared for. But I certainly didn't expect it to happen so soon.

NORA: [*gripping him by the arm*] What have you found out? Doctor Rank, you must tell me. 260

RANK: [*sitting down by the stove*] It's all up with me. And it can't be helped.

NORA: [*with a sigh of relief*] Is it about yourself?

RANK: Who else? It's no use lying to one's self. I am the most wretched of all my patients, Mrs. Helmer. Lately I've been taking stock of my internal economy. Bankrupt! Probably within a month I shall lie rotting in the churchyard. 265

NORA: What an ugly thing to say!

RANK: The thing itself is cursedly ugly, and the worst of it is that I'll have to face so much more that is ugly before that. I'll only make one more examination of myself; when I have done that, I'll know pretty certainly when the horrors of dissolution will begin. There's something I want to tell you. Helmer's sensitivity makes him disgusted at 270 everything that is ugly; I won't have him in my sickroom.

NORA: Oh, but, Doctor Rank—

RANK: I won't have him there. Not on any account. I bar my door to him. As soon as I'm quite certain that the worst has come, I'll send you my card with a black cross on it, and then you will know that the loathsome end has begun. 275

NORA: You are quite absurd to-day. And I wanted you so much to be in a really good humour.

RANK: With death stalking beside me?—To have to pay this penalty for another man's sin! Is there any justice in that? And in every single family, in one way or another, some such inexorable retribution is being exacted— 280

NORA: [*putting her hands over her ears*] Rubbish! Do talk of something cheerful.

RANK: Oh, it's a mere laughing matter, the whole thing. My poor innocent spine has to suffer for my father's youthful amusements.

NORA: [*sitting at the table on the left*] I suppose you mean that he was too partial to asparagus and paté de foie gras, don't you? 285

RANK: Yes, and to truffles.

NORA: Truffles, yes. And oysters, too, I suppose?

RANK: Oysters, of course, that goes without saying.

NORA: And heaps of port and champagne. It is sad that all these nice things should take their revenge on our bones. 290

RANK: Especially that they should revenge themselves on the unlucky bones of those who have not had the satisfaction of enjoying them.

NORA: Yes, that's the saddest part of it all.

RANK: [*with a searching look at her*] Hm!—

NORA: [*after a short pause*] Why did you smile? 295

RANK: No, it was you that laughed.

NORA: No, it was you that smiled, Doctor Rank!

RANK: [*rising*] You're a bigger tease than I thought.

NORA: I'm in a silly mood to-day.

RANK: So it seems. 300

NORA: [*putting her hands on his shoulders*] Dear, dear Doctor Rank, death mustn't take you away from Torvald and me.

RANK: It's a loss you would easily recover from. Those who are gone are soon forgotten.

NORA: [*looking at him anxiously*] Do you believe that?

RANK: People form new ties, and then— 305

NORA: Who will form new ties?

RANK: Both you and Helmer, when I'm gone. You yourself are already on the high road to it, I think. What did Mrs. Linde want here last night?

NORA: Oho!—you don't mean to say you're jealous of poor Christine?

RANK: Yes, I am. She'll be my successor in this house. When I'm done for, this woman 310 will—

NORA: Hush! don't speak so loud. She's in that room.

RANK: To-day again. There, you see.

NORA: She's only come to sew my costume for me. Bless my soul, how unreasonable you are! [*sits down on the sofa*] Be nice now, Doctor Rank, and to-morrow you will see 315 how beautifully I shall dance, and you can imagine I'm doing it all for you—and for Torvald, too, of course. [*takes various things out of the box*] Doctor Rank, come and sit down here, and I'll show you something.

RANK: [*sitting down*] What is it?

NORA: Just look at those! 320

RANK: Silk stockings.

NORA: Flesh-coloured. Aren't they lovely? It is so dark here now, but to-morrow—. No, no, no! you must only look at the feet. Oh well, you may have leave to look at the legs, too.

RANK: Hm!— 325

NORA: Why are you looking so critical? Don't you think they will fit me?

RANK: I have no means of forming an opinion about that.

NORA: [*looks at him for a moment*] For shame! [*hits him lightly on the ear with the stockings*] That's to punish you. [*folds them up again*]

RANK: And what other nice things am I to be allowed to see? 330

NORA: Not a single thing more, for being so naughty. [*She looks among the things, humming to herself.*]

RANK: [*after a short silence*] When I'm sitting here, talking to you as intimately as this, I can't imagine for a moment what would have become of me if I had never come into this house. 335

NORA: [*smiling*] I believe you do feel thoroughly at home with us.

RANK: [*in a lower voice, looking straight in front of him*] And to be obliged to leave it all—

NORA: Nonsense, you're not going to leave it.

RANK: [*as before*] And not be able to leave behind one the slightest token of one's gratitude, scarcely even a fleeting regret—nothing but an empty place which the first comer 340 can fill as well as any other.

NORA: And if I asked you now for a—? No!

RANK: For what?

NORA: For a big proof of your friendship—

RANK: Yes, yes! 345

NORA: I mean a tremendously big favour—

RANK: Would you really make me so happy for once?

NORA: Ah, but you don't know what it is yet.

RANK: No—but tell me.

NORA: I really can't, Doctor Rank. It's something out of all reason; it means advice, and 350 help, and a favour—

RANK: The bigger the better. I can't conceive what it is you mean. Do tell me. Haven't I your confidence?

NORA: More than anyone else. I know you are my truest and best friend, and so I'll tell you what it is. Well, Doctor Rank, it's something you must help me to prevent. You 355 know how devotedly, how inexpressibly deeply Torvald loves me; he would never for a moment hesitate to give his life for me.

RANK: [*leaning towards her*] Nora—do you think he is the only one—?

NORA: [*with a slight start*] The only one—?

RANK: The only one who would gladly give his life for your sake. 360

NORA: [*sadly*] Is that it?

RANK: I was determined you should know it before I went away, and there'll never be a better opportunity than this. Now you know it, Nora. And now you know, too, that you can trust me as you would trust no one else.

NORA: [*rises, deliberately and quietly*] Let me pass. 365

RANK: [*makes room for her to pass him, but sits still*] Nora!

NORA: [*at the hall door*] Helen, bring in the lamp. [*goes over to the stove*] Dear Doctor Rank, that was really horrid of you.

RANK: To have loved you as much as anyone else does? Was that horrid?

NORA: No, but to go and tell me so. There was really no need— 370

RANK: What do you mean? Did you know—? [MAID *enters with lamp, puts it down on the table, and goes out.*] Nora—Mrs. Helmer—tell me, had you any idea of this?

NORA: Oh, how do I know whether I had or whether I hadn't? I really can't tell you—To think you could be so clumsy, Doctor Rank! We were getting on so nicely.

RANK: Well, at all events you know now that you can command me, body and soul. So 375 won't you speak out?

NORA: [*looking at him*] After what happened?

RANK: I beg you to let me know what it is.

NORA: I can't tell you anything now.

RANK: Yes, yes. You mustn't punish me in that way. Let me have permission to do for you   380
whatever a man may do.

NORA: You can do nothing for me now. Besides, I really don't need any help at all. You will
find the whole thing is merely fancy on my part. It really is so—of course it is! [*Sits
down in the rocking chair, and looks at him with a smile.*] You are a nice man, Doctor
Rank!—don't you feel ashamed of yourself, now the lamp has come!   385

RANK: Not a bit. But perhaps I had better go—for ever?

NORA: No, indeed, you shall not. Of course you must come here just as before. You know
very well Torvald can't do without you.

RANK: Yes, but you?

NORA: Oh I'm always tremendously pleased when you come.   390

RANK: It's just that, that put me on the wrong track. You are a riddle to me. I've often
thought that you'd almost as soon be in my company as in Helmer's.

NORA: Yes—you see there are some people one loves best, and others whom one would
almost always rather have as companions.

RANK: Yes, there is something in that.   395

NORA: When I was at home, of course I loved papa best. But I always thought it tremendous fun if I could steal down into the maids' room, because they never moralised at
all, and talked to each other about such entertaining things.

RANK: I see—it is their place I have taken.

NORA: [*jumping up and going to him*] Oh, dear, nice Doctor Rank, I never meant that at   400
all. But surely you can understand that being with Torvald is a little like being with
papa—

[*Enter* MAID *from the hall.*]

MAID: If you please, ma'am. [*whispers and hands her a card*]

NORA: [*glancing at the card*] Oh! [*puts it in her pocket*]

RANK: Is there anything wrong?   405

NORA: No, no, not in the least. It's only something—it's my new dress—

RANK: What? Your dress is lying there.

NORA: Oh, yes, that one; but this is another. I ordered it. Torvald mustn't know about
it—

RANK: Oho! Then that was the great secret.   410

NORA: Of course. Just go in to him; he is sitting in the inner room. Keep him as long
as—

RANK: Make your mind easy; I won't let him escape. [*goes into* HELMER'*s room*]

NORA: [*to the* MAID] And he's waiting in the kitchen?

MAID: Yes; he came up the back stairs.   415

NORA: But didn't you tell him no one was in?

MAID: Yes, but it was no good.

NORA: He won't go away?

MAID: No; he says he won't until he has seen you, ma'am.

NORA: Well, let him come in—but quietly. Helen, you mustn't say anything about it to   420
anyone. It's a surprise for my husband.

MAID: Yes, ma'am, I quite understand. [*exit*]

NORA: This dreadful thing is going to happen! It will happen in spite of me! No, no, no,
it can't happen—it shan't happen! [*She bolts the door of* HELMER'*s room. The* MAID
opens the hall door for KROGSTAD *and shuts it after him. He is wearing a fur coat, high*   425
boots, and a fur cap.]

NORA: [*advancing towards him*] Speak low—my husband is at home.

KROGSTAD: No matter about that!

NORA: What do you want of me?

KROGSTAD: An explanation. 430

NORA: Make haste then. What is it?

KROGSTAD: You know, I suppose, that I've got my dismissal.

NORA: I couldn't prevent it, Mr. Krogstad. I fought as hard as I could on your side, but it was no good.

KROGSTAD: Does your husband love you so little, then? He knows what I can expose you 435 to, and yet he ventures—

NORA: How can you suppose that he has any knowledge of the sort?

KROGSTAD: I didn't suppose so at all. It would not be the least like our dear Torvald Helmer to show so much courage—

NORA: Mr. Krogstad, a little respect for my husband, please. 440

KROGSTAD: Certainly—all the respect he deserves. But since you have kept the matter so carefully to yourself, I make bold to suppose that you have a little clearer idea, than you had yesterday, of what it actually is that you have done?

NORA: More than you could ever teach me.

KROGSTAD: Yes, bad lawyer that I am. 445

NORA: What is it you want of me?

KROGSTAD: Only to see how you were, Mrs. Helmer. I have been thinking about you all day long. A mere cashier, hackwriter, a—well, a man like me—even he has a little of what is called feeling, you know.

NORA: Show it, then; think of my little children. 450

KROGSTAD: Have you and your husband thought of mine? But never mind about that. I only wanted to tell you that you need not take this matter too seriously. In the first place there will be no accusation made on my part.

NORA: No, of course not; I was sure of that.

KROGSTAD: The whole thing can be arranged amicably; there is no reason why anyone 455 should know anything about it. It will remain a secret between us three.

NORA: My husband must never get to know anything about it.

KROGSTAD: How will you be able to prevent it? Am I to understand that you can pay the balance that's owing?

NORA: No, not just at present. 460

KROGSTAD: Or perhaps that you have some means of raising the money soon?

NORA: None that I mean to make use of.

KROGSTAD: Well, in any case, it would've been of no use to you now. If you stood there with ever so much money in your hand, I would never part with your bond.

NORA: Tell me what purpose you mean to put it to. 465

KROGSTAD: I shall only preserve it—keep it in my possession. No one who is not concerned in the matter shall have the slightest hint of it. So that if the thought of it has driven you to any desperate resolution—

NORA: It has.

KROGSTAD: If you had it in your mind to run away from your home— 470

NORA: I had.

KROGSTAD: Or even something worse—

NORA: How could you know that?

KROGSTAD: Give up the idea.

NORA: How did you know I had thought of *that*? 475

KROGSTAD: Most of us think of that at first. I did, too—but I hadn't the courage.

NORA: [*faintly*] No more had I.

KROGSTAD: [*in a tone of relief*] No, that's it, isn't it—you hadn't the courage, either?

NORA: No, I haven't—I haven't.

KROGSTAD: Besides, it would have been a great piece of folly. Once the first storm at   480
home is over—. I have a letter for your husband in my pocket.

NORA: Telling him everything?

KROGSTAD: In as lenient a manner as I possibly could.

NORA: [*quickly*] He mustn't get that letter. Tear it up. I will find some means of getting
money.   485

KROGSTAD: Excuse me, Mrs. Helmer, but I think I told you just now—

NORA: I am not speaking of what I owe you. Tell me what sum you are asking my husband
for, and I will get the money.

KROGSTAD: I am not asking your husband for a penny.

NORA: What do you want, then?   490

KROGSTAD: I will tell you. I want to rehabilitate myself, Mrs. Helmer; I want to get on;
and in that your husband must help me. For the last year and a half I have not had
a hand in anything dishonourable, and all that time I have been struggling in most
restricted circumstances. I was content to work my way up step by step. Now I'm
turned out, and I'm not going to be satisfied with merely being taken into favour   495
again. I want to get on, I tell you. I want to get into the Bank again, in a higher
position. Your husband must make a place for me—

NORA: That he will never do!

KROGSTAD: He will; I know him; he dare not protest. And as soon as I'm in there again
with him, then you will see! Within a year I shall be the manager's right hand. It will   500
be Nils Krogstad and not Torvald Helmer who manages the Bank.

NORA: That's a thing you will never see!

KROGSTAD: Do you mean that you will—?

NORA: I have courage enough for it now.

KROGSTAD: Oh, you can't frighten me. A fine, spoilt lady like you—   505

NORA: You'll see, you'll see.

KROGSTAD: Under the ice, perhaps? Down into the cold, coal-black water? And then, in
the spring, to float up to the surface, all horrible and unrecognisable, with your hair
fallen out—

NORA: You can't frighten me.   510

KROGSTAD: Nor you me. People don't do such things, Mrs. Helmer. Besides, what use
would it be? I should have him completely in my power all the same.

NORA: Afterwards? When I am no longer—

KROGSTAD: Have you forgotten that it is I who have the keeping of your reputation?
[*Nora stands speechlessly looking at him.*] Well, now, I've warned you. Don't do any-   515
thing foolish. When Helmer has received my letter, I shall expect a message from
him. And be sure you remember that it's your husband himself who has forced me
into such ways as this again. I'll never forgive him for that. Good-bye, Mrs. Helmer.
[*exit through the hall*]

NORA: [*goes to the hall door, opens it slightly and listens*] He's going. He's not putting the   520
letter in the box. Oh no, no! that's impossible! [*opens the door by degrees*] What's
that? He's standing outside. He's not going downstairs. Is he hesitating? Can he—?
[*A letter drops into the box; then* KROGSTAD's *footsteps are heard, till they die away
as he goes downstairs.* NORA *utters a stifled cry, and runs across the room to the table
by the sofa. A short pause.*]   525

NORA: In the mail box. [*steals across to the hall door*] There it lies—Torvald, Torvald, there
is no hope for us now!

[MRS. LINDE *comes in from the room on the left, carrying the dress.*]

MRS. LINDE: There, I can't see anything more to mend now. Would you like to try it on—?

NORA: [*in a hoarse whisper*] Christine, come here. 530

MRS. LINDE: [*throwing the dress down on the sofa*] What's the matter with you? You look so upset.

NORA: Come here. Do you see that letter? There, look—you can see it through the glass in the box.

MRS. LINDE: Yes, I see it. 535

NORA: That letter is from Krogstad.

MRS. LINDE: Nora—it was Krogstad who lent you the money!

NORA: Yes, and now Torvald will know all about it.

MRS. LINDE: Believe me, Nora, that's the best thing for both of you.

NORA: You don't know all. I forged a name. 540

MRS. LINDE: Good heavens—!

NORA: I only want to say this to you, Christine—you must be my witness.

MRS. LINDE: Your witness? What do you mean? What am I to—?

NORA: If I should go out of my mind—and it might easily happen—

MRS. LINDE: Nora! 545

NORA: Or if anything else should happen to me—anything, for instance, that might prevent my being here—

MRS. LINDE: Nora! Nora! You're quite out of your mind.

NORA: And if it should happen that there were someone who wanted to take all the responsibility, all the blame, you understand— 550

MRS. LINDE: Yes, yes—but how can you suppose—?

NORA: Then you must be my witness, that it's not true, Christine. I'm not out of my mind at all. I'm in my right senses now, and I tell you no one else has known anything about it; I, and I alone, did the whole thing. Remember that.

MRS. LINDE: I will, indeed. But I don't understand all this. 555

NORA: How should you understand it? A miracle is going to happen.

MRS. LINDE: A miracle?

NORA: Yes, a miracle.—But it's so terrible, Christine; it *mustn't* happen, not for all the world.

MRS. LINDE: I will go at once and see Krogstad.

NORA: Don't go to him; he will do you some harm. 560

MRS. LINDE: There was a time when he would gladly do anything for my sake.

NORA: He?

MRS. LINDE: Where does he live?

NORA: How should I know—? Yes [*feeling in her pocket*] here is his card. But the letter, the letter—! 565

HELMER: [*calls from his room, knocking at the door*] Nora!

NORA: [*cries out anxiously*] Oh, what's that? What do you want?

HELMER: Don't be so frightened. We are not coming in; you have locked the door. Are you trying on your dress?

NORA: Yes, that's it. I look so nice, Torvald. 570

MRS. LINDE: [*who has read the card*] I see he lives at the corner here.

NORA: Yes, but it's no use. It's hopeless. The letter is lying there in the box.

MRS. LINDE: And your husband keeps the key?

NORA: Yes, always.

MRS. LINDE: Krogstad must ask for his letter back unread, he must find some pretence— 575

NORA: But it's just at this time that Torvald generally—

MRS. LINDE: You must delay him. Go in to him in the meantime. I'll come back as soon as I can. [*She goes out hurriedly through the hall door.*]

NORA: [*goes to* HELMER'*s door, opens it and peeps in*] Torvald!

HELMER: [*from the inner room*] Well? May I venture at last to come into my own room   580
    again? Come along, Rank, now you'll see—[*halting in the doorway*] But what is this?

NORA: What is what, dear?

HELMER: Rank led me to expect a splendid transformation.

RANK: [*in the doorway*] I understood so, but evidently I was mistaken.

NORA: Yes, nobody is to have the chance of admiring me in my costume until to-morrow.   585

HELMER: But, my dear Nora, you look so worn out. Have you been practising too much?

NORA: No, I have not practised at all.

HELMER: But you will need to—

NORA: Yes, indeed I shall, Torvald. But I can't get on a bit without you to help me; I have
    absolutely forgotten the whole thing.   590

HELMER: Oh, we'll soon work it up again.

NORA: Yes, help me, Torvald. Promise that you will! I'm so nervous about it—all the people.
    You must give yourself up to me entirely this evening. Not the tiniest bit of business—
    you mustn't even take a pen in your hand. Will you promise, Torvald dear?

HELMER: I promise: This evening I'll be wholly and absolutely at your service, you helpless   595
    little thing. But, first of all I'll just—[*goes towards the hall door*]

NORA: What are you going to do there?

HELMER: Only see if any letters have come.

NORA: No, no! Don't do that, Torvald!

HELMER: Why not?   600

NORA: Torvald, please don't. There is nothing there.

HELMER: Well, let me look. [*Turns to go to the letterbox.* NORA, *at the piano, plays the first
    bars of the Tarantella.* HELMER *stops in the doorway.*] Aha!

NORA: I can't dance to-morrow if I don't practise with you.

HELMER: [*going up to her*] Are you really so afraid of it, dear?   605

NORA: Yes, so dreadfully afraid of it. Let me practise at once; there is time now, before we
    go to dinner. Sit down and play for me, Torvald dear; coach me, and correct me as
    you play.

HELMER: With great pleasure, if you wish me to. [*sits down at the piano*]

NORA: [*Takes out of the box a tambourine and a long variegated shawl. She hastily drapes the*   610
    shawl round her. Then she springs to the front of the stage and calls out.] Now play for
    me! I'm going to dance!

    [HELMER *plays and* NORA *dances.* RANK *stands by the piano behind* HELMER,
    and looks on.]

HELMER: [*as he plays*] Slower, slower!

NORA: I can't do it any other way.

HELMER: Not so violently, Nora!   615

NORA: This is the way.

HELMER: [*stops playing*] No, no—that's not a bit right.

NORA: [*laughing and swinging the tambourine*] Didn't I tell you so?

RANK: Let me play for her.

HELMER: [*getting up*] Yes, do. I can correct her better then.   620

    [RANK *sits down at the piano and plays.* NORA *dances more and more wildly.*
    HELMER *has taken up a position beside the stove, and during her dance gives her*
    frequent instructions. She does not seem to hear him; her hair comes down and
    falls over her shoulders; she pays no attention to it, but goes on dancing. Enter
    MRS. LINDE.]

MRS. LINDE: [*standing as if spellbound in the doorway*] Oh!—

NORA: [*as she dances*] Such fun, Christine!

HELMER: My dear darling Nora, you are dancing as if your life depended on it.

NORA: So it does.

HELMER: Stop, Rank; this is sheer madness. Stop, I tell you! [RANK *stops playing, and*   625
NORA *suddenly stands still.* HELMER *goes up to her.*] I could never have believed it.
You have forgotten everything I taught you.

NORA: [*throwing away the tambourine*] There, you see.

HELMER: You'll want a lot of coaching.

NORA: Yes, you see how much I need it. You must coach me up to the last minute. Promise   630
me that, Torvald!

HELMER: You can depend on me.

NORA: You must not think of anything but me, either to-day or to-morrow; you mustn't
open a single letter—not even open the mail box—

HELMER: Ah, you're still afraid of that fellow—   635

NORA: Yes, indeed I am.

HELMER: Nora, I tell from your looks that there is a letter from him lying there.

NORA: I don't know; I think there is; but you must not read anything of that kind now.
Nothing horrid must come between us till this is all over.

RANK: [*whispers to* HELMER] You mustn't contradict her.   640

HELMER: [*taking her in his arms*] The child shall have her way. But to-morrow night, after
you've danced—

NORA: Then you will be free. [*The* MAID *appears in the doorway to the right.*]

MAID: Dinner is served, ma'am.

NORA: We will have champagne, Helen.   645

MAID: Very good, ma'am. [*exit*]

HELMER: Hullo!—are we going to have a banquet?

NORA: Yes, a champagne banquet till the small hours. [*calls out*] And a few macaroons,
Helen—lots, just for once!

HELMER: Come, come, don't be so wild and nervous. Be my own little skylark.   650

NORA: Yes, dear, I will. But go in now and you, too, Doctor Rank. Christine, you must
help me to do up my hair.

RANK: [*whispers to* HELMER *as they go out*] I suppose there's nothing—she is not expecting
anything?

HELMER: Far from it, my dear fellow; it is simply nothing more than this childish nervous-   655
ness I was telling you of. [*They go into the right-hand room.*]

NORA: Well!

MRS. LINDE: Gone out of town.

NORA: I could tell from your face.

MRS. LINDE: He's coming home to-morrow evening. I wrote a note for him.   660

NORA: You should have let it alone; you must prevent nothing. After all, it is splendid to
be waiting for a wonderful thing to happen.

MRS. LINDE: What is it that you are waiting for?

NORA: Oh, you wouldn't understand. Go in to them, I will come in a moment. [MRS.
LINDE *goes into the dining room.* NORA *stands still for a little while, as if to compose*   665
herself. Then she looks at her watch.] Five o'clock. Seven hours till midnight; and then
twenty-four hours till the next midnight. Then the Tarantella will be over. Twenty-
four and seven? Thirty-one hours to live.

HELMER: [*from the doorway on the right*] Where's my little skylark?

NORA: [*going to him with her arms outstretched*] Here she is!   670

ACT III

THE SAME SCENE——*The table has been placed in the middle of the stage, with chairs round it. A lamp is burning on the table. The door into the hall stands open. Dance music is heard in the room above. MRS. LINDE is sitting at the table idly turning over the leaves of a book she tries to read, but does not seem able to collect her thoughts. Every now and then she listens intently for a sound at the outer door.*

MRS. LINDE: [*looking at her watch*] Not yet—and the time is nearly up. If only he doesn't—. [*listens again*] Ah, there he is. [*Goes into the hall and opens the outer door carefully. Light footsteps are heard on the stairs. She whispers.*] Come in. There's no one here.

KROGSTAD: [*in the doorway*] I found a note from you at home. What does this mean?

MRS. LINDE: It's absolutely necessary that I have a talk with you. 5

KROGSTAD: Really! And is it absolutely necessary that it should be here?

MRS. LINDE: It's impossible where I live; there's no private entrance to my rooms. Come in; we're quite alone. The maid's asleep and the Helmers are at the dance upstairs.

KROGSTAD: [*coming into the room*] Are the Helmers really at a dance to-night?

MRS. LINDE: Yes, why not? 10

KROGSTAD: Certainly—why not?

MRS. LINDE: Now, Nils, let's have a talk.

KROGSTAD: Can we two have anything to talk about.

MRS. LINDE: We have a great deal to talk about.

KROGSTAD: I shouldn't have thought so. 15

MRS. LINDE: No, you have never properly understood me.

KROGSTAD: Was there anything else to understand except what was obvious to all the world—a heartless woman jilts a man when a better catch turns up.

MRS. LINDE: Do you believe I'm as absolutely heartless as all that? And do you believe that I did it with a light heart? 20

KROGSTAD: Didn't you?

MRS. LINDE: Nils, did you really think that?

KROGSTAD: If it were as you say, why did you write to me as you did at that time?

MRS. LINDE: I could do nothing else. As I had to break with you, it was my duty also to put an end to all that you felt for me. 25

KROGSTAD: [*wringing his hands*] So that was it. And all this—only for the sake of money!

MRS. LINDE: You must not forget that I had a helpless mother and two little brothers. We couldn't wait for you, Nils; your prospects seemed hopeless then.

KROGSTAD: That may be so, but you had no right to throw me over for any one else's sake.

MRS. LINDE: Indeed I don't know. Many a time did I ask myself if I had the right to do it. 30

KROGSTAD: [*more gently*] When I lost you, it was as if all the solid ground went from under my feet. Look at me now—I'm a shipwrecked man clinging to a bit of wreckage.

MRS. LINDE: But help may be near.

KROGSTAD: It *was* near; but then you came and stood in my way.

MRS. LINDE: Unintentionally, Nils. It was only to-day that I learned it was your place I was going to take in the Bank. 35

KROGSTAD: I believe you, if you say so. But now that you know it, are you not going to give it up to me?

MRS. LINDE: No, because that would not benefit you in the least.

KROGSTAD: Oh, benefit, benefit—I would have done it whether or no. 40

MRS. LINDE: I have learned to act prudently. Life, and hard, bitter necessity have taught me that.

KROGSTAD: And life has taught me not to believe in fine speeches.

MRS. LINDE: Then life has taught you something very reasonable. But deeds you must believe in? 45

KROGSTAD: What do you mean by that?

MRS. LINDE: You said you were like a shipwrecked man clinging to some wreckage.

KROGSTAD: I had good reason to say so.

MRS. LINDE: Well, I am like a shipwrecked woman clinging to some wreckage—no one to mourn for, no one to care for. 50

KROGSTAD: It was your own choice.

MRS. LINDE: There was no other choice—then.

KROGSTAD: Well, what now?

MRS. LINDE: Nils, how would it be if we two shipwrecked people could join forces?

KROGSTAD: What are you saying? 55

MRS. LINDE: Two on the same piece of wreckage would stand a better chance than each on their own.

KROGSTAD: Christine!

MRS. LINDE: What do you suppose brought me to town?

KROGSTAD: Do you mean that you gave me a thought? 60

MRS. LINDE: I couldn't endure life without work. All my life, as long as I can remember, I have worked, and it's been my greatest and only pleasure. But now I'm quite alone in the world—my life is so dreadfully empty and I feel so forsaken. There is not the least pleasure in working for one's self. Nils, give me someone and something to work for.

KROGSTAD: I don't trust that. It's nothing but a woman's overstrained sense of generosity 65 that prompts you to make such an offer of yourself.

MRS. LINDE: Have you ever noticed anything of the sort in me?

KROGSTAD: Could you really do it? Tell me—do you know all about my past life?

MRS. LINDE: Yes.

KROGSTAD: And do you know what they think of me here? 70

MRS. LINDE: You seemed to me to imply that with me you might have been quite another man.

KROGSTAD: I'm certain of it.

MRS. LINDE: Is it too late now?

KROGSTAD: Christine, are you saying this deliberately? Yes, I'm sure you are. I see it in 75 your face. Have you really the courage, then—?

MRS. LINDE: I want to be a mother to someone, and your children need a mother. We two need each other. Nils, I have faith in your real character—I can dare anything together with you.

KROGSTAD: [*grasps her hand*] Thanks, thanks, Christine! Now I shall find a way to clear 80 myself in the eyes of the world. Ah, but I forgot—

MRS. LINDE: [*listening*] Hush! The Tarantella! Go, go!

KROGSTAD: Why? What is it?

MRS. LINDE: Do you hear them up there? When that is over, we may expect them back.

KROGSTAD: Yes, yes—I will go. But it's all no use. Of course you're not aware what steps 85 I've taken in the matter of the Helmers.

MRS. LINDE: Yes, I know all about that.

KROGSTAD: And in spite of that have you the courage to—?

MRS. LINDE: I understand very well to what lengths a man like you might be driven by despair. 90

KROGSTAD: If I could only undo what I've done!

MRS. LINDE: You cannot. Your letter is lying in the mail box now.

KROGSTAD: Are you sure of that?

MRS. LINDE: Quite sure, but—

KROGSTAD: [*with a searching look at her*] Is that what it all means?—that you want to save   95
    your friend at any cost? Tell me frankly. Is that it?

MRS. LINDE: Nils, a woman who has once sold herself for another's sake, doesn't do it a
    second time.

KROGSTAD: I'll ask for my letter back.

MRS. LINDE: No, no.   100

KROGSTAD: Yes, of course I will. I'll wait here till Torvald comes; I will tell him he must give
    me my letter back—that it only concerns my dismissal—that he's not to read it.

MRS. LINDE: No, Nils, you must not recall your letter.

KROGSTAD: But, tell me, wasn't it for that very purpose that you asked me to meet you
    here?   105

MRS. LINDE: In my first moment of fright, it was. But twenty-four hours have elapsed
    since then, and in that time I've witnessed incredible things in this house. Torvald
    must know all about it. This unhappy secret must be disclosed; they must have a
    complete understanding between them, which is impossible with all this conceal-
    ment and falsehood going on.   110

KROGSTAD: Very well, if you will take the responsibility. But there's one thing I can do in
    any case, and I shall do it at once.

MRS. LINDE: [*listening*] You must be quick and go! The dance is over; we are not safe a
    moment longer.

KROGSTAD: I'll wait for you below.   115

MRS. LINDE: Yes, do. You must see me back to my door.

KROGSTAD: I have never had such an amazing piece of good fortune in my life! [*goes out
    through the outer door. The door between the room and the hall remains open.*]

MRS. LINDE: [*tidying up the room and laying her hat and cloak ready*] What a difference!
    What a difference! Someone to work for and live for—a home to bring comfort into.   120
    That I will do, indeed. I wish they would be quick and come—[*listens*] Ah, there
    they are now. I must put on my things. [*Takes up her hat and cloak.* HELMER's and
    NORA's *voices are heard outside; a key is turned, and* HELMER *brings* NORA *almost
    by force into the hall. She is in an Italian costume with a large black shawl around her;
    he is in evening dress, and a black cloak which is flying open.*]   125

NORA: [*hanging back in the doorway, and struggling with him*] No, no, no!—don't take me
    in. I want to go upstairs again; I don't want to leave so early.

HELMER: But, my dearest Nora—

NORA: Please, Torvald dear—please, *please*—only an hour more.

HELMER: Not a single minute, my sweet Nora. You know that was our agreement. Come   130
    along into the room; you are catching cold standing there. [*He brings her gently into
    the room, in spite of her resistance.*]

MRS. LINDE: Good-evening.

NORA: Christine!

HELMER: You here, so late, Mrs. Linde?   135

MRS. LINDE: Yes, you must excuse me; I was so anxious to see Nora in her dress.

NORA: Have you been sitting here waiting for me?

MRS. LINDE: Yes, unfortunately I came too late; you had already gone upstairs, and I
    thought I couldn't go away again without having seen you.

HELMER: [*taking off* NORA's *shawl*] Yes, take a good look at her. I think she's worth look-   140
    ing at. Isn't she charming, Mrs. Linde?

MRS. LINDE: Yes, indeed she is.

HELMER: Doesn't she look remarkably pretty? Everyone thought so at the dance. But she is terribly self-willed, this sweet little person. What are we to do with her? You will hardly believe that I had almost to bring her away by force. 145

NORA: Torvald, you will repent not having let me stay, even if it were only for half an hour.

HELMER: Listen to her, Mrs. Linde! She had danced her Tarantella, and it had been a tremendous success, as it deserved—although possibly the performance was a trifle too realistic—a little more so, I mean, than was strictly compatible with propriety. 150
But never mind about that! The chief thing is, she had made a success—she had made a tremendous success. Do you think I was going to let her remain there after that, and spoil the effect? No, indeed! I took my charming little Capri maiden—my capricious little Capri maiden, I should say—on my arm; took one quick turn around the room; a curtsy on either side, and, as they say in novels, the beautiful 155
apparition disappeared. An exit ought always to be effective, Mrs. Linde; but that's what I cannot make Nora understand. Pooh! this room is hot. [*throws his cloak on a chair, and opens the door of his room*] Hullo! it's all dark in here. Oh, of course—excuse me—[*He goes in, and lights some candles.*]

NORA: [*in a hurried and breathless whisper*] Well? 160

MRS. LINDE: [*in a low voice*] I have had a talk with him.

NORA: Yes, and—

MRS. LINDE: Nora, you must tell your husband all about it.

NORA: [*in an expressionless voice*] I knew it.

MRS. LINDE: You have nothing to be afraid of as far as Krogstad is concerned; but you 165
must tell him.

NORA: I won't tell him.

MRS. LINDE: Then the letter will.

NORA: Thank you, Christine. Now I know what I must do. Hush—!

HELMER: [*coming in again*] Well, Mrs. Linde, have you admired her? 170

MRS. LINDE: Yes, and now I will say good-night.

HELMER: What, already? Is this yours, this knitting?

MRS. LINDE: [*taking it*] Yes, thank you, I had very nearly forgotten it.

HELMER: So you knit?

MRS. LINDE: Of course. 175

HELMER: Do you know, you ought to embroider.

MRS. LINDE: Really? Why?

HELMER: Yes, it's far more becoming. Let me show you. You hold the embroidery thus in your left hand, and use the needle with the right—like this—with a long, easy sweep. Do you see? 180

MRS. LINDE: Yes, perhaps.

HELMER: But in the case of knitting—that can never be anything but ungraceful; look here—the arms close together, the knitting-needles going up and down—it has a sort of Chinese effect. That was really excellent champagne they gave us.

MRS. LINDE: Well—good-night, Nora, and don't be stubborn any more. 185

HELMER: That's right, Mrs. Linde.

MRS. LINDE: Good-night, Mr. Helmer.

HELMER: [*accompanying her to the door*] Good-night, good-night. I hope you'll get home all right. I should be very happy to—but you haven't any great distance to go. Good-night, good-night. [*She goes out; he shuts the door after her, and comes in again.*] Ah!— 190
at last we have got rid of her. She is a frightful bore, that woman.

NORA: Aren't you very tired, Torvald?

HELMER: No, not in the least.

NORA: Nor sleepy?

HELMER: Not a bit. On the contrary, I feel extraordinarily lively. And you?—you really 195
look both tired and sleepy.

NORA: Yes, I'm very tired. I want to go to sleep at once.

HELMER: There, you see it was quite right of me not to let you stay there any longer.

NORA: Everything you do is quite right, Torvald.

HELMER: [*kissing her on the forehead*] Now my little skylark is speaking reasonably. Did 200
you notice what good spirits Rank was in this evening?

NORA: Really? Was he? I didn't speak to him at all.

HELMER: And I very little, but I haven't seen him in such good form for a long time. [*looks
for a while at her and then goes nearer to her*] It's delightful to be at home by ourselves
again, to be all alone with you—you fascinating, charming little darling! 205

NORA: Don't look at me like that, Torvald.

HELMER: Why shouldn't I look at my dearest treasure?—at all the beauty that's mine, all
mine?

NORA: [*going to the other side of the table*] You mustn't say things like that to me to-night.

HELMER: [*following her*] You have still got the Tarantella in your blood, I see. And it makes 210
you more captivating than ever. Listen—the guests are beginning to leave now. [*in
a lower voice*] Nora—soon the whole house will be quiet.

NORA: Yes, I hope so.

HELMER: Yes, my own darling Nora. Do you know when I'm out at a party with you like
this, why I speak so little to you, keep away from you, and only send a stolen glance 215
in your direction now and then?—do you know why I do that? It's because I make
believe that we are secretly in love, and you are my secretly promised bride, and that
no one suspects there is anything between us.

NORA: Yes, yes—I know very well you're thinking about me all the time.

HELMER: And when we are leaving, and I am putting the shawl over your beautiful young 220
shoulders—on your lovely neck—then I imagine that you are my bride and that
we have just come from the wedding, and I am bringing you for the first time into
our home—to be alone with you for the first time—quite alone with my shy little
darling! All this evening I have longed for nothing but you. When I watched the
seductive figures of the Tarantella, my blood was on fire; I could endure it no longer, 225
and that was why I brought you down so early—

NORA: Go away, Torvald! You must let me go. I won't—

HELMER: What's that? You're teasing, my little Nora! You won't—you won't? Am I not your
husband? [*A knock is heard at the outer door.*]

NORA: [*starting*] Did you hear—? 230

HELMER: [*going into the hall*] Who is it?

RANK: [*outside*] It is I. May I come in for a moment?

HELMER: [*in a fretful whisper*]. Oh, what does he want now? [*aloud*] Wait a minute?
[*unlocks the door*] Come, that's kind of you not to pass by our door.

RANK: I thought I heard your voice, and felt as if I should like to look in. [*with a swift* 235
glance round] Ah, yes!—these dear familiar rooms. You are very happy and cozy in
here, you two.

HELMER: It seems to me that you looked after yourself pretty well upstairs, too.

RANK: Excellently. Why shouldn't I? Why shouldn't one enjoy everything in this world?—
at any rate as much as one can, and as long as one can. The wine was capital— 240

HELMER: Especially the champagne.

RANK: So you noticed that, too? It's almost incredible how much I managed to put away!

NORA: Torvald drank a great deal of champagne to-night, too.

RANK: Did he?

NORA: Yes, and he is always in such good spirits afterwards. 245

RANK: Well, why should one not enjoy a merry evening after a well-spent day?

HELMER: Well spent: I'm afraid I can't take credit for that.

RANK: [*clapping him on the back*] But I can, you know!

NORA: Doctor Rank, you must have been occupied with some scientific investigation today. 250

RANK: Exactly.

HELMER: Just listen!—little Nora talking about scientific investigations!

NORA: And may I congratulate you on the result?

RANK: Indeed you may.

NORA: Was it favourable, then? 255

RANK: The best possible, for both doctor and patient—certainty.

NORA: [*quickly and searchingly*] Certainty?

RANK: Absolute certainty. So wasn't I entitled to make a merry evening of it after that?

NORA: Yes, you certainly were, Doctor Rank.

HELMER: I think so, too, so long as you don't have to pay for it in the morning. 260

RANK: Oh well, one can't have anything in this life without paying for it.

NORA: Doctor Rank—are you fond of masked balls?

RANK: Yes, if there's a fine lot of pretty costumes.

NORA: Tell me—what shall we two wear at the next?

HELMER: Little featherbrain!—are you thinking of the next already? 265

RANK: We two? Yes. I can tell you. You shall go as a good fairy—

HELMER: Yes, but what do you suggest as an appropriate costume for that?

RANK: Let your wife go dressed just as she is in everyday life.

HELMER: That was really very prettily turned. But can't you tell us what you'll be?

RANK: Yes, my dear friend, I have quite made up my mind about that. 270

HELMER: Well?

RANK: At the next fancy-dress ball I shall be invisible.

HELMER: That's a good joke!

RANK: There is a big black hat—have you never heard of hats that make you invisible? If you put one on, no one can see you. 275

HELMER: [*suppressing a smile*] Yes, you're quite right.

RANK: But I am clean forgetting what I came for. Helmer, give me a cigar—one of the dark Havanas.

HELMER: With the greatest pleasure. [*offers him his case*]

RANK: [*takes a cigar and cuts off the end*] Thanks. 280

NORA: [*striking a match*] Let me give you a light.

RANK: Thank you. [*She holds the match for him to light his cigar.*] And now good-bye!

HELMER: Good-bye, good-bye, dear old man!

NORA: Sleep well, Doctor Rank.

RANK: Thank you for that wish. 285

NORA: Wish me the same.

RANK: You? Well, if you want me to sleep well! And thanks for the light. [*He nods to them both and goes out.*]

HELMER: [*in a subdued voice*] He has drunk more than he ought.

NORA: [*absently*] Maybe. [HELMER *takes a bunch of keys out of his pocket and goes into the hall.*] Torvald! what are you going to do there? 290

HELMER: Empty the mail box; it's quite full; there will be no room for the newspaper, to-morrow morning.

NORA: Are you going to work to-night?

HELMER: You know quite well I'm not. What is this? Some one has been at the lock.

NORA: At the lock—?   295

HELMER: Yes, someone has. What can it mean? I should never have thought the maid—. Here is a broken hairpin. Nora, it is one of yours.

NORA: [*quickly*] Then it must have been the children—

HELMER: Then you must get them out of those ways. There, at last I have got it open. [*takes out the contents of the mail box, and calls to the kitchen*] Helen! Helen, put out   300 the light over the front door. [*goes back into the room and shuts the door into the hall. He holds out his hand full of letters.*] Look at that—look what a heap of them there are. [*turning them over*] What on earth is that?

NORA: [*at the window*] The letter—No! Torvald, no!

HELMER: Two cards—of Rank's.   305

NORA: Of Doctor Rank's?

HELMER: [*looking at them*] Doctor Rank. They were on the top. He must have put them in when he went out.

NORA: Is there anything written on them?

HELMER: There is a black cross over the name. Look there—what an uncomfortable idea!   310 It looks as if he were announcing his own death.

NORA: It's just what he's doing.

HELMER: What? Do you know anything about it? Has he said anything to you?

NORA: Yes. He told me that when the cards came it would be his leave-taking from us. He means to shut himself up and die.   315

HELMER: My poor old friend. Certainly I knew we should not have him very long with us. But so soon! And so he hides himself away like a wounded animal.

NORA: If it has to happen, it's best it should be without a word—don't you think so, Torvald?

HELMER: [*walking up and down*] He had so grown into our lives. I can't think of him as   320 having gone out of them. He, with his sufferings and his loneliness, was like a cloudy background to our sunlit happiness. Well, perhaps it's best so. For him, anyway. [*standing still*] And perhaps for us, too, Nora. We two are thrown quite upon each other now. [*puts his arms round her*] My darling wife, I don't feel as if I could hold you tight enough. Do you know, Nora, I've often wished that you might be threatened   325 by some great danger, so I might risk my life's blood, and everything, for your sake.

NORA: [*disengages herself, and says firmly and decidedly*] Now you must read your letters, Torvald.

HELMER: No, no; not to-night. I want to be with you, my darling wife.

NORA: With the thought of your friend's death—   330

HELMER: You are right, it has affected us both. Something ugly has come between us—the thought of the horrors of death. We must try and rid our minds of that. Until then— we'll each go to our own room.

NORA: [*hanging on his neck*] Good-night, Torvald—Good-night!

HELMER: [*kissing her on the forehead*] Good-night, my little singing-bird. Sleep sound,   335 Nora. Now I'll read my letters through. [*He takes his letters and goes into his room, shutting the door after him.*]

NORA: [*gropes distractedly about, seizes* HELMER's *cloak, throws it round her, while she says in quick, hoarse, spasmodic whispers*] Never to see him again. Never! Never! [*puts her shawl over her head*] Never to see my children again, either—never again. Never!   340 Never!—Ah! the icy, black water—the unfathomable depths—if only it were over!

He has got it now—now he is reading it. Good-bye, Torvald and my children! [*She is about to rush out through the hall, when* HELMER *opens his door hurriedly and stands with an open letter in his hand.*]

HELMER: Nora! 345

NORA: Ah!—

HELMER: What's this? Do you know what's in this letter?

NORA: Yes, I know. Let me go! Let me get out!

HELMER: [*holding her back*] Where are you going?

NORA: [*trying to get free*] You shan't save me, Torvald! 350

HELMER: [*reeling*] True? Is this true, that I read here? Horrible! No, no—it's impossible that it can be true.

NORA: It's true. I have loved you above everything else in the world.

HELMER: Oh, don't let us have any silly excuses.

NORA: [*taking a step towards him*] Torvald—! 355

HELMER: Miserable creature—what have you done?

NORA: Let me go. You shall not suffer for my sake. You shall not take it upon yourself.

HELMER: No tragedy airs, please. [*locks the hall door*] Here you shall stay and give me an explanation. Do you understand what you've done? Answer me? Do you understand what you've done? 360

NORA: [*looks steadily at him and says with a growing look of coldness in her face*] Yes, now I am beginning to understand thoroughly.

HELMER: [*walking about the room*] What a horrible awakening! All these eight years—she who was my joy and pride—a hypocrite, a liar—worse, worse—a criminal! The unutterable ugliness of it all!—For shame! For shame! [NORA *is silent and looks* 365 *steadily at him. He stops in front of her.*] I ought to have suspected that something of the sort would happen. I ought to have foreseen. All your father's lack of princi- ple—be silent!—all your father's lack of principle has come out in you. No religion, no morality, no sense of duty—. How I'm punished for having winked at what he did! I did it for your sake, and this is how you repay me. 370

NORA: Yes, that's just it.

HELMER: Now you have destroyed all my happiness. You've ruined my entire future. It is horrible to think of! I'm in the power of an unscrupulous man; he can do what he likes with me, ask anything he likes of me, give me any orders he pleases—I dare not refuse. And I must sink to such miserable depths because of a silly woman! 375

NORA: When I'm out of the way, you'll be free.

HELMER: No fine speeches, please. Your father had always plenty of those ready, too. What good would it be to me if you were out of the way, as you say? Not the slightest. He can make the affair known everywhere; and if he does, I may be falsely suspected of having been a party to your criminal action. Very likely people will think I was 380 behind it all—that it was I who prompted you! and I have to thank you for all this— you whom I have cherished during the whole of our married life. Do you understand now what it is you have done to me?

NORA: [*coldly and quietly*] Yes.

HELMER: It's so incredible that I can't take it in. But we must come to some understanding. 385 Take off that shawl. Take it off, I tell you. I must try and appease him some way or another. The matter must be hushed up at any cost. And as for you and me, it must appear as if everything between us were just as before—but naturally only in the eyes of the world. You will still remain in my house, that is a matter of course. But I shall not allow you to bring up the children; I dare not trust them to you. To 390 think that I should be obliged to say so to one whom I have loved dearly, and whom I still—. No, that's all over. From this moment happiness is not the question; all that concerns us is to save the remains, the fragments, the appearance—

[*A ring is heard at the front-door bell.*]

HELMER: [*with a start*] What's that? So late? Can the worst—? Can he—? Hide yourself, Nora. Say you are ill.   395

[NORA *stands motionless.* HELMER *goes and unlocks the hall door.*]

MAID: [*half-dressed, comes to the door*] A letter for the mistress.

HELMER: Give it to me. [*takes the letter, and shuts the door*] Yes, it's from him. You shall not have it; I will read it myself.

NORA: Yes, read it.

HELMER: [*standing by the lamp*] I scarcely have the courage to do it. It may mean ruin for   400
both of us. No, I must know. [*tears open the letter, runs his eye over a few lines, looks at a paper enclosed, and gives a shout of joy*] Nora! [*She looks at him questioningly.*] Nora!—No, I must read it once again—. Yes, it's true! I'm saved! Nora, I'm saved!

NORA: And I?

HELMER: You, too, of course; we are both saved, both you and I. Look, he sends you your   405
bond back. He says he regrets and repents—that a happy change in his life—never mind what he says! We are saved, Nora! No one can do anything to you. Oh, Nora, Nora!—no, first I must destroy these hateful things. Let me see—. [*takes a look at the bond*] No, no, I won't look at it. The whole thing shall be nothing but a bad dream to me. [*tears up the bond and both letters, throws them all into the stove, and watches   410
them burn*] There—now it doesn't exist any longer. He says that since Christmas Eve you—. These must have been three dreadful days for you, Nora.

NORA: I have fought a hard fight these three days.

HELMER: And suffered agonies, and seen no way out but—. No, we won't call any of the horrors to mind. We'll only shout with joy, and keep saying, "It's all over! It's all   415
over!" Listen to me, Nora. You don't seem to realise that it is all over. What is this?—such a cold, set face! My poor little Nora, I quite understand; you don't feel that I have forgiven you. But it's true, Nora, I swear it; I've forgiven you everything. I know that what you did, you did out of love for me.

NORA: That's true.   420

HELMER: You have loved me as a wife ought to love her husband. Only you hadn't sufficient knowledge to judge of the means you used. But do you suppose you are any the less dear to me, because you don't understand how to act on your own responsibility? No, no; only lean on me; I will advise you and direct you. I should not be a man if this womanly helplessness did not just give you a double attractiveness in my eyes.   425
You mustn't think any more about the hard things I said in my first moment of consternation, when I thought everything was going to overwhelm me. I've forgiven you, Nora; I swear to you I've forgiven you.

NORA: Thank you for your forgiveness. [*She goes out through to the door to the right.*]

HELMER: No, don't go—[*looks in*] What are you doing in there?   430

NORA: [*from within*] Taking off my costume.

HELMER: [*standing at the open door*] Yes, do. Try and calm yourself, and make your mind easy again, my frightened little singing-bird. Be at rest, and feel secure; I have broad wings to shelter you under. [*walks up and down by the door*] How warm and cozy our home is, Nora. Here is shelter for you; here I'll protect you like a hunted dove that   435
I have saved from a hawk's claws: I'll bring peace to your poor beating heart. It will come, little by little, Nora, believe me. To-morrow morning you will look upon it all

quite differently; soon everything will be just as it was before. Very soon you won't need me to assure you that I've forgiven you; you will feel the certainty that I've done so. Can you suppose I should ever think of such a thing as repudiating you, or even reproaching you? You have no idea what a true man's heart is like, Nora. There is something so indescribably sweet and satisfying, to a man, in the knowledge that he has forgiven his wife—forgiven her freely, and with all his heart. It seems as if that had made her, as it were, doubly his own; he has given her a new life, so to speak; and she has in a way become both wife and child to him. So you shall be for me after this, my little scared, helpless darling. Have no anxiety about anything, Nora; only be frank and open with me, and I'll serve as will and conscience both to you—. What's this? Not gone to bed? Have you changed your clothes?

NORA: [*in everyday dress*] Yes, Torvald, I have changed my clothes now.

HELMER: But what for?—so late as this.

NORA: I shall not sleep to-night.

HELMER: But, my dear Nora—

NORA: [*looking at her watch*] It's not so very late. Sit down here, Torvald. You and I have much to say to one another. [*She sits down at one side of the table.*]

HELMER: Nora—what's this?—this cold, set face!

NORA: Sit down. It'll take some time; I have a lot to talk over with you.

HELMER: [*sits down at the opposite side of the table*] You alarm me, Nora!—and I don't understand you.

NORA: No, that's just it. You don't understand me, and I've never understood you either—before to-night. No, you mustn't interrupt me. You must simply listen to what I say. Torvald, this is a settling of accounts.

HELMER: What do you mean by that?

NORA: [*after a short silence*] Isn't there any thing that strikes you as strange in our sitting here like this?

HELMER: What is that?

NORA: We've been married now eight years. Doesn't it occur to you that this is the first time we two, you and I, husband and wife, have had a serious conversation?

HELMER: What do you mean by "serious"?

NORA: In all these eight years—longer than that—from the beginning of our acquaintance, we've never exchanged a word on any serious subject.

HELMER: Was it likely that I would be continually and for ever telling you about worries that you couldn't help me with?

NORA: I'm not speaking about business matters. I say that we have never sat down in earnest together to try and get at the bottom of anything.

HELMER: But, dearest Nora, would it have been any good to you?

NORA: That's just it; you've never understood me. I have been greatly wronged, Torvald—first by papa and then by you.

HELMER: What! By us two—by us two, who've loved you better than anyone else in the world?

NORA: [*shaking her head*] You've never loved me. You've only thought it pleasant to be in love with me.

HELMER: Nora, what do I hear you saying?

NORA: It's perfectly true, Torvald. When I was at home with papa, he told me his opinion about everything, and so I had the same opinions; and if I differed from him I concealed the fact, because he wouldn't have liked it. He called me his doll-child, and he played with me just as I used to play with my dolls. And when I came to live with you—

HELMER: What sort of an expression is that to use about our marriage?

NORA: [*undisturbed*] I mean that I was simply transferred from papa's hands into yours. You arranged everything according to your own taste, and so I got the same tastes as you—or else I pretended to. I'm really not quite sure which—I think sometimes the one and sometimes the other. When I look back on it, it seems to me as if I'd been living here like a poor woman—just from hand to mouth. I've existed merely to perform tricks for you, Torvald. But you would have it so. You and papa have committed a great sin against me. It's your fault that I have made nothing of my life.   490   495

HELMER: How unreasonable and how ungrateful you are, Nora! Have you not been happy here?

NORA: No, I have never been happy. I thought I was, but it's never really been so.

HELMER: Not—not happy!

NORA: No, only merry. And you've always been so kind to me. But our home has been nothing but a playroom. I've been your doll-wife, just as at home I was papa's doll-child; and here the children have been my dolls. I thought it great fun when you played with me, just as they thought it great fun when I played with them. That's what our marriage has been, Torvald.   500

HELMER: There is some truth in what you say—exaggerated and strained as your view of it is. But for the future it'll be different. Playtime shall be over, and lesson-time shall begin.   505

NORA: Whose lessons? Mine, or the children's?

HELMER: Both yours and the children's, my darling Nora.

NORA: Alas, Torvald, you're not the man to educate me into being a proper wife for you.   510

HELMER: And you can say that?

NORA: And I—how am I fitted to bring up the children?

HELMER: Nora!

NORA: Didn't you say so yourself a little while ago—that you dare not trust me to bring them up?   515

HELMER: In a moment of anger! Why do you pay any heed to that?

NORA: Indeed, you were perfectly right. I'm not fit for the task. There is another task I must undertake first. I must try and educate myself—you're not the man to help me in that. I must do that for myself. And that's why I'm going to leave you now.

HELMER: [*springing up*] What do you say?   520

NORA: I must stand quite alone, if I'm to understand myself and everything about me. It's for that reason that I cannot remain with you any longer.

HELMER: Now, Nora!

NORA: I'm going away from here now, at once. I'm sure Christine will take me in for the night—   525

HELMER: You're out of your mind! I won't allow it! I forbid you!

NORA: It's no use forbidding me anything any longer. I'll take with me what belongs to myself. I'll take nothing from you, either now or later.

HELMER: What sort of madness is this!

NORA: To-morrow I'll go home—I mean, to my old home. It will be easiest for me to find something to do there.   530

HELMER: You blind, foolish woman!

NORA: I must try and get some sense, Torvald.

HELMER: To desert your home, your husband, and your children! And you don't consider what people will say!   535

NORA: I can't consider that at all. I only know that it is necessary for me.

HELMER: It's shocking. This is how you would neglect your most sacred duties.

NORA: What do you consider my most sacred duties?

HELMER: Do I need to tell you that? Are they not your duties to your husband and your children? 540

NORA: I have other duties just as sacred.

HELMER: That you have not. What duties could those be?

NORA: Duties to myself.

HELMER: Before all else, you are a wife and a mother.

NORA: I don't believe that any longer. I believe that before all else I'm a reasonable human 545
being, just as you are—or, at all events, that I must try and become one. I know
quite well, Torvald, that most people would think you right, and that views of that
kind are to be found in books; but I can no longer content myself with what most
people say, or with what's found in books. I must think over things for myself and
get to understand them. 550

HELMER: Can't you understand your place in your own home? Haven't you a reliable guide
in such matters as that?—have you no religion?

NORA: I'm afraid, Torvald, I do not exactly know what religion is.

HELMER: What're you saying?

NORA: I know nothing but what the clergyman said, when I went to be confirmed. He 555
told us that religion was this, and that, and the other. When I'm away from all this,
and am alone, I'll look into that matter, too. I'll see if what the clergyman said is
true, or at all events if it is true for me.

HELMER: This is unheard of in a woman of your age! But if religion cannot touch you, let
me try and awaken your conscience. I suppose you have some moral sense? Or— 560
answer me—am I to think you have none?

NORA: I assure you, Torvald, that is not an easy question to answer. I really don't know.
The thing puzzles me altogether. I only know that you and I look at it in quite a
different light. I'm learning, too, that the law is quite another thing from what I
supposed; but I find it impossible to convince myself that the law is right. According 565
to it a woman has no right to spare her old dying father, or to save her husband's
life. I can't believe that.

HELMER: You talk like a child. You don't understand the conditions of the world in which
you live.

NORA: No, I don't. But now I'm going to try. I'm going to see if I can make out who is 570
right, the world or I.

HELMER: You're ill, Nora; you're delirious; I almost think you're out of your mind.

NORA: I've never felt my mind so clear and certain as to-night.

HELMER: And is it with a clear and certain mind that you forsake your husband and your
children? 575

NORA: Yes, it is.

HELMER: Then there is only one possible explanation.

NORA: What is that?

HELMER: You don't love me any more.

NORA: No, that's just it. 580

HELMER: Nora!—and you can say that?

NORA: It gives me great pain, Torvald, for you have always been so kind to me, but I can't
help it. I don't love you any more.

HELMER: [regaining his composure] Is that a clear and certain conviction, too?

NORA: Yes, absolutely clear and certain. That's the reason why I'll not stay here any longer. 585

HELMER: And can you tell me what I've done to forfeit your love?

NORA: Yes, indeed I can. It was to-night, when the wonderful thing did not happen; then
I saw you were not the man I had thought you.

HELMER: Explain yourself better—I don't understand you.

NORA: I've waited so patiently for eight years; for, goodness knows, I knew very well that wonderful things don't happen every day. Then this horrible misfortune came upon me; and then I felt quite certain that the wonderful thing was going to happen at last. When Krogstad's letter was lying out there, never for a moment did I imagine that you would consent to accept this man's conditions. I was so absolutely certain that you would say to him: Publish the thing to the whole world. And when that was done—

HELMER: Yes, what then?—when I had exposed my wife to shame and disgrace?

NORA: When that was done, I was so absolutely certain, you would come forward and take everything upon yourself, and say I'm the guilty one.

HELMER: Nora—!

NORA: You mean that I would never have accepted such a sacrifice on your part? No, of course not. But what would my assurances have been worth against yours? That was the wonderful thing which I hoped for and feared; and it was to prevent that, that I wanted to kill myself.

HELMER: I would gladly work night and day for you, Nora—bear sorrow and want for your sake. But no man would sacrifice his honour for the one he loves.

NORA: Millions of women have done it.

HELMER: Oh, you think and talk like a heedless child.

NORA: Maybe. But you neither think nor talk like the man I could bind myself to. As soon as your fear was over—and it was not fear for what threatened me, but for what might happen to you—when the whole thing was past, as far as you were concerned it was exactly as if nothing at all had happened. Exactly as before, I was your little skylark, your doll, which you would in future treat with doubly gentle care, because it was so brittle and fragile. [*getting up*] Torvald—it was then it dawned on me that for eight years I'd been living here with a strange man, and had borne him three children—. Oh, I can't bear to think of it! I could tear myself into little bits!

HELMER: [*sadly*] I see, I see. An abyss has opened between us—there's no denying it. But, Nora, wouldn't it be possible to fill it up?

NORA: As I am now, I'm no wife for you.

HELMER: I have it in me to become a different man.

NORA: Perhaps—if your doll is taken away from you.

HELMER: But to part!—to part from you! No, no. Nora, I can't understand that idea.

NORA: [*going out to the right*] That makes it all the more certain that it must be done. [*She comes back with her cloak and hat and a small bag, which she puts on a chair by the table.*]

HELMER: Nora, Nora, not now! Wait till to-morrow.

NORA: [*putting on her cloak*] I can't spend the night in a strange man's room.

HELMER: But can't we live here like brother and sister?

NORA: [*putting on her hat*] You know very well that wouldn't last long. [*puts the shawl round her*] Good-bye, Torvald. I won't see the little ones. I know they are in better hands than mine. As I am now, I can be of no use to them.

HELMER: But some day, Nora—some day?

NORA: How can I tell? I have no idea what is going to become of me.

HELMER: But you are my wife, whatever becomes of you.

NORA: Listen, Torvald. I have heard that when a wife deserts her husband's house, as I'm doing now, he is legally freed from all obligations towards her. In any case I set you free from all your obligations. You're not to feel yourself bound in the slightest way, any more than I shall. There must be perfect freedom on both sides. See, here is your ring back. Give me mine.

HELMER: That, too?

NORA: That, too. 640

HELMER: Here it is.

NORA: That's right. Now it's all over. I've put the keys here. The maids know all about everything in the house—better than I do. To-morrow, after I've left her, Christine will come here and pack up my own things that I brought with me from home. I'll have them sent to me. 645

HELMER: All over! all over!—Nora, shall you never think of me again?

NORA: I know I'll often think of you and the children and this house.

HELMER: May I write to you, Nora?

NORA: No—never. You must not do that.

HELMER: But at least let me send you— 650

NORA: Nothing—nothing—

HELMER: Let me help you if you're in want.

NORA: No. I can receive nothing from a stranger.

HELMER: Nora—can I never be anything more than a stranger to you? 655

NORA: [*taking her bag*] Ah, Torvald, the most miraculous thing of all would have to happen.

HELMER: Tell me what that would be!

NORA: Both you and I would have to be so changed that—Oh, Torvald, I don't believe any longer in miracles happening.

HELMER: But I will believe in it. Tell me? So changed that—? 660

NORA: That our life together would be a real wedlock. Good-bye. [*She goes out through the hall.*]

HELMER: [*sinks down on a chair at the door and buries his face in his hands*] Nora! Nora! [*looks round, and rises*] Empty. She is gone. [*A hope flashes across his mind.*] The most miraculous thing of all—? 665

[*The sound of a door shutting is heard from below.*]

The Importance of Being Earnest (1895)

ate-nineteenth- and early-twentieth-century movements in art and literature (symbolism, expressionism, and surrealism, for example) valued the subjective vision of artists and writers to interpret subjects rather than to reproduce them realistically. Many of these movements innovatively used abstraction and distortion to create evocative impressions or effects. In England, Walter Pater set forth the basic ideas of English aestheticism, which advocated the liberation of art from any function except to live life intensely and to provide sensuous pleasure ("art for art's sake"). But it was Oscar Wilde who became English aestheticism's best-known playwright and its most eloquent spokesman. In his 1889 essay, "The Decay of Lying," Wilde expresses the imaginative power of art to create independent of reality:

> Art is a veil rather than a mirror. She has flowers that no forests know of, birds that no woodland possesses. She makes and unmakes many worlds, and can draw the moon from heaven with a scarlet thread. Hers are the forms more real than living man . . .

The Importance of Being Earnest is Wilde's most successful play. Whereas some critics have seen the play as a flimsy farce that serves as an excuse for Wilde's witty epigrams, others have seen it as a penetratingly insightful social comedy. Wilde's earlier plays were somewhat conventional domestic comedies, featuring a secret being hidden from polite society, typified characters, somewhat clichéd dramatic situations, and sensational last-minute revelations. Although *The Importance of Being Earnest* uses these same devices, it lifts them to ridiculous levels.

The characters are obsessed with surface appearances, and Wilde both celebrates and satirizes their shallowness. He pokes fun at the pillars of society, the nobility, and the clergy (Lady Bracknell and Canon Chasuble) and exposes their moral standards as dull and hypocritical. Wilde contrasts these figures with delightful characters who, as Wilde advocates as the proper aim of art in "The Decay of Lying," tell beautiful untrue things—which later become true.

Algernon invents a friend named "Bunbury," so that he may have an excuse to avoid dull social responsibilities. Jack invents a wicked brother named "Ernest" for much the same purpose and lives as Ernest in London, where he has become engaged to Gwendolen. Jack's ward Cecily invents (in her diary) a romance, engagement, break-up, and reconciliation with the irresistibly wicked Ernest, whom she has never met. Her fiction so appeals to her that when she meets Algernon, pretending to be Ernest, she accepts the events that she imagined as actually having taken place. When Gwendolen meets Cecily at Jack's country estate, confusion arises over who is engaged to "Ernest." Upon discovering that neither man is truly "Ernest," the women refuse to wed them until they are appropriately rechristened. By a delightfully contrived turn of events, Jack eventually proves to be named Ernest. The imagination's power to create models for life to imitate (rather than art imitating life) is clearly portrayed as the deceptions in the play, superior to truths, become true.

261

The Importance of Being Earnest

Characters
JOHN WORTHING, J.P.[1]
LADY BRACKNELL
ALGERNON MONCRIEFF
HON. GWENDOLEN FAIRFAX[2]
REV. CANON CHASUBLE, D.D.[3]
CECILY CARDEW
MERRIMAN, *butler*
MISS PRISM, *governess*
LANE, *manservant*

ACT I ALGERNON MONCRIEFF'S *Flat in Half-Moon Street, W.*
ACT II *The Garden at the Manor House, Woolton*
ACT III *Drawing-Room of the Manor House, Woolton*

——————————————————— **ACT I** ———————————————————

SCENE————*Morning-room in* ALGERNON'S *flat in Half-Moon Street. The room is luxuriously and artistically furnished. The sound of a piano is heard in the adjoining room.* LANE *is arranging afternoon tea on the table, and after the music has ceased,* ALGERNON *enters.*

ALGERNON: Did you hear what I was playing, Lane?
LANE: I didn't think it polite to listen, sir.
ALGERNON: I'm sorry for that, for your sake. I don't play accurately—anyone can play accurately—but I play with wonderful expression. As far as the piano is concerned, sentiment is my forte. I keep science for Life.   5
LANE: Yes, sir.
ALGERNON: And, speaking of the science of Life, have you got the cucumber sandwiches cut for Lady Bracknell?
LANE: Yes, sir. [*hands them on a salver*]

———————————————

[1] **J.P.** Justice of the Peace; indicates a country gentleman with extensive property.
[2] **Hon. Gwendolen Fairfax** identifies her as nobility and her father as a peer. Although "Bracknell" is the family, her surname is Fairfax.
[3] **Rev. Canon Chasuble, D.D.** identifies him as Rector of an Anglo-Catholic church with a Doctorate in theology.

ALGERNON: [*inspects them, takes two, and sits down on the sofa*] Oh! . . . by the way, Lane, I see   10
    from your book that on Thursday night, when Lord Shoreman and Mr. Worthing were
    dining with me, eight bottles of champagne are entered as having been consumed.

LANE: Yes, sir; eight bottles and a pint.

ALGERNON: Why is it that at a bachelor's establishment the servants invariably drink the
    champagne? I ask merely for information.   15

LANE: I attribute it to the superior quality of the wine, sir. I have often observed that in
    married households the champagne is rarely of a first-rate brand.

ALGERNON: Good heavens! Is marriage so demoralizing as that?

LANE: I believe it *is* a very pleasant state, sir. I have had very little experience of it myself
    up to the present. I have only been married once. That was in consequence of a   20
    misunderstanding between myself and a young woman.

ALGERNON: [*languidly*] I don't know that I am much interested in your family life, Lane.

LANE: No, sir; it is not a very interesting subject. I never think of it myself.

ALGERNON: Very natural, I am sure. That will do, Lane, thank you.

LANE: Thank you, sir. [LANE *goes out.*]   25

ALGERNON: Lane's views on marriage seem somewhat lax. Really, if the lower orders don't
    set us a good example, what on earth is the use of them? They seem, as a class, to
    have absolutely no sense of moral responsibility.

      [*Enter* LANE.]

LANE: Mr. Ernest Worthing.

      [*Enter* JACK. LANE *goes out.*]

ALGERNON: How are you, my dear Ernest? What brings you up to town?   30

JACK: Oh, pleasure, pleasure! What else should bring one anywhere? Eating as usual, I see,
    Algy!

ALGERNON: [*stiffly*] I believe it is customary in good society to take some slight refresh-
    ment at five o'clock. Where have you been since last Thursday?

JACK: [*sitting down on the sofa*] In the country.   35

ALGERNON: What on earth do you do there?

JACK: [*pulling off his gloves*] When one is in town one amuses oneself. When one is in the
    country one amuses other people. It is excessively boring.

ALGERNON: And who are the people you amuse?

JACK: [*airily*] Oh, neighbors, neighbors.   40

ALGERNON: Got nice neighbors in your part of Shropshire?

JACK: Perfectly horrid! Never speak to one of them.

ALGERNON: How immensely you must amuse them! [*goes over and takes sandwich*] By the
    way, Shropshire is your county, is it not?

JACK: Eh? Shropshire? Yes, of course. Hallo! Why all these cups? Why cucumber sand-   45
    wiches? Why such reckless extravagance in one so young? Who is coming to tea?

ALGERNON: Oh! merely Aunt Augusta and Gwendolen.

JACK: How perfectly delightful!

ALGERNON: Yes, that is all very well; but I am afraid Aunt Augusta won't quite approve
    of your being here.   50

JACK: May I ask why?

ALGERNON: My dear fellow, the way you flirt with Gwendolen is perfectly disgraceful. It
    is almost as bad as the way Gwendolen flirts with you.

JACK: I am in love with Gwendolen. I have come up to town expressly to propose to her.

ALGERNON: I thought you had come up for pleasure? . . . I call that business.   55

JACK: How utterly unromantic you are!

ALGERNON: I really don't see anything romantic in proposing. It is very romantic to be in love. But there is nothing romantic about a definite proposal. Why, one may be accepted. One usually is, I believe. Then the excitement is all over. The very essence of romance is uncertainty. If ever I get married, I'll certainly try to forget the fact.   60

JACK: I have no doubt about that, dear Algy. The Divorce Court was specially invented for people whose memories are so curiously constituted.

ALGERNON: Oh! there is no use speculating on that subject. Divorces are made in Heaven—[JACK *puts out his hand to take a sandwich,* ALGERNON *at once interferes.*] Please don't touch the cucumber sandwiches. They are ordered specially for Aunt   65
Augusta. [*takes one and eats it*]

JACK: Well, you have been eating them all the time.

ALGERNON: That is quite a different matter. She is my aunt. [*takes plate from below*] Have some bread and butter. The bread and butter is for Gwendolen. Gwendolen is devoted to bread and butter.   70

JACK: [*advancing to table and helping himself*] And very good bread and butter it is too.

ALGERNON: Well, my dear fellow, you need not eat as if you were going to eat it all. You behave as if you were married to her already. You are not married to her already, and I don't think you will ever be.

JACK: Why on earth do you say that?   75

ALGERNON: Well, in the first place girls never marry the men they flirt with. Girls don't think it right.

JACK: Oh, that is nonsense!

ALGERNON: It isn't. It is a great truth. It accounts for the extraordinary number of bachelors that one sees all over the place. In the second place, I don't give my consent.   80

JACK: Your consent!

ALGERNON: My dear fellow, Gwendolen is my first cousin. And before I allow you to marry her, you will have to clear up the whole question of Cecily. [*rings bell*]

JACK: Cecily! What on earth do you mean? What do you mean, Algy, by Cecily? I don't know anyone of the name of Cecily.   85

    [*Enter* LANE.]

ALGERNON: Bring me that cigarette case Mr. Worthing left in the smoking-room the last time he dined here.

LANE: Yes, sir. [LANE *goes out.*]

JACK: Do you mean to say you have had my cigarette case all this time? I wish to goodness you had let me know. I have been writing frantic letters to Scotland Yard about it. I   90
was very nearly offering a large reward.

ALGERNON: Well, I wish you would offer one. I happen to be more than usually hard up.

JACK: There is no good offering a large reward now that the thing is found.

    [*Enter* LANE *with the cigarette case on a salver.* ALGERNON *takes it at once.* LANE *goes out.*]

ALGERNON: I think that is rather mean of you, Ernest, I must say. [*opens case and examines it*] However, it makes no matter, for, now that I look at the inscription, I find that   95
the thing isn't yours after all.

JACK: Of course it's mine. [*moving to him*] You have seen me with it a hundred times, and you have no right whatsoever to read what is written inside. It is a very ungentlemanly thing to read a private cigarette case.

ALGERNON: Oh! it is absurd to have a hard-and-fast rule about what one should read and   100 what one shouldn't. More than half of modern culture depends on what one shouldn't read.

JACK: I am quite aware of the fact, and I don't propose to discuss modern culture. It isn't the sort of thing one should talk of in private. I simply want my cigarette case back.

ALGERNON: Yes; but this isn't your cigarette case. This cigarette case is a present from   105
someone of the name of Cecily, and you said you didn't know anyone of that name.

JACK: Well, if you want to know, Cecily happens to be my aunt.

ALGERNON: Your aunt!

JACK: Yes. Charming old lady she is, too. Lives at Tunbridge Wells. Just give it back to
me, Algy.   110

ALGERNON: [*retreating to back of sofa*] But why does she call herself little Cecily if she is your aunt and lives at Tunbridge Wells? [*reading*] "From little Cecily with her fondest love."

JACK: [*moving to sofa and kneeling upon it*] My dear fellow, what on earth is there in that? Some aunts are tall, some aunts are not tall. That is a matter that surely an aunt may   115
be allowed to decide for herself. You seem to think that every aunt should be exactly like your aunt! That is absurd! For Heaven's sake give me back my cigarette case. [*follows* ALGERNON *round the room*]

ALGERNON: Yes. But why does your aunt call you her uncle? "From little Cecily, with her fondest love to her dear Uncle Jack." There is no objection, I admit, to an aunt being   120
a small aunt, but why an aunt, no matter what her size may be, should call her own nephew her uncle, I can't quite make out. Besides, your name isn't Jack at all; it's Ernest.

JACK: It isn't Ernest; it's Jack.

ALGERNON: You have always told me it was Ernest. I have introduced you to everyone as   125
Ernest. You answer to the name of Ernest. You look as if your name was Ernest. You are the most earnest-looking person I ever saw in my life. It is perfectly absurd your saying that your name isn't Ernest. It's on your cards. Here is one of them. [*taking it from case*] "Mr. Ernest Worthing, B 4, The Albany." I'll keep this as a proof your name is Ernest if ever you attempt to deny it to me, or to Gwendolen, or to anyone   130
else. [*puts the card in his pocket*]

JACK: Well, my name is Ernest in town and Jack in the country, and the cigarette case was given to me in the country.

ALGERNON: Yes, but that does not account for the fact that your small Aunt Cecily, who lives at Tunbridge Wells, calls you her dear uncle. Come, old boy, you had much   135
better have the thing out at once.

JACK: My dear Algy, you talk exactly as if you were a dentist. It is very vulgar to talk like a dentist when one isn't a dentist. It produces a false impression.

ALGERNON: Well, that is exactly what dentists always do. Now, go on! Tell me the whole thing. I may mention that I have always suspected you of being a confirmed and   140
secret Bunburyist; and I am quite sure of it now.

JACK: Bunburyist? What on earth do you mean by a Bunburyist?

ALGERNON: I'll reveal to you the meaning of that incomparable expression as soon as you are kind enough to inform me why you are Ernest in town and Jack in the country.

JACK: Well, produce my cigarette case first.   145

ALGERNON: Here it is. [*hands cigarette case*] Now produce your explanation, and pray make it improbable. [*sits on sofa*]

JACK: My dear fellow, there is nothing improbable about my explanation at all. In fact it's perfectly ordinary. Old Mr. Thomas Cardew, who adopted me when I was a little boy, made me in his will guardian to his grand-daughter, Miss Cecily Cardew. Cecily, who   150 addresses me as her uncle from motives of respect that you could not possibly appreciate, lives at my place in the country under the charge of her admirable governess, Miss Prism.

ALGERNON: Where is that place in the country, by the way?

JACK: That is nothing to you, dear boy. You are not going to be invited. . . . I may tell you   155
candidly that the place is not in Shropshire.

ALGERNON: I suspected that, my dear fellow! I have Bunburyed all over Shropshire on two separate occasions. Now, go on. Why are you Ernest in town and Jack in the country?

JACK: My dear Algy, I don't know whether you will be able to understand my real motives. You are hardly serious enough. When one is placed in the position of   160
guardian, one has to adopt a very high moral tone on all subjects. It's one's duty to do so. And as a high moral tone can hardly be said to conduce very much to either one's health or one's happiness, in order to get up to town I have always pretended to have a younger brother of the name of Ernest, who lives in the Albany, and gets into the most dreadful scrapes. That, my dear Algy, is the whole   165
truth pure and simple.

ALGERNON: The truth is rarely pure and never simple. Modern life would be very tedious if it were either, and modern literature a complete impossibility!

JACK: That wouldn't be at all a bad thing.

ALGERNON: Literary criticism is not your forte, my dear fellow. Don't try it. You should   170
leave that to people who haven't been at a University. They do it so well in the daily papers. What you really are is a Bunburyist. I was quite right in saying you were a Bunburyist. You are one of the most advanced Bunburyists I know.

JACK: What on earth do you mean?

ALGERNON: You have invented a very useful younger brother called Ernest, in order that   175
you may be able to come up to town as often as you like. I have invented an invaluable permanent invalid called Bunbury, in order that I may be able to go down into the country whenever I choose. Bunbury is perfectly invaluable. If it wasn't for Bunbury's extraordinary bad health, for instance, I wouldn't be able to dine with you at Willis' to-night, for I have been really engaged to Aunt Augusta for more than   180
a week.

JACK: I haven't asked you to dine with me anywhere to-night.

ALGERNON: I know. You are absurdly careless about sending out invitations. It is very foolish of you. Nothing annoys people so much as not receiving invitations.

JACK: You had much better dine with your Aunt Augusta.   185

ALGERNON: I haven't the smallest intention of doing anything of the kind. To begin with, I dined there on Monday, and once a week is quite enough to dine with one's own relatives. In the second place, whenever I do dine there I am always treated as a member of the family, and sent down with either no woman at all, or two. In the third place, I know perfectly well whom she will place me next to, to-night. She will   190
place me next Mary Farquhar, who always flirts with her own husband across the dinner-table. That is not very pleasant. Indeed, it is not even decent . . . and that sort of thing is enormously on the increase. The amount of women in London who flirt with their own husbands is perfectly scandalous. It looks so bad. It is simply washing one's clean linen in public. Besides, now that I know you to be a con-   195
firmed Bunburyist I naturally want to talk to you about Bunburying. I want to tell you the rules.

JACK: I'm not a Bunburyist at all. If Gwendolen accepts me, I am going to kill my brother. Indeed, I think I'll kill him in any case. Cecily is a little too much interested in him. It is rather a bore. So I am going to get rid of Ernest. And I strongly advise you to   200 do the same with Mr. . . . with your invalid friend who has the absurd name.

ALGERNON: Nothing will induce me to part with Bunbury, and if you ever get married, which seems to me extremely problematic, you will be very glad to know Bunbury. A man who marries without knowing Bunbury has a very tedious time of it.

JACK: That is nonsense. If I marry a charming girl like Gwendolen, and she is the only girl   205
I ever saw in my life that I would marry, I certainly won't want to know Bunbury.

ALGERNON: Then your wife will. You don't seem to realize, that in married life three is company and two is none.

JACK: [*sentenciously*] That, my dear young friend, is the theory that the corrupt French
Drama[4] has been propounding for the last fifty years.   210

ALGERNON: Yes; and that the happy English home has proved in half the time.

JACK: For heaven's sake, don't try to be cynical. It's perfectly easy to be cynical.

ALGERNON: My dear fellow, it isn't easy to be anything now-a-days. There's such a lot of beastly competition about. [*The sound of an electric bell is heard.*] Ah! that must be Aunt Augusta. Only relatives, or creditors, ever ring in that Wagnerian[5] manner.   215
Now, if I get her out of the way for ten minutes, so that you can have an opportunity for proposing to Gwendolen, may I dine with you to-night at Willis'?

JACK: I suppose so, if you want to.

ALGERNON: Yes, but you must be serious about it. I hate people who are not serious about meals. It is so shallow of them.   220

    [*Enter* LANE.]

LANE: Lady Bracknell and Miss Fairfax.

    [ALGERNON *goes forward to meet them. Enter* LADY BRACKNELL *and*
    GWENDOLEN.]

LADY BRACKNELL: Good afternoon, dear Algernon, I hope you are behaving very well.

ALGERNON: I'm feeling very well, Aunt Augusta.

LADY BRACKNELL: That's not quite the same thing. In fact the two things rarely go together. [*Sees* JACK *and bows to him with icy coldness.*]   225

ALGERNON: [*to* GWENDOLEN] Dear me, you are smart![6]

GWENDOLEN: I am always smart! Aren't I, Mr. Worthing?

JACK: You're quite perfect, Miss Fairfax.

GWENDOLEN: Oh! I hope I am not that. It would leave no room for developments, and I intend to develop in many directions.   230

    [GWENDOLEN *and* JACK *sit down together in the corner.*]

LADY BRACKNELL: I'm sorry if we are a little late, Algernon, but I was obliged to call on dear Lady Harbury. I hadn't been there since her poor husband's death. I never saw a woman so altered; she looks quite twenty years younger. And now I'll have a cup of tea, and one of those nice cucumber sandwiches you promised me.

ALGERNON: Certainly, Aunt Augusta. [*goes over to tea-table*]   235

LADY BRACKNELL: Won't you come and sit here, Gwendolen?

GWENDOLEN: Thanks, mamma, I'm quite comfortable where I am.

---

[4] **corrupt French Drama** the French were less adamant in censoring plays dealing with sexual misconduct than were the English.
[5] **Wagnerian** pertaining to the operas of Richard Wagner (1813–1883), sometimes musically characterized as heavily dramatic and perhaps even imperious
[6] **smart** stylishly dressed

ALGERNON: [*picking up empty plate in horror*] Good heavens! Lane! Why are there no cucumber sandwiches? I ordered them specially.

LANE: [*gravely*] There were no cucumbers in the market this morning, sir. I went down twice.   240

ALGERNON: No cucumbers!

LANE: No, sir. Not even for ready money.

ALGERNON: That will do, Lane, thank you.

LANE: Thank you, sir. [*goes out*]

ALGERNON: I am greatly distressed, Aunt Augusta, about there being no cucumbers, not   245
even for ready money.

LADY BRACKNELL: It really makes no matter, Algernon. I had some crumpets with Lady Harbury, who seems to me to be living entirely for pleasure now.

ALGERNON: I hear her hair has turned quite gold from grief.

LADY BRACKNELL: It certainly has changed its color. From what cause I, of course, cannot   250
say. [ALGERNON *crosses and hands tea.*] Thank you. I've quite a treat for you to-night, Algernon. I am going to send you down with Mary Farquhar. She is such a nice woman, and so attentive to her husband. It's delightful to watch them.

ALGERNON: I am afraid, Aunt Augusta, I shall have to give up the pleasure of dining with you to-night after all.   255

LADY BRACKNELL: [*frowning*] I hope not, Algernon. It would put my table completely out.[7] Your uncle would have to dine upstairs. Fortunately he is accustomed to that.

ALGERNON: It is a great bore, and, I need hardly say, a terrible disappointment to me, but the fact is I have just had a telegram to say that my poor friend Bunbury is very ill again. [*He exchanges glances with* JACK.] They seem to think I should be with him.   260

LADY BRACKNELL: It is very strange. This Mr. Bunbury seems to suffer from curiously bad health.

ALGERNON: Yes; poor Bunbury is a dreadful invalid.

LADY BRACKNELL: Well, I must say, Algernon, that I think it is high time that Mr. Bunbury made up his mind whether he was going to live or to die. This shilly-shallying with   265
the question is absurd. Nor do I in any way approve of the modern sympathy with invalids. I consider it morbid. Illness of any kind is hardly a thing to be encouraged in others. Health is the primary duty of life. I am always telling that to your poor uncle, but he never seems to take much notice . . . as far as any improvement in his ailments goes. I should be much obliged if you would ask Mr. Bunbury, from me,   270
to be kind enough not to have a relapse on Saturday, for I rely on you to arrange my music for me. It is my last reception and one wants something that will encourage conversation, particularly at the end of the season when everyone has practically said whatever they had to say, which, in most cases, was probably not much.

ALGERNON: I'll speak to Bunbury, Aunt Augusta, if he is still conscious, and I think I can   275
promise you he'll be all right by Saturday. Of course the music is a great difficulty. You see, if one plays good music, people don't listen, and if one plays bad music people don't talk. But I'll run over the program I've drawn out, if you will kindly come into the next room for a moment.

LADY BRACKNELL: Thank you, Algernon. It is very thoughtful of you. [*rising, and following*   280
ALGERNON] I'm sure the program will be delightful, after a few expurgations. French songs I cannot possibly allow. People always seem to think that they are improper, and either look shocked, which is vulgar, or laugh, which is worse. But German sounds a thoroughly respectable language, and indeed, I believe is so. Gwendolen, you will accompany me.   285

---

[7] **put my table completely out** ruin the symmetry of the seating arrangements by creating an uneven number of men and women at the table

GWENDOLEN: Certainly, mamma.

> [LADY BRACKNELL *and* ALGERNON *go into the music-room,* GWENDOLEN *remains behind.*]

JACK: Charming day it has been, Miss Fairfax.

GWENDOLEN: Pray don't talk to me about the weather, Mr. Worthing. Whenever people talk to me about the weather, I always feel quite certain that they mean something else. And that makes me so nervous. 290

JACK: I do mean something else.

GWENDOLEN: I thought so. In fact, I am never wrong.

JACK: And I would like to be allowed to take advantage of Lady Bracknell's temporary absence . . .

GWENDOLEN: I would certainly advise you to do so. Mamma has a way of coming back 295 suddenly into a room that I have often had to speak to her about.

JACK: [*nervously*] Miss Fairfax, ever since I met you I have admired you more than any girl . . . I have ever met since . . . I met you.

GWENDOLEN: Yes, I am quite aware of the fact. And I often wish that in public, at any rate, you had been more demonstrative. For me you have always had an irresistible 300 fascination. Even before I met you I was far from indifferent to you. [JACK *looks at her in amazement.*] We live, as I hope you know, Mr. Worthing, in an age of ideals. The fact is constantly mentioned in the more expensive monthly magazines, and has reached the provincial pulpits I am told: and my ideal has always been to love some one of the name of Ernest. There is something in that name that inspires absolute 305 confidence. The moment Algernon first mentioned to me that he had a friend called Ernest, I knew I was destined to love you.

JACK: You really love me, Gwendolen?

GWENDOLEN: Passionately!

JACK: Darling! You don't know how happy you've made me. 310

GWENDOLEN: My own Ernest!

JACK: But you don't really mean to say that you couldn't love me if my name wasn't Ernest?

GWENDOLEN: But your name is Ernest.

JACK: Yes, I know it is. But supposing it was something else? Do you mean to say you 315 couldn't love me then?

GWENDOLEN: [*glibly*] Ah! that is clearly a metaphysical speculation, and like most metaphysical speculations has very little reference at all to the actual facts of real life, as we know them.

JACK: Personally, darling, to speak quite candidly, I don't much care about the name of 320 Ernest . . . I don't think the name suits me at all.

GWENDOLEN: It suits you perfectly. It is a divine name. It has a music of its own. It produces vibrations.

JACK: Well, really, Gwendolen, I must say that I think there are lots of other much nicer names. I think Jack, for instance, a charming name. 325

GWENDOLEN: Jack? . . . No, there is very little music in the name Jack, if any at all, indeed. It does not thrill. It produces absolutely no vibrations . . . I have known several Jacks, and they all, without exception, were more than usually plain. Besides, Jack is a notorious domesticity for John! And I pity any woman who is married to a man called John. She would probably never be allowed to know the entrancing 330 pleasure of a single moment's solitude. The only really safe name is Ernest.

JACK: Gwendolen, I must get christened at once—I mean we must get married at once. There is no time to be lost.

GWENDOLEN: Married, Mr. Worthing?

JACK: [*astounded*] Well . . . surely. You know that I love you, and you led me to believe,   335
Miss Fairfax, that you were not absolutely indifferent to me.

GWENDOLEN: I adore you. But you haven't proposed to me yet. Nothing has been said at
all about marriage. The subject has not even been touched on.

JACK: Well . . . may I propose to you now?

GWENDOLEN: I think it would be an admirable opportunity. And to spare you any pos-   340
sible disappointment, Mr. Worthing, I think it only fair to tell you quite frankly
beforehand that I am fully determined to accept you.

JACK: Gwendolen!

GWENDOLEN: Yes, Mr. Worthing, what have you got to say to me?

JACK: You know what I have got to say to you.   345

GWENDOLEN: Yes, but you don't say it.

JACK: Gwendolen, will you marry me? [*goes on his knees*]

GWENDOLEN: Of course I will, darling. How long you have been about it! I am afraid you
have had very little experience in how to propose.

JACK: My own one, I have never loved anyone in the world but you.   350

GWENDOLEN: Yes, but men often propose for practice. I know my brother Gerald does.
All my girl-friends tell me so. What wonderfully blue eyes you have, Ernest! They are
quite, quite blue. I hope you will always look at me just like that, especially when
there are other people present.

　　　　[*Enter* LADY BRACKNELL.]

LADY BRACKNELL: Mr. Worthing! Rise, sir, from this semi-recumbent posture. It is most   355
indecorous.

GWENDOLEN: Mamma! [*He tries to rise; she restrains him.*] I must beg you to retire. This
is no place for you. Besides, Mr. Worthing has not quite finished yet.

LADY BRACKNELL: Finished what, may I ask?

GWENDOLEN: I am engaged to Mr. Worthing, mamma. [*They rise together.*]   360

LADY BRACKNELL: Pardon me, you are not engaged to anyone. When you do become
engaged to someone, I, or your father, should his health permit him, will inform you
of the fact. An engagement should come on a young girl as a surprise, pleasant or
unpleasant, as the case may be. It is hardly a matter that she could be allowed to
arrange for herself. . . . And now I have a few questions to put to you, Mr. Worthing.   365
While I am making these inquiries, you, Gwendolen, will wait for me below in the
carriage.

GWENDOLEN: [*reproachfully*] Mamma!

LADY BRACKNELL: In the carriage, Gwendolen! [GWENDOLEN *goes to the door. She and*
JACK *blow kisses to each other behind* LADY BRACKNELL's *back.* LADY BRACKNELL   370
*looks vaguely about as if she could not understand what the noise was. Finally turns
round.*] Gwendolen, the carriage!

GWENDOLEN: Yes, mamma. [*goes out, looking back at* JACK]

LADY BRACKNELL: [*sitting down*] You can take a seat, Mr. Worthing. [*looks in her pocket
for note-book and pencil*]   375

JACK: Thank you, Lady Bracknell, I prefer standing.

LADY BRACKNELL: [*pencil and note-book in hand*] I feel bound to tell you that you are not
down on my list of eligible young men, although I have the same list as the dear
Duchess of Bolton has. We work together, in fact. However, I am quite ready to enter
your name, should your answers be what a really affectionate mother requires. Do   380
you smoke?

JACK: Well, yes, I must admit I smoke.

LADY BRACKNELL: I am glad to hear it. A man should always have an occupation of some kind. There are far too many idle men in London as it is. How old are you?

JACK: Twenty-nine. 385

LADY BRACKNELL: A very good age to be married at. I have always been of opinion that a man who desires to get married should know either everything or nothing. Which do you know?

JACK: [*after some hesitation*] I know nothing, Lady Bracknell.

LADY BRACKNELL: I am pleased to hear it. I do not approve of anything that tampers with 390 natural ignorance. Ignorance is like a delicate exotic fruit; touch it and the bloom is gone. The whole theory of modern education is radically unsound. Fortunately in England, at any rate, education produces no effect whatsoever. If it did, it would prove a serious danger to the upper classes, and probably lead to acts of violence in Grosvenor Square. What is your income? 395

JACK: Between seven and eight thousand a year.

LADY BRACKNELL: [*makes a note in her book*] In land, or in investments?

JACK: In investments, chiefly.

LADY BRACKNELL: That is satisfactory. What between the duties expected of one during one's lifetime, and the duties[8] exacted from one after one's death, land has ceased to 400 be either a profit or a pleasure. It gives one position, and prevents one from keeping it up. That's all that can be said about land.

JACK: I have a country house with some land, of course, attached to it, about fifteen hundred acres, I believe; but I don't depend on that for my real income. In fact, as far as I can make out, the poachers are the only people who make anything out of it. 405

LADY BRACKNELL: A country house! How many bedrooms? Well, that point can be cleared up afterwards. You have a town house, I hope? A girl with a simple, unspoiled nature, like Gwendolen, could hardly be expected to reside in the country.

JACK: Well, I own a house in Belgrave Square, but it is let by the year to Lady Bloxham. Of course, I can get it back whenever I like, at six months' notice. 410

LADY BRACKNELL: Lady Bloxham? I don't know her.

JACK: Oh, she goes about very little. She is a lady considerably advanced in years.

LADY BRACKNELL: Ah, now-a-days that is no guarantee of respectability of character. What number in Belgrave Square?

JACK: 149. 415

LADY BRACKNELL: [*shaking her head*] The unfashionable side. I thought there was something. However, that could easily be altered.

JACK: Do you mean the fashion, or the side?

LADY BRACKNELL: [*sternly*] Both, if necessary, I presume. What are your politics?

JACK: Well, I am afraid I really have none. I am a Liberal Unionist.[9] 420

LADY BRACKNELL: Oh, they count as Tories. They dine with us. Or come in the evening, at any rate. Now to minor matters. Are your parents living?

JACK: I have lost both my parents.

LADY BRACKNELL: Both? . . . That seems like carelessness. Who was your father? He was evidently a man of some wealth. Was he born in what the Radical papers call the 425 purple of commerce, or did he rise from the ranks of the aristocracy?

JACK: I am afraid I really don't know. The fact is, Lady Bracknell, I said I had lost my parents. It would be nearer the truth to say that my parents seem to have lost me . . .

---

[8] **duties estate taxes**; Wilde uses "duties" to set the two meanings of the word [responsibilities and taxes] off against each other

[9] **Liberal Unionist** member of the Liberal Party who opposed its leader, Gladstone, on many of his policies; therefore acceptable to the opposition party, the Tories

I don't actually know who I am by birth. I was . . . well, I was found.

LADY BRACKNELL: Found! 430

JACK: The late Mr. Thomas Cardew, an old gentleman of a very charitable and kindly disposition, found me, and gave me the name of Worthing, because he happened to have a first-class ticket for Worthing in his pocket at the time. Worthing is a place in Sussex. It is a seaside resort.

LADY BRACKNELL: Where did the charitable gentleman who had a first-class ticket for this 435 seaside resort find you?

JACK: [*gravely*] In a hand-bag.[10]

LADY BRACKNELL: A hand-bag?

JACK: [*very seriously*] Yes, Lady Bracknell. I was in a hand-bag—a somewhat large, black leather hand-bag, with handles to it—an ordinary hand-bag in fact. 440

LADY BRACKNELL: In what locality did this Mr. James, or Thomas, Cardew come across this ordinary hand-bag?

JACK: In the cloak-room at Victoria Station. It was given to him in mistake for his own.

LADY BRACKNELL: The cloak-room at Victoria Station?

JACK: Yes. The Brighton line. 445

LADY BRACKNELL: The line is immaterial. Mr. Worthing, I confess I feel somewhat bewildered by what you have just told me. To be born, or at any rate bred, in a hand-bag, whether it had handles or not, seems to me to display a contempt for the ordinary decencies of family life that remind one of the worst excesses of the French Revolution. And I presume you know what that unfortunate movement led to? As for the particular 450 locality in which the hand-bag was found, a cloak-room at a railway station might serve to conceal a social indiscretion—has probably, indeed, been used for that purpose before now—but it could hardly be regarded as an assured basis for a recognized position in good society.

JACK: May I ask you then what you would advise me to do? I need hardly say I would do 455 anything in the world to ensure Gwendolen's happiness.

LADY BRACKNELL: I would strongly advise you, Mr. Worthing, to try and acquire some relations as soon as possible, and to make a definite effort to produce at any rate one parent, of either sex, before the season is quite over.

JACK: Well, I don't see how I could possibly manage to do that. I can produce the hand-bag 460 at any moment. It is in my dressing-room at home. I really think that should satisfy you, Lady Bracknell.

LADY BRACKNELL: Me, sir! What has it to do with me? You can hardly imagine that I and Lord Bracknell would dream of allowing our only daughter—a girl brought up with the utmost care—to marry into a cloak-room, and form an alliance with a parcel? Good 465 morning, Mr. Worthing! [**LADY BRACKNELL** *sweeps out in majestic indignation.*]

JACK: Good morning!

[**ALGERNON**, *from the other room, strikes up the Wedding March.* **JACK** *looks perfectly furious and goes to the door.*]

JACK: For goodness' sake don't play that ghastly tune, Algy! How idiotic you are!

[*The music stops and* **ALGERNON** *enters cheerily.*]

ALGERNON: Didn't it go off all right, old boy? You don't mean to say Gwendolen refused you? I know it is a way she has. She is always refusing people. I think it is most ill- 470 natured of her.

---

[10] **hand-bag** refers to a medium-size traveling bag (not a lady's small purse)

JACK: Oh, Gwendolen is as right as a trivet.[11] As far as she is concerned, we are engaged. Her mother is perfectly unbearable. Never met such a Gorgon . . . .[12] I don't really know what a Gorgon is like, but I am quite sure that Lady Bracknell is one. In any case, she is a monster, without being a myth, which is rather unfair. . . . I beg your pardon, Algy, I suppose I shouldn't talk about your own aunt in that way before you. 475

ALGERNON: My dear boy, I love hearing my relations abused. It is the only thing that makes me put up with them at all. Relations are simply a tedious pack of people, who haven't got the remotest knowledge of how to live, nor the smallest instinct about when to die. 480

JACK: Oh, that is nonsense!

ALGERNON: It isn't!

JACK: Well, I won't argue about the matter. You always want to argue about things.

ALGERNON: That is exactly what things were originally made for.

JACK: Upon my word, if I thought that, I'd shoot myself . . . . [*a pause*] You don't think there is any chance of Gwendolen becoming like her mother in about a hundred and fifty years, do you, Algy? 485

ALGERNON: All women become like their mothers. That is their tragedy. No man does. That's his.

JACK: Is that clever? 490

ALGERNON: It is perfectly phrased! and quite as true as any observation in civilized life should be.

JACK: I am sick to death of cleverness. Everybody is clever now-a-days. You can't go anywhere without meeting clever people. The thing has become an absolute public nuisance. I wish to goodness we had a few fools left. 495

ALGERNON: We have.

JACK: I should extremely like to meet them. What do they talk about?

ALGERNON: The fools? Oh! about the clever people, of course.

JACK: What fools!

ALGERNON: By the way, did you tell Gwendolen the truth about your being Ernest in town, and Jack in the country? 500

JACK: [*in a very patronizing manner*] My dear fellow, the truth isn't quite the sort of thing one tells to a nice, sweet, refined girl. What extraordinary ideas you have about the way to behave to a woman!

ALGERNON: The only way to behave to a woman is to make love to her, if she is pretty, and to someone else if she is plain. 505

JACK: Oh, that is nonsense.

ALGERNON: What about your brother? What about the profligate Ernest?

JACK: Oh, before the end of the week I shall have got rid of him. I'll say he died in Paris of apoplexy. Lots of people die of apoplexy, quite suddenly, don't they? 510

ALGERNON: Yes, but it's hereditary, my dear fellow. It's a sort of thing that runs in families. You had much better say a severe chill.

JACK: You are sure a severe chill isn't hereditary, or anything of that kind?

ALGERNON: Of course it isn't!

JACK: Very well, then. My poor brother Ernest is carried off suddenly in Paris, by a severe chill. That gets rid of him. 515

---

[11] **right as a trivet** perfectly fine; stable and reliable
[12] **Gorgon** in Greek mythology, the Gorgons were three sisters so hideous that to look upon any one of them turned a man into stone

ALGERNON: But I thought you said that . . . Miss Cardew was a little too much interested in your poor brother Ernest? Won't she feel his loss a good deal?

JACK: Oh, that is all right. Cecily is not a silly, romantic girl, I am glad to say. She has got a capital appetite, goes for long walks, and pays no attention at all to her lessons.   520

ALGERNON: I would rather like to see Cecily.

JACK: I will take very good care you never do. She is excessively pretty, and she is only just eighteen.

ALGERNON: Have you told Gwendolen yet that you have an excessively pretty ward who is only just eighteen?   525

JACK: Oh! one doesn't blurt these things out to people. Cecily and Gwendolen are perfectly certain to be extremely great friends. I'll bet you anything you like that half an hour after they have met, they will be calling each other sister.

ALGERNON: Women only do that when they have called each other a lot of other things first. Now, my dear boy, if we want to get a good table at Willis', we really must go   530
and dress. Do you know it is nearly seven?

JACK: [*irritably*] Oh! it always is nearly seven.

ALGERNON: Well, I'm hungry.

JACK: I never knew you when you weren't . . . .

ALGERNON: What shall we do after dinner? Go to a theatre?   535

JACK: Oh, no! I loathe listening.

ALGERNON: Well, let us go to the Club?

JACK: Oh, no! I hate talking.

ALGERNON: Well, we might trot round to the Empire[13] at ten?

JACK: Oh, no! I can't bear looking at things. It is so silly.   540

ALGERNON: Well, what shall we do?

JACK: Nothing!

ALGERNON: It is awfully hard work doing nothing. However, I don't mind hard work where there is no definite object of any kind.

[*Enter* LANE.]

LANE: Miss Fairfax.   545

[*Enter* GWENDOLEN. LANE *goes out.*]

ALGERNON: Gwendolen, upon my word!

GWENDOLEN: Algy, kindly turn your back. I have something very particular to say to Mr. Worthing.

ALGERNON: Really, Gwendolen, I don't think I can allow this at all.

GWENDOLEN: Algy, you always adopt a strictly immoral attitude towards life. You are not   550
quite old enough to do that.

[ALGERNON *retires to the fireplace.*]

JACK: My own darling!

GWENDOLEN: Ernest, we may never be married. From the expression on mamma's face I fear we never shall. Few parents now-a-days pay any regard to what their children say to them. The old-fashioned respect for the young is fast dying out. Whatever influ-   555
ence I ever had over mamma, I lost at the age of three. But although she may prevent

---

[13] **Empire** theatre specializing in popular music and farce

us from becoming man and wife, and I may marry someone else, and marry often, nothing that she can possibly do can alter my eternal devotion to you.

JACK: Dear Gwendolen!

GWENDOLEN: The story of your romantic origin, as related to me by mamma, with   560
unpleasing comments, has naturally stirred the deeper fibers of my nature. Your Christian name[14] has an irresistible fascination. The simplicity of your character makes you exquisitely incomprehensible to me. Your town address at the Albany I have. What is your address in the country?

JACK: The Manor House, Woolton, Hertfordshire.   565

[ALGERNON, *who has been carefully listening, smiles to himself, and writes the address on his shirt-cuff. Then picks up the Railway Guide.*]

GWENDOLEN: There is a good postal service, I suppose? It may be necessary to do something desperate. That, of course, will require serious consideration. I will communicate with you daily.

JACK: My own one!

GWENDOLEN: How long do you remain in town?   570

JACK: Till Monday.

GWENDOLEN: Good! Algy, you may turn round now.

ALGERNON: Thanks, I've turned round already.

GWENDOLEN: You may also ring the bell.

JACK: You will let me see you to your carriage, my own darling?   575

GWENDOLEN: Certainly.

JACK: [*to* LANE, *who now enters.*] I will see Miss Fairfax out.

LANE: Yes, sir.

[JACK *and* GWENDOLEN *go off.* LANE *presents several letters on a salver to* ALGERNON. *It is to be surmised that they are bills, as* ALGERNON, *after looking at the envelopes, tears them up.*]

ALGERNON: A glass of sherry, Lane.

LANE: Yes, sir.   580

ALGERNON: To-morrow, Lane, I'm going Bunburying.

LANE: Yes, sir.

ALGERNON: I shall probably not be back till Monday. You can put up my dress clothes, my smoking jacket, and all the Bunbury suits . . .

LANE: Yes, sir. [*handing sherry*]   585

ALGERNON: I hope to-morrow will be a fine day, Lane.

LANE: It never is, sir.

ALGERNON: Lane, you're a perfect pessimist.

LANE: I do my best to give satisfaction, sir.

[*Enter* JACK. LANE *goes off.*]

JACK: There's a sensible, intellectual girl! the only girl I ever cared for in my life. [ALGERNON   590
is laughing immoderately.] What on earth are you so amused at?

ALGERNON: Oh, I'm a little anxious about poor Bunbury, that's all.

JACK: If you don't take care, your friend Bunbury will get you into a serious scrape some day.

---

[14] **Your Christian name** first name given in the sacrament of baptism (christening)

ALGERNON: I love scrapes. They are the only things that are never serious.
JACK: Oh, that's nonsense, Algy. You never talk anything but nonsense. 595
ALGERNON: Nobody ever does.

> [JACK *looks indignantly at him, and leaves the room.* ALGERNON *lights a cigarette, reads his shirt-cuff, and smiles.*]

CURTAIN

ACT II

SCENE————*Garden at the Manor House. A flight of gray stone steps leads up to the house. The garden, an old-fashioned one, full of roses. Time of year, July. Basket chairs, and a table covered with books, are set under a large yew tree.* MISS PRISM *discovered seated at the table.* CECILY *is at the back watering flowers.*

MISS PRISM: [*calling*] Cecily, Cecily! Surely such a utilitarian occupation as the watering of flowers is rather Moulton's duty than yours? Especially at a moment when intellectual pleasures await you. Your German grammar is on the table. Pray open it at page fifteen. We will repeat yesterday's lesson.
CECILY: [*coming over very slowly*] But I don't like German. It isn't at all a becoming language. 5
I know perfectly well that I look quite plain after my German lesson.
MISS PRISM: Child, you know how anxious your guardian is that you should improve yourself in every way. He laid particular stress on your German, as he was leaving for town yesterday. Indeed, he always lays stress on your German when he is leaving for town.
CECILY: Dear Uncle Jack is so very serious! Sometimes he is so serious that I think he 10
cannot be quite well.
MISS PRISM: [*drawing herself up*] Your guardian enjoys the best of health, and his gravity of demeanor is especially to be commended in one so comparatively young as he is. I know no one who has a higher sense of duty and responsibility.
CECILY: I suppose that is why he often looks a little bored when we three are together. 15
MISS PRISM: Cecily! I am surprised at you. Mr. Worthing has many troubles in his life. Idle merriment and triviality would be out of place in his conversation. You must remember his constant anxiety about that unfortunate young man, his brother.
CECILY: I wish Uncle Jack would allow that unfortunate young man, his brother, to come down here sometimes. We might have a good influence over him, Miss Prism. I am 20
sure you certainly would. You know German, and geology, and things of that kind influence a man very much. [CECILY *begins to write in her diary.*]
MISS PRISM: [*shaking her head*] I do not think that even I could produce any effect on a character that, according to his own brother's admission, is irretrievably weak and vacillating. Indeed, I am not sure that I would desire to reclaim him. I am not in 25
favor of this modern mania for turning bad people into good people at a moment's notice. As a man sows so let him reap. You must put away your diary, Cecily. I really don't see why you should keep a diary at all.

CECILY: I keep a diary in order to enter the wonderful secrets of my life. If I didn't write them down I should probably forget all about them.   30

MISS PRISM: Memory, my dear Cecily, is the diary that we all carry about with us.

CECILY: Yes, but it usually chronicles the things that have never happened, and couldn't possibly have happened. I believe that Memory is responsible for nearly all the three-volume novels that Mudie[15] sends us.

MISS PRISM: Do not speak slightingly of the three-volume novel, Cecily. I wrote one   35
myself in earlier days.

CECILY: Did you really, Miss Prism? How wonderfully clever you are! I hope it did not end happily? I don't like novels that end happily. They depress me so much.

MISS PRISM: The good ended happily, and the bad unhappily. That is what Fiction means.   40

CECILY: I suppose so. But it seems very unfair. And was your novel ever published?

MISS PRISM: Alas! no. The manuscript unfortunately was abandoned. I use the word in the sense of lost or mislaid. To your work, child, these speculations are profitless.

CECILY: [*smiling*] But I see dear Dr. Chasuble coming up through the garden.

MISS PRISM: [*rising and advancing*] Dr. Chasuble! This is indeed a pleasure.   45

[*Enter* CANON CHASUBLE.]

CHASUBLE: And how are we this morning? Miss Prism, you are, I trust, well?

CECILY: Miss Prism has just been complaining of a slight headache. I think it would do her so much good to have a short stroll with you in the park, Dr. Chasuble.

MISS PRISM: Cecily, I have not mentioned anything about a headache.

CECILY: No, dear Miss Prism, I know that, but I felt instinctively that you had a headache.   50
Indeed I was thinking about that, and not about my German lesson when the Rector came in.

CHASUBLE: I hope, Cecily, you are not inattentive.

CECILY: Oh, I am afraid I am.

CHASUBLE: That is strange. Were I fortunate enough to be Miss Prism's pupil, I would   55
hang upon her lips. [MISS PRISM *glares*.] I spoke metaphorically.—My metaphor was drawn from bees. Ahem! Mr. Worthing, I suppose, has not returned from town yet?

MISS PRISM: We do not expect him till Monday afternoon.

CHASUBLE: Ah yes, he usually likes to spend his Sunday in London. He is not one of those whose sole aim is enjoyment, as, by all accounts, that unfortunate young man,   60
his brother, seems to be. But I must not disturb Egeria[16] and her pupil any longer.

MISS PRISM: Egeria? My name is Lætitia, Doctor.

CHASUBLE: [*bowing*] A classical allusion merely, drawn from the Pagan authors. I shall see you both no doubt at Evensong.

MISS PRISM: I think, dear Doctor, I will have a stroll with you. I find I have a headache   65
after all, and a walk might do it good.

CHASUBLE: With pleasure, Miss Prism, with pleasure. We might go as far as the schools and back.

MISS PRISM: That would be delightful. Cecily, you will read your Political Economy in my absence. The chapter on the Fall of the Rupee you may omit. It is somewhat too   70
sensational. Even these metallic problems have their melodramatic side. [*goes down the garden with* DR. CHASUBLE]

---

[15] **Mudie** popular lending-library service of the day
[16] **Egeria** according to Roman legend, a water-nymph goddess who inspired and guided Numa Pompilius (the successor of Romulus) in the kingship of Rome; she taught him wise legislation.

CECILY: [*picks up books and throws them back on table*] Horrid Political Economy! Horrid Geography! Horrid, horrid German!

[*Enter* MERRIMAN *with a card on a salver.*]

MERRIMAN: Mr. Ernest Worthing has just driven over from the station. He has brought   75
his luggage with him.

CECILY: [*takes the card and reads it*] "Mr. Ernest Worthing, B 4, The Albany, W." Uncle Jack's brother! Did you tell him Mr. Worthing was in town?

MERRIMAN: Yes, Miss. He seemed very much disappointed. I mentioned that you and Miss Prism were in the garden. He said he was anxious to speak to you privately for   80
a moment.

CECILY: Ask Mr. Ernest Worthing to come here. I suppose you had better talk to the housekeeper about a room for him.

MERRIMAN: Yes, Miss. [MERRIMAN *goes off.*]

CECILY: I have never met any really wicked person before. I feel rather frightened. I am so   85
afraid he will look just like everyone else.

[*Enter* ALGERNON, *very gay and debonair.*]

He does!

ALGERNON: [*raising his hat*] You are my little Cousin Cecily, I'm sure.

CECILY: You are under some strange mistake. I am not little. In fact, I am more than usually tall for my age. [ALGERNON *is rather taken aback.*] But I am your Cousin Cecily.   90
You, I see from your card, are Uncle Jack's brother, my Cousin Ernest, my wicked Cousin Ernest.

ALGERNON: Oh! I am not really wicked at all, Cousin Cecily. You mustn't think that I am wicked.

CECILY: If you are not, then you have certainly been deceiving us all in a very inexcusable   95
manner. I hope you have not been leading a double life, pretending to be wicked and being really good all the time. That would be hypocrisy.

ALGERNON: [*looks at her in amazement*] Oh! Of course I have been rather reckless.

CECILY: I am glad to hear it.

ALGERNON: In fact, now you mention the subject, I have been very bad in my own small   100
way.

CECILY: I don't think you should be so proud of that, though I am sure it must have been very pleasant.

ALGERNON: It is much pleasanter being here with you.

CECILY: I can't understand how you are here at all. Uncle Jack won't be back till Monday   105
afternoon.

ALGERNON: That is a great disappointment. I am obliged to go up by the first train on Monday morning. I have a business appointment that I am anxious . . . to miss.

CECILY: Couldn't you miss it anywhere but in London?

ALGERNON: No; the appointment is in London.   110

CECILY: Well, I know, of course, how important it is not to keep a business engagement, if one wants to retain any sense of the beauty of life, but still I think you had better wait till Uncle Jack arrives. I know he wants to speak to you about your emigrating.

ALGERNON: About my what?

CECILY: Your emigrating. He has gone up to buy your outfit.   115

ALGERNON: I certainly wouldn't let Jack buy my outfit. He has no taste in neckties at all.

CECILY: I don't think you will require neckties. Uncle Jack is sending you to Australia.

ALGERNON: Australia! I'd sooner die.

CECILY: Well, he said at dinner on Wednesday night, that you would have to choose
between this world, the next world, and Australia.   120
ALGERNON: Oh, well! The accounts I have received of Australia and the next world, are
not particularly encouraging. This world is good enough for me, Cousin Cecily.
CECILY: Yes, but are you good enough for it?
ALGERNON: I'm afraid I'm not that. That is why I want you to reform me. You might
make that your mission, if you don't mind, Cousin Cecily.   125
CECILY: I'm afraid I've not time, this afternoon.
ALGERNON: Well, would you mind my reforming myself this afternoon?
CECILY: That is rather quixotic of you. But I think you should try.
ALGERNON: I will. I feel better already.
CECILY: You are looking a little worse.   130
ALGERNON: That is because I am hungry.
CECILY: How thoughtless of me. I should have remembered that when one is going to lead
an entirely new life, one requires regular and wholesome meals. Won't you come in?
ALGERNON: Thank you. Might I have a buttonhole[17] first? I never have any appetite unless
I have a buttonhole first.   135
CECILY: A Maréchal Niel?[18] [picks up scissors]
ALGERNON: No, I'd sooner have a pink rose.
CECILY: Why? [cuts a flower]
ALGERNON: Because you are like a pink rose, Cousin Cecily.
CECILY: I don't think it can be right for you to talk to me like that. Miss Prism never says   140
such things to me.
ALGERNON: Then Miss Prism is a short-sighted old lady. [CECILY puts the rose in his button-
hole.] You are the prettiest girl I ever saw.
CECILY: Miss Prism says that all good looks are a snare.
ALGERNON: They are a snare that every sensible man would like to be caught in.   145
CECILY: Oh! I don't think I would care to catch a sensible man. I shouldn't know what to
talk to him about.

[They pass into the house. MISS PRISM and DR. CHASUBLE return.]

MISS PRISM: You are too much alone, dear Dr. Chasuble. You should get married. A misanthrope I can understand—a womanthrope,[19] never!
CHASUBLE: [with a scholar's shudder] Believe me, I do not deserve so neologistic a phrase. The   150
precept as well as the practice of the Primitive Church was distinctly against matrimony.
MISS PRISM: [sententiously] That is obviously the reason why the Primitive Church has not
lasted up to the present day. And you do not seem to realize, dear Doctor, that by
persistently remaining single, a man converts himself into a permanent public temp-
tation. Men should be careful; this very celibacy leads weaker vessels astray.   155
CHASUBLE: But is a man not equally attractive when married?
MISS PRISM: No married man is ever attractive except to his wife.
CHASUBLE: And often, I've been told, not even to her.
MISS PRISM: That depends on the intellectual sympathies of the woman. Maturity can always
be depended on. Ripeness can be trusted. Young women are green. [CHASUBLE starts.]   160
I spoke horticulturally. My metaphor was drawn from fruits. But where is Cecily?
CHASUBLE: Perhaps she followed us to the schools.

---

[17] **buttonhole** flower worn in the lapel
[18] **Maréchal Niel** pale yellow rose named in honor of a French general
[19] **Womanthrope** Ms. Prism's word for one who hates women; a "misanthrope" hates all human kind.

[*Enter* JACK *slowly from the back of the garden. He is dressed in the deepest mourning, with crape hat-band and black gloves.*]

MISS PRISM: Mr. Worthing!

CHASUBLE: Mr. Worthing?

MISS PRISM: This is indeed a surprise. We did not look for you till Monday afternoon.   165

JACK: [*Shakes* MISS PRISM*'s hand in a tragic manner.*] I have returned sooner than I expected. Dr. Chasuble, I hope you are well?

CHASUBLE: Dear Mr. Worthing, I trust this garb of woe does not betoken some terrible calamity?

JACK: My brother.   170

MISS PRISM: More shameful debts and extravagance?

CHASUBLE: Still leading his life of pleasure?

JACK: [*shaking his head*] Dead.

CHASUBLE: Your brother Ernest dead?

JACK: Quite dead.   175

MISS PRISM: What a lesson for him! I trust he will profit by it.

CHASUBLE: Mr. Worthing, I offer you my sincere condolence. You have at least the consolation of knowing that you were always the most generous and forgiving of brothers.

JACK: Poor Ernest! He had many faults, but it is a sad, sad blow.

CHASUBLE: Very sad indeed. Were you with him at the end?   180

JACK: No. He died abroad; in Paris, in fact. I had a telegram last night from the manager of the Grand Hotel.

CHASUBLE: Was the cause of death mentioned?

JACK: A severe chill, it seems.

MISS PRISM: As a man sows, so shall he reap.   185

CHASUBLE: [*raising his hand*] Charity, dear Miss Prism, charity! None of us are perfect. I myself am peculiarly susceptible to draughts. Will the interment take place here?

JACK: No. He seems to have expressed a desire to be buried in Paris.

CHASUBLE: In Paris! [*shakes his head*] I fear that hardly points to any very serious state of mind at the last. You would no doubt wish me to make some slight allusion to this   190
tragic domestic affliction next Sunday. [JACK *presses his hand convulsively.*] My sermon on the meaning of the manna[20] in the wilderness can be adapted to almost any occasion, joyful, or, as in the present case, distressing. [*All sigh.*] I have preached it at harvest celebrations, christenings, confirmations, on days of humiliation and festal days. The last time I delivered it was in the Cathedral, as a charity sermon on   195
behalf of the Society for the Prevention of Discontent among the Upper Orders. The Bishop, who was present, was much struck by some of the analogies I drew.

JACK: Ah, that reminds me, you mentioned christenings I think, Dr. Chasuble? I suppose you know how to christen all right? [CHASUBLE *looks astounded.*] I mean, of course, you are continually christening, aren't you?   200

MISS PRISM: It is, I regret to say, one of the Rector's most constant duties in this parish. I have often spoken to the poorer classes on the subject. But they don't seem to know what thrift is.

CHASUBLE: But is there any particular infant in whom you are interested, Mr. Worthing? Your brother was, I believe, unmarried, was he not?   205

JACK: Oh, yes.

---

[20] **manna** miraculous "bread from heaven" (Exodus 16)

MISS PRISM: [*bitterly*] People who live entirely for pleasure usually are.

JACK: But it is not for any child, dear Doctor. I am very fond of children. No! the fact is, I would like to be christened myself, this afternoon, if you have nothing better to do.

CHASUBLE: But surely, Mr. Worthing, you have been christened already? 210

JACK: I don't remember anything about it.

CHASUBLE: But have you any grave doubts on the subject?

JACK: I certainly intend to have. Of course, I don't know if the thing would bother you in any way, or if you think I am a little too old now.

CHASUBLE: Not at all. The sprinkling, and, indeed, the immersion of adults is a perfectly 215 canonical practice.

JACK: Immersion!

CHASUBLE: You need have no apprehensions. Sprinkling is all that is necessary, or indeed I think advisable. Our weather is so changeable. At what hour would you wish the ceremony performed? 220

JACK: Oh, I might trot round about five if that would suit you.

CHASUBLE: Perfectly, perfectly! In fact I have two similar ceremonies to perform at that time. A case of twins that occurred recently in one of the outlying cottages on your own estate. Poor Jenkins the carter, a most hard-working man.

JACK: Oh! I don't see much fun in being christened along with other babies. It would be 225 childish. Would half-past five do?

CHASUBLE: Admirably! Admirably! [*takes out watch*] And now, dear Mr. Worthing, I will not intrude any longer into a house of sorrow. I would merely beg you not to be too much bowed down by grief. What seem to us bitter trials at the moment are often blessings in disguise. 230

MISS PRISM: This seems to me a blessing of an extremely obvious kind.

[*Enter* CECILY *from the house.*]

CECILY: Uncle Jack! Oh, I am pleased to see you back. But what horrid clothes you have on! Do go and change them.

MISS PRISM: Cecily!

CHASUBLE: My child! My child! 235

[CECILY *goes towards* JACK; *he kisses her brow in a melancholy manner.*]

CECILY: What is the matter, Uncle Jack? Do look happy! You look as if you had a toothache and I have such a surprise for you. Who do you think is in the dining-room? Your brother!

JACK: Who?

CECILY: Your brother Ernest. He arrived about half an hour ago. 240

JACK: What nonsense! I haven't got a brother.

CECILY: Oh, don't say that. However badly he may have behaved to you in the past, he is still your brother. You couldn't be so heartless as to disown him. I'll tell him to come out. And you will shake hands with him, won't you, Uncle Jack? [*runs back into the house*]

CHASUBLE: These are very joyful tidings. 245

MISS PRISM: After we had all been resigned to his loss, his sudden return seems to me peculiarly distressing.

JACK: My brother is in the dining-room? I don't know what it all means. I think it is perfectly absurd.

[*Enter* ALGERNON *and* CECILY *hand in hand. They come slowly up to* JACK.]

JACK: Good heavens! [*motions* ALGERNON *away*] 250

ALGERNON: Brother John, I have come down from town to tell you that I am very sorry for all the trouble I have given you, and that I intend to lead a better life in the future.

[JACK *glares at him and does not take his hand.*]

CECILY: Uncle Jack, you are not going to refuse your own brother's hand?

JACK: Nothing will induce me to take his hand. I think his coming down here disgraceful.   255
He knows perfectly well why.

CECILY: Uncle Jack, do be nice. There is some good in everyone. Ernest has just been telling me about his poor invalid friend Mr. Bunbury, whom he goes to visit so often.
And surely there must be much good in one who is kind to an invalid, and leaves the
pleasures of London to sit by a bed of pain.   260

JACK: Oh! he has been talking about Bunbury, has he?

CECILY: Yes, he has told me all about poor Mr. Bunbury, and his terrible state of health.

JACK: Bunbury! Well, I won't have him talk to you about Bunbury or about anything else.
It is enough to drive one perfectly frantic.

ALGERNON: Of course I admit that the faults were all on my side. But I must say that I   265
think that Brother John's coldness to me is peculiarly painful. I expected a more
enthusiastic welcome, especially considering it is the first time I have come here.

CECILY: Uncle Jack, if you don't shake hands with Ernest I will never forgive you.

JACK: Never forgive me?

CECILY: Never, never, never!   270

JACK: Well, this is the last time I shall ever do it. [*shakes hands with* ALGERNON *and*
glares]

CHASUBLE: It's pleasant, is it not, to see so perfect a reconciliation? I think we might leave
the two brothers together.

MISS PRISM: Cecily, you will come with us.   275

CECILY: Certainly, Miss Prism. My little task of reconciliation is over.

CHASUBLE: You have done a beautiful action to-day, dear child.

MISS PRISM: We must not be premature in our judgments.

CECILY: I feel very happy.

[*They all go off except* JACK *and* ALGERNON.]

JACK: You young scoundrel, Algy, you must get out of this place as soon as possible. I don't   280
allow any Bunburying here.

[*Enter* MERRIMAN.]

MERRIMAN: I have put Mr. Ernest's things in the room next to yours, sir. I suppose that
is all right?

JACK: What?

MERRIMAN: Mr. Ernest's luggage, sir. I have unpacked it and put it in the room next to   285
your own.

JACK: His luggage?

MERRIMAN: Yes, sir. Three portmanteaus, a dressing-case, two hat-boxes, and a large
luncheon-basket.

ALGERNON: I am afraid I can't stay more than a week this time.   290

JACK: Merriman, order the dog-cart[21] at once. Mr. Ernest has been suddenly called back
to town.

MERRIMAN: Yes, sir. [*goes back into the house*]

---

[21] **dog-cart** small, horse-drawn open carriage

ALGERNON: What a fearful liar you are, Jack. I have not been called back to town at all.

JACK: Yes, you have. 295

ALGERNON: I haven't heard anyone call me.

JACK: Your duty as a gentleman calls you back.

ALGERNON: My duty as a gentleman has never interfered with my pleasures in the smallest degree.

JACK: I can quite understand that. 300

ALGERNON: Well, Cecily is a darling.

JACK: You are not to talk of Miss Cardew like that. I don't like it.

ALGERNON: Well, I don't like your clothes. You look perfectly ridiculous in them. Why on earth don't you go up and change? It is perfectly childish to be in deep mourning for a man who is actually staying for a whole week with you in your house as a guest. 305 I call it grotesque.

JACK: You are certainly not staying with me for a whole week as a guest or anything else. You have got to leave . . . by the four-five train.

ALGERNON: I certainly won't leave you so long as you are in mourning. It would be most unfriendly. If I were in mourning you would stay with me, I suppose. I should think 310 it very unkind if you didn't.

JACK: Well, will you go if I change my clothes?

ALGERNON: Yes, if you are not too long. I never saw anybody take so long to dress, and with such little result.

JACK: Well, at any rate, that is better than being always over-dressed as you are. 315

ALGERNON: If I am occasionally a little over-dressed, I make up for it by being always immensely over-educated.

JACK: Your vanity is ridiculous, your conduct an outrage, and your presence in my garden utterly absurd. However, you have got to catch the four-five, and I hope you will have a pleasant journey back to town. This Bunburying, as you call it, has not been 320 a great success for you. [*goes into the house*]

ALGERNON: I think it has been a great success. I'm in love with Cecily, and that is everything.

> [*Enter* CECILY *at the back of the garden. She picks up the can and begins to water the flowers.*]

But I must see her before I go, and make arrangements for another Bunbury. Ah, there she is.

CECILY: Oh, I merely came back to water the roses. I thought you were with Uncle Jack. 325

ALGERNON: He's gone to order the dog-cart for me.

CECILY: Oh, is he going to take you for a nice drive?

ALGERNON: He's going to send me away.

CECILY: Then have we got to part?

ALGERNON: I am afraid so. It's a very painful parting. 330

CECILY: It is always painful to part from people whom one has known for a very brief space of time. The absence of old friends one can endure with equanimity. But even a momentary separation from anyone to whom one has just been introduced is almost unbearable.

ALGERNON: Thank you. 335

> [*Enter* MERRIMAN.]

MERRIMAN: The dog-cart is at the door, sir.

> [ALGERNON *looks appealingly at* CECILY.]

CECILY: It can wait, Merriman . . . for . . . five minutes.

MERRIMAN: Yes, Miss. [*Exit* MERRIMAN.]

ALGERNON: I hope, Cecily, I shall not offend you if I state quite frankly and openly that you seem to me to be in every way the visible personification of absolute perfection.   340

CECILY: I think your frankness does you great credit, Ernest. If you will allow me I will copy your remarks into my diary. [*goes over to table and begins writing in diary*]

ALGERNON: Do you really keep a diary? I'd give anything to look at it. May I?

CECILY: Oh, no. [*puts her hand over it*] You see, it is simply a very young girl's record of her own thoughts and impressions, and consequently meant for publication. When   345 it appears in volume form I hope you will order a copy. But pray, Ernest, don't stop. I delight in taking down from dictation. I have reached "absolute perfection." You can go on. I am quite ready for more.

ALGERNON: [*somewhat taken aback*] Ahem! Ahem!

CECILY: Oh, don't cough, Ernest. When one is dictating one should speak fluently and not   350 cough. Besides, I don't know how to spell a cough. [*writes as* ALGERNON *speaks*]

ALGERNON: [*speaking very rapidly*] Cecily, ever since I first looked upon your wonderful and incomparable beauty, I have dared to love you wildly, passionately, devotedly, hopelessly.

CECILY: I don't think that you should tell me that you love me wildly, passionately, devotedly,   355 hopelessly. Hopelessly doesn't seem to make much sense, does it?

ALGERNON: Cecily!

[*Enter* MERRIMAN.]

MERRIMAN: The dog-cart is waiting, sir.

ALGERNON: Tell it to come round next week, at the same hour.

MERRIMAN: [*looks at* CECILY, *who makes no sign*] Yes, sir. [MERRIMAN *retires*]   360

CECILY: Uncle Jack would be very much annoyed if he knew you were staying on till next week, at the same hour.

ALGERNON: Oh, I don't care about Jack. I don't care for anybody in the whole world but you. I love you, Cecily. You will marry me, won't you?

CECILY: You silly boy! Of course. Why, we have been engaged for the last three months.   365

ALGERNON: For the last three months?

CECILY: Yes, it will be exactly three months on Thursday.

ALGERNON: But how did we become engaged?

CECILY: Well, ever since dear Uncle Jack first confessed to us that he had a younger brother who was very wicked and bad, you of course have formed the chief topic of conver-   370 sation between myself and Miss Prism. And of course a man who is much talked about is always very attractive. One feels there must be something in him after all. I daresay it was foolish of me, but I fell in love with you, Ernest.

ALGERNON: Darling! And when was the engagement actually settled?

CECILY: On the 14th of February last. Worn out by your entire ignorance of my existence,   375 I determined to end the matter one way or the other, and after a long struggle with myself I accepted you under this dear old tree here. The next day I bought this little ring in your name, and this is the little bangle with the true lovers' knot I promised you always to wear.

ALGERNON: Did I give you this? It's very pretty, isn't it?   380

CECILY: Yes, you've wonderfully good taste, Ernest. It's the excuse I've always given for your leading such a bad life. And this is the box in which I keep all your dear letters. [*kneels at table, opens box, and produces letters tied up with blue ribbon*]

ALGERNON: My letters! But my own sweet Cecily, I have never written you any letters.

CECILY: You need hardly remind me of that, Ernest. I remember only too well that I was forced   385 to write your letters for you. I wrote always three times a week, and sometimes oftener.

ALGERNON: Oh, do let me read them, Cecily?

CECILY: Oh, I couldn't possibly. They would make you far too conceited. [*replaces box*] The three you wrote me after I had broken off the engagement are so beautiful, and so badly spelled, that even now I can hardly read them without crying a little.   390

ALGERNON: But was our engagement ever broken off?

CECILY: Of course it was. On the 22nd of last March. You can see the entry if you like. [*shows diary*] "To-day I broke off my engagement with Ernest. I feel it is better to do so. The weather still continues charming."

ALGERNON: But why on earth did you break it off? What had I done? I had done nothing   395
at all. Cecily, I am very much hurt indeed to hear you broke it off. Particularly when the weather was so charming.

CECILY: It would hardly have been a really serious engagement if it hadn't been broken off at least once. But I forgave you before the week was out.

ALGERNON: [*crossing to her, and kneels*] What a perfect angel you are, Cecily.   400

CECILY: You dear romantic boy. [*He kisses her, she puts her fingers through his hair.*] I hope your hair curls naturally, does it?

ALGERNON: Yes, darling, with a little help from others.

CECILY: I am so glad.

ALGERNON: You'll never break off our engagement again, Cecily?   405

CECILY: I don't think I could break it off now that I have actually met you. Besides, of course, there is the question of your name.

ALGERNON: [*nervously*] Yes, of course.

CECILY: You must not laugh at me, darling, but it had always been a girlish dream of mine to love someone whose name was Ernest.   410

    [ALGERNON *rises,* CECILY *also.*]

There is something in that name that seems to inspire absolute confidence. I pity any poor married woman whose husband is not called Ernest.

ALGERNON: But, my dear child, do you mean to say you could not love me if I had some other name?

CECILY: But what name?   415

ALGERNON: Oh, any name you like—Algernon, for instance . . . .

CECILY: But I don't like the name of Algernon.

ALGERNON: Well, my own dear, sweet, loving little darling, I really can't see why you should object to the name of Algernon. It is not at all a bad name. In fact, it is rather an aristo-cratic name. Half of the chaps who get into the Bankruptcy Court are called Algernon.   420
But seriously, Cecily . . . [*moving to her*] . . . if my name was Algy, couldn't you love me?

CECILY: [*rising*] I might respect you, Ernest, I might admire your character, but I fear that I should not be able to give you my undivided attention.

ALGERNON: Ahem! Cecily! [*picking up hat*] Your Rector here is, I suppose, thoroughly experienced in the practice of all the rites and ceremonials of the Church?   425

CECILY: Oh, yes. Dr. Chasuble is a most learned man. He has never written a single book, so you can imagine how much he knows.

ALGERNON: I must see him at once on a most important christening—I mean on most important business.

CECILY: Oh!   430

ALGERNON: I shan't be away more than half an hour.

CECILY: Considering that we have been engaged since February the 14th, and that I only met you to-day for the first time, I think it is rather hard that you should leave me for so long a period as half an hour. Couldn't you make it twenty minutes?

ALGERNON: I'll be back in no time. [*kisses her and rushes down the garden*]   435

CECILY: What an impetuous boy he is! I like his hair so much. I must enter his proposal in my diary.

> [*Enter* MERRIMAN.]

MERRIMAN: A Miss Fairfax has just called to see Mr. Worthing. On very important business, Miss Fairfax states.

CECILY: Isn't Mr. Worthing in his library?   440

MERRIMAN: Mr. Worthing went over in the direction of the Rectory some time ago.

CECILY: Pray ask the lady to come out here; Mr. Worthing is sure to be back soon. And you can bring tea.

MERRIMAN: Yes, Miss. [*goes out*]

CECILY: Miss Fairfax! I suppose one of the many good elderly women who are associated   445
with Uncle Jack in some of his philanthropic work in London. I don't quite like women who are interested in philanthropic work. I think it is so forward of them.

> [*Enter* MERRIMAN.]

MERRIMAN: Miss Fairfax.

> [*Enter* GWENDOLEN. *Exit* MERRIMAN.]

CECILY: [*advancing to meet her*] Pray let me introduce myself to you. My name is Cecily Cardew.   450

GWENDOLEN: Cecily Cardew? [*moving to her and shaking hands*] What a very sweet name! Something tells me that we are going to be great friends. I like you already more than I can say. My first impressions of people are never wrong.

CECILY: How nice of you to like me so much after we have known each other such a comparatively short time. Pray sit down.   455

GWENDOLEN: [*still standing up*] I may call you Cecily, may I not?

CECILY: With pleasure!

GWENDOLEN: And you will always call me Gwendolen, won't you?

CECILY: If you wish.

GWENDOLEN: Then that is all quite settled, is it not?   460

CECILY: I hope so. [*a pause; they both sit down together*]

GWENDOLEN: Perhaps this might be a favorable opportunity for my mentioning who I am. My father is Lord Bracknell. You have never heard of papa, I suppose?

CECILY: I don't think so.

GWENDOLEN: Outside the family circle, papa, I am glad to say, is entirely unknown. I   465
think that is quite as it should be. The home seems to me to be the proper sphere for the man. And certainly once a man begins to neglect his domestic duties he becomes painfully effeminate, does he not? And I don't like that. It makes men so very attractive. Cecily, mamma, whose views on education are remarkably strict, has brought me up to be extremely short-sighted; it is part of her system; so do you mind my   470
looking at you through my glasses?

CECILY: Oh! not at all, Gwendolen. I am very fond of being looked at.

GWENDOLEN: [*after examining* CECILY *carefully through a lorgnette*[22]] You are here on a short visit, I suppose.

CECILY: Oh, no, I live here.   475

GWENDOLEN: [*severely*] Really? Your mother, no doubt, or some female relative of advanced years, resides here also?

---

[22] **lorgnette** opera glasses mounted on a handle

CECILY: Oh, no. I have no mother, nor, in fact, any relations.

GWENDOLEN: Indeed?

CECILY: My dear guardian, with the assistance of Miss Prism, has the arduous task of   480
looking after me.

GWENDOLEN: Your guardian?

CECILY: Yes, I am Mr. Worthing's ward.

GWENDOLEN: Oh! It is strange he never mentioned to me that he had a ward. How secre-
tive of him! He grows more interesting hourly. I am not sure, however, that the news   485
inspires me with feelings of unmixed delight. [*rising and going to her*] I am very
fond of you, Cecily; I have liked you ever since I met you. But I am bound to state
that now that I know that you are Mr. Worthing's ward, I cannot help expressing a
wish you were—well, just a little older than you seem to be—and not quite so very
alluring in appearance. In fact, if I may speak candidly—   490

CECILY: Pray do! I think that whenever one has anything unpleasant to say, one should
always be quite candid.

GWENDOLEN: Well, to speak with perfect candor, Cecily, I wish that you were fully forty-
two, and more than usually plain for your age. Ernest has a strong upright nature.
He is the very soul of truth and honor. Disloyalty would be as impossible to him as   495
deception. But even men of the noblest possible moral character are extremely susceptible to the influence of the physical charms of others. Modern, no less than
Ancient History, supplies us with most painful examples of what I refer to. If it were
not so, indeed, History would be quite unreadable.

CECILY: I beg your pardon, Gwendolen, did you say Ernest?   500

GWENDOLEN: Yes.

CECILY: Oh, but it is not Mr. Ernest Worthing who is my guardian. It is his brother—his
elder brother.

GWENDOLEN: [*sitting down again*] Ernest never mentioned to me that he had a brother.

CECILY: I am sorry to say they have not been on good terms for a long time.   505

GWENDOLEN: Ah! that accounts for it. And now that I think of it I have never heard any
man mention his brother. The subject seems distasteful to most men. Cecily, you
have lifted a load from my mind. I was growing almost anxious. It would have been
terrible if any cloud had come across a friendship like ours, would it not? Of course
you are quite, quite sure that it is not Mr. Ernest Worthing who is your guardian?   510

CECILY: Quite sure. [*a pause*] In fact, I am going to be his.

GWENDOLEN: [*enquiringly*] I beg your pardon?

CECILY: [*rather shy and confidingly*] Dearest Gwendolen, there is no reason why I should
make a secret of it to you. Our little county newspaper is sure to chronicle the fact
next week. Mr. Ernest Worthing and I are engaged to be married.   515

GWENDOLEN: [*quite politely, rising*] My darling Cecily, I think there must be some slight
error. Mr. Ernest Worthing is engaged to me. The announcement will appear in the
'Morning Post' on Saturday at the latest.

CECILY: [*very politely, rising*] I am afraid you must be under some misconception. Ernest
proposed to me exactly ten minutes ago. [*shows diary*]   520

GWENDOLEN: [*examines diary through her lorgnette carefully*] It is certainly very curious,
for he asked me to be his wife yesterday afternoon at 5:30. If you would care to
verify the incident, pray do so. [*produces diary of her own*] I never travel without my
diary. One should always have something sensational to read in the train. I am so
sorry, dear Cecily, if it is any disappointment to you, but I am afraid *I* have the   525
prior claim.

CECILY: It would distress me more than I can tell you, dear Gwendolen, if it caused you
any mental or physical anguish, but I feel bound to point out that since Ernest proposed to you he clearly has changed his mind.

GWENDOLEN: [*meditatively*] If the poor fellow has been entrapped into any foolish prom-   530
    ise I shall consider it my duty to rescue him at once, and with a firm hand.

CECILY: [*thoughtfully and sadly*] Whatever unfortunate entanglement my dear boy may
    have got into, I will never reproach him with it after we are married.

GWENDOLEN: Do you allude to me, Miss Cardew, as an entanglement? You are presump-
    tuous. On an occasion of this kind it becomes more than a moral duty to speak one's   535
    mind. It becomes a pleasure.

CECILY: Do you suggest, Miss Fairfax, that I entrapped Ernest into an engagement? How
    dare you? This is no time for wearing the shallow mask of manners. When I see a
    spade I call it a spade.

GWENDOLEN: [*satirically*] I am glad to say that I have never seen a spade. It is obvious that   540
    our social spheres have been widely different.

> [*Enter* MERRIMAN, *followed by the footman. He carries a salver, tablecloth, and*
> *plate stand.* CECILY *is about to retort. The presence of the servants exercises a*
> *restraining influence, under which both girls chafe.*]

MERRIMAN: Shall I lay tea here as usual, Miss?

CECILY: [*sternly, in a calm voice*] Yes, as usual.

> [MERRIMAN *begins to clear and lay cloth. A long pause.* CECILY *and* GWEN-
> DOLEN *glare at each other.*]

GWENDOLEN: Are there many interesting walks in the vicinity, Miss Cardew?

CECILY: Oh, yes, a great many. From the top of one of the hills quite close one can see five   545
    counties.

GWENDOLEN: Five counties! I don't think I should like that. I hate crowds.

CECILY: [*sweetly*] I suppose that is why you live in town?

> [GWENDOLEN *bites her lip, and beats her foot nervously with her parasol.*]

GWENDOLEN: [*looking round*] Quite a well-kept garden this is, Miss Cardew.

CECILY: So glad you like it, Miss Fairfax.   550

GWENDOLEN: I had no idea there were any flowers in the country.

CECILY: Oh, flowers are as common here, Miss Fairfax, as people are in London.

GWENDOLEN: Personally I cannot understand how anybody manages to exist in the country,
    if anybody who is anybody does. The country always bores me to death.

CECILY: Ah! This is what the newspapers call agricultural depression, is it not? I believe the   555
    aristocracy are suffering very much from it just at present. It is almost an epidemic
    amongst them, I have been told. May I offer you some tea, Miss Fairfax?

GWENDOLEN: [*with elaborate politeness*] Thank you. [*aside*] Detestable girl! But I require tea!

CECILY: [*sweetly*] Sugar?

GWENDOLEN: [*superciliously*] No, thank you. Sugar is not fashionable any more.   560

> [CECILY *looks angrily at her, takes up the tongs and puts four lumps of sugar into*
> *the cup.*]

CECILY: [*severely*] Cake or bread and butter?

GWENDOLEN: [*in a bored manner*] Bread and butter, please. Cake is rarely seen at the best
    houses nowadays.

CECILY: [*cuts a very large slice of cake, and puts it on the tray*] Hand that to Miss Fairfax.

> [MERRIMAN *does so, and goes out with footman.* GWENDOLEN *drinks the tea*
> *and makes a grimace. Puts down cup at once, reaches out her hand to the bread*
> *and butter, looks at it, and finds it is cake. Rises in indignation.*]

GWENDOLEN: You have filled my tea with lumps of sugar, and though I asked most dis-   565
tinctly for bread and butter, you have given me cake. I am known for the gentleness
of my disposition, and the extraordinary sweetness of my nature, but I warn you,
Miss Cardew, you may go too far.

CECILY: [*rising*] To save my poor, innocent, trusting boy from the machinations of any
other girl there are no lengths to which I would not go.   570

GWENDOLEN: From the moment I saw you I distrusted you. I felt that you were false and
deceitful. I am never deceived in such matters. My first impressions of people are
invariably right.

CECILY: It seems to me, Miss Fairfax, that I am trespassing on your valuable time. No doubt
you have many other calls of a similar character to make in the neighborhood.   575

[*Enter* JACK.]

GWENDOLEN: [*catching sight of him*] Ernest! My own Ernest!

JACK: Gwendolen! Darling! [*offers to kiss her*]

GWENDOLEN: [*drawing back*] A moment! May I ask if you are engaged to be married to
this young lady? [*points to* CECILY]

JACK: [*laughing*] To dear little Cecily! Of course not! What could have put such an idea   580
into your pretty little head?

GWENDOLEN: Thank you. You may. [*offers her cheek*]

CECILY: [*very sweetly*] I knew there must be some misunderstanding, Miss Fairfax.
The gentleman whose arm is at present around your waist is my dear guardian,
Mr. John Worthing.   585

GWENDOLEN: I beg your pardon?

CECILY: This is Uncle Jack.

GWENDOLEN: [*receding*] Jack! Oh!

[*Enter* ALGERNON.]

CECILY: Here is Ernest.

ALGERNON: [*Goes straight over to* CECILY *without noticing anyone else.*] My own love!   590
[*offers to kiss her*]

CECILY: [*drawing back*] A moment, Ernest! May I ask you—are you engaged to be married
to this young lady?

ALGERNON: [*looking round*] To what young lady? Good heavens! Gwendolen!

CECILY: Yes, to good heavens, Gwendolen, I mean to Gwendolen.   595

ALGERNON: [*laughing*] Of course not! What could have put such an idea into your pretty
little head?

CECILY: Thank you. [*presenting her cheek to be kissed*] You may. [ALGERNON *kisses her.*]

GWENDOLEN: I felt there was some slight error, Miss Cardew. The gentleman who is now
embracing you is my cousin, Mr. Algernon Moncrieff.   600

CECILY: [*breaking away from* ALGERNON] Algernon Moncrieff! Oh! [*The two girls move
towards each other and put their arms round each other's waist as if for protection.*] Are
you called Algernon?

ALGERNON: I cannot deny it.

CECILY: Oh!   605

GWENDOLEN: Is your name really John?

JACK: [*standing rather proudly*] I could deny it if I liked. I could deny anything if I liked.
But my name certainly is John. It has been John for years.

CECILY: [*to* GWENDOLEN] A gross deception has been practiced on both of us.

GWENDOLEN: My poor wounded Cecily!   610

CECILY: My sweet wronged Gwendolen!

GWENDOLEN: [*slowly and seriously*] You will call me sister, will you not? [*They embrace.* JACK *and* ALGERNON *groan and walk up and down.*]

CECILY: [*rather brightly*] There is just one question I would like to be allowed to ask my guardian. 615

GWENDOLEN: An admirable idea! Mr. Worthing, there is just one question I would like to be permitted to put to you. Where is your brother Ernest? We are both engaged to be married to your brother Ernest, so it is a matter of some importance to us to know where your brother Ernest is at present.

JACK: [*slowly and hesitatingly*] Gwendolen—Cecily—it is very painful for me to be forced 620 to speak the truth. It is the first time in my life that I have ever been reduced to such a painful position, and I am really quite inexperienced in doing anything of the kind. However, I will tell you quite frankly that I have no brother Ernest. I have no brother at all. I never had a brother in my life, and I certainly have not the smallest intention of ever having one in the future. 625

CECILY: [*surprised*] No brother at all?

JACK: [*cheerily*] None!

GWENDOLEN: [*severely*] Had you never a brother of any kind?

JACK: [*pleasantly*] Never. Not even of any kind.

GWENDOLEN: I am afraid it is quite clear, Cecily, that neither of us is engaged to be married 630 to anyone.

CECILY: It is not a very pleasant position for a young girl suddenly to find herself in. Is it?

GWENDOLEN: Let us go into the house. They will hardly venture to come after us there.

CECILY: No, men are so cowardly, aren't they?

[*They retire into the house with scornful looks.*]

JACK: This ghastly state of things is what you call Bunburying, I suppose? 635

ALGERNON: Yes, and a perfectly wonderful Bunbury it is. The most wonderful Bunbury I have ever had in my life.

JACK: Well, you've no right whatsoever to Bunbury here.

ALGERNON: That is absurd. One has a right to Bunbury anywhere one chooses. Every serious Bunburyist knows that. 640

JACK: Serious Bunburyist! Good heavens!

ALGERNON: Well, one must be serious about something, if one wants to have any amusement in life. I happen to be serious about Bunburying. What on earth you are serious about I haven't got the remotest idea. About everything, I should fancy. You have such an absolutely trivial nature. 645

JACK: Well, the only small satisfaction I have in the whole of this wretched business is that your friend Bunbury is quite exploded. You won't be able to run down to the country quite so often as you used to do, dear Algy. And a very good thing too.

ALGERNON: Your brother is a little off color, isn't he, dear Jack? You won't be able to disappear to London quite so frequently as your wicked custom was. And not a bad thing either. 650

JACK: As for your conduct towards Miss Cardew, I must say that your taking in a sweet, simple, innocent girl like that is quite inexcusable. To say nothing of the fact that she is my ward.

ALGERNON: I can see no possible defense at all for your deceiving a brilliant, clever, thoroughly experienced young lady like Miss Fairfax. To say nothing of the fact that she 655 is my cousin.

JACK: I wanted to be engaged to Gwendolen, that is all. I love her.

ALGERNON: Well, I simply wanted to be engaged to Cecily. I adore her.

JACK: There is certainly no chance of your marrying Miss Cardew.

ALGERNON: I don't think there is much likelihood, Jack, of you and Miss Fairfax being   660
united.

JACK: Well, that is no business of yours.

ALGERNON: If it was my business, I wouldn't talk about it. [*begins to eat muffins*] It is very
vulgar to talk about one's business. Only people like stockbrokers do that, and then
merely at dinner parties.   665

JACK: How can you sit there, calmly eating muffins, when we are in this horrible trouble,
I can't make out. You seem to me to be perfectly heartless.

ALGERNON: Well, I can't eat muffins in an agitated manner. The butter would probably
get on my cuffs. One should always eat muffins quite calmly. It is the only way to
eat them.   670

JACK: I say it's perfectly heartless your eating muffins at all, under the circumstances.

ALGERNON: When I am in trouble, eating is the only thing that consoles me. Indeed,
when I am in really great trouble, as anyone who knows me intimately will tell you,
I refuse everything except food and drink. At the present moment I am eating muffins because I am unhappy. Besides, I am particularly fond of muffins. [*rising*]   675

JACK: [*rising*] Well, that is no reason why you should eat them all in that greedy way. [*takes
muffins from* ALGERNON]

ALGERNON: [*offering tea-cake*] I wish you would have tea-cake instead. I don't like tea-cake.

JACK: Good heavens! I suppose a man may eat his own muffins in his own garden.

ALGERNON: But you have just said it was perfectly heartless to eat muffins.   680

JACK: I said it was perfectly heartless of you, under the circumstances. That is a very different thing.

ALGERNON: That may be. But the muffins are the same. [*He seizes the muffin-dish from*
JACK.]

JACK: Algy, I wish to goodness you would go.   685

ALGERNON: You can't possibly ask me to go without having some dinner. It's absurd. I
never go without my dinner. No one ever does, except vegetarians and people like
that. Besides I have just made arrangements with Dr. Chasuble to be christened at a
quarter to six under the name of Ernest.

JACK: My dear fellow, the sooner you give up that nonsense the better. I made arrangements   690
this morning with Dr. Chasuble to be christened myself at 5:30, and I naturally will
take the name of Ernest. Gwendolen would wish it. We can't both be christened
Ernest. It's absurd. Besides, I have a perfect right to be christened if I like. There
is no evidence at all that I ever have been christened by anybody. I should think it
extremely probable I never was, and so does Dr. Chasuble. It is entirely different in   695
your case. You have been christened already.

ALGERNON: Yes, but I have not been christened for years.

JACK: Yes, but you have been christened. That is the important thing.

ALGERNON: Quite so. So I know my constitution can stand it. If you are not quite sure
about your ever having been christened, I must say I think it rather dangerous your   700
venturing on it now. It might make you very unwell. You can hardly have forgotten
that someone very closely connected with you was very nearly carried off this week
in Paris by a severe chill.

JACK: Yes, but you said yourself that a severe chill was not hereditary.

ALGERNON: It usen't to be, I know—but I daresay it is now. Science is always making   705
wonderful improvements in things.

JACK: [*picking up the muffin-dish*] Oh, that is nonsense; you are always talking nonsense.

ALGERNON: Jack, you are at the muffins again! I wish you wouldn't. There are only two
left. [*takes them*] I told you I was particularly fond of muffins.

JACK: But I hate tea-cake.   710

ALGERNON: Why on earth then do you allow tea-cake to be served up for your guests? What ideas you have of hospitality!

JACK: Algernon! I have already told you to go. I don't want you here. Why don't you go?

ALGERNON: I haven't quite finished my tea yet, and there is still one muffin left.

[JACK *groans, and sinks into a chair.* ALGERNON *continues eating.*]

CURTAIN

────────────────── **ACT III** ──────────────────

SCENE─────*Morning-room at the Manor House.* GWENDOLEN *and* CECILY *are at the window, looking out into the garden.*

GWENDOLEN: The fact that they did not follow us at once into the house, as anyone else would have done, seems to me to show that they have some sense of shame left.

CECILY: They have been eating muffins. That looks like repentance.

GWENDOLEN: [*after a pause*] They don't seem to notice us at all. Couldn't you cough?

CECILY: But I haven't a cough.   5

GWENDOLEN: They're looking at us. What effrontery!

CECILY: They're approaching. That's very forward of them.

GWENDOLEN: Let us preserve a dignified silence.

CECILY: Certainly. It's the only thing to do now.

[*Enter* JACK *followed by* ALGERNON. *They whistle some dreadful popular air from a British Opera.*]

GWENDOLEN: This dignified silence seems to produce an unpleasant effect.   10

CECILY: A most distasteful one.

GWENDOLEN: But we will not be the first to speak.

CECILY: Certainly not.

GWENDOLEN: Mr. Worthing, I have something very particular to ask you. Much depends on your reply.   15

CECILY: Gwendolen, your common sense is invaluable. Mr. Moncrieff, kindly answer me the following question. Why did you pretend to be my guardian's brother?

ALGERNON: In order that I might have an opportunity of meeting you.

CECILY: [*to* GWENDOLEN] That certainly seems a satisfactory explanation, does it not?

GWENDOLEN: Yes, dear, if you can believe him.   20

CECILY: I don't. But that does not affect the wonderful beauty of his answer.

GWENDOLEN: True. In matters of grave importance, style, not sincerity is the vital thing. Mr. Worthing, what explanation can you offer to me for pretending to have a brother? Was it in order that you might have an opportunity of coming up to town to see me as often as possible?   25

JACK: Can you doubt it, Miss Fairfax?

GWENDOLEN: I have the gravest doubts upon the subject. But I intend to crush them.

This is not the moment for German skepticism.[23] [*moving to* CECILY] Their explanations appear to be quite satisfactory, especially Mr. Worthing's. That seems to me to have the stamp of truth upon it. 30

CECILY: I am more than content with what Mr. Moncrieff said. His voice alone inspires one with absolute credulity.

GWENDOLEN: Then you think we should forgive them?

CECILY: Yes. I mean no.

GWENDOLEN: True! I had forgotten. There are principles at stake that one cannot surrender. 35
Which of us should tell them? The task is not a pleasant one.

CECILY: Could we not both speak at the same time?

GWENDOLEN: An excellent idea! I nearly always speak at the same time as other people. Will you take the time from me?

CECILY: Certainly. [GWENDOLEN *beats time with uplifted finger.*] 40

GWENDOLEN and CECILY: [*speaking together*] Your Christian names are still an insuperable barrier. That is all!

JACK and ALGERNON: [*speaking together*] Our Christian names! Is that all? But we are going to be christened this afternoon.

GWENDOLEN: [*to* JACK] For my sake you are prepared to do this terrible thing? 45

JACK: I am.

CECILY: [*to* ALGERNON] To please me you are ready to face this fearful ordeal?

ALGERNON: I am.

GWENDOLEN: How absurd to talk of the equality of the sexes! Where questions of self-sacrifice are concerned, men are infinitely beyond us. 50

JACK: We are. [*clasps hands with* ALGERNON]

CECILY: They have moments of physical courage of which we women know absolutely nothing.

GWENDOLEN: [*to* JACK] Darling!

ALGERNON: [*to* CECILY] Darling! 55

[*They fall into each other's arms. Enter* MERRIMAN. *When he enters he coughs loudly, seeing the situation.*]

MERRIMAN: Ahem! Ahem! Lady Bracknell!

JACK: Good heavens!

[*Enter* LADY BRACKNELL. *The couples separate in alarm. Exit* MERRIMAN.]

LADY BRACKNELL: Gwendolen! What does this mean?

GWENDOLEN: Merely that I am engaged to be married to Mr. Worthing, mamma.

LADY BRACKNELL: Come here. Sit down. Sit down immediately. Hesitation of any kind 60
is a sign of mental decay in the young, of physical weakness in the old. [*turns to* JACK] Apprised, sir, of my daughter's sudden flight by her trusty maid, whose confidence I purchased by means of a small coin, I followed her at once by a luggage train. Her unhappy father is, I am glad to say, under the impression that she is attending a more than usually lengthy lecture by the University Extension Scheme 65
on the influence of a permanent income on thought. I do not propose to undeceive him. Indeed I have never undeceived him on any question. I would consider it wrong. But of course, you will clearly understand that all communication between

---

[23] **German skepticism** nineteenth-century German philosophical movements which called into question the first principles of religion and ethics

yourself and my daughter must cease immediately from this moment. On this point, as indeed on all points, I am firm.   70

JACK: I am engaged to be married to Gwendolen, Lady Bracknell!

LADY BRACKNELL: You are nothing of the kind, sir. And now, as regards Algernon. . . . Algernon!

ALGERNON: Yes, Aunt Augusta.

LADY BRACKNELL: May I ask if it is in this house that your invalid friend Mr. Bunbury   75
resides?

ALGERNON: [*stammering*] Oh, Bunbury doesn't live here. Bunbury is somewhere else at present. In fact, Bunbury is dead.

LADY BRACKNELL: Dead! When did Mr. Bunbury die? His death must have been extremely sudden.   80

ALGERNON: [*airily*] Oh, I killed Bunbury this afternoon. I mean poor Bunbury died this afternoon.

LADY BRACKNELL: What did he die of?

ALGERNON: Bunbury? Oh, he was quite exploded.

LADY BRACKNELL: Exploded! Was he the victim of a revolutionary outrage? I was not   85
aware that Mr. Bunbury was interested in social legislation. If so, he is well punished for his morbidity.

ALGERNON: My dear Aunt Augusta, I mean he was found out! The doctors found out that Bunbury could not live, that is what I mean—so Bunbury died.

LADY BRACKNELL: He seems to have had great confidence in the opinion of his physicians.   90
I am glad, however, that he made up his mind at the last to some definite course of action, and acted under proper medical advice. And now that we have finally got rid of this Mr. Bunbury, may I ask, Mr. Worthing, who is that young person whose hand my nephew Algernon is now holding in what seems to me a peculiarly unnecessary manner?   95

JACK: That lady is Miss Cecily Cardew, my ward.

[LADY BRACKNELL *bows coldly to* CECILY.]

ALGERNON: I am engaged to be married to Cecily, Aunt Augusta.

LADY BRACKNELL: I beg your pardon?

CECILY: Mr. Moncrieff and I are engaged to be married, Lady Bracknell.

LADY BRACKNELL: [*with a shiver, crossing to the sofa and sitting down*] I do not know   100
whether there is anything peculiarly exciting in the air in this particular part of Hertfordshire, but the number of engagements that go on seems to me considerably above the proper average that statistics have laid down for our guidance. I think some preliminary enquiry on my part would not be out of place. Mr. Worthing, is Miss Cardew at all connected with any of the larger railway stations in London? I   105
merely desire information. Until yesterday I had no idea that there were any families or persons whose origin was a Terminus.

[JACK *looks perfectly furious, but restrains himself.*]

JACK: [*in a clear, cold voice*] Miss Cardew is the granddaughter of the late Mr. Thomas Cardew of 149, Belgrave Square, S.W.; Gervase Park, Dorking, Surrey; and the Sporran, Fifeshire, N.B.[24]   110

LADY BRACKNELL: That sounds not unsatisfactory. Three addresses always inspire confidence, even in tradesmen. But what proof have I of their authenticity?

---

[24] **N.B.** North Britain, a snobbish English term for Scotland

JACK: I have carefully preserved the Court Guides of the period. They are open to your inspection, Lady Bracknell.

LADY BRACKNELL: [*grimly*] I have known strange errors in that publication. 115

JACK: Miss Cardew's family solicitors are Messrs. Markby, Markby, and Markby.

LADY BRACKNELL: Markby, Markby, and Markby! A firm of the very highest position in their profession. Indeed I am told that one of the Mr. Markbys is occasionally to be seen at dinner parties. So far I am satisfied.

JACK: [*very irritably*] How extremely kind of you, Lady Bracknell! I have also in my pos- 120 session, you will be pleased to hear, certificates of Miss Cardew's birth, baptism, whooping cough, registration, vaccination, confirmation, and the measles; both the German and the English variety.

LADY BRACKNELL: Ah! A life crowded with incident, I see; though perhaps somewhat too exciting for a young girl. I am not myself in favor of premature experiences. [*rises,* 125 *looks at her watch*] Gwendolen! the time approaches for our departure. We have not a moment to lose. As a matter of form, Mr. Worthing, I had better ask you if Miss Cardew has any little fortune?

JACK: Oh, about a hundred and thirty thousand pounds in the Funds.[25] That is all. Good- bye, Lady Bracknell. So pleased to have seen you. 130

LADY BRACKNELL: [*sitting down again*] A moment, Mr. Worthing. A hundred and thirty thousand pounds! And in the Funds! Miss Cardew seems to me a most attractive young lady, now that I look at her. Few girls of the present day have any really solid qualities, any of the qualities that last, and improve with time. We live, I regret to say, in an age of surfaces. [*to* CECILY] Come over here, dear. [CECILY *goes across.*] 135 Pretty child! your dress is sadly simple, and your hair seems almost as Nature might have left it. But we can soon alter all that. A thoroughly experienced French maid produces a really marvelous result in a very brief space of time. I remember recom- mending one to young Lady Lancing, and after three months her own husband did not know her. 140

JACK: [*to himself*] And after six months nobody knew her.

LADY BRACKNELL: [*Glares at* JACK *for a few moments. Then bends, with a practiced smile, to* CECILY.] Kindly turn round, sweet child. [CECILY *turns completely round.*] No, the side view is what I want. [CECILY *presents her profile.*] Yes, quite as I expected. There are distinct social possibilities in your profile. The two weak points in our age are 145 its want of principle and its want of profile. The chin a little higher, dear. Style largely depends on the way the chin is worn. They are worn very high, just at present. Algernon!

ALGERNON: Yes, Aunt Augusta!

LADY BRACKNELL: There are distinct social possibilities in Miss Cardew's profile. 150

ALGERNON: Cecily is the sweetest, dearest, prettiest girl in the whole world. And I don't care two-pence about social possibilities.

LADY BRACKNELL: Never speak disrespectfully of society, Algernon. Only people who can't get into it do that. [*to* CECILY] Dear child, of course you know that Algernon has nothing but his debts to depend upon. But I do not approve of mercenary marriages. 155 When I married Lord Bracknell I had no fortune of any kind. But I never dreamed for a moment of allowing that to stand in my way. Well, I suppose I must give my consent.

ALGERNON: Thank you, Aunt Augusta.

---

[25]**a hundred and thirty thousand pounds in the Funds** tremendous sum of money held in conservative govern- ment bonds

LADY BRACKNELL: Cecily, you may kiss me! 160

CECILY: [*kisses her*] Thank you, Lady Bracknell.

LADY BRACKNELL: You may also address me as Aunt Augusta for the future.

CECILY: Thank you, Aunt Augusta.

LADY BRACKNELL: The marriage, I think, had better take place quite soon.

ALGERNON: Thank you, Aunt Augusta. 165

CECILY: Thank you, Aunt Augusta.

LADY BRACKNELL: To speak frankly, I am not in favor of long engagements. They give people the opportunity of finding out each other's character before marriage, which I think is never advisable.

JACK: I beg your pardon for interrupting you, Lady Bracknell, but this engagement is quite 170
out of the question. I am Miss Cardew's guardian, and she cannot marry without my consent until she comes of age. That consent I absolutely decline to give.

LADY BRACKNELL: Upon what grounds, may I ask? Algernon is an extremely, I may almost say an ostentatiously, eligible young man. He has nothing, but he looks everything. What more can one desire? 175

JACK: It pains me very much to have to speak frankly to you, Lady Bracknell, about your nephew, but the fact is that I do not approve at all of his moral character. I suspect him of being untruthful.

[ALGERNON and CECILY *look at him in indignant amazement.*]

LADY BRACKNELL: Untruthful! My nephew Algernon? Impossible! He is an Oxonian.[26]

JACK: I fear there can be no possible doubt about the matter. This afternoon, during my 180
temporary absence in London on an important question of romance, he obtained admission to my house by means of the false pretense of being my brother. Under an assumed name he drank, I've just been informed by my butler, an entire pint bottle of my Perrier-Jouet, Brut, '89; a wine I was specially reserving for myself. Continuing his disgraceful deception, he succeeded in the course of the afternoon 185
in alienating the affections of my only ward. He subsequently stayed to tea, and devoured every single muffin. And what makes his conduct all the more heartless is, that he was perfectly well aware from the first that I have no brother, that I never had a brother, and that I don't intend to have a brother, not even of any kind. I distinctly told him so myself yesterday afternoon. 190

LADY BRACKNELL: Ahem! Mr. Worthing, after careful consideration I have decided entirely to overlook my nephew's conduct to you.

JACK: That is very generous of you, Lady Bracknell. My own decision, however, is unalterable. I decline to give my consent.

LADY BRACKNELL: [*to* CECILY] Come here, sweet child. [CECILY *goes over*] How old are 195
you, dear?

CECILY: Well, I am really only eighteen, but I always admit to twenty when I go to evening parties.

LADY BRACKNELL: You are perfectly right in making some slight alteration. Indeed, no woman should ever be quite accurate about her age. It looks so calculating. . . . [*in a* 200
meditative manner] Eighteen, but admitting to twenty at evening parties. Well, it will not be very long before you are of age and free from the restraints of tutelage. So I don't think your guardian's consent is, after all, a matter of any importance.

JACK: Pray excuse me, Lady Bracknell, for interrupting you again, but it is only fair to tell you that according to the terms of her grandfather's will Miss Cardew does not come 205
legally of age till she is thirty-five.

---

[26] **Oxonian** Oxford graduate

LADY BRACKNELL: That does not seem to me to be a grave objection. Thirty-five is a very attractive age. London society is full of women of the very highest birth who have, of their own free choice, remained thirty-five for years. Lady Dumbleton is an instance in point. To my own knowledge she has been thirty-five ever since she arrived at the age of forty, which was many years ago now. I see no reason why our dear Cecily should not be even still more attractive at the age you mention than she is at present. There will be a large accumulation of property. 210

CECILY: Algy, could you wait for me till I was thirty-five?

ALGERNON: Of course I could, Cecily. You know I could. 215

CECILY: Yes, I felt it instinctively, but I couldn't wait all that time. I hate waiting even five minutes for anybody. It always makes me rather cross. I am not punctual myself, I know, but I do like punctuality in others, and waiting, even to be married, is quite out of the question.

ALGERNON: Then what is to be done, Cecily? 220

CECILY: I don't know, Mr. Moncrieff.

LADY BRACKNELL: My dear Mr. Worthing, as Miss Cardew states positively that she cannot wait till she is thirty-five—a remark which I am bound to say seems to me to show a somewhat impatient nature—I would beg of you to reconsider your decision.

JACK: But my dear Lady Bracknell, the matter is entirely in your own hands. The moment 225
you consent to my marriage with Gwendolen, I will most gladly allow your nephew to form an alliance with my ward.

LADY BRACKNELL: [*rising and drawing herself up*] You must be quite aware that what you propose is out of the question.

JACK: Then a passionate celibacy is all that any of us can look forward to. 230

LADY BRACKNELL: That is not the destiny I propose for Gwendolen. Algernon, of course, can choose for himself. [*pulls out her watch*] Come dear; [GWENDOLEN *rises.*] we have already missed five, if not six, trains. To miss any more might expose us to comment on the platform.

[*Enter* CHASUBLE.]

CHASUBLE: Everything is quite ready for the christenings. 235

LADY BRACKNELL: The christenings, sir! Is not that somewhat premature?

CHASUBLE: [*looking rather puzzled, and pointing to* JACK *and* ALGERNON] Both these gentlemen have expressed a desire for immediate baptism.

LADY BRACKNELL: At their age? The idea is grotesque and irreligious! Algernon, I forbid you to be baptized. I will not hear of such excesses. Lord Bracknell would be highly 240
displeased if he learned that that was the way in which you wasted your time and money.

CHASUBLE: Am I to understand then that there are to be no christenings at all this afternoon?

JACK: I don't think that, as things are now, it would be of much practical value to either of 245
us, Dr. Chasuble.

CHASUBLE: I am grieved to hear such sentiments from you, Mr. Worthing. They savor of the heretical views of the Anabaptists,[27] views that I have completely refuted in four of my unpublished sermons. However, as your present mood seems to be one peculiarly secular, I will return to the church at once. Indeed, I have just been informed 250
by the pew-opener that for the last hour and a half Miss Prism has been waiting for me in the vestry.

LADY BRACKNELL: [*starting*] Miss Prism! Did I hear you mention a Miss Prism?

---

[27] **Anabaptists** Christian sect advocating adult baptism even for those already baptized as infants

CHASUBLE: Yes, Lady Bracknell. I am on my way to join her.

LADY BRACKNELL: Pray allow me to detain you for a moment. This matter may prove to   255
be one of vital importance to Lord Bracknell and myself. Is this Miss Prism a female
of repellent aspect, remotely connected with education?

CHASUBLE: [*somewhat indignantly*] She is the most cultivated of ladies, and the very picture of respectability.

LADY BRACKNELL: It is obviously the same person. May I ask what position she holds in   260
your household?

CHASUBLE: [*severely*] I am a celibate, madam.

JACK: [*interposing*] Miss Prism, Lady Bracknell, has been for the last three years Miss
Cardew's esteemed governess and valued companion.

LADY BRACKNELL: In spite of what I hear of her, I must see her at once. Let her be sent for.   265

CHASUBLE: [*looking off*] She approaches; she is nigh.

> [*Enter* MISS PRISM *hurriedly.*]

MISS PRISM: I was told you expected me in the vestry, dear Canon. I have been waiting
for you there for an hour and three-quarters. [*Catches sight of* LADY BRACKNELL,
who has fixed her with a stony glare. MISS PRISM *grows pale and quails. She looks
anxiously round as if desirous to escape.*]   270

LADY BRACKNELL: [*in a severe, judicial voice*] Prism! [MISS PRISM *bows her head in shame.*]
Come here, Prism! [MISS PRISM *approaches in a humble manner.*] Prism! Where is
that baby?

> [*General consternation. The* CANON *starts back in horror.* ALGERNON *and*
> JACK *pretend to be anxious to shield* CECILY *and* GWENDOLEN *from hearing
> the details of a terrible public scandal.*]

Twenty-eight years ago, Prism, you left Lord Bracknell's house, Number 104, Upper
Grosvenor Street, in charge of a perambulator that contained a baby of the male   275
sex. You never returned. A few weeks later, through the elaborate investigations of
the Metropolitan police, the perambulator was discovered at midnight, standing by
itself in a remote corner of Bayswater. It contained the manuscript of a three-volume
novel of more than usually revolting sentimentality. [MISS PRISM *starts in involuntary
indignation.*] But the baby was not there! [*Everyone looks at* MISS PRISM.] Prism,   280
where is that baby? [*a pause*]

MISS PRISM: Lady Bracknell, I admit with shame that I do not know. I only wish I did.
The plain facts of the case are these. On the morning of the day you mention, a day
that is forever branded on my memory, I prepared as usual to take the baby out in
its perambulator. I had also with me a somewhat old, but capacious hand-bag in   285
which I had intended to place the manuscript of a work of fiction that I had written
during my few unoccupied hours. In a moment of mental abstraction, for which I
never can forgive myself, I deposited the manuscript in the bassinette, and placed
the baby in the hand-bag.

JACK: [*who has been listening attentively*] But where did you deposit the hand-bag?   290

MISS PRISM: Do not ask me, Mr. Worthing.

JACK: Miss Prism, this is a matter of no small importance to me. I insist on knowing where
you deposited the hand-bag that contained that infant.

MISS PRISM: I left it in the cloak-room of one of the larger railway stations in London.

JACK: What railway station?   295

MISS PRISM: [*quite crushed*] Victoria. The Brighton line. [*sinks into a chair*]

JACK: I must retire to my room for a moment. Gwendolen, wait here for me.

GWENDOLEN: If you are not too long, I will wait here for you all my life.

[*Exit* JACK *in great excitement.*]

CHASUBLE: What do you think this means, Lady Bracknell?

LADY BRACKNELL: I dare not even suspect, Dr. Chasuble. I need hardly tell you that in   300
families of high position strange coincidences are not supposed to occur. They are
hardly considered the thing.

[*Noises heard overhead as if someone was throwing trunks about. Everyone looks up.*]

CECILY: Uncle Jack seems strangely agitated.

CHASUBLE: Your guardian has a very emotional nature.

LADY BRACKNELL: This noise is extremely unpleasant. It sounds as if he was having   305
an argument. I dislike arguments of any kind. They are always vulgar, and often
convincing.

CHASUBLE: [*looking up*] It has stopped now. [*The noise is redoubled.*]

LADY BRACKNELL: I wish he would arrive at some conclusion.

GWENDOLEN: This suspense is terrible. I hope it will last.   310

[*Enter* JACK *with a hand-bag of black leather in his hand.*]

JACK: [*rushing over to* MISS PRISM] Is this the hand-bag, Miss Prism? Examine it carefully
before you speak. The happiness of more than one life depends on your answer.

MISS PRISM: [*calmly*] It seems to be mine. Yes, here is the injury it received through the
upsetting of a Gower Street omnibus in younger and happier days. Here is the stain
on the lining caused by the explosion of a temperance beverage, an incident that   315
occurred at Leamington. And here, on the lock, are my initials. I had forgotten that
in an extravagant mood I had had them placed there. The bag is undoubtedly mine.
I am delighted to have it so unexpectedly restored to me. It has been a great incon-
venience being without it all these years.

JACK: [*in a pathetic voice*] Miss Prism, more is restored to you than this hand-bag. I was   320
the baby you placed in it.

MISS PRISM: [*amazed*] You?

JACK: [*embracing her*] Yes . . . mother!

MISS PRISM: [*recoiling in indignant astonishment*] Mr. Worthing! I am unmarried!

JACK: Unmarried! I do not deny that is a serious blow. But after all, who has the right to   325
cast a stone against one who has suffered? Cannot repentance wipe out an act of
folly? Why should there be one law for men, and another for women? Mother, I
forgive you. [*tries to embrace her again*]

MISS PRISM: [*Still more indignant*] Mr. Worthing, there is some error. [*pointing to* LADY
BRACKNELL] There is the lady who can tell you who you really are.   330

JACK: [*after a pause*] Lady Bracknell, I hate to seem inquisitive, but would you kindly
inform me who I am?

LADY BRACKNELL: I am afraid that the news I have to give you will not altogether please
you. You are the son of my poor sister, Mrs. Moncrieff, and consequently Algernon's
elder brother.   335

JACK: Algy's elder brother? Then I have a brother after all. I knew I had a brother! I always
said I had a brother! Cecily—how could you have ever doubted that I had a brother?
[*seizes hold of* ALGERNON] Dr. Chasuble, my unfortunate brother. Miss Prism, my
unfortunate brother. Gwendolen, my unfortunate brother. Algy, you young scoundrel, you will have to treat me with more respect in the future. You have never   340
behaved to me like a brother in all your life.

ALGERNON: Well, not till to-day, old boy, I admit. I did my best, however, though I was
out of practice. [*shakes hands*]

GWENDOLEN: [*to* JACK] My own! But what own are you? What is your Christian name, now that you have become someone else? 345

JACK: Good heavens! . . . I had quite forgotten that point. Your decision on the subject of my name is irrevocable, I suppose?

GWENDOLEN: I never change, except in my affections.

CECILY: What a noble nature you have, Gwendolen!

JACK: Then the question had better be cleared up at once. Aunt Augusta, a moment. At 350 the time when Miss Prism left me in the hand-bag, had I been christened already?

LADY BRACKNELL: Every luxury that money could buy, including christening, had been lavished on you by your fond and doting parents.

JACK: Then I was christened! That is settled. Now, what name was I given? Let me know the worst. 355

LADY BRACKNELL: Being the eldest son you were naturally christened after your father.

JACK: [*irritably*] Yes, but what was my father's Christian name?

LADY BRACKNELL: [*meditatively*] I cannot at the present moment recall what the General's Christian name was. But I have no doubt he had one. He was eccentric, I admit. But only in later years. And that was the result of the Indian climate, and marriage, and 360 indigestion, and other things of that kind.

JACK: Algy! Can't you recollect what our father's Christian name was?

ALGERNON: My dear boy, we were never even on speaking terms. He died before I was a year old.

JACK: His name would appear in the Army Lists of the period, I suppose, Aunt Augusta? 365

LADY BRACKNELL: The General was essentially a man of peace, except in his domestic life. But I have no doubt his name would appear in any military directory.

JACK: The Army Lists of the last forty years are here. These delightful records should have been my constant study. [*rushes to bookcase and tears the books out*] M. Generals . . . Mallam, Maxbohm, Magley, what ghastly names they have—Markby, Migsby, Moss, 370 Moncrieff! Lieutenant 1840, Captain, Lieutenant-Colonel, Colonel, General 1869, Christian names, Ernest John. [*puts book very quietly down and speaks quite calmly*] I always told you, Gwendolen, my name was Ernest, didn't I? Well, it is Ernest after all. I mean it naturally is Ernest.

LADY BRACKNELL: Yes, I remember that the General was called Ernest. I knew I had some 375 particular reason for disliking the name.

GWENDOLEN: Ernest! My own Ernest! I felt from the first that you could have no other name!

JACK: Gwendolen, it is a terrible thing for a man to find out suddenly that all his life he has been speaking nothing but the truth. Can you forgive me? 380

GWENDOLEN: I can. For I feel that you are sure to change.

JACK: My own one!

CHASUBLE: [*to* MISS PRISM] Lætitia! [*embraces her*]

MISS PRISM: [*enthusiastically*] Frederick! At last!

ALGERNON: Cecily! [*embraces her*] At last! 385

JACK: Gwendolen! [*embraces her*] At last!

LADY BRACKNELL: My nephew, you seem to be displaying signs of triviality.

JACK: On the contrary, Aunt Augusta, I've now realized for the first time in my life the vital Importance of Being Earnest.

[*tableau*]

CURTAIN

"The Hairy Ape"
(1921)

ugene O'Neill was the first American dramatist to win widespread international fame. He experimented with many dramatic forms and styles in his twenty-five full-length plays. Included among these are *Anna Christie* (1920), *Strange Interlude* (1928), and *Long Day's Journey into Night* (published in 1941 and first performed in 1956), each of which won the Pulitzer Prize for drama. In *"The Hairy Ape"* O'Neill adopted many conventions of expressionism, an artistic movement that emerged in Germany just prior to World War I. The expressionists proclaimed the supreme importance of the human spirit, which they believed was being crushed or distorted by materialism and industrialism.

"The Hairy Ape" shows the influence of expressionism on American drama. The unity of the play derives from a central theme: humanity's frustrated search for identity in a hostile environment. In the first scene, Yank is confident that he and his fellow stokers are the only ones who belong on the ship because it is they who make the ship go. "What's dem slobs in de foist cabin got to do wit us? We're better men dan dey are, ain't we?" By extension, Yank asserts the value of common workers in the factories of the industrialized world and demeans those who benefit from their labor but don't share in it. However, when Yank is told that the pampered, anemic daughter of one of the shipowners (who represents power, money, and influence) sees him as "a hairy ape," his confidence is shattered. Seeking to reestablish his identity and value, Yank first visits Fifth Avenue, the home territory of the rich and powerful. There, he asserts his physical superiority, accosting high-society women and men who ignore him until they're inconvenienced by him and call for the police. Thrown into jail, Yank decides that the answer lies in destroying the steel and machinery over which he originally thought he had power. While in jail, Yank learns that the International Workers of the World (IWW) opposes the owners of factories and ships. After his release, Yank goes to the IWW headquarters and offers to blow up its enemies. But the IWW secretary first rejects Yank as a spy sent to undo the organization's efforts and, later, simply dismisses him as "a brainless ape." Finally, Yank visits a gorilla at the zoo with whom he identifies, but when he releases the gorilla from the cage the gorilla crushes him, and he dies without having achieved the sense of belonging he sought. Yank is symbolic of modern humanity in an industrialized society cut off from a past when human beings had an integral relationship with the natural environment but are now little better than cogs in an industrial machine.

"The Hairy Ape" is representative of the outlook and techniques of expressionism. The episodic structure and distorted visual and aural elements are typical of the movement, as is the longing for fulfillment, which suggests the need to change society so that the individual can find a coherent, satisfying relationship within it.

Eugene O'Neill

"The Hairy Ape"

Characters

ROBERT SMITH, "YANK"

PADDY

LONG

MILDRED DOUGLAS

HER AUNT

SECOND ENGINEER

A GUARD

A SECRETARY OF AN ORGANIZATION

STOKERS, LADIES, GENTLEMEN, ETC.

Scenes

SCENE I: *The firemen's forecastle of an ocean liner—an hour after sailing from New York.*
SCENE II: *Section of promenade deck, two days out—morning.*
SCENE III: *The stokehole. A few minutes later.*
SCENE IV: *Same as Scene I. Half an hour later.*
SCENE V: *Fifth Avenue, New York. Three weeks later.*
SCENE VI: *An island near the city. The next night.*
SCENE VII: *In the city. About a month later.*
SCENE VIII: *In the city. Twilight of the next day.*

SCENE I

The firemen's forecastle of a transatlantic liner an hour after sailing from New York for the voyage across. Tiers of narrow, steel bunks, three deep, on all sides. An entrance in rear. Benches on the floor before the bunks. The room is crowded with men, shouting, cursing, laughing, singing—a confused, inchoate uproar swelling into a sort of unity, a meaning—the bewildered, furious, baffled defiance of a beast in a cage. Nearly all the men are drunk. Many bottles are passed from hand to hand. All are dressed in dungaree pants, heavy, ugly shoes. Some wear singlets, but the majority are stripped to the waist.

The treatment of this scene, or of any other scene in the play, should by no means be naturalistic. The effect sought after is a cramped space in the bowels of a ship, imprisoned by white steel. The lines of bunks, the uprights supporting them, cross each other like the steel framework of a cage. The ceiling crushes down upon the men's heads. They cannot stand upright. This accentuates the natural stooping posture which shoveling coal and the resultant overdevelopment of back and shoulder muscles have given them. The men themselves should resemble those pictures in which the appearance of Neanderthal Man is guessed at. All are hairy-chested, with long arms of tremendous power, and low, receding brows above their small, fierce, resentful eyes. All the civilized white races are represented, but except for the slight differentiation in color of hair, skin, eyes, all these men are alike.

The curtain rises on a tumult of sound. YANK *is seated in the foreground. He seems broader, fiercer, more truculent, more powerful, more sure of himself than the rest. They respect his superior strength—the grudging respect of fear. Then, too, he represents to them a self-expression, the very last word in what they are, their most highly developed individual.*

VOICES: Gif me trink dere, you!
    'Ave a wet!
    Salute!
    Gesundheit!
    Skoal!   5
    Drunk as a lord, God stiffen you!
    Here's how!
    Luck!
    Pass back that bottle, damn you!
    Pourin' it down his neck!   10
    Ho, Froggy! Where the devil have you been?
    La Touraine.
    I hit him smash in yaw, py Gott!
    Jenkins—the First—he's a rotten swine
    And the coppers nabbed him—and I run—   15
    I like peer better. It don't pig head gif you.
    A slut, I'm sayin'! She robbed me aslape—
    To hell with 'em all!
    You're a bloody liar!
    Say dot again!   20

        [*Commotion. Two men about to fight are pulled apart.*]

    No scrappin' now!
    Tonight—
    See who's the best man!
    Bloody Dutchman!
    Tonight on the for'ard square.   25
    I'll bet on Dutchy.
    He packa da wallop, I tella you!
    Shut up, Wop!
    No fightin', maties. We're all chums, ain't we?

        [*A voice starts bawling a song.*]

       Beer, beer, glorious beer!   30
       Fill yourselves right up to here.
YANK: [*for the first time seeming to take notice of the uproar about him, turns around threateningly—in a tone of contemptuous authority*] Choke off dat noise! Where d'yuh get dat beer stuff? Beer, hell! Beer's for goils—and Dutchmen. Me for somep'n wit a kick to it! Gimme a drink, one of youse guys. [*Several bottles are eagerly offered. He takes a*   35 *tremendous gulp at one of them; then, keeping the bottle in his hand, glares belligerently at the owner, who hastens to acquiesce in this robbery by saying*] All righto, Yank. Keep it and have another. [YANK *contemptuously turns his back on the crowd again. For a second there is an embarrassed silence. Then—*]

VOICES: We must be passing the Hook. 40
      She's beginning to roll to it.
      Six days in hell—and then Southampton.
      Py Yesus, I vish somepody take my first vatch for me!
      Gittin seasick, Square-head?
      Drink up and forget it! 45
      What's in your bottle?
      Gin.
      Dot's nigger trink.
      Absinthe? It's doped. You'll go off your chump, Froggy!
      Cochon! 50
      Whisky, that's the ticket!
      Where's Paddy?
      Going asleep.
      Sing us that whisky song, Paddy.

      [*They all turn to an old, wizened Irishman who is dozing, very drunk, on the benches forward. His face is extremely monkey-like with all the sad, patient pathos of that animal in his small eyes.*]

      Singa da song, Caruso Pat! 55
      He's gettin' old. The drink is too much for him.
      He's too drunk.
PADDY: [*blinking about him, starts to his feet resentfully, swaying, holding on to the edge of a bunk*] I'm never too drunk to sing. 'Tis only when I'm dead to the world I'd be wishful to sing at all. [*with a sort of sad contempt*] "Whisky Johnny," ye want? A chanty, 60
ye want? Now that's a queer wish from the ugly like of you, God help you. But no matther. [*He starts to sing in a thin, nasal, doleful tone.*]
      Oh, whisky is the life of man!
      Whisky! O Johnny! [*They all join in on this.*]
      Oh, whisky is the life of man! 65
      Whisky for my Johnny! [*Again chorus.*]
      Oh, whisky drove my old man mad!
      Whisky! O Johnny!
      Oh, whisky drove my old man mad!
      Whisky for my Johnny! 70
YANK: [*again turning around scornfully*] Aw hell! Nix on dat old sailing ship stuff! All dat bull's dead, see? And you're dead, too, yuh damned old Harp, on'y yuh don't know it. Take it easy, see. Give us a rest. Nix on de loud noise. [*with a cynical grin*] Can't youse see I'm tryin to t'ink?
ALL: [*repeating the word after him as one with the same cynical amused mockery*] Think! [*The* 75
chorused word has a brazen metallic quality as if their throats were phonograph horns. It is followed by a general uproar of hard, barking laughter.]
VOICES: Don't be cracking your head wit ut, Yank.
      You gat headache, py yingo!
      One thing about it—it rhymes with drink! 80
      Ha, ha, ha!
      Drink, don't think!
      Drink, don't think!
      Drink, don't think!

      [*A whole chorus of voices has taken up this refrain, stamping on the floor, pounding on the benches with fists.*]

YANK: [*taking a gulp from his bottle—good-naturedly*] Aw right. Can de noise. I got yuh de   85
foist time. [*The uproar subsides. A very drunken sentimental tenor begins to sing.*]
> Far away in Canada,
> Far across the sea,
> There's a lass who fondly waits
> Making a home for me—   90

YANK: [*fiercely contemptuous*] Shut up, yuh lousy boob! Where d'yuh get dat tripe? Home?
Home, hell! I'll make a home for yuh! I'll knock yuh dead. Home! T'hell wit home!
Where d'yuh get dat tripe? Dis is home, see? What d'yuh want wit home? [*proudly*]
I runned away from mine when I was a kid. On'y too glad to beat it, dat was me.
Home was lickings for me, dat's all. But yuh can bet your shoit no one ain't never
licked me since! Wanter try it, any of youse? Huh! I guess not. [*in a more placated
but still contemptuous tone*] Goils waitin' for yuh, huh? Aw, hell! Dat's all tripe. Dey   95
don't wait for no one. Dey'd double-cross yuh for a nickel. Dey're all tarts, get me?
Treat 'em rough, dat's me. To hell wit 'em. Tarts, dat's what, de whole bunch of 'em.

LONG: [*very drunk, jumps on a bench excitedly, gesticulating with a bottle in his hand*] Listen 'ere,
Comrades! Yank 'ere is right. 'E says this 'ere stinkin' ship is our 'ome. And 'e says as
'ome is 'ell. And 'e's right! This is 'ell. We lives in 'ell, Comrades—and right enough we'll   100
die in it. [*raging*] And who's ter blame, I arsks yer? We ain't. We wasn't born this
rotten way. All men is born free and ekal. That's in the bleedin' Bible, maties. But
what d'they care for the Bible—them lazy, bloated swine what travels firstcabin?
Them's the ones. They dragged us down 'til we're on'y wage slaves in the bowels
of a bloody ship, sweatin', burnin' up, eatin' coal dust! Hit's them's ter blame—the   105
damned Capitalist clarss!

> [*There had been a gradual murmur of contemptuous resentment rising among the
> men until now he is interrupted by a storm of catcalls, hisses, boos, hard laughter.*]

VOICES: Turn it off!
> Shut up!
> Sit down!
> Closa da face!   110
> Tamn fool! [*Etc.*]

YANK: [*standing up and glaring at* LONG] Sit down before I knock yuh down! [LONG *makes
haste to efface himself.* YANK *goes on contemptuously.*] De Bible, huh? De Cap'tlist class,
huh? Aw nix on dat Salvation Army–Socialist bull. Git a soapbox! Hire a hall!
Come and be saved, huh? Jerk us to Jesus, huh? Aw g'wan! I've listened to lots of guys   115
like you, see. Yuh're all wrong. Wanter know what I t'ink? Yuh ain't no good for no
one. Yuh're de bunk. Yuh ain't got no noive, get me? Yuh're yellow, dat's what. Yellow, dat's you. Say! What's dem slobs in de foist cabin got to do wit us? We're better
men dan dey are, ain't we? Sure! One of us guys could clean up de whole mob wit
one mitt. Put one of 'em down here for one watch in de stokehole, what'd happen?   120
Dey'd carry him off on a stretcher. Dem boids don't amount to nothin'. Dey're just
baggage. Who makes dis old tub run? Ain't it us guys? Well den, we belong, don't
we? We belong and dey don't. Dat's all. [*A loud chorus of approval.* YANK *goes on.*] As
for dis bein' hell—aw, nuts! Yuh lost your noive, dat's what. Dis is a man's job, get me?
It belongs. It runs dis tub. No stiffs need apply. But yuh're a stiff, see? Yuh're yellow,   125
dat's you.

VOICES: [*with a great hard pride in them*]
> Righto!
> A man's job!
> Talk is cheap, Long.   130
> He never could hold up his end.

Divil take him!
Yank's right. We make it go.
Py Gott, Yank say right ting!
We don't need no one cryin' over us.   135
Makin' speeches.
Throw him out!
Yellow!
Chuck him overboard!
I'll break his jaw for him!   140

[*They crowd around* LONG *threateningly.*]

YANK: [*half good-natured again—contemptuously*] Aw, take it easy. Leave him alone. He ain't
woith a punch. Drink up. Here's how, whoever owns dis. [*He takes a long swallow
from his bottle. All drink with him. In a flash all is hilarious amiability again, back-
slapping, loud talk, etc.*]

PADDY: [*who has been sitting in a blinking, melancholy daze—suddenly cries out in a voice*   145
full of old sorrow] We belong to this, you're saying? We make the ship to go, you're
saying? Yerra then, that Almighty God have pity on us! [*His voice runs into the wail
of a keen, he rocks back and forth on his bench. The men stare at him, startled and
impressed in spite of themselves.*] Oh, to be back in the fine days of my youth, ochone!
Oh, there was fine beautiful ships them days—clippers wid tall masts fine strong men   150
in them—men that was sons of the sea as if 'twas the mother that bore them. Oh,
the clean skins of them, and the clear eyes, the straight backs and full chests of them!
Brave men they was, and bold men surely! We'd be sailing out, bound down round
the Horn maybe. We'd be making sail in the dawn, with a fair breeze, singing a
chanty song wid no care to it. And astern the land would be sinking low and dying   155
out, but we'd give it no heed but a laugh, and never a look behind. For the day that
was, was enough, for we was free men—and I'm thinking 'tis only slaves do be
giving heed to the day that's gone or the day to come—until they're old like me.
[*with a sort of religious exaltation*] Oh, to be scudding south again wid the power
of the Trade Wind driving her on steady through the nights and the days! Full sail   160
on her! Nights and days! Nights when the foam of the wake would be flaming wid
fire, when the sky'd be blazing and winking wid stars. Or the full of the moon maybe.
Then you'd see her driving through the gray night, her sails stretching aloft all silver
and white, not a sound on the deck, the lot of us dreaming dreams, till you'd believe
'twas no real ship at all you was on but a ghost ship like the Flying Dutchman they   165
say does be roaming the seas forevermore widout touching a port. And there was the
days, too. A warm sun on the clean decks. Sun warming the blood of you, and wind
over the miles of shiny green ocean like strong drink to your lungs. Work—aye, hard
work—but who'd mind that at all? Sure, you worked under the sky and 'twas work
wid skill and daring to it. And wid the day done, in the dog watch, smoking me pipe   170
at ease, the lookout would be raising land maybe, and we'd see the mountains of
South Americy wid the red fire of the setting sun painting their white tops and the
clouds floating by them! [*His tone of exaltation ceases. He goes on mournfully.*] Yerra,
what's the use of talking? 'Tis a dead man's whisper. [*to* YANK *resentfully*] 'Twas them
days men belonged to ships, not now. 'Twas them days a ship was part of the sea, and   175
a man was part of a ship, and the sea joined all together and made it one. [*scornfully*]
Is it one wid this you'd be, Yank—black smoke from the funnels smudging the sea,
smudging the decks—the bloody engines pounding and throbbing and shaking—wid
divil a sight of sun or a breath of clean air—choking our lungs wid coal dust—breaking
our backs and hearts in the hell of the stokehole—feeding the bloody furnace—feed-   180

ing our lives along wid the coal, I'm thinking—caged in by steel from a sight of the sky like bloody apes in the zoo! [*with a harsh laugh*] Ho-ho, divil mend you! Is it to belong to that you're wishing? Is it a flesh and blood wheel of the engines you'd be?

YANK: [*who has been listening with a contemptuous sneer, barks out the answer*] Sure ting! Dat's me. What about it? 185

PADDY: [*as if to himself—with great sorrow*] Me time is past due. That a great wave wid sun in the heart of it may sweep me over the side sometime I'd be dreaming of the days that's gone!

YANK: Aw, yuh crazy Mick! [*He springs to his feet and advances on Paddy threateningly—then stops, fighting some queer struggle within himself—lets his hands fall to his sides—contemptuously.*] Aw, take it easy. Yuh're aw right, at dat. Yuh're bugs, dat's all—nutty as a cuckoo. All dat tripe yuh been pullin'—Aw, dat's all right. On'y it's dead, get me? Yuh don't belong no more, see. Yuh don't got de stuff. Yuh're too old. [*disgustedly*] But aw say, come up for air onct in a while, can't yuh? See what's happened since yuh croaked. [*He suddenly bursts forth vehemently, growing more and more excited.*] Say! Sure! Sure I meant it! What de hell—Say, lemme talk! Hey! Hey, you old Harp! Hey, youse guys! Say, listen to me—wait a moment—I gotter talk, see. I belong and he don't. He's dead but I'm livin'. Listen to me! Sure I'm part of de engines! Why de hell not! Dey move, don't dey? Dey're speed, ain't dey? Dey smash trou, don't dey! Twenty-five knots a hour! Dat's goin' some! Dat's new stuff! 200
Dat belongs! But him, he's too old. He gets dizzy. Say, listen. All dat crazy tripe about nights and days; all dat crazy tripe about stars and moons; all dat crazy tripe about suns and winds, fresh air and de rest of it—Aw hell, dat's all a dope dream! Hittin' de pipe of de past, dat's what he's doin'. He's old and don't belong no more. But me, I'm young! I'm in de pink! I move wit it! It, get me! I mean de ting dat's de guts of 205
all dis. It ploughs trou all de tripe he's been sayin'. It blows dat up! It knocks dat dead! It slams dat offen de face of de Oith! It, get me! De engines and de coal and de smoke and all de rest of it! He can't breathe and swallow coal dust, but I kin, see? Dat's fresh air for me! Dat's food for me! I'm new, get me? Hell in de stokehole? Sure! It takes a man to work in hell. Hell, sure, dat's my fav'rite climate. I eat it up! I git fat on it! It's 210
me makes it hot! It's me makes it roar! It's me makes it move! Sure, on'y for me everyting stops. It all goes dead, get me? De noise and smoke and all de engines movin' de woild, dey stop. Dere ain't nothin' no more! Dat's what I'm sayin'. Everyting else dat makes de woild move, somep'n makes it move. It can't move without somep'n else, see? Den yuh get down to me. I'm at de bottom, get me! Dere ain't 215
nothin' foither. I'm de end! I'm de start! I start somep'n and de woild moves! It—dat's me!—de new dat's moiderin' de old! I'm de ting in coal dat makes it boin; I'm steam and oil for de engines; I'm de ting in noise dat makes yuh hear it; I'm smoke and express trains and steamers and factory whistles; I'm de ting in gold dat makes it money! And I'm what makes iron into steel! Steel, dat stands for de whole ting! And 220
I'm steel—steel—steel! I'm de muscles in steel, de punch behind it! [*As he says this he pounds with his fist against the steel bunks. All the men, roused to a pitch of frenzied self-glorification by his speech, do likewise. There is a deafening metallic roar, through which* YANK's *voice can be heard bellowing.*] Slaves, hell. We run de whole woiks. All de rich guys dat tink dey're somep'n, dey ain't nothin'! Dey don't belong. But us 225
guys, we're in de move, we're at de bottom, de whole ting is us! [PADDY *from the start of* YANK's *speech has been taking one gulp after another from his bottle, at first frightenedly, as if he were afraid to listen, then desperately, as if to drown his senses, but finally has achieved complete indifferent, even amused, drunkenness.* YANK *sees his lips moving. He quells the uproar with a shout.*] Hey, youse guys, take it easy! Wait a 230
moment! De nutty Harp is sayin' somep'n.

PADDY: [*is heard now—throws his head back a mocking burst of laughter*] Ho-ho-ho-ho-ho—

YANK: [*drawing back his fist, with a snarl*] Aw! Look out who yuh're givin' the bark!

PADDY: [*begins to sing the "Miller of Dee" with enormous good nature*]
>   I care for nobody, no, not I,   235
>   And nobody cares for me.

YANK: [*good-natured himself in a flash, interrupts Paddy with a slap on the bare back like a report*] Dat's de stuff! Now yuh're gettin' wise to somep'n. Care for nobody, dat's de dope! To hell wit 'em all. And nix on nobody else carin'. I kin care for myself, get me! [*Eight bells sound, muffled, vibrating through the steel walls as if some enormous* 240 *brazen gong were imbedded in the heart of the ship. All the men jump up mechanically, file through the door silently close upon each other's heels in what is very like a prisoners' lockstep.* YANK *slaps* PADDY *on the back.*] Our watch, yuh old Harp! [*mockingly*] Come on down in hell. Eat up de coal dust. Drink in de heat. It's it, see! Act like yuh liked it, yuh better—or croak yuhself.   245

PADDY: [*with jovial defiance*] To the divil wid it! I'll not report this watch. Let thim log me and be damned. I'm no slave the like of you. I'll be sittin' here at me ease, and drink-ing, and thinking, and dreaming dreams.

YANK: [*contemptuously*] Tinkin' and dreamin', what'll that get yuh? What's tinkin' got to do wit it? We move, don't we? Speed, ain't it? Fog, dat's all you stand for. But we 250 drive trou dat, don't we? We split dat up and smash trou—twenty-five knots a hour! [*turns his back on* PADDY *scornfully*] Aw, yuh make me sick! Yuh don't belong! [*He strides out the door in rear.* PADDY *hums to himself, blinking drowsily.*]

CURTAIN

SCENE II

Two days out. A section of the promenade deck, MILDRED DOUGLAS *and her aunt are discovered reclining in deck chairs. The former is a girl of twenty, slender, delicate, with a pale, pretty face marred by a self-conscious expression of disdainful superiority. She looks fretful, nervous, and discontented, bored by her own anemia. Her aunt is a pompous and proud—and fat—old lady. She is a type even to the point of a double chin and lorgnettes. She is dressed pretentiously, as if afraid her face alone would never indicate her position in life.* MILDRED *is dressed all in white.*

The impression to be conveyed by this scene is one of the beautiful, vivid life of the sea all about— sunshine on the deck in a great flood, the fresh sea wind blowing across it. In the midst of this, these two incongruous, artificial figures, inert and disharmonious, the elder like a gray lump of dough touched up with rouge, the younger looking as if the vitality of her stock had been sapped before she was conceived, so that she is the expression not of its life energy but merely of the artificialities that energy had won for itself in the spending.

MILDRED: [*looking up with affected dreaminess*] How the black smoke swirls back against the sky! Is it not beautiful?   255

AUNT: [*without looking up*] I dislike smoke of any kind.

MILDRED: My great-grandmother smoked a pipe—a clay pipe.

AUNT: [*ruffling*] Vulgar!

MILDRED: She was too distant a relative to be vulgar. Time mellows pipes.

AUNT: [*pretending boredom but irritated*] Did the sociology you took up at college teach 260
you that—to play the ghoul on every possible occasion, excavating old bones? Why
not let your great-grandmother rest in her grave?

MILDRED: [*dreamily*] With her pipe beside her—puffing in Paradise.

AUNT: [*with spite*] Yes, you are a natural-born ghoul. You are even getting to look like one,
my dear. 265

MILDRED: [*in a passionless tone*] I detest you, Aunt. [*looking at her critically*] Do you
know what you remind me of? Of a cold pork pudding against a background of
linoleum tablecloth in the kitchen of a—but the possibilities are wearisome. [*She
closes her eyes.*]

AUNT: [*with a bitter laugh*] Merci for your candor. But since I am and must be your 270
chaperon—in appearance, at least—let us patch up some sort of armed truce. For
my part you are quite free to indulge any pose of eccentricity that beguiles you—as
long as you observe the amenities—

MILDRED: [*drawling*] The inanities?

AUNT: [*going on as if she hadn't heard*] After exhausting the morbid thrills of social service 275
work on New York's East Side—how they must have hated you, by the way, the
poor that you made so much poorer in their own eyes!—you are now bent on making your slumming international. Well, I hope Whitechapel will provide the needed
nerve tonic. Do not ask me to chaperon you there, however. I told your father
I would not. I loathe deformity. We will hire an army of detectives and you may 280
investigate everything—they allow you to see.

MILDRED: [*protesting with a trace of genuine earnestness*] Please do not mock at my
attempts to discover how the other half lives. Give me credit for some sort of groping sincerity in that at least. I would like to help them. I would like to be some
use in the world. Is it my fault I don't know how? I would like to be sincere, to 285
touch life somewhere.[*with weary bitterness*] But I'm afraid I have neither the
vitality nor integrity. All that was burnt out in our stock before I was born. Grandfather's blast furnaces, flaming to the sky, melting steel, making millions—then
father keeping those home fires burning, making more millions—and little me at
the tail-end of it all. I'm a waste product in the Bessemer process—like the millions. 290
Or rather, I inherit the acquired trait of the by-product, wealth, but none of the
energy, none of the strength of the steel that made it. I am sired by gold and
damned by it, as they say at the race track—damned in more ways than one. [*She
laughs mirthlessly.*]

AUNT: [*unimpressed—superciliously*] You seem to be going in for sincerity today. It isn't 295
becoming to you, really—except as an obvious pose. Be as artificial as you are, I
advise. There's a sort of sincerity in that, you know. And, after all, you must confess
you like that better.

MILDRED: [*again affected and bored*] Yes, I suppose I do. Pardon me for my outburst.
When a leopard complains of its spots, it must sound rather grotesque. [*in a mocking 300
tone*] Purr, little leopard. Purr, scratch, tear, kill, gorge yourself and be happy—
only stay in the jungle where your spots are camouflage. In a cage they make you
conspicuous.

AUNT: I don't know what you are talking about.

MILDRED: It would be rude to talk about anything to you. Let's just talk. [*She looks at her 305
wristwatch.*] Well, thank goodness, it's about time for them to come for me. That
ought to give me a new thrill, Aunt.

AUNT: [*affectedly troubled*] You don't mean to say you're really going? The dirt—the heat
must be frightful—

MILDRED: Grandfather started as a puddler. I should have inherited an immunity to heat   310
    that would make a salamander shiver. It will be fun to put it to the test.

AUNT: But don't you have to have the captain's—or someone's—permission to visit the
    stokehole?

MILDRED: [*with a triumphant smile*] I have it—both his and the chief engineer's. Oh, they
    didn't want to at first, in spite of my social service credentials. They didn't seem a bit   315
    anxious that I should investigate how the other half lives and works on a ship. So
    I had to tell them that my father, the president of Nazareth Steel, chairman of the
    board of directors of this line, had told me it would be all right.

AUNT: He didn't.

MILDRED: How naïve age makes one! But I said he did, Aunt. I even said he had given me   320
    a letter to them—which I had lost. And they were afraid to take the chance that I
    might be lying. [*excitedly*] So it's ho! for the stokehole. The second engineer is to
    escort me. [*looking at her watch again*] It's time. And here he comes, I think.

        [*The* SECOND ENGINEER *enters. He is a husky, fine-looking man of thirty-five
        or so. He stops before the two and tips his cap, visibly embarrassed and ill-at-ease.*]

SECOND ENGINEER: Miss Douglas?

MILDRED: Yes. [*throwing off her rugs and getting to her feet*] Are we all ready to start?   325

SECOND ENGINEER: In just a second, ma'am. I'm waiting for the Fourth. He's coming
    along.

MILDRED: [*with a scornful smile*] You don't care to shoulder this responsibility alone, is
    that it?

SECOND ENGINEER: [*forcing a smile*] Two are better than one. [*disturbed by her eyes, glances*   330
    out to sea—blurts out] A fine day we're having.

MILDRED: Is it?

SECOND ENGINEER: A nice warm breeze—

MILDRED: It feels cold to me.

SECOND ENGINEER: But it's hot enough in the sun—   335

MILDRED: Not hot enough for me. I don't like Nature. I was never athletic.

SECOND ENGINEER: [*forcing a smile*] Well, you'll find it hot enough where you're going.

MILDRED: Do you mean hell?

SECOND ENGINEER: [*flabbergasted, decides to laugh*] Ho-ho! No, I mean the stokehole.

MILDRED: My grandfather was a puddler. He played with boiling steel.   340

SECOND ENGINEER: [*all at sea—uneasily*] Is that so? Hum, you'll excuse me, ma'am, but
    are you intending to wear that dress?

MILDRED: Why not?

SECOND ENGINEER: You'll likely rub against oil and dirt. It can't be helped.

MILDRED: It doesn't matter. I have lots of white dresses.   345

SECOND ENGINEER: I have an old coat you might throw over—

MILDRED: I have fifty dresses like this. I will throw this one into the sea when I come back.
    That ought to wash it clean, don't you think?

SECOND ENGINEER: [*doggedly*] There's ladders to climb down that are none too clean—
    and dark alleyways—   350

MILDRED: I will wear this very dress and none other.

SECOND ENGINEER: No offense meant. It's none of my business. I was only warning
    you—

MILDRED: Warning? That sounds thrilling.

SECOND ENGINEER: [*looking down the deck—with a sigh of relief*] There's the Fourth now.   355
    He's waiting for us. If you'll come—

MILDRED: Go on. I'll follow you. [*He goes.* MILDRED *turns a mocking smile on her aunt.*]

An oaf—but a handsome, virile oaf.

AUNT: [*scornfully*] Poser!

MILDRED: Take care. He said there were dark alleyways— 360

AUNT: [*in the same tone*] Poser!

MILDRED: [*biting her lips angrily*] You are right. But would that my millions were not so anemically chaste!

AUNT: Yes, for a fresh pose I have no doubt you would drag the name of Douglas in the gutter! 365

MILDRED: From which it sprang. Good-by, Aunt. Don't pray too hard that I may fall into the fiery furnace.

AUNT: Poser!

MILDRED: [*viciously*] Old hag! [*She slaps her aunt insultingly across the face and walks off, laughing gaily.*] 370

AUNT: [*screams after her*] I said "poser"!

CURTAIN

SCENE III

The stokehole. In the rear, the dimly outlined bulks of the furnaces and boilers. High overhead one hanging electric bulb sheds just enough light through the murky air laden with coal dust to pile up masses of shadows everywhere. A line of men, stripped to the waist, is before the furnace doors. They bend over, looking neither to right nor left, handling their shovels as if they were part of their bodies, with a strange, awkward, swinging rhythm. They use the shovels to throw open the furnace doors. Then from these fiery round holes in the black a flood of terrific light and heat pours full upon the men who are outlined in silhouette in the crouching, inhuman attitudes of chained gorillas. The men shovel with a rhythmic motion, swinging as on a pivot from the coal which lies in heaps on the floor behind to hurl it into the flaming mouths before them. There is a tumult of noise—the brazen clang of the furnace doors as they are flung open or slammed shut, the grating, teeth-gritting grind of steel against steel, of crunching coal. This clash of sounds stuns one's ears with its rending dissonance. But there is order in it, rhythm, a mechanical regulated recurrence, a tempo. And rising above all, making the air hum with the quiver of liberated energy, the roar of leaping flames in the furnaces, the monotonous throbbing beat of the engines.

As the curtain rises, the furnace doors are shut. The men are taking a breathing spell. One or two are arranging the coal behind them, pulling it into more accessible heaps. The others can be dimly made out leaning on their shovels in relaxed attitudes of exhaustion.

PADDY: [*from somewhere in the line—plaintively*] Yerra, will this divil's own watch nivir end? Me back is broke. I'm destroyed entirely.

YANK: [*from the center of the line—with exuberant scorn*] Aw, yuh make me sick! Lie down and croak, why don't yuh? Always beefin', dat's you! Say, dis is a cinch! Dis was made 375 for me! It's my meat, get me! [*A whistle is blown—a thin, shrill note from somewhere overhead in the darkness.* YANK *curses without resentment.*] Dere's de damn engineer crackin' de whip. He tinks we're loafin'.

PADDY: [*vindictively*] God stiffen him!

YANK: [*in an exultant tone of command*] Come on, youse guys! Git into de game! She's git-   380
tin' hungry. Pile some grub in her. Trow it into her belly! Come on now, all of youse!
Open her up!

> [*At this last all the men, who have followed his movements of getting into position,
> throw open their furnace doors with a deafening clang. The fiery light floods over
> their shoulders as they bend round for the coal. Rivulets of sooty sweat have traced
> maps on their backs. The enlarged muscles form bunches of highlight and shadow.*]

YANK: [*chanting a count as he shovels without seeming effort*] One—two—tree—[*his voice
rising exultantly in the joy of battle*] Dat's de stuff! Let her have it! All togedder now!
Sling it into her! Let her ride! Shoot de piece now! Call de toin on her! Drive her into   385
it! Feel her move! Watch her smoke! Speed, dat's her middle name! Give her coal,
youse guys! Coal, dat's her booze! Drink it up, baby! Let's see yuh sprint! Dig in and
gain a lap! Dere she go-o-es.

> [*This last in the chanting formula of the gallery gods at the six-day bike race. He
> slams his furnace door shut. The others do likewise with as much unison as their
> wearied bodies will permit. The effect is of one fiery eye after another, being blot-
> ted out with a series of accompanying bangs.*]

PADDY: [*groaning*] Me back is broke. I'm bate out—bate—

> [*There is a pause. Then the inexorable whistle sounds again from the dim regions
> above the electric light. There is a growl of cursing rage from all sides.*]

YANK: [*shaking his fist upward—contemptuously*] Take it easy dere, you! Who d'yuh tink's   390
runnin' dis game, me or you? When I git ready, we move. Not before! When I git
ready, get me!
VOICES: [*approvingly*]
That's the stuff!
Yank tal him, py golly!   395
Yank ain't affeerd.
Goot poy, Yank!
Give 'im hell!
Tell 'im 'e's a bloody swine!
Bloody slave-driver!   400
YANK: [*contemptuously*] He ain't got no noive. He's yellow, get me? All de engineers
is yellow. Dey got streaks a mile wide. Aw, to hell wit him! Let's move, youse
guys. We had a rest. Come on, she needs it! Give her pep! It ain't for him. Him
and his whistle, dey don't belong. But we belong, see! We gotter feed de baby!
Come on!   405

> [*He turns and flings his furnace door open. They all follow his lead. At this
> instant the SECOND and FOURTH ENGINEERS enter from the darkness on the
> left with MILDRED between them. She starts, turns paler, her pose is crumbling,
> she shivers with fright in spite of the blazing heat, but forces herself to leave the
> ENGINEERS and take a few steps nearer the men. She is right behind YANK. All
> this happens quickly while the men have their backs turned.*]

YANK: Come on, youse guys! [*He is turning to get coal when the whistle sounds again in a
peremptory, irritating note. This drives YANK into a sudden fury. While the other men
have turned full around and stopped dumbfounded by the spectacle of MILDRED
standing there in her white dress, YANK does not turn far enough to see her. Besides, his*

head is thrown back, he blinks upward through the murk trying to find the owner of the   410
whistle, he brandishes his shovel murderously over his head in one hand, pounding on
his chest, gorilla-like, with the other, shouting.] Toin off dat whistle! Come down outa
dere, yuh yellow, brass-buttoned, Belfast bum, yuh! Come down and I'll knock
yer brains out! Yuh lousy, stinkin', yellow mutt of a Catholic-moiderin' bastard!
Come down and I'll moider yuh! Pullin' dat whistle on me, huh? I'll show yuh! I'll   415
crash yer skull in! I'll drive yer teet' down yer troat! I'll slam yer nose trou de back
of yer head! I'll cut yer guts out for a nickel, yuh lousy boob, yuh dirty crummy,
muck-eatin' son of a—[*Suddenly he becomes conscious of all the other men staring at*
something directly behind his back. He whirls defensively with a snarling, murderous
growl, crouching to spring, his lips drawn back over his teeth, his small eyes gleaming   420
ferociously. He sees MILDRED, *like a white apparition in the full light from the open fur-*
nace doors. He glares into her eyes, turned to stone. As for her, during his speech she has lis-
tened, paralyzed with horror, terror, her whole personality crushed, beaten in, collapsed, by
the terrific impact of this unknown, abysmal brutality, naked and shameless. As she looks
at his gorilla face, as his eyes bore into hers, she utters a low, choking cry and shrinks away   425
from him, putting both hands up before her eyes to shut out the sight of his face, to protect
her own. This startles YANK *to a reaction. His mouth falls open, his eyes grow bewildered.*]
MILDRED: [*about to faint—to the* ENGINEERS, *who now have her one by each arm—whim-*
peringly] Take me away! Oh, the filthy beast!

      [*She faints. They carry her quickly back, disappearing in the darkness at the left, rear.*
      An iron door clangs shut. Rage and bewildered fury rush back on YANK. *He feels*
      himself insulted in some unknown fashion in the very heart of his pride. He roars.]

YANK: God damn yuh! [*And hurls his shovel after them at the door which has just closed. It*   430
hits the steel bulkhead with a clang and falls clattering on the steel floor. From overhead
the whistle sounds again in a long, angry, insistent command.]

CURTAIN

SCENE IV

The firemen's forecastle. YANK'*s watch has just come off duty and had dinner. Their faces and bodies*
shine from a soap-and-water scrubbing but around their eyes, where a hasty dousing does not touch, the
coal dust sticks like black makeup, giving them a queer, sinister expression. YANK *has not washed either*
face or body. He stands out in contrast to them, a blackened, brooding figure. He is seated forward
on a bench in the exact attitude of Rodin's "The Thinker." The others, most of them smoking pipes,
are staring at YANK *half-apprehensively, as if fearing an outburst; half-amusedly as if they saw a joke*
somewhere that tickled them.

VOICES: He ain't ate nothin'
    Py golly, a fallar gat to gat grub in him.
    Divil a lie.   435
    Yank feeda da fire, no feeda da face.
    Ha-ha.

He ain't even washed hisself.
He's forgot.
Hey, Yank you forgot to wash. 440
YANK: [*sullenly*] Forgot nothin'! To hell wit washin'.
VOICES: It'll stick to you.
It'll get under your skin.
Give yer the bleedin' itch, that's wot.
It makes spots on you—like a leopard. 445
Like a piebald nigger, you mean.
Better wash up, Yank.
You sleep better.
Wash up, Yank.
Wash up! Wash up! 450
YANK: [*resentfully*] Aw say, youse guys. Lemme alone. Can't youse see I'm tryin' to tink?
ALL: [*repeating the word after him as one with cynical mockery*] Think! [*The word has a bra-zen, metallic quality as if their throats were phonograph horns. It is followed by a chorus of hard, barking laughter.*]
YANK: [*springing to his feet and glaring at them belligerently*] Yes, tink! Tink, dat's what I said! 455
What about it?

[*They are silent, puzzled by his sudden resentment at what used to be one of his jokes.* YANK *sits down again in the same attitude of "The Thinker."*]

VOICES: Leave him alone.
He's got a grouch on.
Why wouldn't he?
PADDY: [*with a wink at the others*] Sure I know what's the matther. 'Tis aisy to see. He's 460
fallen in love, I'm telling you.
ALL: [*repeating the word after him as one with cynical mockery*] Love! [*The word has a brazen, metallic quality as if their throats were phonograph horns. It is followed by a chorus of hard, barking laughter.*]
YANK: [*with a contemptuous snort*] Love, hell! Hate, dat's what. I've fallen in hate, get me? 465
PADDY: [*philosophically*] 'Twould take a wise man to tell one from the other. [*with a bitter, ironical scorn, increasing as he goes on*] But I'm telling you it's love that's in it. Sure what else but love for us poor bastes in the stokehole would be bringing a fine lady, dressed like a white quane, down a mile of ladders and steps to be havin' a look at us? [*A growl of anger goes up from all sides.*] 470
LONG: [*jumping on a bench—hectically*] Hinsultin' us! Hinsultin' us, the bloody cow! And them bloody engineers! What right 'as they got to be exhibitin' us's if we was bleedin' monkeys in a menagerie? Did we sign for hinsults to our dignity as 'onest workers? Is that in the ship's articles? You kin bloody well bet it ain't! But I knows why they done it. I arsked a deck steward 'o she was and 'e told me. 'Er old man's a bleedin' millionaire, 475
a bloody Capitalist! 'E's got enuf bloody gold to sink this bleedin' ship! 'E makes arf the bloody steel in the world! 'E owns this bloody boat! And you and me, Comrades, we're 'is slaves! And the skipper and mates and engineers, they're 'is slaves! And she's 'is bloody daughter and we're all 'er slaves, too! And she gives 'er orders as 'ow she wants to see the bloody animals below decks and down they takes 'er! 480

[*There is a roar of rage from all sides.*]

YANK: [*blinking at him bewilderedly*] Say! Wait a moment! Is all dat straight goods?
LONG: Straight as string! The bleedin' steward as waits on 'em, 'e told me about 'er. And what're we goin' ter do, I arsks yer? 'Ave we got ter swaller 'er hinsults like dogs? It ain't in the ship's articles. I tell yer we got a case. We kin go to law—

YANK: [*with abysmal contempt*] Hell! Law!   485

ALL: [*repeating the word after him as one with cynical mockery*] Law! [*The word has a brazen, metallic quality as if their throats were phonograph horns. It is followed by a chorus of hard, barking laughter.*]

LONG: [*feeling the ground slipping from under his feet—desperately*] As voters and citizens we kin force the bloody governments—   490

YANK: [*with abysmal contempt*] Hell! Governments!

ALL: [*repeating the word after him as one with cynical mockery*] Governments! [*The word has a brazen, metallic quality as if their throats were phonograph horns. It is followed by a chorus of hard, barking laughter.*]

LONG: [*hysterically*] We're free and equal in the sight of God—   495

YANK: [*with abysmal contempt*] Hell! God!

ALL: [*repeating the word after him as one with cynical mockery*] God! [*The word has a brazen, metallic quality as if their throats were phonograph horns. It is followed by a chorus of hard, barking laughter.*]

YANK: [*witheringly*] Aw, join de Salvation Army!   500

ALL: Sit down! Shut up! Damn fool! Sea-lawyer!

[**LONG** *slinks back out of sight.*]

PADDY: [*continuing the trend of his thoughts as if he had never been interrupted—bitterly*] And there she was standing behind us, and the Second pointing at us like a man you'd hear in a circus would be saying: In this cage is a queerer kind of baboon than ever you'd find in darkest Africy. We roast them in their own sweat—and be damned   505
if you won't hear some of thim saying they like it! [*He glances scornfully at* **YANK**.]

YANK: [*with a bewildered uncertain growl*] Aw!

PADDY: And there was Yank roarin' curses and turning round wid his shovel to brain her— and she looked at him, and him at her—

YANK: [*slowly*] She was all white. I tought she was a ghost. Sure.   510

PADDY: [*with heavy, biting sarcasm*] 'Twas love at first sight, divil a doubt of it! If you'd seen the endearin' look on her pale mug when she shriveled away with her hands over her eyes to shut out the sight of him! Sure, 'twas as if she'd seen a great hairy ape escaped from the zoo!

YANK: [*stung—with a growl of rage*] Aw!   515

PADDY: And the loving way Yank heaved his shovel at the skull of her, only she was out the door! [*a grin breaking over his face*] 'Twas touching, I'm telling you! It put the touch of home, swate home in the stokehole. [*There is a roar of laughter from all.*]

YANK: [*glaring at* **PADDY** *menacingly*] Aw, choke dat off, see!

PADDY: [*not heeding him—to the others*] And her grabbin' at the Second's arm for protec-   520
tion. [*with a grotesque imitation of a woman's voice*] Kiss me, Engineer dear, for it's dark down here and me old man's in Wall Street making money! Hug me tight, darlin', for I'm afeerd in the dark and me mother's on deck makin' eyes at the skip- per! [*Another roar of laughter.*]

YANK: [*threateningly*] Say! What yuh tryin' to do, kid me, yuh old Harp?   525

PADDY: Divil a bit! Ain't I wishin' myself you'd brained her?

YANK: [*fiercely*] I'll brain her! I'll brain her yet, wait 'n' see! [*coming over to* **PADDY**—*slowly*] Say, is dat what she called me—a hairy ape?

PADDY: She looked it at you if she didn't say the word itself.

YANK: [*grinning horribly*] Hairy ape, huh? Sure! Dat's de way she looked at me, aw right.   530
Hairy ape! So dat's me, huh? [*bursting into rage—as if she were still in front of him*] Yuh skinny tart! Yuh white-faced bum, yuh! I'll show yuh who's a ape! [*turning to the others, bewilderment seizing him again*] Say, youse guys. I was bawlin' him out for pullin' de whistle on us. You heard me. And den I seen youse lookin' at somep'n

and I tought he'd sneaked down to come up in back of me, and I hopped round to knock   535
him dead wit de shovel. And dere she was wit de light on her! Christ, yuh coulda
pushed me over with a finger! I was scared, get me? Sure! I tought she was a ghost,
see? She was all in white like dey wrap around stiffs. You seen her. Kin yuh blame
me? She didn't belong, dat's what. And den when I come to and seen it was a real
skoit and seen de way she was lookin' at me—like Paddy said—Christ, I was sore,   540
get me? I don't stand for dat stuff from nobody. And I flung de shovel—on'y she'd
beat it. [*furiously*] I wished it'd banged her! I wished it'd knocked her block off!
LONG: And be 'anged for murder or 'lectrocuted? She ain't bleedin' well worth it.
YANK: I don't give a damn what! I'd be square wit her, wouldn't I? Tink I wanter let her put
somep'n over on me? Tink I'm goin' to let her git away wit dat stuff? Yuh don't know   545
me! No one ain't never put nothin' over on me and got away wit it, see!—not dat
kind of stuff—no guy and no skoit neither! I'll fix her! Maybe she'll come down
again—
VOICE: No chance, Yank. You scared her out of a year's growth.
YANK: I scared her? Why de hell should I scare her? Who de hell is she? Ain't she de same   550
as me? Hairy ape, huh? [*with his old confident bravado*] I'll show her I'm better'n her,
if she on'y knew it. I belong and she don't, see! I move and she's dead! Twenty-five
knots a hour, dat's me! Dat carries her but I make dat. She's on'y baggage. Sure!
[*again bewilderedly*] But, Christ, she was funny lookin'! Did yuh pipe her hands?
White and skinny. Yuh could see de bones through 'em. And her mush, dat was dead   555
white, too. And her eyes, dey was like dey'd seen a ghost. Me, dat was! Sure! Hairy
ape! Ghost, huh? Look at dat arm! [*He extends his right arm, swelling out the great
muscles.*] I coulda took her wit dat, wit just my little finger even, and broke her in
two. [*again bewilderedly*] Say, who is dat skoit, huh? What is she? What's she come
from? Who made her? Who give her de noive to look at me like dat? Dis ting's got   560
my goat right. I don't get her. She's new to me. What does a skoit like her mean,
huh? She don't belong, get me! I can't see her. [*with growing anger*] But one ting I'm
wise to, aw right, aw right! Youse all kin bet your shoits I'll git even wit her. I'll show
her if she tinks she—She grinds de organ and I'm on de string, huh? I'll fix her! Let
her come down again and I'll fling her in de furnace! She'll move den! She won't   565
shiver at nothin', den! Speed, dat'll be her! She'll belong den! [*He grins horribly.*]
PADDY: She'll never come. She's had her bellyful, I'm telling you. She'll be in bed now, I'm
thinking, wid ten doctors and nurses feedin' her salts to clean the fear out of her.
YANK: [*enraged*] Yuh tink I made her sick, too, do yuh? Just lookin' at me, huh? Hairy ape,
huh? [*in a frenzy of rage*] I'll fix her! I'll tell her where to git off! She'll git down on   570
her knees and take it back or I'll bust de face offen her! [*shaking one fist upward and
beating on his chest with the other*] I'll find yuh! I'm comin', d'yuh hear? I'll fix yuh,
God damn yuh! [*He makes a rush for the door.*]
VOICES: Stop him!
    He'll get shot!   575
    He'll murder her!
    Trip him up!
    Hold him!
    He's gone crazy!
    Gott, he's strong!   580
    Hold him down!
    Look out for a kick!
    Pin his arms!

[*They have all piled on him and, after a fierce struggle, by sheer weight of numbers have borne him to the floor just inside the door.*]

PADDY: [*who has remained detached*] Kape him down till he's cooled off. [*scornfully*] Yerra, Yank, you're a great fool. Is it payin' attention at all you are to the like of that skinny   585
    sow widout one drop of rale blood in her?

YANK: [*frenziedly, from the bottom of the heap*] She done me doit! She done me doit, didn't she? I'll get square wit her! I'll get her some way! Git offen me, youse guys! Lemme up! I'll show her who's a ape!

CURTAIN

SCENE V

Three weeks later. A corner of Fifth Avenue in the Fifties on a fine Sunday morning. A general atmosphere of clean, well-tidied, wide street; a flood of mellow, tempered sunshine; gentle, genteel breezes. In the rear, the show windows of two shops, a jewelry establishment on the corner, a furrier's next to it. Here the adornments of extreme wealth are tantalizingly displayed. The jeweler's window is gaudy with glittering diamonds, emeralds, rubies, pearls, etc., fashioned in ornate tiaras, crowns, necklaces, collars, etc. From each piece hangs an enormous tag from which a dollar sign and numerals in intermittent electric lights wink out the incredible prices. The same in the furrier's. Rich furs of all varieties hang there bathed in a downpour of artificial light. The general effect is of a background of magnificence cheapened and made grotesque by commercialism, a background in tawdry disharmony with the clear light and sunshine on the street itself.
    Up the side street YANK and LONG come swaggering. LONG is dressed in shore clothes, wears a black Windsor tie, cloth cap. YANK is in his dirty dungarees. A fireman's cap with black peak is cocked defiantly on the side of his head. He has not shaved for days and around his fierce, resentful eyes—as around those of LONG to a lesser degree—the black smudge of coal dust still sticks like makeup. They hesitate and stand together at the corner, swaggering, looking about them with a forced, defiant contempt.

LONG: [*indicating it all with an oratorical gesture*] Well, 'ere we are, Fif' Avenoo. This 'ere's   590
    their bleedin private lane, as yer might say. [*bitterly*] We're trespassers 'ere. Proletarians keep orf the grass!

YANK: [*dully*] I don't see no grass, yuh boob. [*staring at the sidewalk*] Clean, ain't it? Yuh could eat a fried egg offen it. The white wings got some job sweepin' dis up. [*looking up and down the avenue—surlily*] Where's all de white-collar stiffs yuh said was   595
    here—and de skoits—her kind?

LONG: In church, blast 'em! Arskin' Jesus to give 'em more money.

YANK: Choich, huh? I uster go to choich onct—sure—when I was a kid. Me old man and woman, dey made me. Dey never went demselves, dough. Always got too big a head on Sunday mornin', dat was dem. [*with a grin*] Dey was scrappers for fair,   600
    bot' of dem. On Satiday nights when dey bot' got a skinful dey could put up a bout oughter been staged at de Garden. When dey got trough dere wasn't a chair or table wit a leg under it. Or else dey bot' jumped on me for somep'n. Dat was where I loined to take punishment. [*with a grin and a swagger*] I'm a chip offen de old block, get me?   605

LONG: Did yer old man follow the sea?

YANK: Naw. Worked along shore. I runned away when me old lady croaked wit de tremens. I helped at truckin' and in de market. Den I shipped in de stokehole. Sure. Dat belongs. De rest was nothin'. [*looking around him*] I ain't never seen dis before. De Brooklyn waterfront, dat was where I was dragged up. [*taking a deep breath*] Dis ain't so bad at dat, huh?   610

LONG: Not bad? Well, we pays for it wiv our bloody sweat, if yer wants to know!

YANK: [*with sudden angry disgust*] Aw, hell! I don't see no one, see—like her. All dis gives me a pain. It don't belong. Say, ain't dere a back room around dis dump? Let's go shoot a ball. All dis is too clean and quiet and dolled-up, get me! It gives me a pain.   615

LONG: Wait and yer'll bloody well see—

YANK: I don't wait for no one. I keep on de move. Say, what yuh drag me up here for, anyway? Tryin' to kid me, yuh simp, yuh?

LONG: Yer wants to get back at 'er, don't yer? That's what yer been sayin' every bloomin' hour since she hinsulted yer.   620

YANK: [*vehemently*] Sure ting I do! Didn't I try to get even wit her in Southampton? Didn't I sneak on de dock and wait for her by de gangplank? I was goin' to spit in her pale mug, see! Sure, right in her pop-eyes! Dat woulda made me even, see? But no chanct. Dere was a whole army of plainclothes bulls around. Dey spotted me and gimme de bum's rush. I never seen her. But I'll git square wit her yet, you watch! [*furiously*] De lousy tart! She tinks she kin get away wit moider—but not wit me! I'll fix her! I'll tink of a way!   625

LONG: [*as disgusted as he dares to be*] Ain't that why I brought yer up 'ere—to show yer? Yer been lookin' at this 'ere 'ole affair wrong. Yer been actin' an' talkin' 's if it was all a bleedin' personal matter between yer and that bloody cow. I wants to convince yer she was on'y a representative of 'er clarss. I wants to awaken yer bloody clarss consciousness. Then yer'll see it's 'er clarss yer've got to fight, not 'er alone. There's a 'ole mob of 'em like 'er, Gawd blind 'em!   630

YANK: [*spitting on his hands—belligerently*] De more de merrier when I gits started. Bring on de gang!   635

LONG: Yer'll see 'em in arf a mo', when that church lets out. [*He turns and sees the window display in the two stores for the first time.*] Blimey! Look at that, will yer? [*They both walk back and stand looking in the jeweler's.* LONG *flies into a fury.*] Just look at this 'ere bloomin' mess! Just look at it! Look at the bleedin' prices on 'em—more 'n our 'ole bloody stokehole makes in ten voyages sweatin' in 'ell! And they—'er and 'er bloody clarss—buys 'em for toys to dangle on 'em! One of these 'ere would buy scoff for a starvin' family for a year!   640

YANK: Aw, cut de sob stuff! T'hell wit de starvin' family. Yuh'll be passin' de hat to me next. [*with naïve admiration*] Say, dem tings is pretty, huh? Bet yuh dey'd hock for a piece of change aw right. [*then turning away, bored*] But, aw hell, what good are dey? Let her have 'em. Dey don't belong no more'n she does. [*with a gesture of sweeping the jeweler's into oblivion*] All dat don't count, get me?   645

LONG: [*who has moved to the furrier's—indignantly*] And I s'pose this 'ere don't, neither—skins of poor, 'armless animals slaughtered so as 'er and 'ers can keep their bleedin' noses warm!   650

YANK: [*who has been staring at something inside—with queer excitement*] Take a slant at dat! Give it de once-over! Monkey fur—two t'ousand bucks! [*bewilderedly*] Is dat straight goods—monkey fur? What de hell?

LONG: [*bitterly*] It's straight enuf. [*with grim humor*] They wouldn't bloody well pay that for a 'airy ape's skin—no, nor for the 'ole livin' ape with all 'is 'ead, and body, and soul thrown in!   655

YANK: [*clenching his fists, his face growing pale with rage as if the skin in the window were a personal insult*] Trowin' it up in my face! Christ! I'll fix her!

LONG: [*excitedly*] Church is out. 'Ere they come, the bleedin' swine. [*after a glance at* YANK'*s lowering face—uneasily*] Easy goes, Comrade. Keep yer bloomin' temper.   660

Remember force defeats itself. It ain't our weapon. We must impress our demands through peaceful means—the votes of the onmarching proletarians of the bloody world!

YANK: [*with abysmal contempt*] Votes, hell! Votes is a joke, see. Votes for women! Let dem do it! 665

LONG: [*still more uneasily*] Calm, now. Treat 'em wiv the proper contempt. Observe the bleedin' parasites but 'old yer 'orses.

YANK: [*angrily*] Git away from me! Yuh're yellow, dat's what. Force, dat's me! De punch, dat's me every time, see!

> [*The crowd from church enter from the right, sauntering slowly and affectedly, their heads held stiffly up, looking neither to right nor left, talking in toneless, simpering voices. The women are rouged, calcimined, dyed, overdressed to the nth degree. The men are in Prince Alberts, high hats, spats, canes, etc. A procession of gaudy marionettes, yet with something of the relentless horror of Frankensteins in their detached, mechanical unawareness.*]

VOICES: Dear Doctor Caiaphas! He is so sincere! 670
What was the sermon? I dozed off.
About the radicals, my dear—and the false doctrines that are being preached.
We must organize a hundred percent American bazaar.
And let everyone contribute one one-hundredth percent of their income tax.
What an original idea! 675
We can devote the proceeds to rehabilitating the veil of the temple.
But that has been done so many times.

YANK: [*glaring from one to the other of them—with an insulting snort of scorn*] Huh! Huh! [*Without seeming to see him, they make wide detours to avoid the spot where he stands in the middle of the sidewalk.*] 680

LONG: [*frightenedly*] Keep yer bloomin' mouth shut, I tells yer.

YANK: [*viciously*] G'wan! Tell it to Sweeney! [*He swaggers away and deliberately lurches into a top-hatted gentleman, then glares at him pugnaciously.*] Say, who d'yuh tink yuh're bumpin'? Tink yuh own de Oith?

GENTLEMAN: [*coldly and affectedly*] I beg your pardon. [*He has not looked at* YANK *and* 685 *passes on without a glance, leaving him bewildered.*]

LONG: [*rushing up and grabbing* YANK's *arm*] 'Ere! Come away! This wasn't what I meant. Yer'll 'ave the bloody coppers down on us.

YANK: [*savagely—giving him a push that sends him sprawling*] G'wan!

LONG: [*picks himself up—hysterically*] I'll pop orf then. This ain't what I meant. And what- 690 ever 'appens, yer can't blame me. [*He slinks off left.*]

YANK: T' hell wit youse! [*He approaches a lady—with a vicious grin and a smirking wink.*] Hello, Kiddo. How's every little ting? Got anyting on for tonight? I know an old boiler down to de docks we kin crawl into. [*The lady stalks by without a look, without a change of pace.* YANK *turns to others—insultingly.*] Holy smokes, 695 what a mug! Go hide yuhself before de horses shy at yuh. Gee, pipe de heinie on dat one! Say, youse, yuh look like de stoin of a ferryboat. Paint and powder! All dolled up to kill! Yuh look like stiffs laid out for de boneyard! Aw, g'wan, de lot of youse! Yuh give me de eye-ache. Yuh don't belong, get me! Look at me, why don't youse dare? I belong, dat's me! [*pointing to a skyscraper across the street which* 700 *is in process of construction—with bravado*] See dat building goin' up dere? See de steel work? Steel, dat's me! Youse guys lives on it and tink yuh're somep'n. But I'm in it, see! I'm de hoistin' engine dat makes it go up! I'm it—de inside and bottom of it! Sure! I'm steel and steam and smoke and de rest of it! It moves—speed—twenty-five stories up—and me at de top and bottom—movin'! Youse 705 simps don't move. Yuh're on'y dolls I winds up to see 'm spin. Yuh're de garbage, get me—de leavins—de ashes we dump over de side! Now, what 'a' yuh gotta say? [*But as they seem neither to see nor hear him, he flies into a fury.*] Bums! Pigs! Tarts! Bitches! [*He turns in a rage on the men, bumping viciously into them but not jarring them the least bit. Rather it is he who recoils after each collision. He keeps*   710 *growling.*] Git off de Oith! G'wan, yuh bum! Look where yuh're goin', can't yuh? Git outa here! Fight, why don't yuh? Put up yer mitts! Don't be a dog! Fight or I'll knock yuh dead!

> [*But, without seeming to see him, they all answer with mechanical affected politeness:*] I beg your pardon. [*Then at a cry from one of the women, they all scurry to the furrier's window.*]

THE WOMAN: [*ecstatically, with a gasp of delight*] Monkey fur! [*The whole crowd of men and women chorus after her in the same tone of affected delight.*] Monkey fur!   715
YANK: [*with a jerk of his head back on his shoulders, as if he had received a punch full in the face—raging*] I see yuh, all in white! I see yuh, yuh white-faced tart, yuh! Hairy ape, huh? I'll hairy ape yuh!

> [*He bends down and grips at the street curbing as if to pluck it out and hurl it. Foiled in this, snarling with passion, he leaps to the lamppost on the corner and tries to pull it up for a club. Just at that moment a bus is heard rumbling up. A fat, high-hatted, spatted gentleman runs out from the side street. He calls out plaintively:*] Bus! Bus! Stop there! [*and runs full tilt into the bending, straining* YANK, *who is bowled off his balance*]

YANK: [*seeing a fight—with a roar of joy as he springs to his feet*] At last! Bus, huh? I'll bust yuh! [*He lets drive a terrific swing, his fist landing full on the fat gentleman's face. But*   720 *the gentleman stands unmoved as if nothing had happened.*]
GENTLEMAN: I beg your pardon. [*then irritably*] You have made me lose my bus. [*He claps his hands and begins to scream.*] Officer! Officer!

> [*Many police whistles shrill out on the instant and a whole platoon of policemen rush in on* YANK *from all sides. He tries to fight but is clubbed to the pavement and fallen upon. The crowd at the window have not moved or noticed this disturbance. The clanging gong of the patrol wagon approaches with a clamoring din.*]

CURTAIN

SCENE VI

Night of the following day. A row of cells in the prison on Blackwells Island. The cells extend back diagonally from right front to left rear. They do not stop, but disappear in the dark background as if they ran on, numberless, into infinity. One electric bulb from the low ceiling of the narrow corridor sheds its light through the heavy steel bars of the cell at the extreme front and reveals part of the interior. YANK *can be seen within, crouched on the edge of his cot in the attitude of Rodin's "The Thinker." His face is spotted with black and blue bruises. A blood-stained bandage is wrapped around his head.*

YANK: [*suddenly starting as if awakening from a dream, reaches out and shakes the bars—aloud to himself, wonderingly*] Steel. Dis is de zoo, huh? [*A burst of hard, barking laughter comes from the unseen occupants of the cells, runs back down the tier, and abruptly ceases.*] 725

VOICES: [*mockingly*] The zoo? That's a new name for this coop—a damn good name! Steel, eh? You said a mouthful. This is the old iron house. Who is that boob talkin'? 730 He's the bloke they brung in out of his head. The bulls had beat him up fierce.

YANK: [*dully*] I musta been dreamin'. I tought I was in a cage at de zoo—but de apes don't talk, do dey?

VOICES: [*with mocking laughter*] You're in a cage aw right. A coop! 735 A pen! A sty! A kennel! [*hard laughter—a pause*] Say, guy! Who are you? No, never mind lying. What are you? Yes, tell us your sad story. What's your game? 740 What did they jug yuh for?

YANK: [*dully*] I was a fireman—stokin' on de liners. [*then with sudden rage, rattling his cell bars*] I'm a hairy ape, get me? And I'll bust youse all in de jaw if yuh don't lay off kiddin' me.

VOICES: Huh! You're a hard-boiled duck, ain't you! 745 When you spit, it bounces! [*laughter*] Aw, can it. He's a regular guy. Ain't you? What did he say he was—a ape?

YANK: [*defiantly*] Sure ting! Ain't dat what youse all are—apes?

[*A silence. Then a furious rattling of bars from down the corridor.*]

A VOICE: [*thick with rage*] I'll show yuh who's a ape, yuh bum! 750
VOICES: Ssshh! Nix! Can de noise! Piano! You'll have the guard down on us!

YANK: [*scornfully*] De guard? Yuh mean de keeper, don't yuh? 755

[*angry exclamations from all the cells*]

VOICE: [*placatingly*] Aw, don't pay no attention to him. He's off his nut from the beatin'-up he got. Say, you guy! We're waitin' to hear what they landed you for—or ain't yuh tellin'?

YANK: Sure, I'll tell youse. Sure! Why de hell not? On'y—youse won't get me. Nobody gets me but me, see? I started to tell de judge and all he says was: "Toity days to tink it 760 over." Tink it over! Christ, dat's all I been doin' for weeks! [*after a pause*] I was tryin' to git even wit someone, see?—someone dat done me doit.

VOICES: [*cynically*] De old stuff, I bet. Your goil, huh? Give yuh the double-cross, huh? That's them every time! 765 Did yuh beat up de odder guy?

YANK: [*disgustedly*] Aw, yuh're all wrong! Sure dere was a skoit in it—but not what youse mean, not dat old tripe. Dis was a new kind of skoit. She was dolled up all in white— in de stokehole. I tought she was a ghost. Sure. [*A pause.*]

VOICES: [*whispering*] Gee, he's still nutty. 770 Let him rave. It's fun listenin'.

YANK: [*unheeding—groping in his thoughts*] Her hands—dey was skinny and white like dey wasn't real but painted on somep'n. Dere was a million miles from me to her— twenty-five knots a hour. She was like some dead ting de cat brung in. Sure, dat's what. She didn't belong. She belonged in de window of a toy store, or on de top of a garbage can, see! Sure! [*He breaks out angrily.*] But would yuh believe it, she had de noive to do me doit. She lamped me like she was seein' somep'n broke loose from de menagerie. Christ, yuh'd oughter seen her eyes! [*He rattles the bars of his cell furiously.*] But I'll get back at her yet, you watch! And if I can't find her I'll take it out on de gang she runs wit. I'm wise to where dey hangs out now. I'll show her who belongs! I'll show her who's in de move and who ain't. You watch my smoke! 775 780

VOICES: [*serious and joking*] Dat's de talkin'!
Take her for all she's got!
What was this dame anyway? Who was she, eh? 785

YANK: I dunno. First cabin stiff. Her old man's a millionaire, dey says—name of Douglas.

VOICES: Douglas? That's the president of the Steel Trust, I bet.
Sure. I seen his mug in de papers.
He's filthy with dough.

VOICE: Hey, feller, take a tip from me. If you want to get back at that dame, you better join the Wobblies. You'll get some action then. 790

YANK: Wobblies? What de hell's dat?

VOICE: Ain't you ever heard of the I.W.W.?

YANK: Naw. What is it?

VOICE: A gang of blokes—a tough gang. I been readin' about 'em today in the paper. The guard give me the *Sunday Times*. There's a long spiel about 'em. It's from a speech made in the Senate by a guy named Senator Queen. [*He is in the cell next to* YANK's. *There is a rustling of paper.*] Wait'll I see if I got light enough and I'll read you. Listen. [*He reads.*] "There is a menace existing in the country today which threatens the vitals of our fair Republic—as foul a menace against the very life-blood of the American Eagle as was the foul conspiracy of Cataline against the eagles of ancient Rome!" 795 800

VOICE: [*disgustedly*] Aw, hell! Tell him to salt de tail of dat eagle!

VOICE: [*reading*] "I refer to that devil's brew of rascals, jailbirds, murderers and cutthroats who libel all honest working men by calling themselves the Industrial Workers of the World; but in the light of their nefarious plots, I call them the Industrious *Wreckers* of the World!" 805

YANK: [*with vengeful satisfaction*] Wreckers, dat's de right dope! Dat belongs! Me for dem!

VOICE: Ssshh! [*reading*] "This fiendish organization is a foul ulcer on the fair body of our Democracy—" 810

VOICE: Democracy, hell! Give him the boid, fellers—the raspberry! [*They do.*]

VOICE: Ssshh! [*reading*] "Like Cato I say to this Senate, the I.W.W. must be destroyed! For they represent an ever-present dagger pointed at the heart of the greatest nation the world has ever known, where all men are born free and equal, with equal opportunities to all, where the Founding Fathers have guaranteed to each one happiness, where Truth, Honor, Liberty, Justice, and the Brotherhood of Man are a religion absorbed with one's mother's milk, taught at our father's knee, sealed, signed, and stamped upon the glorious Constitution of these United States!" [*a perfect storm of hisses, catcalls, boos, and hard laughter*] 815

VOICES: [*scornfully*] Hurrah for de Fort' of July! 820
Pass de hat!
Liberty!
Justice!
Honor!

Opportunity! 825
Brotherhood!
ALL: [*with abysmal scorn*] Aw, hell!
VOICE: Give that Queen Senator guy the bark! All togedder now—one—two—tree—

[*a terrific chorus of barking and yapping*]

GUARD: [*from a distance*] Quiet there, youse—or I'll git the hose.

[*The noise subsides.*]

YANK: [*with growling rage*] I'd like to catch dat senator guy alone for a second. I'd loin him 830
some trute!
VOICE: Ssshh! Here's where he gits down to cases on the Wobblies. [*reads*] "They plot with
fire in one hand and dynamite in the other. They stop not before murder to gain
their ends, nor at the outraging of defenseless womanhood. They would tear down
society, put the lowest scum in the seats of the mighty, turn Almighty God's revealed 835
plan for the world topsy-turvy, and make of our sweet and lovely civilization a
shambles, a desolation where man, God's masterpiece, would soon degenerate back
to the ape!"
VOICE: [*to* YANK] Hey, you guy. There's your ape stuff again.
YANK: [*with a growl of fury*] I got him. So dey blow up tings, do dey? Dey turn tings round, 840
do dey? Hey, lend me dat paper, will yuh?
VOICE: Sure. Give it to him. On'y keep it to yourself, see. We don't wanter listen to no
more of that slop.
VOICE: Here you are. Hide it under your mattress.
YANK: [*reaching out*] Tanks. I can't read much but I kin manage. [*He sits, the paper in the* 845
hand at his side, in the attitude of Rodin's "The Thinker." A pause. Several snores from
down the corridor. Suddenly YANK *jumps to his feet with a furious groan as if some*
appalling thought had crashed on him—bewilderedly.] Sure—her old man—president
of de Steel Trust—makes half de steel in de world—steel—where I tought I
belonged—drivin' trou—movin'—in dat—to make *her*—and cage me in for her to 850
spit on! Christ! [*He shakes the bars of his cell door till the whole tier trembles. Irritated,*
protesting exclamations from those awakened or trying to get to sleep.] He made dis—dis
cage! Steel! *It* don't belong, dat's what! Cages, cells, locks, bolts, bars—dat's what it
means!—holdin' me down wit him at de top! But I'll drive trou! Fire, dat melts it!
I'll be fire—under de heap—fire dat never goes out—hot as hell—breakin' out in 855
de night—[*While he has been saying this last he has shaken his cell door to a clanging*
accompaniment. As he comes to the "breakin' out" he seizes one bar with both hands and,
putting his two feet up against the others so that his position is parallel to the floor like a
monkey's, he gives a great wrench backwards. The bar bends like a licorice stick under
his tremendous strength. Just at this moment the PRISON GUARD *rushes in, dragging* 860
a hose behind him.]
GUARD: [*angrily*] I'll loin youse bums to wake me up! [*sees* YANK] Hello, it's you, huh? Got
the D.Ts., hey? Well, I'll cure 'em. I'll drown your snakes for yuh! [*noticing the bar*]
Hell, look at dat bar bended! On'y a bug is strong enough for dat!
YANK: [*glaring at him*] Or a hairy ape, yuh big yellow bum! Look out! Here I come! [*He* 865
grabs another bar.]
GUARD: [*scared now—yelling off left*] Toin de hose on, Ben—Full pressure! And call de
others—and a straitjacket!

[*The curtain is falling. As it hides* YANK *from view, there is a splattering smash*
as the stream of water hits the steel of YANK's *cell.*]

CURTAIN

SCENE VII

Nearly a month later. An I.W.W. local near the waterfront, showing the interior of a front room on the ground floor, and the street outside. Moonlight on the narrow street, buildings massed in black shadow. The interior of the room, which is general assembly room, office, and reading room, resembles some dingy settlement boys' club. A desk and high stool are in one corner. A table with papers, stacks of pamphlets, chairs about it, is at center. The whole is decidedly cheap, banal, commonplace and unmysterious as a room could well be. The SECRETARY *is perched on the stool making entries in a large ledger. An eye shade casts his face into shadows. Eight or ten men, longshoremen, ironworkers, and the like, are grouped about the table. Two are playing checkers. One is writing a letter. Most of them are smoking pipes. A big signboard is on the wall at the rear, "Industrial Workers of the World—Local No. 57."*

> [YANK *comes down the street outside. He is dressed as in Scene Five. He moves cautiously, mysteriously. He comes to a point opposite the door; tiptoes softly up to it, listens, is impressed by the silence within, knocks carefully, as if he were guessing at the password to some secret rite. Listens. No answer. Knocks again a bit louder. No answer. Knocks impatiently, much louder.*]

SECRETARY: [*turning around on his stool*] What the hell is that—someone knocking? [*shouts*] Come in, why don't you? 870

> [*All the men in the room look up.* YANK *opens the door slowly, gingerly, as if afraid of an ambush. He looks around for secret doors, mystery, is taken aback by the commonplaceness of the room and the men in it, thinks he may have gotten in the wrong place, then sees the signboard on the wall and is reassured.*]

YANK: [*blurts out*] Hello.
MEN: [*reservedly*] Hello.
YANK: [*more easily*] I tought I'd bumped into de wrong dump.
SECRETARY: [*scrutinizing him carefully*] Maybe you have. Are you a member?
YANK: Naw, not yet. Dat's what I come for—to join. 875
SECRETARY: That's easy. What's your job—longshore?
YANK: Naw. Fireman—stoker on de liners.
SECRETARY: [*with satisfaction*] Welcome to our city. Glad to know you people are waking up at last. We haven't got many members in your line.
YANK: Naw. Dey're all dead to de woild. 880
SECRETARY: Well, you can help to wake 'em. What's your name? I'll make out your card.
YANK: [*confused*] Name? Lemme tink.
SECRETARY: [*sharply*] Don't you know your own name?
YANK: Sure; but I been just Yank for so long—Bob, dat's it—Bob Smith.
SECRETARY: [*writing*] Robert Smith. [*fills out the rest of card*] Here you are. Cost you half 885 a dollar.
YANK: Is dat all—four bits? Dat's easy. [*gives the* SECRETARY *the money*]
SECRETARY: [*throwing it in drawer*] Thanks. Well, make yourself at home. No introductions needed. There's literature on the table. Take some of those pamphlets with you to distribute aboard ship. They may bring results. Sow the seed, only go about it 890 right. Don't get caught and fired. We got plenty out of work. What we need is men who can hold their jobs—and work for us at the same time.
YANK: Sure. [*But he still stands, embarrassed and uneasy.*]
SECRETARY: [*looking at him—curiously*] What did you knock for? Think we had a coon in uniform to open doors? 895
YANK: Naw. I tought it was locked—and dat yuh'd wanter give me the once-over trou a peep-hole or somep'n to see if I was right.

SECRETARY: [*alert and suspicious but with an easy laugh*] Think we were running a crap game? That door is never locked. What put that in your nut?

YANK: [*with a knowing grin, convinced that this is all camouflage, a part of the secrecy*] Dis 900
burg is full of bulls, ain't it?

SECRETARY: [*sharply*] What have the cops got to do with us? We're breaking no laws.

YANK: [*with a knowing wink*] Sure. Youse wouldn't for woilds. Sure. I'm wise to dat.

SECRETARY: You seem to be wise to a lot of stuff none of us knows about.

YANK: [*with another wink*] Aw, dat's aw right, see. [*then made a bit resentful by the suspicious 905
glances from all sides*] Aw, can it! Youse needn't put me trou de toid degree. Can't
youse see I belong? Sure! I'm reg'lar. I'll stick, get me? I'll shoot de woiks for youse.
Dat's why I wanted to join in.

SECRETARY: [*breezily, feeling him out*] That's the right spirit. Only are you sure you understand what you've joined? It's all plain and above board; still, some guys get a wrong 910
slant on us. [*sharply*] What's your notion of the purpose of the I.W.W.?

YANK: Aw, I know all about it.

SECRETARY: [*sarcastically*] Well, give us some of your valuable information.

YANK: [*cunningly*] I know enough not to speak outa my toin. [*then resentfully again*] Aw,
say! I'm reg'lar. I'm wise to de game. I know yuh got to watch your step wit a 915
stranger. For all youse know, I might be a plainclothes dick, or somep'n, dat's what
yuh're tinkin', huh? Aw, forget it! I belong, see? Ask any guy down to de docks if I
don't.

SECRETARY: Who said you didn't?

YANK: After I'm 'nitiated, I'll show yuh. 920

SECRETARY: [*astounded*] Initiated? There's no initiation.

YANK: [*disappointed*] Ain't there no password—no grip nor nothin'?

SECRETARY: What'd you think this is—the Elks—or the Black Hand?

YANK: De Elks, hell! De Black Hand, dey're a lot of yellow back-stickin' Ginees. Naw. Dis
is a man's gang, ain't it? 925

SECRETARY: You said it! That's why we stand on our two feet in the open. We got no
secrets.

YANK: [*surprised but admiringly*] Yuh mean to say yuh always run wide open—like dis?

SECRETARY: Exactly.

YANK: Den yuh sure got your noive wit youse! 930

SECRETARY: [*sharply*] Just what was it made you want to join us? Come out with that
straight.

YANK: Yuh call me? Well, I got noive, too! Here's my hand. Yuh wanter blow tings up, don't
yuh? Well, dat's me! I belong!

SECRETARY: [*with pretended carelessness*] You mean change the unequal conditions of soci- 935
ety by legitimate direct action—or with dynamite?

YANK: Dynamite! Blow it offen de Oith—steel—all de cages—all de factories, steamers,
buildings, jails—de Steel Trust and all dat makes it go.

SECRETARY: So—that's your idea, eh? And did you have any special job in that line you
wanted to propose to us? [*He makes a sign to the men, who get up cautiously one by 940
one and group behind* YANK.]

YANK: [*boldly*] Sure, I'll come out wit it. I'll show youse I'm one of de gang. Dere's dat
millionaire guy, Douglas—

SECRETARY: President of the Steel Trust, you mean? Do you want to assassinate him?

YANK: Naw, dat don't get yuh nothin'. I mean blow up de factory, de woiks, where he 945
makes de steel. Dat's what I'm after—to blow up de steel, knock all de steel in de
woild up to de moon. Dat'll fix tings! [*eagerly, with a touch of bravado*] I'll do it by
me lonesome! I'll show yuh! Tell me where his woiks is, how to get there, all de dope.
Gimme de stuff, de old butter—and watch me do de rest! Watch de smoke and see it
move! I don't give a damn if dey nab me—long as it's done! I'll soive life for it—and 950

give 'em de laugh! [*half to himself*] And I'll write her a letter and tell her de hairy ape done it. Dat'll square tings.

SECRETARY: [*stepping away from* YANK] Very interesting. [*He gives a signal. The men, huskies all, throw themselves on* YANK *and before he knows it they have his legs and arms pinioned. But he is too flabbergasted to make a struggle, anyway. They feel him over for weapons.*] 955

MAN: No gat, no knife. Shall we give him what's what and put the boots to him?

SECRETARY: No. He isn't worth the trouble we'd get into. He's too stupid. [*He comes closer and laughs mockingly in* YANK's *face.*] Ho-ho! By God, this is the biggest joke they've put up on us yet. Hey, you Joke! Who sent you—Burns or Pinkerton? 960 No, by God, you're such a bonehead I'll bet you're in the Secret Service! Well, you dirty spy, you rotten agent-provocator, you can go back and tell whatever skunk is paying you blood-money for betraying your brothers that he's wasting his coin. You couldn't catch a cold. And tell him that all he'll ever get on us, or ever has got, is just his own sneaking plots that he's framed up to put us in jail. We are what our 965 manifesto says we are, neither more nor less—and we'll give him a copy of that any time he calls. And as for you—[*He glares scornfully at* YANK, *who is sunk in an oblivious stupor.*] Oh, hell, what's the use of talking? You're a brainless ape.

YANK: [*aroused by the word to fierce-but-futile struggles*] What's dat, yuh Sheeny bum, yuh!

SECRETARY: Throw him out, boys. 970

[*In spite of his struggles, this is done with gusto and éclat. Propelled by several parting kicks,* YANK *lands sprawling in the middle of the narrow cobbled street. With a growl he starts to get up and storm the closed door, but stops bewildered by the confusions in his brain, pathetically impotent. He sits there brooding, in as near to the attitude of Rodin's "The Thinker" as he can get in his position.*]

YANK: [*bitterly*] So dem boids don't tink I belong, neider. Aw, to hell wit 'em! Dey're in de wrong pew—de same old bull—soapboxes and Salvation Army—no guts! Cut out an hour offen de job a day and make me happy! Gimme a dollar more a day and make me happy! Tree square a day, and cauliflowers in de front yard—ekal rights— a woman and kids—a lousy vote—and I'm all fixed for Jesus, huh? Aw, hell! What 975 does dat get yuh? Dis ting's in your inside, but it ain't your belly. Feedin' your face—sinkers and coffee—dat don't touch it. It's way down—at de bottom. Yuh can't grab it, and yuh can't stop it. It moves, and everything moves. It stops and de whole woild stops. Dat's me now—I don't tick, see?—I'm a busted Ingersoll, dat's what. Steel was me, and I owned de woild. Now I ain't steel, and de woild owns me. 980 Aw, hell! I can't see—it's all dark, get me? It's all wrong! [*He turns a bitter mocking face up like an ape gibbering at the moon.*] Say, youse up dere, Man in de Moon, yuh look so wise, gimme de answer, huh? Slip me de inside dope, de information right from de stable—where do I get off at, huh?

POLICEMAN: [*who has come up the street in time to hear this last—with grim humor*] You'll 985 get off at the station, you boob, if you don't get up out of that and keep movin'.

YANK: [*looking up at him—with a hard, bitter laugh*] Sure! Lock me up! Put me in a cage! Dat's de on'y answer yuh know. G'wan, lock me up!

POLICEMAN: What you been doin'?

YANK: Enuf to gimme life for! I was born, see? Sure, dat's de charge. Write it in de blotter. 990 I was born, get me!

POLICEMAN: [*jocosely*] God pity your old woman! [*then matter-of-fact*] But I've no time for kidding. You're soused. I'd run you in but it's too long a walk to the station. Come on now, get up, or I'll fan your ears with this club! Beat it now! [*He hauls* YANK *to his feet.*]

YANK: [*in a vague mocking tone*] Say, where do I go from here? 995
POLICEMAN: [*giving him a push—with a grin, indifferently*] Go to hell.

CURTAIN

SCENE VIII

Twilight of the next day. The monkey house at the zoo. One spot of clear gray light falls on the front of one cage so that the interior can be seen. The other cages are vague, shrouded in shadow from which chatterings pitched in a conversational tone can be heard. On the one cage a sign from which the word "gorilla" stands out. The gigantic animal himself is seen squatting on his haunches on a bench in much the same attitude as Rodin's "The Thinker." YANK enters from the left. Immediately a chorus of angry chattering and screeching breaks out. The gorilla turns his eyes but makes no sound or move.

YANK: [*with a hard, bitter laugh*] Welcome to your city, huh? Hail, hail, de gang's all here! [*At the sound of his voice the chattering dies away into an attentive silence.* YANK *walks up to the gorilla's cage and, leaning over the railing, stares in at its occupant, who stares back at him, silent and motionless. There is a pause of dead stillness. Then* YANK 1000 *begins to talk in a friendly, confidential tone, half-mockingly, but with a deep under-current of sympathy.*] Say, yuh're some hard-lookin' guy, ain't yuh? I seen lots of tough nuts dat de gang called gorillas, but yuh're de foist real one I ever seen. Some chest yuh got, and shoulders, and dem arms and mitts! I bet yuh got a punch in eider fist dat'd knock 'em silly! [*This with genuine admiration. The gorilla, as if* 1005 *he understood, stands upright, swelling out his chest and pounding on it with his fist.* YANK *grins sympathetically.*] Sure, I get yuh. Yuh challenge de whole woild, huh? Yuh got what I was sayin' even if yuh muffed de woids. [*then bitterness creeping in*] And why wouldn't yuh get me? Ain't we both members of de same club—de Hairy Apes? [*They stare at each other—a pause—then* YANK *goes on slowly and bitterly.*] So 1010 yuh're what she seen when she looked at me, de white-faced tart! I was you to her, get me? On'y outa de cage—broke out—free to moider her, see? Sure! Dat's what she tought. She wasn't wise dat I was in a cage, too—worser'n yours—sure—a damn sight—'cause you got some chanct to bust loose—but me—[*He grows confused.*] Aw, hell! It's all wrong, ain't it? [*a pause*] I s'pose yuh wanter know what I'm doin' here, 1015 huh? I been warmin' a bench down to de Battery—ever since last night. Sure. I seen de sun come up. Dat was pretty, too—all red and pink and green. I was lookin' at de skyscrapers—steel—and all de ships comin' in, sailin' out, all over de Oith—and dey was steel, too. De sun was warm, dey wasn't no clouds, and dere was a breeze blowin'. Sure, it was great stuff. I got it aw right—what Paddy said about dat bein' 1020 de right dope—on'y I couldn't get *in* it, see? I couldn't belong in dat. It was over my head. And I kept tinkin' and den I beat it up here to see what youse was like. And I waited till dey was all gone to git yuh alone. Say, how d'yuh feel sittin' in dat pen all de time, havin' to stand for 'em comin' and starin' at yuh—de white-faced, skinny tarts and de boobs what marry 'em—makin' fun of yuh, laughin' at yuh, gittin' 1025 scared of yuh—damn 'em! [*He pounds on the rail with his fist. The gorilla rattles the bars of his cage and snarls. All the other monkeys set up an angry chattering in the darkness.* YANK *goes on excitedly.*] Sure! Dat's de way it hits me, too. On'y yuh're lucky, see? Yuh don't belong wit 'em and yuh know it. But me, I belong wit 'em—but I don't, see? Dey don't belong wit me, dat's what. Get me? Tinkin' is hard—[*He* 1030 *passes one hand across his forehead with a painful gesture. The gorilla growls impatiently.* YANK *goes on gropingly.*] It's dis way, what I'm drivin' at. Youse can sit and dope dream in de past, green woods, de jungle, and de rest of it. Den yuh belong and dey don't. Den yuh kin laugh at 'em, see? Yuh're de champ of de woild. But me—I ain't got no past to tink in, nor nothin' dat's comin', on'y what's now—and dat don't 1035 belong. Sure, you're de best off! Yuh can't tink, can yuh? Yuh can't talk, neider. But I kin make a bluff at talkin' and tinkin'—a'most git away wit it—a'most!—and dat's where de joker comes in. [*He laughs.*] I ain't on Oith and I ain't in heaven, get me? I'm in de middle tryin' to separate 'em, takin' all de woise punches from bot' of 'em. Maybe dat's what dey call hell, huh? But you, yuh're at de bottom. You 1040 belong! Sure! Yuh're de on'y one in de woild dat does, yuh lucky stiff! [*The gorilla growls proudly.*] And dat's why dey gotter put yuh in a cage, see? [*The gorilla roars angrily.*] Sure! Yuh get me. It beats it when you try to tink it or talk it—it's way down—deep—behind—you 'n' me we feel it. Sure! Bot' members of dis club! [*He laughs—then in a savage tone.*] What de hell! T' hell wit it! A little action, dat's our 1045 meat! Dat belongs! Knock 'em down and keep bustin' 'em till dey croak yuh wit a gat—wit steel! Sure! Are yuh game? Dey've looked at youse, ain't dey—in a cage? Wanter git even? Wanter wind up like a sport 'stead of croakin' slow in dere? [*The gorilla roars an emphatic affirmative.* YANK *goes on with a sort of furious exultation.*] Sure! Yuh're reg'lar! You'll stick to de finish! Me 'n' you, huh?—bot' members of this 1050 club! We'll put up one last star bout dat'll knock 'em offen deir seats! Dey'll have to make de cages stronger after we're trou! [*The gorilla is straining at his bars, growling, hopping from one foot to the other.* YANK *takes a jimmy from under his coat and forces the lock on the cage door. He throws this open.*] Pardon from de governor! Step out and shake hands. I'll take yuh for a walk down Fif' Avenoo. We'll knock 'em offen de 1055 Oith and croak wit' de band playin'. Come on, Brother. [*The gorilla scrambles gingerly out of his cage. Goes to* YANK *and stands looking at him.* YANK *keeps his mocking tone—holds out his hand.*] Shake—de secret grip of our order. [*Something, the tone of mockery, perhaps, suddenly outrages the animal. With a spring he wraps his huge arms around* YANK *in a murderous hug. There is a cracking snap of crushed ribs—a gasping* 1060 *cry, still mocking, from* YANK.] Hey, I didn't say kiss me! [*The gorilla lets the crushed body slip to the floor, stands over it uncertainly, considering; then picks it up, throws it in the cage, shuts the door, and shuffles off menacingly into the darkness at left. A great uproar of frightened chattering and whimpering comes from the other cages. Then* YANK *moves, groaning, opening his eyes, and there is silence. He mutters painfully.*] Say—dey 1065 oughter match him—wit Zybszko. He got me, aw right. I'm trou. Even him didn't tink I belonged. [*then, with sudden passionate despair*] Christ, where do I get off at? Where do I fit in? [*checking himself as suddenly*] Aw, what de hell! No squawkin', see! No quittin', get me! Croak wit your boots on! [*He grabs hold of the bars of the cage and hauls himself painfully to his feet—looks around him bewilderedly—forces a mock-* 1070 *ing laugh.*] In de cage, huh? [*in the strident tones of a circus broker*] Ladies and gents, step forward and take a slant at de one and only—[*his voice weakening*]—one and original—Hairy Ape from de wilds of—

[*He slips in a heap on the floor and dies. The monkeys set up a chattering, whimpering wail. And, perhaps, the Hairy Ape at last belongs.*]

CURTAIN

Cat on a Hot Tin Roof (1955)

For several years following World War II, the most successful American plays were written in a style that can be called modified realism. Influenced by modernism and by the "New Stagecraft," a design style popularized by Robert Edmond Jones, these plays sought to capture the psychological truth of characters and situations in suggestive rather than scrupulously realistic settings. Tennessee Williams helped to popularize this style with *The Glass Menagerie* (1944), in which scenes and characters are called up out of the narrator-character's memory. The emphasis in *Cat on a Hot Tin Roof* and in Williams' *A Streetcar Named Desire* (1949), both of which won Pulitzer Prizes, is on characters who are struggling to distinguish truth from illusion.

The action in *Cat on a Hot Tin Roof* takes place over the course of a single evening in a bed-sitting room in a large plantation house in Mississippi. Within this restricted time and space, the characters are engulfed in mendacity—deception both of themselves and others. Big Daddy and Brick are forced to face truths that threaten the very core of their being. Big Daddy faces the truth that he is actually dying of cancer even though he has been told he is free of it. Brick faces the truth that he drove his friend Skipper into an early grave when he refused to discuss Skipper's true feelings for him.

Brick's wife, Maggie, and his brother, Gooper (along with Gooper's wife, Mae), are primarily concerned with gaining control over Big Daddy's estate. Maggie, who comes from a far less wealthy family than Brick, describes herself as "consumed with envy an' eaten up with longing." Her description of her position as that of "a cat on a hot tin roof" gives the play its title. In Act Three Maggie falsely announces to the family that she is pregnant because she believes a child will help overcome doubts about Brick's reliability as Big Daddy's heir—doubts raised by his alcoholism. In a desperate bid to make this lie true, Maggie hides all of the alcohol from Brick, promising to return it only after he's slept with her. Her final line of the play asserts her love for Brick, as does Big Mama's last line to Big Daddy. Both Big Daddy and Brick respond to these declarations of love by saying, "Wouldn't it be funny if that was true," thereby underscoring the difficulty of knowing the truth in a world so full of mendacity.

With its powerful psychological portraits, compelling conflicts, and its insights into a world dominated by self-interest, *Cat on a Hot Tin Roof* is an excellent example of postwar modified realism.

329

Cat on a Hot Tin Roof

Characters

MARGARET

BRICK

MAE, *sometimes called Sister Woman*

BIG MAMA

DIXIE, *a little girl*

BIG DADDY

REVEREND TOOKER

GOOPER, *sometimes called Brother Man*

DOCTOR BAUGH, *pronounced "Baw"*

LACEY, *a Negro servant*

SOOKEY, *another Negro servant*

Another little girl and two small boys

The set is the bed-sitting room of a plantation house in the Mississippi Delta. It is along an upstairs gallery that probably runs around the entire house; it has two pairs of very wide doors opening onto the gallery, showing white balustrades against a fair summer sky that fades into dusk and night during the course of the play. . . . The bathroom door, showing only pale-blue tile and silver towel racks, is in one side wall; the hall door in the opposite wall. Two articles of furniture need mention: a big double bed . . . ; and against the wall space between the two huge double doors upstage . . . a huge console combination of radio-phonograph (hi-fi with three speakers), TV set, and liquor cabinet, bearing and containing many glasses and bottles. . . . The walls below the ceiling should dissolve mysteriously into air; the set should be roofed by the sky. . . .

An evening in summer. The action is continuous, with two intermissions.

ACT I

At the rise of the curtain someone is taking a shower in the bathroom, the door of which is half open. A pretty young woman, with anxious lines in her face, enters the bedroom and crosses to the bathroom door.

MARGARET: [*shouting above roar of water*] One of those no-neck monsters hit me with a hot buttered biscuit so I have t' change!

> [MARGARET's *voice is both rapid and drawling. In her long speeches she has the vocal tricks of a priest delivering a liturgical chant, the lines are almost sung, always continuing a little beyond her breath so she has to gasp for another. Sometimes she intersperses the lines with a little wordless singing, such as "DA-DA-DAAAA!"*]

[*Water turns off and* BRICK *calls out to her, but is still unseen. A tone of politely feigned interest, masking indifference, or worse, is characteristic of his speech with* MARGARET.]

BRICK: Wha'd you say, Maggie? Water was on s' loud I couldn't hearya. . . .

MARGARET: Well, I!—just remarked that!—one of th' no-neck monsters messed up m' lovely lace dress so I got t'—cha-a-ange. . . .   5

[*She opens and kicks shut drawers of the dresser.*]

BRICK: Why d'ya call Gooper's kiddies "no-neck monsters"?

MARGARET: Because they've got no necks! Isn't that a good enough reason?

BRICK: Don't they have any necks?

MARGARET: None visible. Their fat little heads are set on their fat little bodies without a bit of connection.   10

BRICK: That's too bad.

MARGARET: Yes, it's too bad because you can't wring their necks if they've got no necks to wring! Isn't that right, honey?

[*She steps out of her dress, stands in a slip of ivory satin and lace.*]

Yep, they're no-neck monsters, all no-neck people are monsters. . . .

[*Children shriek downstairs.*]

Hear them? Hear them screaming? I don't know where their voice boxes are located   15
since they don't have necks. I tell you I got so nervous at that table tonight I thought
I would throw back my head and utter a scream you could hear across the Arkansas
border an' parts of Louisiana an' Tennessee. I said to your charming sister-in-law,
Mae, honey, couldn't you feed those precious little things at a separate table with an
oilcloth cover? They make such a mess an' the lace cloth looks so pretty! She made   20
enormous eyes at me and said, "Ohhh, noooooo! On Big Daddy's birthday? Why,
he would never forgive me!" Well, I want you to know, Big Daddy hadn't been at
the table two minutes with those five no-neck monsters slobbering and drooling
over their food before he threw down his fork an' shouted, "Fo' God's sake, Gooper,
why don't you put them pigs at a trough in th' kitchen?"—Well, I swear, I simply   25
could have di-ieed!

    Think of it, Brick, they've got five of them and number six is coming. They've
brought the whole bunch down here like animals to display at a county fair. Why
they have those children doin' tricks all the time! "Junior, show Big Daddy how you
do this, show Big Daddy how you do that, say your little piece fo' Big Daddy, Sister.   30
Show your dimples, Sugar. Brother, show Big Daddy how you stand on your
head!"—It goes on all the time along, with constant little remarks and innuendos
about the fact that you and I have not produced any children, are totally childless,
and therefore totally useless!—Of course it's comical but it's also disgusting since it's
so obvious what they're up to!   35

BRICK: [*without interest*] What are they up to, Maggie?

MARGARET: Why, you know what they're up to!

BRICK: [*appearing*] No, I don't know what they're up to.

[*He stands there in the bathroom doorway drying his hair with a towel and hanging onto the towel rack because one ankle is broken, plastered and bound. He is
still slim and firm as a boy. His liquor hasn't started tearing him down outside.
He has the additional charm of that cool air of detachment that people have who*

have given up the struggle. But now and then, when disturbed, something flashes behind it, like lightning in a fair sky, which shows that at some deeper level he is far from peaceful. Perhaps in a stronger light he would show some signs of deliquescence, but the fading, still warm, light from the gallery treats him gently.]

MARGARET: I'll tell you what they're up to, boy of mine!—They're up to cutting you out of your father's estate, and—   40

[*She freezes momentarily before her next remark. Her voice drops as if it were somehow a personally embarrassing admission.*]

—Now we know that Big Daddy's dyin' of—*cancer.* . . .

[*There are voices on the lawn below: long-drawn calls across distance.* MARGARET *raises her lovely bare arms and powders her armpits with a light sigh.*]

[*She adjusts the angle of a magnifying mirror to straighten an eyelash, then rises fretfully saying:*]

There's so much light in the room it—
BRICK: [*softly but sharply*] Do we?
MARGARET: Do we what?
BRICK: Know Big Daddy's dyin' of cancer?   45
MARGARET: Got the report today.
BRICK: Oh . . .
MARGARET: [*letting down bamboo blinds which cast long, gold-fretted shadows over the room*] Yep, got th' report just now . . . It didn't surprise me, Baby. . . .

[*Her voice has range and music; sometimes it drops low as a boy's and you have a sudden image of her playing boy's games as a child.*]

I recognized the symptoms soon's we got here last spring and I'm willin' to bet you   50
that Brother Man and his wife were pretty sure of it, too. That more than likely explains why their usual summer migration to the coolness of the Great Smokies was passed up this summer in favor of—hustlin' down here ev'ry whipstitch with their whole screamin' tribe! And why so many allusions have been made to Rainbow Hill lately. You know what Rainbow Hill is? Place that's famous for treatin' alcoholics   55
an' dope fiends in the movies!
BRICK: I'm not in the movies.
MARGARET: No, and you don't take dope. Otherwise you're a perfect candidate for Rainbow Hill, Baby, and that's where they aim to ship you—over my dead body! Yep, over my dead body they'll ship you there, but nothing would please them better. Then Brother   60
Man could get a-hold of the purse strings and dole out remittances to us, maybe get power of attorney and sign checks for us and cut off our credit wherever, whenever he wanted! Son-of-a-bitch!—How'd you like that, Baby?—Well, you've been doin' just about ev'rything in your power to bring it about, you've just been doin' ev'rything you can think of to aid and abet them in this scheme of theirs! Quittin'   65
work, devoting yourself to the occupation of drinkin'!—Breakin' your ankle last night on the high school athletic field: doin' what? Jumpin' hurdles? At two or three in the morning? Just fantastic! Got in the paper. *Clarksdale Register* carried a nice little item about it, human interest story about a well-known former athlete stagin' a one-man track meet on the Glorious Hill High School athletic field last night, but   70
was slightly out of condition and didn't clear the first hurdle! Brother Man Gooper claims he exercised his influence t' keep it from goin' out over AP or UP or every goddam *"P."*
    But, Brick? You still have one big advantage!

[*During the above swift flood of words,* BRICK *has reclined with contrapuntal leisure on the snowy surface of the bed and has rolled over carefully on his side or belly.*]

BRICK: [*wryly*] Did you say something, Maggie?   75

MARGARET: Big Daddy dotes on you, honey. And he can't stand Brother Man and Brother Man's wife, that monster of fertility, Mae; she's downright odious to him! Know how I know? By little expressions that flicker over his face when that woman is holding fo'th on one of her choice topics such as—how she refused twilight sleep!—when the   80 twins were delivered! Because she feels motherhood's an experience that a woman ought to experience fully!—in order to fully appreciate the wonder and beauty of it! HAH!

> [*This loud "HAH!" is accompanied by a violent action such as slamming a drawer shut.*]

—and how she made Brother Man come in an' stand beside her in the delivery room so he would not miss out on the "wonder and beauty" of it, either!—producin' those no-neck monsters. . . .   85

> [*A speech of this kind would be antipathetic from almost anybody but* MARGARET; *she makes it oddly funny, because her eyes constantly twinkle and her voice shakes with laughter which is basically indulgent.*]

—Big Daddy shares my attitude toward those two! As for me, well—I give him a laugh now and then and he tolerates me. In fact!—I sometimes suspect that Big Daddy harbors a little unconscious "lech" fo' me. . . .

BRICK: What makes you think that Big Daddy has a lech for you, Maggie?

MARGARET: Way he always drops his eyes down my body when I'm talkin' to him, drops   90 his eyes to my boobs an' licks his old chops! Ha ha!

BRICK: That kind of talk is disgusting.

MARGARET: Did anyone ever tell you that you're an ass-aching Puritan, Brick? I think it's mighty fine that that ole fellow, on the doorstep of death, still takes in my shape with what I think is deserved appreciation!   95

And you wanta know something else? Big Daddy didn't know how many little Maes and Goopers had been produced! "How many kids have you got?" he asked at the table, just like Brother Man and his wife were new acquaintances to him! Big Mama said he was jokin', but that old boy wasn't jokin', Lord, no!

And when they infawmed him that they had five already and were turning out   100 number six!—the news seemed to come as a sort of unpleasant surprise. . . .

> [*Children yell below.*]

Scream, monsters!

> [*Turns to* BRICK *with a sudden, gay, charming smile which fades as she notices that he is not looking at her but into fading gold space with a troubled expression.*]

> [*It is constant rejection that makes her humor "bitchy."*]

Yes, you should of been at that supper table, Baby.

> [*Whenever she calls him "Baby" the word is a soft caress.*]

Y'know, Big Daddy, bless his ole sweet soul, he's the dearest ole thing in the world, but he does hunch over his food as if he preferred not to notice anything else. Well,   105 Mae an' Gooper were side by side at the table, direckly across from Big Daddy, watchin' his face like hawks while they jawed an' jabbered about the cuteness an' brilliance of th' no-neck monsters!

[*She giggles with a hand fluttering at her throat and her breast and her long throat arched.*]

[*She comes downstage and re-creates the scene with voice and gesture.*]

And the no-neck monsters were ranged around the table, some in high chairs and some on th' *Books of Knowledge*, all in fancy little paper caps in honor of Big Daddy's 110 birthday, and all through dinner, well, I want you to know that Brother Man an' his partner never once, for one moment, stopped exchanging pokes an' pinches an' kicks an' signs an' signals!—Why, they were like a couple of cardsharps fleecing a sucker.—Even Big Mama, bless her ole sweet soul, she isn't th' quickest an' brightest thing in the world, she finally noticed, at last, an' said to Gooper, "Gooper, what 115 are you an' Mae makin' all these signs at each other about?"—I swear t' goodness, I nearly choked on my chicken!

[MARGARET, *back at the dressing table, still doesn't see* BRICK. *He is watching her with a look that is not quite definable—Amused? shocked? contemptuous?— part of those and part of something else.*]

Y'know—your brother Gooper still cherishes the illusion he took a giant step up on the social ladder when he married Miss Mae Flynn of the Memphis Flynns.

[MARGARET, *moves about the room as she talks, stops before the mirror, moves on.*]

But I have a piece of Spanish news for Gooper. The Flynns never had a thing in this 120 world but money and they lost that, they were nothing at all but fairly successful climbers. Of course, Mae Flynn came out in Memphis eight years before I made my debut in Nashville, but I had friends at Ward-Belmont who came from Memphis and they used to come to see me and I used to go to see them for Christmas and spring vacations, and so I know who rates an' who doesn't rate in Memphis society. 125 Why, y'know ole Papa Flynn, he barely escaped doing time in the federal pen for shady manipulations on th' stock market when his chain stores crashed, and as for Mae having been a cotton carnival queen, as they remind us so often, lest we forget, well, that's one honor that I don't envy her for!—Sit on a brass throne on a tacky float an' ride down Main Street, smilin', bowin', and blowin' kisses to all the trash 130 on the street—

[*She picks out a pair of jeweled sandals and rushes to the dressing table.*]

Why, year before last, when Susan McPheeters was singled out fo' that honor, y'know what happened to her? Y'know what happened to poor little Susie McPheeters?
BRICK: [*absently*] No. What happened to little Susie McPheeters?
MARGARET: Somebody spit tobacco juice in her face. 135
BRICK: [*dreamily*] Somebody spit tobacco juice in her face?
MARGARET: That's right, some old drunk leaned out of a window in the Hotel Gayoso and yelled, "Hey, Queen, hey, hey, there, Queenie!" Poor Susie looked up and flashed him a radiant smile and he shot out a squirt of tobacco juice right in poor Susie's face.
BRICK: Well, what d'you know about that. 140
MARGARET: [*gaily*] What do I know about it? I was there, I saw it!
BRICK: [*absently*] Must have been kind of funny.
MARGARET: Susie didn't think so. Had hysterics. Screamed like a banshee. They had to stop th' parade an' remove her from her throne an' go on with—

[*She catches sight of him in the mirror, gasps slightly, wheels about to face him. Count ten.*]

—Why are you looking at me like that?   145

BRICK: [*whistling softly, now*] Like what, Maggie?

MARGARET: [*intensely, fearfully*] The way y' were looking at me just now, befo' I caught
     your eye in the mirror and you started t' whistle! I don't know how t' describe it but
     it froze my blood!—I've caught you lookin' at me like that so often lately. What are
     you thinkin' of when you look at me like that?   150

BRICK: I wasn't conscious of lookin' at you, Maggie.

MARGARET: Well, I was conscious of it! What were you thinkin'?

BRICK: I don't remember thinking of anything, Maggie.

MARGARET: Don't you think I know that—? Don't you—?—Think I know that—?

BRICK: [*coolly*] Know *what*, Maggie?   155

MARGARET: [*struggling for expression*] That I've gone through this—*hideous!*—*transforma-
     tion*, become—*hard! Frantic!*

     [*Then she adds, almost tenderly:*]

—cruel!!

That's what you've been observing in me lately. How could y' help but observe it?
That's all right. I'm not—thin-skinned any more, can't afford t' be thin-skinned   160
any more.

     [*She is now recovering her power.*]

—But Brick? Brick?

BRICK: Did you say something?

MARGARET: I was *goin'* t' say something: that I get—lonely. Very!

BRICK: Ev'rybody gets that. . . .   165

MARGARET: Living with someone you love can be lonelier—than living entirely *alone!*—if
     the one that y' love doesn't love you. . . .

     [*There is a pause.* BRICK *hobbles downstage and asks, without looking at her:*]

BRICK: Would you like to live alone, Maggie?

     [*Another pause: then—after she has caught a quick, hurt breath:*]

MARGARET: No!—*God!—I wouldn't!*

     [*Another gasping breath. She forcibly controls what must have been an impulse to
     cry out. We see her deliberately, very forcibly, going all the way back to the world
     in which you can talk about ordinary matters.*]

Did you have a nice shower?   170

BRICK: Uh-huh.

MARGARET: Was the water cool?

BRICK: No.

MARGARET: But it made y' feel fresh, huh?

BRICK: Fresher. . . .   175

MARGARET: I know something would make y' feel *much* fresher!

BRICK: What?

MARGARET: An alcohol rub. Or cologne, a rub with cologne!

BRICK: That's good after a workout but I haven't been workin' out, Maggie.

MARGARET: You've kept in good shape, though.   180

BRICK: [*indifferently*] You think so, Maggie?

MARGARET: I always thought drinkin' men lost their looks, but I was plainly mistaken.

BRICK: [*wryly*] Why; thanks, Maggie.

MARGARET: You're the only drinkin' man I know that it never seems t' put fat on.

BRICK: I'm gettin' softer, Maggie. 185

MARGARET: Well, sooner or later it's bound to soften you up. It was just beginning to soften up Skipper when—

[*She stops short.*]

I'm sorry. I never could keep my fingers off a sore—I wish you would lose your looks. If you did it would make the martyrdom of Saint Maggie a little more bearable. But no such goddam luck. I actually believe you've gotten better looking since 190 you've gone on the bottle. Yeah, a person who didn't know you would think you'd never had a tense nerve in your body or a strained muscle.

[*There are sounds of croquet on the lawn below: the click of mallets, light voices, near and distant.*]

Of course, you always had that detached quality as if you were playing a game without much concern over whether you won or lost, and now that you've lost the game, not lost but just quit playing, you have that rare sort of charm that usually 195 only happens in very old or hopelessly sick people, the charm of the defeated.—You look so cool, so cool, so enviably cool.

[*Music is heard.*]

They're playing croquet. The moon has appeared and it's white, just beginning to turn a little bit yellow. . . .

    You were a wonderful lover. . . . 200

    Such a wonderful person to go to bed with, and I think mostly because you were really indifferent to it. Isn't that right? Never had any anxiety about it, did it naturally, easily, slowly, with absolute confidence and perfect calm, more like opening a door for a lady or seating her at a table than giving expression to any longing for her. Your indifference made you wonderful at lovemaking—*strange?*—but true. . . . 205

    You know, if I thought you would never, never, never make love to me again— I would go downstairs to the kitchen and pick out the longest and sharpest knife I could find and stick it straight into my heart, I swear that I would!

    But one thing I don't have is the charm of the defeated, my hat is still in the ring, and I am determined to win! 210

[*There is the sound of croquet mallets hitting croquet balls.*]

—What is the victory of a cat on a hot tin roof?—I wish I knew. . . . Just staying on it, I guess, as long as she can. . . .

[*more croquet sounds*]

Later tonight I'm going to tell you I love you an' maybe by that time you'll be drunk enough to believe me. Yes, they're playing croquet. . . .

    Big Daddy is dying of cancer. . . . 215

    What were you thinking of when I caught you looking at me like that? Were you thinking of Skipper?

[**BRICK** *takes up his crutch, rises.*]

Oh, excuse me, forgive me, but laws of silence don't work! No, laws of silence don't work. . . .

[BRICK *crosses to the bar, takes a quick drink, and rubs his head with a towel.*]

Laws of silence don't work. . . .   220
     When something is festering in your memory or your imagination, laws of silence
don't work, it's just like shutting a door and locking it on a house on fire in hope of
forgetting that the house is burning. But not facing a fire doesn't put it out. Silence
about a thing just magnifies it. It grows and festers in silence, becomes malignant. . . .
Get dressed, Brick.   225

     [*He drops his crutch.*]

BRICK: I've dropped my crutch.

     [*He has stopped rubbing his hair dry but still stands hanging onto the towel rack
     in a white towel-cloth robe.*]

MARGARET: Lean on me.
BRICK: No, just give me my crutch.
MARGARET: Lean on my shoulder.
BRICK: I don't want to lean on your shoulder, I want my crutch!   230

     [*This is spoken like sudden lightning.*]

Are you going to give me my crutch or do I have to get down on my knees on the
floor and—
MARGARET: Here, here, take it, take it!

     [*She has thrust the crutch at him.*]

BRICK: [*hobbling out*] Thanks. . . .
MARGARET: We mustn't scream at each other, the walls in this house have ears. . . .   235

     [*He hobbles directly to liquor cabinet to get a new drink.*]

—but that's the first time I've heard you raise your voice in a long time, Brick. A
crack in the wall?—Of composure?
—I think that's a good sign. . . .
A sign of nerves in a player on the defensive!

     [BRICK *turns and smiles at her coolly over his fresh drink.*]

BRICK: It just hasn't happened yet, Maggie.   240
MARGARET: What?
BRICK: The click I get in my head when I've had enough of this stuff to make me
     peaceful. . . .
     Will you do me a favor?
MARGARET: Maybe I will. What favor?   245
BRICK: Just, just keep your voice down!
MARGARET: [*in a hoarse whisper*] I'll do you that favor, I'll speak in a whisper, if not shut
     up completely, if *you* will do *me* a favor and make that drink your last one till after
     the party.
BRICK: What party?   250
MARGARET: Big Daddy's birthday party.
BRICK: Is this Big Daddy's birthday?
MARGARET: You know this is Big Daddy's birthday!
BRICK: No, I don't, I forgot it.

MARGARET: Well, I remembered it for you. . . .   255

[*They are both speaking as breathlessly as a pair of kids after a fight, drawing deep exhausted breaths and looking at each other with faraway eyes, shaking and panting together as if they had broken apart from a violent struggle.*]

BRICK: Good for you, Maggie.
MARGARET: You just have to scribble a few lines on this card.
BRICK: You scribble something, Maggie.
MARGARET: It's got to be your handwriting; it's your present, I've given him my present; it's got to be your handwriting!   260

[*The tension between them is building again, the voices becoming shrill once more.*]

BRICK: I didn't get him a present.
MARGARET: I got one for you.
BRICK: All right. You write the card, then.
MARGARET: And have him know you didn't remember his birthday?
BRICK: I didn't remember his birthday.   265
MARGARET: You don't have to prove you didn't!
BRICK: I don't want to fool him about it.
MARGARET: Just write "Love, Brick!" for God's—
BRICK: No.
MARGARET: You've *got* to!   270
BRICK: I don't have to do anything I don't want to do. You keep forgetting the conditions on which I agreed to stay on living with you.
MARGARET: [*out before she knows it*] I'm not living with you. We occupy the same cage.
BRICK: You've got to remember the conditions agreed on.
MARGARET: They're impossible conditions!   275
BRICK: Then why don't you—?
MARGARET: HUSH! Who is out there? Is somebody at the door?

[*There are footsteps in hall.*]

MAE: [*outside*] May I enter a moment?
MARGARET: Oh, you! Sure. Come in, Mae.

[MAE *enters bearing aloft the bow of a young lady's archery set.*]

MAE: Brick, is this thing yours?   280
MARGARET: Why, Sister Woman—that's my Diana Trophy. Won it at the intercollegiate archery contest on the Ole Miss campus.
MAE: It's a mighty dangerous thing to leave exposed round a house full of nawmal rid-blooded children attracted t' weapons.
MARGARET: "Nawmal rid-blooded children attracted t' weapons" ought t' be taught to   285
keep their hands off things that don't belong to them.
MAE: Maggie, honey, if you had children of your own you'd know how funny that is. Will you please lock this up and put the key out of reach?
MARGARET: Sister Woman, nobody is plotting the destruction of your kiddies.—Brick and I still have our special archers' license. We're goin' deer-huntin' on Moon Lake   290
as soon as the season starts. I love to run with dogs through chilly woods, run, run, leap over obstructions—

[*She goes into the closet carrying the bow.*]

MAE: How's the injured ankle, Brick?

BRICK: Doesn't hurt. Just itches.

MAE: Oh my! Brick—Brick, you should've been downstairs after supper! Kiddies put on a   295
show. Polly played the piano, Buster an' Sonny drums, an' then they turned out the
lights an' Dixie an' Trixie puhfawmed a toe dance in fairy costume with *spahkluhs!*
Big Daddy just beamed! He just beamed!

MARGARET: [*from the closet with a sharp laugh*] Oh, I bet. It breaks my heart that we
missed it!   300

[*She reenters.*]

But Mae? Why did y'give dawgs' names to all your kiddies?

MAE: Dogs' names?

[MARGARET *has made this observation as she goes to raise the bamboo blinds,
since the sunset glare has diminished. In crossing she winks at* BRICK.]

MARGARET: [*sweetly*] Dixie, Trixie, Buster, Sonny, Polly!—Sounds like four dogs and a
parrot . . . animal act in a circus!

MAE: Maggie?   305

[MARGARET *turns with a smile.*]

Why are you so catty?

MARGARET: 'Cause I'm a cat! But why can't you take a joke, Sister Woman?

MAE: Nothin' pleases me more than a joke that's funny. You know the real names of our
kiddies. Buster's real name is Robert. Sonny's real name is Saunders. Trixie's real name
is Marlene and Dixie's—   310

[*Someone downstairs calls for her.* "HEY, MAE!"—*She rushes to door, saying:*]

Intermission is over!

MARGARET: [*as* MAE *closes door*] I wonder what Dixie's real name is?

BRICK: Maggie, being catty doesn't help things any. . . .

MARGARET: I know! *WHY!*—Am I so catty?—'Cause I'm consumed with envy an' eaten
up with longing?—Brick, I've laid out your beautiful Shantung silk suit from Rome   315
and one of your monogrammed silk shirts. I'll put your cuff links in it, those lovely
star sapphires I get you to wear so rarely. . . .

BRICK: I can't get trousers on over this plaster cast.

MARGARET: Yes, you can, I'll help you.

BRICK: I'm not going to get dressed, Maggie.   320

MARGARET: Will you just put on a pair of white silk pajamas?

BRICK: Yes, I'll do that, Maggie.

MARGARET: Thank you, thank you *so much!*

BRICK: Don't mention it.

MARGARET: Oh, Brick! How long does it have t' go on? This punishment? Haven't I done   325
time enough, haven't I served my term, can't I apply for a—pardon?

BRICK: Maggie, you're spoiling my liquor. Lately your voice always sounds like you'd been
running upstairs to warn somebody that the house was on fire!

MARGARET: Well, no wonder, no wonder. Y'know what I feel like, Brick?

[*Children's and grown-ups' voices are blended, below, in a loud-but-uncertain
rendition of "My Wild Irish Rose."*]

I feel all the time like a cat on a hot tin roof!   330

BRICK: Then jump off the roof, jump off it, cats can jump off roofs and land on their four
feet uninjured!

MARGARET: Oh, yes!

BRICK: Do it!—Fo' God's sake, do it. . . .

MARGARET: Do what?   335

BRICK: Take a lover!

MARGARET: I can't see a man but you! Even with my eyes closed, I just see you!
Why don't you get ugly, Brick, why don't you please get fat or ugly or something
so I could stand it?

[*She rushes to hall door, opens it, listens.*]

The concert is still going on! Bravo, no-necks, bravo!   340

[*She slams and locks door fiercely.*]

BRICK: What did you lock the door for?

MARGARET: To give us a little privacy for a while.

BRICK: You know better, Maggie.

MARGARET: No, I don't know better. . . .

[*She rushes to gallery doors, draws the rose-silk drapes across them.*]

BRICK: Don't make a fool of yourself.   345

MARGARET: I don't mind makin' a fool of myself over you!

BRICK: I mind, Maggie. I feel embarrassed for you.

MARGARET: Feel embarrassed! But don't continue my torture. I can't live on and on under
these circumstances.

BRICK: You agreed to—   350

MARGARET: I know but—

BRICK: Accept that condition!

MARGARET: I CAN'T! CAN'T! CAN'T!

[*She seizes his shoulder.*]

BRICK: Let go!

[*He breaks away from her and seizes the small boudoir chair and raises it like a
lion-tamer facing a big circus cat.*]

[*Count five. She stares at him with her fist pressed to her mouth, then bursts into
shrill, almost hysterical laughter. He remains grave for a moment, then grins and
puts the chair down.*]

[**BIG MAMA** *calls through closed door.*]

BIG MAMA: Son? Son? Son?   355

BRICK: What is it, Big Mama?

BIG MAMA: [*outside*] Oh, son! We got the most wonderful news about Big Daddy. I just
had t' run up an' tell you right this—

[*She rattles the knob.*]

—What's this door doin', locked, faw? You all think there's robbers in the house?

MARGARET: Big Mama, Brick is dressin', he's not dressed yet.   360

BIG MAMA: That's all right, it won't be the first time I've seen Brick not dressed. Come on,
open this door!

[**MARGARET,** *with a grimace, goes to unlock and open the hall door, as* **BRICK** *hobbles rapidly to the bathroom and kicks the door shut.* BIG MAMA *has disappeared from the hall.*]

MARGARET: Big Mama?

[BIG MAMA *appears through the opposite gallery doors behind* MARGARET, *huffing and puffing like an old bulldog. She is a short, stout woman; her sixty years and 170 pounds have left her somewhat breathless most of the time; she's always tensed like a boxer, or rather, a Japanese wrestler. Her "family" was maybe a little superior to* BIG DADDY's, *but not much. She wears a black or silver lace dress and at least half a million in flashy gems. She is very sincere.*]

BIG MAMA: [*loudly, startling* MARGARET] Here—I come through Gooper's and Mae's gall'ry door. Where's Brick? *Brick*—Hurry on out of there, son, I just have a second and want to give you the news about Big Daddy.—I hate locked doors in a house. . . . 365

MARGARET: [*with affected lightness*] I've noticed you do, Big Mama, but people have got to have *some* moments of privacy, don't they?

BIG MAMA: No, ma'am, not in *my* house. [*without pause*] Whacha took off you' dress faw? I thought that little lace dress was so sweet on yuh, honey. 370

MARGARET: I thought it looked sweet on me, too, but one of m' cute little table partners used it for a napkin so—!

BIG MAMA: [*picking up stockings on floor*] What?

MARGARET: You know, Big Mama, Mae and Gooper's so touchy about those children— thanks, Big Mama . . . 375

[BIG MAMA *has thrust the picked-up stockings in* MARGARET's *hand with a grunt.*]

—that you just don't dare to suggest there's any room for improvement in their—

BIG MAMA: Brick, hurry out!—Shoot, Maggie, you just don't like children.

MARGARET: I do SO like children! Adore them!—well brought up!

BIG MAMA: [*gentle—loving*] Well, why don't you have some and bring them up well, then, instead of all the time pickin' on Gooper's an' Mae's? 380

GOOPER: [*shouting up the stairs*] Hey, hey, Big Mama, Betsy an' Hugh got to go, waitin' t' tell yuh g'by!

BIG MAMA: Tell 'em to hold their hawses, I'll be right down in a jiffy!

[*She turns to the bathroom door and calls out.*]

Son? Can you hear me in there? 385

[*There is a muffled answer.*]

We just got the full report from the laboratory at the Ochsner Clinic, completely negative, son, ev'rything negative, right on down the line! Nothin' a-tall's wrong with him but some little functional thing called a spastic colon. Can you hear me, son?

MARGARET: He can hear you, Big Mama.

BIG MAMA: Then why don't he say something? God Almighty, a piece of news like that should make him shout. It made me shout, I can tell you. I shouted and sobbed and fell right down on my knees!—Look! 390

[*She pulls up her skirt.*]

See the bruises where I hit my kneecaps? Took both doctors to haul me back on my feet!

[*She laughs—she always laughs like hell at herself.*]

Big Daddy was furious with me! But ain't that wonderful news?   395

[*Facing bathroom again, she continues:*]

After all the anxiety we been through to git a report like that on Big Daddy's birthday? Big Daddy tried to hide how much of a load that news took off his mind, but didn't fool *me*. He was mighty close to crying about it *himself!*

[*Goodbyes are shouted downstairs, and she rushes to door.*]

Hold those people down there, don't let them go!—Now, git dressed, we're all comin' up to this room fo' Big Daddy's birthday party because of your ankle.—How's his   400
ankle, Maggie?

MARGARET: Well, he broke it, Big Mama.

BIG MAMA: I know he broke it.

[*A phone is ringing in hall. A Negro voice answers:* "Mistuh Polly's res'dence."]

I mean does it hurt him much still.

MARGARET: I'm afraid I can't give you that information, Big Mama. You'll have to ask   405
Brick if it hurts much still or not.

SOOKEY: [*in the hall*] It's Memphis, Mizz Polly, it's Miss Sally in Memphis.

BIG MAMA: Awright, Sookey.

[BIG MAMA *rushes into the hall and is heard shouting on the phone:*]

Hello, Miss Sally. How are you, Miss Sally?—Yes, well, I was just gonna call you
about it. *Shoot!*—   410

[*She raises her voice to a bellow.*]

*Miss Sally? Don't ever call me from the Gayoso Lobby, too much talk goes on in that hotel
lobby, no wonder you can't hear me!* Now listen, Miss Sally. They's nothin' serious
wrong with Big Daddy. We got the report just now, they's nothin' wrong but a thing
called a—spastic! *SPASTIC!*—colon. . . .

[*She appears at the hall door and calls to* MARGARET.]

—Maggie, come out here and talk to that fool on the phone. I'm shouted breathless!   415

MARGARET: [*goes out and is heard sweetly at phone*] Miss Sally? This is Brick's wife, Maggie.
So nice to hear your voice. Can you hear mine? Well, good!—Big Mama just wanted
you to know that they've got the report from the Ochsner Clinic and what Big
Daddy has is a spastic colon. Yes. Spastic colon, Miss Sally. That's right, spastic colon.
G'bye, Miss Sally, hope I'll see you real soon!   420

[*Hangs up a little before* MISS SALLY *was probably ready to terminate the talk.
She returns through the hall door.*]

She heard me perfectly. I've discovered with deaf people the thing to do is not shout
at them but just enunciate clearly. My rich old Aunt Cornelia was deaf as the dead
but I could make her hear me just by sayin' each word slowly, distinctly, close to
her ear. I read her the *Commercial Appeal* ev'ry night, read her the classified ads in
it, even, she never missed a word of it. But was she a mean ole thing! Know what I   425
got when she died? Her unexpired subscriptions to five magazines and the Book-of-
the-Month Club and a LIBRARY full of ev'ry dull book ever written! All else went
to her hellcat of a sister . . . meaner than she was, even!

[BIG MAMA *has been straightening things up in the room during this speech.*]

BIG MAMA: [*closing closet door on discarded clothes*] Miss Sally sure is a case! Big Daddy says
she's always got her hand out fo' something. He's not mistaken. That poor ole thing   430
always has her hand out fo' somethin'. I don't think Big Daddy gives her as much
as he should.

[*Somebody shouts for her downstairs and she shouts:*]

I'm comin'!

[*She starts out. At the hall door, turns and jerks a forefinger, first toward the
bathroom door, then toward the liquor cabinet, meaning: "Has Brick been
drinking?" MARGARET pretends not to understand, cocks her head and raises her
brows as if the pantomimic performance was completely mystifying to her.*]

[BIG MAMA *rushes back to* MARGARET:]

Shoot! Stop playin' so dumb!—I mean has he been drinkin' that stuff much yet?
MARGARET: [*with a little laugh*] Oh! I think he had a highball after supper.   435
BIG MAMA: Don't laugh about it!—Some single men stop drinkin' when they git married
and others start! Brick never touched liquor before he—!
MARGARET: [*crying out*] *THAT'S NOT FAIR!*
BIG MAMA: Fair or not fair I want to ask you a question, one question: D'you make Brick
happy in bed?   440
MARGARET: Why don't you ask if he makes *me* happy in bed?
BIG MAMA: Because I know that—
MARGARET: It works both ways!
BIG MAMA: Something's not right! You're childless and my son drinks!

[*Someone has called her downstairs and she has rushed to the door on the line
above. She turns at the door and points at the bed.*]

When a marriage goes on the rocks, the rocks are *there*, right *there!*   445
MARGARET: That's—

[BIG MAMA *has swept out of the room and slammed the door.*]

—not *fair* . . .

[MARGARET *is alone, completely alone, and she feels it. She draws in, hunches her
shoulders, raises her arms with fists clenched, shuts her eyes tight as a child about to
be stabbed with a vaccination needle. When she opens her eyes again, what she sees
is the long oval mirror and she rushes straight to it, stares into it with a grimace and
says: "Who are you?"—Then she crouches a little and answers herself in a different
voice which is high, thin, mocking: "I am Maggie the Cat!"—Straightens quickly
as bathroom door opens a little and* BRICK *calls out to her.*]

BRICK: Has Big Mama gone?
MARGARET: She's gone.

[*He opens the bathroom door and hobbles out, with his liquor glass now empty,
straight to the liquor cabinet. He is whistling softly.* MARGARET's *head pivots on
her long, slender throat to watch him.*]

[*She raises a hand uncertainly to the base of her throat, as if it was difficult for
her to swallow, before she speaks:*]

You know, our sex life didn't just peter out in the usual way, it was cut off short, long   450
before the natural time for it to, and it's going to revive again, just as sudden as that.
I'm confident of it. That's what I'm keeping myself attractive for. For the time when
you'll see me again like other men see me. Yes, like other men see me. They still see
me, Brick, and they like what they see. Uh-huh. Some of them would give their—
    Look, Brick!   455

[*She stands before the long oval mirror, touches her breast and then her hips with
her two hands.*]

How high my body stays on me!—Nothing has fallen on me—not a fraction. . . .

[*Her voice is soft and trembling: a pleading child's. At this moment as he turns to
glance at her—a look which is like a player passing a ball to another player, third
down and goal to go—she has to capture the audience in a grip so tight that she
can hold it till the first intermission without any lapse of attention.*]

Other men still want me. My face looks strained, sometimes, but I've kept my
figure as well as you've kept yours, and men admire it. I still turn heads on the
street. Why, last week in Memphis everywhere that I went men's eyes burned holes
in my clothes, at the country club and in restaurants and department stores, there   460
wasn't a man I met or walked by that didn't just eat me up with his eyes and turn
around when I passed him and look back at me. Why, at Alice's party for her New
York cousins, the best-lookin' man in the crowd—followed me upstairs and tried to
force his way in the powder room with me, followed me to the door and tried
to force his way in!   465
BRICK: Why didn't you let him, Maggie?
MARGARET: Because I'm not that common, for one thing. Not that I wasn't almost
    tempted to. You like to know who it was? It was Sonny Boy Maxwell, that's who!
BRICK: Oh, yeah, Sonny Boy Maxwell, he was a good end-runner but had a little injury
    to his back and had to quit.   470
MARGARET: He has no injury now and has no wife and still has a lech for me!
BRICK: I see no reason to lock him out of a powder room in that case.
MARGARET: And have someone catch me at it? I'm not that stupid. Oh, I might sometime
    cheat on you with someone, since you're so insultingly eager to have me do it!—But
    if I do, you can be damned sure it will be in a place and time where no one but me   475
    and the man could possibly know. Because I'm not going to give you any excuse to
    divorce me for being unfaithful or anything else. . . .
BRICK: Maggie, I wouldn't divorce you for being unfaithful or anything else. Don't you
    know that? Hell. I'd be relieved to know that you'd found yourself a lover.
MARGARET: Well, I'm taking no chances. No, I'd rather stay on this hot tin roof.   480
BRICK: A hot tin roof's 'n uncomfo'table place t' stay on. . . .

[*He starts to whistle softly.*]

MARGARET: [*through his whistle*] Yeah, but I can stay on it just as long as I have to.
BRICK: You could leave me, Maggie.

[*He resumes whistle. She wheels about to glare at him.*]

MARGARET: Don't want to and will not! Besides if I did, you don't have a cent to pay for
    it but what you get from Big Daddy and he's dying of cancer!   485

[*For the first time a realization of* **BIG DADDY**'*s doom seems to penetrate to*

BRICK's *consciousness, visibly, and he looks at* MARGARET.]

BRICK: Big Mama just said he *wasn't*, that the report was okay.

MARGARET: That's what she thinks because she got the same story that they gave Big Daddy. And was just as taken in by it as he was, poor ole things. . . .

But tonight they're going to tell her the truth about it. When Big Daddy goes to bed, they're going to tell her that he is dying of cancer.   490

[*She slams the dresser drawer.*]

—It's malignant and it's terminal.

BRICK: Does Big Daddy know it?

MARGARET: Hell, do they *ever* know it? Nobody says, "You're dying." You have to fool them. They have to fool *themselves*.

BRICK: Why?   495

MARGARET: Why? Because human beings dream of life everlasting, that's the reason! But most of them want it on earth and not in heaven.

[*He gives a short, hard laugh at her touch of humor.*]

Well. . . . [*She touches up her mascara.*] That's how it is, anyhow. . . . [*She looks about.*] Where did I put down my cigarette? Don't want to burn up the home place, at least not with Mae and Gooper and their five monsters in it!   500

[*She has found it and sucks at it greedily. Blows out smoke and continues:*]

So this is Big Daddy's last birthday. And Mae and Gooper, they know it, oh, *they* know it, all right. They got the first information from the Ochsner Clinic. That's why they rushed down here with their no-neck monsters. Because. Do you know something? Big Daddy's made no will? Big Daddy's never made out any will in his life, and so this campaign's afoot to impress him, forcibly as possible, with the fact   505
that you drink and I've borne no children!

[*He continues to stare at her a moment, then mutters something sharp but not audible and hobbles rather rapidly out onto the long gallery in the fading, much faded, gold light.*]

MARGARET: [*continuing her liturgical chant*] Y'know, I'm *fond* of Big Daddy, I am genuinely fond of that old man, I really *am*, you know. . . .

BRICK: [*faintly, vaguely*] Yes, I know you are. . . .

MARGARET: I've always sort of admired him in spite of his coarseness, his four-letter   510
words, and so forth. Because Big Daddy *is* what he *is,* and he makes no bones about it. He hasn't turned gentleman farmer, he's still a Mississippi redneck, as much of a redneck as he must have been when he was just overseer here on the old Jack Straw and Peter Ochello place. But he got hold of it an' built it into th' biggest an' finest plantation in the Delta.—I've always *liked* Big Daddy. . . .   515

[*She crosses to the proscenium.*]

Well, this is Big Daddy's last birthday. I'm sorry about it. But I'm facing the facts. It takes money to take care of a drinker and that's the office that I've been elected to lately.

BRICK: You don't have to take care of me.

MARGARET: Yes, I do. Two people in the same boat have got to take care of each other. At   520
least you want money to buy more Echo Spring when this supply is exhausted, or will you be satisfied with a ten-cent beer?

Mae an' Gooper are plannin' to freeze us out of Big Daddy's estate because you drink and I'm childless. But we can defeat that plan. We're going to defeat that plan!

Brick, y'know, I've been so goddam disgustingly poor all my life!—That's the truth, Brick! 525

BRICK: I'm not sayin' it isn't.

MARGARET: Always had to suck up to people I couldn't stand because they had money and I was poor as Job's turkey. You don't know what that's like. Well, I'll tell you, it's like you would feel a thousand miles away from Echo Spring!—And had to get back 530 to it on that broken ankle . . . without a crutch!

That's how it feels to be as poor as Job's turkey and have to suck up to relatives that you hated because they had money and all you had was a bunch of hand-me-down clothes and a few old moldly three-percent government bonds. My daddy loved his liquor, he fell in love with his liquor the way you've fallen in love with Echo 535 Spring!—And my poor Mama, having to maintain some semblance of social position, to keep appearances up, on an income of one hundred and fifty dollars a month on those old government bonds!

When I came out, the year that I made my debut, I had just two evening dresses! One Mother made me from a pattern in *Vogue,* the other a hand-me-down 540 from a snotty rich cousin I hated!

—The dress that I married you in was my grandmother's weddin' gown. . . . So that's why I'm like a cat on a hot tin roof!

[BRICK *is still on the gallery. Someone below calls up to him in a warm Negro voice,* "Hiya, Mistuh Brick, how yuh feelin'?" BRICK *raises his liquor glass as if that answered the question.*]

MARGARET: You can be young without money, but you can't be old without it. You've got to be old *with* money because to be old without it is just too awful, you've got to be 545 one or the other, either *young* or *with money,* you can't be old and *without* it.—That's the *truth,* Brick. . . .

[BRICK *whistles softly, vaguely.*]

Well, now I'm dressed, I'm all dressed, there's nothing else for me to do.

[*forlornly, almost fearfully*]

I'm dressed, all dressed, nothing else for me to do. . . .

[*She moves about restlessly, aimlessly, and speaks, as if to herself.*]

I know when I made my mistake.—What am I—? Oh!—my bracelets. . . . 550

[*She starts working a collection of bracelets over her hands onto her wrists, about six on each, as she talks.*]

I've thought a whole lot about it and now I know when I made my mistake. Yes, I made my mistake when I told you the truth about that thing with Skipper. Never should have confessed it, a fatal error, tellin' you about that thing with Skipper.

BRICK: Maggie, shut up about Skipper. I mean it, Maggie; you got to shut up about Skipper.

MARGARET: You ought to understand that Skipper and I— 555

BRICK: You don't think I'm serious, Maggie? You're fooled by the fact that I am saying this quiet? Look, Maggie. What you're doing is a dangerous thing to do. You're—you're—you're—

MARGARET: This time I'm going to finish what I have to say to you. Skipper and I made love, if love you could call it, because it made both of us feel a little bit closer to you. 560 You see, you son of a bitch, you asked too much of people, of me, of him, of all the unlucky poor damned sons of bitches that happen to love you, and there was a whole pack of them, yes, there was a pack of them besides me and Skipper, you asked too goddam much of people that loved you, you—superior creature!—you godlike being!—And so we made love to each other to dream it was you, both of us! Yes, 565 yes, yes! Truth, truth! What's so awful about it? I like it, I think the truth is—yeah! I shouldn't have told you. . . .

BRICK: [*holding his head unnaturally still and uptilted a bit*] It was Skipper that told me about it. Not you, Maggie.

MARGARET: I told you! 570

BRICK: After he told me!

MARGARET: What does it matter who?

[**BRICK** *turns suddenly out upon the gallery and calls:*]

BRICK: Little girl! Hey, little girl!

LITTLE GIRL: [*at a distance*] What, Uncle Brick?

BRICK: Tell the folks to come up!—Bring everybody upstairs! 575

MARGARET: I can't stop myself! I'd go on telling you this in front of them all, if I had to!

BRICK: Little girl! Go on, go on, will you? Do what I told you, call them!

MARGARET: Because it's got to be told and you, you!—you never let me!

[*She sobs, then controls herself, and continues almost calmly.*]

It was one of those beautiful, ideal things they tell about in the Greek legends, it couldn't be anything else, you being you, and that's what made it so sad, that's what 580 made it so awful, because it was love that never could be carried through to anything satisfying or even talked about plainly. Brick, I tell you, you got to believe me, Brick, I *do* understand all about it! I—I think it was—*noble!* Can't you tell I'm sincere when I say I respect it? My only point, the only point that I'm making, is life has got to be allowed to continue even after the *dream* of life is—all—over. . . . 585

[**BRICK** *is without his crutch. Leaning on furniture, he crosses to pick it up as she continues as if possessed by a will outside herself:*]

Why, I remember when we double-dated at college, Gladys Fitzgerald and I and you and Skipper, it was more like a date between you and Skipper. Gladys and I were just sort of tagging along as if it was necessary to chaperone you!—to make a good public impression—

BRICK: [*turns to face her, half lifting his crutch*] Maggie, you want me to hit you with this 590 crutch? Don't you know I could kill you with this crutch?

MARGARET: Good Lord, man, d' you think I'd care if you did?

BRICK: One man has one great good true thing in his life. One great good thing which is true!—I had friendship with Skipper.—You are naming it dirty!

MARGARET: I'm not naming it dirty! I am naming it clean. 595

BRICK: Not love with you, Maggie, but friendship with Skipper was that one great true thing, and you are naming it dirty!

MARGARET: Then you haven't been listenin', not understood what I'm saying! I'm naming it so damn clean that it killed poor Skipper!—You two had something that had to be kept on ice, yes, incorruptible, yes!—and death was the only icebox where you could 600 keep it. . . .

BRICK: I married you, Maggie. Why would I marry you, Maggie, if I was—?

MARGARET: Brick, don't brain me yet, let me finish!—I know, believe me I know, that it was only Skipper that harbored even any *unconscious* desire for anything not perfectly pure between you two!—Now let me skip a little. You married me early that summer we graduated out of Ole Miss, and we were happy, weren't we, we were blissful, yes, hit heaven together ev'ry time that we loved! But that fall you an' Skipper turned down wonderful offers of jobs in order to keep on bein' football heroes—pro football heroes. You organized the Dixie Stars that fall, so you could keep on bein' teammates forever! But somethin' was not right with it!—*Me included!*—between you. Skipper began hittin' the bottle . . . you got a spinal injury—couldn't play the Thanksgivin' game in Chicago, watched it on TV from a traction bed in Toledo. I joined Skipper. The Dixie Stars lost because poor Skipper was drunk. We drank together that night all night in the bar of the Blackstone and when cold day was comin' up over the lake an' we were comin' out drunk to take a dizzy look at it, I said, "SKIPPER! STOP LOVIN' MY HUSBAND OR TELL HIM HE'S GOT TO LET YOU ADMIT IT TO HIM!"—one way or another!

HE SLAPPED ME HARD ON THE MOUTH!—then turned and ran without stopping once, I am sure, all the way back into his room at the Blackstone. . . .

—When I came to his room that night, with a little scratch like a shy little mouse at his door, he made that pitiful, ineffectual little attempt to prove that what I had said wasn't true. . . .

[BRICK *strikes at her with crutch, a blow that shatters the gemlike lamp on the table.*]

—In this way, I destroyed him, by telling him truth that he and his world which he was born and raised in, yours and his world, had told him could not be told?

—From then on Skipper was nothing at all but a receptacle for liquor and drugs. . . .

Who shot Cock Robin? I with my—

[*She throws back her head with tight shut eyes.*]

—*merciful arrow!*

[BRICK *strikes at her; misses.*]

Missed me!—Sorry—I'm not tryin' to whitewash my behavior, Christ, no! Brick, I'm not good. I don't know why people have to pretend to be good, nobody's good. The rich or the well-to-do can afford to respect moral patterns, conventional moral patterns, but I could never afford to, yeah, but—I'm honest! Give me credit for just that, will you *please?*—Born poor, raised poor, expect to die poor unless I manage to get us something out of what Big Daddy leaves when he dies of cancer! But Brick?!—*Skipper is dead! I'm alive!* Maggie the Cat is—

[BRICK *hops awkwardly forward and strikes at her again with his crutch.*]

—alive! I am alive, alive! I am . . .

[*He hurls the crutch at her, across the bed she took refuge behind, and pitches forward on the floor as she completes her speech.*]

—alive!

[*A little girl,* DIXIE, *bursts into the room, wearing an Indian war bonnet and firing a cap pistol at* MARGARET *and shouting:* "Bang, bang, bang!"]

[*Laughter downstairs floats through the open hall door.* MARGARET *had crouched gasping to bed at child's entrance. She now rises and says with cool fury:*]

Little girl, your mother or someone should teach you—[*gasping*]—to knock at a door before you come into a room. Otherwise people might think that you—lack—good breeding. . . .   640

DIXIE: Yanh, yanh, yanh, what is Uncle Brick doin' on th' floor?

BRICK: I tried to kill your Aunt Maggie, but I failed—and I fell. Little girl, give me my crutch so I can get up off th' floor.

MARGARET: Yes, give your uncle his crutch, he's a cripple, honey, he broke his ankle last night jumping hurdles on the high school athletic field!   645

DIXIE: What were you jumping hurdles for, Uncle Brick?

BRICK: Because I used to jump them, and people like to do what they used to do, even after they've stopped being able to do it. . . .

MARGARET: That's right, that's your answer, now go away, little girl.

[DIXIE *fires cap pistol at* MARGARET *three times.*]

Stop, you stop that, monster! You little no-neck monster!   650

[*She seizes the cap pistol and hurls it through gallery doors.*]

DIXIE: [*with a precocious instinct for the cruelest thing*] You're *jealous!*—You're just jealous because you can't have babies!

[*She sticks out her tongue at* MARGARET *as she sashays past her with her stomach stuck out, to the gallery.* MARGARET *slams the gallery doors and leans panting against them. There is a pause.* BRICK *has replaced his spilt drink and sits, far-away, on the great four-poster bed.*]

MARGARET: You see?—they gloat over us being childless, even in front of their five little no-neck monsters!

[*Pause. Voices approach on the stairs.*]

Brick?—I've been to a doctor in Memphis, a—a gynecologist. . . .   655
I've been completely examined, and there is no reason why we can't have a child whenever we want one. And this is my time by the calendar to conceive. Are you listening to me? Are you? Are you LISTENING TO ME!

BRICK: Yes. I hear you, Maggie.

[*His attention returns to her inflamed face.*]

—But how in hell on Earth do you imagine—that you're going to have a child by a   660
man that can't stand you?

MARGARET: That's a problem that I will have to work out.

[*She wheels about to face the hall door.*]

Here they come!

[*The lights dim.*]

CURTAIN

ACT II

There is no lapse of time. MARGARET *and* BRICK *are in the same positions they held at the end of Act I.*

MARGARET: [*at door*]: *Here they come!*

> [BIG DADDY *appears first, a tall man with a fierce, anxious look, moving carefully not to betray his weakness even, or especially, to himself.*]

BIG DADDY: Well, Brick.
BRICK: Hello, Big Daddy.—Congratulations!
BIG DADDY: —Crap. . . .

> [*Some of the people are approaching through the hall, others along the gallery: voices from both directions.* GOOPER *and* REVEREND TOOKER *become visible outside gallery doors, and their voices come in clearly.*]

> [*They pause outside as* GOOPER *lights a cigar.*]

REVEREND TOOKER: [*vivaciously*] Oh, but St. Paul's in Grenada has three memorial   5
  windows, and the latest one is a Tiffany stained-glass window that cost twenty-five
  hundred dollars, a picture of Christ the Good Shepherd with a Lamb in His arms.
GOOPER: Who give that window, Preach?
REVEREND TOOKER: Clyde Fletcher's widow. Also presented St. Paul's with a baptismal
  font.   10
GOOPER: Y'know what somebody ought t' give your church is a *coolin'* system, Preach.
REVEREND TOOKER: Yes, siree, Bob! And y'know what Gus Hamma's family gave in his
  memory to the church at Two Rivers? A complete new stone parish-house with a
  basketball court in the basement and a—
BIG DADDY: [*uttering a loud barking laugh, which is far from truly mirthful*] Hey, Preach!   15
  What's all this talk about memorials, Preach? Y' think somebody's about t' kick off
  around here? 'S that it?

> [*Startled by this interjection,* REVEREND TOOKER *decides to laugh at the question almost as loud as he can.*]

> [*How he would answer the question we'll never know, as he's spared that embarrassment by the voice of* GOOPER's *wife,* MAE, *rising high and clear as she appears with* "DOC" BAUGH, *the family doctor, through the hall door.*]

MAE: [*almost religiously*]—Let's see now, they've had their *tyyy*-phoid shots, and their teta-
  nus shots, their diphtheria shots and their hepatitis shots and their polio shots, they
  got *those* shots every month from May through September and—Gooper? Hey!   20
  Gooper!—What all have the kiddies been shot faw?
MARGARET: [*overlapping a bit*] Turn on the hi-fi, Brick! Let's have some music t' start off
  th' party with!

> [*The talk becomes so general that the room sounds like a great aviary of chattering birds. Only* BRICK *remains unengaged, leaning upon the liquor cabinet with his faraway smile, an ice cube in a paper napkin with which he now and then rubs his forehead. He doesn't respond to* MARGARET's *command. She bounds forward and stoops over the instrument panel of the console.*]

GOOPER: We gave 'em that thing for a third anniversary present, got three speakers in it.

[*The room is suddenly blasted by the climax of a Wagnerian opera or a Beethoven symphony.*]

BIG DADDY: Turn that dam thing off! 25

[*Almost instant silence, almost instantly broken by the shouting charge of* BIG MAMA, *entering through hall door like a charging rhino.*]

BIG MAMA: Wha's my Brick, wha's mah precious baby!!
BIG DADDY: Sorry! Turn it back on!

[*Everyone laughs very loud.* BIG DADDY *is famous for his jokes at* BIG MAMA's *expense, and nobody laughs louder at these jokes than* BIG MAMA *herself, though sometimes they're pretty cruel and* BIG MAMA *has to pick up or fuss with something to cover the hurt that the loud laugh doesn't quite cover.*]

[*On this occasion, a happy occasion because the dread in her heart has also been lifted by the false report on* BIG DADDY's *condition, she giggles, grotesquely, coyly, in* BIG DADDY's *direction and bears down upon* BRICK, *all very quick and alive.*]

BIG MAMA: Here he is, here's my precious baby! What's that you've got in your hand? You put that liquor down, son, your hand was made fo' holdin' somethin' better than that! 30
GOOPER: Look at Brick put it down!

[BRICK *has obeyed* BIG MAMA *by draining the glass and handing it to her. Again everyone laughs, some high, some low.*]

BIG MAMA: Oh, you bad boy, you're my bad little boy. Give Big Mama a kiss, you bad boy, you!—Look at him shy away, will you? Brick never liked bein' kissed or made a fuss over, I guess because he's always had too much of it!
Son, you turn that thing off! 35

[BRICK *has switched on the TV set.*]

I can't stand TV, radio was bad enough but TV has gone it one better, I mean— [*plops wheezing in chair*]—one worse, ha ha! Now what'm I sittin' down here faw? I want t' sit next to my sweetheart on the sofa, hold hands with him and love him up a little!

[BIG MAMA *has on a black-and-white–figured chiffon. The large irregular patterns, like the markings of some massive animal, the luster of her great diamonds and many pearls, the brilliants set in the silver frames of her glasses, her riotous voice, booming laugh, have dominated the room since she entered.* BIG DADDY *has been regarding her with a steady grimace of chronic annoyance.*]

BIG MAMA: [*still louder*] Preacher, Preacher, hey, Preach! Give me you' hand an' help me up from this chair! 40
REVEREND TOOKER: None of your tricks, Big Mama!
BIG MAMA: What tricks? You give me you' hand so I can get up an'—

[REVEREND TOOKER *extends her his hand. She grabs it and pulls him into her lap with a shrill laugh that spans an octave in two notes.*]

Ever seen a preacher in a fat lady's lap? Hey, hey, folks! Ever seen a preacher in a fat lady's lap? 45

[BIG MAMA *is notorious throughout the Delta for this sort of inelegant horseplay.* MARGARET *looks on with indulgent humor, sipping Dubonnet "on the rocks" and watching* BRICK, *but* MAE *and* GOOPER *exchange signs of humorless anxiety over these antics, the sort of behavior which* MAE *thinks may account for their failure to quite get in with the smartest young married set in Memphis, despite all. One of the negroes,* LACY *or* SOOKEY, *peeks in, cackling. They are waiting for a sign to bring in the cake and champagne. But* BIG DADDY's *not amused. He doesn't understand why, in spite of the infinite mental relief he's received from the doctor's report, he still has these same old fox teeth in his guts. "This spastic thing sure is something," he says to himself, but aloud he roars at* BIG MAMA:]

BIG DADDY: BIG MAMA, WILL YOU QUIT HORSIN'?—You're too old an' too fat fo' that sort of crazy kid stuff an' besides a woman with your blood pressure—she had two hundred last spring!—is riskin' a stroke when you mess around like that. . . .

BIG MAMA: Here comes Big Daddy's birthday!   50

[*Negroes in white jackets enter with an enormous birthday cake ablaze with candles and carrying buckets of champagne with satin ribbons about the bottle necks.*]

[MAE *and* GOOPER *strike up song, and everybody, including the Negroes and* CHILDREN, *joins in. Only* BRICK *remains aloof.*]

EVERYONE:
Happy birthday to you.
Happy birthday to you.
Happy birthday, Big Daddy

[*Some sing:* "Dear, Big Daddy!"]

Happy birthday to you.

[*Some sing:* "How old are you?"]

[MAE *has come down center and is organizing her children like a chorus. She gives them a barely audible:* "One, two, three!" *and they are off in the new tune.*]

CHILDREN:
Skinamarinka—dinka—dink   55
Skinamarinka—do
We love you.
Skinamarinka—dinka—dink
Skinamarinka—do.

[*All together, they turn to* BIG DADDY.]

Big Daddy, you!   60

[*They turn back front, like a musical comedy chorus.*]

We love you in the morning;
We love you in the night.
We love you when we're with you,
And we love you out of sight.
Skinamarinka—dinka—dink   65
Skinamarinka—do.

[MAE *turns to* BIG MAMA.]

Big Mama, too!

[BIG MAMA *bursts into tears. The Negroes leave.*]

BIG DADDY: Now Ida, what the hell is the matter with you?

MAE: She's just so happy.

BIG MAMA: I'm just so happy, Big Daddy, I have to cry or something. 70

[*Sudden and loud in the hush:*]

Brick, do you know the wonderful news that Doc Baugh got from the clinic about Big Daddy? Big Daddy's one hundred percent!

MARGARET: Isn't that wonderful?

BIG MAMA: He's just one hundred percent. Passed the examination with flying colors. Now that we know there's nothing wrong with Big Daddy but a spastic colon, I can tell 75 you something. I was worried sick, half out of my mind, for fear that Big Daddy might have a thing like—

[MARGARET *cuts through this speech, jumping up and exclaiming shrilly:*]

MARGARET: Brick, honey, aren't you going to give Big Daddy his birthday present?

[*Passing by him, she snatches his liquor glass from him.*]

[*She picks up a fancily wrapped package.*]

Here it is, Big Daddy, this is from Brick!

BIG MAMA: This is the biggest birthday Big Daddy's ever had, a hundred presents and 80 bushels of telegrams from—

MAE: [*at same time*] What is it, Brick?

GOOPER: I bet 500 to 50 that Brick don't know what it is.

BIG MAMA: The fun of presents is not knowing what they are till you open the package. Open your present, Big Daddy. 85

BIG DADDY: Open it you'self. I want to ask Brick somethin'! Come here, Brick.

MARGARET: Big Daddy's callin' you, Brick.

[*She is opening the package.*]

BRICK: Tell Big Daddy I'm crippled.

BIG DADDY: I see you're crippled. I want to know how you got crippled.

MARGARET: [*making diversionary tactics*] *Oh, look, oh, look, why, it's a cashmere robe!* 90

[*She holds the robe up for all to see.*]

MAE: You sound surprised, Maggie.

MARGARET: I never saw one before.

MAE: That's funny.—*Hah!*

MARGARET: [*turning on her fiercely, with a brilliant smile*] Why is it funny? All my family ever had was family—and luxuries such as cashmere robes still surprise me! 95

BIG DADDY: [*ominously*] Quiet!

MAE: [*heedless in her fury*] I don't see how you could be so surprised when you bought it yourself at Loewenstein's in Memphis last Saturday. You know how I know?

BIG DADDY: I said, "Quiet!"

MAE: —I know because the salesgirl that sold it to you waited on me and said, "Oh, Mrs. 100 Pollitt, your sister-in-law just bought a cashmere robe for your husband's father!"

MARGARET: Sister Woman! Your talents are wasted as a housewife and mother, you really ought to be with the FBI or—

BIG DADDY: QUIET!

> [**REVEREND TOOKER**'s *reflexes are slower than the others'. He finishes a sentence after the bellow.*]

REVEREND TOOKER: [*to* DOC BAUGH]—the Stork and the Reaper are running neck   105
and neck!

> [*He starts to laugh gaily when he notices the silence and* **BIG DADDY**'s *glare. His laugh dies falsely.*]

BIG DADDY: Preacher, I hope I'm not butting in on more talk about memorial stained-
glass windows, am I, Preacher?

> [**REVEREND TOOKER** *laughs feebly, then coughs dryly in the embarrassed silence.*]

Preacher?

BIG MAMA: Now, Big Daddy, don't you pick on Preacher!   105

BIG DADDY: [*raising his voice*] You ever hear that expression "all hawk and no spit"? You bring
that expression to mind with that little dry cough of yours, all hawk an' no spit. . . .

> [*The pause is broken only by a short startled laugh from* MARGARET, *the only one there who is conscious of and amused by the grotesque.*]

MAE: [*raising her arms and jangling her bracelets*] I wonder if the mosquitoes are active
tonight?

BIG DADDY: What's that, Little Mama? Did you make some remark?   115

MAE: Yes, I said I wondered if the mosquitoes would eat us alive if we went out on the
gallery for a while.

BIG DADDY: Well, if they do, I'll have your bones pulverized for fertilizer!

BIG MAMA: [*quickly*] Last week we had an airplane spraying the place and I think it done
some good, at least I haven't had a—   120

BIG DADDY: [*cutting her speech*] Brick, they tell me, if what they tell me is true, that you
done some jumping last night on the high school athletic field?

BIG MAMA: Brick, Big Daddy is talking to you, son.

BRICK: [*smiling vaguely over his drink*] What was that, Big Daddy?

BIG DADDY: They said you done some jumping on the high school track field last night.   125

BRICK: That's what they told me, too.

BIG DADDY: Was it jumping or humping that you were doing out there? What were you
doing out there at three A.M., layin' a woman on that cinder track?

BIG MAMA: Big Daddy, you are off the sick-list, now, and I'm not going to excuse you for
talkin' so—   130

BIG DADDY: Quiet!

BIG MAMA: —*nasty* in front of Preacher and—

BIG DADDY: QUIET!—I ast you, Brick, if you was cuttin' you'self a piece o' poon-tang last
night on that cinder track? I thought maybe you were chasin poon-tang on that
track an' tripped over something in the heat of the chase—'sthat it?   135

> [GOOPER *laughs, loud and false, others nervously following suit.* BIG MAMA *stamps her foot, and purses her lips, crossing to* MAE *and whispering something to her as* BRICK *meets his father's hard, intent, grinning stare with a slow, vague smile that he offers all situations from behind the screen of his liquor.*]

BRICK: No, sir, I don't think so. . . .

MAE: [*at the same time, sweetly*] Reverend Tooker, let's you and I take a stroll on the widow's walk.

[*She and the preacher go out on the gallery as* BIG DADDY *says:*]

BIG DADDY: Then what the hell were you doing out there at three o'clock in the morning?

BRICK: Jumping the hurdles, Big Daddy, runnin' and jumpin' the hurdles, but those high hurdles have gotten too high for me, now.   140

BIG DADDY: 'Cause you was drunk?

BRICK: [*his vague smile fading a little*] Sober I wouldn't have tried to jump the *low* ones. . . .

BIG MAMA: [*quickly*] Big Daddy, blow out the candles on your birthday cake!   145

MARGARET: [*at the same time*] I want to propose a toast to Big Daddy Pollitt on his sixty-fifth birthday, the biggest cotton planter in—

BIG DADDY: [*bellowing with fury and disgust*] I told you to stop it, now stop it, quit this!

BIG MAMA: [*coming in front of* BIG DADDY *with the cake*] Big Daddy, I will not allow you to talk that way, not even on your birthday, I—   150

BIG DADDY: I'll talk like I want to on my birthday, Ida, or any other goddam day of the year and anybody here that don't like it knows what they can do!

BIG MAMA: You don't mean that!

BIG DADDY: What makes you think I don't mean it?

[*Meanwhile various discreet signals have been exchanged and* **GOOPER** *has also gone out on the gallery.*]

BIG MAMA: I just know you don't mean it.   155

BIG DADDY: You don't know a goddam thing and you never did!

BIG MAMA: Big Daddy, you don't mean that.

BIG DADDY: Oh, yes, I do, oh, yes, I do, I mean it! I put up with a whole lot of crap around here because I thought I was dying. And you thought I was dying and you started taking over, well, you can stop taking over now, Ida, because I'm not gonna   160
die, you can just stop now this business of taking over because you're not taking over because I'm not dying, I went through the laboratory and the goddam exploratory operation and there's nothing wrong with me but a spastic colon. And I'm not dying of cancer which you thought I was dying of. Ain't that so? Didn't you think that I was dying of cancer, Ida?   165

[*Almost everybody is out on the gallery but the two old people glaring at each other across the blazing cake.*]

[**BIG MAMA**'s *chest heaves and she presses a fat fist to her mouth.*]

[**BIG DADDY** *continues, hoarsely:*]

Ain't that so, Ida? Didn't you have an idea I was dying of cancer and now you could take control of this place and everything on it? I got that impression, I seemed to get that impression. Your loud voice everywhere, your fat old body butting in here and there!

BIG MAMA: Hush! The preacher!   170

BIG DADDY: Rut the goddam preacher!

[**BIG MAMA** *gasps loudly and sits down on the sofa, which is almost too small for her.*]

Did you hear what I said? I said rut the goddam preacher!

[*Somebody closes the gallery doors from outside just as there is a burst of fireworks and excited cries from the children.*]

BIG MAMA: I never seen you act like this before and I can't think what's got in you!

BIG DADDY: I went through all that laboratory and operation and all just so I would know if you or me was boss here! Well, now it turns out that I am and you ain't—and that's   175
my birthday present—and my cake and champagne!—because for three years now you been gradually taking over. Bossing. Talking. Sashaying your fat old body around the place I made! I made this place! I was overseer on it! I was the overseer on the old Straw and Ochello plantation. I quit school at ten! I quit school at ten   180
years old and went to work like a nigger in the fields. And I rose to be overseer of the Straw and Ochello plantation. And old Straw died and I was Ochello's partner and the place got bigger and bigger and bigger and bigger and bigger! I did all that myself with no goddam help from you, and now you think you're just about to take over. Well, I am just about to tell you that you are not just about to take over, you are not   185
just about to take over a goddam thing. Is that clear to you, Ida? Is that very plain to you, now? Is that understood completely? I been through the laboratory from A to Z. I've had the goddam exploratory operation, and nothing is wrong with me but a spastic colon—made spastic, I guess, by *disgust!* By all the goddam lies and liars that I have had to put up with, and all the goddam hypocrisy that I lived with all these forty years that we been livin' together!   190

Hey! Ida!! Blow out the candles on the birthday cake! Purse up your lips and draw a deep breath and blow out the goddam candles on the cake!

BIG MAMA: Oh, Big Daddy, oh, oh, oh, Big Daddy!

BIG DADDY: What's the matter with you?

BIG MAMA: In all these years you never believed that I loved you??   195

BIG DADDY: Huh?

BIG MAMA: And I did, I did so much, I did love you!—I even loved your hate and your hardness, Big Daddy!

[*She sobs and rushes awkwardly out onto the gallery.*]

BIG DADDY: [*to himself*] Wouldn't it be funny if that was true. . . .

[*A pause is followed by a burst of light in the sky from the fireworks.*]

BRICK! HEY, BRICK   200

[*He stands over his blazing birthday cake.*]

[*After some moments,* BRICK *hobbles in on his crutch, holding his glass.*]

[MARGARET *follows him with a bright, anxious smile.*]

I didn't call you, Maggie. I called Brick.

MARGARET: I'm just delivering him to you.

[*She kisses* BRICK *on the mouth, which he immediately wipes with the back of his hand. She flies girlishly back out.* BRICK *and his father are alone.*]

BIG DADDY: Why did you do that?

BRICK: Do what, Big Daddy?

BIG DADDY: Wipe her kiss off your mouth like she'd spit on you.   205

BRICK: I don't know. I wasn't conscious of it.

BIG DADDY: That woman of yours has a better shape on her than Gooper's but somehow or other they got the same look about them.

BRICK: What sort of look is that, Big Daddy?

BIG DADDY: I don't know how to describe it but it's the same look.   210

BRICK: They don't look peaceful, do they?

BIG DADDY: No, they sure in hell don't.

BRICK: They look nervous as cats?

BIG DADDY: That's right, they look nervous as cats.

BRICK: Nervous as a couple of cats on a hot tin roof?   215

BIG DADDY: That's right, boy, they look like a couple of cats on a hot tin roof. It's funny
    that you and Gooper being so different would pick out the same type of woman.

BRICK: Both of us married into society, Big Daddy.

BIG DADDY: Crap . . . I wonder what gives them both that look?

BRICK: Well. They're sittin' in the middle of a big piece of land, Big Daddy, twenty-eight   220
    thousand acres is a pretty big piece of land and so they're squaring off on it, each
    determined to knock off a bigger piece of it than the other whenever you let it go.

BIG DADDY: I got a surprise for those women. I'm not gonna let it go for a long time yet
    if that's what they're waiting for.

BRICK: That's right, Big Daddy. You just sit tight and let them scratch each other's eyes   225
    out. . . .

BIG DADDY: You bet your life I'm going to sit tight on it and let those sons of bitches
    scratch their eyes out, ha ha ha. . . .
        But Gooper's wife's a good breeder, you got to admit she's fertile. Hell, at sup-
    per tonight she had them all at the table and they had to put a couple of extra leafs   230
    in the table to make room for them, she's got five head of them, now, and another
    one's comin'.

BRICK: Yep, number six is comin'. . . .

BIG DADDY: Brick, you know, I swear to God, I don't know the way it happens?

BRICK: The way what happens, Big Daddy?   235

BIG DADDY: You git you a piece of land, by hook or crook, an' things start growin' on it,
    things accumulate on it, and the first thing you know it's completely out of hand,
    completely out of hand!

BRICK: Well, they say nature hates a vacuum, Big Daddy.

BIG DADDY: That's what they say, but sometimes I think that a vacuum is a hell of a lot   240
    better than some of the stuff that nature replaces it with.
        Is someone out there by that door?

BRICK: Yep.

BIG DADDY: Who?

[*He has lowered his voice.*]

BRICK: Someone int'rested in what we say to each other.   245

BIG DADDY: Gooper?—*GOOPER!*

[*After a discreet pause,* MAE *appears in the gallery door.*]

MAE: Did you call Gooper, Big Daddy?

BIG DADDY: Aw, it was you.

MAE: Do you want Gooper, Big Daddy?

BIG DADDY: No, and I don't want you. I want some privacy here, while I'm having a   250
    confidential talk with my son Brick. Now it's too hot in here to close them doors,
    but if I have to close those rutten doors in order to have a private talk with my son
    Brick, just let me know and I'll close 'em. Because I hate eavesdroppers, I don't like
    any kind of sneakin' an' spyin'.

MAE: Why, Big Daddy—   255

BIG DADDY: You stood on the wrong side of the moon, it threw your shadow!

MAE: I was just—

BIG DADDY: You was just nothing but *spyin'* an' you *know* it!

MAE: [*begins to sniff and sob*] Oh, Big Daddy, you're so unkind for some reason to those that really love you! 260

BIG DADDY: Shut up, shut up, shut up! I'm going to move you and Gooper out of that room next to this! It's none of your goddam business what goes on in here at night between Brick an' Maggie. You listen at night like a couple of rutten peekhole spies and go and give a report on what you hear to Big Mama an' she comes to me and says they say such and such and so and so about what they heard goin' on between 265 Brick an' Maggie, and Jesus, it makes me sick. I'm goin' to move you an' Gooper out of that room, I can't stand sneakin' an' spyin', it makes me sick. . . .

> [MAE *throws back her head and rolls her eyes heavenward and extends her arms as if invoking God's pity for this unjust martyrdom; then she presses a handkerchief to her nose and flies from the room with a loud swish of skirts.*]

BRICK: [*now at the liquor cabinet*] They listen, do they?

BIG DADDY: Yeah. They listen and give reports to Big Mama on what goes on in here between you and Maggie. They say that— 270

> [*He stops as if embarrassed.*]

—You won't sleep with her, that you sleep on the sofa. Is that true or not true? If you don't like Maggie, get rid of Maggie!—What are you doin' there now?

BRICK: Fresh'nin' up my drink.

BIG DADDY: Son, you know you got a real liquor problem?

BRICK: Yes, sir, yes, I know. 275

BIG DADDY: Is that why you quit sports announcing, because of this liquor problem?

BRICK: Yes, sir, yes, sir, I guess so.

> [*He smiles vaguely and amiably at his father across his replenished drink.*]

BIG DADDY: Son, don't guess about it, it's too important.

BRICK: [*vaguely*] Yes, sir.

BIG DADDY: And listen to me, don't look at the damn chandelier. . . . 280

> [*Pause.* BIG DADDY*'s voice is husky.*]

—Somethin' else we picked up at th' big fire sale in Europe.

> [*another pause*]

Life is important. There's nothing else to hold onto. A man that drinks is throwing his life away. Don't do it, hold onto your life. There's nothing else to hold onto. . . .
  Sit down over here so we don't have to raise our voices, the walls have ears in this place. 285

BRICK: [*hobbling over to sit on the sofa beside him*] All right, Big Daddy.

BIG DADDY: Quit!—how'd that come about? Some disappointment?

BRICK: I don't know. Do you?

BIG DADDY: I'm askin' you, goddam it! How in hell would I know if you don't?

BRICK: I just got out there and found that I had a mouth full of cotton. I was always two 290 or three beats behind what was goin' on on the field and so I—

BIG DADDY: Quit!

BRICK: [*amiably*] Yes, quit.

BIG DADDY: Son?

BRICK: Huh? 295

BIG DADDY: [*inhales loudly and deeply from his cigar; then bends suddenly a little forward, exhaling loudly and raising a hand to his forehead*]

—Whew!—ha ha!—I took in too much smoke, it made me a little light-headed. . . .

[*The mantel clock chimes.*]

Why is it so damn hard for people to talk?

BRICK: Yeah. . . . 300

[*The clock goes on sweetly chiming till it has completed the stroke of ten.*]

—Nice peaceful-soundin' clock, I like to hear it all night. . . .

[*He slides low and comfortable on the sofa;* BIG DADDY *sits up straight and rigid with some unspoken anxiety. All his gestures are tense and jerky as he talks. He wheezes and pants and sniffs through his nervous speech, glancing quickly, shyly, from time to time, at his son.*]

BIG DADDY: We got that clock the summer we wint to Europe, me an' Big Mama on that damn Cook's Tour, never had such an awful time in my life, I'm tellin' you, son, those gooks over there, they gouge your eyeballs out in their grand hotels. And Big Mama bought more stuff than you could haul in a couple of boxcars, that's no crap. 305 Everywhere she wint on this whirlwind tour, she bought, bought, bought. Why, half that stuff she bought is still crated up in the cellar, under water last spring!

[*He laughs.*]

That Europe is nothin' on earth but a great big auction, that's all it is, that bunch of worn-out places, it's just a big fire sale, the whole rutten thing, an' Big Mama wint wild in it, why, you couldn't hold that woman with a mule's harness! Bought, bought, 310 bought!—lucky I'm a rich man, yes, siree, Bob, an' half that stuff is mildewin' in th' basement. It's lucky I'm a rich man, it sure is lucky, well, I'm a rich man, Brick, yep, I'm a mighty rich man.

[*His eyes light up for a moment.*]

Y'know how much I'm worth? Guess, Brick! Guess how much I'm worth!

[BRICK *smiles vaguely over his drink.*]

Close on ten million in cash an' blue-chip stocks, outside, mind you, of twenty-eight 315 thousand acres of the richest land this side of the valley Nile!

[*A puff and crackle and the night sky blooms with an eerie greenish glow. Children shriek on the gallery.*]

But a man can't buy his life with it, he can't buy back his life with it when his life has been spent, that's one thing not offered in the Europe fire sale or in the American markets or any markets on earth, a man can't buy his life with it, he can't buy back his life when his life is finished. . . . 320

That's a sobering thought, a very sobering thought, and that's a thought that I was turning over in my head, over and over and over—until today. . . .

I'm wiser and sadder, Brick, for this experience which I just gone through. They's one thing else that I remember in Europe.

BRICK: What is that, Big Daddy? 325

BIG DADDY: The hills around Barcelona in the country of Spain and the children running over those bare hills in their bare skins beggin' like starvin' dogs with howls and screeches, and how fat the priests are on the streets of Barcelona, so many of them and so fat and so pleasant, ha ha!—Y'know I could feed that country? I got money enough to feed that goddam country, but the human animal is a selfish beast and I don't reckon the money I passed out there to those howling children in the hills around Barcelona would more than upholster one of the chairs in this room, I mean pay to put a new cover on this chair! 330

Hell, I threw them money like you'd scatter feed corn for chickens, I threw money at them just to get rid of them long enough to climb back into th' car and— drive away. . . . 335

And then in Morocco, them Arabs, why, prostitution begins at four or five, that's no exaggeration, why, I remember one day in Marrakech, that old walled Arab city, I set on a broken-down wall to have a cigar, it was fearful hot there and this Arab woman stood in the road and looked at me till I was embarrassed, she stood stock still in the dusty hot road and looked at me till I was embarrassed. But listen to this. She had a naked child with her, a little naked girl with her, barely able to toddle, and after a while she set this child on the ground and give her a push and whispered something to her. 340

This child come toward me, barely able t' walk, come toddling up to me and— Jesus, it makes you sick t' remember a thing like this! 345

It stuck out its hand and tried to unbutton my trousers!

That child was not yet five! Can you believe me? Or do you think that I am making this up? I wint back to the hotel and said to Big Mama, "Git packed! We're clearing out of this country." . . .

BRICK: Big Daddy, you're on a talkin' jag tonight. 350

BIG DADDY: [*ignoring this remark*] Yes, sir, that's how it is, the human animal is a beast that dies but the fact that he's dying don't give him pity for others, no, sir, it— —Did you say something?

BRICK: Yes.

BIG DADDY: What? 355

BRICK: Hand me over that crutch so I can get up.

BIG DADDY: Where you goin'?

BRICK: I'm takin' a little short trip to Echo Spring.

BIG DADDY: To where?

BRICK: Liquor cabinet. . . . 360

BIG DADDY: Yes, sir, boy—

[*He hands* BRICK *the crutch.*]

—the human animal is a beast that dies and if he's got money he buys and buys and buys and I think the reason he buys everything he can buy is that in the back of his mind he has the crazy hope that one of his purchases will be life everlasting!—Which it never can be. . . . The human animal is a beast that— 365

BRICK: [*at the liquor cabinet*] Big Daddy, you sure are shootin' th' breeze here tonight.

[*There is a pause and voices are heard outside.*]

BIG DADDY: I been quiet here lately, spoke not a word, just sat and stared into space. I had something heavy weighing on my mind but tonight that load was took off me. That's why I'm talking.—The sky looks diff'rent to me. . . .

BRICK: You know what I like to hear most? 370

BIG DADDY: What?

BRICK: Solid quiet. Perfect unbroken quiet.
BIG DADDY: Why?
BRICK: Because it's more peaceful.
BIG DADDY: Man, you'll hear a lot of that in the grave.   375

[*He chuckles agreeably.*]

BRICK: Are you through talkin' to me?
BIG DADDY: Why are you so anxious to shut me up?
BRICK: Well, sir, ever so often you say to me, "Brick, I want to have a talk with you," but
    when we talk, it never materializes. Nothing is said. You sit in a chair and gas about
    this and that and I look like I listen. I try to look like I listen, but I don't listen, not   380
    much. Communication is—awful hard between people an'—somehow between you
    and me, it just don't—
BIG DADDY: Have you ever been scared? I mean have you ever felt downright terror of
    something?

[*He gets up.*]

Just one moment. I'm going to close these doors. . . .   385

[*He closes doors on gallery as if he were going to tell an important secret.*]

BRICK: What?
BIG DADDY: Brick?
BRICK: Huh?
BIG DADDY: Son, I thought I had it!
BRICK: Had what? Had what, Big Daddy?   390
BIG DADDY: Cancer!
BRICK: Oh . . .
BIG DADDY: I thought the old man made out of bones had laid his cold and heavy hand
    on my shoulder!
BRICK: Well, Big Daddy, you kept a tight mouth about it.   395
BIG DADDY: A pig squeals. A man keeps a tight mouth about it, in spite of a man not
    having a pig's advantage.
BRICK: What advantage is that?
BIG DADDY: Ignorance—of mortality—is a comfort. A man don't have that comfort, he's
    the only living thing that conceives of death, that knows what it is. The others go   400
    without knowing, which is the way that anything living should go, go without
    knowing, without any knowledge of it, and yet a pig squeals, but a man sometimes,
    he can keep a tight mouth about it. Sometimes he—

[*There is a deep, smoldering ferocity in the old man.*]

—can keep a tight mouth about it. I wonder if—
BRICK: What, Big Daddy?   405
BIG DADDY: A whiskey highball would injure this spastic condition?
BRICK: No, sir, it might do it good.
BIG DADDY: [*grins suddenly, wolfishly*] Jesus, I can't tell you! The sky is open! Christ it's
    open again! It's open, boy, it's open!

[BRICK *looks down at his drink.*]

BRICK: You feel better, Big Daddy?   410

BIG DADDY: Better? Hell! I can breathe!—All of my life I been like a doubled-up fist. . . .

[*He pours a drink.*]

—Poundin', smashin', drivin'!—now I'm going to loosen these doubled-up hands and touch things easy with them. . . .

[*He spreads his hands as if caressing the air.*]

You know what I'm contemplating? 415
BRICK: [*vaguely*] No, sir. What are you contemplating?
BIG DADDY: Ha ha!—*Pleasure!*—pleasure with *women!*

[BRICK's *smile fades a little but lingers.*]

Brick, this stuff burns me!—
—Yes, boy. I'll tell you something that you might not guess. I still have desire for women and this is my sixty-fifth birthday. 420
BRICK: I think that's mighty remarkable, Big Daddy.
BIG DADDY: Remarkable?
BRICK: Admirable, Big Daddy.
BIG DADDY: You're damn right it is, remarkable and admirable both. I realize now that I never had me enough. I let many chances slip by because of scruples about it, scruples, 425 convention—crap. . . . All that stuff is bull, bull, bull!—It took the shadow of death to make me see it. Now that shadow's lifted, I'm going to cut loose and have, what is it they call it, have me a—ball!
BRICK: A ball, huh?
BIG DADDY: That's right, a ball, a ball! Hell!—I slept with Big Mama till, let's see, five years 430 ago, till I was sixty and she was fifty-eight, and never even liked her, never did!

[*The phone has been ringing down the hall.* BIG MAMA *enters, exclaiming.*]

BIG MAMA: Don't you men hear that phone ring? I heard it way out on the gall'ry.
BIG DADDY: There's five rooms off this front gall'ry that you could go through. Why do you go through this one?

[BIG MAMA *makes a playful face as she bustles out the hall door.*]

Hunh!—Why, when Big Mama goes out of a room, I can't remember what that 435 woman looks like, but when Big Mama comes back into the room, boy, then I see what she looks like, and I wish I didn't!

[*Bends over laughing at this joke till it hurts his guts and he straightens with a grimace. The laugh subsides to a chuckle as he puts the liquor glass a little distrustfully down on the table.*]

[BRICK *has risen and hobbled to the gallery doors.*]

Hey! Where you goin'?
BRICK: Out for a breather.
BIG DADDY: Not yet you ain't. Stay here till this talk is finished, young fellow. 440
BRICK: I thought it was finished, Big Daddy.
BIG DADDY: It ain't even begun.
BRICK: My mistake. Excuse me. I just wanted to feel that river breeze.
BIG DADDY: Turn on the ceiling fan and set back down in that chair.

[BIG MAMA's *voice rises, carrying down the hall.*]

BIG MAMA: Miss Sally, you're a case! You're a caution, Miss Sally. Why didn't you give me   445
a chance to explain it to you?

BIG DADDY: Jesus, she's talking to my old maid sister again.

BIG MAMA: Well, goodbye, now, Miss Sally. You come down real soon, Big Daddy's dying
to see you! Yaisss, goodbye, Miss Sally. . . .

[*She hangs up and bellows with mirth.* BIG DADDY *groans and covers his ears as
she approaches.*]

[*Bursting in:*]

Big Daddy, that was Miss Sally callin' from Memphis again! You know what she   450
done, Big Daddy? She called her doctor in Memphis to git him to tell her what
that spastic thing is! Ha-*HAAAA!*—And called back to tell me how relieved she was
that—Hey! Let me in!

[BIG DADDY *has been holding the door half closed against her.*]

BIG DADDY: Naw I ain't. I told you not to come and go through this room. You just back
out and go through those five other rooms.   455

BIG MAMA: Big Daddy? Big Daddy? Oh, Big Daddy!—You didn't mean those things you
said to me, did you?

[*He shuts door firmly against her but she still calls.*]

Sweetheart? Sweetheart? Big Daddy? You didn't mean those awful things you said to
me?—I know you didn't. I know you didn't mean those things in your heart. . . .

[*The childlike voice fades with a sob and her heavy footsteps retreat down the hall.*
BRICK *has risen once more on his crutches and starts for the gallery again.*]

BIG DADDY: All I ask of that woman is that she leave me alone. But she can't admit to   460
herself that she makes me sick. That comes of having slept with her too many years.
Should of quit much sooner but that old woman she never got enough of it—and
I was good in bed. . . . I never should of wasted so much of it on her. . . . They say
you got just so many and each one is numbered. Well, I got a few left in me, a few,
and I'm going to pick me a good one to spend 'em on! I'm going to pick me a choice   465
one, I don't care how much she costs, I'll smother her in—minks! Ha ha! I'll strip
her naked and smother her in minks and choke her with diamonds! Ha ha! I'll strip
her naked and choke her with diamonds and smother her with minks and hump her
from hell to breakfast. *Ha aha ha ha ha!*

MAE: [*gaily at door*] Who's that laughin' in there?   470

GOOPER: Is Big Daddy laughin' in there?

BIG DADDY: Crap!—them two—*drips.* . . .

[*He goes over and touches* BRICK's *shoulder.*]

Yes, son. Brick, boy.—I'm—*happy!* I'm happy, son, I'm happy!

[*He chokes a little and bites his under lip, pressing his head quickly, shyly against
his son's head and then, coughing with embarrassment, goes uncertainly back to
the table where he set down the glass. He drinks and makes a grimace as it burns
his guts.* BRICK *sighs and rises with effort.*]

What makes you so restless? Have you got ants in your britches?

BRICK: Yes, sir. . . .   475
BIG DADDY: Why?
BRICK: —Something—hasn't happened. . . .
BIG DADDY: Yeah? What is that!
BRICK: [*sadly*]—the click. . . .
BIG DADDY: Did you say "click"?   480
BRICK: Yes, click.
BIG DADDY: What click?
BRICK: A click that I get in my head that makes me peaceful.
BIG DADDY: I sure in hell don't know what you're talking about, but it disturbs me.
BRICK: It's just a mechanical thing.   485
BIG DADDY: What is a mechanical thing?
BRICK: This click that I get in my head that makes me peaceful. I got to drink till I get it.
    It's just a mechanical thing, something like a—like a—like a—
BIG DADDY: Like a—
BRICK: Switch clicking off in my head, turning the hot light off and the cool night on   490
    and—

> [*He looks up, smiling sadly.*]

—all of a sudden there's—peace!
BIG DADDY: [*whistles long and soft with astonishment; he goes back to* BRICK *and clasps his
    son's two shoulders*] Jesus! I didn't know it had gotten that bad with you. Why, boy,
    you're—*alcoholic!*   495
BRICK: That's the truth, Big Daddy. I'm alcoholic.
BIG DADDY: This shows how I—let things go!
BRICK: I have to hear that little click in my head that makes me peaceful. Usually I hear it
    sooner than this, sometimes as early as—noon, but—
    —Today it's—dilatory. . . .   500
    —I just haven't got the right level of alcohol in my bloodstream yet!

> [*This last statement is made with energy as he freshens his drink.*]

BIG DADDY: Uh—huh. Expecting death made me blind. I didn't have no idea that a son
    of mine was turning into a drunkard under my nose.
BRICK: [*gently*] Well, now you do, Big Daddy, the news has penetrated.
BIG DADDY: Uh-huh, yes, now I do, the news has—penetrated. . . .   505
BRICK: And so if you'll excuse me—
BIG DADDY: No, I won't excuse you.
BRICK: —I'd better sit by myself till I hear that click in my head, it's just a mechanical
    thing but it don't happen except when I'm alone or talking to no one. . . .
BIG DADDY: You got a long, long time to sit still, boy, and talk to no one, but now you're   510
    talkin' to me. At least I'm talking to you. And you set there and listen until I tell you
    the conversation is over!
BRICK: But this talk is like all the others we've ever had together in our lives! It's nowhere,
    nowhere!—it's—it's *painful*, Big Daddy. . . .
BIG DADDY: All right, then let it be painful, but don't you move from that chair!—I'm   515
    going to remove that crutch. . . .

> [*He seizes the crutch and tosses it across room.*]

BRICK: I can hop on one foot, and if I fall, I can crawl!
BIG DADDY: If you ain't careful you're gonna crawl off this plantation and then, by Jesus,
    you'll have to hustle your drinks along Skid Row!

BRICK: That'll come, Big Daddy.   520
BIG DADDY: Naw, it won't. You're my son and I'm going to straighten you out; now that
    I'm straightened out, I'm going to straighten out you!
BRICK: Yeah?
BIG DADDY: Today the report come in from Ochsner Clinic. Y'know what they told me?

    [*His face glows with triumph.*]

The only thing that they could detect with all the instruments of science in that   525
great hospital is a little spastic condition of the colon! And nerves torn to pieces by
all that worry about it.

    [*A little girl bursts into room with a sparkler clutched in each fist, hops and
    shrieks like a monkey gone mad and rushes back out again as* BIG DADDY *strikes
    at her.*]

    [*Silence. The two men stare at each other. A woman laughs gaily outside.*]

I want you to know I breathed a sigh of relief almost as powerful as the Vicksburg
tornado!
BRICK: You weren't ready to go?   530
BIG DADDY: GO WHERE?—crap. . . .
    —When you are gone from here, boy, you are long gone and no where! The
human machine is not no different from the animal machine or the fish machine
or the bird machine or the reptile machine or the insect machine! It's just a whole
goddam lot more complicated and consequently more trouble to keep together. Yep.   535
I thought I had it. The earth shook under my foot, the sky come down like the black
lid of a kettle and I couldn't breathe!—Today!!—that lid was lifted, I drew my first
free breath in—how many years?—*God!*—three. . . .

    [*There is laughter outside, running footsteps, the soft, plushy sound and light of
    exploding rockets.*]

    [BRICK *stares at him soberly for a long moment; then makes a sort of startled sound
    in his nostrils and springs up on one foot and hops across the room to grab his crutch,
    swinging on the furniture for support. He gets the crutch and flees as if in horror for
    the gallery. His father seizes him by the sleeve of his white silk pajamas.*]

Stay here, you son of a bitch!—till I say go!
BRICK: I can't.   540
BIG DADDY: You sure in hell will, goddamn it.
BRICK: No, I can't. We talk, you talk, in—circles! We get no where, no where! It's always the
    same, you say you want to talk to me and don't have a ruttin' thing to say to me!
BIG DADDY: Nothin' to say when I'm tellin' you I'm going to live when I thought I was
    dying?!   545
BRICK: Oh—*that!*—Is that what you have to say to me?
BIG DADDY: Why, you son of a bitch! Ain't that, ain't that—*important?!*
BRICK: Well, you said that, that's said, and now I—
BIG DADDY: Now you set back down.
BRICK: You're all balled up, you—   550
BIG DADDY: I ain't balled up!
BRICK: You are, you're all balled up!
BIG DADDY: Don't tell me what I am, you drunken whelp! I'm going to tear this coat sleeve
    off if you don't set down!
BRICK: Big Daddy—   555

BIG DADDY: Do what I tell you! I'm the boss here, now! I want you to know I'm back in the driver's seat now!

[BIG MAMA *rushes in, clutching her great heaving bosom.*]

What in hell do you want in here, Big Mama?

BIG MAMA: Oh, Big Daddy! Why are you shouting like that? I just cain't *stainnnnnnnd—it.* . . .   560

BIG DADDY: [*raising the back of his hand above his head*] GIT!—outa here.

[*She rushes back out, sobbing.*]

BRICK: [*softly, sadly*] Christ. . . .

BIG DADDY: [*fiercely*] Yeah! Christ!—is right. . . .

[BRICK *breaks loose and hobbles toward the gallery.*]

[BIG DADDY *jerks his crutch from under* BRICK *so he steps with the injured ankle. He utters a hissing cry of anguish, clutches a chair and pulls it over on top of him on the floor.*]

Son of a—tub of—hog fat. . . .

BRICK: Big Daddy! Give me my crutch.   565

[BIG DADDY *throws the crutch out of reach.*]

Give me that crutch, Big Daddy.

BIG DADDY: Why do you drink?

BRICK: Don't know, give me my crutch!

BIG DADDY: You better think why you drink or give up drinking!

BRICK: Will you please give me my crutch so I can get up off this floor?   570

BIG DADDY: First you answer my question. Why do you drink? Why are you throwing your life away, boy, like somethin' disgusting you picked up on the street?

BRICK: [*getting onto his knees*] Big Daddy, I'm in pain, I stepped on that foot.

BIG DADDY: Good! I'm glad you're not too numb with the liquor in you to feel some pain!   575

BRICK: You—spilled my—drink. . . .

BIG DADDY: I'll make a bargain with you. You tell me why you drink and I'll hand you one. I'll pour you the liquor myself and hand it to you.

BRICK: Why do I drink?

BIG DADDY: Yea! Why?   580

BRICK: Give me a drink and I'll tell you.

BIG DADDY: Tell me first!

BRICK: I'll tell you in one word.

BIG DADDY: What word?

BRICK: DISGUST!   585

[*The clock chimes softly, sweetly.* BIG DADDY *gives it a short, outraged glance.*]

Now how about that drink?

BIG DADDY: What are you disgusted with? You got to tell me that, first. Otherwise being disgusted don't make no sense!

BRICK: Give me my crutch.

BIG DADDY: You heard me, you got to tell me what I asked you first.   590

BRICK: I told you, I said to kill my disgust!

BIG DADDY: DISGUST WITH WHAT!

BRICK: You strike a hard bargain.

BIG DADDY: What are you disgusted with?—an' I'll pass you the liquor.

BRICK: I can hop on one foot, and if I fall, I can crawl.   595

BIG DADDY: You want liquor that bad?

BRICK: [*dragging himself up, clinging to bedstead*] Yeah, I want it that bad.

BIG DADDY: If I give you a drink, will you tell me what it is you're disgusted with, Brick?

BRICK: Yes, sir, I will try to.

> [*The old man pours him a drink and solemnly passes it to him.*]

> [*There is silence as* BRICK *drinks.*]

Have you ever heard the word "mendacity"?   600

BIG DADDY: Sure. Mendacity is one of them five-dollar words that cheap politicians throw
    back and forth at each other.

BRICK: You know what it means?

BIG DADDY: Don't it mean lying and liars?

BRICK: Yes, sir, lying and liars.   605

BIG DADDY: Has someone been lying to you?

CHILDREN: [*chanting in chorus offstage*]
    We want Big Dad-dee!
    We want Big Dad-dee!

> [GOOPER *appears in the gallery door.*]

GOOPER: Big Daddy, the kiddies are shouting for you out there.   610

BIG DADDY: [*fiercely*] Keep out, Gooper!

GOOPER: 'Scuse *me!*

> [BIG DADDY *slams the doors after* GOOPER.]

BIG DADDY: Who's been lying to you, has Margaret been lying to you, has your wife been
    lying to you about something, Brick?

BRICK: Not her. That wouldn't matter.   615

BIG DADDY: Then who's been lying to you, and what about?

BRICK: No one single person and no one lie. . . .

BIG DADDY: Then what, what then, for Christ's sake?

BRICK: The whole, the whole—thing. . . .

BIG DADDY: Why are you rubbing your head? You got a headache?   620

BRICK: No, I'm tryin' to—

BIG DADDY: —Concentrate, but you can't because your brain's all soaked with liquor, is
    that the trouble? Wet brain!

> [*He snatches the glass from* BRICK'*s hand.*]

What do you know about this mendacity thing? Hell! I could write a book on it!
Don't you know that? I could write a book on it and still not cover the subject? Well,   625
I could, I could write a goddam book on it and still not cover the subject anywhere
near enough!!—Think of all the lies I got to put up with!—Pretenses! Ain't that
mendacity? Having to pretend stuff you don't think or feel or have any idea of?
Having for instance to act like I care for Big Mama!—I haven't been able to stand
the sight, sound, or smell of that woman for forty years now!—even when I *laid*   630
her!—regular as a piston. . . .

Pretend to love that son of a bitch of a Gooper and his wife Mae and those five same screechers out there like parrots in a jungle? Jesus! Can't stand to look at 'em!

Church!—it bores the bejesus out of me but I go!—I go an' sit there and listen to the fool preacher! 635

Clubs!—Elks! Masons! Rotary!—*crap!*

[*A spasm of pain makes him clutch his belly. He sinks into a chair and his voice is softer and hoarser.*]

You I *do* like for some reason, did always have some kind of real feeling for—affection—respect yes, always. . . .

You and being a success as a planter is all I ever had any devotion to in my whole life and that's the truth. . . . 640

I don't know why, but it is!

I've lived with mendacity!—Why can't *you* live with it? Hell, you *got* to live with it, there's nothing *else* to *live* with except mendacity, is there?

BRICK: Yes, sir. Yes, sir, there is something else that you can live with!

BIG DADDY: What? 645

BRICK: [*lifting his glass*] This!—Liquor. . . .

BIG DADDY: That's not living, that's dodging away from life.

BRICK: I want to dodge away from it.

BIG DADDY: Then why don't you kill yourself, man?

BRICK: I like to drink. . . . 650

BIG DADDY: Oh, God, I can't talk to you. . . .

BRICK: I'm sorry, Big Daddy.

BIG DADDY: Not as sorry as I am. I'll tell you something. A little while back when I thought my number was up—

[*This speech should have torrential pace and fury.*]

—before I found out it was just this—spastic—colon. I thought about you. Should I 655 or should I not, if the jig was up, give you this place when I go—since I hate Gooper an' Mae an' know that they hate me, and since all five same monkeys are little Maes an' Goopers.—And I thought, No!—Then I thought, Yes!—I couldn't make up my mind. I hate Gooper and his five same monkeys and that bitch Mae! Why should I turn over twenty-eight thousand acres of the richest land this side of the valley Nile 660 to not my kind?—But why in hell, on the other hand, Brick—should I subsidize a goddam fool on the bottle?—Liked or not liked, well, maybe even—*loved!*—Why should I do that?—Subsidize worthless behavior? Rot? Corruption?

BRICK: [*smiling*] I understand.

BIG DADDY: Well, if you do, you're smarter than I am, goddam it, because I don't understand. 665 And this I will tell you frankly. I didn't make up my mind at all on that question and still to this day I ain't made out no will!—Well, now I don't have to. The pressure is gone. I can just wait and see if you pull yourself together or if you don't.

BRICK: That's right, Big Daddy.

BIG DADDY: You sound like you thought I was kidding. 670

BRICK: [*rising*] No, sir, I know you're not kidding.

BIG DADDY: But you don't care—?

BRICK: [*hobbling toward the gallery door*] No, sir, I don't care. . . .

Now how about taking a look at your birthday fireworks and getting some of that cool breeze off the river? 675

[*He stands in the gallery doorway as the night sky turns pink and green and gold with successive flashes of light.*]

BIG DADDY: WAIT!—Brick. . . .

> [*His voice drops. Suddenly there is something shy, almost tender, in his restraining gesture.*]

Don't let's—leave it like this, like them other talks we've had, we've always—talked around things, we've—just talked around things for some rutten reason, I don't know what, it's always like something was left not spoken, something avoided because neither of us was honest enough with the—other. . . .   680

BRICK: I never lied to you, Big Daddy.

BIG DADDY: Did I ever to *you?*

BRICK: No, sir. . . .

BIG DADDY: Then there is at least two people that never lied to each other.

BRICK: But we've never *talked* to each other.   685

BIG DADDY: We can *now.*

BRICK: Big Daddy, there don't seem to be anything much to say.

BIG DADDY: You say that you drink to kill your disgust with lying.

BRICK: You said to give you a reason.

BIG DADDY: Is liquor the only thing that'll kill this disgust?   690

BRICK: Now. Yes.

BIG DADDY: But not once, huh?

BRICK: Not when I was still young an' believing. A drinking man's someone who wants to forget he isn't still young an' believing.

BIG DADDY: Believing what?   695

BRICK: Believing. . . .

BIG DADDY: Believing *what?*

BRICK: [*stubbornly evasive*] Believing. . . .

BIG DADDY: I don't know what the hell you mean by "believing" and I don't think you know what you mean by "believing" but if you still got sports in your blood, go back   700
to sports announcing and—

BRICK: Sit in a glass box watching games I can't play? Describing what I can't do while players do it? Sweating out their disgust and confusion in contests I'm not fit for? Drinkin' a Coke, half bourbon, so I can stand it? That's no goddam good any more, no help—time just outran me, Big Daddy—got there first. . . .   705

BIG DADDY: I think you're passing the buck.

BRICK: You know many drinkin' men?

BIG DADDY: [*with a slight, charming smile*] I have known a fair number of that species.

BRICK: Could any of them tell you why he drank?

BIG DADDY: Yep, you're passin' the buck to things like time and disgust with "mendacity"   710
and—crap!—if you got to use that kind of language about a thing, it's ninety-proof bull, and I'm not buying any.

BRICK: I had to give you a reason to get a drink!

BIG DADDY: You started drinkin' when your friend Skipper died.

> [*Silence for five beats. Then* BRICK *makes a startled movement, reaching for his crutch.*]

BRICK: What are you suggesting?   715

BIG DADDY: I'm suggesting nothing.

> [*The shuffle and clop of* BRICK's *rapid hobble away from his father's steady, grave attention.*]

—But Gooper an' Mae suggested that there was something not right exactly in your—

BRICK: [*stopping short downstage as if backed to a wall*] "Not right"?
BIG DADDY: Not, well, exactly normal in your friendship with— 720
BRICK: They suggested that, too? I thought that was Maggie's suggestion.

[BRICK'*s detachment is at last broken through. His heart is accelerated; his forehead sweat-beaded; his breath becomes more rapid and his voice hoarse. The thing
they're discussing, timidly and painfully on the side of* BIG DADDY, *fiercely,
violently on* BRICK'*s side, is the inadmissible thing that Skipper died to disavow
between them. The fact that if it existed it had to be disavowed to "keep face" in
the world they lived in, may be at the heart of the "mendacity" that* BRICK *drinks
to kill his disgust with. It may be the root of his collapse. Or maybe it is only a
single manifestation of it, not even the most important. The bird that I hope to
catch in the net of this play is not the solution of one man's psychological problem.
I'm trying to catch the true quality of experience in a group of people, that cloudy,
flickering, evanescent—fiercely charged!—interplay of live human beings in the
thundercloud of a common crisis. Some mystery should be left in the revelation of
character in a play, just as a great deal of mystery is always left in the revelation of
character in life, even in one's own character to himself. This does not absolve the
playwright of his duty to observe and probe as clearly and deeply as he legitimately
can: but it should steer him away from "pat" conclusions, facile definitions which
make a play just a play, not a snare for the truth of human experience.*]

[*The following scene should be played with great concentration, with most of the
power leashed but palpable in what is left unspoken.*]

Who else's suggestion is it, is it yours? How many others thought that Skipper and
I were—
BIG DADDY: [*gently*] Now, hold on, hold on a minute, son.—I knocked around in my time.
BRICK: What's that got to do with— 725
BIG DADDY: I said "Hold on!"—I bummed, I bummed this country till I was—
BRICK: Whose suggestion, who else's suggestion is it?
BIG DADDY: Slept in hobo jungles and railroad Y's and flophouses in all cities before I—
BRICK: Oh, *you* think so, too, you call me your son and a queer. Oh! Maybe that's why you
put Maggie and me in this room that was Jack Straw's and Peter Ochello's, in which 730
that pair of old sisters slept in a double bed where both of 'em died!
BIG DADDY: Now just don't go throwing rocks at—

[*Suddenly* REVEREND TOOKER *appears in the gallery doors, his head slightly,
playfully, fatuously cocked, with a practiced clergyman's smile, sincere as a bird call
blown on a hunter's whistle, the living embodiment of the pious, conventional lie.*]

[BIG DADDY *gasps a little at this perfectly timed, but incongruous, apparition.*]

—What're you lookin' for, Preacher?
REVEREND TOOKER: The gentleman's lavatory, ha ha!—heh, heh . . .
BIG DADDY: [*with strained courtesy*]—Go back out and walk down to the other end of the 735
gallery, Reverend Tooker, and use the bathroom connected with my bedroom, and
if you can't find it, ask them where it is!
REVEREND TOOKER: Ah, thanks.

[*He goes out with a deprecatory chuckle.*]

BIG DADDY: It's hard to talk in this place. . . .
BRICK: Son of a—! 740

BIG DADDY: [*leaving a lot unspoken*]—I seen all things and understood a lot of them, till 1910. Christ, the year that—I had worn my shoes through, hocked my—I hopped off a yellow dog freight car half a mile down the road, slept in a wagon of cotton outside the gin—Jack Straw an' Peter Ochello took me in. Hired me to manage this place which grew into this one. When Jack Straw died—why, old Peter Ochello quit   745 eatin' like a dog does when its master's dead, and died, too!

BRICK: Christ!

BIG DADDY: I'm just saying I understand such—

BRICK: [*violently*] Skipper is dead. I have not quit eating!

BIG DADDY: No, but you started drinking.   750

[BRICK *wheels on his crutch and hurls his glass across the room shouting.*]

BRICK: YOU THINK SO, TOO?

BIG DADDY: Shhh!

[*Footsteps run on the gallery. There are women's calls.*]

[BIG DADDY *goes toward the door.*]

Go way!—Just broke a glass. . . .

[BRICK *is transformed, as if a quiet mountain blew suddenly up in volcanic flame.*]

BRICK: You think so, too? You think so, too? You think me an' Skipper did, did, did!— *sodomy!*—together?   755

BIG DADDY: Hold—!

BRICK: That what you—

BIG DADDY: —*ON*—a minute!

BRICK: You think we did dirty things between us, Skipper an'—

BIG DADDY: Why are you shouting like that? Why are you—   760

BRICK: —Me, is that what you think of Skipper, is that—

BIG DADDY: —so excited? I don't think nothing. I don't know nothing. I'm simply telling you what—

BRICK: You think that Skipper and me were a pair of dirty old men?

BIG DADDY: Now that's—   765

BRICK: Straw? Ochello? A couple of—

BIG DADDY: Now just—

BRICK: —ducking sissies? Queers? Is that what you—

BIG DADDY: Shhh.

BRICK: —think?   770

[*He loses his balance and pitches to his knees without noticing the pain. He grabs the bed and drags himself up.*]

BIG DADDY: Jesus!—Whew. . . . Grab my hand!

BRICK: Naw, I don't want your hand. . . .

BIG DADDY: Well, I want yours. Git up!

[*He draws him up, keeps an arm about him with concern and affection.*]

You broken out in a sweat! You're panting like you'd run a race with—

BRICK: [*freeing himself from his father's hold*] Big Daddy, you shock me, Big Daddy, you,   775 you—shock me! Talkin' so—

[*He turns away from his father.*]

—casually!—about a—thing like that. . . .

—Don't you know how people *feel* about things like that? How, how *disgusted* they are by things like that? Why, at Ole Miss when it was discovered a pledge to our fraternity, Skipper's and mine, did a, attempted to do a, unnatural thing with— 780
We not only dropped him like a hot rock!—We told him to git off the campus, and he did, he got!—All the way to—

[*He halts, breathless.*]

BIG DADDY: —Where?

BRICK: —North Africa, last I heard!

BIG DADDY: Well, I have come back from further away than that, I have just now returned 785 from the other side of the moon, death's country, son, and I'm not easy to shock by anything here.

[*He comes downstage and faces out.*]

Always, anyhow, lived with too much space around me to be infected by ideas of other people. One thing you can grow on a big place more important than cotton!— is *tolerance!*—I grown it. 790

[*He returns toward* BRICK.]

BRICK: Why can't exceptional friendship, *real, real, deep, deep friendship!* between two men be respected as something clean and decent without being thought of as—

BIG DADDY: It can, it is, for God's sake.

BRICK: —*Fairies.* . . .

[*In his utterance of this word, we gauge the wide and profound reach of the conventional mores he got from the world that crowned him with early laurel.*]

BIG DADDY: I told Mae an' Gooper— 795

BRICK: Frig Mae and Gooper, frig all dirty lies and liars!—Skipper and me had a clean, true thing between us!—had a clean friendship, practically all our lives, till Maggie got the idea you're talking about. Normal? No!—It was too rare to be normal, any true thing between two people is too rare to be normal. Oh, once in a while he put his hand on my shoulder or I'd put mine on his, oh, maybe even, when we were 800 touring the country in pro football an' shared hotel rooms we'd reach across the space between the two beds and shake hands to say goodnight, yeah, one or two times we—

BIG DADDY: Brick, nobody thinks that that's not normal!

BRICK: Well, they're mistaken, it was! It was a pure an' true thing an' that's not normal. 805

[*They both stare straight at each other for a long moment. The tension breaks and both turn away as if tired.*]

BIG DADDY: Yeah, it's—hard t'—talk. . . .

BRICK: All right, then, let's—let it go. . . .

BIG DADDY: Why did Skipper crack up? Why have you?

[BRICK *looks back at his father again. He has already decided, without knowing that he has made this decision, that he is going to tell his father that he is dying of cancer. Only this could even the score between them: one inadmissible thing in return for another.*]

BRICK: [*ominously*] All right. You're asking for it, Big Daddy. We're finally going to have that real true talk you wanted. It's too late to stop it, now, we got to carry it through 810 and cover every subject.

[*He hobbles back to the liquor cabinet.*]

Uh-huh.

[*He opens the ice bucket and picks up the silver tongs with slow admiration of their frosty brightness.*]

Maggie declares that Skipper and I went into pro football after we left Ole Miss because we were scared to grow up. . . .

[*He moves downstage with the shuffle and clop of a cripple on a crutch. As* MAR-GARET *did when her speech became "recitative," he looks out into the house, commanding its attention by his direct, concentrated gaze—a broken, "tragically elegant" figure telling simply as much as he knows of "the Truth":*]

—Wanted to—keep on tossing—those long, long!—high, high!—passes that— 815
couldn't be intercepted except by time, the aerial attack that made us famous! And so we did, we did, we kept it up for one season, that aerial attack, we held it high!— Yeah, but—

  —that summer, Maggie, she laid the law down to me, said, Now or never, and so I married Maggie. . . . 820

BIG DADDY: How was Maggie in bed?

BRICK: [*wryly*] Great! the greatest!

  [BIG DADDY *nods as if he thought so.*]

She went on the road that fall with the Dixie Stars. Oh, she made a great show of being the world's best sport. She wore a—wore a—tall bearskin cap! A "shako," they call it, a dyed moleskin coat, a moleskin coat dyed red!—Cut up crazy! Rented 825
hotel ballrooms for victory celebrations, wouldn't cancel them when it—turned out—defeat. . . .

MAGGIE THE CAT! Ha ha!

  [BIG DADDY *nods.*]

—But Skipper, he had some fever which came back on him which doctors couldn't explain and I got that injury—turned out to be just a shadow on the X-ray plate— 830
and a touch of bursitis. . . .

  I lay in a hospital bed, watched our games on TV, saw Maggie on the bench next to Skipper when he was hauled out of a game for stumbles, fumbles!—Burned me up the way she hung on his arm!—Y'know, I think that Maggie had always felt sort of left out because she and me never got any closer together than two people just 835
get in bed, which is not much closer than two cats on a—fence humping. . . .

  So! She took this time to work on poor dumb Skipper. He was a less-than-average student at Ole Miss, you know that, don't you?!—Poured in his mind the dirty, false idea that what we were, him and me, was a frustrated case of that ole pair of sisters that lived in this room, Jack Straw and Peter Ochello!—He, poor Skipper, 840
went to bed with Maggie to prove it wasn't true, and when it didn't work out, he thought it was true!—Skipper broke in two like a rotten stick—nobody ever turned so fast to a lush—or died of it so quick. . . .

  —Now are you satisfied?

  [BIG DADDY *has listened to this story, dividing the grain from the chaff. Now he looks at his son.*]

BIG DADDY: Are *you* satisfied? 845

BRICK: With what?

BIG DADDY: That half-ass story!

BRICK: What's half-ass about it?

BIG DADDY: Something's left out of that story. What did you leave out?

> [*The phone has started ringing in the hall. As if it reminded him of something,* BRICK *glances suddenly toward the sound and says:*]

BRICK: Yes!—I left out a long-distance call which I had from Skipper, in which he made a   850
drunken confession to me and on which I hung up!—last time we spoke to each
other in our lives. . . .

> [*Muted ring stops as someone answers phone in a soft, indistinct voice in hall.*]

BIG DADDY: You hung up?

BRICK: Hung up. Jesus! Well—

BIG DADDY: Anyhow now!—we have tracked down the lie with which you're disgusted   855
and which you are drinking to kill your disgust with, Brick. You been passing the
buck. This disgust with mendacity is disgust with yourself.
You!—dug the grave of your friend and kicked him in it!—before you'd face
truth with him!

BRICK: His truth, not *mine!*   860

BIG DADDY: His truth, okay! But you wouldn't face it with him!

BRICK: Who *can* face truth? Can *you?*

BIG DADDY: Now don't start passin' the rotten buck again, boy!

BRICK: How about these birthday congratulations, these many, many happy returns of the
day, when ev'rybody but you knows there won't be any!   865

> [*Whoever has answered the hall phone lets out a high, shrill laugh; the voice becomes audible saying: "No, no, you got it all wrong! Upside down! Are you crazy?"*]

> [BRICK *suddenly catches his breath as he realizes that he has made a shocking disclosure. He hobbles a few paces, then freezes, and without looking at his father's shocked face, says:*]

Let's let's—go out, now, and—

> [BIG DADDY *moves suddenly forward and grabs hold of the boy's crutch like it was a weapon for which they were fighting for possession.*]

BIG DADDY: Oh, no, no! No one's going out! What did you start to say?

BRICK: I don't remember.

BIG DADDY: "Many happy returns when they know there won't be any"?

BRICK: Aw, hell, Big Daddy, forget it. Come on out on the gallery and look at the fireworks   870
they're shooting off for your birthday. . . .

BIG DADDY: First you finish that remark you were makin' before you cut off. "Many happy
returns when they know there won't be any"?—Ain't that what you just said?

BRICK: Look, now. I can get around without that crutch if I have to but it would be a lot
easier on the furniture an' glassware if I didn' have to go swinging along like Tarzan   875
of th'—

BIG DADDY: FINISH! WHAT YOU WAS SAYIN'!

> [*An eerie green glow shows in sky behind him.*]

BRICK: [*sucking the ice in his glass, speech becoming thick*] Leave th' place to Gooper and
Mae an' their five little same little monkeys. All I want is—

BIG DADDY: "LEAVE TH' PLACE," did you say?   880

BRICK: [*vaguely*] All twenty-eight thousand acres of the richest land this side of the valley Nile.

BIG DADDY: Who said I was "leaving the place" to Gooper or anybody? This is my sixty-fifth birthday! I got fifteen years or twenty years left in me! I'll outlive *you!* I'll bury you an' have to pay for your coffin!   885

BRICK: Sure. Many happy returns. Now let's go watch the fireworks, come on, let's—

BIG DADDY: Lying, have they been lying? About the report from th'—clinic? did they, did they—find something?—*Cancer.* Maybe?

BRICK: Mendacity is a system that we live in. Liquor is one way out an' death's the other. . . .

> [*He takes the crutch from* BIG DADDY'*s loose grip and swings out on the gallery leaving the doors open.*]

> [*A song, "Pick a Bale of Cotton," is heard.*]

MAE: [*appearing in door*] Oh, Big Daddy, the field hands are singin' fo' you!   890

BIG DADDY: [*shouting hoarsely*] BRICK! BRICK!

MAE: He's outside drinkin', Big Daddy.

BIG DADDY: BRICK!

> [MAE *retreats, awed by the passion of his voice. Children call "Brick" in tones mocking* BIG DADDY. *His face crumbles like broken yellow plaster about to fall into dust.*]

> [*There is a glow in the sky.* BRICK *swings back through the doors, slowly, gravely, quite soberly.*]

BRICK: I'm sorry, Big Daddy. My head don't work any more and it's hard for me to understand how anybody could care if he lived or died or was dying or cared about any thing but whether or not there was liquor left in the bottle and so I said what I said without thinking. In some ways I'm no better than the others, in some ways worse because I'm less alive. Maybe it's being alive that makes them lie, and being almost not alive makes me sort of accidentally truthful—I don't know but—anyway—we've been friends. . . .   895, 900

    —And being friends is telling each other the truth. . . .

> [*There is a pause.*]

You told *me!* I told *you!*

> [*A child rushes into the room and grabs a fistful of firecrackers and runs out again.*]

CHILD: [*screaming*] Bang, bang, bang, bang, bang, bang, bang, bang, bang!

BIG DADDY: [*slowly and passionately*] CHRIST—DAMN—ALL—LYING SONS OF—LYING BITCHES!   905

> [*He straightens at last and crosses to the inside door. At the door he turns and looks back as if he had some desperate question he couldn't put into words. Then he nods reflectively and says in a hoarse voice:*]

Yes, all liars, all liars, all lying dying liars!

> [*This is said slowly, slowly, with a fierce revulsion. He goes on out.*]

—Lying! Dying! Liars!

[*His voice dies out. There is a sound of a child being slapped. It rushes, hideously bawling, through room and out the hall door.*]

[**BRICK** *remains motionless as the lights dim out and the curtain falls.*]

CURTAIN

ACT III

There is no lapse of time. MAE *enters with* REVEREND TOOKER.

MAE: Where is Big Daddy! Big Daddy?
BIG MAMA: [*entering*] Too much smell of burnt fireworks makes me feel a little bit sick at
    my stomach.—Where is Big Daddy?
MAE: That's what I want to know, where has Big Daddy gone?
BIG MAMA: He must have turned in, I reckon he went to baid. . . .   5

      [GOOPER *enters.*]

GOOPER: Where is Big Daddy?
MAE: We don't know where he is!
BIG MAMA: I reckon he's gone to baid.
GOOPER: Well, then, now we can talk.
BIG MAMA: What *is* this talk, *what* talk?   10

      [MARGARET *appears on gallery, talking to* DR. BAUGH.]

MARGARET: [*musically*] My family freed their slaves ten years before abolition, my great-
    great-grandfather gave his slaves their freedom five years before the War between the
    States started!
MAE: Oh, for God's sake! Maggie's climbed back up in her family tree!
MARGARET: [*sweetly*] What, Mae?—Oh, where's Big Daddy?!   15

      [*The pace must be very quick. Great Southern animation.*]

BIG MAMA: [*addressing them all*] I think Big Daddy was just worn out. He loves his family,
    he loves to have them around him, but it's a strain on his nerves. He wasn't himself
    tonight, Big Daddy wasn't himself, I could tell he was all worked up.
REVEREND TOOKER: I think he's remarkable.
BIG MAMA: Yaisss! Just remarkable. Did you all notice the food he ate at that table? Did   20
    you all notice the supper he put away? Why, he ate like a hawss!
GOOPER: I hope he doesn't regret it.
BIG MAMA: Why, that man—ate a huge piece of cawn-bread with molasses on it! Helped
    himself twice to hoppin' john.
MARGARET: Big Daddy loves hoppin' john.—We had a real country dinner.   25
BIG MAMA: [*overlapping* MARGARET] Yais, he simply adores it! An' candied yams? That
    man put away enough food at that table to stuff a nigger *field* hand!

GOOPER: [*with grim relish*] I hope he don't have to pay for it later on. . . .

BIG MAMA: [*fiercely*] What's *that*, Gooper?

MAE: Gooper says he hopes Big Daddy doesn't suffer tonight.   30

BIG MAMA: Oh, shoot, Gooper says, Gooper says! Why should Big Daddy suffer for satisfying a normal appetite? There's nothin' wrong with that man but nerves, he's
sound as a dollar! And now he knows he is an' that's why he ate such a supper. He
had a big load off his mind, knowin' he wasn't doomed t'—what he thought he was
doomed to. . . .   35

MARGARET: [*sadly and sweetly*] Bless his old sweet soul. . . .

BIG MAMA: [*vaguely*] Yais, bless his heart, where's Brick?

MAE: Outside.

GOOPER: —Drinkin' . . .

BIG MAMA: I know he's drinkin'. You all don't have to keep tellin' *me* Brick is drinkin'. 40
Cain't I see he's drinkin' without you continually tellin' me that boy's drinkin'?

MARGARET: Good for you, Big Mama!

[*She applauds.*]

BIG MAMA: Other people *drink* and *have* drunk an' will *drink*, as long as they make that
stuff an' put it in bottles.

MARGARET: That's the truth. I never trusted a man that didn't drink.   45

MAE: Gooper never drinks. Don't you trust Gooper?

MARGARET: Why, Gooper, don't you drink? If I'd known you didn't drink, I wouldn't of
made that remark—

BIG MAMA: Brick?

MARGARET: —at least not in your presence.   50

[*She laughs sweetly.*]

BIG MAMA: Brick!

MARGARET: He's still on the gall'ry. I'll go bring him in so we can talk.

BIG MAMA: [*worriedly*] I don't know what this mysterious family conference is about.

[*Awkward silence.* BIG MAMA *looks from face to face, then belches slightly and
mutters, "Excuse me. . . . " She opens an ornamental fan suspended about her
throat, a black lace fan to go with her black lace gown, and fans her wilting corsage, sniffing nervously and looking from face to face in the uncomfortable silence
as* MARGARET *calls "Brick?" and* BRICK *sings to the moon on the gallery.*]

I don't know what's wrong here, you all have such long faces! Open that door on the
hall and let some air circulate through here, will you please, Gooper?   55

MAE: I think we'd better leave that door closed, Big Mama, till after the talk.

BIG MAMA: Reveren' Tooker, will *you* please open that door?!

REVEREND TOOKER: I sure will, Big Mama.

MAE: I just didn't think we ought t' take any chance of Big Daddy hearin' a word of this
discussion.   60

BIG MAMA: I *swan!* Nothing's going to be said in Big Daddy's house that he cain't hear if
he wants to!

GOOPER: Well, Big Mama, it's—

[MAE *gives him a quick, hard poke to shut him up. He glares at her fiercely as she
circles before him like a burlesque ballerina, raising her skinny bare arms over her
head, jangling her bracelets, exclaiming:*]

MAE: *A breeze! A breeze!*

REVEREND TOOKER: I think this house is the coolest house in the Delta.—Did you all   65
     know that Halsey Banks' widow put air-conditioning units in the church and rectory
     at Friar's Point in memory of Halsey?

> [*General conversation has resumed; everybody is chatting so that the stage sounds
> like a big bird cage.*]

GOOPER: Too bad nobody cools your church off for you. I bet you sweat in that pulpit
     these hot Sundays, Reverend Tooker.
REVEREND TOOKER: Yes, my vestments are drenched.   70
MAE: [*at the same time to* DR. BAUGH] You think those vitamin B$_{12}$ injections are what
     they're cracked up t' be, Doc Baugh?
DOCTOR BAUGH: Well, if you want to be stuck with something I guess they're as good to
     be stuck with as anything else.
BIG MAMA: [*at gallery door*] *Maggie, Maggie, aren't you comin' with Brick?*   75
MAE: [*suddenly and loudly, creating a silence*] *I have a strange feeling, I have a peculiar
     feeling!*
BIG MAMA: [*turning from gallery*] What feeling?
MAE: That Brick said somethin' he shouldn't of said t' Big Daddy.
BIG MAMA: Now what on earth could Brick of said t' Big Daddy that he shouldn't say?   80
GOOPER: Big Mama, there's somethin'—
MAE: NOW, WAIT!

> [*She rushes up to* BIG MAMA *and gives her a quick hug and kiss.* BIG MAMA
> *pushes her impatiently off as the* REVEREND TOOKER'*s voice rises serenely in a
> little pocket of silence:*]

REVEREND TOOKER: Yes, last Sunday the gold in my chasuble faded into th' purple. . . .
GOOPER: Reveren', you must of been preachin' hell's fire last Sunday!

> [*He guffaws at this witticism but the* REVEREND *is not sincerely amused. At the
> same time* BIG MAMA *has crossed over to* DR. BAUGH *and is saying to him:*]

BIG MAMA: [*her breathless voice rising high-pitched above the others*]   85
     In my day they had what they call the Keeley cure for heavy drinkers. But now I
     understand they just take some kind of tablets, they call them "Annie Bust" tablets.
     But *Brick* don't need to take *nothin'.*

> [BRICK *appears in gallery doors with* MARGARET *behind him.*]

BIG MAMA: [*unaware of his presence behind her*] That boy is just broken up over Skipper's
     death. You know how poor Skipper died. They gave him a big, big dose of that   90
     sodium amytal stuff at his home and then they called the ambulance and give him
     another big, big dose of it at the hospital and that and all of the alcohol in his system
     fo' months an' months an' months just proved too much for his heart. . . . I'm scared
     of needles! I'm more scared of a needle than the knife. . . . I think more people have
     been needled out of this world than—   95

> [*She stops short and wheels about.*]

OH!—here's Brick! My precious baby—

> [*She turns upon* BRICK *with short, fat arms extended, at the same time uttering a
> loud, short sob, which is both comic and touching.*]

> [BRICK *smiles and bows slightly, making a burlesque gesture of gallantry for*

MAGGIE *to pass before him into the room. Then he hobbles on his crutch directly to the liquor cabinet and there is absolute silence, with everybody looking at* BRICK *as everybody has always looked at* BRICK *when he spoke or moved or appeared. One by one he drops ice cubes in his glass, then suddenly, but not quickly, looks back over his shoulder with a wry, charming smile, and says:*]

BRICK: I'm sorry! Anyone else?

BIG MAMA: [*sadly*] No, son. I *wish* you wouldn't!

BRICK: I wish I didn't have to, Big Mama, but I'm still waiting for that click in my head which makes it all smooth out! 100

BIG MAMA: Aw, Brick, you—BREAK MY HEART!

MARGARET: [*at the same time*] Brick, go sit with Big Mama!

BIG MAMA: I just cain't *staiiiiiiiii-nnnnnd*—it. . . .

[*She sobs.*]

MAE: Now that we're all assembled—

GOOPER: We kin talk. . . . 105

BIG MAMA: Breaks my heart. . . .

MARGARET: Sit with Big Mama, Brick, and hold her hand.

[BIG MAMA *sniffs very loudly three times, almost like three drum beats in the pocket of silence.*]

BRICK: You do that, Maggie. I'm a restless cripple. I got to stay on my crutch.

[BRICK *hobbles to the gallery door; leans there as if waiting.* MAE *sits beside* BIG MAMA, *while* GOOPER *moves in front and sits on the end of the couch, facing her.* REVEREND TOOKER *moves nervously into the space between them; on the other side,* DR. BAUGH *stands looking at nothing in particular and lights a cigar.* MARGARET *turns away.*]

BIG MAMA: Why're you all *surroundin'* me—like this? Why're you all starin' at me like this an' makin' signs at each other? 110

[REVEREND TOOKER *steps back startled.*]

MAE: Calm yourself, Big Mama.

BIG MAMA: Calm you'self, *you'self*, Sister Woman. How could I calm myself with everyone starin' at me as if big drops of blood had broken out on m' face? What's this all about, annh! What?

[GOOPER *coughs and takes a center position.*]

GOOPER: Now, Doc Baugh. 115

MAE: Doc Baugh?

BRICK: [*suddenly*] SHHH!

[*Then he grins and chuckles and shakes his head regretfully.*]

—Naw!—that wasn't th' click.

GOOPER: Brick, shut up or stay out there on the gallery with your liquor! We got to talk about a serious matter. Big Mama wants to know the complete truth about the report we got today from the Ochsner Clinic. 120

MAE: [*eagerly*]—on Big Daddy's condition!

GOOPER: Yais, on Big Daddy's condition, we got to face it.

DOCTOR BAUGH: Well. . . .

BIG MAMA: [*terrified, rising*] Is there? Something? Something that I? Don't—Know?   125

> [*In these few words, this startled, very soft, question,* BIG MAMA *reviews the history of her forty-five years with* BIG DADDY, *her great, almost embarrassingly true-hearted and simple-minded devotion to* BIG DADDY, *who must have had something* BRICK *has, who made himself loved so much by the "simple expedient" of not loving enough to disturb his charming detachment, also once coupled, like* BRICK's, *with virile beauty.*]

> [BIG MAMA *has a dignity at this moment: she almost stops being fat.*]

DOCTOR BAUGH: [*after a pause, uncomfortably*] Yes?—Well—

BIG MAMA: I!!!—want to—*knowwwwwww*. . . .

> [*Immediately she thrusts her fist to her mouth as if to deny that statement.*]

> [*Then, for some curious reason, she snatches the withered corsage from her breast and hurls it on the floor and steps on it with her short, fat feet.*]

> —Somebody must be *lyin'!*—I want to know!

MAE: Sit down, Big Mama, sit down on this sofa.

MARGARET: [*quickly*] Brick, go sit with Big Mama.   130

BIG MAMA: What is it, what is it?

DOCTOR BAUGH: I never have seen a more thorough examination than Big Daddy Pollitt was given in all my experience with the Ochsner Clinic.

GOOPER: It's one of the best in the country.

MAE: It's *THE* best in the country—bar *none!*   135

> [*For some reason she gives* GOOPER *a violent poke as she goes past him. He slaps at her hand without removing his eyes from his mother's face.*]

DOCTOR BAUGH: Of course, they were ninety-nine and nine-tenths percent sure before they even started.

BIG MAMA: Sure of what, sure of what, sure of—*what?*—*what!*

> [*She catches her breath in a startled sob.* MAE *kisses her quickly. She thrusts* MAE *fiercely away from her, staring at the doctor.*]

MAE: Mommy, be a brave girl!

BRICK: [*in the doorway, softly*]   140
>   "By the light, by the light,
>   Of the sil-ve-ry mo-ooo-n . . . "

GOOPER: Shut up!—Brick.

BRICK: —Sorry. . . .

> [*He wanders out on the gallery.*]

DOCTOR BAUGH: But now, you see, Big Mama, they cut a piece off this growth, a specimen   145
of the tissue and—

BIG MAMA: Growth? You told Big Daddy—

DOCTOR BAUGH: Now wait.

BIG MAMA: [*fiercely*] You told me and Big Daddy there wasn't a thing wrong with him but—

MAE: Big Mama, they always—   150

GOOPER: Let Doc Baugh talk, will yuh?

BIG MAMA: —little spastic condition of—

> [*Her breath gives out in a sob.*]

DOCTOR BAUGH: Yes, that's what we told Big Daddy. But we had this bit of tissue run through the laboratory and I'm sorry to say the test was positive on it. It's—well— malignant. . . .   155

[*Pause.*]

BIG MAMA: —Cancer?! Cancer?!

[DR. BAUGH *nods gravely.*]

[BIG MAMA *gives a long gasping cry.*]

MAE AND GOOPER: Now, now, now, Big Mama, you had to know. . . .
BIG MAMA: *WHY DIDN'T THEY CUT IT OUT OF HIM? HANH? HANH?*
DOCTOR BAUGH: Involved too much, Big Mama, too many organs affected.
MAE: Big Mama, the liver's affected and so's the kidneys, both! It's gone way past what they   160
call a—
GOOPER: A Surgical risk.
MAE: —Uh-huh. . . .

[BIG MAMA *draws a breath like a dying gasp.*]

REVEREND TOOKER: Tch, tch, tch, tch, tch!
DOCTOR BAUGH: Yes, it's gone past the knife.   165
MAE: That's why he's turned yellow, Mommy!
BIG MAMA: Git away from me, git away from me, Mae!

[*She rises abruptly.*]

   I want Brick! Where's Brick? Where is my only son?
MAE: Mama! Did she say "*only* son"?
GOOPER: What does that make *me?*   170
MAE: A sober responsible man with five precious children!—*Six!*
BIG MAMA: I want Brick to tell me! Brick! Brick!
MARGARET: [*rising from her reflections in a corner*] Brick was so upset he went back out.
BIG MAMA: Brick!
MARGARET: Mama, let *me* tell you!
BIG MAMA: No, no, leave me alone, you're not my blood!   175
GOOPER: Mama, I'm your son! Listen to *me!*
MAE: Gooper's your son, Mama, he's your first-born!
BIG MAMA: Gooper never liked Daddy.
MAE: [*as if terribly shocked*] *That's not TRUE!*

[*There is a pause. The minister coughs and rises.*]

REVEREND TOOKER: [*to* MAE] I think I'd better slip away at this point.   180
MAE: [*sweetly and sadly*] Yes, Doctor Tooker, you go.
REVEREND TOOKER: [*discreetly*] Goodnight, goodnight, everybody, and God bless you all
   . . . on this place. . . .

[*He slips out.*]

DOCTOR BAUGH: That man is a good man but lacking in tact. Talking about people giving memorial windows—if he mentioned one memorial window, he must have   185
spoke of a dozen, and saying how awful it was when somebody died intestate, the
legal wrangles, and so forth.

[MAE *coughs, and points at* BIG MAMA.]

DOCTOR BAUGH: Well, Big Mama. . . .

[*He sighs.*]

BIG MAMA: It's all a mistake, I know it's just a bad dream.
DOCTOR BAUGH: We're gonna keep Big Daddy as comfortable as we can.   190
BIG MAMA: Yes, it's just a bad dream, that's all it is, it's just an awful dream.
GOOPER: In my opinion Big Daddy is having some pain but won't admit that he has it.
BIG MAMA: Just a dream, a bad dream.
DOCTOR BAUGH: That's what lots of them do, they think if they don't admit they're
    having the pain they can sort of escape the fact of it.   195
GOOPER: [*with relish*] Yes, they get sly about it, they get real sly about it.
MAE: Gooper and I think—
GOOPER: Shut up, Mae!—Big Daddy ought to be started on morphine.
BIG MAMA: Nobody's going to give Big Daddy morphine.
DOCTOR BAUGH: Now, Big Mama, when that pain strikes it's going to strike mighty hard   200
    and Big Daddy's going to need the needle to bear it.
BIG MAMA: I tell you, nobody's going to give him morphine.
MAE: Big Mama, you don't want to see Big Daddy suffer, you know you—

[GOOPER *standing beside her gives her a savage poke.*]

DOCTOR BAUGH: [*placing a package on the table*] I'm leaving this stuff here, so if there's a
    sudden attack you all won't have to send out for it.   205
MAE: I know how to give a hypo.
GOOPER: Mae took a course in nursing during the war.
MARGARET: Somehow I don't think Big Daddy would want Mae to give him a hypo.
MAE: You think he'd want *you* to do it?

[DR. BAUGH *rises.*]

GOOPER: Doctor Baugh is goin'.   210
DOCTOR BAUGH: Yes, I got to be goin'. Well, keep your chin up, Big Mama.
GOOPER: [*with jocularity*] She's gonna keep *both* chins up, aren't you, Big Mama?

[BIG MAMA *sobs.*]

Now stop that, Big Mama.
MAE: Sit down with me, Big Mama.
GOOPER: [*at door with* DR. BAUGH] Well, Doc, we sure do appreciate all you done. I'm   215
    telling you, we're surely obligated to you for—

[DR. BAUGH *has gone out without a glance at him.*]

GOOPER: I guess that doctor has got a lot on his mind but it wouldn't hurt him to act a
    little more human. . . .

[BIG MAMA *sobs.*]

Now be a brave girl, Mommy.
BIG MAMA: It's not true, I know that it's just not true!   220
GOOPER: Mama, those tests are infallible!
BIG MAMA: Why are you so determined to see your father daid?
MAE: Big Mama!
MARGARET: [*gently*] I know what Big Mama means.
MAE: [*fiercely*] Oh, do you?   225
MARGARET: [*quietly and very sadly*] Yes, I think I do.

MAE: For a newcomer in the family you sure do show a lot of understanding.

MARGARET: Understanding is needed on this place.

MAE: I guess you must have needed a lot of it in your family, Maggie, with your father's liquor problem and now you've got Brick with his! 230

MARGARET: Brick does not have a liquor problem at all. Brick is devoted to Big Daddy. This thing is a terrible strain on him.

BIG MAMA: Brick is Big Daddy's boy, but he drinks too much and it worries me and Big Daddy, and, Margaret, you've got to cooperate with us, you've got to cooperate with Big Daddy and me in getting Brick straightened out. Because it will break Big Daddy's 235 heart if Brick don't pull himself together and take hold of things.

MAE: Take hold of *what* things, Big Mama?

BIG MAMA: The place.

[*There is a quick violent look between* MAE *and* GOOPER.]

GOOPER: Big Mama, you've had a shock.

MAE: Yais, we've all had a shock, but . . . 240

GOOPER: Let's be realistic—

MAE: —Big Daddy would never, would never, be foolish enough to—

GOOPER: —put this place in irresponsible hands!

BIG MAMA: Big Daddy ain't going to leave the place in anybody's hands; Big Daddy is *not* going to die. I want you to get that in your heads, all of you! 245

MAE: Mommy, Mommy, Big Mama, we're just as hopeful an' optimistic as you are about Big Daddy's prospects, we have faith in *prayer*—but nevertheless there are certain matters that have to be discussed an' dealt with, because otherwise—

GOOPER: Eventualities have to be considered and now's the time. . . . Mae, will you please get my briefcase out of our room? 250

MAE: Yes, honey.

[*She rises and goes out through the hall door.*]

GOOPER: [*standing over* BIG MAMA] Now, Big Mom. What you said just now was not at all true and you know it. I've always loved Big Daddy in my own quiet way. I never made a show of it, and I know that Big Daddy has always been fond of me in a quiet way, too, and he never made a show of it, neither. 255

[MAE *returns with* GOOPER'*s briefcase.*]

MAE: Here's your briefcase, Gooper, honey.

GOOPER: [*handing the briefcase back to her*] Thank you. . . . Of ca'use, my relationship with Big Daddy is different from Brick's.

MAE: You're eight years older'n Brick an' always had t' carry a bigger load of th' responsibilities than Brick ever had t' carry. He never carried a thing in his life but a football or 260 a highball.

GOOPER: Mae, will y' let me talk, please?

MAE: Yes, honey.

GOOPER: Now, a twenty-eight-thousand-acre plantation's a mighty big thing t' run.

MAE: Almost singlehanded. 265

[MARGARET *has gone out onto the gallery, and can be heard calling softly* BRICK.]

BIG MAMA: You never had to run this place! What are you talking about? As if Big Daddy was dead and in his grave, you had to run it? Why, you just helped him out with a few business details and had your law practice at the same time in Memphis!

MAE: Oh, Mommy, Mommy, Big Mommy! Let's be fair! Why, Gooper has given himself

body and soul to keeping this place up for the past five years since Big Daddy's health 270
started failing. Gooper won't say it, Gooper never thought of it as a duty, he just
did it. And what did Brick do? Brick kept living in his past glory at college! Still a
football player at twenty-seven!

MARGARET: [*returning alone*] Who are you talking about, now? Brick? A football player?
He isn't a football player and you know it. Brick is a sports announcer on TV and 275
one of the best-known ones in the country!

MAE: I'm talking about what he was.

MARGARET: Well, I wish you would just stop talking about my husband.

GOOPER: I've got a right to discuss my brother with other members of MY OWN family
which don't include *you*. Why don't you go out there and drink with Brick? 280

MARGARET: I've never seen such malice toward a brother.

GOOPER: How about his for me? Why, he can't stand to be in the same room with me!

MARGARET: This is a deliberate campaign of vilification for the most disgusting and sor-
did reason on earth, and I know what it is! It's *avarice, avarice, greed, greed!*

BIG MAMA: Oh, I'll scream! I will scream in a moment unless this stops! 285

> [GOOPER *has stalked up to* MARGARET *with clenched fists at his sides as if*
> *he would strike her.* MAE *distorts her face again into a hideous grimace behind*
> MARGARET*'s back.*]

MARGARET: We only remain on the place because of Big Mom and Big Daddy. If it is true
what they say about Big Daddy we are going to leave here just as soon as it's over.
Not a moment later.

BIG MAMA: [*sobs*] Margaret. Child. Come here. Sit next to Big Mama.

MARGARET: Precious Mommy. I'm sorry, I'm so sorry, I—! 290

> [*She bends her long graceful neck to press her forehead to* BIG MAMA*'s bulging*
> *shoulder under its black chiffon.*]

GOOPER: How beautiful, how touching, this display of devotion!

MAE: Do you know why she's childless? She's childless because that big beautiful athlete
husband of hers won't go to bed with her!

GOOPER: You jest won't let me do this in a nice way, will yah? Aw right—Mae and I have
five kids with another one coming! I don't give a goddam if Big Daddy likes me or 295
don't like me or did or never did or will or will never! I'm just appealing to a sense
of common decency and fair play. I'll tell you the truth. I've resented Big Daddy's
partiality to Brick ever since Brick was born, and the way I've been treated like I was
just barely good enough to spit on and sometimes not even good enough for that.
Big Daddy is dying of cancer, and it's spread all through him and it's attacked all his 300
vital organs including the kidneys and right now he is sinking into uremia, and you
all know what uremia is, it's poisoning of the whole system due to the failure of the
body to eliminate its poisons.

MARGARET: [*to herself, downstage, hissingly*] *Poisons, poisons! Venomous thoughts and words!*
In hearts and minds!—That's poisons! 305

GOOPER: [*overlapping her*] I am asking for a square deal, and I expect to get one. But if I
don't get one, if there's any peculiar shenanigans going on around here behind my
back, or before me, well, I'm not a corporation lawyer for nothing, I know how to
protect my own interests.—*OH! A late arrival!*

> [BRICK *enters from the gallery with a tranquil, blurred smile, carrying an empty*
> *glass with him.*]

MAE: Behold the conquering hero comes! 310

GOOPER: The fabulous Brick Pollitt! Remember him?—Who could forget him!

MAE: He looks like he's been injured in a game!

GOOPER: Yep, I'm afraid you'll have to warm the bench at the Sugar Bowl this year, Brick!

> [MAE *laughs shrilly.*]

Or was it the Rose Bowl that he made that famous run in?

MAE: The punch bowl, honey. It was in the punch bowl, the cut-glass punch bowl! 315

GOOPER: Oh, that's right, I'm getting the bowls mixed up!

MARGARET: Why don't you stop venting your malice and envy on a sick boy?

BIG MAMA: *Now you two hush, I mean it, hush, all of you, hush!*

GOOPER: All right, Big Mama. A family crisis brings out the best and the worst in every member of it. 320

MAE: *That's* the truth.

MARGARET: *Amen!*

BIG MAMA: I said, "hush!" I won't tolerate any more catty talk in my house.

> [MAE *gives* GOOPER *a sign indicating briefcase.*]

> [BRICK's *smile has grown both brighter and vaguer. As he prepares a drink, he sings softly:*]

BRICK:
> *Show me the way to go home,*
> *I'm tired and I wanta go to bed,* 325
> *I had a little drink about an hour ago—*

GOOPER: [*at the same time*] Big Mama, you know it's necessary for me t' go back to Memphis in th' mornin' t' represent the Parker estate in a lawsuit.

> [MAE *sits on the bed and arranges papers she has taken from the briefcase.*]

BRICK: [*continuing the song*]
> *Wherever I may roam,* 330
> *On land or sea or foam.*

BIG MAMA: Is it, Gooper?

MAE: Yaiss.

GOOPER: That's why I'm forced to—to bring up a problem that—

MAE: Somethin' that's too important t' be put off! 335

GOOPER: If Brick was sober, he ought to be in on this.

MARGARET: Brick is present; we're here.

GOOPER: Well, good. I will now give you this outline my partner, Tom Bullitt, an' me have drawn up—a sort of dummy—trusteeship.

MARGARET: Oh, that's it! You'll be in charge an' dole out remittances, will you? 340

GOOPER: This we did as soon as we got the report on Big Daddy from th' Ochsner Laboratories. We did this thing, I mean we drew up this dummy outline with the advice and assistance of the Chairman of the Boa'd of Directors of th' Southern Plantahs Bank and Trust Company in Memphis, C.C. Bellowes, a man who handles estates for all th' prominent fam'lies in West Tennessee and th' Delta. 345

BIG MAMA: Gooper?

GOOPER: [*crouching in front of* BIG MAMA] Now this is not—not final, or anything like it. This is just a preliminary outline. But it does provide a basis—a design—a— possible, feasible—*plan!*

MARGARET: Yes, I'll bet. 350

MAE: It's a plan to protect the biggest estate in the Delta from irresponsibility an'—

BIG MAMA: Now you listen to me, all of you, you listen here! They's not goin' to be any more catty talk in my house! And Gooper, you put that away before I grab it out of your hand and tear it right up! I don't know what the hell's in it, and I don't want to know what the hell's in it. I'm talkin' in Big Daddy's language now; I'm his *wife*, not his *widow*, I'm still his *wife!* And I'm talkin' to you in his language an'—   355

GOOPER: Big Mama, what I have here is—

MAE: Gooper explained that it's just a plan. . . .

BIG MAMA: I don't care what you got there. Just put it back where it came from, an' don't let me see it again, not even the outside of the envelope of it! Is that understood? 360 Basis! Plan! Preliminary! Design! I say—what is it Big Daddy always says when he's disgusted?

BRICK: [*from the bar*] Big Daddy says "crap" when he's disgusted.

BIG MAMA: [*rising*] That's right—*CRAP!* I say *CRAP*, too, like Big Daddy!

MAE: Coarse language doesn't seem called for in this—   365

GOOPER: Somethin' in me is *deeply outraged* by hearin' you talk like this.

BIG MAMA: *Nobody's goin' to take nothin'!*—till Big Daddy lets go of it, and maybe, just possibly, not—not even then! No, not even then!

BRICK: *You can always hear me singin' this song,*
                                  Show me the way to go home.   370

BIG MAMA: Tonight Brick looks like he used to look when he was a little boy, just like he did when he played wild games and used to come home all sweaty and pink-cheeked and sleepy, with his—red curls shining. . . .

> [*She comes over to him and runs her fat shaky hand through his hair. He draws aside as he does from all physical contact and continues the song in a whisper, opening the ice bucket and dropping in the ice cubes one by one as if he were mixing some important chemical formula.*]

BIG MAMA: [*continuing*] Time goes by so fast. Nothin' can outrun it. Death commences too early—almost before you're half acquainted with life—you meet with the other. . . . 375 Oh, you know we just got to love each other an' stay together, all of us, just as close as we can, especially now that such a *black* thing has come and moved into this place without invitation.

> [*Awkwardly embracing* BRICK, *she presses her head to his shoulder.*]

> [GOOPER *has been returning papers to* MAE, *who has restored them to briefcase with an air of severely tried patience.*]

GOOPER: Big Mama? Big Mama?

> [*He stands behind her, tense with sibling envy.*]

BIG MAMA: [*oblivious of* GOOPER] Brick, you hear me, don't you?   380

MARGARET: Brick hears you, Big Mama, he understands what you're saying.

BIG MAMA: Oh, Brick, son of Big Daddy! Big Daddy does so love you! Y'know what would be his fondest dream come true? If before he passed on, if Big Daddy has to pass on, you gave him a child of yours, a grandson as much like his son as his son is like Big Daddy!   385

MAE: [*zipping briefcase shut: an incongruous sound*] Such a pity that Maggie an' Brick can't oblige!

MARGARET: [*suddenly and quietly but forcefully*] Everybody listen.

> [*She crosses to the center of the room, holding her hands rigidly together.*]

MAE: Listen to what, Maggie?

MARGARET: I have an announcement to make.

GOOPER: A sports announcement, Maggie?

MARGARET: Brick and I are going to—*have a child!*   390

[BIG MAMA *catches her breath in a loud gasp.*]

[*Pause.* BIG MAMA *rises.*]

BIG MAMA: Maggie! Brick! This is too good to believe!

MAE: That's right, too good to believe.

BIG MAMA: Oh, my, my! This is Big Daddy's dream, his dream come true! I'm going to
tell him right now before he—

MARGARET: We'll tell him in the morning. Don't disturb him now.   395

BIG MAMA: I want to tell him before he goes to sleep, I'm going to tell him his dream's
come true this minute! And Brick! A child will make you pull yourself together and
quit this drinking!

[*She seizes the glass from his hand.*]

The responsibilities of a father will—

[*Her face contorts and she makes an excited gesture; bursting into sobs, she rushes
out, crying.*]

I'm going to tell Big Daddy right this minute!   400

[*Her voice fades out down the hall.*]

[BRICK *shrugs slightly and drops an ice cube into another glass.* MARGARET
*crosses quickly to his side, saying something under her breath, and she pours the
liquor for him, staring up almost fiercely into his face.*]

BRICK: [*coolly*] Thank you, Maggie, that's a nice big shot.

[MAE *has joined* GOOPER *and she gives him a fierce poke, making a low hissing
sound and a grimace of fury.*]

GOOPER: [*pushing her aside*] Brick, could you possibly spare me one small shot of that
liquor?

BRICK: Why, help yourself, Gooper boy.

GOOPER: I will.   405

MAE: [*shrilly*] Of course we know that this is—

GOOPER: Be still, Mae!

MAE: I won't be still! I know she's made this up!

GOOPER: Goddam it, I said to shut up!

MARGARET: Gracious! I didn't know that my little announcement was going to provoke   410
such a storm!

MAE: *That* woman isn't *pregnant!*

GOOPER: Who said she was?

MAE: *She* did.

GOOPER: The doctor didn't. Doc Baugh didn't.   415

MARGARET: I haven't gone to Doc Baugh.

GOOPER: Then who'd you go to, Maggie?

MARGARET: One of the best gynecologists in the South.

GOOPER: Uh huh, uh huh!—I see. . . .

[*He takes out pencil and notebook.*]

—May we have his name, please?   420

MARGARET: No, you may not, Mister Prosecuting Attorney!

MAE: He doesn't have any name, he doesn't exist!

MARGARET: Oh, he exists all right, and so does my child, Brick's baby!

MAE: You can't conceive a child by a man that won't sleep with you unless you think
  you're—   425

[**BRICK** *has turned on the phonograph. A scat song cuts* **MAE**'*s speech.*]

GOOPER: *Turn that off!*

MAE: We know it's a lie because we hear you in here; he won't sleep with you, we hear you!
  So don't imagine you're going to put a trick over on us, to fool a dying man with a—

[*A long drawn cry of agony and rage fills the house.* **MARGARET** *turns phonograph down to a whisper.*]

[*The cry is repeated.*]

MAE: [*awed*] Did you hear that, Gooper, did you hear that?

GOOPER: Sounds like the pain has struck.   430

MAE: Go see, Gooper!

GOOPER: Come along and leave these lovebirds together in their nest!

[*He goes out first.* **MAE** *follows but turns at the door, contorting her face and hissing at* **MARGARET**.]

MAE: Liar!

[*She slams the door.*]

[**MARGARET** *exhales with relief and moves a little unsteadily to catch hold of*
  BRICK'*s arm.*]

MARGARET: Thank you for—keeping still. . . .

BRICK: Okay, Maggie.   435

MARGARET: It was gallant of you to save my face!

BRICK: —It hasn't happened yet.

MARGARET: What?

BRICK: The click. . . .

MARGARET: —the click in your head that makes you peaceful, honey?   440

BRICK: Uh-huh. It hasn't happened. . . . I've got to make it happen before I can
  sleep. . . .

MARGARET: —I—know what you—mean. . . .

BRICK: Give me that pillow in the big chair, Maggie.

MARGARET: I'll put it on the bed for you.   445

BRICK: No, put it on the sofa, where I sleep.

MARGARET: Not tonight, Brick.

BRICK: I want it on the sofa. That's where I sleep.

[*He has hobbled to the liquor cabinet. He now pours down three shots in quick
  succession and stands waiting, silent. All at once he turns with a smile and says:*]

There!

MARGARET: What?

BRICK: The *click.* . . .   450

[*His gratitude seems almost infinite as he hobbles out on the gallery with a drink. We hear his crutch as he swings out of sight. Then, at some distance, he begins singing to himself a peaceful song.*]

[MARGARET *holds the big pillow forlornly as if it were her only companion, for a few moments, then throws it on the bed. She rushes to the liquor cabinet, gathers all the bottles in her arms, turns about undecidedly, then runs out of the room with them, leaving the door ajar on the dim yellow hall.* BRICK *is heard hobbling back along the gallery, singing his peaceful song. He comes back in, sees the pillow on the bed, laughs lightly, sadly, picks it up. He has it under his arm as* MARGARET *returns to the room.* MARGARET *softly shuts the door and leans against it, smiling softly at* BRICK.]

MARGARET: Brick, I used to think that you were stronger than me and I didn't want to be overpowered by you. But now, since you've taken to liquor—you know what?—I guess it's bad, but now I'm stronger than you and I can love you more truly! Don't move that pillow. I'll move it right back if you do!
—Brick? 455

[*She turns out all the lamps but a single rose-silk-shaded one by the bed.*]

I really have been to a doctor and I know what to do and—Brick?—this is my time by the calendar to conceive!
BRICK: Yes, I understand, Maggie. But how are you going to conceive a child by a man in love with his liquor?
MARGARET: By locking his liquor up and making him satisfy my desire before I unlock it! 460
BRICK: Is that what you've done, Maggie?
MARGARET: Look and see. That cabinet's mighty empty compared to before!
BRICK: Well, I'll be a son of a—

[*He reaches for his crutch but she beats him to it and rushes out on the gallery, hurls the crutch over the rail and comes back in, panting.*]

[*There are running footsteps.* BIG MAMA *bursts into the room, her face all awry, gasping, stammering.*]

BIG MAMA: Oh, my God, oh, my God, oh, my God, where is it?
MARGARET: Is this what you want, Big Mama? 465

[MARGARET *hands her the package left by the doctor.*]

BIG MAMA: I can't bear it, oh, God! Oh, Brick! Brick, baby!

[*She rushes at him. He averts his face from her sobbing kisses.* MARGARET *watches with a tight smile.*]

My son, Big Daddy's boy! Little Father!

[*The groaning cry is heard again. She runs out, sobbing.*]

MARGARET: And so tonight we're going to make the lie true, and when that's done, I'll bring the liquor back here and we'll get drunk together, here, tonight, in this place that death has come into. . . .
—What do you say? 470
BRICK: I don't say anything. I guess there's nothing to say.
MARGARET: Oh, you weak people, you weak, beautiful people!—who give up.—What you want is someone to—

[*She turns out the rose-silk lamp.*]

—take hold of you.—Gently, gently, with love! And—   475

[*The curtain begins to fall slowly.*]

I *do* love you, Brick, I *do!*
BRICK: [*smiling with charming sadness*] Wouldn't it be funny if that was true?

CURTAIN—THE END

The Strong Breed
(1964)

n *The Strong Breed*, the dramatic action focuses on a ritual that in one form or another is found in various societies—the selection and expulsion of a scapegoat. This theme exists in *Oedipus Rex*, as well as many other plays. In Soyinka's play, the protagonist Eman's mistake lies in thinking the ritual is observed everywhere as it was in his own community, where someone willingly allowed the troubles and cares of the village to be loaded into a symbolic vessel that a "carrier" then took away down the river, thereby cleansing the community in preparation for the new year. In Eman's village, the carrier was honored for his strength, courage, and wisdom. However, in the village to which Eman has recently come, the carrier himself becomes the object of loathing and is driven from the village permanently. In this village, outsiders are chosen as carriers and then are drugged, hypnotized, and subjected to beatings and curses as well as other forms of abuse. As one of only two outsiders present in the village, Eman quickly becomes an obvious candidate to serve as the carrier.

In the first part of the play, little is revealed about Eman's past or why he is here. But as the villagers begin to close in on him, Eman relives his past and his attempt to escape its unpleasantness. In a flashback, his father reminds him that he comes from a family of carriers (the strong breed) and that he cannot escape his fate. Eventually, the villagers track down Eman and kill him, but the act fills most of them with shame and makes them question following their leaders blindly.

The Strong Breed develops a number of themes common in Soyinka's plays: the conflict between the traditional and the modern; the ongoing need to save society from its tendency to follow custom and mistaken belief unquestioningly; and the special individual, who through dedication and vision awakens the people and leads them toward better ways, even though he may become a victim of the society he seeks to benefit.

In this and his other plays, Soyinka draws his material from native sources but reinterprets it, often showing the conflict between traditional customs and modern consciousness. Soyinka, a strong advocate for peace and reconciliation in postcolonial Africa, has sought a balance between appreciation for the culture of the past and the need to alter conditions to achieve a just society. In addition to being a playwright, Soyinka is also an acclaimed poet, novelist, and essay writer. His many accomplishments were acknowledged when he became the first African dramatist to win the Nobel Prize for Literature.

The Strong Breed

Characters

EMAN, *a stranger*
SUNMA, *Jaguna's daughter*
IFADA, *an idiot*
GIRL
JAGUNA
ORAGE
THE VILLAGERS, *attendants stalwarts*

from EMAN'S *past—*
OLD MAN, *his father*
OMAE, *his betrothed*
TUTOR
PRIEST
THE VILLAGERS, *attendants*

The scenes are described briefly, but very often a darkened stage with lit areas will not only suffice but is necessary. Except for the one indicated place, there can be no break in the action. A distracting scene-change would be ruinous.

A mud house, with space in front of it. EMAN, *in light buba and trousers stands at the window, looking out. Inside,* SUNMA *is clearing the table of what looks like a modest clinic, putting the things away in the cupboard. Another rough table in the room is piled with exercise books, two or three worn text-books, etc.* SUNMA *appears agitated. Outside, just below the window crouches* IFADA. *He looks up with a shy smile from time to time, waiting for* EMAN *to notice him.*

SUNMA: [*hesitant*] You will have to make up your mind soon Eman. The lorry leaves very shortly.

> [As EMAN *does not answer,* SUNMA *continues her work, more nervously. Two villagers, obvious travellers, pass hurriedly in front of the house; the man has a small raffia sack, the woman a cloth-covered basket; the man enters first, turns and urges the woman who is just emerging to hurry.*]

SUNMA: [*Seeing them, her tone is more intense.*] Eman, are we going or aren't we? You will leave it till too late.
EMAN: [*quietly*] There is still time—if you want to go.
SUNMA: If I want to go . . . and you?

> [EMAN *makes no reply.*]

SUNMA: [*bitterly*] You don't really want to leave here. You never want to go away—even for a minute.

> [IFADA *continues his antics.* EMAN *eventually pats him on the head and the boy grins happily. Leaps up suddenly and returns with a basket of oranges which he offers to* EMAN.]

EMAN: My gift for today's festival enh?

392

[IFADA *nods, grinning.*]

EMAN: They look ripe—that's a change.　　　　　　　　　　　　　　　10

SUNMA: [*She has gone inside the room. Looks round the door.*] Did you call me?

EMAN: No. [*She goes back.*] And what will you do tonight Ifada? Will you take part in the dancing? Or perhaps you will mount your own masquerade?

[IFADA *shakes his head, regretfully.*]

EMAN: You won't? So you haven't any? But you would like to own one.

[IFADA *nods eagerly.*]

EMAN: Then why don't you make your own?　　　　　　　　　　　　15

[IFADA *stares, puzzled by this idea.*]

EMAN: Sunma will let you have some cloth you know. And bits of wool . . .

SUNMA: [*coming out*] Who are you talking to Eman?

EMAN: Ifada. I am trying to persuade him to join the young maskers.

SUNMA: [*losing control*] What does he want here? Why is he hanging around us?

EMAN: [*amazed*] What . . . ? I said Ifada, Ifada.　　　　　　　　　20

SUNMA: Just tell him to go away. Let him go and play somewhere else!

EMAN: What is this? Hasn't he always played here?

SUNMA: I don't want him here. [*rushes to the window*] Get away idiot. Don't bring your foolish face here any more, do you hear? Go on, go away from here . . .

EMAN: [*restraining her*] Control yourself Sunma. What on earth has got into you?　　25

[IFADA, *hurt and bewildered, backs slowly away.*]

SUNMA: He comes crawling around here like some horrible insect. I never want to lay my eyes on him again.

EMAN: I don't understand. It *is* Ifada you know. Ifada! The unfortunate one who runs errands for you and doesn't hurt a soul.

SUNMA: I cannot bear the sight of him.　　　　　　　　　　　　　30

EMAN: You can't do what? It can't be two days since he last fetched water for you.

SUNMA: What else can he do except that? He is useless. Just because we have been kind to him . . . Others would have put him in an asylum.

EMAN: You are not making sense. He is not a madman, he is just a little more unlucky than other children. [*looks keenly at her*] But what is the matter?　　　　　35

SUNMA: It's nothing. I only wish we had sent him off to one of those places for creatures like him.

EMAN: He is quite happy here. He doesn't bother anyone and he makes himself useful.

SUNMA: Useful! Is that one of any use to anybody? Boys of his age are already earning a living but all he can do is hang around and drool at the mouth.　　　　40

EMAN: But he does work. You know he does a lot for you.

SUNMA: Does he? And what about the farm you started for him! Does he ever work on it? Or have you forgotten that it was really for Ifada you cleared that brush. Now you have to go and work it yourself. You spend all your time on it and you have no room for anything else.　　　　　　　　　　　　　　　　　45

EMAN: That wasn't his fault. I should first have asked him if he was fond of farming.

SUNMA: Oh, so he can choose? As if he shouldn't be thankful for being allowed to live.

EMAN: Sunma!

SUNMA: He does not like farming but he knows how to feast his dumb mouth on the fruits.　　　　　　　　　　　　　　　　　　　　　　50

EMAN: But I want him to. I encourage him.

SUNMA: Well keep him. I don't want to see him any more.

EMAN: [*after some moments*] But why? You cannot be telling all the truth. What has he done?

SUNMA: The sight of him fills me with revulsion.

EMAN: [*goes to her and holds her*] What really is it? [SUNMA *avoids his eyes.*] It is almost as 55
    if you are forcing yourself to hate him. Why?

SUNMA: That is not true. Why should I?

EMAN: Then what is the secret? You've even played with him before.

SUNMA: I have always merely tolerated him. But I cannot any more. Suddenly my disgust
    won't take him any more. Perhaps . . . perhaps it is the new year. Yes, yes, it must 60
    be the new year.

EMAN: I don't believe that.

SUNMA: It must be. I am a woman, and these things matter. I don't want a mis-shape near
    me. Surely for one day in the year, I may demand some wholesomeness.

EMAN: I do not understand you. 65

    [SUNMA *is silent.*]

It was cruel of you. And to Ifada who is helpless and alone. We are the only friends
he has.

SUNMA: No, just you. I have told you, with me it has always been only an act of kindness.
    And now I haven't any pity left for him.

EMAN: No. He is not a wholesome being. 70

    [*He turns back to looking through the window.*]

SUNMA: [*half-pleading*] Ifada can rouse your pity. And yet if anything, I need more kindness
    from you. Every time my weakness betrays me, you close your mind against me . . .
    Eman . . . Eman . . .

    [*A* GIRL *comes in view, dragging an effigy by a rope attached to one of its legs.*
    She stands for a while gazing at EMAN. IFADA, *who has crept back shyly to his*
    accustomed position, becomes somewhat excited when he sees the effigy. The GIRL
    is unsmiling. She possesses in fact, a kind of inscrutability which does not make
    her hard but is unsettling.]

GIRL: Is the teacher in?

EMAN: [*smiling*] No. 75

GIRL: Where is he gone?

EMAN: I really don't know. Shall I ask?

GIRL: Yes, do.

EMAN: [*turning slightly*] Sunma, a girl outside wants to know . . .

    [SUNMA *turns away, goes into the inside room.*]

EMAN: Oh. [*returns to the* GIRL, *but his slight gaiety is lost*] There is no one at home who 80
    can tell me.

GIRL: Why are you not in?

EMAN: I don't really know. Maybe I went somewhere.

GIRL: All right. I will wait until you get back.

    [*She pulls the effigy to her, sits down.*]

EMAN: [*slowly regaining his amusement*] So you are all ready for the new year. 85

GIRL: [*without turning around*] I am not going to the festival.

EMAN: Then why have you got that?

GIRL: Do you mean my carrier? I am unwell you know. My mother says it will take away my sickness with the old year.

EMAN: Won't you share the carrier with your playmates? 90

GIRL: Oh, no. Don't you know I play alone? The other children won't come near me. Their mothers would beat them.

EMAN: But I have never seen you here. Why don't you come to the clinic?

GIRL: My mother said No.

[*gets up, begins to move off*]

EMAN: You are not going away? 95

GIRL: I must not stay talking to you. If my mother caught me . . .

EMAN: All right, tell me what you want before you go.

GIRL: [*Stops. For some moments she remains silent.*] I must have some clothes for my carrier.

EMAN: Is that all? You wait a moment.

[SUNMA *comes out as he takes down a buba from the wall. She goes to the window and glares almost with hatred at the* GIRL. *The* GIRL *retreats hastily, still impassive.*]

By the way Sunma, do you know who that girl is? 100

SUNMA: I hope you don't really mean to give her that.

EMAN: Why not? I hardly ever use it.

SUNMA: Just the same don't give it to her. She is not a child. She is as evil as the rest of them.

EMAN: What has got into you today?

SUNMA: All right, all right. Do what you wish. 105

[*She withdraws. Baffled,* EMAN *returns to the window.*]

EMAN: Here . . . will this do? Come and look at it.

GIRL: Throw it.

EMAN: What is the matter? I am not going to eat you.

GIRL: No one lets me come near them.

EMAN: But I am not afraid of catching your disease. 110

GIRL: Throw it.

[EMAN *shrugs and tosses the buba. She takes it without a word and slips it on the effigy, completely absorbed in the task.* EMAN *watches for a while, then joins* SUNMA *in the inner room.*]

GIRL: [*after a long, cool survey of* IFADA] You have a head like a spider's egg, and your mouth dribbles like a roof. But there is no one else. Would you like to play?

[IFADA *nods eagerly, quite excited.*]

GIRL: You will have to get a stick.

[IFADA *rushes around, finds a big stick and whirls it aloft, bearing down on the carrier.*]

GIRL: Wait. I don't want you to spoil it. If it gets torn I shall drive you away. Now, let me 115 see how you are going to beat it.

[IFADA *hits it gently.*]

GIRL: You may hit harder than that. As long as there is something left to hang at the end.

[*She appraises him up and down.*]

You are not very tall . . . will you be able to hang it from a tree?

[IFADA *nods, grinning happily.*]

GIRL: You will hang it up and I will set fire to it. [*then, with surprising venom*] But just because you are helping me, don't think it is going to cure you. I am the one who 120
will get well at midnight, do you understand? It is my carrier and it is for me alone.

[*She pulls at the rope to make sure that it is well attached to the leg.*]

Well don't stand there drooling. Let's go.

[*She begins to walk off, dragging the effigy in the dust.* IFADA *remains where he is for some moments, seemingly puzzled. Then his face breaks into a large grin and he leaps after the procession, belabouring the effigy with all his strength. The stage remains empty for some moments. Then the horn of a lorry is sounded and* SUNMA *rushes out. The hooting continues for some time with a rhythmic pattern.* EMAN *comes out.*]

EMAN: I am going to the village . . . I shan't be back before nightfall.
SUNMA: [*blankly*] Yes.
EMAN: [*hesitates*] Well what do you want me to do? 125
SUNMA: The lorry was hooting just now.
EMAN: I didn't hear it.
SUNMA: It will leave in a few minutes. And you did promise we could go away.
EMAN: I promised nothing. Will you go home by yourself or shall I come back for you?
SUNMA: You don't even want me here? 130
EMAN: But you have to go home haven't you?
SUNMA: I had hoped we would watch the new year together—in some other place.
EMAN: Why do you continue to distress yourself?
SUNMA: Because you will not listen to me. Why do you continue to stay where nobody wants you? 135
EMAN: That is not true.
SUNMA: It is. You are wasting your life on people who really want you out of their way.
EMAN: You don't know what you are saying.
SUNMA: You think they love you? Do you think they care at all for what you—or I—do for them? 140
EMAN: *Them?* These are your own people. Sometimes you talk as if you were a stranger too.
SUNMA: I wonder if I really sprang from here. I know they are evil and I am not. From, the oldest to the smallest child, they are nourished in evil and unwholesomeness in which I have no part.
EMAN: You knew this when you returned? 145
SUNMA: You reproach me for trying at all?
EMAN: I reproach you with nothing? But you must leave me out of your plans. I can have no part in them.
SUNMA: [*nearly pleading*] Once I could have run away. I would have gone and never looked back. 150
EMAN: I cannot listen when you talk like that.
SUNMA: I swear to you, I do not mind what happens afterwards. But you must help me tear myself away from here. I can no longer do it myself . . . It is only a little thing. And we have worked so hard this past year . . . surely we can go away for a week . . . even a few days would be enough. 155
EMAN: I have told you Sunma . . .

SUNMA: [*desperately*] Two days Eman. Only two days.

EMAN: [*distressed*] But I tell you I have no wish to go.

SUNMA: [*suddenly angry*] Are you so afraid then?

EMAN: Me? Afraid of what? 160

SUNMA: You think you will not want to come back.

EMAN: [*pitying*] You cannot dare me that way.

SUNMA: Then why won't you leave here, even for an hour? If you are so sure that your life is settled here, why are you afraid to do this thing for me? What is so wrong that you will not go into the next town for a day or two? 165

EMAN: I don't want to. I do not have to persuade you, or myself about anything. I simply have no desire to go away.

SUNMA: [*His quiet confidence appears to incense her.*] You are afraid. You accuse me of losing my sense of mission, but you are afraid to put yours to the test.

EMAN: You are wrong Sunma. I have no sense of mission. But I have found peace here and 170 I am content with that.

SUNMA: I haven't. For a while I thought that too, but I found there could be no peace in the midst of so much cruelty. Eman, tonight at least, the last night of the old year . . .

EMAN: No Sunma. I find this too distressing; you should go home now. 175

SUNMA: It is the time for making changes in one's life Eman. Let's breathe in the new year away from here.

EMAN: You are hurting yourself.

SUNMA: Tonight. Only tonight. We will come back tomorrow as early as you like. But let us go away for this one night. Don't let another year break on me in this place . . . 180 you don't know how important it is to me, but I will tell you, I will tell you on the way . . . but we must not be here today, Eman, do this one thing for me.

EMAN: [*sadly*] I cannot.

SUNMA: [*suddenly calm*] I was a fool to think it would be otherwise. The whole village may use you as they will but for me there is nothing. Sometimes I think you believe that 185 doing anything for me makes you unfaithful to some part of your life. If it was a woman then I pity her for what she must have suffered.

[EMAN *winces and hardens slowly.* SUNMA *notices nothing.*]

Keeping faith with so much is slowly making you inhuman.
[*seeing the change in* EMAN] Eman. Eman. What is it?

[*As she goes towards him,* EMAN *goes into the house.*]

SUNMA: [*apprehensive, follows him*] What did I say? Eman. Forgive me, forgive me please. 190

[EMAN *remains facing into the slow darkness of the room.* SUNMA, *distressed, cannot decide what to do.*]

I swear I didn't know . . . I would not have said it for all the world.

[*A lorry is heard taking off somewhere nearby. The sound comes up and slowly fades away into the distance.* SUNMA *starts visibly, goes slowly to the window.*]

SUNMA: [*as the sound dies off, to herself*] What happens now?

EMAN: [*joining her at the window*] What did you say?

SUNMA: Nothing.

EMAN: Was that not the lorry going off? 195

SUNMA: It was.

EMAN: I am sorry I couldn't help you.

[SUNMA, *about to speak, changes her mind.*]

EMAN: I think you ought to go home now.

SUNMA: No, don't send me away. It's the least you can do for me. Let me stay here until all the noise is over. 200

EMAN: But are you not needed at home? You have a part in the festival.

SUNMA: I have renounced it; I am Jaguna's eldest daughter only in name.

EMAN: Renouncing one's self is not so easy—surely you know that.

SUNMA: I don't want to talk about it. Will you at least let us be together tonight?

EMAN: But . . . 205

SUNMA: Unless you are afraid my father will accuse you of harbouring me.

EMAN: All right, we will go out together.

SUNMA: Go out? I want us to stay here?

EMAN: When there is so much going on outside?

SUNMA: Some day you will wish that you went away when I tried to make you. 210

EMAN: Are we going back to that?

SUNMA: No. I promise you I will not recall it again. But you must know that it was also for your sake that I tried to get us away.

EMAN: For me? How?

SUNMA: By yourself you can do nothing here. Have you not noticed how tightly we shut 215 out strangers? Even if you lived here for a lifetime, you would remain a stranger.

EMAN: Perhaps that is what I like. There is peace in being a stranger.

SUNMA: For a while perhaps. But they would reject you in the end. I tell you it is only I who stand between you and contempt. And because of this you have earned their hatred. I don't know why I say this now, except that somehow, I feel that it no longer 220 matters. It is only I who have stood between you and much humiliation.

EMAN: Think carefully before you say any more. I am incapable of feeling indebted to you. This will make no difference at all.

SUNMA: I ask for nothing. But you must know it all the same. It is true I hadn't the strength to go by myself. And I must confess this now, if you had come with me, I would have 225 done everything to keep you from returning.

EMAN: I know that.

SUNMA: You see, I bare myself to you. For days I had thought it over, this was to be a new beginning for us. And I placed my fate wholly in your hands. Now the thought will not leave me, I have a feeling which will not be shaken off, that in some way, you 230 have tonight totally destroyed my life.

EMAN: You are depressed, you don't know what you are saying.

SUNMA: Don't think I am accusing you. I say all this only because I cannot help it.

EMAN: We must not remain shut up here. Let us go and be part of the living.

SUNMA: No leave me alone. 235

EMAN: Surely you don't want to stay indoors when the whole town is alive with rejoicing.

SUNMA: Rejoicing! Is that what it seems to you? No, let us remain here. Whatever happens I must not go out until all this is over.

[*There is silence. It has grown much darker.*]

EMAN: I shall light the lamp.

SUNMA: [*eager to do something*] No, let me do it. 240

[*She goes into the inner room.* EMAN *paces the room, stops by a shelf and toys with the seed in an "ayo" board, takes down the whole board and places it on a table,*

[*playing by himself. The* GIRL *is now seen coming back, still dragging her "carrier."* IFADA *brings up the rear as before. As she comes round the corner of the house two men emerge from the shadows. A sack is thrown over* IFADA'*s head, the rope is pulled tight rendering him instantly helpless. The* GIRL *has reached the front of the house before she turns round at the sound of the scuffle. She is in time to see* IFADA *thrown over the shoulders and borne away. Her face betraying no emotion at all, the* GIRL *backs slowly away, turns and flees, leaving the "carrier" behind.* SUNMA *enters, carrying two kerosene lamps. She hangs one up from the wall.*]

EMAN: One is enough.
SUNMA: I want to leave one outside.

[*She goes out, hangs the lamp from a nail just above the door. As she turns she sees the effigy and gasps.* EMAN *rushes out.*]

EMAN: What is it? Oh, is that what frightened you?
SUNMA: I thought . . . I didn't really see it properly.

[EMAN *goes towards the object, stoops to pick it up.*]

EMAN: It must belong to that sick girl.   245
SUNMA: Don't touch it.
EMAN: Let's keep it for her.
SUNMA: Leave it alone. Don't touch it Eman.
EMAN: [*shrugs and goes back*] You are very nervous.
SUNMA: Let's go in.   250
EMAN: Wait. [*He detains her by the door, under the lamp.*] I know there is something more than you've told me. What are you afraid of tonight?
SUNMA: I was only scared by that thing. There is nothing else.
EMAN: I am not blind Sunma. It is true I would not run away when you wanted me to, but that doesn't mean I do not feel things. What does tonight really mean that it makes you   255
    so helpless?
SUNMA: It is only a mood. And your indifference to me . . . let's go in.

[EMAN *moves aside and she enters; he remains there for a moment and then follows. She fiddles with the lamp, looks vaguely round the room, then goes and shuts the door, bolting it. When she turns, it is to meet* EMAN'*s eyes, questioning.*]

SUNMA: There is a cold wind coming in.

[EMAN *keeps his gaze on her.*]

SUNMA: It was getting cold.

[*She moves guiltily to the table and stands by the "ayo" board, rearranging the seed.* EMAN *remains where he is a few moments, then brings a stool and sits opposite her. She sits down also and they begin to play in silence.*]

SUNMA: What brought you here at all, Eman? And what makes you stay?   260

[*There is another silence.*]

SUNMA: I am not trying to share your life. I know you too well by now. But at least we have worked together since you came. Is there nothing at all I deserve to know?
EMAN: Let me continue a stranger—especially to you. Those who have much to give fulfill themselves only in total loneliness.

SUNMA: Then there is no love in what you do.   265

EMAN: There is. Love comes to me more easily with strangers.

SUNMA: That is unnatural.

EMAN: Not for me. I know I find consummation only when I have spent myself for a total
stranger.

SUNMA: It seems unnatural to me. But then I am a woman. I have a woman's longings and   270
weaknesses. And the ties of blood are very strong in me.

EMAN: [*smiling*] You think I have cut loose from all these—ties of blood.

SUNMA: Sometimes you are so inhuman.

EMAN: I don't know what that means. But I am very much my father's son.

> [*They play in silence. Suddenly* EMAN *pauses listening.*]

EMAN: Did you hear that?   275

SUNMA: [*quickly*] I heard nothing . . . it's your turn.

EMAN: Perhaps some of the mummers are coming this way.

> [EMAN *about to play, leaps up suddenly.*]

SUNMA: What is it? Don't you want to play any more?

> [EMAN *moves to the door.*]

SUNMA: No. Don't go out Eman.

EMAN: If it's the dancers I want to ask them to stay. At least we won't have to miss everything.   280

SUNMA: No, no. Don't open the door. Let us keep out everyone tonight.

> [*A terrified and disordered figure bursts suddenly around the corner, past the win-
> dow and begins hammering at the door. It is* IFADA. *Desperate with terror, he
> pounds madly at the door, dumb-moaning all the while.*]

EMAN: Isn't that Ifada?

SUNMA: They are only fooling about. Don't pay any attention.

EMAN: [*looks round the window*] That is Ifada. [*begins to unbolt the door*]

SUNMA: [*pulling at his hands*] It is only a trick they are playing on you. Don't take any   285
notice Eman.

EMAN: What are you saying? The boy is out of his senses with fear.

SUNMA: No, no. Don't interfere Eman. For God's sake don't interfere.

EMAN: Do you know something of this then?

SUNMA: You are a stranger here Eman. Just leave us alone and go your own way. There is   290
nothing you can do.

EMAN: [*He tries to push her out of the way but she clings fiercely to him.*] Have you gone mad?
I tell you the boy must come in.

SUNMA: Why won't you listen to me Eman? I tell you it's none of your business. For your
own sake do as I say.   295

> [EMAN *pushes her off, unbolts the door.* IFADA *rushes in, clasps* EMAN *round the
> knees, dumb-moaning against his legs.*]

EMAN: [*manages to re-bolt the door*] What is it Ifada? What is the matter?

> [*Shouts and voices are heard coming nearer the house.*]

SUNMA: Before it's too late, let him go. For once Eman, believe what I tell you. Don't
harbour him or you will regret it all your life.

[EMAN *tries to calm* IFADA *who becomes more and more abject as the outside voices get nearer.*]

EMAN: What have they done to him? At least tell me that. What is going on Sunma?

SUNMA: [*with sudden venom*] Monster! Could you not take yourself somewhere else? 300

EMAN: Stop talking like that.

SUNMA: He could have run into the bush couldn't he? Toad! Why must he follow us with his own disasters!

VOICES OUTSIDE: It's here . . . Round the back . . . Spread, spread . . . this way . . . no, head him off . . . use the bush path and head him off . . . get some more lights . . . 305

[EMAN *listens. Lifts* IFADA *bodily and carries him into the inner room. Returns at once, shutting the door behind him.*]

SUNMA: [*slumps into a chair, resigned*] You always follow your own way.

JAGUNA: [*comes round the corner followed by* OROGE *and three men, one bearing a torch*] I knew he would come here.

OROGE: I hope our friend won't make trouble.

JAGUNA: He had better not. You, recall all the men and tell them to surround the house. 310

OROGE: But he may not be in the house after all.

JAGUNA: I know he is here . . . [*to the men*] . . . go on, do as I say.

[*He bangs on the door.*]

Teacher, open your door . . . you two stay by the door. If I need you I will call you.

[EMAN *opens the door.*]

JAGUNA: [*speaks as he enters*] We know he is here.

EMAN: Who? 315

JAGUNA: Don't let us waste time. We are grown men, teacher. You understand me and I understand you. But we must take back the boy.

EMAN: This is my house.

JAGUNA: Daughter, you'd better tell your friend. I don't think he quite knows our ways. Tell him why he must give up the boy. 320

SUNMA: Father, I . . .

JAGUNA: Are you going to tell him or aren't you?

SUNMA: Father, I beg you, leave us alone tonight . . .

JAGUNA: I thought you might be a hindrance. Go home then if you will not use your sense.

SUNMA: But there are other ways . . . 325

JAGUNA: [*turning to the men*] See that she gets home. I no longer trust her. If she gives trouble carry her. And see that the women stay with her until this is all over.

[SUNMA *departs, accompanied by one of the men.*]

JAGUNA: Now teacher . . .

OROGE: [*restrains him*] You see, Mister Eman, it is like this. Right now, nobody knows that Ifada has taken refuge here. No one except us and our men—and they know 330 how to keep their mouths shut. We don't want to have to burn down the house you see, but if the word gets around, we would have no choice.

JAGUNA: In fact, it may be too late already. A carrier should end up in the bush, not in a house. Anyone who doesn't guard his door when the carrier goes by has himself to blame. A contaminated house should be burnt down. 335

OROGE: But we are willing to let it pass. Only, you must bring him out quickly.

EMAN: All right. But at least you will let me ask you something.

JAGUNA: What is there to ask? Don't you understand what we have told you?

EMAN: Yes. But why did you pick on a helpless boy. Obviously he is not willing.

JAGUNA: What is the man talking about? Ifada is a godsend. Does he have to be willing?   340

EMAN: In my home we believe that a man should be willing.

OROGE: Mister Eman, I don't think you quite understand. This is not a simple matter at
all. I don't know what you do, but here, it is not a cheap task for anybody. No one
in his senses would do such a job. Why do you think we give refuge to idiots like
him? We don't know where he came from. One morning, he is simply there, just like   345
that. From nowhere at all. You see, there is purpose in that.

JAGUNA: We only waste time.

OROGE: Jaguna, be patient. After all, the man has been with us for some time now and
deserves to know. The evil of the old year is no light thing to load on any man's head.   350

EMAN: I know something about that.

OROGE: You do? [*turns to* JAGUNA *who snorts impatiently*] You see I told you so didn't I?
From the moment you came I saw you were one of the knowing ones.

JAGUNA: Then let him behave like a man and give back the boy.

EMAN: It is you who are not behaving like men.

JAGUNA: [*advances aggressively*] That is a quick mouth you have . . .   355

OROGE: Patience Jaguna . . . if you want the new year to cushion the land there must be
no deeds of anger. What did you mean my friend?

EMAN: It is a simple thing. A village which cannot produce its own carrier contains no
men.

JAGUNA: Enough. Let there be no more talk or this business will be ruined by some rash-   360
ness. You . . . come inside. Bring the boy out, he must be in the room there.

EMAN: Wait.

[*The men hesitate.*]

JAGUNA: [*hitting the nearer one and propelling him forward*] Go on. Have you changed
masters now that you listen to what he says?

OROGE: [*sadly*] I am sorry you would not understand Mister Eman. But you ought to know   365
that no carrier may return to the village. If he does, the people will stone him to death.
It has happened before. Surely it is too much to ask a man to give up his own soil.

EMAN: I know others who have done more.

[IFADA *is brought out, abjectly dumb-moaning.*]

EMAN: You can see him with your own eyes. Does it really have meaning to use one as
unwilling as that.   370

OROGE: [*smiling*] He shall be willing. Not only willing but actually joyous. I am the one
who prepares them all, and I have seen worse. This one escaped before I began to
prepare him for the event. But you will see him later tonight, the most joyous creature in the festival. Then perhaps you will understand.

EMAN: Then it is only a deceit. Do you believe the spirit of a new year is so easily fooled?   375

JAGUNA: Take him out. [*The men carry out* IFADA.] You see, it is so easy to talk. You say there
are no men in this village because they cannot provide a willing carrier. And yet I
heard Oroge tell you we only use strangers. There is only one other stranger in the
village, but I have not heard him offer himself [*spits*] It is so easy to talk, is it not?

[*He turns his back on him. They go off, taking* IFADA *with them, limp and
silent. The only sign of life is that he strains his neck to keep his eyes on* EMAN
till the very moment that he disappears from sight. EMAN *remains where they left
him, staring after the group.*]

[*A blackout lasting no more than a minute. The lights come up slowly and* IFADA *is seen returning to the house. He stops at the window and looks in. Seeing no one, he bangs on the sill. Appears surprised that there is no response. He slithers down on his favourite spot, then sees the effigy still lying where the* GIRL *had dropped it in her flight. After some hesitation, he goes towards it, begins to strip it of the clothing. Just then the* GIRL *comes in.*]

GIRL: Hey, Leave that alone. You know it's mine.   380

[IFADA *Pauses, then speeds up his action.*]

GIRL: I said it is mine. Leave it where you found it.

[*She rushes at him and begins to struggle for possession of the "carrier."*]

GIRL: Thief! Thief! Let it go, it is mine. Let it go. You animal, just because I let you play with it. Idiot! Idiot!

[*The struggle becomes quite violent. The* GIRL *is hanging onto the effigy and* IFADA *lifts her with it, flinging her all about. The* GIRL *hangs on grimly.*]

GIRL: You are spoiling it . . . why don't you get your own? Thief! Let it go you thief!

[SUNMA *comes in walking very fast, throwing apprehensive glances over her shoulder. Seeing the two children, she becomes immediately angry. Advances on them.*]

SUNMA: So you've made this place your playground. Get away you untrained pigs. Get out   385
of here.

[IFADA *flees at once, the* GIRL *retreats also, retaining possession of the "carrier."* SUNMA *goes to the door. She has her hand on the door when the significance of* IFADA'*s presence strikes her for the first time. She stands rooted to the spot, then turns slowly around.*]

SUNMA: Ifada! What are you doing here?

[IFADA *is bewildered.* SUNMA *turns suddenly and rushes into the house, flying into the inner room and out again.*]

Eman! Eman! Eman!

[*She rushes outside.*]

Where did he go? Where did they take him?

[IFADA *distressed, points.* SUNMA *seizes him by the arm, drags him off.*]

Take me there at once. God help you if we are too late. You loathsome thing, if you   390
let him suffer . . .

[*Her voice fades into other shouts, running footsteps, banged tins, bells, dogs, etc., rising in volume.*]

[*It is a narrow passageway between two mud-houses. At the far end one man after another is seen running across the entry, the noise dying off gradually. About half-way down the passage,* EMAN *is crouching against the wall, tense with apprehension. As the noise dies off, he seems to relax, but the alert hunted look is still in his eyes, which are ringed in a reddish colour. The rest of his body has been whitened with a floury substance. He is naked down to the waist, wears a baggy pair of trousers, calf-length, and around both feet are bangles.*]

EMAN: I will simply stay here till dawn. I have done enough. [*A window is thrown open and a* WOMAN *empties some slop from a pail. With a startled cry* EMAN *leaps aside to avoid it and the* WOMAN *puts out her head.*]

WOMAN: Oh, my head. What have I done? Forgive me neighbour . . . Eh, it's the carrier!   395

> [*Very rapidly she clears her throat and spits on him, flings the pail at him and runs off, shouting.*]

He's here. The carrier is hiding in the passage. Quickly, I have found the carrier!

> [*The cry is taken up and* EMAN *flees down the passage. Shortly afterwards his pursuers come pouring down the passage in full cry. After the last of them come* JAGUNA *and* OROGE.]

OROGE: Wait, wait. I cannot go so fast.

JAGUNA: We will rest a little then. We can do nothing anyway.

OROGE: If only he had let me prepare him.

JAGUNA: They are the ones who break first, these fools who think they were born to carry   400
suffering like a hat. What are we to do now?

OROGE: When they catch him I must prepare him.

JAGUNA: He? It will be impossible now. There can be no joy left in that one.

OROGE: Still, it took him by surprise. He was not expecting what he met.

JAGUNA: Why then did he refuse to listen? Did he think he was coming to sit down to a   405
feast. He had not even gone through one compound before he bolted. Did he think
he was taken round the people to be blessed? A woman, that is all he is.

OROGE: No, no. He took the beating well enough. I think he is the kind who would let
himself be beaten from night till dawn and not utter a sound. He would let himself
be stoned until he dropped dead.   410

JAGUNA: Then what made him run like a coward?

OROGE: I don't know. I really don't know. It is a night of curses Jaguna. It is not many
unprepared minds will remain unhinged under the load.

JAGUNA: We must find him. It is a poor beginning for a year when our own curses remain
hovering over our homes because the carrier refused to take them.   415

> [*They go. The scene changes.* EMAN *is crouching beside some shrubs, torn and bleeding.*]

EMAN: They are even guarding my house . . . as if I would go there, but I need water . . . they
could at least grant me that . . . I can be thirsty too . . . [*He pricks his ears.*] . . . there
must be a stream near by . . . [*As he looks round him, his eyes widen at a scene he encoun-
ters. An* OLD MAN, *short and vigorous looking is seated on a stool. He is also wearing calf-
length baggy trousers, white. On his head, a white cap. An* ATTENDANT *is engaged in*   420
rubbing his body with oil. Round his eyes, two white rings have already been marked.]

OLD MAN: Have they prepared the boat?

ATTENDANT: They are making the last sacrifice.

OLD MAN: Good. Did you send for my son?

ATTENDANT: He's on his way.   425

OLD MAN: I have never met the carrying of the boat with such a heavy heart. I hope nothing comes of it.

ATTENDANT: The gods will not desert us on that account.

OLD MAN: A man should be at his strongest when he takes the boat my friend. To be
weighed down inside and out is not a wise thing. I hope when the moment comes I   430
shall have found my strength.

[*Enter* EMAN, *a wrapper round his waist and a "danski" (a brief Yoruba attire) over it.*]

OLD MAN: I meant to wait until after my journey to the river, but my mind is so burdened with my own grief and yours I could not delay it. You know I must have all my strength. But I sit here, feeling it all eaten slowly away by my unspoken grief. It helps to say it out. It even helps to cry sometimes. 435

[*He signals to the* ATTENDANT *to leave them.*]

Come nearer . . . we will never meet again son. Not on this side of the flesh. What I do not know is whether you will return to take my place.

EMAN: I will never come back.

OLD MAN: Do you know what you are saying? Ours is a strong breed, my son. It is only a strong breed that can take this boat to the river year after year and wax stronger on it. I 440 have taken down each year's evils for over twenty years. I hoped you would follow me.

EMAN: My life here died with Omae.

OLD MAN: Omae died giving birth to your child and you think the world is ended. Eman, my pain did not begin when Omae died. Since you sent her to stay with me, son, I lived with the burden of knowing that this child would die bearing your son. 445

EMAN: Father . . .

OLD MAN: Don't you know it was the same with you? And me? No woman survives the bearing of the strong ones. Son, it is not the mouth of the boaster that says he belongs to the strong breed. It is the tongue that is red with pain and black with sorrow. Twelve years you were away my son, and for those twelve years I knew the love of an old man 450 for his daughter and the pain of a man helplessly awaiting his loss.

EMAN: I wish I had stayed away. I wish I never came back to meet her.

OLD MAN: It had to be. But you know now what slowly ate away my strength. I awaited your return with love and fear. Forgive me then if I say that your grief is light. It will pass. This grief may drive you now from home. But you must return. 455

EMAN: You do not understand. It is not grief alone.

OLD MAN: What is it then? Tell me I can still learn.

EMAN: I was away twelve years. I changed much in that time.

OLD MAN: I am listening.

EMAN: I am unfitted for your work, father. I wish to say no more. But I am totally unfitted 460 for your call.

OLD MAN: It is only time you need son. Stay longer and you will answer the urge of your blood.

EMAN: That I stayed at all was because of Omae. I did not expect to find her waiting. I would have taken her away, but hard as you claim to be, it would have killed you. 465 And I was a tired man. I needed peace. Because Omae was peace, I stayed. Now nothing holds me here.

OLD MAN: Other men would rot and die doing this task year after year. It is strong medicine which only we can take. Our blood is strong like no other. Anything you do in life must be less than this, son. 470

EMAN: That is not true father.

OLD MAN: I tell you it is true. Your own blood will betray you son, because you cannot hold it back. If you make it do less than this, it will rush to your head and burst it open. I say what I know my son.

EMAN: There are other tasks in life father. This one is not for me. There are even greater 475 things you know nothing of.

OLD MAN: I am very sad. You only go to give others what rightly belongs to us. You will
    use your strength among thieves. They are thieves because they take what is ours,
    they have no claim of blood to it. They will even lack the knowledge to use it wisely.
    Truth is my companion at this moment my son. I know everything I say will surely   480
    bring the sadness of truth.
EMAN: I am going father.
OLD MAN: Call my attendant. And be with me in your strength for this last journey. A-ah,
    did you hear that? It came out without my knowing it; this is indeed my last journey.
    But I am not afraid.   485

> [EMAN *goes out. A few moments later, the* ATTENDANT *enters.*]

ATTENDANT: The boat is ready.
OLD MAN: So am I.

> [*He sits perfectly still for several moments. Drumming begins somewhere in the dis-*
> *tance, and the* OLD MAN *sways his head almost imperceptibly. Two men come in*
> *bearing a miniature boat, containing an indefinable mound. They rush it in and*
> *set it briskly down near the* OLD MAN, *and stand well back. The* OLD MAN *gets*
> *up slowly, the* ATTENDANT *watching him keenly. He signs to the men, who lift the*
> *boat quickly onto the* OLD MAN'*s head. As soon as it touches his head, he holds it*
> *down with both hands and runs off, the men give him a start, then follow at a trot.*
>   *As the last man disappears* OROGE *limps in and comes face to face with*
> EMAN—*as carrier—who is now seen still standing beside the shrubs, staring into*
> *the scene he has just witnessed.* OROGE, *struck by the look on* EMAN'*s face, looks*
> *anxiously behind him to see what has engaged* EMAN'*s attention.* EMAN *notices*
> *him then, and the pair stare at each other.* JAGUNA *enters, sees him and shouts,*
> *Here he is, rushes at* EMAN *who is whipped back to the immediate and flees,*
> JAGUNA *in pursuit. Three or four others enter and follow them.* OROGE *remains*
> *where he is, thoughtful.*]

JAGUNA: [*re-enters*] They have closed in on him now, we'll get him this time.
OROGE: It is nearly midnight.
JAGUNA: You were standing there looking at him as if he was some strange spirit. Why   490
    didn't you shout?
OROGE: You shouted didn't you? Did that catch him?
JAGUNA: Don't worry. We have him now. But things have taken a bad turn. It is no longer
    enough to drive him past every house. There is too much contamination about already.
OROGE: [*not listening*] He saw something. Why may I not know what it was?   495
JAGUNA: What are you talking about?
OROGE: Hm. What is it?
JAGUNA: I said there is too much harm done already. The year will demand more from this
    carrier than we thought.
OROGE: What do you mean?   500
JAGUNA: Do we have to talk with the full mouth?
OROGE: S-sh . . . look!

> [JAGUNA *turns just in time to see* SUNMA *fly at him, clawing at his face like a*
> *crazed tigress.*]

SUNMA: Murderer! What are you doing to him. Murderer! Murderer!

> [JAGUNA *finds himself struggling really hard to keep off his daughter, he succeeds*

in pushing her off and striking her so hard on the face that she falls to her knees. He moves on her to hit her again.]

OROGE: [*comes between*] Think what you are doing Jaguna, she is your daughter.

JAGUNA: My daughter! Does this one look like my daughter? Let me cripple the harlot   505
for life.

OROGE: That is a wicked thought Jaguna.

JAGUNA: Don't come between me and her.

OROGE: Nothing in anger—do you forget what tonight is?

JAGUNA: Can you blame me for forgetting?   510

[*Draws his hand across his cheek—it is covered with blood.*]

OROGE: This is an unhappy night for us all. I fear what is to come of it.

JAGUNA: Let's go. I cannot restrain myself in this creature's presence. My own daughter . . .
and for a stranger . . .

[*They go off.* IFADA, *who came in with* SUNMA *and had stood apart, horror-stricken, comes shyly forward. He helps* SUNMA *up. They go off, he holding* SUNMA *bent and sobbing.*]

[*Enter* EMAN—*as carrier. He is physically present in the bounds of this next scene, a side of a round thatched hut. A young girl, about fourteen, runs in, stops beside the hut. She looks carefully to see that she is not observed, puts her mouth to a little hole in the wall.*]

OMAE: Eman . . . Eman . . .

[EMAN—*as carrier—responds, as he does throughout the scene, but they are unaware of him.*]

EMAN: [*from inside*] Who is it?   515

OMAE: It is me, Omae.

EMAN: How dare you come here!

[*Two hands appear at the hole and, pushing outwards, create a much larger hole through which* EMAN *puts out his head. It is* EMAN *as a boy, the same age as the girl.*]

Go away at once. Are you trying to get me in trouble!

OMAE: What is the matter?

EMAN: You. Go away.   520

OMAE: But I came to see you.

EMAN: Are you deaf? I say I don't want to see you. Now go before my tutor catches you.

OMAE: All right. Come out.

EMAN: Do what!

OMAE: Come out.   525

EMAN: You must be mad.

OMAE: [*sits on the ground*] All right, if you don't come out I shall simply stay here until
your tutor arrives.

EMAN: [*about to explode, thinks better of it and the head disappears. A moment later he emerges
from behind the hut.*] What sort of evil has got into you?   530

OMAE: None. I just wanted to see you.

EMAN: [*His mimicry is nearly hysterical.*] None. I just wanted to see you. Do you think this
place is the stream where you can go and molest innocent people?

OMAE: [*coyly*] Aren't you glad to see me?
EMAN: I am not.   535
OMAE: Why?
EMAN: Why? Do you really ask me why? Because you are a woman and a most troublesome
    woman. Don't you know anything about this at all. We are not meant to see any
    woman. So go away before more harm is done.
OMAE: [*flirtatious*] What is so secret about it anyway? What do they teach you.   540
EMAN: Nothing any woman can understand.
OMAE: Ha ha. You think we don't know eh? You've all come to be circumcised.
EMAN: Shut up. You don't know anything.
OMAE: Just think, all this time you haven't been circumcised, and you dared make eyes at
    us women.   545
EMAN: Thank you—woman. Now go.
OMAE: Do they give you enough to eat?
EMAN: [*testily*] No. We are so hungry that when silly girls like you turn up, we eat them.
OMAE: [*feigning tears*] Oh, oh, oh, he's abusing me. He's abusing me.
EMAN: [*alarmed*] Don't try that here. Go quickly if you are going to cry.   550
OMAE: All right, I won't cry.
EMAN: Cry or no cry, go away and leave me alone. What do you think will happen if my
    tutor turns up now.
OMAE: He won't.
EMAN: [*mimicking*] He won't. I suppose you are his wife and he tells you where he goes. 555
    In fact this is just the time he comes round to our huts. He could be at the next hut
    this very moment.
OMAE: Ha-ha. You're lying. I left him by the stream, pinching the girls' bottoms. Is that
    the sort of thing he teaches you?
EMAN: Don't say anything against him or I shall beat you. Isn't it you loose girls who tease 560
    him, wiggling your bottoms under his nose?
OMAE: [*going tearful again*] A-ah, so I am one of those girls eh?
EMAN: Now don't you start accusing me of things I didn't say.
OMAE: But you said it. You said it.
EMAN: I didn't. Look Omae, someone will hear you and I'll be in disgrace. Why don't you 565
    go before anything happens.
OMAE: It's all right. My friends have promised to hold your old rascal tutor till I get back.
EMAN: Then you go back right now. I have work to do. [*going in*]
OMAE: [*runs after and tries to hold him.* EMAN *leaps back, genuinely scared.*] What is the
    matter? I was not going to bite you.   570
EMAN: Do you know what you nearly did? You almost touched me!
OMAE: Well?
EMAN: Well! Isn't it enough that you let me set my eyes on you? Must you now totally
    pollute me with your touch? Don't you understand anything?
OMAE: Oh, that.   575
EMAN: [*nearly screaming*] It is not "oh that." Do you think this is only a joke or a little visit
    like spending the night with your grandmother? This is an important period of my life.
    Look, these huts, we built them with our own hands. Every boy builds his own. We
    learn things, do you understand? And we spend much time just thinking. At least, I
    do. It is the first time I have had nothing to do except think. Don't you see, I am 580
    becoming a man. For the first time, I understand that I have a life to fulfil. Has that
    thought ever worried you?
OMAE: You are frightening me.

EMAN: There. That is all you can say. And what use will that be when a man finds himself alone—like that? [*points to the hut*] A man must go on his own, go where no one can help him, and test his strength. Because he may find himself one day sitting alone in a wall round as that. In there, my mind could hold no other thought. I may never have such moments again to myself. Don't dare come to steal any more of it.

OMAE: [*this time genuinely tearful*] Oh, I know you hate me. You only want to drive me away.

EMAN: [*impatiently*] Yes, yes, I know I hate you—but go.

OMAE: [*going, all tears. Wipes her eyes, suddenly all mischief.*] Eman.

EMAN: What now?

OMAE: I only want to ask one thing . . . do you promise to tell me?

EMAN: Well, what is it?

OMAE: [*gleefully*] Does it hurt?

> [*She turns instantly and flees, landing straight into the arms of the returning tutor.*]

TUTOR: Te-he-he . . . what have we here? What little mouse leaps straight into the beak of the wise old owl eh?

> [OMAE *struggles to free herself, flies to the opposite side, grimacing with distaste.*]

TUTOR: I suppose you merely came to pick some fruits eh? You did not sneak here to see any of my children.

OMAE: Yes, I came to steal your fruits.

TUTOR: Te-he-he . . . I thought so. And that dutiful son of mine over there. He saw you and came to chase you off my fruit trees didn't he? Te-he-he . . . I'm sure he did, isn't that so my young Eman?

EMAN: I was talking to her.

TUTOR: Indeed you were. Now be good enough to go into your hut until I decide your punishment. [EMAN *withdraws.*] Te-he-he . . . now my little daughter, you need not be afraid of me.

OMAE: [*spiritedly*] I am not.

TUTOR: Good. Very good. We ought to be friendly. [*His voice becomes leering.*] Now this is nothing to worry you my daughter . . . a very small thing indeed. Although of course if I were to let it slip that your young Eman had broken a strong taboo, it might go hard on him you know. I am sure you would not like that to happen, would you?

OMAE: No.

TUTOR: Good. You are sensible my girl. Can you wash clothes?

OMAE: Yes.

TUTOR: Good. If you will come with me now to my hut, I shall give you some clothes to wash, and then we will forget all about this matter eh? Well, come on.

OMAE: I shall wait here. You go and bring the clothes.

TUTOR: Eh? What is that? Now now, don't make me angry. You should know better than to talk back to your elders. Come now.

> [*He takes her by the arm, and tries to drag her off.*]

OMAE: No no, I won't come to your hut. Leave me. Leave me alone you shameless old man.

TUTOR: If you don't come I shall disgrace the whole family of Eman, and yours too.

> [EMAN *re-enters with a small bundle.*]

EMAN: Leave her alone. Let us go Omae.

TUTOR: And where do you think you are going?

EMAN: Home.

TUTOR: Te-he-he . . . As easy as that eh? You think you can leave here at any time you please? Get right back inside that hut!

[EMAN *takes* OMAE *by the arm and begins to walk off.*]

TUTOR: Come back at once.   630

[*He goes after him and raises his stick.* EMAN *catches it, wrenches it from him and throws it away.*]

OMAE: [*hopping delightedly*] Kill him. Beat him to death.

TUTOR: Help! Help! He is killing me! Help!

[*Alarmed,* EMAN *clamps his hand over his mouth.*]

EMAN: Old tutor, I don't mean you any harm, but you mustn't try to harm me either. [*He removes his hand.*]

TUTOR: You think you can get away with your crime. My report shall reach the elders   635
before you ever get into town.

EMAN: You are afraid of what I will say about you? Don't worry. Only if you try to shame me, then will I speak. I am not going back to the village anyway. Just tell them I have gone, no more. If you say one word more then I shall hear of it the same day and I shall come back.   640

TUTOR: You are telling me what to do? But don't think to come back here even ten years from now. And don't send your children.

[*Goes off with threatening gestures.*]

EMAN: I won't come back.

OMAE: Smoked vulture! But Eman, he says you cannot return next year. What will you do?

EMAN: It is a small thing one can do in the big towns.   645

OMAE: I thought you were going to beat him that time. Why didn't you crackle his dirty hide?

EMAN: Listen carefully Omae . . . I am going on a journey.

OMAE: Come on. Tell me about it on the way.

EMAN: No, I go that way. I cannot return to the village.   650

OMAE: Because of that wretched man? Anyway you will first talk to your father.

EMAN: Go and see him for me. Tell him I have gone away for some time. I think he will know.

OMAE: But Eman . . .

EMAN: I haven't finished. You will go and live with him till I get back. I have spoken to him   655
about you. Look after him!

OMAE: But what is this journey? When will you come back?

EMAN: I don't know. But this is a good moment to go. Nothing ties me down.

OMAE: But Eman, you want to leave me.

EMAN: Don't forget all I said. I don't know how long I will be. Stay in my father's house as   660
long as you remember me. When you become tired of waiting, you must do as you please. You understand? You must do as you please.

OMAE: I cannot understand anything Eman. I don't know where you are going or why. Suppose you never came back! Don't go, Eman. Don't leave me by myself.

EMAN: I must go. Now let me see you on your way.   665

OMAE: I shall come with you.

EMAN: Come with me! And who will look after you? Me? You will only be in my way, you know that! You will hold me back and I shall desert you in a strange place. Go home and do as I say. Take care of my father and let him take care of you.

[*He starts going but* OMAE *clings to him.*]

OMAE: But Eman, stay the night at least. You will only lose your way. Your father Eman,   670
what will he say? I won't remember what you said . . . come back to the village . . . I cannot return alone Eman . . . come with me as far as the crossroads.

[*His face set,* EMAN *strides off and* OMAE *loses balance as he increases his pace. Falling, she quickly wraps her arms around his ankle, but* EMAN *continues unchecked, dragging her along.*]

OMAE: Don't go Eman . . . Eman, don't leave me, don't leave me . . . don't leave your Omae . . . don't go Eman . . . don't leave your Omae . . .

[EMAN—*as carrier—makes a nervous move as if he intends to go after the vanished pair. He stops but continues to stare at the point where he last saw them. There is stillness for a while. Then the* GIRL *enters from the same place and remains looking at* EMAN. *Startled,* EMAN *looks apprehensively round him. The* GIRL *goes nearer but keeps beyond arm's length.*]

GIRL: Are you the carrier?   675
EMAN: Yes. I am Eman.
GIRL: Why are you hiding?
EMAN: I really came for a drink of water . . . er . . . is there anyone in front of the house?
GIRL: No.
EMAN: But there might be people in the house. Did you hear voices?   680
GIRL: There is no one here.
EMAN: Good. Thank you. [*he is about to go, stops suddenly*] Er . . . would you . . . you will find a cup on the table. Could you bring me the water out here? The water-pot is in a corner. [*The* GIRL *goes. She enters the house, then, watching* EMAN *carefully, slips out and runs off.*]   685
EMAN: [*sitting*] Perhaps they have all gone home. It will be good to rest. [*He hears voices and listens hard.*] Too late. [*moves cautiously nearer the house*] Quickly girl, I can hear people coming. Hurry up. [*looks through the window*] Where are you? Where is she? [*The truth dawns on him suddenly and he moves off, sadly.*]

[*Enter* JAGUNA *and* OROGE, *led by the* GIRL.]

GIRL: [*pointing*]: He was there.   690
JAGUNA: Ay, he's gone now. He is a sly one is your friend. But it won't save him for ever.
OROGE: What was he doing when you saw him?
GIRL: He asked me for a drink of water.
JAGUNA, OROGE: Ah! [*They look at each other.*]
OROGE: We should have thought of that.   695
JAGUNA: He is surely finished now. If only we had thought of it earlier.
OROGE: It is not too late. There is still an hour before midnight.
JAGUNA: We must call back all the men. Now we need only wait for him—in the right place.
OROGE: Everyone must be told. We don't want anyone heading him off again.   700
JAGUNA: And it works so well. This is surely the help of the gods themselves Oroge. Don't you know at once what is on the path to the stream?

OROGE: The sacred trees.

JAGUNA: I tell you it is the very hand of the gods. Let us go.

[*An overgrown part of the village.* EMAN *wanders in, aimlessly, seemingly uncaring of discovery. Beyond him, an area lights up, revealing a group of people clustered round a spot, all the heads are bowed. One figure stands away and separate from them. Even as* EMAN *looks, the group breaks up and the people disperse, coming down and past him. Only three people are left, a man (*EMAN*) whose back is turned, the village* PRIEST, *and the isolated one. They stand on opposite sides of the grave, the man on the mound of earth. The* PRIEST *walks round to the man's side and lays a hand on his shoulder.*]

PRIEST: Come.   705

EMAN: I will. Give me a few moments here alone.

PRIEST: Be comforted.

[*They fall silent.*]

EMAN: I was gone twelve years but she waited. She whom I thought had too much of the laughing child in her. Twelve years I was a pilgrim, seeking the vain shrine of secret strength. And all the time, strange knowledge, this silent strength of my child-woman.   710

PRIEST: We all saw it. It was a lesson to us; we did not know that such goodness could be found among us.

EMAN: Then why? Why the wasted years if she had to perish giving birth to my child? [*They are both silent.*] I do not really know for what great meaning I searched. When I returned, I could not be certain I had found it. Until I reached my home and I   715
found her a full-grown woman, still a child at heart. When I grew to believe it, I thought this, after all, is what I sought. It was here all the time. And I threw away my new-gained knowledge. I buried the part of me that was formed in strange places. I made a home in my birthplace.

PRIEST: That was as it should be.   720

EMAN: Any truth of that was killed in the cruelty of her brief happiness.

PRIEST: [*looks up and sees the figure standing away from them, the child in his arms. He is totally still.*] Your father—he is over there.

EMAN: I knew he would come. Has he my son with him?

PRIEST: Yes.   725

EMAN: He will let no one take the child. Go and comfort him priest. He loved Omae like a daughter, and you all know how well she looked after him. You see how strong we really are. In his heart of hearts the old man's love really awaited a daughter. Go and comfort him. His grief is more than mine.

[*The* PRIEST *goes. The* OLD MAN *has stood well away from the burial group. His face is hard and his gaze unswerving from the grave. The* PRIEST *goes to him, pauses, but sees that he can make no dent in the man's grief. Bowed, he goes on his way.*]

[EMAN, *as carrier, walking towards the graveside, the other* EMAN *having gone. His feet sink into the mound and he breaks slowly onto his knees, scooping up the sand in his hands and pouring it on his head. The scene blacks out slowly.*]

[*Enter* JAGUNA *and* OROGE.]

OROGE: We have only a little time.   730

JAGUNA: He will come. All the wells are guarded. There is only the stream left him. The animal must come to drink.

OROGE: You are sure it will not fail—the trap I mean.

JAGUNA: When Jaguna sets the trap, even elephants pay homage—their trunks downwards and one leg up in the sky. When the carrier steps on the fallen twigs, it is up in the sacred trees with him. 735

OROGE: I shall breathe again when this long night is over.

[*They go out.*]

[*Enter* EMAN—*as carrier—from the same direction as the last two entered. In front of him is still a figure, the* OLD MAN *as he was, carrying the dwarf boat.*]

EMAN: [*joyfully*] Father.

[*The figure does not turn round.*]

EMAN: It is your son. Eman. [*He moves nearer.*] Don't you want to look at me? It is I, Eman. [*He moves nearer still.*] 740

OLD MAN: You are coming too close. Don't you know what I carry on my head?

EMAN: But father, I am your son.

OLD MAN: Then go back. We cannot give the two of us.

EMAN: Tell me first where you are going.

OLD MAN: Do you ask that? Where else but to the river? 745

EMAN: [*visibly relieved*] I only wanted to be sure. My throat is burning. I have been looking for the stream all night.

OLD MAN: It is the other way.

EMAN: But you said . . .

OLD MAN: I take the longer way, you know how I must do this. It is quicker if you take the other way. Go now. 750

EMAN: No, I will only get lost again. I shall go with you.

OLD MAN: Go back my son. Go back.

EMAN: Why? Won't you even look at me?

OLD MAN: Listen to your father. Go back. 755

EMAN: But father!

[*He makes to hold him. Instantly the* OLD MAN *breaks into a rapid trot.* EMAN *hesitates, then follows, his strength nearly gone.*]

EMAN: Wait father. I am coming with you . . . wait . . . wait for me father . . .

[*There is a sound of twigs breaking, of a sudden trembling in the branches. Then silence.*]

[*The front of* EMAN's *house. The effigy is hanging from the sheaves. Enter* SUNMA, *still supported by* IFADA, *she stands transfixed as she sees the hanging figure.* IFADA *appears to go mad, rushes at the object and tears it down.* SUNMA, *her last bit of will gone, crumbles against the wall. Some distance away from them, partly hidden, stands the* GIRL, *impassively watching.* IFADA *hugs the effigy to him, stands above* SUNMA. *The* GIRL *remains where she is, observing.*
　　Almost at once, the villagers begin to return, subdued and guilty. They walk across the front, skirting the house as widely as they can. No word is exchanged. JAGUNA, *who is leading, sees* SUNMA *as soon as he comes in view. He stops at once, retreating slightly.*]

OROGE: [*almost whispering*] What is it?

JAGUNA: The viper.

[OROGE *looks cautiously at the woman.*]

OROGE: I don't think she will even see you. 760

JAGUNA: Are you sure? I am in no frame of mind for another meeting with her.

OROGE: Let's go home.

JAGUNA: I am sick to the heart of the cowardice I have seen tonight.

OROGE: That is the nature of men.

JAGUNA: Then it is a sorry world to live in. We did it for them. It was all for their own 765
common good. What did it benefit me whether the man lived or died. But did you
see them? One and all they looked up at the man and words died in their throats.

OROGE: It was no common sight.

JAGUNA: Women could not have behaved so shamefully. One by one they crept off like
sick dogs. Not one could raise a curse. 770

OROGE: It was not only him they fled. Do you see how unattended we are?

JAGUNA: There are those who will pay for this night's work!

OROGE: Ay, let us go home.

[*They go off.* SUNMA, IFADA *and the* GIRL *remain as they are, the light fading
slowly on them.*]

THE END

Ma Rainey's Black Bottom (1984)

M A RAINEY'S BLACK BOTTOM was the first in a cycle of plays that August Wilson wrote about the black experience in twentieth-century America— one play for each decade. *Ma Rainey's Black Bottom* is the only one of these plays not set in Pittsburgh, where Wilson was raised. The play takes its title character from the legendary blues queen of the same name, whose song, *Ma Rainey's Black Bottom*, referred to a popular dance of the 1920s. Set in Chicago in 1927, the play's action is confined to a recording studio where white managers have arranged to record Ma Rainey and her band.

As the play develops, it becomes clear that the white managers have little respect for the black musicians or their music. Rather, they are interested primarily in exploiting the blacks and seek to dictate both what is to be recorded and how it is to be done. All of the musicians in the band, except for the newcomer, Levee, are used to doing what they are told in order to avoid stirring up trouble. But Ma Rainey recognizes that she also has an important weapon, for although the white managers may not respect her, they cannot proceed without her cooperation. Through small demands (for a soft drink, that her nephew introduce her song—even though he has a persistent stutter, etc.), she gradually establishes her power and is able to maintain the integrity of her music.

All might have concluded peaceably were it not for Levee, who has little respect for Ma Rainey's music and has reached a tentative agreement with the white managers to follow his advice on today's recording, as well as to record some of Levee's own music, which he considers a great improvement over the blues popular at the time. When it becomes clear to the managers that Levee is both out of favor with Ma Rainey and a potential troublemaker, they back out of their promise to him. His disappointment and frustration lead Levee to provoke a fight with one of the band members, whom he stabs to death.

The relationship between whites and blacks in the play is symbolic of that in the larger society outside the recording studio. Virtually powerless, blacks like Ma Rainey have learned to defend their integrity in subtle and roundabout ways. But as the relationship between Levee and the other musicians indicates, not all have that ability, and the price they pay is high.

Wilson was perhaps one of the most successful American playwrights of the last quarter of the twentieth century, writing numerous award-winning plays including Pulitzer Prize winners *Fences* and *The Piano Lesson*.

Ma Rainey's Black Bottom

Characters

STURDYVANT, *studio owner*
IRVIN, *Ma Rainey's manager*
CUTLER, *guitar and trombone player*
TOLEDO, *piano player*
SLOW DRAG, *bass player*
LEVEE, *trumpet player*
MA RAINEY, *blues singer*
POLICEMAN
DUSSIE MAE, *Ma Rainey's companion*
SYLVESTER, *Ma Rainey's nephew*

> *They tore the railroad down*
>
> *so the Sunshine Special can't run*
>
> *I'm going away baby*
>
> *build me a railroad of my own*
>
> —Blind Lemon Jefferson

THE SETTING

There are two playing areas: what is called the "band room," and the recording studio. The band room is at stage left and is in the basement of the building. It is entered through a door up left. There are benches and chairs scattered about, a piano, a row of lockers, and miscellaneous paraphernalia stacked in a corner and long since forgotten. A mirror hangs on a wall with various posters.

The studio is upstairs at stage right, and resembles a recording studio of the late 1920s. The entrance is from a hall on the right wall. A small control booth is at the rear and its access is gained by means of a spiral staircase. Against one wall there is a line of chairs, and a horn through which the control room communicates with the performers. A door in the rear wall allows access to the band room.

THE PLAY

It is early March in Chicago, 1927. There is a bit of a chill in the air. Winter has broken but the wind coming off the lake does not carry the promise of spring. The people of the city are bundled and brisk in their defense against such misfortunes as the weather, and the business of the city proceeds largely undisturbed.

Chicago in 1927 is a rough city, a bruising city, a city of millionaires and derelicts, gangsters and roughhouse dandies, whores and Irish grandmothers who move through its streets fingering long black rosaries. Somewhere a man is wrestling with the taste of a woman in his cheek. Somewhere a dog is barking. Somewhere the moon has fallen through a window and broken into thirty pieces of silver.

It is one o'clock in the afternoon. Secretaries are returning from their lunch, the noon Mass at St. Anthony's is over, and the priest is mumbling over his vestments while the altar boys practice their Latin. The procession of cattle cars through the stockyards continues unabated. The busboys in Mac's Place are cleaning away the last of the corned beef and cabbage, and on the city's Southside, sleepy-eyed negroes move lazily toward their small cold-water flats and rented rooms to await the onslaught of night, which will find them crowded in the bars and juke joints both dazed and dazzling in their rapport with life. It is with these negroes that our concern lies most heavily: their values, their attitudes, and particularly their music.

It is hard to define this music. Suffice it to say that it is music that breathes and touches. That connects. That is in itself a way of being, separate and distinct from any other. This music is called blues. Whether this music came from Alabama or Mississippi or other parts of the South doesn't matter anymore. The men and women who make this music have learned it from the narrow crooked streets of East St. Louis, or the streets of the city's Southside, and the Alabama or Mississippi roots have been strangled by the northern manners and customs of free men of definite and sincere worth, men for whom this music often lies at the forefront of their conscience and concerns. Thus they are laid open to be consumed by it; its warmth and redress, its braggadocio and roughly poignant comments, its vision and prayer, which would instruct and allow them to reconnect, to reassemble and gird up for the next battle in which they would be both victim and the ten thousand slain.

ACT I

The lights come up in the studio. IRVIN *enters, carrying a microphone. He is a tall, fleshy man who prides himself on his knowledge of blacks and his ability to deal with them. He hooks up the microphone, blows into it, taps it, etc. He crosses over to the piano, opens it, and fingers a few keys.* STURDYVANT *is visible in the control booth. Preoccupied with money, he is insensitive to black performers and prefers to deal with them at arm's length. He puts on a pair of earphones.*

STURDYVANT: [*over speaker*] Irv . . . let's crack that mike, huh? Let's do a check on it.
IRVIN: [*crosses to mike, speaks into it*] Testing . . . one . . . two . . . three . . .

[*There is a loud feedback.* STURDYVANT *fiddles with the dials.*]

Testing . . . one . . . two . . . three . . . testing. How's that Mel?

[STURDYVANT *doesn't respond.*]

Testing . . . one . . . two . . .

STURDYVANT: [*taking off the earphones*] Okay . . . that checks. We got a good reading.   5
    [*Pause.*] You got that list, Irv?

IRVIN: Yeah . . . yeah, I got it. Don't worry about nothing.

STURDYVANT: Listen, Irv . . . you keep her in line, okay? I'm holding you responsible for
    her . . . If she starts any of her . . .

IRVIN: Mel, what's with the goddamn horn? You wanna talk to me . . . okay! I can't talk to   10
    you over the goddamn horn . . . Christ!

STURDYVANT: I'm not putting up with any shenanigans. You hear, Irv?

      [IRVIN *crosses over to the piano and mindlessly runs his fingers over the keys.*]

I'm just not gonna stand for it. I want you to keep her in line. Irv?

      [STURDYVANT *enters from the control booth.*]

Listen, Irv . . . you're her manager . . . she's your responsibility . . .

IRVIN: Okay, okay, Mel . . . let me handle it.   15

STURDYVANT: She's your responsibility. I'm not putting up with any Royal Highness . . .
    Queen of the Blues bullshit!

IRVIN: Mother of the Blues, Mel. Mother of the Blues.

STURDYVANT: I don't care what she calls herself. I'm not putting up with it. I just want
    to get her in here . . . record those songs on that list . . . and get her out. Just like   20
    clockwork, huh?

IRVIN: Like clockwork, Mel. You just stay out of the way and let me handle it.

STURDYVANT: Yeah . . . yeah . . . You handled it last time. Remember? She marches in
    here like she owns the damn place . . . doesn't like the songs we picked out . . . says
    her throat is sore . . . doesn't want to do more than one take . . .   25

IRVIN: Okay . . . okay . . . I was here! I know all about it.

STURDYVANT: Complains about the building being cold . . . and then . . . trips over the
    mike wire and threatens to sue me. That's taking care of it?

IRVIN: I've got it all worked out this time. I talked with her last night. Her throat is fine . . .
    We went over the songs together . . . I got everything straight, Mel.   30

STURDYVANT: Irv, that horn player . . . the one who gave me those songs . . . is he gonna
    be here today? Good. I want to hear more of that sound. Times are changing. This
    is a tricky business now. We've got to jazz it up . . . put in something different. You
    know, something wild . . . with a lot of rhythm. [*Pause.*] You know what we put out
    last time, Irv? We put out garbage last time. It was garbage. I don't even know why I   35
    bother with this anymore.

IRVIN: You did all right last time, Mel. Not as good as you did before, but you did all right.

STURDYVANT: You know how many records we sold in New York? You wanna see the
    sheet? And you know what's in New York, Irv? Harlem. Harlem's in New York, Irv.

IRVIN: Okay, so they didn't sell in New York. But look at Memphis . . . Birmingham . . .   40
    Atlanta. Christ, you made a bundle.

STURDYVANT: It's not the money, Irv. You know I couldn't sleep last night? This business
    is bad for my nerves. My wife is after me to slow down and take a vacation. Two more
    years and I'm gonna get out . . . get into something respectable. Textiles. That's a
    respectable business. You know what you could do with a shipload of textiles from   45
    Ireland?

      [*A buzzer is heard offstage.*]

IRVIN: Why don't you go upstairs and let me handle it, Mel?

STURDYVANT: Remember . . . you're responsible for her.

[*STURDYVANT exits to the control booth.* IRVIN *crosses to get the door.* CUTLER, SLOW DRAG, *and* TOLEDO *enter.* CUTLER *is in his mid-fifties, as are most of the others. He plays guitar and trombone and is the leader of the group, possibly because he is the most sensible. His playing is solid and almost totally unembellished. His understanding of his music is limited to the chord he is playing at the time he is playing it. He has all the qualities of a loner except the introspection.* SLOW DRAG, *the bass player, is perhaps the one most bored by life. He resembles* CUTLER, *but lacks* CUTLER's *energy. He is deceptively intelligent, though, as his name implies, he appears to be slow. He is a rather large man with a wicked smile. Innate African rhythms underlie everything he plays, and he plays with an ease that is at times startling.* TOLEDO *is the piano player. In control of his instrument, he understands and recognizes that its limitations are an extension of himself. He is the only one in the group who can read. He is self-taught but misunderstands and misapplies his knowledge, though he is quick to penetrate to the core of a situation and his insights are thought-provoking. All of the men are dressed in a style of clothing befitting the members of a successful band of the era.*]

IRVIN: How you boys doing, Cutler? Come on in. [*Pause.*] Where's Ma? Is she with you?
CUTLER: I don't know, Mr. Irvin. She told us to be here at one o'clock. That's all I know. 50
IRVIN: Where's . . . huh . . . the horn player? Is he coming with Ma?
CUTLER: Levee's supposed to be here same as we is. I reckon he'll be here in a minute. I can't rightly say.
IRVIN: Well, come on . . . I'll show you to the band room, let you get set up and rehearsed. You boys hungry? I'll call over to the deli and get some sandwiches. Get you fed and 55
ready to make some music. Cutler . . . here's the list of songs we're gonna record.
STURDYVANT: [*over speaker*] Irvin, what's happening? Where's Ma?
IRVIN: Everything under control, Mel. I got it under control.
STURDYVANT: Where's Ma? How come she isn't with the band?
IRVIN: She'll be here in a minute, Mel. Let me get these fellows down to the band room, 60
huh?

[*They exit the studio. The lights go down in the studio and up in the band room.* IRVIN *opens the door and allows them to pass as they enter.*]

You boys go ahead and rehearse. I'll let you know when Ma comes.

[IRVIN *exits.* CUTLER *hands* TOLEDO *the list of songs.*]

CUTLER: What we got here, Toledo?
TOLEDO: [*reading*] We got . . . "Prove It on Me" . . . "Hear Me Talking to You" . . . "Ma Rainey's Black Bottom" . . . and "Moonshine Blues." 65
CUTLER: Where Mr. Irvin go? Them ain't the songs Ma told me.
SLOW DRAG: I wouldn't worry about it if I were you, Cutler. They'll get it straightened out. Ma will get it straightened out.
CUTLER: I just don't want no trouble about these songs, that's all. Ma ain't told me them songs. She told me something else. 70
SLOW DRAG: What she tell you?
CUTLER: This "Moonshine Blues" wasn't in it. That's one of Bessie's songs.
TOLEDO: Slow Drag's right . . . I wouldn't worry about it. Let them straighten it up.
CUTLER: Levee know what time he supposed to be here?
SLOW DRAG: Levee gone out to spend your four dollars. He left the hotel this morning 75
talking about he was gonna go buy some shoes. Say it's the first time he ever beat you shooting craps.

CUTLER: Do he know what time he supposed to be here? That's what I wanna know. I ain't thinking about no four dollars.

SLOW DRAG: Levee sure was thinking about it. That four dollars liked to burn a hole in   80
his pocket.

CUTLER: Well, he's supposed to be here at one o'clock. That's what time Ma said. That nigger get out in the streets with that four dollars and ain't no telling when he's liable to show. You ought to have seen him at the club last night, Toledo. Trying to talk to some gal Ma had with her.   85

TOLEDO: You ain't got to tell me. I know how Levee do.

[*Buzzer is heard offstage.*]

SLOW DRAG: Levee tried to talk to that gal and got his feelings hurt. She didn't want no part of him. She told Levee he'd have to turn his money green before he could talk with her.

CUTLER: She out for what she can get. Anybody could see that.   90

SLOW DRAG: That's why Levee run out to buy some shoes. He's looking to make an impression on that gal.

CUTLER: What the hell she gonna do with his shoes? She can't do nothing with the nigger's shoes.

[SLOW DRAG *takes out a pint bottle and drinks.*]

TOLEDO: Let me hit that, Slow Drag.   95

SLOW DRAG: [*handing him the bottle*] This some of that good Chicago bourbon!

[*The door opens and* LEVEE *enters, carrying a shoe box. In his early thirties,* LEVEE *is younger than the other men. His flamboyance is sometimes subtle and sneaks up on you. His temper is rakish and bright. He lacks fuel for himself and is somewhat of a buffoon. But it is an intelligent buffoonery, clearly calculated to shift control of the situation to where he can grasp it. He plays trumpet. His voice is strident and totally dependent on his manipulation of breath. He plays wrong notes frequently. He often gets his skill and talent confused with each other.*]

CUTLER: Levee . . . where Mr. Irvin go?

LEVEE: Hell, I don't know. I ain't none of his keeper.

SLOW DRAG: What you got there, Levee?

LEVEE: Look here, Cutler . . . I got me some shoes!   100

CUTLER: Nigger, I ain't studying you.

[LEVEE *takes the shoes out of the box and starts to put them on.*]

TOLEDO: How much you pay for something like that, Levee?

LEVEE: Eleven dollars. Four dollars of it belong to Cutler.

SLOW DRAG: Levee say if it wasn't for Cutler . . . he wouldn't have no new shoes.

CUTLER: I ain't thinking about Levee or his shoes. Come on . . . let's get ready to rehearse.   105

SLOW DRAG: I'm with you on that score, Cutler. I wanna get out of here. I don't want to be around here all night. When it comes time to go up there and record them songs . . . I just wanna go up there and do it. Last time it took us all day and half the night.

TOLEDO: Ain't but four songs on the list. Last time we recorded six songs.

SLOW DRAG: It felt like it was sixteen!   110

LEVEE: [*finishes with his shoes*] Yeah! Now I'm ready! I can play some good music now!

[*He goes to put up his old shoes and looks around the room.*]

Damn! They done changed things around. Don't never leave well enough alone.

TOLEDO: Everything changing all the time. Even the air you breathing change. You got, monoxide, hydrogen . . . changing all the time. Skin changing . . . different molecules and everything. 115

LEVEE: Nigger, what is you talking about? I'm talking about the room. I ain't talking about no skin and air. I'm talking about something I can see! Last time the band room was upstairs. This time it's downstairs. Next time it be over there. I'm talking about what I can see. I ain't talking about no molecules or nothing.

TOLEDO: Hell, I know what you talking about. I just said everything changin'. I know what you talking about, but you don't know what I'm talking about. 120

LEVEE: That door! Nigger, you see that door? That's what I'm talking about. That door wasn't there before.

CUTLER: Levee, you wouldn't know your right from your left. This is where they used to keep the recording horns and things . . . and damn if that door wasn't there. How in hell else you gonna get in here? Now, if you talking about they done switched rooms, you right. But don't go telling me that damn door wasn't there! 125

SLOW DRAG: Damn the door and let's get set up. I wanna get out of here.

LEVEE: Toledo started all that about the door. I'm just saying that things change.

TOLEDO: What the hell you think I was saying? Things change. The air and everything. Now you gonna say you was saying it. You gonna fit two propositions on the same track . . . run them into each other, and because they crash, you gonna say it's the same train. 130

LEVEE: Now this nigger talking about trains! We done went from the air to the skin to the door . . . and now trains. Toledo, I'd just like to be inside your head for five minutes. Just to see how you think. You done got more shit piled up and mixed up in there than the devil got sinners. You been reading too many goddamn books. 135

TOLEDO: What you care about how much I read? I'm gonna ignore you 'cause you ignorant.

[LEVEE *takes off his coat and hangs it in the locker.*]

SLOW DRAG: Come on, let's rehearse the music.

LEVEE: You ain't gotta rehearse that . . . ain't nothing but old jug-band music. They need one of them jug bands for this. 140

SLOW DRAG: Don't make me no difference. Long as we get paid.

LEVEE: That ain't what I'm talking about, nigger. I'm talking about art!

SLOW DRAG: What's drawing got to do with it?

LEVEE: Where you get this nigger from, Cutler? He sound like one of them Alabama niggers. 145

CUTLER: Slow Drag's all right. It's you talking all that weird shit about art. Just play the piece, nigger. You wanna be one of them . . . what you call . . . virtuoso or something, you in the wrong place. You ain't no Buddy Bolden or King Oliver . . . you just an old trumpet player come a dime a dozen. Talking about art. 150

LEVEE: What is you? I don't see your name in lights.

CUTLER: I just play the piece. Whatever they want. I don't go talking about art and criticizing other people's music.

LEVEE: I ain't like you, Cutler. I got talent! Me and this horn . . . we's tight. If my daddy knowed I was gonna turn out like this, he would've named me Gabriel. I'm gonna 155 get me a band and make me some records. I done give Mr. Sturdyvant some of my songs I wrote and he say he's gonna let me record them when I get my band together. [*Takes some papers out of his pocket.*] I just gotta finish the last part of this song. And Mr. Sturdyvant want me to write another part to this song.

SLOW DRAG: How you learn to write music, Levee? 160

LEVEE: I just picked it up . . . like you pick up anything. Miss Eula used to play the piano . . .

she learned me a lot. I knows how to play *real* music . . . not this old jug-band shit. I got style!

TOLEDO: Everybody got style. Style ain't nothing but keeping the same idea from beginning to end. Everybody got it.   165

LEVEE: But everybody can't play like I do. Everybody can't have their own band.

CUTLER: Well, until you get your own band where you can play what you want, you just play the piece and stop complaining. I told you when you came on here, this ain't none of them hot bands. This is an accompaniment band. You play Ma's music when you here.   170

LEVEE: I got sense enough to know that. Hell, I can look at you all and see what kind of band it is. I can look at Toledo and see what kind of band it is.

TOLEDO: Toledo ain't said nothing to you now. Don't let Toledo get started. You can't even spell music, much less play it.

LEVEE: What you talking about? I can spell music. I got a dollar say I can spell it! Put your   175
dollar up. Where your dollar?

[TOLEDO *waves him away.*]

Now come on. Put your dollar up. Talking about I can't spell music.

[LEVEE *peels a dollar off his roll and slams it down on the bench beside*
TOLEDO.]

TOLEDO: All right, I'm gonna show you. Cutler. Slow Drag. You hear this? The nigger betting me a dollar he can spell music. I don't want no shit now!

[TOLEDO *lays a dollar down besides* LEVEE*'s.*]

All right. Go ahead. Spell it.   180

LEVEE: It's a bet then. Talking about I can't spell music.

TOLEDO: Go ahead, then. Spell it. Music. Spell it.

LEVEE: I can spell it, nigger! M-U-S-I-K. There!

[*He reaches for the money.*]

TOLEDO: Naw! Naw! Leave the money alone! You ain't spelled it.

LEVEE: What you mean I ain't spelled it? I said M-U-S-I-K!   185

TOLEDO: That ain't how you spell it! That ain't how you spell it! It's M-U-S-I-C! C, nigger. Not K! C! M-U-S-I-C!

LEVEE: What you mean, C? Who say it's C?

TOLEDO: Cutler. Slow Drag. Tell this fool.

[*They look at each other and then away.*]

Well, I'll be a monkey's uncle!   190

[TOLEDO *picks up the money and hands* LEVEE *his dollar back.*]

Here's your dollar back, Levee. I done won it, you understand. I done won the dollar. But if don't nobody know but me, how am I gonna prove it to you?

LEVEE: You just mad 'cause I spelled it.

TOLEDO: Spelled what! M-U-S-I-K don't spell nothing. I just wish there was some way I could show you the right and wrong of it. How you gonna know something if the   195
other fellow don't know if you're right or not? Now I can't even be sure that I'm spelling it right.

LEVEE: That's what I'm talking about. You don't know it. Talking about C. You ought to give me that dollar I won from you.

TOLEDO: All right. All right. I'm gonna show you how ridiculous you sound. You know 200
the Lord's Prayer?

LEVEE: Why? You wanna bet a dollar on that?

TOLEDO: Just answer the question. Do you know the Lord's Prayer or don't you?

LEVEE: Yeah, I know it. What of it?

TOLEDO: Cutler? 205

CUTLER: What you Cutlering me for? I ain't got nothing to do with it.

TOLEDO: I just want to show the man how ridiculous he is.

CUTLER: Both of you all sound like damn fools. Arguing about something silly. Yeah, I
know the Lord's Prayer. My daddy was a deacon in the church. Come asking me if I
know the Lord's Prayer. Yeah, I know it. 210

TOLEDO: Slow Drag?

SLOW DRAG: Yeah.

TOLEDO: All right. Now I'm gonna tell you a story to show just how ridiculous he sound.
There was these two fellows, see. So, the one of them go up to this church and commence to taking up the church learning. The other fellow see him out on the road and 215
he say, "I done heard you taking up the church learning," say, "Is you learning anything
up there?" The other one say, "Yeah, I done take up the church learning and I's learning all kinds of things about the Bible and what it say and all. Why you be asking?"
The other one say, "Well, do you know the Lord's Prayer?" And he say "Why, sure I
know the Lord's Prayer, I'm taking up learning at the church ain't I? I know the Lord's 220
Prayer backwards and forewards." And the other fellow says, "I bet you five dollars you
don't know the Lord's Prayer, 'cause I don't think you knows it. I think you be going
up to the church 'cause the Widow Jenkins be going up there and you just wanna be
sitting in the same room with her when she cross them big, fine, pretty legs she got."
And the other one say, "Well, I'm gonna prove you wrong and I'm gonna bet you that 225
five dollars." So he say, "Well, go on and say it then." So he commenced to saying the
Lord's Prayer. He say, "Now I lay me down to sleep, I pray the Lord my soul to keep."
The other one say, "Here's your five dollars. I didn't think you knew it."

[*They all laugh.*]

Now that's just how ridiculous Levee sound. Only 'cause I knowed how to spell
music, I still got my dollar. 230

LEVEE: That don't prove nothing. What's that supposed to prove?

[**TOLEDO** *takes a newspaper out of his back pocket and begins to read.*]

TOLEDO: I'm through with it.

SLOW DRAG: Is you all gonna rehearse this music or ain't you?

[**CUTLER** *takes out some papers and starts to roll a reefer.*]

LEVEE: How many times you done played them songs? What you gotta rehearse for?

SLOW DRAG: This a recording session. I wanna get it right the first time and get on out 235
of here.

CUTLER: Slow Drag's right. Let's go on and rehearse and get it over with.

LEVEE: You all go and rehearse, then. I got to finish this song for Mr. Sturdyvant.

CUTLER: Come on, Levee . . . I don't want no shit now. You rehearse like everybody else.
You in the band like everybody else. Mr. Sturdyvant just gonna have to wait. You 240
got to do that on your own time. This is the band's time.

LEVEE: Well, what is you doing? You sitting there rolling a reefer talking about let's rehearse.
Toledo reading a newspaper. Hell, I'm ready if you wanna rehearse. I just say there
ain't no point in it. Ma ain't here. What's the point in it?

CUTLER: Nigger, why you gotta complain all the time? 245

TOLEDO: Levee would complain if a gal ain't laid across his bed just right.

CUTLER: That's what I know. That's what I try to tell him just play the music and forget about it. It ain't no big thing.

TOLEDO: Levee ain't got an eye for that. He wants to tie on to some abstract component and sit down on the elemental. 250

LEVEE: This is get-on-Levee time, huh? Levee ain't said nothing except this some old jug-band music.

TOLEDO: Under the right circumstances you'd play anything. If you know music, then you play it. Straight on or off to the side. Ain't nothing abstract about it.

LEVEE: Toledo, you sound like you got a mouth full of marbles. You the only cracker- 255 talking nigger I know.

TOLEDO: You ought to have learned yourself to read . . . then you'd understand the basic understanding of everything.

SLOW DRAG: Both of you all gonna drive me crazy with that philosophy bullshit. Cutler, give me a reefer. 260

CUTLER: Ain't you got some reefer? Where's your reefer? Why you all the time asking me?

SLOW DRAG: Cutler, how long I done known you? How long we been together? Twenty-two years. We been doing this together for twenty-two years. All up and down the back roads, the side roads, the front roads . . . We done played the juke joints, the whore-houses, the barn dances, and city sit-downs . . . I done lied for you and lied with 265 you . . . We done laughed together, fought together, slept in the same bed together, done sucked on the same titty . . . and now you don't wanna give me no reefer.

CUTLER: You see this nigger trying to talk me out of my reefer, Toledo? Running all that about how long he done knowed me and how we done sucked on the same titty. Nigger, you *still* ain't getting none of my reefer! 270

TOLEDO: That's African.

SLOW DRAG: What? What you talking about? What's African?

LEVEE: I know he ain't talking about me. You don't see me running around in no jungle with no bone between my nose.

TOLEDO: Levee, you worse than ignorant. You ignorant without a premise. [*Pauses.*] Now, 275 what I was saying is what Slow Drag was doing is African. That's what you call an African conceptualization. That's when you name the gods or call on the ancestors to achieve whatever your desires are.

SLOW DRAG: Nigger, I ain't no African! I ain't doing no African nothing!

TOLEDO: Naming all those things you and Cutler done together is like trying to solicit 280 some reefer based on a bond of kinship. That's African. An ancestral retention. Only you forgot the name of the gods.

SLOW DRAG: I ain't forgot nothing, I was telling the nigger how cheap he is. Don't come talking that African nonsense to me.

TOLEDO: You just like Levee. No eye for taking an abstract and fixing it to a specific. 285 There's so much that goes on around you and you can't even see it.

CUTLER: Wait a minute . . . wait a minute. Toledo, now when this nigger . . . when an African do all them things you say and name all the gods and whatnot . . . then what happens?

TOLEDO: Depends on if the gods is sympathetic with his cause for which he is calling them with the right names. Then his success comes with the right proportion of his naming. 290 That's the way that go.

CUTLER: [*taking out a reefer*] Here, Slow Drag. Here's a reefer. You done talked yourself up on that one.

SLOW DRAG: Thank you. You ought to have done that in the first place and saved me all the aggravation. 295

CUTLER: What I wants to know is . . . what's the same titty we done sucked on. That's what I want to know.

SLOW DRAG: Oh, I just threw that in there to make it sound good.

[*They all laugh.*]

CUTLER: Nigger, you ain't right.

SLOW DRAG: I knows it.   300

CUTLER: Well, come on . . . let's get it rehearsed. Time's wasting.

[*The musicians pick up their instruments.*]

Let's do it. "Ma Rainey's Black Bottom." One . . . two . . . you know what to do.

[*They begin to play.* LEVEE *is playing something different. He stops.*]

LEVEE: Naw! Naw! We ain't doing it that way.

[TOLEDO *stops playing, then* SLOW DRAG.]

We doing my version. It say so right there on that piece of paper you got. Ask Toledo. That's what Mr. Irvin told me . . . say it's on the list he gave you.   305

CUTLER: Let me worry about what's on the list and what ain't on the list. How you gonna tell me what's on the list?

LEVEE: 'Cause I know what Mr. Irvin told me! Ask Toledo!

CUTLER: Let me worry about what's on the list. You just play the song I say.

LEVEE: What kind of sense it make to rehearse the wrong version of the song? That's what   310
I wanna know. Why you wanna rehearse that version.

SLOW DRAG: You supposed to rehearse what you gonna play. That's the way they taught me. Now, *whatever* version we gonna play . . . let's go on and rehearse it.

LEVEE: That's what I'm trying to tell the man.

CUTLER: You trying to tell me what we is and ain't gonna play. And that ain't none of your   315
business. Your business is to play what I say.

LEVEE: Oh, I see now. You done got jealous cause Mr. Irvin using my version. You done got jealous cause I proved I know something about music.

CUTLER: What the hell . . . nigger, you talk like a fool! What the hell I got to be jealous of you about? The day I get jealous of you I may as well lay down and die.   320

TOLEDO: Levee started all that 'cause he too lazy to rehearse. [*to* LEVEE] You ought to just go on and play the song . . . What difference does it make?

LEVEE: Where's the paper? Look at the paper! Get the paper and look at it! See what it say. Gonna tell me I'm too lazy to rehearse.

CUTLER: We ain't talking about the paper. We talking about you understanding where you   325
fit in when you around here. You just play what I say.

LEVEE: Look . . . I don't care what you play! All right? It don't matter to me. Mr. Irvin gonna straighten it up! I don't care what you play.

CUTLER: Thank you. [*Pauses.*] Let's play this "Hear Me Talking to You" till we find out what's happening with the "Black Bottom." Slow Drag, you sing Ma's part. [*Pauses.*]   330
"Hear Me Talking to You." Let's do it. One . . . Two . . . You know what to do.

[*They play.*]

SLOW DRAG: [*Singing*]

> Rambling man makes no change in me
> I'm gonna ramble back to my used-to-be
> Ah, you hear me talking to you   335
> I don't bite my tongue

You wants to be my man
You got to fetch it with you when you come.

Eve and Adam in the garden taking a chance
Adam didn't take time to get his pants   340
Ah, you hear me talking to you
I don't bite my tongue
You wants to be my man
You got to fetch it with you when you come.

Our old cat swallowed a ball of yarn   345
When the kittens were born they had sweaters on
Ah, you hear me talking to you
I don't bite my tongue
You wants to be my man
You got to fetch it with you when you come.   350

[IRVIN *enters. The musicians stop playing.*]

IRVIN: Any of you boys know what's keeping Ma?
CUTLER: Can't say, Mr. Irvin. She'll be along directly, I reckon. I talked to her this morn-
ing, she say she'll be here in time to rehearse.
IRVIN: Well, you boys go ahead.

[*He starts to exit.*]

CUTLER: Mr. Irvin, about these songs . . . Levee say . . .   355
IRVIN: Whatever's on the list, Cutler. You got that list I gave you?
CUTLER: Yessir, I got it right here.
IRVIN: Whatever's on there. Whatever that says.
CUTLER: I'm asking about this "Black Bottom" piece . . . Levee say . . .
IRVIN: Oh, it's on the list. "Ma Rainey's Black Bottom" on the list.   360
CUTLER: I know it's on the list. I wanna know what version. We got two versions of that
song.
IRVIN: Oh, Levee's arrangement. We're using Levee's arrangement.
CUTLER: Ok. I got that straight. Now, this "Moonshine Blues" . . .
IRVIN: We'll work it out with Ma, Cutler. Just rehearse whatever's on the list and use   365
Levee's arrangement on that "Black Bottom" piece.

[*He exits.*]

LEVEE: See, I told you! It don't mean nothing when I say it. You got to wait for Mr. Irvin
to say it. Well, I told you the way it is.
CUTLER: Levee, the sooner you understand it ain't what you say, or what Mr. Irvin say . . .
it's what Ma say that counts.   370
SLOW DRAG: Don't nobody say when it come to Ma. She's gonna do what she wants to
do. Ma says what happens with her.
LEVEE: Hell, the man's the one putting out the record! He's gonna put out what he wanna
put out!
SLOW DRAG: He's gonna put out what Ma want him to put out.   375
LEVEE: You heard what the man told you . . . "Ma Rainey's Black Bottom," Levee's arrange-
ment. There you go! That's what he told you.
SLOW DRAG: What you gonna do, Cutler?

CUTLER: Ma ain't told me what version. Let's go on and play it Levee's way.

TOLEDO: See, now . . . I'll tell you something. As long as the colored man look to white 380
folks to put the crown on what he say . . . as long as he looks to white folks for
approval . . . then he ain't never gonna find out who he is and what he's about. He's
just gonna be about what white folks want him to be about. That's one sure thing.

LEVEE: I'm just trying to show Cutler where he's wrong.

CUTLER: Cutler don't need you to show him nothing. 385

SLOW DRAG: [*irritated*] Come on, let's get this shit rehearsed! You all can bicker afterward!

CUTLER: Levee's confused about who the boss is. He don't know Ma's the boss.

LEVEE: Ma's the boss on the road! We at a recording session. Mr. Sturdyvant and Mr. Irvin say
what's gonna be here! We's in Chicago, we ain't in Memphis! I don't know why you all
wanna pick me about it, shit! I'm with Slow Drag . . . Let's go on and get it rehearsed. 390

CUTLER: All right. All right. I know how to solve this. "Ma Rainey's Black Bottom."
Levee's version. Let's do it. Come on.

TOLEDO: How that first part go again, Levee?

LEVEE: It go like this. [*He plays.*] That's to get the people's attention to the song. That's
when you and Slow Drag come in with the rhythm part. Me and Cutler play on the 395
breaks. [*Becoming animated.*] Now we gonna dance it . . . but we ain't gonna coun-
trify it. This ain't no barn dance. We gonna play it like . . .

CUTLER: The man ask you how the first part go. He don't wanna hear all that. Just tell him
how the piece go.

TOLEDO: I got it. I got it. Let's go. I know how to do it. 400

CUTLER: "Ma Rainey's Black Bottom." One . . . two . . . You know what to do.

[*They begin to play.* LEVEE *stops.*]

LEVEE: You all got to keep up now. You playing in the wrong time. Ma come in over the
top. She got to find her own way in.

CUTLER: Nigger, will you let us play this song? When you get your own band . . . then you
tell them that nonsense. We know how to play the piece. I was playing music before 405
you was born. Gonna tell me how to play . . . All right. Let's try it again.

SLOW DRAG: Cutler, wait till I fix this. This string started to unravel. [*Playfully.*] And you
know I want to play Levee's music right.

LEVEE: If you was any kind of musician, you'd take care of your instrument. Keep it in
tip-top order. If you was any kind of musician, I'd let you be in my band. 410

SLOW DRAG: Shhheeeeet!

[*He crosses to get his string and steps on* LEVEE*'s shoes.*]

LEVEE: Damn, Slow Drag! Watch them big-ass shoes you got.

SLOW DRAG: Boy, ain't nobody done nothing to you.

LEVEE: You done stepped on my shoes.

SLOW DRAG: Move them the hell out the way, then. You was in my way . . . I wasn't in 415
your way.

[CUTLER *lights up another reefer.* SLOW DRAG *rummages around in his
belongings for a string.* LEVEE *takes out a rag and begins to shine his shoes.*]

You can shine these when you get done, Levee.

CUTLER: If I had them shoes Levee got, I could buy me a whole suit of clothes.

LEVEE: What kind of difference it make what kind of shoes I got? Ain't nothing wrong with
having nice shoes. I ain't said nothing about your shoes. Why you wanna talk about 420
me and my Florsheims?

CUTLER: Any man who takes a whole week's pay and puts it on some shoes—you understand what I mean, what you walk around on the ground with—is a fool! And I don't
mind telling you.

LEVEE: [*irritated*] What difference it make to you, Cutler?   425

SLOW DRAG: The man ain't said nothing about your shoes. Ain't nothing wrong with having nice shoes. Look at Toledo.

TOLEDO: What about Toledo?

SLOW DRAG: I said ain't nothing wrong with having nice shoes.

LEVEE: Nigger got them clodhoppers! Old brogans! He ain't nothing but a sharecropper.   430

TOLEDO: You can make all the fun you want. It don't mean nothing. I'm satisfied with
them and that's what counts.

LEVEE: Nigger, why don't you get some decent shoes? Got nerve to put on a suit and tie
with them farming boots.

CUTLER: What you just tell me? It don't make no difference about the man's shoes. That's   435
what you told me.

LEVEE: Aw, hell, I don't care what the nigger wear. I'll be honest with you. I don't care if
he went barefoot. [SLOW DRAG *has put his string on the bass and is tuning it.*] Play
something for me, Slow Drag. [SLOW DRAG *plays.*] A man got to have some shoes
to dance like this! You can't dance like this with them clodhoppers Toledo got.   440

> [LEVEE *sings.*]
>
> *Hello Central give me Doctor Jazz*
> *He's got just what I need I'll say he has*
> *When the world goes wrong and I have got the blues*
> *He's the man who makes me get on my dancing shoes.*

TOLEDO: That's the trouble with colored folks . . . always wanna have a good time. Good   445
times done got more niggers killed than God got ways to count. What the hell having
a good time mean? That's what I wanna know.

LEVEE: Hell, nigger . . . it don't need explaining. Ain't you never had no good time before?

TOLEDO: The more niggers get killed having a good time, the more good times niggers
wanna have.   450

> [SLOW DRAG *stops playing.*]

There's more to life than having a good time. If there ain't, then this is piss-poor life
we're having . . . if that's all there is to be got out of it.

SLOW DRAG: Toledo, just 'cause you like to read them books and study and whatnot . . .
that's your good time. People get other things they likes to do to have a good time.
Ain't no need you picking them about it.   455

CUTLER: Niggers been having a good time before you was born, and they gonna keep
having a good time after you gone.

TOLEDO: Yeah, but what else they gonna do? Ain't nobody talking about making the lot
of the colored man better for him here in America.

LEVEE: Now you gonna be Booker T. Washington.   460

TOLEDO: Everybody worried about having a good time. Ain't nobody thinking about what
kind of world they gonna leave their youngens. "Just give me the good time, that's
all I want." It just makes me sick.

SLOW DRAG: Well, the colored man's gonna be all right. He got through slavery, and he'll
get through whatever else the white man put on him. I ain't worried about that.   465
Good times is what makes life worth living. Now, you take the white man . . . The
white man don't know how to have a good time. That's why he's troubled all the time.

He don't know how to have a good time. He don't know how to laugh at life.

LEVEE: That's what the problem is with Toledo . . . reading all them books and things. He done got to the point where he forgot how to laugh and have a good time. Just like the white man. 470

TOLEDO: I know how to have a good time as well as the next man. I said, there's got to be more to life than having a good time. I said the colored man ought to be doing more than just trying to have a good time all the time.

LEVEE: Well, what is you doing, nigger? Talking all them highfalutin ideas about making a better world for the colored man. What is you doing to make it better? You playing the music and looking for your next piece of pussy same as we is. What is you doing? That's what I wanna know. Tell him, Cutler. 475

CUTLER: You all leave Cutler out of this. Cutler ain't got nothing to do with it.

TOLEDO: Levee, you just about the most ignorant nigger I know. Sometimes I wonder why I ever bother to try and talk with you. 480

LEVEE: Well, what is you doing? Talking that shit to me about I'm ignorant! What is you doing? You just a whole lot of mouth. A great big windbag. Thinking you smarter than everybody else. What is you doing, huh?

TOLEDO: It ain't just me, fool! It's everybody! What you think . . . I'm gonna solve the colored man's problems by myself? I said, we. You understand that? We. That's every living colored man in the world got to do his share. Got to do his part. I ain't talking about what I'm gonna do . . . or what you or Cutler or Slow Drag or anybody else. I'm talking about all of us together. What all of us is gonna do. That's what I'm talking about, nigger! 485

490

LEVEE: Well, why didn't you say that, then?

CUTLER: Toledo, I don't know why you waste your time on this fool.

TOLEDO: That's what I'm trying to figure out.

LEVEE: Now there go Cutler with his shit. Calling me a fool. You wasn't even in the conversation. Now you gonna take sides and call me a fool. 495

CUTLER: Hell, I was listening to the man. I got sense enough to know what he was saying. I could tell it straight back to you.

LEVEE: Well, you go on with it. But I'll tell you this . . . I ain't gonna be too many more of your fools. I'll tell you that. Now you put that in your pipe and smoke it.

CUTLER: Boy, ain't nobody studying you. Telling me what to put in my pipe. Who's you to tell me what to do? 500

LEVEE: All right, I ain't nobody. Don't pay me no mind. I ain't nobody.

TOLEDO: Levee, you ain't nothing but the devil.

LEVEE: There you go! That's who I am. I'm the devil. I ain't nothing but the devil.

CUTLER: I can see that. That's something you know about. You know all about the devil. 505

LEVEE: I ain't saying what I know. I know plenty. What you know about the devil? Telling me what I know. What you know?

SLOW DRAG: I know a man sold his soul to the devil.

LEVEE: There you go! That's the only thing I ask about the devil . . . to see him coming so I can sell him this one I got. 'Cause if there's a god up there, he done went to sleep. 510

SLOW DRAG: Sold his soul to the devil himself. Name of Eliza Cotter. Lived in Tuscaloosa County, Alabama. The devil came by and he done upped and sold him his soul.

CUTLER: How you know the man done sold his soul to the devil, nigger? You talking that old-woman foolishness.

SLOW DRAG: Everybody know. It wasn't no secret. He went around working for the devil and everybody knowed it. Carried him a bag . . . one of them carpetbags. Folks say he carried the devil's papers and whatnot where he put your fingerprint on the paper with blood. 515

LEVEE: Where he at now? That's what I want to know. He can put my whole handprint if   520
he want to!

CUTLER: That's the damnedest thing I ever heard! Folks kill me with that talk.

TOLEDO: Oh, that's real enough, all right. Some folks go arm in arm with the devil, shoulder to shoulder, and talk to him all the time. That's real, ain't nothing wrong in
believing that.

SLOW DRAG: That's what I'm saying. Eliza Cotter is one of them. All right. The man living   525
up in an old shack on Ben Foster's place, shoeing mules and horses, making them
charms and things in secret. He done hooked up with the devil, showed up one day
all fancied out with just the finest clothes you ever seen on a colored man . . . dressed
just like one of them crackers . . . and carrying this bag with them papers and things.
All right. Had a pocketful of money, just living the life of a rich man. Ain't done   530
no more work or nothing. Just had him a string of women he run around with and
throw his money away on. Bought him a big fine house . . . Well, it wasn't all that
big, but it did have one of them white picket fences around it. Used to hire a man
once a week just to paint that fence. Messed around there and one of the fellows of
them gals he was messing with got fixed on him wrong and Eliza killed him. And   535
he laughed about it. Sheriff come and arrest him, and then let him go. And he went
around in that town laughing about killing this fellow. Trial come up, and the judge
cut him loose. He must have been in converse with the devil too . . . 'cause he cut
him loose and give him a bottle of whiskey! Folks ask what done happened to make
him change, and he'd tell them straight out he done sold his soul to the devil and   540
ask them if they wanted to sell theirs 'cause he could arrange it for them. Preacher
see him coming, used to cross on the other side of the road. He'd just stand there
and laugh at the preacher and call him a fool to his face.

CUTLER: Well, whatever happened to this fellow? What come of him? A man who, as you
say, done sold his soul to the devil is bound to come to a bad end.   545

TOLEDO: I don't know about that. The devil's strong. The devil ain't no pushover.

SLOW DRAG: Oh, the devil had him under his wing, all right. Took good care of him. He
ain't wanted for nothing.

CUTLER: What happened to him? That's what I want to know.

SLOW DRAG: Last I heard, he headed north with that bag of his, handing out hundred-   550
dollar bills on the spot to whoever wanted to sign on with the devil. That's what I
hear tell of him.

CUTLER: That's a bunch of fool talk. I don't know how you fix your mouth to tell that
story. I don't believe that.

SLOW DRAG: I ain't asking you to believe it. I'm just telling you the facts of it.   555

LEVEE: I sure wish I knew where he went. He wouldn't have to convince me long. Hell, I'd
even help him sign people up.

CUTLER: Nigger, God's gonna strike you down with that blasphemy you talking.

LEVEE: Oh, shit! God don't mean nothing to me. Let him strike me! Here I am, standing
right here. What you talking about he's gonna strike me? Here I am! Let him strike   560
me! I ain't scared of him. Talking that stuff to me.

CUTLER: All right. You gonna be sorry. You gonna fix yourself to have bad luck. Ain't
nothing gonna work for you.

[*Buzzer sounds offstage.*]

LEVEE: Bad luck? What I care about some bad luck? You talking simple. I ain't knowed
nothing but bad luck all my life. Couldn't get no worse. What the hell I care about   565
some bad luck? Hell, I eat it every day for breakfast! You dumber than I thought you
was . . . talking about bad luck.

CUTLER: All right, nigger, you'll see! Can't tell a fool nothing. You'll see!

IRVIN: [IRVIN *enters the studio, checks his watch, and calls down the stairs.*] Cutler . . . you boys' sandwiches are up here . . . Cutler? 570

CUTLER: Yessir, Mr. Irvin . . . be right there.

TOLEDO: I'll walk up there and get them.

> [TOLEDO *exits. The lights go down in the band room and up in the studio.* IRVIN *paces back and forth in an agitated manner.* STURDYVANT *enters.*]

STURDYVANT: Irv, what's happening? Is she here yet? Was that her?

IRVIN: It's the sandwiches, Mel. I told you . . . I'll let you know when she comes, huh?

STURDYVANT: What's keeping her? Do you know what time it is? Have you looked at the 575 clock? You told me she'd be here. You told me you'd take care of it.

IRVIN: Mel, for Chrissakes! What do you want from me? What do you want me to do?

STURDYVANT: Look what time it is, Irv. You told me she'd be here.

IRVIN: She'll be here, okay? I don't know what's keeping her. You know they're always late, Mel. 580

STURDYVANT: You should have went by the hotel and made sure she was on time. You should have taken care of this. That's what you told me, huh? "I'll take care of it."

IRVIN: Okay! Okay! I didn't go by the hotel! What do you want me to do? She'll be here, okay? The band's here . . . she'll be here. 585

STURDYVANT: Okay, Irv. I'll take your word. But if she doesn't come . . . if she doesn't come . . .

> [STURDYVANT *exits to the control booth as* TOLEDO *enters.*]

TOLEDO: Mr. Irvin . . . I come up to get the sandwiches.

IRVIN: Say . . . uh . . . look . . . one o'clock, right? She said one o'clock.

TOLEDO: That's what time she told us. Say be here at one o'clock. 590

IRVIN: Do you know what's keeping her? Do you know why she ain't here?

TOLEDO: I can't say, Mr Irvin. Told us one o'clock.

> [*The buzzer sounds.* IRVIN *goes to the door. There is a flurry of commotion as* MA RAINEY *enters, followed closely by the* POLICEMAN, DUSSIE MAE, *and* SYLVESTER. MA RAINEY *is a short, heavy woman. She is dressed in a fulllength fur coat with matching hat, an emerald-green dress, and several strands of pearls of varying lengths. Her hair is secured by a headband that matches her dress. Her manner is simple and direct, and she carries herself in a royal fashion.* DUSSIE MAE *is a young, dark-skinned woman whose greatest asset is the sensual energy which seems to flow from her. She is dressed in a fur jacket and a tightfitting canary-yellow dress.* SYLVESTER *is an Arkansas country boy, the size of a fullback. He wears a new suit and coat, in which he is obviously uncomfortable. Most of the time, he stutters when he speaks.*]

MA RAINEY: Irvin . . . you better tell this man who I am! You better get him straight!

IRVIN: Ma, do you know what time it is? Do you have any idea? We've been waiting . . .

DUSSIE MAE: [*to* SYLVESTER] If you was watching where you was going . . . 595

SYLVESTER: I was watching . . . What you mean?

IRVIN: [*notices* POLICEMAN] What's going on here? Officer, what's the matter?

MA RAINEY: Tell the man who he's messing with!

POLICEMAN : Do you know this lady?

MA RAINEY: Just tell the man who I am! That's all you gotta do. 600

POLICEMAN: Lady, will you let me talk, huh?

MA RAINEY: Tell the man who I am!

IRVIN: Wait a minute . . . wait a minute! Let me handle it. Ma, will you let me handle it?

MA RAINEY: Tell him who he's messing with!

IRVIN: Okay! Okay! Give me a chance! Officer, this is one of our recording artists . . .　605
Ma Rainey.

MA RAINEY: Madame Rainey! Get it straight! Madame Rainey! Talking about taking me
to jail!

IRVIN: Look, Ma . . . give me a chance, okay? Here . . . sit down. I'll take care of it. Officer,
what's the problem?　610

DUSSIE MAE: [to SYLVESTER] It's all your fault.

SYLVESTER: I ain't done nothing . . . Ask Ma.

POLICEMAN: Well . . . when I walked up on the incident . . .

DUSSIE MAE: Sylvester wrecked Ma's car.

SYLVESTER: I d-d-did not! The m-m-man ran into me!　615

POLICEMAN: [to IRVIN] Look, buddy . . . if you want it in a nutshell, we got her charged
with assault and battery.

MA RAINEY: Assault and what for what!

DUSSIE MAE: See . . . we was trying to get a cab . . . and so Ma . . .

MA RAINEY: Wait a minute! I'll tell you if you wanna know what happened. [She points to　620
SYLVESTER.] Now, that's Sylvester. That's my nephew. He was driving my car . . .

POLICEMAN: Lady, we don't know whose car he was driving.

MA RAINEY: That's my car!

DUSSIE MAE AND SYLVESTER: That's Ma's car!

MA RAINEY: What you mean you don't know whose car it is? I bought and paid for that car.　625

POLICEMAN: That's what you say, lady . . . We still gotta check. [to IRVIN] They hit a car
on Market Street. The guy said the kid ran a stoplight.

SYLVESTER: What you mean? The man c-c-come around the corner and hit m-m-me!

POLICEMAN: While I was calling a paddy wagon to haul them to the station, they try to
hop into a parked cab. The cabbie said he was waiting on a fare . . .　630

MA RAINEY: The man was just sitting there. Wasn't waiting for nobody. I don't know why
he wanna tell that lie.

POLICEMAN: Look, lady . . . will you let me tell the story?

MA RAINEY: Go ahead and tell it then. But tell it right!

POLICEMAN: Like I say . . . she tries to get in this cab. The cabbie's waiting on a fare. She　635
starts creating a disturbance. The cabbie gets out to try to explain the situation to
her . . . and she knocks him down.

DUSSIE MAE: She ain't hit him! He just fell!

SYLVESTER: He just s-s-s-slipped!

MA RAINEY: If that don't beat all to hell. I ain't touched the man! The man was trying to　640
reach around me to keep his car door closed. I opened the door and it hit him and
he fell down. I ain't touched the man!

IRVIN: Okay. Okay . . . I got it straight now, Ma. You didn't touch him. All right? Officer,
can I see you for a minute?

DUSSIE MAE: Ma was just trying to open the door.　645

SYLVESTER: He j-j-just got in t-t-the way!

MA RAINEY: Said he wasn't gonna haul no colored folks . . . if you want to know the truth
of it.

IRVIN: Okay, Ma . . . I got it straight now . . . Officer?

[IRVIN *pulls the* POLICEMAN *off to the side.*]

MA RAINEY: [*noticing* TOLEDO] Toledo, Cutler and everybody here?　650

TOLEDO: Yeah, they down in the band room. What happened to your car?

STURDYVANT: [*entering*] Irv, what's the problem? What's going on? Officer . . .

IRVIN: Mel, let me take care of it. I can handle it.

STURDYVANT: What's happening? What the hell's going on?

IRVIN: Let me handle it, Mel, huh? 655

[STURDYVANT *crosses over to* MA RAINEY.]

STURDYVANT: What's going on, Ma. What'd you do?

MA RAINEY: Sturdyvant, get on away from me! That's the last thing I need . . . to go through some of your shit!

IRVIN: Mel, I'll take care of it. I'll explain it all to you. Let me handle it, huh?

[STURDYVANT *reluctantly returns to the control booth.*]

POLICEMAN: Look, buddy, like I say . . . we got her charged with assault and battery . . . 660 and the kid with threatening the cabbie.

SYLVESTER: I ain't done n-n-nothing!

MA RAINEY: You leave the boy out of it. He ain't done nothing. What's he supposed to have done?

POLICEMAN: He threatened the cabbie, lady! You just can't go around threatening people! 665

SYLVESTER: I ain't done nothing to him! He's the one talking about he g-g-gonna get a b-b-baseball bat on me! I just told him what I'd do with it. But I ain't done nothing 'cause he didn't get the b-b-bat!

IRVIN: [*Pulling the* POLICEMAN *aside.*] Officer . . . look here . . .

POLICEMAN: We was on our way down to the precinct . . . but I figured I'd do you a favor 670 and bring her by here. I mean, if she's as important as she says she is . . .

IRVIN: [*slides a bill from his pocket*] Look, Officer . . . I'm Madame Rainey's manager . . . It's good to meet you. [*He shakes the* POLICEMAN'*s hand and passes him the bill.*] As soon as we're finished with the recording session, I'll personally stop by the precinct house and straighten up this misunderstanding. 675

POLICEMAN: Well . . . I guess that's all right. As long as someone is responsible for them.

[*He pockets the bill and winks at* IRVIN.]

No need to come down . . . I'll take care of it myself. Of course, we wouldn't want nothing like this to happen again.

IRVIN: Don't worry, Officer . . . I'll take care of everything. Thanks for your help.

[IRVIN *escorts the* POLICEMAN *to the door and returns. He crosses over to* MA RAINEY.]

Here, Ma . . . let me take your coat. [*to* SYLVESTER] I don't believe I know you. 680

MA RAINEY: That's my nephew, Sylvester.

IRVIN: I'm very pleased to meet you. Here . . . you can give me your coat.

MA RAINEY: That there is Dussie Mae.

IRVIN: Hello . . .

[DUSSIE MAE *hands* IRVIN *her coat.*]

Listen, Ma, just sit there and relax. The boys are in the band room rehearsing. You 685 just sit and relax a minute.

MA RAINEY: I ain't for no sitting. I ain't never heard of such. Talking about taking me to jail. Irvin, call down there and see about my car.

IRVIN: Okay, Ma . . . I'll take care of it. You just relax.

[IRVIN *exits with the coats.*]

MA RAINEY: Why you all keep it so cold in here? Sturdyvant try and pinch every penny he 690
can. You all wanna make some records, you better put some heat on in here or give
me back my coat.

IRVIN: [*entering*] We got the heat turned up, Ma. It's warming up. It'll be warm in a minute.

DUSSIE MAE: [*whispering to* MA RAINEY] Where's the bathroom?

MA RAINEY: It's in the back. Down the hall next to Sturdyvant's office. Come on, I'll show 695
you where it is. Irvin, call down there and see about my car. I want my car fixed today.

IRVIN: I'll take care of everything, Ma.

[*He notices* TOLEDO.]

Say . . . uh . . . uh . . .

TOLEDO: Toledo.

IRVIN: Yeah . . . Toledo. I got the sandwiches, you can take down to the rest of the boys. 700
We'll be ready to go in a minute. Give you boys a chance to eat and then we'll be
ready to go.

[IRVIN *and* TOLEDO *exit. The lights go down in the studio and come up in the
band room.*]

LEVEE: Slow Drag, you ever been to New Orleans?

SLOW DRAG: What's in New Orleans that I want?

LEVEE: How you call yourself a musician and ain't never been to New Orleans. 705

SLOW DRAG: You ever been to Fat Back, Arkansas? [*Pauses.*] All right, then. Ain't never
been nothing in New Orleans that I couldn't get in Fat Back.

LEVEE: That's why you backwards. You just an old country boy talking about Fat Back,
Arkansas, and New Orleans in the same breath.

CUTLER: I been to New Orleans. What about it? 710

LEVEE: You ever been to Lula White's?

CUTLER: Lula White's? I ain't never heard of it.

LEVEE: Man, they got some gals in there just won't wait! I seen a man get killed in there once.
Got drunk and grabbed one of the gals wrong . . . I don't know what the matter of it
was. But he grabbed her and she stuck a knife in him all the way up to the hilt. He ain't 715
even fell. He just stood there and choked on his own blood. I was just asking Slow
Drag 'cause I was gonna take him to Lula White's when we get down to New Orleans
and show him a good time. Introduce him to one of them gals I know down there.

CUTLER: Slow Drag don't need you to find him no pussy. He can take care of his own self.
Fact is . . . you better watch your gal when Slow Drag's around. They don't call him 720
Slow Drag for nothing. [*He laughs.*] Tell him how you got your name Slow Drag.

SLOW DRAG: I ain't thinking about Levee.

CUTLER: Slow Drag break a woman's back when he dance. They had this contest one time
in this little town called Bolingbroke about a hundred miles outside of Macon. We
was playing for this dance and they was giving twenty dollars to the best slow drag- 725
gers. Slow Drag looked over the competition, got down off the bandstand, grabbed
hold of one of them gals, and stuck to her like a fly to jelly. Like wood to glue. Man
had that gal whooping and hollering so . . . everybody stopped to watch. This fellow come in . . . this gal's fellow . . . and pulled a knife a foot long on Slow Drag.
'Member that, Slow Drag? 730

SLOW DRAG: Boy that mama was hot! The front of her dress was wet as a dishrag!

LEVEE: So what happened? What the man do?

CUTLER: Slow Drag ain't missed a stroke. The gal, she just look at her man with that sweet dizzy look in her eye. She ain't about to stop! Folks was clearing out, ducking and hiding under tables, figuring there's gonna be a fight. Slow Drag just looked over the   735
gal's shoulder at the man and said, "Mister, if you'd quit hollering and wait a minute . . . you'll see I'm doing you a favor. I'm helping this gal win ten dollars so she can buy you a gold watch." The man just stood there and looked at him, all the while stroking that knife. Told Slow Drag, say, "All right, then, nigger. You just better make damn sure you win." That's when folks started calling him Slow Drag. The   740
women got to hanging around him so bad after that, them fellows in that town ran us out of there.

[TOLEDO *enters, carrying a small cardboard box with the sandwiches.*]

LEVEE: Yeah . . . well, them gals in Lula White's will put a harness on his ass.
TOLEDO: Ma's up there. Some kind of commotion with the police.
CUTLER: Police? What the police up there for?   745
TOLEDO: I couldn't get it straight. Something about her car. They gone now . . . she's all right. Mr. Irvin sent some sandwiches.

[LEVEE *springs across the room.*]

LEVEE: Yeah, all right. What we got here?

[*He takes two sandwiches out of the box.*]

TOLEDO: What you doing grabbing two? There ain't but five in there . . . How you figure you get two?   750
LEVEE: 'Cause I grabbed them first. There's enough for everybody . . . What you talking about? It ain't like I'm taking food out of nobody's mouth.
CUTLER: That's all right. He can have mine too. I don't want none.

[LEVEE *starts toward the box to get another sandwich.*]

TOLEDO: Nigger, you better get out of here. Slow Drag, you want this?
SLOW DRAG: Naw, you can have it.   755
TOLEDO: With Levee around, you don't have to worry about no leftovers. I can see that.
LEVEE: What's the matter with you? Ain't you eating two sandwiches? Then why you wanna talk about me? Talking about there won't be no leftovers with Levee around. Look at your own self before you look at me.
TOLEDO: That's what you is. That's what we all is. A leftover from history. You see now,   760
I'll show you.
LEVEE: Aw, shit . . . I done got the nigger started now.
TOLEDO: Now, I'm gonna show how this goes . . . where you just a leftover from history. Everybody come from different places in Africa, right? Come from different tribes and things. Soonawhile they began to make one big stew. You had the carrots, the   765
peas, and potatoes and whatnot over here. And over there you had the meat, the nuts, the okra, corn . . . and then you mix it up and let it cook right through to get the flavors flowing together . . . then you got one thing. You got a stew.
   Now you take and eat the stew. You take and make your history with that stew. All right, Now it's over. Your history's over and you done ate the stew. But you look   770
around and you see some carrots over here, some potatoes over there. That stew's still there. You done made your history and it's still there. You can't eat it all. So what you got? You got some leftovers. That's what it is. You got leftovers and you can't do nothing with it. You already making you another history . . . cooking you another meal, and you don't need them leftovers no more. What to do?   775

See, we's the leftovers. The colored man is the leftovers. Now, what's the colored man gonna do with himself? That's what we waiting to find out. But first we gotta know we the leftovers. Now, who knows that? You find me a nigger that knows that and I'll turn any whichaway you want me to. I'll bend over for you. You ain't gonna find that. And that's what the problem is. The problem ain't with the white man. The white man knows you just a leftover. 'Cause he the one who done the eating and he know what he done ate. But we don't know that we been took and made history out of. Done went and filled the white man's belly and now he's full and tired and wants you to get out the way and let him be by himself. Now, I know what I'm talking about. And if you wanna find out, you just ask Mr. Irvin what he had for supper yesterday. And if he's an honest white man . . . which is asking for a whole heap of a lot . . . he'll tell you he done ate your black ass and if you please I'm full up with you . . . so go on and get off the plate and let me eat something else.

SLOW DRAG: What that mean? What's eating got to do with how the white man treat you? He don't treat you no different according to what he ate.

TOLEDO: I ain't said it had nothing to do with how he treat you.

CUTLER: The man's trying to tell you something, fool!

SLOW DRAG: What he trying to tell me? Ain't you here. Why you say he was trying to tell *me* something? Wasn't he trying to tell you too?

LEVEE: He was trying all right. He was trying a whole heap. I'll say that for him. But trying ain't worth a damn. I got lost right there trying to figure out who puts nuts in their stew.

SLOW DRAG: I knowed that before. My grandpappy used to put nuts in his stew. He and my grandmama both. That ain't nothing new.

TOLEDO: They put nuts in their stew all over Africa. But the stew they eat, and the stew your grandpappy made, and all the stew that you and me eat, and the stew Mr. Irvin eats . . . ain't in no way the same stew. That's the way that go. I'm through with it. That's the last you know me to ever try and explain something to you.

CUTLER: [*after a pause*] Well, time's getting along . . . Come on, let's finish rehearsing.

LEVEE: [*stretching out on a bench*] I don't feel like rehearsing. I ain't nothing but a left over. You go and rehearse with Toledo . . . He's gonna teach you how to make a stew.

SLOW DRAG: Cutler, what you gonna do? I don't want to be around here all day.

LEVEE: I know my part. You all go on and rehearse your part. You all need some rehearsal.

CUTLER: Come on, Levee, get up off your ass and rehearse the songs.

LEVEE: I already know them songs . . . What I wanna rehearse them for?

SLOW DRAG: You in the band, ain't you? You supposed to rehearse when the band rehearse.

TOLEDO: Levee think he the king of the barnyard. He thinks he's the only rooster know how to crow.

LEVEE: All right! All right! Come on, I'm gonna show you I know them songs. Come on, let's rehearse. I bet you the first one mess be Toledo. Come on . . . I wanna see if he know how to crow.

CUTLER: "Ma Rainey's Black Bottom," Levee's version. Let's do it.

[*They begin to rehearse. The lights go down in the band room and up in the studio.* MA RAINEY *sits and takes off her shoe, rubs her feet.* DUSSIE MAE *wanders about looking at the studio.* SYLVESTER *is over by the piano.*]

MA RAINEY: [*singing to herself*]

> Oh, Lord, these dogs of mine 820
> They sure do worry me all the time
> The reason why I don't know
> Lord, I beg to be excused
> I can't wear me no sharp-toed shoes.
> I went for a walk 825
> I stopped to talk
> Oh, how my corns did bark.

DUSSIE MAE: It feels kinda spooky in here. I ain't never been in no recording studio before. Where's the band at?

MA RAINEY: They off somewhere rehearsing. I don't know where Irvin went to. All this 830 hurry up and he goes off back there with Sturdyvant. I know he better come on 'cause Ma ain't gonna be waiting. Come here . . . let me see that dress.

[DUSSIE MAE *crosses over.* MA RAINEY *tugs at the dress around the waist, appraising the fit.*]

That dress looks nice. I'm gonna take you tomorrow and get you some more things before I take you down to Memphis. They got clothes up here you can't get in Memphis. I want you to look nice for me. If you gonna travel with the show you 835 got to look nice.

DUSSIE MAE: I need me some more shoes. These hurt my feet.

MA RAINEY: You get you some shoes that fit your feet. Don't you be messing around with no shoes that pinch your feet. Ma know something about bad feet. Hand me my slippers out my bag over yonder. 840

[DUSSIE MAE *brings the slippers.*]

DUSSIE MAE: I just want to get a pair of them yellow ones. About a half-size bigger.

MA RAINEY: We'll get you whatever you need. Sylvester, too . . . I'm gonna get him some more clothes. Sylvester, tuck your clothes in. Straighten them up and look nice. Look like a gentleman.

DUSSIE MAE: Look at Sylvester with that hat on. 845

MA RAINEY: Sylvester, take your hat off inside. Act like your mama taught you something. I know she taught you better than that.

[SYLVESTER *bangs on the piano.*]

Come on over here and leave that piano alone.

SYLVESTER: I ain't d-d-doing nothing to the p-p-piano. I'm just l-l-looking at it.

MA RAINEY: Well. Come on over here and sit down. As soon as Mr. Irvin comes back, I'll 850 have him take you down and introduce you to the band.

[SYLVESTER *comes over.*]

He's gonna take you down there and introduce you in a minute . . . have Cutler show you how your part go. And when you get your money, you gonna send some of it home to your mama. Let her know you doing all right. Make her feel good to know you doing all right in the world. 855

[DUSSIE MAE *wanders about the studio and opens the door leading to the band room. The strains of* LEVEE'*s version of "Ma Rainey's Black Bottom" can be heard.* IRVIN *enters.*]

IRVIN: Ma, I called down to the garage and checked on your car. It's just a scratch. They'll have it ready for you this afternoon. They're gonna send it over with one of their fellows.

MA RAINEY: They better have my car fixed right too. I ain't going for that. Brand-new car . . . they better fix it like new.   860

IRVIN: It was just a scratch on the fender, Ma . . . They'll take care of it . . . don't worry . . . they'll have it like new.

MA RAINEY: Irvin, what is that I hear? What is that the band's rehearsing? I know they ain't rehearsing Levee's "Black Bottom." I know I ain't hearing that?

IRVIN: Ma, listen . . . that's what I wanted to talk to you about. Levee's version of that   865
song . . . it's got a nice arrangement . . . a nice horn intro . . . It really picks it up . . .

MA RAINEY: I ain't studying Levee nothing. I know what he done to that song and I don't like to sing it that way. I'm doing it the old way. That's why I brought my nephew to do the voice intro.

IRVIN: Ma, that's what the people want now. They want something they can dance to.   870
Times are changing. Levee's arrangement gives the people what they want. It gets them excited . . . makes them forget about their troubles.

MA RAINEY: I don't care what you say, Irvin. Levee ain't messing up my song. If he got what the people want, let him take it somewhere else. I'm singing Ma Rainey's song. I ain't singing Levee's song. Now that's all there is to it. Carry my nephew on down there   875
and introduce him to the band. I promised my sister I'd look out for him and he's gonna do the voice intro on the song my way.

IRVIN: Ma, we just figured that . . .

MA RAINEY: Who's this "we"? What you mean "we"? I ain't studying Levee nothing. Come talking this "we" stuff. Who's "we"?   880

IRVIN: Me and Sturdyvant. We decided that it would . . .

MA RAINEY: You decided, huh? I'm just a bump on the log. I'm gonna go which ever way the river drift. Is that it? You and Sturdyvant decided.

IRVIN: Ma, it was just that we thought it would be better.

MA RAINEY: I ain't got good sense. I don't know nothing about music. I don't know what's   885
a good song and what ain't. You know more about my fans than I do.

IRVIN: It's not that, Ma. It would just be easier to do. It's more what the people want.

MA RAINEY: I'm gonna tell you something, Irvin . . . and you go on up there and tell Sturdyvant. What you all say don't count with me. You understand? Ma listens to her heart. Ma listens to the voice inside her. That's what counts with Ma. Now, you   890
carry my nephew on down there . . . tell Cutler he's gonna do the voice intro on that "Black Bottom" song and that Levee ain't messing up my song with none of his music shit. Now, if that don't set right with you and Sturdyvant . . . then I can carry my black bottom on back down South to my tour, 'cause I don't like it up here no ways.   895

IRVIN: Okay, Ma . . . I don't care. I just thought . . .

MA RAINEY: Damn what you thought! What you look like telling me how to sing my song? This Levee and Sturdyvant nonsense . . . I ain't going for it! Sylvester, go on down there and introduce yourself. I'm through playing with Irvin.

SYLVESTER: Which way you go? Where they at?   900

MA RAINEY: Here . . . I'll carry you down there myself.

DUSSIE MAE: Can I go? I wanna see the band.

MA RAINEY: You stay your behind up here. Ain't no cause in you being down there. Come on, Sylvester.

IRVIN: Okay, Ma. Have it your way. We'll be ready to go in fifteen minutes.   905

MA RAINEY: We'll be ready to go when Madame says we're ready. That's the way it goes around here.

[MA RAINEY *and* SYLVESTER *exit. The lights go down in the studio and up in the band room.* MA RAINEY *enters with* SYLVESTER.]

Cutler, this here is my nephew Sylvester. He's gonna do that voice intro on the "Black Bottom" song using the old version.

LEVEE: What you talking about? Mr. Irvin says he's using my version. What you talking   910
about?

MA RAINEY: Levee, I ain't studying you or Mr. Irvin. Cutler, get him straightened out on how to do his part. I ain't thinking about Levee. These folks done messed with the wrong person this day. Sylvester, Cutler gonna teach you your part. You go ahead and get it straight. Don't worry about what nobody else say.   915

[MA RAINEY *exits.*]

CUTLER: Well, come on in, boy. I'm Cutler. You got Slow Drag . . . Levee . . . and that's Toledo over there. Sylvester, huh?

SYLVESTER: Sylvester Brown.

LEVEE: I done wrote a version of that song what picks it up and sets it down in the people's lap! Now she come talking this! You don't need that old circus bullshit! I know what   920
I'm talking about. You gonna mess up the song Cutler and you know it.

CUTLER: I ain't gonna mess up nothing. Ma say . . .

LEVEE: I don't care what Ma say! I'm talking about what the intro gonna do to the song. The peoples in the North ain't gonna buy all that tent-show nonsense. They wanna hear some music!   925

CUTLER: Nigger, I done told you time and again . . . you just in the band. You plays the piece . . . whatever they want! Ma says what to play! Not you! You ain't here to be doing no creating. Your job is to play whatever Ma says!

LEVEE: I might not play nothing! I might quit!

CUTLER: Nigger, don't nobody care if you quit. Whose heart you gonna break?   930

TOLEDO: Levee ain't gonna quit. He got to make some money to keep him in shoe polish.

LEVEE: I done told you all . . . you all don't know me. You don't know what I'll do.

CUTLER: I don't think nobody too much give a damn! Sylvester, here's the way your part go. The band plays the intro . . . I'll tell you where to come in. The band plays the intro and then you say, "All right, boys, you done seen the rest . . . Now I'm gonna   935
show you the best. Ma Rainey's gonna show you her black bottom." You got that? [SYLVESTER *nods.*] Let me hear you say it one time.

SYLVESTER: "All right, boys, you done s-s-seen the rest n-n-now I'm gonna show you the best. M-m-m-m-m-ma Rainey's gonna s-s-show you her black b-b-bottom."

LEVEE: What kind of . . . All right, Cutler! Let me see you fix that! You straighten that out!   940
You hear that shit, Slow Drag? How in the hell the boy gonna do the part and he can't even talk!

SYLVESTER: W-w-w-who's you to tell me what to do, nigger! This ain't your band! Ma tell me to d-d-d-do it and I'm gonna do it. You can go to hell, n-n-n-nigger!

LEVEE: B-b-b-boy, ain't nobody studying you. You go on and fix that one, Cutler. You fix   945
that one and I'll . . . I'll shine your shoes for you. You go on and fix that one!

TOLEDO: You say you Ma's nephew, huh?

SYLVESTER: Yeah. So w-w-what that mean?

TOLEDO: Oh, I ain't mean nothing . . . I was just asking.

SLOW DRAG: Well, come on and let's rehearse so the boy can get it right.   950

LEVEE: I ain't rehearsing nothing! You just wait till I get my band. I'm gonna record that song and show you how it supposed to go!

CUTLER: We can do it without Levee. Let him sit on over there. Sylvester, you remember your part?

SYLVESTER: I remember it pretty g-g-g-good.   955

CUTLER: Well, come on, let's do it, then.

> [*The band begins to play.* LEVEE *sits and pouts.* STURDYVANT *enters the band room.*]

STURDYVANT: Good . . . you boys are rehearsing, I see.

LEVEE: [*Jumping up.*] Yessir! We rehearsing. We know them songs real good.

STURDYVANT: Good! Say, Levee, did you finish that song?

LEVEE: Yessir, Mr. Sturdyvant. I got it right here. I wrote that other part just like you say.   960
It go like:

> *You can shake it, you can break it*
> *You can dance at any hall*
> *You can slide across the floor*
> *You'll never have to stall*   965
> *My jelly, my roll*
> *Sweet Mama, don't you let it fall.*

Then I put that part in there for the people to dance, like you say, for them to forget about their troubles.

STURDYVANT: Good! Good! I'll just take this. I wanna see you about your songs as soon   970
as I get the chance.

LEVEE: Yessir! As soon as you get the chance, Mr. Sturdyvant.

> [STURDYVANT *exits.*]

CUTLER: You hear, Levee? You hear this nigger? "Yessuh, we's rehearsing, boss."

SLOW DRAG: I heard him. Seen him too. Shuffling them feet.

TOLEDO: Aw, Levee can't help it none. He's like all of us. Spooked up with the white man.   975

LEVEE: I'm spooked up with him, all right. You let one of them crackers fix on me wrong.
I'll show you how spooked up I am with him.

TOLEDO: That's the trouble of it. You wouldn't know if he was fixed on you wrong or not.
You so spooked up by him you ain't had the time to study him.

LEVEE: I studies the white man. I got him studied good. The first time one fixes on me   980
wrong, I'm gonna let him know just how much I studied. Come telling me I'm
spooked up with the white man. You let one of them mess with me, I'll show you
how spooked up I am.

CUTLER: You talking out your hat. The man come in here, call you a boy, tell you to get up
off your ass and rehearse, and you ain't had nothing to say to him, except "Yessir!"   985

LEVEE: I can say "yessir" to whoever I please. What you got to do with it? I know how to
handle white folks. I been handling them for thirty-two years, and now you gonna
tell me how to do it. Just 'cause I say "yessir" don't mean I'm spooked up with him.
I know what I'm doing. Let me handle him my way.

CUTLER: Well, go on and handle it, then.   990

LEVEE: Toledo, you always messing with somebody! Always agitating somebody with that
old philosophy bullshit you be talking. You stay out of my way about what I do and
say. I'm my own person. Just let me alone.

TOLEDO: You right, Levee. I apologize. It ain't none of my business that you spooked up by the white man. 995

LEVEE: All right! See! That's the shit I'm talking about. You all back up and leave Levee alone.

SLOW DRAG: Aw, Levee, we was all just having fun. Toledo ain't said nothing about you he ain't said about me. You just taking it all wrong.

TOLEDO: I ain't meant nothing by it Levee. [*Pauses.*] Cutler, you ready to rehearse? 1000

LEVEE: Levee got to be Levee! And he don't need nobody messing with him about the white man—cause you don't know nothing about me. You don't know Levee. You don't know nothing about what kind of blood I got! What kind of heart I got beating here! [*He pounds his chest.*] I was eight years old when I watched a gang of white mens come into my daddy's house and have to do with my mama any way they wanted. 1005 [*Pauses.*] We was living in Jefferson County, about eighty miles outside of Natchez. My daddy's name was Memphis . . . Memphis Lee Green . . . had him near fifty acres of good farming land. I'm talking about good land! Grow anything you want! He done gone off of shares and bought this land from Mr. Hallie's widow woman after he done passed on. Folks called him an uppity nigger 'cause he done saved and 1010 borrowed to where he could buy this land and be independent. [*Pauses.*] It was coming on planting time and my daddy went into Natchez to get him some seed and fertilizer. Called me, say, "Levee you the man of the house now. Take care of your mama while I'm gone." I wasn't but a little boy, eight years old. [*Pauses.*] My mama was frying up some chicken when them mens come in that house. Must have been 1015 eight or nine of them. She standing there frying that chicken and them mens come and took hold of her just like you take hold of a mule and make him do what you want. [*Pauses.*] There was my mama with a gang of white mens. She tried to fight them off, but I could see where it wasn't gonna do her any good, I didn't know what they were doing to her . . . but I figured whatever it was they may as well do to me 1020 too. My daddy had a knife that he kept around there for hunting and working and whatnot. I knew where he kept it and I went and got it.

I'm gonna show you how spooked up I was by the white man. I tried my damndest to cut one of them's throat! I hit him on the shoulder with it. He reached back and grabbed hold of that knife and whacked me across the chest with it. 1025

[LEVEE *raises his shirt to show a long ugly scar.*]

That's what made them stop. They was scared I was gonna bleed to death. My mama wrapped a sheet around me and carried me two miles down to the Furlow place and they drove me up to Doc Albans. He was waiting on a calf to be born, and say he ain't had time to see me. They carried me up to Miss Etta, the midwife, and she fixed me up. 1030

My daddy came back and acted like he done accepted the facts of what happened. But he got the names of them mens from mama. He found out who they was and then we announced we was moving out of that county. Said good-bye to everybody . . . all the neighbors. My daddy went and smiled in the face of one of them crackers who had been with my mama. Smiled in his face and sold him our land. We moved over with 1035 relations in Caldwell. He got us settled in and then he took off one day. I ain't never seen him since. He sneaked back, hiding up in the woods, laying to get them eight or nine men. [*Pauses.*] He got four of them before they got him. They tracked him down in the woods. Caught up with him and hung him and set him afire. [*Pauses.*] My daddy wasn't spooked up by the white man. No sir! And that taught me how to 1040 handle them. I seen my daddy go up and grin in this cracker's face . . . smile in his face and sell him his land. All the while he's planning how he's gonna get him and what he's gonna do to him. That taught me how to handle them. So you all just back up and leave Levee alone about the white man. I can smile and say yessir to whoever I please. I got time coming to me. You all just leave Levee alone about the white man.   1045

[*There is a long pause.* SLOW DRAG *begins playing on the bass and sings.*]

SLOW DRAG: [*singing*]

> *If I had my way*
> *If I had my way*
> *If I had my way*
> *I would tear this old building down.*   1050

ACT II

[*The lights come up in the studio. The musicians are setting up their instruments.* MA RAINEY *walks about shoeless, singing softly to herself.* LEVEE *stands near* DUSSIE MAE, *who hikes up her dress and crosses her leg.* CUTLER *speaks to* IRVIN *off to the side.*]

CUTLER: Mr. Irvin, I don't know what you gonna do. I ain't got nothing to do with it, but the boy can't do the part. He stutters. He can't get it right. He stutters right through it every time.

IRVIN: Christ! Okay. We'll . . . Shit! We'll just do it like we planned. We'll do Levee's version. I'll handle it, Cutler. Come on, let's go. I'll think of something.   5

[*He exits to the control booth.*]

MA RAINEY: [*calling* CUTLER *over*] Levee's got his eyes in the wrong place. You better school him, Cutler.

CUTLER: Come on, Levee . . . let's get ready to play! Get your mind on your work!

IRVIN: [*over speaker*] Okay, boys, we're gonna do "Moonshine Blues" first. "Moonshine Blues," Ma.   10

MA RAINEY: I ain't doing no "Moonshine" nothing. I'm doing the "Black Bottom" first. Come on, Sylvester. [*to* IRVIN] Where's Sylvester's mike? You need a mike for Sylvester. Irvin . . . get him a mike.

IRVIN: Uh . . . Ma, the boys say he can't do it. We'll have to do Levee's version.

MA RAINEY: What you mean he can't do it? Who say he can't do it? What boys say he can't do it?   15

IRVIN: The band, Ma . . . the boys in the band.

MA RAINEY: What band? The band work for me! I say what goes! Cutler, what's he talking about? Levee, this some of your shit?

IRVIN: He stutters, Ma. They say he stutters.   20

MA RAINEY: I don't care if he do. I promised the boy he could do the part . . . and he's gonna do it! That's all there is to it. He don't stutter all the time. Get a microphone down here for him.

IRVIN: Ma, we don't have time. We can't . . .

MA RAINEY: If you wanna make a record, you gonna find time. I ain't playing with you, 25
Irvin. I can walk out of here and go back to my tour. I got plenty fans. I don't need
to go through all of this. Just go and get the boy a microphone.

[IRVIN *and* STURDYVANT *consult in the booth,* IRVIN *exits.*]

STURDYVANT: All right, Ma . . . we'll get him a microphone. But if he messes up . . . He's
only getting one chance . . . The cost . . .
MA RAINEY: Damn the cost. You always talking about the cost. I make more money for 30
this outfit than anybody else you got put together. If he messes up he'll just do it
till he gets it right. Levee, I know you had something to do with this. You better
watch yourself.
LEVEE: It was Cutler!
SYLVESTER: It was you! You the only one m-m-mad about it. 35
LEVEE: The boy stutter. He can't do the part. Everybody see that. I don't know why you
want the boy to do the part no ways.
MA RAINEY: Well, can or can't . . . he's gonna do it! You ain't got nothing to do with it!
LEVEE: I don't care what you do! He can sing the whole goddamned song for all I care!
MA RAINEY: Well, all right. Thank you. 40

[IRVIN *enters with a microphone and hooks it up. He exits to the control booth.*]

MA RAINEY: Come on, Sylvester. You just stand here and hold your hands like I told you.
Just remember the words and say them . . . That's all there is to it. Don't worry about
messing up. If you mess up, we'll do it again. Now, let me hear you say it. Play for
him, Cutler.
CUTLER: One . . . two . . . you know what to do. 45

[*The band begins to play and* SYLVESTER *curls his fingers and clasps his hands
together in front of his chest, pulling in opposite directions as he says his lines.*]

SYLVESTER: "All right, boys, you d-d-done s-s-seen the best . . .

[LEVEE *stops playing.*]

Now I'm g-g-g-gonna show you the rest . . . Ma R-r-rainey's gonna show you her
b-b-black b-b-bottom."

[*The rest of the band stops playing.*]

MA RAINEY: That's all right. That's real good. You take your time, you'll get it right.
STURDYVANT: [*Over speaker*] Listen, Ma . . . now, when you come in, don't wait so long 50
to come in. Don't take so long on the intro, huh?
MA RAINEY: Sturdyvant, don't you go trying to tell me how to sing. You just take care of
that up there and let me take care of this down here. Where's my Coke?
IRVIN: Okay, Ma. We're all set up to go up here. "Ma Rainey's Black Bottom," boys.
MA RAINEY: Where's my Coke? I need a Coke. You ain't got no Coke down here? Where's 55
my Coke?
IRVIN: What's the matter, Ma? What's . . .
MA RAINEY: Where's my Coke? I need a Coca-Cola.
IRVIN: Uh . . . Ma, look, I forgot the Coke, huh? Let's do it without it, huh? Just this one
song. What say, boys? 60
MA RAINEY: Damn what the band say! You know I don't sing nothing without my
Coca-Cola!
STURDYVANT: We don't have any, Ma. There's no Coca-Cola here. We're all set up and
we'll just go ahead and . . .

MA RAINEY: You supposed to have Coca-Cola. Irvin knew that. I ain't singing nothing   65
without my Coca-Cola!

> [*She walks away from the mike, singing to herself.* STURDYVANT *enters from the control booth.*]

STURDYVANT: Now, just a minute here, Ma. You come in an hour late . . . we're way
behind schedule as it is . . . the band is set up and ready to go . . . I'm burning my
lights . . . I've turned up the heat . . . We're ready to make a record and what? You   70
decide you want a Coca-Cola?

MA RAINEY: Sturdyvant, get out of my face.

> [IRVIN *enters.*]

Irvin . . . I told you keep him away from me.

IRVIN: Mel, I'll handle it.

STURDYVANT: I'm tired of her nonsense, Irv. I'm not gonna put up with this!

IRVIN: Let me handle it, Mel. I know how to handle her. [IRVIN *to* MA RAINEY.] Look,   75
Ma. . . I'll call down to the deli and get you a Coke. But let's get started, huh? Sylvester's standing there ready to go . . . the band's set up . . . let's do this one song, huh?

MA RAINEY: If you too cheap to buy me a Coke, I'll buy my own. Slow Drag! Sylvester, go
with Slow Drag and get me a Coca-Cola.

> [SLOW DRAG *comes over.*]

Slow Drag, walk down to that store on the corner and get me three bottles of Coca-   80
Cola. Get out of my face, Irvin. You all just wait until I get my Coke. It ain't gonna
kill you.

IRVIN: Okay, Ma. Get your Coke, for Chrissakes! Get your Coke!

> [IRVIN *and* STURDYVANT *exit into the hallway followed by* SLOW DRAG *and*
> SYLVESTER. TOLEDO, CUTLER, *and* LEVEE *head for the band room.*]

MA RAINEY: Cutler, come here a minute. I want to talk to you.

> [CUTLER *crosses over somewhat reluctantly.*]

What's all this about "the boys in the band say"? I tells you what to do. I says what   85
the matter is with the band. I say who can and can't do what.

CUTLER: We just say 'cause the boy stutter . . .

MA RAINEY: I know he stutters. Don't you think I know he stutters. This is what's gonna
help him.

CUTLER: Well, how can he do the part if he stutters? You want him to stutter through it?   90
We just thought it be easier to go on and let Levee do it like we planned.

MA RAINEY: I don't care if he stutters or not! He's doing the part and I don't wanna hear
any more of this shit about what the band says. And I want you to find somebody
to replace Levee when we get to Memphis. Levee ain't nothing but trouble.

CUTLER: Levee's all right. He plays good music when he puts his mind to it. He knows   95
how to write music too.

MA RAINEY: I don't care what he know. He ain't nothing but bad news. Find somebody
else. I know it was his idea about who to say who can do what.

> [DUSSIE MAE *wanders over to where they are sitting.*]

Dussie Mae, go sit your behind down somewhere and quit flaunting yourself around.

DUSSIE MAE: I ain't doing nothing.   100

MA RAINEY: Well, just go on somewhere and stay out of the way.

CUTLER: I been meaning to ask you, Ma . . . about these songs. This "Moonshine Blues" . . . that's one of them songs Bessie Smith sang, I believes.

MA RAINEY: Bessie what? Ain't nobody thinking about Bessie. I taught Bessie. She ain't doing nothing but imitating me. What I care about Bessie? I don't care if she sell a million records. She got her people and I got mine. I don't care what nobody else do. Ma was the *first* and don't you forget it! 105

CUTLER: Ain't nobody said nothing about that. I just said that's the same song she sang.

MA RAINEY: I been doing this a long time. Ever since I was a little girl. I don't care what nobody else do. That's what gets me so mad with Irvin. White folks try to be put out with you all the time. Too cheap to buy me a Coca-Cola. I lets them know it, though. Ma don't stand for no shit. Wanna take my voice and trap it in them fancy boxes with all them buttons and dials . . . and then too cheap to buy me a Coca-Cola. And it don't cost but a nickle a bottle. 110

CUTLER: I knows what you mean about that. 115

MA RAINEY: They don't care nothing about me. All they want is my voice. Well, I done learned that, and they gonna treat me like I want to be treated no matter how much it hurt them. They back there now calling me all kinds of names . . . calling me everything but a child of god. But they can't do nothing else. They ain't got what they wanted yet. As soon as they get my voice down on them recording machines, then it's just like if I'd be some whore and they roll over and put their pants on. Ain't got no use for me then. I know what I'm talking about. You watch. Irvin right there with the rest of them. He don't care nothing about me either. He's been my manager for six years, always talking about sticking together, and the only time he had me in his house was to sing for some of his friends. 120

125

CUTLER: I know how they do.

MA RAINEY: If you colored and can make them some money, then you all right with them. Otherwise, you just a dog in the alley. I done made this company more money from my records than all other recording artists they got put together. And they wanna balk about how much this session is costing them. 130

CUTLER: I don't see where it's costing them all what they say.

MA RAINEY: It ain't! I don't pay that kind of talk no mind.

[*The lights go down on the studio and come up on the band room.* TOLEDO *sits reading a newspaper.* LEVEE *sings and hums his song.*]

LEVEE: [*singing*]

> *You can shake it, you can break it*
> *You can dance at any hall* 135
> *You can slide across the floor*
> *You'll never have to stall*
> *My jelly, my roll,*
> *Sweet Mama, don't you let it fall.*

Wait till Sturdyvant hear me play that! I'm talking about some real music, Toledo! 140
I'm talking about *real* music!

[*The door opens and* DUSSIE MAE *enters.*]

Hey, mama! Come on in.

DUSSIE MAE: Oh, hi! I just wanted to see what it looks like down here.

LEVEE: Well, come on in . . . I don't bite.

DUSSIE MAE: I didn't know you could really write music. I thought you was just jiving me   145
at the club last night.

LEVEE: Naw, baby . . . I knows how to write music. I done give Mr. Sturdyvant some of
my songs and he says he's gonna let me record them. Ask Toledo. I'm gonna have my
own band! Toledo, ain't I give Mr. Sturdyvant some of my songs I wrote?

TOLEDO: Don't get Toledo mixed up in nothing.   150

[*He exits.*]

DUSSIE MAE: You gonna get your own band sure enough?

LEVEE: That's right! Levee Green and his Footstompers.

DUSSIE MAE: That's real nice.

LEVEE: That's what I was trying to tell you last night. A man what's gonna get his own band   155
need to have a woman like you.

DUSSIE MAE: A woman like me wants somebody to bring it and put it in my hand. I don't
need nobody wanna get something for nothing and leave me standing in my door.

LEVEE: That ain't Levee's style sugar. I got more style than that. I knows how to treat a
woman. Buy her presents and things . . . treat her like she wants to be treated.

DUSSIE MAE: That's what they all say . . . till it come time to be buying the presents.   160

LEVEE: When we get down to Memphis, I'm gonna show you what I'm talking about. I'm
gonna take you out and show you a good time. Show you Levee knows how to treat
a woman.

DUSSIE MAE: When you getting your own band?

LEVEE: [*moves closer to slip his arm around her*] Soon as Mr. Sturdyvant say. I done got my   165
fellows already picked out. Getting me some good fellows know how to play real
sweet music.

DUSSIE MAE: [*moves away*] Go on now, I don't go for all that pawing and stuff. When you
get your own band, maybe we can see about this stuff you talking.

LEVEE: [*moving toward her*] I just wanna show you I know what the women like. They   170
don't call me Sweet Lemonade for nothing.

[LEVEE *takes her in his arms and attempts to kiss her.*]

DUSSIE MAE: Stop it now. Somebody's gonna come in here.

LEVEE: Naw they ain't. Look here, sugar . . . what I wanna know is . . . can I introduce my
red rooster to your brown hen?

DUSSIE MAE: You get your band, then we'll see if that rooster know how to crow.   175

[*He grinds up against her and feels her buttocks.*]

LEVEE: Now I know why my grandpappy sat on the back porch with his straight razor
when grandma hung out the wash.

DUSSIE MAE: Nigger, you crazy!

LEVEE: I bet you sound like the midnight train from Alabama when it crosses the Mason-
Dixon line.   180

DUSSIE MAE: How's you get so crazy?

LEVEE: It's women like you . . . drives me that way.

[*He moves to kiss her as the lights go down in the band room and up in the studio.* MA RAINEY *sits with* CUTLER *and* TOLEDO.]

MA RAINEY: It sure done got quiet in here. I never could stand no silence. I always got to
have some music going on in my head somewhere. It keeps things balanced. Music
will do that. It fills things up. The more music you got in the world, the fuller it is.   185

CUTLER: I can agree with that. I got to have my music too.

MA RAINEY: White folks don't understand about the blues. They hear it come out, but they don't know how it got there. They don't understand that's life's way of talking. You don't sing to feel better. You sing 'cause that's a way of understanding life.

CUTLER: That's right. You get that understanding and you done got a grip on life to where   190
you can hold your head up and go on to see what else life got to offer.

MA RAINEY: The blues help you get out of bed in the morning. You get up knowing you ain't alone. There's something else in the world. Something's been added by that song. This be an empty world without the blues. I take that emptiness and try to fill it up with something.   195

TOLEDO: You fill it up with something people can't be without, Ma. That's why they call you the Mother of the Blues. You fill up that emptiness in a way ain't nobody ever thought of doing before. And now they can't be without it.

MA RAINEY: I ain't started the blues way of singing. The blues always been here.

CUTLER: In the church sometimes you find that way of singing. They got blues in the church.   200

MA RAINEY: They say I started it . . . but I didn't. I just helped it out. Filled up that empty space a little bit. That's all. But if they wanna call me the Mother of the Blues, that's all right with me. It don't hurt none.

[SLOW DRAG *and* SYLVESTER *enter with the Cokes.*]

It sure took you long enough. That store ain't but on the corner.

SLOW DRAG: That one was closed. We had to find another one.   205

MA RAINEY: Sylvester, go and find Mr. Irvin and tell him we ready to go.

[SYLVESTER *exits. The lights in the band room come up while the lights in the studio stay on.* LEVEE *and* DUSSIE MAE *are kissing.* SLOW DRAG *enters. They break their embrace.* DUSSIE MAE *straightens up her clothes.*]

SLOW DRAG: Cold out. I just wanted to warm up with a little sip.

[*He goes to his locker, takes out his bottle and drinks.*]

Ma got her Coke, Levee. We about ready to start.

[SLOW DRAG *exits.* LEVEE *attempts to kiss* DUSSIE MAE *again.*]

DUSSIE MAE: No . . . Come on! I got to go. You gonna get me in trouble.

[*She pulls away and exits up the stairs.* LEVEE *watches after her.*]

LEVEE: Good God! Happy birthday to the lady with the cakes!   210

[*The lights go down in the band room and come up in the studio.* MA RAINEY *drinks her Coke.* LEVEE *enters from the band room. The musicians take their places.* SYLVESTER *stands by his mike.* IRVIN *and* STURDYVANT *look on from the control booth.*]

IRVIN: We're all set up here, Ma. We're all set to go. You ready down there?

MA RAINEY: Sylvester you just remember your part and say it. That's all there is to it. [*To* IRVIN.] Yeah, we ready.

IRVIN: Okay, boys. "Ma Rainey's Black Bottom." Take one.

CUTLER: One . . . two . . . You know what to do.   215

[*The band plays.*]

SYLVESTER: All right boys, you d-d-done s-s-seen the rest . . .

IRVIN: Hold it!

[*The band stops.* STURDYVANT *changes the recording disk and nods to* IRVIN.]

Okay. Take two.

CUTLER: One . . . two . . . You know what to do.

[*The band plays.*]

SYLVESTER: All right, boys, you done seen the rest . . . now I'm gonna show you the best.   220
Ma Rainey's g-g-g-gonna s-s-show you her b-b-black bottom.

IRVIN: Hold it! Hold it!

[*The band stops.* STURDYVANT *changes the recording disk.*]

Okay. Take three. Ma, let's do it without the intro, huh? No voice intro . . . you
just come in singing.

MA RAINEY: Irvin, I done told you . . . the boy's gonna do the part. He don't stutter all the   225
time. Just give him a chance. Sylvester, hold your hands like I told you and just relax.
Just relax and concentrate.

IRVIN: All right. Take three.

CUTLER: One . . . two . . . You know what to do.

[*The band plays.*]

SYLVESTER: All right, boys, you done seen the rest . . . now, I'm gonna show you the best.   230
Ma Rainey's gonna show you her black bottom.

MA RAINEY: [*Singing*]

> *Way down south in Alabamy*
> *I got a friend they call dancing Sammy*
> *Who's crazy about all the latest dances*   235
> *Black Bottom stomping, two babies prancing*
>
> *The other night at a swell affair*
> *As soon as the boys found out that I was there*
> *They said, come on, Ma, let's go to the cabaret.*
> *When I got there, you ought to hear them say,*   240
>
> *I want to see the dance you call the black bottom*
> *I want to learn that dance*
> *I want to see the dance you call your big black bottom*
> *It'll put you in a trance.*
>
> *All the boys in the neighborhood*   245
> *They say your black bottom is really good*
> *Come on and show me your black bottom*
> *I want to learn that dance*
>
> *I want to see the dance you call the black bottom*
> *I want to learn that dance*   250
> *Come on and show the dance you call your big black bottom*
> *It puts you in a trance.*
>
> *Early last morning about the break of day*
> *Grandpa told my grandma, I heard him say,*
> *Get up and show your old man your black bottom*   255
> *I want to learn that dance.*

[*Instrumental break.*]

I done showed you all my black bottom
You ought to learn that dance.

IRVIN: Okay, that's good Ma. That sounded great! Good job, boys!

MA RAINEY: [*to* SYLVESTER] See! I told you. I knew you could do it. You just have to put your mind to it. Didn't he do good, Cutler? Sound real good. I told him he could do it. 260

CUTLER: He sure did. He did better than I thought he was gonna do.

IRVIN: [*entering to remove* SYLVESTER's *mike*] Okay, boys . . . Ma . . . let's do "Moonshine Blues" next, huh? "Moonshine Blues," boys.

STURDYVANT: [*over speaker*] Irv! Something's wrong down there. We don't have it right. 265

IRVIN: What? What's the matter Mel . . .

STURDYVANT: We don't have it right. Something happened. We don't have the goddamn song recorded!

IRVIN: What's the matter? Mel, what happened? You sure you don't have nothing?

STURDYVANT: Check that mike, huh, Irv. It's the kid's mike. Something's wrong with the mike. We've got everything all screwed up here. 270

IRVIN: Christ almighty! Ma, we got to do it again. We don't have it. We didn't record the song.

MA RAINEY: What you mean you didn't record it? What was you and Sturdyvant doing up there? 275

IRVIN: [*following the mike wire*] Here . . . Levee must have kicked the plug out.

LEVEE: I ain't done nothing. I ain't kicked nothing!

SLOW DRAG: If Levee had his mind on what he's doing . . .

MA RAINEY: Levee, if it ain't one thing, it's another. You better straighten yourself up!

LEVEE: Hell . . . it ain't my fault. I ain't done nothing! 280

STURDYVANT: What's the matter with that mike, Irv? What's the problem?

IRVIN: It's the cord, Mel. The cord's all chewed up. We need another cord.

MA RAINEY: This is the most disorganized . . . Irvin, I'm going home! Come on. Come on, Dussie.

[MA RAINEY *walks past* STURDYVANT *as he enters from the control booth. She exits offstage to get her coat.*]

STURDYVANT: [*to* IRVIN] Where's she going? 285

IRVIN: She said she's going home.

STURDYVANT: Irvin, you get her! If she walks out of here . . .

[MA RAINEY *enters carrying her and* DUSSIE MAE's *coats.*]

MA RAINEY: Come on, Sylvester.

IRVIN: [*helping her with her coat*] Ma . . . Ma . . . listen. Fifteen minutes! All I ask is fifteen minutes! 290

MA RAINEY: Come on, Sylvester, get your coat.

STURDYVANT: Ma, if you walk out of this studio . . .

IRVIN: Fifteen minutes, Ma!

STURDYVANT: You'll be through . . . washed up! If you walk out on me . . .

IRVIN: Mel, for Chrissakes, shut up and let me handle it! 295

[*He goes after* MA RAINEY, *who has started for the door.*]

Ma, listen. These records are gonna be hits! They're gonna sell like crazy! Hell, even Sylvester will be a star. Fifteen minutes. That's all I'm asking! Fifteen minutes.

MA RAINEY: [*Crossing to a chair and sits with her coat on.*] Fifteen minutes! You hear me, Irvin? Fifteen minutes . . . and then I'm gonna take my black bottom on back down to Georgia. Fifteen minutes. Then Madame Rainey is leaving! 300

IRVIN: [*kisses her*] All right, Ma . . . fifteen minutes. I promise. [*to the band*] You boys go ahead and take a break. Fifteen minutes and we'll be ready to go.

CUTLER: Slow Drag, you got any of that bourbon left?

SLOW DRAG: Yeah, there's some down there.

CUTLER: I could use a little nip.   305

> [CUTLER *and* SLOW DRAG *exit to the band room, followed by* LEVEE, *and* TOLEDO. *The lights go down in the studio and up in the band room.*]

SLOW DRAG: Don't make no difference if she leave or not. I was kinda hoping she would leave.

CUTLER: I'm like Mr. Irvin . . . After all this time we done put in here, it's best to go ahead and get something out of it.

TOLEDO: Ma gonna do what she wanna do, that's for sure. If I was Mr. Irvin, I'd best go   310
on and get them cords and things hooked up right. And I wouldn't take no longer than fifteen minutes doing it.

CUTLER: If Levee had his mind on his work, we wouldn't be in this fix. We'd be up there finishing up. Now we got to go back and see if that boy get that part right. Ain't no telling if he ever get that right again in his life.   315

LEVEE: Hey, Levee ain't done nothing!

SLOW DRAG: Levee up there got one eye on the gal and the other on his trumpet.

CUTLER: Nigger, don't you know that's Ma's gal?

LEVEE: I don't care whose gal it is. I ain't done nothing to her. I just talk to her like I talk   320
to anybody else.

CUTLER: Well, that being Ma's gal, and that being that boy's gal, is one and two different things. The boy is liable to kill you . . . but you' ass gonna be out there scraping the concrete looking for a job if you messing with Ma's gal.

LEVEE: How am I messing with her? I ain't done nothing to the gal. I just asked her her name. Now, if you telling me I can't do that, then Ma will just have to go to hell.   325

CUTLER: All I can do is warn you.

SLOW DRAG: Let him hang himself, Cutler. Let him string his neck out.

LEVEE: I ain't done nothing to the gal! You all talk like I done went and done something to her. Leave me go with my business.

CUTLER: I'm through with it. Try and talk to a fool . . .   330

TOLEDO: Some mens got it worse than others . . . this foolishness I'm talking about. Some mens is excited to be fools. That excitement is something else. I know about it. I done experienced it. It makes you feel good to be a fool. But it don't last long. It's over in a minute. Then you got to tend with the consequences. You got to tend with what comes after. That's when you wish you had learned something about it.   335

LEVEE: That's the best sense you made all day. Talking about being a fool. That's the only sensible thing you said today. Admitting you was a fool.

TOLEDO: I admits it, all right. Ain't nothing wrong with it. I done been a little bit of everything.

LEVEE: Now you're talking. You's as big a fool as they make.   340

TOLEDO: Gonna be a bit more things before I'm finished with it. Gonna be foolish again. But I ain't never been the same fool twice. I might be a different kind of fool, but I ain't gonna be the same fool twice. That's where we parts ways.

SLOW DRAG: Toledo, you done been a fool about a woman?

TOLEDO: Sure. Sure I have. Same as everybody.   345

SLOW DRAG: Hell, I ain't never seen you mess with no woman. I thought them books was your woman.

TOLEDO: Sure I messed with them. Done messed with a whole heap of them. And gonna mess with some more. But I ain't gonna be no fool about them. What you think? I done come in the world full-grown, with my head in a book? I done been young. Married. Got kids. I done been around and I done loved women to where you shake in your shoes just at the sight of them. Feel it all up and down your spine. 350

SLOW DRAG: I didn't know you was married.

TOLEDO: Sure. Legally. I been married legally. Got the papers and all. I done been through life. Made my marks. Followed some signs on the road. Ignored some others. I done been all through it. I touched and been touched by it. But I ain't never been the same fool twice. That's what I can say. 355

LEVEE: But you been a fool. That's what counts. Talking about I'm a fool for asking the gal her name and here you is one yourself.

TOLEDO: Now, I married a woman. A good woman. To this day I can't say she wasn't a good woman. I can't say nothing bad about her. I married that woman with all the good graces and intentions of being hooked up and bound to her for the rest of my life. I was looking for her to put me in my grave. But, you see . . . it ain't all the time what you' intentions and wishes are. She went out and joined the church. All right. There ain't nothing wrong with that. A good Christian woman going to church and wanna do right by her god. There ain't nothing wrong with that. But she got up there, got to seeing them good Christian mens and wonder why I ain't like that. Soon she figure she got a heathen on her hands. She figured she couldn't live like that. The church was more important than I was. So she left. Packed up one day and moved out. To this day I ain't never said another word to her. Come home one day and my house was empty! And I sat down and figured out that I was a fool not to see that she needed something that I wasn't giving her. Else she wouldn't have been up there at the church in the first place. I ain't blaming her. I just said it wasn't gonna happen to me again. So, yeah, Toledo been a fool about a woman. That's part of making life. 360 365 370

CUTLER: Well, yeah, I been a fool too. Everybody done been a fool once or twice. But, you see, Toledo, what you call a fool and what I call a fool is two different things. I can't see where you was being a fool for that. You ain't done nothing foolish. You can't help what happened, and I wouldn't call you a fool for it. A fool is responsible for what happens to him. A fool cause it to happen. Like Levee . . . if he keeps messing with Ma's gal and his feet be out there scraping the ground. That's a fool. 375 380

LEVEE: Ain't nothing gonna happen to Levee. Levee ain't gonna let nothing happen to him. Now, I'm gonna say it again. I asked the gal her name. That's all I done. And if that's being a fool, then you looking at the biggest fool in the world . . . 'cause I sure as hell asked her.

SLOW DRAG: You just better not let Ma see you ask her. That's what the man's trying to tell you. 385

LEVEE: I don't need nobody to tell me nothing.

CUTLER: Well, Toledo, all I gots to say is that from the looks of it . . . from your story . . . I don't think life did you fair.

TOLEDO: Oh, life is fair. It's just in the taking what it gives you. 390

LEVEE: Life ain't shit. You can put it in a paper bag and carry it around with you. It ain't got no balls. Now, death . . . death got some style! Death will kick your ass and make you wish you never been born! That's how bad death is! But you can rule over life. Life ain't nothing.

TOLEDO: Cutler, how's your brother doing? 395

CUTLER: Who, Nevada? Oh, he's doing all right. Staying in St. Louis. Got a bunch of kids, last I heard.

TOLEDO: Me and him was all right with each other. Done a lot of farming together down in Plattsville.

CUTLER: Yeah, I know you all was tight. He in St. Louis now. Running an elevator, last I 400
hear about it.

SLOW DRAG: That's better than stepping in muleshit.

TOLEDO: Oh, I don't know now. I liked farming. Get out there in the sun . . . smell that dirt. Be out there by yourself . . . nice and peaceful. Yeah, farming was all right by me. Sometimes I think I'd like to get me a little old place . . . but I done got too old 405
to be following behind one of them balky mules now.

LEVEE: Nigger talking about life is fair. And ain't got a pot to piss in.

TOLEDO: See, now, I'm gonna tell you something. A nigger gonna be dissatisfied no matter what. Give a nigger some bread and butter . . . and he'll cry 'cause he ain't got no jelly. Give him some jelly, and he'll cry 'cause he ain't got no knife to put it on with. 410
If there's one thing I done learned in this life, it's that you can't satisfy a nigger no matter what you do. A nigger's gonna make his own dissatisfaction.

LEVEE: Niggers got a right to be dissatisfied. Is you gonna be satisfied with a bone somebody done throwed you when you see them eating the whole hog?

TOLEDO: You lucky they let you be an entertainer. They ain't got to accept your way of 415
entertaining. You lucky and you don't even know it. You's entertaining and the rest of the people is hauling wood. That's the only kind of job for the colored man.

SLOW DRAG: Ain't nothing wrong with hauling wood. I done hauled plenty wood. My daddy used to haul wood. Ain't nothing wrong with that. That's honest work.

LEVEE: That ain't what I'm talking about. I ain't talking about hauling no wood. I'm talk- 420
ing about being satisfied with a bone somebody done throwed you. That's what's the matter with you all. You satisfied sitting in one place. You got to move on down the road from where you sitting . . . and all the time you got to keep an eye out for that devil who's looking to buy up souls. And hope you get lucky and find him!

CUTLER: I done told you about that blasphemy. Talking about selling your soul to the devil. 425

TOLEDO: We done the same thing, Cutler. There ain't no difference. We done sold Africa for the price of tomatoes. We done sold ourselves to the white man in order to be like him. Look at the way you dressed . . . That ain't African. That's the white man. We trying to be just like him. We done sold who we are in order to become someone else. We's imitation white men. 430

CUTLER: What else we gonna be, living over here?

LEVEE: I'm Levee. Just me. I ain't no imitation nothing!

SLOW DRAG: You change who you are by how you dress. That's what I got to say.

TOLEDO: It ain't all how you dress. It's how you act, how you see the world. It's how you 435
follow life.

LEVEE: It don't matter what you talking about. I ain't no imitation white man. And I don't want to be no white man. As soon as I get my band together and make them records like Mr. Sturdyvant done told me I can make, I'm gonna be like Ma and tell the white man just what he can do. Ma tell Mr. Irvin she gonna leave . . . and Mr. Irvin get down on his knees and beg her to stay! That's the way I'm gonna be! Make the 440
white man respect me!

CUTLER: The white man don't care nothing about Ma. The colored folks made Ma a star. White folks don't care nothing about who she is . . . what kind of music she make.

SLOW DRAG: That's the truth about that. You let her go down to one of them white-folks hotels and see how big she is. 445

CUTLER: Hell, she ain't got to do that. She can't even get a cab up here in the North. I'm gonna tell you something. Reverend Gates . . . you know Reverend Gates? . . . Slow

Drag know who I'm talking about. Reverend Gates . . . now I'm gonna show you how this go where the white man don't care a thing about who you is. Reverend Gates was coming from Tallahassee to Atlanta, going to see his sister, who was sick at that time with the consumption. The train come up through Thomasville, then past Moultrie, and stopped in this little town called Sigsbee . . . 450

LEVEE: You can stop telling that right there! That train don't stop in Sigsbee. I know what train you talking about. That train got four stops before it reach Macon to go on to Atlanta. One in Thomasville, one in Moultrie, one in Cordele . . . and it stop in Centerville. 455

CUTLER: Nigger, I know what I'm talking about. You gonna tell me where the train stop?

LEVEE: Hell, yeah, if you talking about it stop in Sigsbee. I'm gonna tell you the truth.

CUTLER: I'm talking about *this* train! I don't know what train you been riding. I'm talking about *this* train!

LEVEE: Ain't but one train. Ain't but one train come out of Tallahassee heading north to Atlanta, and it don't stop at Sigsbee. Tell him, Toledo . . . that train don't stop at Sigsbee. The only train that stops at Sigsbee is the Yazoo Delta, and you have to transfer at Moultrie to get it! 460

CUTLER: Well, hell, maybe that what he done! I don't know. I'm just telling you the man got off the train at Sigsbee . . . 465

LEVEE: All right . . . you telling it. Tell it your way. Just make up anything.

SLOW DRAG: Levee, leave the man alone and let him finish.

CUTLER: I ain't paying Levee no never mind.

LEVEE: Go on and tell it your way.

CUTLER: Anyway . . . Reverend Gates got off his train in Sigsbee. The train done stopped there and he figured he'd get off and check the schedule to be sure he arrive in time for somebody to pick him up. All right. While he's there checking the schedule, it come upon him that he had to go to the bathroom. Now, they ain't had no colored rest rooms at the station. The only colored rest room is an outhouse they got sitting way back two hundred yards or so from the station. All right. He in the outhouse and train go off and leave him there. He don't know nothing about this town. Ain't never been there before—in fact, ain't never even heard of it before. 470 475

LEVEE: I heard of it! I know just where it's at . . . and he ain't got off no train coming out of Tallahassee in Sigsbee!

CUTLER: The man standing there, trying to figure out what he's gonna do . . . where this train done left him in this strange town. It started getting dark. He see where the sun's getting low in the sky and he's trying to figure out what he's gonna do, when he noticed a couple of white fellows standing across the street from this station. Just standing there, watching him. And then two or three more come up and joined the other one. He look around, ain't seen no colored folks nowhere. He didn't know what was getting in these here fellows' minds, so he commence to walking. He ain't knowed where he was going. He just walking down the railroad tracks when he hear them call him. "Hey, nigger!" See, just like that. "Hey, nigger!" He kept on walking. They called him some more and he just keep walking. Just going down the tracks. And then he heard a gunshot where somebody done fired a gun in the air. He stopped then, you know. 480 485 490

TOLEDO: You don't even have to tell me no more. I know the facts of it. I done heard the same story a hundred times. It happened to me too. Same thing.

CUTLER: Naw, I'm gonna show how the white folks don't care nothing about who or what you is. They crowded around him. These gang of mens made a circle around him. Now, he's standing there, you understand . . . got his cross around his neck like them preachers wear. Had his little Bible with him what he carry all the time. So they 495 crowd on around him and one of them ask who he is. He told them he was Reverend Gates and that he was going to see his sister who was sick and the train left without him. And they said, "Yeah, nigger . . . but can you dance?" He looked at them and commenced to dancing. One of them reached up and tore his cross off his neck. Said he was committing a heresy by dancing with a cross and Bible. Took his Bible and tore it up and had him dancing till they got tired of watching him. 500

SLOW DRAG: White folks ain't never had no respect for the colored minister.

CUTLER: That's the only way he got out of there alive . . . was to dance. Ain't even had no respect for a man of God! Wanna make him into a clown. Reverend Gates sat right in my house and told me that story from his own mouth. So . . . the white folks don't care nothing about Ma Rainey. She's just another nigger who they can use to make some money. 505

LEVEE: What I wants to know is . . . if he's a man of God, then where the hell was God when all of this was going on? Why wasn't God looking out for him. Why didn't God strike down them crackers with some this lightning you talk about to me? 510

CUTLER: Levee, you gonna burn in hell.

LEVEE: What I care about burning in hell? You talk like a fool . . . burning in hell. Why didn't God strike some of them crackers down? Tell me that! That's the question! Don't come telling me this burning-in-hell shit! He a man of God . . . why didn't God strike some of them crackers down? I'll tell you why! I'll tell you the truth! It's sitting out there as plain as day! 'Cause he a white man's God. That's why! God ain't never listened to no nigger's prayers. God take a nigger's prayers and throw them in the garbage. God don't pay niggers no mind. In fact . . . God hate niggers! Hate them with all the fury in his heart. Jesus don't love you, nigger! Jesus hate your black ass! Come talking that shit to me. Talking about burning in hell! God can kiss my ass. 515 520

[CUTLER *can stand no more. He jumps up and punches* LEVEE *in the mouth. The force of the blow knocks* LEVEE *down and* CUTLER *jumps on him.*]

CUTLER: You worthless . . . That's my God! That's my God! That's my God! You wanna blaspheme my God! 525

[TOLEDO *and* SLOW DRAG *grab* CUTLER *and try to pull him off* LEVEE.]

SLOW DRAG: Come on, Cutler . . . let it go! It don't mean nothing!

[CUTLER *has* LEVEE *down on the floor and pounds on him with a fury.*]

CUTLER: Wanna blaspheme my God! You worthless . . . talking about my God!

[TOLEDO *and* SLOW DRAG *succeed in pulling* CUTLER *off* LEVEE, *who is bleeding at the nose and mouth.*]

LEVEE: Naw, let him go! Let him go!

[*He pulls out a knife.*]

That's your God, huh? That's your God, huh? Is that right? Your God, huh? All right. I'm gonna give your God a chance. I'm gonna give him a chance to save your black ass. 530

[LEVEE *circles* CUTLER *with the knife.* CUTLER *picks up a chair to protect himself.*]

TOLEDO: Come on, Levee . . . put the knife up!

LEVEE: Stay out of this, Toledo!

TOLEDO: That ain't no way to solve nothing.

[LEVEE *alternately swipes at* CUTLER *during the following.*]

LEVEE: I'm calling Cutler's God! I'm talking to Cutler's God! You hear me? Cutler's God! 535
I'm calling Cutler's God. Come on and save this nigger! Strike me down before I
cut his throat!

SLOW DRAG: Watch him, Cutler! Put that knife up, Levee!

LEVEE: [*to* CUTLER] I'm calling your God! I'm gonna give him a chance to save you! I'm
calling your God! We gonna find out whose God he is! 540

CUTLER: You gonna burn in hell, nigger!

LEVEE: Cutler's God! Come on and save this nigger! Come on and save him like you did
my mama! Save him like you did my mama! I heard her when she called you! I heard
her when she said, "Lord, have mercy! Jesus, help me! Please, God, have mercy on
me, Lord Jesus, help me!" And did you turn your back? Did you turn your back, 545
motherfucker? Did you turn your back?

[LEVEE *becomes so caught up in his dialogue with God that he forgets about*
CUTLER *and begins to stab upward in the air, trying to reach God.*]

Come on! Come on and turn your back on me! Turn your back on me! Come on!
Where is you? Come on and turn your back on me! Turn your back on me, motherfucker! I'll cut your heart out! Come on, turn your back on me! Come on! What's
the matter? Where is you? Come on and turn your back on me! Come on, what you 550
scared of? Turn your back on me! Come on! Coward, motherfucker?

[LEVEE *folds his knife and stands triumphantly.*]

Your God ain't shit, Cutler.

[*The lights fade to black.*]

MA RAINEY: [*Singing*]

> Ah, you hear me talking to you
> I don't bite my tongue 555
> You wants to be my man
> You got to fetch it with you when you come.

[*Lights come up in the studio. The last bars of the last song of the session are
dying out.*]

IRVIN: [*over speaker*] Good! Wonderful! We have that, boys. Good session. That's great,
Ma. We've got ourselves some winners.

TOLEDO: Well, I'm glad that's over. 560

MA RAINEY: Slow Drag, where you learn to play the bass at? You had it singing! I heard
you! Had that bass jumping all over the place.

SLOW DRAG: I was following Toledo. Nigger got them long fingers striding all over the
piano. I was trying to keep up with him.

TOLEDO: That's what you supposed to do, ain't it? Play the music. Ain't nothing abstract 565
about it.

MA RAINEY: Cutler, you hear Slow Drag on that bass? He make it do what he want it to
do! Spank it just like you spank a baby.

CUTLER: Don't be telling him that. Nigger's head get so big his hat won't fit him.

SLOW DRAG: If Cutler tune that guitar up, we would really have something! 570

CUTLER: You wouldn't know what a tuned-up guitar sounded like if you heard one.

TOLEDO: Cutler was talking. I heard him moaning. He was all up in it.

MA RAINEY: Levee . . . what is that you doing? Why you playing all them notes? You play ten notes for every one you supposed to play. It don't call for that.

LEVEE: You supposed to improvise on the theme. That's what I was doing. 575

MA RAINEY: You supposed to play the song the way I sing it. The way everybody else play it. You ain't supposed to go off by yourself and play what you want.

LEVEE: I was playing the song. I was playing it the way I felt it.

MA RAINEY: I couldn't keep up with what was going on. I'm trying to sing the song and you up there messing up my ear. That's what you was doing. Call yourself playing 580 music.

LEVEE: Hey . . . I know what I'm doing. I know what I'm doing, all right. I know how to play music. You all back up and leave me alone about my music.

CUTLER: I done told you . . . it ain't about *your* music. It's about *Ma's* music.

MA RAINEY: That's all right, Cutler. I done told you what to do. 585

LEVEE: I don't care what you do. You supposed to improvise on the theme. Not play note for note the same thing over and over again.

MA RAINEY: You just better watch yourself. You hear me?

LEVEE: What I care what you or Cutler do? Come telling me to watch myself. What's that supposed to mean? 590

MA RAINEY: All right . . . you gonna find out what it means.

LEVEE: Go ahead and fire me. I don't care. I'm gonna get my own band anyway.

MA RAINEY: You keep messing with me.

LEVEE: Ain't nobody studying you. You ain't gonna do nothing to me. Ain't nobody gonna do nothing to Levee. 595

MA RAINEY: All right, nigger . . . you fired!

LEVEE: You think I care about being fired? I don't care nothing about that. You doing me a favor.

MA RAINEY: Cutler, Levee's out! He don't play in my band no more.

LEVEE: I'm fired . . . Good! Best thing that ever happened to me. I don't need this shit! 600

[LEVEE *exits to the band room.* IRVIN *enters from the control booth.*]

MA RAINEY: Cutler, I'll see you back at the hotel.

IRVIN: Okay, boys . . . you can pack up. I'll get your money for you.

CUTLER: That's cash money, Mr. Irvin. I don't want no check.

IRVIN: I'll see what I can do. I can't promise you nothing.

CUTLER: As long as it ain't no check. I ain't got no use for a check. 605

IRVIN: I'll see what I can do, Cutler.

[CUTLER, TOLEDO, *and* SLOW DRAG *exit to the band room.*]

Oh, Ma, listen . . . I talked to Sturdyvant, and he said . . . Now, I tried to talk him out of it . . . He said the best he can do is to take your twenty-five dollars of your money and give it to Sylvester.

MA RAINEY: Take what and do what? If I wanted the boy to have twenty-five dollars of my 610 money, I'd give it to him. He supposed to get his own money. He supposed to get paid like everybody else.

IRVIN: Ma, I talked to him . . . He said . . .

MA RAINEY: Go talk to him again! Tell him if he don't pay that boy, he'll never make another record of mine again. Tell him that. You supposed to be my manager. All this talk 615 about sticking together. Start sticking! Go on up there and get that boy his money!

IRVIN: Okay, Ma . . . I'll talk to him again. I'll see what I can do.

MA RAINEY: Ain't no see about it! You bring that boy's money back here!

[IRVIN *exits. The lights stay on in the studio and come up in the band room. The* *men have their instruments packed and sit waiting for* IRVIN *to come and pay* *them.* SLOW DRAG *has a pack of cards.*]

SLOW DRAG: Come on, Levee, let me show you a card trick.

LEVEE: I don't need want to see no card trick. What you wanna show me for? Why you 620
    wanna bother me with that?

SLOW DRAG: I was just trying to be nice.

LEVEE: I don't need you to be nice to me. What I need you to be nice to me for? I ain't
    gonna be nice to you. I ain't even gonna let you be in my band no more.

SLOW DRAG: Toledo, let me show you a card trick. 625

CUTLER: I just hope Mr. Irvin don't bring no check down here. What the hell I'm gonna
    do with a check?

SLOW DRAG: All right now . . . pick a card. Any card . . . go on . . . take any of them. I'm
    gonna show you something.

TOLEDO: I agrees with you, Cutler. I don't want no check either. 630

CUTLER: It don't make no sense to give a nigger a check.

SLOW DRAG: Okay, now. Remember your card. Remember which one you got. Now . . .
    put it back in the deck. Anywhere you want. I'm gonna show you something.

[TOLEDO *puts the card in the deck.*]

You remember your card? All right. Now I'm gonna shuffle the deck. Now . . . I'm
gonna show you what card you picked. Don't say nothing now. I'm gonna tell you 635
what card you picked.

CUTLER: Slow Drag, that trick is as old as my mama.

SLOW DRAG: Naw, naw . . . wait a minute! I'm gonna show him his card . . . There it go!
    The six of diamonds. Ain't that your card? Ain't that it?

TOLEDO: Yeah, that's it . . . the six of diamonds. 640

SLOW DRAG: Told you! Told you I'd show him what it was!

[*The lights fade in the band room and come up full on the studio.* STURDYVANT *enters with* IRVIN.]

STURDYVANT: Ma, is there something wrong? Is there a problem?

MA RAINEY: Sturdyvant, I want you to pay that boy his money.

STURDYVANT: Sure, Ma. I got it right here. Two hundred for you and twenty-five for the
    kid, right? 645

[STURDYVANT *hands the money to* IRVIN, *who hands it to* MA RAINEY *and* SYLVESTER.]

Irvin misunderstood me. It was all a mistake. Irv made a mistake.

MA RAINEY: A mistake, huh?

IRVIN: Sure, Ma. I made a mistake. He's paid, right? I straightened it out.

MA RAINEY: The only mistake was when you found out I hadn't signed the release forms.
    That was the mistake. Come on, Sylvester. 650

[*She starts to exit.*]

STURDYVANT: Hey, Ma . . . come on, sign the forms, huh?

IRVIN: Ma . . . come on now.

MA RAINEY: Get your coat, Sylvester. Irvin, where's my car?

IRVIN: It's right out front, Ma. Here . . . I got the keys right here. Come on, sign the
    forms, huh? 655

MA RAINEY: Irvin, give me my car keys!

IRVIN: Sure, Ma . . . just sign the forms, huh?

[*He gives her the keys, expecting a trade-off.*]

MA RAINEY: Send them to my address and I'll get around to them.
IRVIN: Come on, Ma . . . I took care of everything, right? I straightened everything out.
MA RAINEY: Give me the pen, Irvin.   660

[*She signs the forms.*]

You tell Sturdyvant . . . one more mistake like that and I can make my records
someplace else.

[*She turns to exit.*]

Sylvester, straighten up your clothes. Come on, Dussie Mae.

[*She exits, followed by* DUSSIE MAE *and* SYLVESTER. *The lights go down in the
studio and come up on the band room.*]

CUTLER: I know what's keeping him so long. He up there writing out checks. You watch.
I ain't gonna stand for it. He ain't gonna bring me no check down here. If he do, he's   665
gonna take it right back upstairs and get some cash.
TOLEDO: Don't get yourself all worked up about it. Wait and see. Think positive.
CUTLER: I am thinking positive. He positively gonna give me some cash. Man give me a
check last time . . . you remember . . . we went all over Chicago trying to get it cashed.
See a nigger with a check, the first thing they think is he done stole it someplace.   670
LEVEE: I ain't had no trouble cashing mine.
CUTLER: I don't visit no whorehouses.
LEVEE: You don't know about my business. So don't start nothing. I'm tired of you as it is.
I ain't but two seconds off your ass no way.
TOLEDO: Don't you all start nothing now.   675
CUTLER: What the hell I care what you tired of. I wasn't even talking to you. I was talking
to this man right here.

[IRVIN *and* STURDYVANT *enter.*]

IRVIN: Okay boys. Mr. Sturdyvant has your pay.
CUTLER: As long as it's cash money, Mr. Sturdyvant. 'Cause I have too much trouble trying
to cash a check.   680
STURDYVANT: Oh, yes . . . I'm aware of that. Mr. Irvin told me you boys prefer cash, and
that's what I have for you.

[*He starts handing out money.*]

That was a good session you boys put in . . . That's twenty-five for you. Yessir, you
boys really know your business and we are going to . . . Twenty-five for you . . . We
are going to get you back in here real soon . . . twenty-five . . . and have another ses-   685
sion so you can make some more money . . . and twenty-five for you. Okay, thank
you, boys. You can get your things together and Mr. Irvin will make sure you find
your way out.
IRVIN: I'll be out front when you get your things together, Cutler.

[IRVIN *exits,* STURDYVANT *starts to follow.*]

LEVEE: Mr. Sturdyvant, sir. About them songs I give you? . . .   690
STURDYVANT: Oh, yes, . . . uh . . . Levee. About them songs you gave me. I've thought
about it and I just don't think the people will buy them. They're not the type of songs
we're looking for.
LEVEE: Mr. Sturdyvant, sir . . . I done got my band picked out and they's real good fel-

lows. They knows how to play real good. I know if the peoples hear the music,   695
they'll buy it.

STURDYVANT: Well, Levee, I'll be fair with you . . . but they're just not the right songs.

LEVEE: Mr. Sturdyvant, you got to understand about that music. That music is what the
people is looking for. They's tired of jug-band music. They wants something that
excites them. Something with some fire to it.   700

STURDYVANT: Okay, Levee. I'll tell you what I'll do. I'll give you five dollars a piece for
them. Now that's the best I can do.

LEVEE: I don't want no five dollars, Mr. Sturdyvant. I wants to record them songs, like
you say.

STURDYVANT: Well, Levee, like I say . . . they just aren't the kind of songs we're looking for.   705

LEVEE: Mr. Sturdyvant, you asked me to write them songs. Now, why didn't you tell me
that before when I first gave them to you? You told me you was gonna let me record
them. What's the difference between then and now?

STURDYVANT: Well, look . . . I'll pay you for your trouble . . .

LEVEE: What's the difference, Mr. Sturdyvant? That's what I wanna know.   710

STURDYVANT: I had my fellows play your songs, and when I heard them, they just didn't
sound like the kind of songs I'm looking for right now.

LEVEE: You got to hear *me* play them, Mr. Sturdyvant! You ain't heard *me* play them. That's
what's gonna make them sound right.

STURDYVANT: Well, Levee, I don't doubt that really. It's just that . . . well, I don't think   715
they'd sell like Ma's records. But I'll take them off your hands for you.

LEVEE: The people's tired of jug-band music, Mr. Sturdyvant. They wants something that's
gonna excite them! They wants something with some fire! I don't know what fellows
you had playing them songs . . . but if I could play them! I'd set them down in the
people's lap! Now you told me I could record them songs!   720

STURDYVANT: Well, there's nothing I can do about that. Like I say, it's five dollars a piece.
That's what I'll give you. I'm doing you a favor. Now, if you write any more, I'll help
you out and take them off your hands. The price is five dollars a piece. Just like now.

> [*He attempts to hand* LEVEE *the money, finally shoves it in* LEVEE's *coat pocket
> and is gone in a flash.* LEVEE *follows him to the door and it slams in his face. He
> takes the money from his pocket, balls it up and throws it on the floor. The other
> musicians silently gather up their belongings.* TOLEDO *walks past* LEVEE *and
> steps on his shoe.*]

LEVEE: Hey! Watch it . . . Shit Toledo! You stepped on my shoe!

TOLEDO: Excuse me there, Levee.   725

LEVEE: Look at that! Look at that! Nigger, you stepped on my shoe. What you do that
for?

TOLEDO: I said I'm sorry.

LEVEE: Nigger gonna step on my goddamn shoe! You done fucked up my shoe! Look at
that! Look at what you done to my shoe, nigger! I ain't stepped on your shoe! What   730
you wanna step on my shoe for?

CUTLER: The man said he's sorry.

LEVEE: Sorry! How the hell he gonna be sorry after he gone ruin my shoe! Come talking
about sorry!

> [*Turns his attention back to* TOLEDO.]

Nigger, you stepped on my shoe! You know that!   735

> [LEVEE *snatches his shoe off his foot and holds it up for* TOLEDO *to see.*]

See what you done?

TOLEDO: What you want me to do about it? It's done now. I said excuse me.

LEVEE: Wanna go and fuck up my shoe like that. I ain't done nothing to your shoe. Look at this!

[TOLEDO *turns and continues to gather up his things.* LEVEE *spins him around by his shoulder.*]

LEVEE: Naw . . . naw . . . look what you done! 740

[*He shoves the shoe in* TOLEDO*'s face.*]

Look at that! That's my shoe! Look at that! You did it! You did it! You fucked up my shoe! You stepped on my shoe with them raggedy-ass clodhoppers!

TOLEDO: Nigger, ain't nobody studying you and your shoe! I said excuse me. If you can't accept that, then the hell with it. What you want me to do?

[LEVEE *is in near rage, breathing hard. He is trying to get a grip on himself, as even he senses, or perhaps only he senses, he is about to lose control. He looks around, uncertain of what to do.* TOLEDO *has gone back to packing, as have* CUTLER *and* SLOW DRAG. *They purposefully avoid looking at* LEVEE *in hopes he'll calm down if he doesn't have an audience. All the weight in the world suddenly falls on* LEVEE *and he rushes at* TOLEDO *with his knife in his hand.*]

LEVEE: Nigger, you stepped on my shoe! 745

[*He plunges the knife into* TOLEDO*'s back up to the hilt.* TOLEDO *lets out a sound of surprise and agony.* CUTLER *and* SLOW DRAG *freeze.* TOLEDO *falls backward with* LEVEE, *his hand still on the knife, holding him up.* LEVEE *is suddenly faced with the realization of what he has done. He shoves* TOLEDO *forward and takes a step back.* TOLEDO *slumps to the floor.*]

He . . . he stepped on my shoe. He did. Honest, Cutler, he stepped on my shoe. What he do that for? Toledo, what you do that for? Cutler, help me. He stepped on my shoe, Cutler.

[*He turns his attention to* TOLEDO.]

Toledo! Toledo, get up.

[*He crosses to* TOLEDO *and tries to pick him up.*]

It's okay, Toledo. Come on . . . I'll help you. Come on, stand up now. Levee'll 750 help you.

[TOLEDO *is limp and heavy and awkward. He slumps back to the floor.* LEVEE *gets mad at him.*]

Don't look at me like that! Toledo! Nigger, don't look at me like that! I'm warning you nigger! Close your eyes! Don't you look at me like that! [*He turns to* CUTLER.] Tell him to close his eyes. Cutler. Tell him don't look at me like that.

CUTLER: Slow Drag, get Mr. Irvin down here. 755

[*The sound of a trumpet is heard,* LEVEE*'s trumpet, a muted trumpet struggling for the highest of possibilities and blowing pain and warning.*]

BLACK OUT.

How I Learned to Drive (1997)

OW I LEARNED TO DRIVE draws a parallel between learning to drive a car and learning to make one's way through the difficulties of growing up. This parallel is particularly meaningful to the play's central character, Li'l Bit, who was taught to drive by her uncle—a pedophile who used her driving lessons as an opportunity to seduce her. The situation is made especially complex because the would-be seducer, Uncle Peck, is treated somewhat sympathetically. Uncle Peck seems to love his niece, Li'l Bit, and has far more concern for her than do members of her family, who constantly tease her and make her miserable with comments about the size of her breasts. The play strongly suggests that Uncle Peck himself has been a victim of pedophilia and that he honestly sees in Li'l Bit some hope for emotional fulfillment.

How I Learned to Drive is basically a memory play. It moves easily back and forth through time as Li'l Bit recalls her adolescent years and her relationship with Uncle Peck. The playwright frames the scenes through the use of captions, which Vogel suggests should be spoken in the type of voice heard in driver education films. Most of these captions are related to driving lessons such as "Idling in the Neutral Gear," "Shifting Forward from First to Second Gear," "You and the Reverse Gear," and "Driving in Today's World." Li'l Bit and Uncle Peck are the only clearly developed characters. All of the other roles in the play are performed by what the script labels the "Greek Chorus"—one male and two female actors who change identities quickly to become family members, students, waiters, and others needed to make the script function effectively. This choice by the playwright focuses our attention and sympathies on Uncle Peck and Li'l Bit.

Li'l Bit and Uncle Peck share a deep emotional relationship that is always more painful than fulfilling, one that can never be forgotten. As Li'l Bit says of her first understanding of what was happening between them: "That day was the last day I lived in my body. I retreated above the neck, and I've lived inside the 'fire' in my head ever since. . . . The nearest sensation I feel—of flight in the body—I guess I feel when I'm driving." And at the end of the play as she prepares to drive, she recalls and obeys all the rules that Uncle Peck taught her. At this point she seems near acceptance of what happened in the past and as close to reconciliation as is possible.

How I Learned to Drive won the Pulitzer Prize for Drama in 1998.

Paula Vogel

How I Learned to Drive

Characters

LI'L BIT—*A woman who ages forty-something to eleven years old. (See Notes on the New York Production.)*

PECK—*Attractive man in his forties. Despite a few problems, he should be played by an actor one might cast in the role of Atticus in To Kill a Mockingbird.*

THE GREEK CHORUS—*If possible, these three members should be able to sing three-part harmony.*

MALE GREEK CHORUS—*Plays Grandfather, Waiter, High School Boys. Thirties–Forties. (See Notes on the New York Production.)*

FEMALE GREEK CHORUS—*Plays Mother, Aunt Mary, High School Girls. Thirty–Fifty. (See Notes on the New York Production.)*

TEENAGE GREEK CHORUS—*Plays Grandmother, High School Girls, and the voice of eleven-year-old Li'l Bit. Note on the casting of this actor: I would strongly recommend casting a young woman who is of "legal age;" that is, twenty-one to twenty-five years old who can look as close to eleven as possible. The contrast with the other cast members will help. If the actor is too young, the audience may feel uncomfortable. (See Notes on the New York Production.)*

PRODUCTION NOTES

I urge directors to use the Greek Chorus in staging as environment and, well, part of the family—with the exception of the Teenage Greek Chorus member who, after the last time she appears onstage, should perhaps disappear.

As for music: Please have fun. I wrote sections of the play listening to music like Roy Orbison's "Dream Baby" and The Mamas and the Papas' "Dedicated to the One I Love." The vaudeville sections go well to the Tijuana Brass or any music that sounds like a Laugh-In soundtrack. Other sixties music is rife with pedophilish (?) reference: the "You're Sixteen" genre hits; The Beach Boys' "Little Surfer Girl"; Gary Puckett and the Union Gap's "This Girl Is a Woman Now"; "Come Back When You Grow Up," etc.

And whenever possible, please feel free to punctuate the action with traffic signs: "No Passing," "Slow Children," "Dangerous Curves," "One Way," and the visual signs for children, deer crossings, hills, school buses, etc. (See Notes on the New York Production.)

This script uses the notion of slides and projections, which were not used in the New York production of the play.

On titles: Throughout the script there are boldfaced titles. In production these should be spoken in a neutral voice (the type of voice that driver education films employ). In the New York production these titles were assigned to various members of the Greek Chorus and were done live.

NOTES ON THE NEW YORK PRODUCTION

The role of Li'l Bit was originally written as a character who is forty-something. When we cast Mary-Louise Parker in the role of Li'l Bit, we cast the Greek Chorus members with younger actors as the Female Greek and the Male Greek, and cast the Teenage Greek with an older (that is, mid-twenties) actor as well. There is a great deal of flexibility in age. Directors should change the age in the last monologue for Li'l Bit ("And before you know it, I'll be thirty-five . . .") to reflect the actor's age who is playing Li'l Bit.

As the house lights dim, a VOICE announces:

Safety first—You and Driver Education.

[*Then the sound of a key turning the ignition of a car.* LI'L BIT *steps into a spotlight on the stage; "well-endowed," she is a softer-looking woman in the present time than she was at seventeen.*]

LI'L BIT: Sometimes to tell a secret, you first have to teach a lesson. We're going to start our lesson tonight on an early, warm summer evening.
  In a parking lot overlooking the Beltsville Agricultural Farms in suburban Maryland.   5
Less than a mile away, the crumbling concrete of U.S. One wends its way past one-room revival churches, the porno drive-in, and boarded up motels with For Sale signs tumbling down.
  Like I said, it's a warm summer evening.
Here on the land the Department of Agriculture owns, the smell of sleeping farm   10
animal is thick in the air. The smells of clover and hay mix in with the smells of the leather dashboard. You can still imagine how Maryland used to be, before the malls took over. This countryside was once dotted with farmhouses—from their porches you could have witnessed the Civil War raging in the front fields.
  Oh yes. There's a moon over Maryland tonight, that spills into the car where I   15
sit beside a man old enough to be—did I mention how still the night is? Damp soil and tranquil air. It's the kind of night that makes a middle-aged man with a mortgage feel like a country boy again.
  It's 1969. And I am very old, very cynical of the world, and I know it all. In short, I am seventeen years old, parking off a dark lane with a married man on an   20
early summer night.

  [*Lights up on two chairs facing front—or a Buick Riviera, if you will. Waiting patiently, with a smile on his face,* PECK *sits sniffing the night air.* LI'L BIT *climbs in beside him, seventeen years old and tense. Throughout the following, the two sit facing directly front. They do not touch. Their bodies remain passive. Only their facial expressions emote.*]

PECK: Ummm. I love the smell of your hair.
LI'L BIT: Uh-huh.
PECK: Oh, Lord. Ummmm. [*beat*] A man could die happy like this.
LI'L BIT: Well, *don't.*   25
PECK: What shampoo is this?
LI'L BIT: Herbal Essence.
PECK: Herbal Essence. I'm gonna buy me some. Herbal Essence. And when I'm all alone in the house, I'm going to get into the bathtub, and uncap the bottle and—
LI'L BIT: —Be good.   30
PECK: What?
LI'L BIT: Stop being . . . bad.
PECK: What did you think I was going to say? What do you think I'm going to do with the shampoo?
LI'L BIT: I don't want to know. I don't want to hear it.   35

PECK: I'm going to wash my hair. That's all.

LI'L BIT: Oh.

PECK: What did you think I was going to do?

LI'L BIT: Nothing . . . I don't know. Something . . . nasty.

PECK: With shampoo? Lord, gal—your mind! 40

LI'L BIT: And whose fault is it?

PECK: Not mine. I've got the mind of a boy scout.

LI'L BIT: Right. A horny boy scout.

PECK: Boy scouts are always horny. What do you think the first Merit Badge is for?

LI'L BIT: There. You're going to be nasty again. 45

PECK: Oh, no. I'm good. Very good.

LI'L BIT: It's getting late.

PECK: Don't change the subject. I was talking about how good I am. [*beat*] Are you ever
gonna let me show you how good I am?

LI'L BIT: Don't go over the line now. 50

PECK: I won't. I'm not gonna do anything you don't want me to do.

LI'L BIT: That's right.

PECK: And I've been good all week.

LI'L BIT: You have?

PECK: Yes. All week. Not a single drink. 55

LI'L BIT: Good boy.

PECK: Do I get a reward? For not drinking?

LI'L BIT: A small one. It's getting late.

PECK: Just let me undo you. I'll do you back up.

LI'L BIT: All right. But be quick about it. [PECK *pantomimes undoing* LI'L BIT'*s brassiere* 60
with one hand.] You know, that's amazing. The way you can undo the hooks through
my blouse with one hand.

PECK: Years of practice.

LI'L BIT: You would make an incredible brain surgeon with that dexterity.

PECK: I'll bet Clyde—what's the name of the boy taking you to the prom? 65

LI'L BIT: Claude Souders.

PECK: Claude Souders. I'll bet it takes him two hands, lights on, and you helping him on
to get to first base.

LI'L BIT: Maybe.

[*beat*]

PECK: Can I . . . kiss them? Please? 70

LI'L BIT: I don't know.

PECK: Don't make a grown man beg.

LI'L BIT: Just one kiss.

PECK: I'm going to lift your blouse.

LI'L BIT: It's a little cold. 75

[PECK *laughs gently.*]

PECK: That's not why you're shivering. [*They sit, perfectly still, for a long moment of silence.*
PECK *makes gentle, concentric circles with his thumbs in the air in front of him.*] How
does that feel?

[LI'L BIT *closes her eyes, carefully keeps her voice calm:*]

LI'L BIT: It's . . . okay.

[*Sacred music, organ music, or a boy's choir swells beneath the following.*]

PECK: I tell you, you can keep all the cathedrals of Europe. Just give me a second with   80
these—these celestial orbs—

[PECK *bows his head as if praying. But he is kissing her nipple.* LI'L BIT, *eyes still closed, rears back her head on the leather Buick car seat.*]

LI'L BIT: Uncle Peck—we've got to go. I've got graduation rehearsal at school tomorrow morning. And you should get on home to Aunt Mary—
PECK: —All right, Li'l Bit.
LI'L BIT: —*Don't* call me that no more. [*calmer*] Any more. I'm a big girl now, Uncle Peck.   85
As you know.

[LI'L BIT *pantomimes refastening her bra behind her back.*]

PECK: That you are. Going on eighteen. Kittens will turn into cats.
[*sighs*] I live all week long for these few minutes with you—you know that?
LI'L BIT: I'll drive.

[A VOICE *cuts in with:*]

Idling in the Neutral Gear.   90

[*Sound of a car revving cuts off the sacred music;* LI'L BIT, *now an adult, rises out of the car and comes to us.*]

LI'L BIT: In most families, relatives get names like "Junior," or "Brother," or "Bubba." In my family, if we call someone "Big Papa," it's not because he's tall. In my family, folks tend to get nicknamed for their genitalia. Uncle Peck, for example. My mama's adage was "the titless wonder," and my cousin Bobby got branded for life as "B.B."

[*In unison with Greek Chorus:*]

LI'L BIT: For blue balls.   95
GREEK CHORUS: For blue balls.
FEMALE GREEK CHORUS: [*as Mother*] And of course, we were so excited to have a baby girl that when the nurse brought you in and said, "It's a girl! It's a baby girl!" I just had to see for myself. So we whipped your diapers down and parted your chubby little legs—and right between your legs there was—   100

[PECK *has come over during the above and chimes along:*]

PECK: Just a little bit.
GREEK CHORUS: Just a little bit.
FEMALE GREEK CHORUS: [*as Mother*] And when you were born, you were so tiny that you fit in Uncle Peck's outstretched hand.

[PECK *stretches his hand out.*]

PECK: Now that's a fact. I held you, one day old, right in this hand.   105

[*A traffic signal is projected of a bicycle in a circle with a diagonal red slash.*]

LI'L BIT: Even with my family background, I was sixteen or so before I realized that pedophilia did not mean people who loved to bicycle . . .

[A VOICE *intrudes:*]

Driving in First Gear.

LI'L BIT: 1969. A typical family dinner.

FEMALE GREEK CHORUS: [*as Mother*] Look, Grandma. Li'l Bit's getting to be as big in   110
    the bust as you are.

LI'L BIT: Mother! Could we please change the subject?

TEENAGE GREEK CHORUS: [*as Grandmother*] Well, I hope you are buying her some
    decent bras. I never had a decent bra, growing up in the Depression, and now my
    shoulders are just crippled—crippled from the weight hanging on my shoulders—   115
    the dents from my bra straps are big enough to put your finger in.—Here, let me
    show you—

      [*as Grandmother starts to open her blouse:*]

LI'L BIT: Grandma! Please don't undress at the dinner table.

PECK: I thought the entertainment came *after* the dinner.

LI'L BIT: [*to the audience*] This is how it always starts. My grandfather, Big Papa, will chime   120
    in next with—

MALE GREEK CHORUS: [*as Grandfather*] Yup. If Li'l Bit gets any bigger, we're gonna
    haveta buy her a wheelbarrow to carry in front of her—

LI'L BIT: —Damn it—

PECK: —How about those Redskins on Sunday, Big Papa?   125

LI'L BIT: [*to the audience*] The only sports Big Papa followed was chasing Grandma around
    the house—

MALE GREEK CHORUS: [*as Grandfather*]—Or we could write to Kate Smith. Ask her for
    somma her used brassieres she don't want anymore—she could maybe give to Li'l Bit
    here—   130

LI'L BIT: —I can't stand it. I can't.

PECK: Now, honey, that's just their way—

FEMALE GREEK CHORUS: [*as Mother*] I tell you, Grandma, Li'l Bit's at that age. She's so
    sensitive, you can't say boo—

LI'L BIT: I'd like some privacy, that's all. Okay? Some goddamn privacy—   135

PECK: —Well, at least she didn't use the savior's name—

LI'L BIT: [*to the audience*] And Big Papa wouldn't let a dead dog lie. No sirree.

MALE GREEK CHORUS: [*as Grandfather*] Well, she'd better stop being so sensitive. 'Cause
    five minutes before Li'l Bit turns the corner, her tits turn first—

LI'L BIT: [*starting to rise from the table*]—That's it. That's it.   140

PECK: Li'l Bit, you can't let him get to you. Then he wins.

LI'L BIT: I hate him. *Hate* him.

PECK: That's fine. But hate him and eat a good dinner at the same time.

      [LI'L BIT *calms down and sits with perfect dignity.*]

LI'L BIT: The gumbo is really good, Grandma.

MALE GREEK CHORUS: [*as Grandfather*] A'course, Li'l Bit's got a big surprise coming for   145
    her when she goes to that fancy college this fall—

PECK: Big Papa—let it go.

MALE GREEK CHORUS: [*as Grandfather*] What does she need a college degree for? She's
    got all the credentials she'll need on her chest—

LI'L BIT: —Maybe I want to learn things. Read. Rise above my cracker background—   150

PECK: —Whoa, now, Li'l Bit—

MALE GREEK CHORUS: [*as Grandfather*] What kind of things do you want to read?

LI'L BIT: There's a whole semester course, for example, on Shakespeare—

[*Greek Chorus, as Grandfather, laughs until he weeps.*]

MALE GREEK CHORUS: [*as Grandfather*] Shakespeare. That's a good one. Shakespeare is really going to help you in life. 155

PECK: I think it's wonderful. And on scholarship!

MALE GREEK CHORUS: [*as Grandfather*] How is Shakespeare going to help her lie on her back in the dark?

[LI'L BIT *is on her feet.*]

LI'L BIT: You're getting old, Big Papa. You are going to die—very, very soon. Maybe even *tonight*. And when you get to heaven, God's going to be a beautiful black woman in 160 a long white robe. She's gonna look at your chart and say: Uh-oh. Fornication. Dog-ugly mean with blood relatives. Oh. Uh-oh. Voted for George Wallace. Well, one last chance: If you can name the play, all will be forgiven. And then she'll quote: "The quality of mercy is not strained." Your answer? Oh, too bad—*Merchant of Venice:* Act IV, Scene iii. And then she'll send your ass to fry in hell with all the other 165 crackers. Excuse me, please.

[*to the audience*] And as I left the house, I would always hear Big Papa say:

MALE GREEK CHORUS: [*as Grandfather*] Lucy, your daughter's got a mouth on her. Well, no sense in wasting good gumbo. Pass me her plate, Mama.

LI'L BIT: And Aunt Mary would come up to Uncle Peck: 170

FEMALE GREEK CHORUS: [*as Aunt Mary*] Peck, go after her, will you? You're the only one she'll listen to when she gets like this.

PECK: She just needs to cool off.

FEMALE GREEK CHORUS: [*as Aunt Mary*] Please, honey—Grandma's been on her feet cooking all day. 175

PECK: All right.

LI'L BIT: And as he left the room, Aunt Mary would say:

FEMALE GREEK CHORUS: [*as Aunt Mary*] Peck's so good with them when they get to be this age.

[LI'L BIT *has stormed to another part of the stage, her back turned, weeping with a teenage fury.* PECK, *cautiously, as if stalking a deer, comes to her. She turns away even more. He waits a bit.*]

PECK: I don't suppose you're talking to family. [*no response*] Does it help that I'm in-law? 180

LI'L BIT: Don't you dare make fun of this.

PECK: I'm not. There's nothing funny about this. [*beat*] Although I'll bet when Big Papa is about to meet his maker, he'll remember *The Merchant of Venice.*

LI'L BIT: I've got to get away from here.

PECK: You're going away. Soon. Here, take this. 185

[PECK *hands her his folded handkerchief.* LI'L BIT *uses it, noisily. Hands it back. Without her seeing, he reverently puts it back.*]

LI'L BIT: I hate this family.

PECK: Your grandfather's ignorant. And you're right—he's going to die soon. But he's family. Family is . . . family.

LI'L BIT: Grown-ups are always saying that. Family.

PECK: Well, when you get a little older, you'll see what we're saying. 190

LI'L BIT: Uh-huh. So family is another acquired taste, like French kissing?

PECK: Come again?

LI'L BIT: You know, at first it really grosses you out, but in time you grow to like it?

PECK: Girl, you are . . . a handful.

LI'L BIT: Uncle Peck—you have the keys to your car?   195

PECK: Where do you want to go?

LI'L BIT: Just up the road.

PECK: I'll come with you.

LI'L BIT: No—please? I just need to . . . to drive for a little bit. Alone.

[PECK *tosses her the keys.*]

PECK: When can I see you alone again?   200

LI'L BIT: Tonight.

[LI'L BIT *crosses to center stage while the lights dim around her.* A VOICE *directs:*]

Shifting Forward from First to Second Gear.

LI'L BIT: There were a lot of rumors about why I got kicked out of that fancy school in
1970. Some say I got caught with a man in my room. Some say as a kid on scholarship I fooled around with a rich man's daughter.   205
[LI'L BIT *smiles innocently at the audience.*] I'm not talking.
    But the real truth was I had a constant companion in my dorm room—who was
less than discrete. Canadian V.O. A fifth a day.
1970. A Nixon recession. I slept on the floors of friends who were out of work themselves. Took factory work when I could find it. A string of dead-end day jobs that   210
didn't last very long.
    What I did, most nights, was cruise the Beltway and the back roads of Mary-
land, where there was still country, past the battlefields and farm houses. Racing in
a 1965 Mustang—and as long as I had gasoline for my car and whiskey for me, the
nights would pass. Fully tanked, I would speed past the churches and the trees on the   215
bend, thinking just one notch of the steering wheel would be all it would take, and
yet some . . . reflex took over. My hands on the wheel in the nine and three o'clock
position—I never so much as got a ticket. He taught me well.

[A VOICE *announces:*]

You and the Reverse Gear.

LI'L BIT: Back up. 1968. On the Eastern Shore. A celebration dinner.   220

[LI'L BIT *joins* PECK *at a table in a restaurant.*]

PECK: Feeling better, missy?

LI'L BIT: The bathroom's really amazing here, Uncle Peck! They have these little soaps—
instead of borax or something—and they're in the shape of shells.

PECK: I'll have to take a trip to the gentlemen's room just to see.

LI'L BIT: How did you know about this place?   225

PECK: This inn is famous on the Eastern Shore—it's been open since the seventeenth
century. And I know how you like history . . .

[LI'L BIT *is shy and pleased.*]

LI'L BIT: It's great.

PECK: And you've just done your first, legal, long-distance drive. You must be hungry.

LI'L BIT: I'm starved.   230

PECK: I would suggest a dozen oysters to start, and the crab imperial . . . [LI'L BIT *is genuinely agog.*] You might be interested to know the town history. When the British sailed up this very river in the dead of night—see outside where I'm pointing?—They were going to bombard the heck out of this town. But the town fathers were ready for them. They crept up all the trees with lanterns so that the British would think they saw the town lights and 235 they aimed their cannons too high. And that's why the inn is still here for business today.

LI'L BIT: That's a great story.

PECK: [*casually*] Would you like to start with a cocktail?

LI'L BIT: You're not . . . you're not going to start drinking, are you, Uncle Peck?

PECK: Not me. I told you, as long as you're with me, I'll never drink. I asked you if *you'd* 240 like a cocktail before dinner. It's nice to have a little something with the oysters.

LI'L BIT: But . . . I'm not . . . legal. We could get arrested. Uncle Peck, they'll never believe I'm twenty-one!

PECK: So? Today we celebrate your driver's license—on the first try. This establishment reminds me a lot of places back home. 245

LI'L BIT: What does that mean?

PECK: In South Carolina, like here on the Eastern Shore, they're . . . [*searches for the right euphemism*] . . . "European." Not so puritanical. And very understanding if gentlemen wish to escort very attractive young ladies who might want a before-dinner cocktail. If you want one, I'll order one. 250

LI'L BIT: Well—sure. Just . . . one.

[*The Female Greek Chorus appears in a spot.*]

FEMALE GREEK CHORUS: [*as Mother*] A Mother's Guide to Social Drinking:
   A lady never gets sloppy—she may, however, get tipsy and a little gay.
   Never drink on an empty stomach. Avail yourself of the bread basket and generous portions of butter. Slather the butter on your bread. 255
Sip your drink, slowly, let the beverage linger in your mouth—interspersed with interesting, fascinating conversation. Sip, never . . . slurp or gulp. Your glass should always be three-quarters full when his glass is empty.
   Stay away from ladies' drinks: drinks like pink ladies, slow gin fizzes, daiquiris, gold cadillacs, Long Island iced teas, margaritas, pina colada, mai tais, planters 260 punch, white Russians, black Russians, red Russians, melon balls, blue balls, hummingbirds, hemorrhages, and hurricanes. In short, avoid anything with sugar, or anything with an umbrella. Get your vitamin C from fruit. Don't order anything with Voodoo or Vixen in the title or sexual positions in the name like Dead Man Screw or the Missionary. [*She sort of titters.*] 265
Believe me, they are lethal . . . I think you were conceived after one of those.
Drink, instead, like a man: straight up or on the rocks, with plenty of water in between.
   Oh, yes. And never mix your drinks. Stay with one all night long, like the man you came in with: bourbon, gin, or tequila till dawn, damn the torpedoes, full 270 speed ahead!

[*As the* FEMALE GREEK CHORUS *retreats, the* MALE GREEK CHORUS *approaches the table as a Waiter.*]

MALE GREEK CHORUS: [*as Waiter*] I hope you all are having a pleasant evening. Is there something I can bring you, sir, before you order?

[LI'L BIT *waits in anxious fear. Carefully, Uncle* PECK *says with command:*]

PECK: I'll have a plain iced tea. The lady would like a drink, I believe.

> [*The* MALE GREEK CHORUS *does a double take; there is a moment when Uncle* PECK *and he are in silent communication.*]

MALE GREEK CHORUS: [*as Waiter*] Very good. What would the . . . lady like? 275

LI'L BIT: [*a bit flushed*] Is there . . . is there any sugar in a martini?

PECK: None that I know of.

LI'L BIT: That's what I'd like then—a dry martini. And could we maybe have some bread?

PECK: A drink fit for a woman of the world.—Please bring the lady a dry martini, be gen- 280
erous with the olives, straight up.

> [*The* MALE GREEK CHORUS *anticipates a large tip.*]

MALE GREEK CHORUS: [*as Waiter*] Right away. Very good, sir.

> [*The* MALE GREEK CHORUS *returns with an empty martini glass which he puts in front of* LI'L BIT.]

PECK: Your glass is empty. Another martini, madam?

LI'L BIT: Yes, thank you.

> [PECK *signals the* MALE GREEK CHORUS, *who nods.*] So why did you leave South 285
Carolina, Uncle Peck?

PECK: I was stationed in D.C. after the war, and decided to stay. Go North, Young Man, someone might have said.

LI'L BIT: What did you do in the service anyway?

PECK: [*suddenly taciturn*] I . . . I did just this and that. Nothing heroic or spectacular. 290

LI'L BIT: But did you see fighting? Or go to Europe?

PECK: I served in the Pacific Theater. It's really nothing interesting to talk about.

LI'L BIT: It is to me. [*The Waiter has brought another empty glass.*] Oh, goody. I love the color of the swizzle sticks. What were we talking about?

PECK: Swizzle sticks. 295

LI'L BIT: Do you ever think of going back?

PECK: To the Marines?

LI'L BIT: No—to South Carolina.

PECK: Well, we do go back. To visit.

LI'L BIT: No, I mean to live. 300

PECK: Not very likely. I think it's better if my mother doesn't have a daily reminder of her disappointment.

LI'L BIT: Are these floorboards slanted?

PECK: Yes, the floor is very slanted. I think this is the original floor.

LI'L BIT: Oh, good. 305

> [*The* FEMALE GREEK CHORUS *as Mother enters swaying a little, a little past tipsy.*]

FEMALE GREEK CHORUS: [*as Mother*] Don't leave your drink unattended when you visit the ladies' room. There is such a thing as white slavery; the modus operandi is to spike an unsuspecting young girl's drink with a "mickey" when she's left the room to powder her nose.

> But if you feel you have had more than your sufficiency in liquor, do go to the 310
ladies' room—often. Pop your head out of doors for a refreshing breath of the night air. If you must, wet your face and head with tap water. Don't be afraid to dunk your head if necessary. A wet woman is still less conspicuous than a drunk woman.

[*The* FEMALE GREEK CHORUS *stumbles a little; conspiratorially.*] When in the course of human events it becomes necessary, go to a corner stall and insert the index and middle finger down the throat almost to the epiglottis. Divulge your stomach contents by such persuasion, and then wait a few moments before rejoining your beau waiting for you at your table.
315

Oh, no. Don't be shy or embarrassed. In the very best of establishments, there's always one or two debutantes crouched in the corner stalls, their beaded purses tossed willy-nilly, sounding like cats in heat, heaving up the contents of their stomachs.
320

[*The* FEMALE GREEK CHORUS *begins to wander off.*] I wonder what it is they do in the men's rooms . . .

LI'L BIT: So why is your mother disappointed in you, Uncle Peck?

PECK: Every mother in Horry County has Great Expectations.
325

LI'L BIT: —Could I have another mar-ti-ni, please?

PECK: I think this is your last one.

> [PECK *signals the Waiter. The Waiter looks at* LI'L BIT *and shakes his head no.* PECK *raises his eyebrow, raises his finger to indicate one more, and then rubs his fingers together. It looks like a secret code. The Waiter sighs, shakes his head sadly, and brings over another empty martini glass. He glares at* PECK.]

LI'L BIT: The name of the county where you grew up is "Horry?" [LI'L BIT, *plastered, begins to laugh. Then she stops.*] I think your mother should be proud of you.

> [PECK *signals for the check.*]

PECK: Well, missy, she wanted me to do—to *be* everything my father was not. She wanted me to amount to something.
330

LI'L BIT: But you have! You've amounted a lot. . . .

PECK: I'm just a very ordinary man.

> [*The Waiter has brought the check and waits.* PECK *draws out a large bill and hands it to the Waiter.* LI'L BIT *is in the soppy stage.*]

LI'L BIT: I'll bet your mother loves you, Uncle Peck.

> [PECK *freezes a bit. To* MALE GREEK CHORUS *as Waiter:*]

PECK: Thank you. The service was exceptional. Please keep the change.
335

MALE GREEK CHORUS: [*as Waiter, in a tone that could freeze*] Thank you, sir. Will you be needing any help?

PECK: I think we can manage, thank you.

> [*Just then, the* FEMALE GREEK CHORUS *as Mother lurches on stage; the* MALE GREEK CHORUS *as Waiter escorts her off as she delivers:*]

FEMALE GREEK CHORUS: [*as Mother*] Thanks to judicious planning and several trips to the ladies' loo, your mother once out-drank an entire regiment of British officers on a goodwill visit to Washington! Every last man of them! Milquetoasts! How'd they ever kick Hitler's cahones, huh? No match for an American lady—I could drink every man in here under the table.
340

[*She delivers one last crucial hint before she is gently "bounced."*] As a last resort, when going out for an evening on the town, be sure to wear a skintight girdle—so tight that only a surgical knife or acetylene torch can get it off you—so that if you do pass out in the arms of your escort, he'll end up with rubber burns on his fingers before he can steal your virtue—
345

[A **VOICE** *punctures the interlude with:*]

Vehicle Failure.

Even with careful maintenance and preventive operation of your automobile, it is 350
all too common for us to experience an unexpected breakdown. If you are driving
at any speed when a breakdown occurs, you must slow down and guide the auto-
mobile to the side of the road.

[**PECK** *is slowly propping up* LI'L BIT *as they work their way to his car in the*
parking lot of the inn.]

PECK: How are you doing, missy?

LI'L BIT: It's so far to the car, Uncle Peck. Like the lanterns in the trees the British fired 355
on . . .

[LI'L BIT *stumbles.* PECK *swoops her up in his arms.*]

PECK: Okay. I think we're going to take a more direct route.
[LI'L BIT *closes her eyes.*] Dizzy? [*She nods her head.*] Don't look at the ground.
Almost there—do you feel sick to your stomach? [LI'L BIT *nods. They reach the "car."*
PECK *gently deposits her on the front seat.*] Just settle here a little while until things 360
stop spinning. [LI'L BIT *opens her eyes.*]

LI'L BIT: What are we doing?

PECK: We're just going to sit here until your tummy settles down.

LI'L BIT: It's such nice upholst'ry—

PECK: Think you can go for a ride, now? 365

LI'L BIT: Where are you taking me?

PECK: Home.

LI'L BIT: You're not taking me—upstairs? There's no room at the inn?

[LI'L BIT *giggles.*]

PECK: Do you want to go upstairs? [LI'L BIT *doesn't answer.*] Or home?

LI'L BIT: —This isn't right, Uncle Peck. 370

PECK: What isn't right?

LI'L BIT: What we're doing. It's wrong. It's very wrong.

PECK: What are we doing? [LI'L BIT *doesn't answer.*] We're just going out to dinner.

LI'L BIT: You know. It's not nice to Aunt Mary.

PECK: You let me be the judge of what's nice and not nice to my wife. 375

[*beat*]

LI'L BIT: Now, you're mad.

PECK: I'm not mad. It's just that I thought you . . . understood me, Li'l Bit. I think you're
the only one who does.

LI'L BIT: Someone will get hurt.

PECK: Have I forced you to do anything? 380

[*There is a long pause as* LI'L BIT *tries to get sober enough to think this through.*]

LI'L BIT: . . . I guess not.

PECK: We're just enjoying each other's company. I've told you, nothing is going to happen
between us until you want it to. Do you know that?

LI'L BIT: Yes.

PECK: Nothing is going to happen until you want it to. [*A second more, with* PECK *staring* 385
ahead at the river while seated at the wheel of his car. Then, softly:] Do you want
something to happen?

> [PECK *reaches over and strokes her face, very gently.* LI'L BIT *softens, reaches for
> him, and buries her head in his neck. Then she kisses him. Then she moves away,
> dizzy again.*]

LI'L BIT: . . . I don't know.

> [PECK *smiles; this has been good news for him—it hasn't been a "no."*]

PECK: Then I'll wait. I'm a very patient man. I've been waiting for a long time. I don't
mind waiting. 390
LI'L BIT: Someone is going to get hurt.
PECK: No one is going to get hurt. [LI'L BIT *closes her eyes.*] Are you feeling sick?
LI'L BIT: Sleepy.

> [*Carefully,* PECK *props* LI'L BIT *up on the seat.*]

PECK: Stay here a second.
LI'L BIT: Where're you going? 395
PECK: I'm getting something from the back seat.
LI'L BIT: [*scared; too loud*] What? What are you going to do?

> [PECK *reappears in the front seat with a lap rug.*]

PECK: Shhhh. [PECK *covers* LI'L BIT. *She calms down.*] There. Think you can sleep?

> [LI'L BIT *nods. She slides over to rest on his shoulder. With a look of happiness,*
> PECK *turns the ignition key. Beat.* PECK *leaves* LI'L BIT *sleeping in the car and
> strolls down to the audience. Wagner's* Flying Dutchman *comes up faintly.*]

> [A VOICE *interjects:*]

Idling in the Neutral Gear.

TEENAGE GREEK CHORUS: Uncle Peck Teaches Cousin Bobby How to Fish. 400
PECK: I get back once or twice a year—supposedly to visit Mama and the family, but the
real truth is to fish. I miss this the most of all. There's a smell in the Low Country—
where the swamp and fresh inlet join the saltwater—a scent of sand and cypress, that
I haven't found anywhere yet.

I don't say this very often up North because it will just play into the stereotype 405
everyone has, but I will tell you: I didn't wear shoes in the summertime until I was
sixteen. It's unnatural down here to pen up your feet in leather. Go ahead—take 'em
off. Let yourself breathe—it really will make you feel better.
We're going to aim for some pompano today—and I have to tell you, they're a very
shy, mercurial fish. Takes patience, and psychology. You have to believe it doesn't 410
matter if you catch one or not.

Sky's pretty spectacular—there's some beer in the cooler next to the crab salad
I packed, so help yourself if you get hungry. Are you hungry? Thirsty? Holler if
you are.

Okay. You don't want to lean over the bridge like that—pompano feed in shal- 415
low water, and you don't want to get too close—they're frisky and shy little things—
wait, check your line. Yep, something's been munching while we were talking.

Okay, look: We take the sand flea and you take the hook like this—right through his little sand flea rump. Sand fleas should always keep their backs to the wall. Okay. Cast it in, like I showed you. That's great! I can taste that pompano now, sautéed with some pecans and butter, a little bourbon—now—let it lie on the bottom—now, reel, jerk, reel, jerk— 420

Look—look at your line. There's something calling, all right. Okay, tip the rod up—not too sharp—hook it—all right, now easy, reel and then rest—let it play. And reel—play it out, that's right—really good! I can't believe it! It's a pompano.—Good work! Way to go! You are an official fisherman now. Pompano are hard to catch. We are going to have a delicious little— 425

What? Well, I don't know how much pain a fish feels—you can't think of that. Oh, no, don't cry, come on now, it's just a fish—the other guys are going to see you.—No, no you're just real sensitive, and I think that's wonderful at your age—look, do you want me to cut it free? You do? 430

Okay, hand me those pliers—look—I'm cutting the hook—okay? And we're just going to drop it in—no I'm not mad. It's just for fun, okay? There—it's going to swim back to its lady friend and tell her what a terrible day it had and she's going to stroke him with her fins until he feels better, and then they'll do something alone together that will make them both feel good and sleepy . . . 435

[PECK *bends down, very earnest.*] I don't want you to feel ashamed about crying. I'm not going to tell anyone, okay? I can keep secrets. You know, men cry all the time. They just don't tell anybody, and they don't let anybody catch them. There's nothing you could do that would make me feel ashamed of you. Do you know that? Okay. [PECK *straightens up, smiles.*] 440

Do you want to pack up and call it a day? I tell you what—I think I can still remember—there's a really neat tree house where I used to stay for days. I think it's still here—it was the last time I looked. But it's a secret place—you can't tell anybody we've gone there—least of all your mom or your sisters.—This is something special just between you and me. Sound good? We'll climb up there and have a beer and some crab salad—okay, B.B.? Bobby? Robert . . . 445

[LI'L BIT *sits at a kitchen table with the two* FEMALE GREEK CHORUS *members.*]

LI'L BIT: [*to the audience*] Three women, three generations, sit at the kitchen table.

On Men, Sex, and Women: Part I:

FEMALE GREEK CHORUS: [*as Mother*] Men only want one thing. 450

LI'L BIT: [*wide-eyed*] But what? What is it they want?

FEMALE GREEK CHORUS: [*as Mother*] And once they have it, they lose all interest. So Don't Give It to Them.

TEENAGE GREEK CHORUS: [*as Grandmother*] I never had the luxury of the rhythm method. Your grandfather is just a big bull. A big bull. Every morning, every evening. 455

FEMALE GREEK CHORUS: [*as Mother, whispers to* LI'L BIT] And he used to come home for lunch every day.

LI'L BIT: My god, Grandma!

TEENAGE GREEK CHORUS: [*as Grandmother*] Your grandfather only cares that I do two things: have the table set and the bed turned down. 460

FEMALE GREEK CHORUS: [*as Mother*] And in all that time, Mother, you never have experienced—?

LI'L BIT: [*to the audience*]—Now my grandmother believed in all the sacraments of the church, to the day she died. She believed in Santa Claus and the Easter Bunny until she was fifteen. But she didn't believe in— 465

TEENAGE GREEK CHORUS: [*as Grandmother*]—Orgasm! That's just something you and Mary have made up! I don't believe you.

FEMALE GREEK CHORUS: [*as Mother*] Mother, it happens to women all the time—

TEENAGE GREEK CHORUS: [*as Grandmother*]—Oh, now you're going to tell me about the G force! 470

LI'L BIT: No, Grandma, I think that's astronauts—

FEMALE GREEK CHORUS: [*as Mother*] Well, Mama, after all, you were a child bride when Big Papa came and got you—you were a married woman and you still believed in Santa Claus.

TEENAGE GREEK CHORUS: [*as Grandmother*] It was legal, what Daddy and I did! I was 475 fourteen and in those days, fourteen was a grown-up woman—

[*Big Papa shuffles in the kitchen for a cookie.*]

MALE GREEK CHORUS: [*as Grandfather*]—Oh, now we're off on Grandma and the Rape of the Sa-bean Women!

TEENAGE GREEK CHORUS: [*as Grandmother*] Well, you were the one in such a big hurry—

MALE GREEK CHORUS: [*as Grandfather to* LI'L BIT]—I picked your grandmother out of 480 that herd of sisters just like a lion chooses the gazelle—the plump, slow, flaky gazelle dawdling at the edge of the herd—your sisters were too smart and too fast and too scrawny—

LI'L BIT: [*to the audience*]—The family story is that when Big Papa came for Grandma, my Aunt Lily was waiting for him with a broom—and she beat him over the head all the 485 way down the stairs as he was carrying out Grandma's hope chest—

MALE GREEK CHORUS: [*as Grandfather*]—And they were *mean*. 'Specially Lily.

FEMALE GREEK CHORUS: [*as Mother*] Well, you were robbing the baby of the family!

TEENAGE GREEK CHORUS: [*as Grandmother*] I still keep a broom handy in the kitchen! And I know how to use it! So get your hand out of the cookie jar and don't you spoil 490 your appetite for dinner—out of the kitchen!

[MALE GREEK CHORUS *as Grandfather leaves chuckling with a cookie.*]

FEMALE GREEK CHORUS: [*as Mother*] Just one thing a married woman needs to know how to use—the rolling pin or the broom. I prefer a heavy cast-iron fry pan—they're great on a man's head, no matter how thick the skull is.

TEENAGE GREEK CHORUS: [*as Grandmother*] Yes, sir, your father is ruled by only two 495 bosses! Mr. Gut and Mr. Peter! And sometimes, first thing in the morning, Mr. Sphincter Muscle!

FEMALE GREEK CHORUS: [*as Mother*] It's true. Men are like children. Just like little boys.

TEENAGE GREEK CHORUS: [*as Grandmother*] Men are bulls! Big bulls! 500

[*The* GREEK CHORUS *is getting aroused.*]

FEMALE GREEK CHORUS: [*as Mother*] They'd still be crouched on their haunches over a fire in a cave if we hadn't cleaned them up!

TEENAGE GREEK CHORUS: [*as Grandmother, flushed*] Coming in smelling of sweat—

FEMALE GREEK CHORUS: [*as Mother*]—Looking at those naughty pictures like boys in a dime store with a dollar in their pockets! 505

TEENAGE GREEK CHORUS: [*as Grandmother; raucous*] No matter to them what they smell like! They've got to have it, right then, on the spot, right there! Nasty!—

FEMALE GREEK CHORUS: [*as Mother*]—Vulgar!—
TEENAGE GREEK CHORUS: [*as Grandmother*] Primitive!—
FEMALE GREEK CHORUS: [*as Mother*]—Hot!—   510
LI'L BIT: And just about then, Big Papa would shuffle in with—
MALE GREEK CHORUS: [*as Grandfather*]—What are you all cackling about in here?
TEENAGE GREEK CHORUS: [*as Grandmother*] Stay out of the kitchen! This is just for girls!

> [*as Grandfather leaves:*]

MALE GREEK CHORUS: [*as Grandfather*] Lucy, you'd better not be filling Mama's head with
    sex! Every time you and Mary come over and start in about sex, when I ask a simple   515
    question like, "What time is dinner going to be ready?," Mama snaps my head off!
TEENAGE GREEK CHORUS: [*as Grandmother*] Dinner will be ready when I'm good and
    ready! Stay out of this kitchen!

> [LI'L BIT *steps out.*]

> [A VOICE *directs:*]

When Making a Left Turn, You Must Downshift While Going Forward.

LI'L BIT: 1979. A long bus trip to Upstate New York. I settled in to read, when a young man   520
    sat beside me.
MALE GREEK CHORUS: [*as Young Man; voice cracking*] "What are you reading?"
LI'L BIT: He asked. His voice broke into that miserable equivalent of vocal acne, not quite
    falsetto and not tenor, either. I glanced a side view. He was appealing in an odd way,
    huge ears at a defiant angle springing forward at ninety degrees. He must have been   525
    shaving, because his face, with a peach sheen, was speckled with nicks and styptic.
    "I have a class tomorrow," I told him.
MALE GREEK CHORUS: [*as Young Man*] "You're taking a class?"
LI'L BIT: "I'm teaching a class." He concentrated on lowering his voice.
MALE GREEK CHORUS: [*as Young Man*] "I'm a senior. Walt Whitman High."   530
LI'L BIT: The light was fading outside, so perhaps he was—with a very high voice. I felt
    his "interest" quicken. Five steps ahead of the hopes in his head, I slowed down,
    waited, pretended surprise, acted at listening, all the while knowing we would get off
    the bus, he would just then seem to think to ask me to dinner, he would chivalrously
    insist on walking me home, he would continue to converse in the street until I would   535
    casually invite him up to my room—and—I was only into the second moment of
    conversation and I could see the whole evening before me.
    And dramaturgically speaking, after the faltering and slightly comical "first act,"
    there was the very briefest of intermissions, and an extremely capable and forceful
    sustained second act. And after the second act climax and a gentle denouement—   540
    before the post-play discussion—I lay on my back in the dark and I thought about you,
    Uncle Peck. Oh. Oh—this is the allure. Being older. Being the first. Being the transla-
    tor, the teacher, the epicure, the already jaded. This is how the giver gets taken.
    [LI'L BIT *changes her tone.*] On Men, Sex, and Women: Part II:

> [LI'L BIT *steps back into the scene as a fifteen year old, gawky and quiet, as the
> gazelle at the edge of the herd.*]

TEENAGE GREEK CHORUS: [*as Grandmother; to* LI'L BIT] You're being mighty quiet, missy.   545
    Cat Got Your Tongue?
LI'L BIT: I'm just listening. Just thinking.
TEENAGE GREEK CHORUS: [*as Grandmother*] Oh, yes, Little Miss Radar Ears? Soaking it
    all in? Little Miss Sponge? Penny for your thoughts?

[LI'L BIT *hesitates to ask but she really wants to know.*]

LI'L BIT: Does it—when you do it—you know, theoretically when I do it and I haven't   550
done it before—I mean—does it hurt?

FEMALE GREEK CHORUS: [*as Mother*] Does what hurt, honey?

LI'L BIT: When a . . . when a girl does it for the first time—with a man—does it hurt?

TEENAGE GREEK CHORUS: [*as Grandmother; horrified*] *That's* what you're thinking
about?   555

FEMALE GREEK CHORUS: [*as Mother; calm*] Well, just a little bit. Like a pinch. And there's
a little blood.

TEENAGE GREEK CHORUS: [*as Grandmother*] Don't tell her that! She's too young to be
thinking those things!

FEMALE GREEK CHORUS: [*as Mother*] Well, if she doesn't find out from me, where is she   560
going to find out? In the street?

TEENAGE GREEK CHORUS: [*as Grandmother*] Tell her it hurts! It's agony! You think you're
going to die! Especially if you do it before marriage!

FEMALE GREEK CHORUS: [*as Mother*] Mama! I'm going to tell her the truth! Unlike you,
you left me and Mary completely in the dark with fairy tales and told us to go to the   565
priest! What does an eighty-year-old priest know about love-making with girls!

LI'L BIT: [*getting upset*] It's not fair!

FEMALE GREEK CHORUS: [*as Mother*] Now, see, she's getting upset—you're scaring her.

TEENAGE GREEK CHORUS: [*as Grandmother*] Good! Let her be good and scared! It hurts!
You bleed like a stuck pig! And you lay there and say, "Why, O Lord, have you for-   570
saken me?!"

LI'L BIT: It's not fair! Why does everything have to hurt for girls? Why is there always blood?

FEMALE GREEK CHORUS: [*as Mother*] It's not a lot of blood—and it feels wonderful after
the pain subsides . . .

TEENAGE GREEK CHORUS: [*as Grandmother*] You're encouraging her to just go out and   575
find out with the first drugstore joe who buys her a milk shake!

FEMALE GREEK CHORUS: [*as Mother*] Don't be scared. It won't hurt you—if the man you
go to bed with really loves you. It's important that he loves you.

TEENAGE GREEK CHORUS: [*as Grandmother*]—Why don't you just go out and rent a
motel room for her, Lucy?   580

FEMALE GREEK CHORUS: [*as Mother*] I believe in telling my daughter the truth! We have
a very close relationship! I want her to be able to ask me anything—I'm not scaring
her with stories about Eve's sin and snakes crawling on their bellies for eternity and
women's bearing children in mortal pain—

TEENAGE GREEK CHORUS: [*as Grandmother*]—If she stops and thinks before she takes   585
her knickers off, maybe someone in this family will finish high school!

[LI'L BIT *knows what is about to happen and starts to retreat from the scene at
this point.*]

FEMALE GREEK CHORUS: [*as Mother*] Mother! If you and Daddy had helped me—I
wouldn't have had to marry that—that no-good-son-of-a—

TEENAGE GREEK CHORUS: [*as Grandmother*]—He was good enough for you on a full
moon! I hold you responsible!   590

FEMALE GREEK CHORUS: [*as Mother*]—You could have helped me! You could have told
me something about the facts of life!

TEENAGE GREEK CHORUS: [*as Grandmother*]—I told you what my mother told me! A
girl with her skirt up can outrun a man with his pants down!

[*The* MALE GREEK CHORUS *enters the fray;* LI'L BIT *edges further downstage.*]

FEMALE GREEK CHORUS: [*as Mother*] And when I turned to you for a little help, all I got   595
    afterwards was—

MALE GREEK CHORUS: [*as Grandfather*] You Made Your Bed; Now Lie On It!

    [*The* GREEK CHORUS *freezes, mouths open, argumentatively.*]

LI'L BIT: [*to the audience*] Oh, please! I still can't bear to listen to it, after all these years—

    [*The* MALE GREEK CHORUS *"unfreezes," but out of his open mouth, as if to his*
    surprise, comes a base refrain from a Motown song.]

MALE GREEK CHORUS: "Do-Bee-Do-Wah!"

    [*The* FEMALE GREEK CHORUS *member is also surprised; but she, too,*
    unfreezes.]

FEMALE GREEK CHORUS: "Shoo-doo-be-doo-be-doo; shoo-doo-be-doo-be-doo."   600

    [*The* MALE *and* FEMALE GREEK CHORUS *members continue with their har-*
    mony, until the TEENAGE *member of the* CHORUS *starts in with Motown*
    lyrics such as "Dedicated to the One I Love," or "In the Still of the Night," or
    "Hold Me"—any Sam Cooke will do. The three modulate down into three-part
    harmony, softly, until they are submerged by the actual recording playing over the
    radio in the car in which Uncle PECK *sits in the driver's seat, waiting.* LI'L BIT
    sits in the passenger seat.]

LI'L BIT: Ahh. That's better.

    [*Uncle* PECK *reaches over and turns the volume down; to* LI'L BIT:]

PECK: How can you hear yourself think?

    [LI'L BIT *does not answer.*]

    [A VOICE *insinuates itself in the pause:*]

Before You Drive.

Always check under your car for obstructions—broken bottles, fallen tree branches,
and the bodies of small children. Each year hundreds of children are crushed   605
beneath the wheels of unwary drivers in their own driveways. Children depend on
***you* to watch them.**

    [*Pause. The* VOICE *continues:*]

You and the Reverse Gear.

    [*In the following section, it would be nice to have slides of erotic photographs*
    of women and cars: women posed over the hood; women draped along the side-
    boards; women with water hoses spraying the car; and the actress playing LI'L BIT
    with a Bel Air or any 1950s car one can find for the finale.]

LI'L BIT: 1967. In a parking lot of the Beltsville Agricultural Farms. The Initiation into a
    Boy's First Love.   610

PECK: [*with a soft look on his face*] Of course, my favorite car will always be the '56 Bel Air
    Sports Coupe. Chevy sold more '55s, but the '56!—a V-8 with Corvette option, 225
    horsepower, went from zero to sixty miles per hour in 8.9 seconds.

LI'L BIT: [*to the audience*] Long after a mother's tits, but before a woman's breasts:

PECK: Super-Turbo-Fire! What a Power Pack—mechanical lifters, twin four-barrel carbs, 615
    lightweight valves, dual exhausts—

LI'L BIT: [*to the audience*] After the milk but before the beer:

PECK: A specific intake manifold, higher-lift camshaft, and the tightest squeeze Chevy had
    ever made—

LI'L BIT: [*to the audience*] Long after he's squeezed down the birth canal but before he's pushed 620
    his way back in: The boy falls in love with the thing that bears his weight with speed.

PECK: I want you to know your automobile inside and out.—Are you there? Li'l Bit?

       [*Slides end here.*]

LI'L BIT: —What?

PECK: You're drifting. I need you to concentrate.

LI'L BIT: Sorry. 625

PECK: Okay. Get into the driver's seat. [LI'L BIT *does.*] Okay. Now. Show me what you're
    going to do before you start the car.

      [LI'L BIT *sits, with her hands in her lap. She starts to giggle.*]

LI'L BIT: I don't know, Uncle Peck.

PECK: Now, come on. What's the first thing you're going to adjust?

LI'L BIT: My bra strap?— 630

PECK: —Li'l Bit. What's the most important thing to have control of on the inside of the car?

LI'L BIT: That's easy. The radio. I tune the radio from Mama's old fart tunes to—

      [LI'L BIT *turns the radio up so we can hear a 1960s tune. With surprising firm-*
      ness, PECK *commands:*]

PECK: —Radio off. Right now. [LI'L BIT *turns the radio off.*] When you are driving your car,
    with your license, you can fiddle with the stations all you want. But when you are driv-
    ing with a learner's permit in my car, I want all your attention to be on the road. 635

LI'L BIT: Yes, sir.

PECK: Okay. Now the seat—forward and up. [LI'L BIT *pushes it forward.*] Do you want a
    cushion?

LI'L BIT: No—I'm good.

PECK: You should be able to reach all the switches and controls. Your feet should be able 640
    to push the accelerator, brake, and clutch all the way down. Can you do that?

LI'L BIT: Yes.

PECK: Okay, the side mirrors. You want to be able to see just a bit of the right side of the
    car in the right mirror—can you?

LI'L BIT: Turn it out more. 645

PECK: Okay. How's that?

LI'L BIT: A little more . . . Okay, that's good.

PECK: Now the left—again, you want to be able to see behind you—but the left lane—
    adjust it until you feel comfortable. [LI'L BIT *does so.*] Next. I want you to check the
    rearview mirror. Angle it so you have a clear vision of the back. [LI'L BIT *does so.*] 650
    Okay. Lock your door. Make sure all the doors are locked.

LI'L BIT: [*making a joke of it*] But then I'm locked in with you.

PECK: Don't fool.

LI'L BIT: All right. We're locked in.

PECK: We'll deal with the air vents and defroster later. I'm teaching you on a manual—once 655
    you learn manual, you can drive anything. I want you to be able to drive any car,

any machine. Manual gives you *control*. In ice, if your brakes fail, if you need more power—okay? It's a little harder at first, but then it becomes like breathing. Now. Put your hands on the wheel. I never want to see you driving with one hand. Always two hands. [LI'L BIT *hesitates*.] What? What is it now?

LI'L BIT: If I put my hands on the wheel—how do I defend myself?

PECK: [*softly*] Now listen. Listen up close. We're not going to fool around with this. This is a serious business. I will never touch you when you are driving a car. Understand?

LI'L BIT: Okay.

PECK: Hands on the nine o'clock and three o'clock position gives you maximum control and turn.

[PECK *goes silent for a while.* LI'L BIT *waits for more instruction.*]

Okay. Just relax and listen to me, Li'l Bit, okay? I want you to lift your hands for a second and look at them. [LI'L BIT *feels a bit silly, but does it.*]

Those are your two hands. When you are driving, your life is in your own two hands. Understand? [LI'L BIT *nods.*]

I don't have any sons. You're the nearest to a son I'll ever have—and I want to give you something. Something that really matters to me.

There's something about driving—when you're in control of the car, just you and the machine and the road—that nobody can take from you. A power. I feel more myself in my car than anywhere else. And that's what I want to give to you.

There's a lot of assholes out there. Crazy men, arrogant idiots, drunks, angry kids, geezers who are blind—and you have to be ready for them. I want to teach you to drive like a man.

LI'L BIT: What does that mean?

PECK: Men are taught to drive with confidence—with aggression. The road belongs to them. They drive defensively—always looking out for the other guy. Women tend to be polite—to hesitate. And that can be fatal.

You're going to learn to think what the other guy is going to do before he does it. If there's an accident, and ten cars pile up, and people get killed, you're the one who's gonna steer through it, put your foot on the gas if you have to, and be the only one to walk away. I don't know how long you or I are going to live, but we're for damned sure not going to die in a car.

So if you're going to drive with me, I want you to take this very seriously.

LI'L BIT: I will, Uncle Peck. I want you to teach me to drive.

PECK: Good. You're going to pass your test on the first try. Perfect score. Before the next four weeks are over, you're going to know this baby inside and out. Treat her with respect.

LI'L BIT: Why is it a "she"?

PECK: Good question. It doesn't have to be a "she"—but when you close your eyes and think of someone who responds to your touch—someone who performs just for you and gives you what you ask for—I guess I always see a "she." You can call her what you like.

LI'L BIT: [*to the audience*] I closed my eyes—and decided not to change the gender.

[*A* VOICE:]

Defensive driving involves defending yourself from hazardous and sudden changes in your automotive environment. By thinking ahead, the defensive driver can adjust to weather, road conditions and road kill. Good defensive driving involves mental and physical preparation. Are you prepared?

[*Another* VOICE *chimes in:*]

You and the Reverse Gear.

LI'L BIT: 1966. The Anthropology of the Female Body in Ninth Grade—Or A Walk Down Mammary Lane.

> [*Throughout the following, there is occasional rhythmic beeping, like a transmitter signaling.* LI'L BIT *is aware of it, but can't figure out where it is coming from. No one else seems to hear it.*]

MALE GREEK CHORUS: In the hallway of Francis Scott Key Middle School.   705

> [*A bell rings; the* GREEK CHORUS *is changing classes and meets in the hall, conspiratorially.*]

TEENAGE GREEK CHORUS: She's coming!

> [LI'L BIT *enters the scene; the* MALE GREEK CHORUS *member has a sudden, violent sneezing and lethal allergy attack.*]

FEMALE GREEK CHORUS: Jerome? Jerome? Are you all right?
MALE GREEK CHORUS: I—don't—know. I can't breathe—get Li'l Bit—
TEENAGE GREEK CHORUS: —He needs oxygen!—
FEMALE GREEK CHORUS: —Can you help us here?   710
LI'L BIT: What's wrong? Do you want me to get the school nurse—

> [*The* MALE GREEK CHORUS *member wheezes, grabs his throat, and sniffs at* LI'L BIT*'s chest, which is beeping away.*]

MALE GREEK CHORUS: No—it's okay—I only get this way when I'm around an allergy trigger—
LI'L BIT: Golly. What are you allergic to?
MALE GREEK CHORUS: [*with a sudden grab of her breast*] Foam rubber.   715

> [*The* GREEK CHORUS *members break up with hilarity; Jerome leaps away from* LI'L BIT*'s kicking rage with agility; as he retreats:*]

LI'L BIT: Jerome! Creep! Cretin! Cro-Magnon!
TEENAGE GREEK CHORUS: Rage is not attractive in a girl.
FEMALE GREEK CHORUS: Really. Get a Sense of Humor.

> [A VOICE *echoes:*]

Good defensive driving involves mental and physical preparation.
Were You Prepared?   720

FEMALE GREEK CHORUS: Gym Class: In the showers.

> [*The sudden sound of water; the* FEMALE GREEK CHORUS *members and* LI'L BIT*, while fully clothed, drape towels across their fronts, miming nudity. They stand, hesitate, at an imaginary shower's edge.*]

LI'L BIT: Water looks hot.
FEMALE GREEK CHORUS: Yesss . . . .

> [FEMALE GREEK CHORUS *members are not going to make the first move. One dips a tentative toe under the water, clutching the towel around her.*]

LI'L BIT: Well, I guess we'd better shower and get out of here.
FEMALE GREEK CHORUS: Yep. You go ahead. I'm still cooling off.   725
LI'L BIT: Okay.—Sally? Are you gonna shower?
TEENAGE GREEK CHORUS: After you—

> [LI'L BIT *takes a deep breath for courage, drops the towel and plunges in: The*
> *two* FEMALE GREEK CHORUS *members look at* LI'L BIT *in the all together,*
> *laugh, gasp, and high-five each other.*]

TEENAGE GREEK CHORUS: Oh my god! Can you believe—
FEMALE GREEK CHORUS: Told you! It's not foam rubber! I win! Jerome owes me fifty cents!

> [A VOICE *editorializes:*]

Were You Prepared?   730

> [LI'L BIT *tries to cover up; she is exposed, as suddenly 1960s Motown fills the*
> *room and we segue into:*]

FEMALE GREEK CHORUS: The Sock Hop.

> [LI'L BIT *stands up against the wall with her female classmates.* TEENAGE
> GREEK CHORUS *is mesmerized by the music and just sways alone, lip-synching*
> *the lyrics.*]

LI'L BIT: I don't know. Maybe it's just me—but—do you ever feel like you're just a walking
   Mary Jane joke?
FEMALE GREEK CHORUS: I don't know what you mean.
LI'L BIT: You haven't heard the Mary Jane jokes? [FEMALE GREEK CHORUS *member*   735
   shakes her head no.] Okay. "Little Mary Jane is walking through the woods, when all
   of a sudden this man who was hiding behind a tree *jumps* out, *rips* open Mary Jane's
   blouse, and *plunges* his hands on her breasts. And Little Mary Jane just laughed and
   laughed because she knew her money was in her shoes."

> [LI'L BIT *laughs; the* FEMALE GREEK CHORUS *does not.*]

FEMALE GREEK CHORUS: You're weird.   740

> [*In another space, in a strange light, Uncle* PECK *stands and stares at* LI'L BIT*'s*
> *body. He is setting up a tripod, but he just stands, appreciative, watching her.*]

LI'L BIT: Well, don't you ever feel . . . self-conscious? Like you're being looked at all the time?
FEMALE GREEK CHORUS: That's not a problem for me.—Oh—look—Greg's coming
   over to ask you to dance.

> [TEENAGE GREEK CHORUS *becomes attentive, flustered.* MALE GREEK CHORUS
> *member, as Greg, bends slightly as a very short young man, whose head is at* LI'L
> BIT*'s chest level. Ardent, sincere, and socially inept, Greg will become a successful*
> *gynecologist.*]

TEENAGE GREEK CHORUS: [*softly*] Hi, Greg.

> [*Greg does not hear. He is intent on only one thing.*]

MALE GREEK CHORUS: [*as Greg, to* LI'L BIT] Good Evening. Would you care to dance?   745
LI'L BIT: [*gently*] Thank you very much, Greg—but I'm going to sit this one out.
MALE GREEK CHORUS: [*as Greg*] Oh. Okay. I'll try my luck later.

> [*He disappears.*]

TEENAGE GREEK CHORUS: Oohhh.

[LI'L BIT *relaxes. Then she tenses, aware of* PECK'*s gaze.*]

FEMALE GREEK CHORUS: Take pity on him. Someone should.
LI'L BIT: But he's so short.   750
TEENAGE GREEK CHORUS: He can't help it.
LI'L BIT: But his head comes up to [LI'L BIT *gestures*] here. And I think he asks me on the fast dances so he can watch me—you know—jiggle.
FEMALE GREEK CHORUS: I wish I had your problems.

[*The tune changes; Greg is across the room in a flash.*]

MALE GREEK CHORUS: [*as Greg*] Evening again. May I ask you for the honor of a spin on   755
the floor?
LI'L BIT: I'm . . . very complimented, Greg. But I . . . I just don't do fast dances.
MALE GREEK CHORUS: [*as Greg*] Oh. No problem. That's okay.

[*He disappears.* TEENAGE GREEK CHORUS *watches him go.*]

TEENAGE GREEK CHORUS: That is just so—*sad.*

[LI'L BIT *becomes aware of* PECK *waiting.*]

FEMALE GREEK CHORUS: You know, you should take it as a compliment that the guys   760
want to watch you jiggle. They're guys. That's what they're supposed to do.
LI'L BIT: I guess you're right. But sometimes I feel like these alien life forces, these two mounds of flesh have grafted themselves onto my chest, and they're using me until they can "propagate" and take over the world and they'll just keep growing, with a mind of their own until I collapse under their weight and they suck all the nourish-   765
ment out of my body and I finally just waste away while they get bigger and bigger and—[LI'L BIT'*s classmates are just staring at her in disbelief.*]
FEMALE GREEK CHORUS: —You are the strangest girl I have ever met.

[LI'L BIT'*s trying to joke but feels on the verge of tears.*]

LI'L BIT: Or maybe someone's implanted radio transmitters in my chest at a frequency I can't hear, that girls can't detect, but they're sending out these signals to men who get   770
mesmerized, like sirens, calling them to dash themselves on these "rocks"—

[*Just then, the music segues into a slow dance, perhaps a Beach Boys tune like Little Surfer, but over the music there's a rhythmic, hypnotic beeping transmitted, which both Greg and* PECK *hear.* LI'L BIT *hears it too, and in horror she stares at her chest. She, too, is almost hypnotized. In a trance, Greg responds to the signals and is called to her side—actually, her front. Like a zombie, he stands in front of her, his eyes planted on her two orbs.*]

MALE GREEK CHORUS: [*as Greg*] This one's a slow dance. I hope your dance card isn't . . . filled?

[LI'L BIT *is aware of* PECK; *but the signals are calling her to him. The signals are no longer transmitters, but an electromagnetic force, pulling* LI'L BIT *to his side, where he again waits for her to join him. She must get away from the dance floor.*]

LI'L BIT: Greg—you really are a nice boy. But I don't like to dance.
MALE GREEK CHORUS: [*as Greg*] That's okay. We don't have to move or anything. I could   775
just hold you and we could just *sway* a little—

LI'L BIT: —No! I'm sorry—but I think I have to leave; I hear someone calling me—

[LI'L BIT *starts across the dance floor, leaving Greg behind. The beeping stops. The lights change, although the music does not. As* LI'L BIT *talks to the audience, she continues to change and prepare for the coming session. She should be wearing a tight tank top or a sheer blouse and very tight pants. To the audience:*]

In every man's home some small room, some zone in his house, is set aside. It might be the attic, or the study, or a den. And there's an invisible sign as if from the old treehouse: Girls Keep Out. 780

Here, away from female eyes, lace doilies and crochet, he keeps his manly toys: the Vargas pinups, the tackle. A scent of tobacco and WD-40. [*She inhales deeply.*] A dash of his Bay Rum. Ahhh . . . [LI'L BIT *savors it for just a moment more.*]

Here he keeps his secrets: a violin or saxophone, drum set or darkroom, and the stacks of Playboy. [*in a whisper*] Here, in my aunt's home, it was the basement. 785 Uncle Peck's turf.

[A VOICE *commands:*]

You and the Reverse Gear.

LI'L BIT: 1965. The Photo Shoot.

[LI'L BIT *steps into the scene as a nervous but curious thirteen year old. Music, from the previous scene, continues to play, changing into something like Roy Orbison later—something seductive with a beat.* PECK *fiddles, all business, with his camera. As in the driving lesson, he is all competency and concentration.* LI'L BIT *stands awkwardly. He looks through the Leica camera on the tripod, adjusts the back lighting, etc.*]

PECK: Are you cold? The lights should heat up some in a few minutes—
LI'L BIT: —Aunt Mary is? 790
PECK: At the National Theatre matinee. With your mother. We have time.
LI'L BIT: But—what if—
PECK: —And so what if they return? I told them you and I were going to be working with my camera. They won't come down. [LI'L BIT *is quiet, apprehensive.*]—Look, are you sure you want to do this? 795
LI'L BIT: I said I'd do it. But—
PECK: —I know. You've drawn the line.
LI'L BIT: [*reassured*] That's right. No frontal nudity.
PECK: Good heavens, girl, where did you pick that up?
LI'L BIT: [*defensive*] I read. 800

[PECK *tries not to laugh.*]

PECK: And I read *Playboy* for the interviews. Okay. Let's try some different music.

[PECK *goes to an expensive reel-to-reel and forwards. Something like "Sweet Dreams" begins to play.*]

LI'L BIT: I didn't know you listened to this.
PECK: I'm not dead, you know. I try to keep up. Do you like this song? [LI'L BIT *nods with pleasure.*] Good. Now listen—at professional photo shoots, they always play music for the models. Okay? I want you to just enjoy the music. Listen to it with your body, 805 and just—respond.
LI'L BIT: Respond to the music with my . . . body?

PECK: Right. Almost like dancing. Here—let's get you on the stool, first. [PECK *comes over and helps her up.*]

LI'L BIT: But nothing showing—   810

> [PECK *firmly, with his large capable hands, brushes back her hair, angles her face.* LI'L BIT *turns to him like a plant to the sun.*]

PECK: Nothing showing. Just a peek.

> [*He holds her by the shoulder, looking at her critically. Then he unbuttons her blouse to the midpoint, and runs his hands over the flesh of her exposed sternum, arranging the fabric, just touching her. Deliberately, calmly. Asexually,* LI'L BIT *quiets, sits perfectly still, and closes her eyes.*]

Okay?

LI'L BIT: Yes.

> [PECK *goes back to his camera.*]

PECK: I'm going to keep talking to you. Listen without responding to what I'm saying; you want to *listen* to the music. Sway, move just your torso or your head—I've got to   815 check the light meter.

LI'L BIT: But—you'll be watching.

PECK: No—I'm not here—just my voice. Pretend you're in your room all alone on a Friday night with your mirror—and the music feels good—just move for me, Li'l Bit—

> [LI'L BIT *closes her eyes. At first self-conscious; then she gets more into the music and begins to sway. We hear the camera start to whir. Throughout the shoot, there can be a slide montage of actual shots of the actor playing* LI'L BIT— *interspersed with other models à la Playboy, Calvin Klein, and Victoriana/Lewis Carroll's Alice Liddell.*]

That's it. That looks great. Okay. Just keep doing that. Lift your head up a bit more,   820 good, good, just keep moving, that a girl—you're a very beautiful young woman. Do you know that? [LI'L BIT *looks up, blushes.* PECK *shoots the camera. The audience should see this shot on the screen.*]

LI'L BIT: No. I don't know that.

PECK: Listen to the music. [LI'L BIT *closes her eyes again.*] Well you are. For a thirteen year   825 old, you have a body a twenty-year-old woman would die for.

LI'L BIT: The boys in school don't think so.

PECK: The boys in school are little Neanderthals in short pants. You're ten years ahead of them in maturity; it's gonna take a while for them to catch up.

> [PECK *clicks another shot; we see a faint smile on* LI'L BIT *on the screen.*]

Girls turn into women long before boys turn into men.   830

LI'L BIT: Why is that?

PECK: I don't know, Li'l Bit. But it's a blessing for men.

> [LI'L BIT *turns silent.*] Keep moving. Try arching your back on the stool, hands behind you, and throw your head back. [*The slide shows a* Playboy *model in this pose.*] Oohh, great. That one was great. Turn your head away, same position. [*whir*]   835 Beautiful.

> [LI'L BIT *looks at him a bit defiantly.*]

LI'L BIT: I think Aunt Mary is beautiful.

[PECK *stands still.*]

PECK: My wife is a very beautiful woman. Her beauty doesn't cancel yours out. [*More casually; he returns to the camera.*] All the women in your family are beautiful. In fact, I think all women are. You're not listening to the music. [PECK *shoots some more film* 840 *in silence.*] All right, turn your head to the left. Good. Now take the back of your right hand and put it on your right cheek—your elbow angled up—now slowly, slowly, stroke your cheek, draw back your hair with the back of your hand. [*another classic* Playboy *or Vargas*] Good. One hand above and behind your head; stretch your body; smile. [*another pose*] 845
Li'l Bit. I want you to think of something that makes you laugh—
LI'L BIT: I can't think of anything.
PECK: Okay. Think of Big Papa chasing Grandma around the living room. [LI'L BIT *lifts her head and laughs. Click. We should see this shot.*] Good. Both hands behind your head. Great! Hold that! [*from behind his camera*] You're doing great work. If we keep 850 this up, in five years we'll have a really professional portfolio.

[LI'L BIT *stops.*]

LI'L BIT: What do you mean in five years?
PECK: You can't submit work to *Playboy* until you're eighteen—

[PECK *continues to shoot; he knows he's made a mistake.*]

LI'L BIT: —Wait a minute. You're joking, aren't you, Uncle Peck?
PECK: Heck, no. You can't get into *Playboy* unless you're the very best. And you are the 855 very best.
LI'L BIT: I would never do that!

[PECK *stops shooting. He turns off the music.*]

PECK: Why? There's nothing wrong with *Playboy*—it's a very classy maga—
LI'L BIT: [*more upset*] But I thought you said I should go to college!
PECK: Wait—Li'l Bit—it's nothing like that. Very respectable women model for *Playboy*— 860 actresses with major careers—women in college—there's an Ivy League issue every—
LI'L BIT: —I'm never doing anything like that! You'd show other people these—other *men*—these—what I'm doing.—Why would you do that?! Any *boy* around here could just pick up, just go into The Stop & Go and *buy*—Why would you ever want 865 to—to share—
PECK: —Whoa, whoa. Just stop a second and listen to me. Li'l Bit. Listen. There's nothing wrong in what we're doing. I'm very proud of you. I think you have a wonderful body and an even more wonderful mind. And of course I want other people to *appreciate* it. It's not anything shameful. 870
LI'L BIT: [*hurt*] But this is something—that I'm only doing for you. This is something—that you said was just between us.
PECK: It is. And if that's how you feel, five years from now, it will remain that way. Okay? I know you're not going to do anything you don't feel like doing.

[*He walks back to the camera.*]

Do you want to stop now? I've got just a few more shots on this roll— 875
LI'L BIT: I don't want anyone seeing this.
PECK: I swear to you. No one will. I'll treasure this—that you're doing this only for me.

[LI'L BIT, *still shaken, sits on the stool. She closes her eyes.*]

Li'l Bit? Open your eyes and look at me. [LI'L BIT *shakes her head no.*] Come on. Just open your eyes, honey.

LI'L BIT: If I look at you—if I look at the camera: You're gonna know what I'm thinking. 880
You'll see right through me—

PECK: —No, I won't. I want you to look at me. All right, then. I just want you to listen. Li'l Bit. [*She waits.*] I love you. [LI'L BIT *opens her eyes; she is startled.* PECK *captures the shot. On the screen we see right through her.* PECK *says softly.*] Do you know that? [LI'L BIT *nods her head yes.*] I have loved you every day since the day you were born. 885

LI'L BIT: Yes.

> [LI'L BIT *and* PECK *just look at each other. Beat. Beneath the shot of herself on screen,* LI'L BIT, *still looking at her uncle, begins to unbutton her blouse.*]

> [*A neutral* VOICE *cuts off the above scene with:*]

Implied Consent.

As an individual operating a motor vehicle in the state of Maryland, you must abide by "Implied Consent." If you do not consent to take the blood alcohol content test, there may be severe penalties: a suspension of license, a fine, community service, and 890 a possible jail sentence.

> [*The* VOICE *shifts tone:*]

Idling in the Neutral Gear.

MALE GREEK CHORUS: [*announcing*] Aunt Mary on behalf of her husband.

> [FEMALE GREEK CHORUS *checks her appearance, and with dignity comes to the front of the stage and sits down to talk to the audience.*]

FEMALE GREEK CHORUS: [*as Aunt Mary*] My husband was such a good man—is. Is such a good man. Every night, he does the dishes. The second he comes home, he's taking 895
out the garbage, or doing yard work, lifting heavy things I can't. Everyone in the neighborhood borrows Peck—it's true—women with husbands of their own, men who just don't have Peck's abilities—there's always a knock on our door for a jump start on cold mornings, when anyone needs a ride, or help shoveling the sidewalk—I look out, and there Peck is, without a coat, pitching in. I know I'm lucky. The man 900
works from dawn to dusk. And the overtime he does every year—my poor sister. She sits every Christmas when I come to dinner with a new stole, or diamonds, or with tickets to Bermuda.

I know he has troubles. And we don't talk about them. I wonder, sometimes, what happened to him during the war. The men who fought World War II didn't 905
have "rap sessions" to talk about their feelings. Men in his generation were expected to be quiet about it and get on with their lives. And sometimes I can feel him just fighting the trouble—whatever has burrowed deeper than the scar tissue—and we don't talk about it. I know he's having a bad spell because he comes looking for me in the house, and just hangs around me until it passes. And I keep my banter light—I 910
discuss a new recipe, or sales, or gossip—because I think domesticity can be a balm for men when they're lost. We sit in the house and listen to the peace of the clocks ticking in his well-ordered living room, until it passes.

[*sharply*] I'm not a fool. I know what's going on. I wish you could feel how hard Peck fights against it—he's swimming against the tide, and what he needs is 915 to see me on the shore, believing in him, knowing he won't go under, he won't give up—

And I want to say this about my niece. She's a sly one, that one is. She knows exactly what she's doing; she's twisted Peck around her little finger and thinks it's all a big secret. Yet another one who's borrowing my husband until it doesn't suit her anymore. 920

Well. I'm counting the days until she goes away to school. And she manipulates someone else. And then he'll come back again, and sit in the kitchen while I bake, or beside me on the sofa when I sew in the evenings. I'm a very patient woman. But I'd like my husband back. 925

I am counting the days.

[A VOICE *repeats:*]

You and the Reverse Gear.

MALE GREEK CHORUS: Li'l Bit's Thirteenth Christmas. Uncle Peck Does the Dishes. Christmas 1964.

[PECK *stands in a dress shirt and tie, nice pants, with an apron. He is washing dishes. He's in a mood we haven't seen. Quiet, brooding.* LI'L BIT *watches him a moment before seeking him out.*]

LI'L BIT: Uncle Peck? [*He does not answer. He continues to work on the pots.*] I didn't know 930 where you'd gone to. [*He nods. She takes this as a sign to come in.*] Don't you want to sit with us for a while?

PECK: No. I'd rather do the dishes.

[*Pause.* LI'L BIT *watches him.*]

LI'L BIT: You're the only man I know who does the dishes. [PECK *says nothing.*] I think it's really nice. 935

PECK: My wife has been on her feet all day. So's your grandmother and your mother.

LI'L BIT: I know. [*beat*] Do you want some help?

PECK: No. [*He softens a bit towards her.*] You can help just by talking to me.

LI'L BIT: Big Papa never does the dishes. I think it's nice.

PECK: I think men should be nice to women. Women are always working for us. There's 940 nothing particularly manly in wolfing down food and then sitting around in a stupor while the women clean up.

LI'L BIT: That looks like a really neat camera that Aunt Mary got you.

PECK: It is. It's a very nice one.

[*Pause, as* PECK *works on the dishes and some demon that* LI'L BIT *intuits.*]

LI'L BIT: Did Big Papa hurt your feelings? 945

PECK: [*tired*] What? Oh, no—it doesn't hurt me. Family is family. I'd rather have him picking on me than—I don't pay him any mind, Li'l Bit.

LI'L BIT: Are you angry with us?

PECK: No, Li'l Bit. I'm not angry.

[*Another pause.*]

LI'L BIT: We missed you at Thanksgiving. . . . I did. I missed you. 950

PECK: Well, there were . . . "things" going on. I didn't want to spoil anyone's Thanksgiving.

LI'L BIT: Uncle Peck? [*very carefully*] Please don't drink anymore tonight.

PECK: I'm not . . . overdoing it.
LI'L BIT: I know. [*beat*] Why do you drink so much?

[PECK *stops and thinks, carefully.*]

PECK: Well, Li'l Bit—let me explain it this way. There are some people who have a . . . a   955
"fire" in the belly. I think they go to work on Wall Street or they run for office. And
then there are people who have a "fire" in their heads—and they become writers or
scientists or historians. [*He smiles a little at her.*] You. You've got a "fire" in the head.
And then there are people like me.
LI'L BIT: Where do you have . . . a fire?   960
PECK: I have a fire in my heart. And sometimes the drinking helps.
LI'L BIT: There's got to be other things that can help.
PECK: I suppose there are.
LI'L BIT: Does it help—to talk to me?
PECK: Yes. It does. [*quiet*] I don't get to see you very much.   965
LI'L BIT: I know. [LI'L BIT *thinks.*] You could talk to me more.
PECK: Oh?
LI'L BIT: I could make a deal with you, Uncle Peck.
PECK: I'm listening.
LI'L BIT: We could meet and talk—once a week. You could just store up whatever's bother-   970
ing you during the week—and then we could talk.
PECK: Would you like that?
LI'L BIT: As long as you don't drink. I'd meet you somewhere for lunch or for a walk—on
the weekends—as long as you stop drinking. And we could talk about whatever you
want.   975
PECK: You would do that for me?
LI'L BIT: I don't think I'd want Mom to know. Or Aunt Mary. I wouldn't want them to
think—
PECK: —No. It would just be us talking.
LI'L BIT: I'll tell Mom I'm going to a girlfriend's. To study. Mom doesn't get home until   980
six, so you can call me after school and tell me where to meet you.
PECK: You get home at four?
LI'L BIT: We can meet once a week. But only in public. You've got to let me—draw the
line. And once it's drawn, you mustn't cross it.
PECK: Understood.   985
LI'L BIT: Would that help?

[PECK *is very moved.*]

PECK: Yes. Very much.
LI'L BIT: I'm going to join the others in the living room now. [LI'L BIT *turns to go.*]
PECK: Merry Christmas, Li'l Bit.

[LI'L BIT *bestows a very warm smile on him.*]

LI'L BIT: Merry Christmas, Uncle Peck.   990

[A VOICE *dictates:*]

Shifting Forward from Second to Third Gear.

[*The* MALE *and* FEMALE GREEK CHORUS *members come forward.*]

MALE GREEK CHORUS: 1969. Days and Gifts: A Countdown:

FEMALE GREEK CHORUS: A note. "September 3, 1969. Li'l Bit: You've only been away two days and it feels like months. Hope your dorm room is cozy. I'm sending you this tape cassette—it's a new model—so you'll have some music in your room. Also   995 that music you're reading about for class—*Carmina Burana*. Hope you enjoy. Only ninety days to go!—Peck."

MALE GREEK CHORUS: September 22. A bouquet of roses. A note: "Miss you like crazy. Sixty-nine days . . ."

TEENAGE GREEK CHORUS: September 25. A box of chocolates. A card: "Don't worry   1000 about the weight gain. You still look great. Got a post office box—write to me there. Sixty-six days.—Love, your candy man."

MALE GREEK CHORUS: October 16. A note: "Am trying to get through the Jane Austen you're reading—*Emma*—here's a book in return: *Liaisons Dangereuses*. Hope you're saving time for me." Scrawled in the margin the number: "47."   1005

FEMALE GREEK CHORUS: November 16. "Sixteen days to go!—Hope you like the perfume.— Having a hard time reaching you on the dorm phone. You must be in the library a lot. Won't you think about me getting you your own phone so we can talk?"

TEENAGE GREEK CHORUS: November 18. "Li'l Bit—got a package returned to the P.O. Box. Have you changed dorms? Call me at work or write to the P.O. Am still on the   1010 wagon. Waiting to see you. Only two weeks more!"

MALE GREEK CHORUS: November 23. A letter. "Li'l Bit. So disappointed you couldn't come home for the turkey. Sending you some money for a nice dinner out—nine days and counting!"

GREEK CHORUS: [*in unison*] November 25th. A letter: 1015

LI'L BIT: "Dear Uncle Peck: I am sending this to you at work. Don't come up next weekend for my birthday. I will not be here—"

[A VOICE *directs:*]

Shifting Forward from Third to Fourth Gear.

MALE GREEK CHORUS: December 10, 1969. A hotel room. Philadelphia. There is no moon tonight.   1020

[PECK *sits on the side of the bed while* LI'L BIT *paces. He can't believe she's in his room, but there's a desperate edge to his happiness.* LI'L BIT *is furious, edgy. There is a bottle of champagne in an ice bucket in a very nice hotel room.*]

PECK: Why don't you sit?

LI'L BIT: I don't want to.—What's the champagne for?

PECK: I thought we might toast your birthday—

LI'L BIT: —I am so pissed off at you, Uncle Peck.

PECK: Why?   1025

LI'L BIT: I mean, are you crazy?

PECK: What did I do?

LI'L BIT: You scared the holy crap out of me—sending me that stuff in the mail—

PECK: —They were gifts! I just wanted to give you some little perks your first semester—

LI'L BIT: —Well, what the hell were those numbers all about! Forty-four days to go—only   1030 two more weeks.—And then just numbers—69—68—67—like some serial killer!

PECK: Li'l Bit! Whoa! This is me you're talking to—I was just trying to pick up your spirits, trying to celebrate your birthday.

LI'L BIT: My *eighteenth* birthday. I'm not a child, Uncle Peck. You were counting down to my eighteenth birthday.   1035

PECK: So?

LI'L BIT: So? So statutory rape is not in effect when a young woman turns eighteen. And you and I both know it.

[PECK *is walking on ice.*]

PECK: I think you misunderstand.

LI'L BIT: I think I understand all too well. I know what you want to do five steps ahead of you doing it. Defensive Driving 101.

PECK: Then why did you suggest we meet here instead of the restaurant?

LI'L BIT: I don't want to have this conversation in public.

PECK: Fine. Fine. We have a lot to talk about.

LI'L BIT: Yeah. We do.

[LI'L BIT *doesn't want to do what she has to do.*] Could I . . . have some of that champagne?

PECK: Of course, madam! [PECK *makes a big show of it.*] Let me do the honors. I wasn't sure which you might prefer—Taittingers or Veuve Clicquot—so I thought we'd start out with an old standard—Perrier Jouet. [*The bottle is popped.*]

Quick—Li'l Bit—your glass! [UNCLE PECK *fills* LI'L BIT's *glass. He puts the bottle back in the ice and goes for a can of ginger ale.*] Let me get some of this ginger ale—my bubbly—and toast you.

[*He turns and sees that* LI'L BIT *has not waited for him.*]

LI'L BIT: Oh—sorry, Uncle Peck. Let me have another. [PECK *fills her glass and reaches for his ginger ale; she stops him.*] Uncle Peck—maybe you should join me in the champagne.

PECK: You want me to—drink?

LI'L BIT: It's not polite to let a lady drink alone.

PECK: Well, missy, if you insist . . . [PECK *hesitates.*]—Just one. It's been a while. [PECK *fills another flute for himself.*] There. I'd like to propose a toast to you and your birthday! [PECK *sips it tentatively.*] I'm not used to this anymore.

LI'L BIT: You don't have anywhere to go tonight, do you?

[PECK *hopes this is a good sign.*]

PECK: I'm all yours.—God, it's good to see you! I've gotten so used to . . . to . . . talking to you in my head. I'm used to seeing you every week—there's so much—I don't quite know where to begin. How's school, Li'l Bit?

LI'L BIT: I—it's hard. Uncle Peck. Harder than I thought it would be. I'm in the middle of exams and papers and—I don't know.

PECK: You'll pull through. You always do.

LI'L BIT: Maybe. I . . . might be flunking out.

PECK: You always think the worse, Li'l Bit, but when the going gets tough—[LI'L BIT *shrugs and pours herself another glass.*]—Hey, honey, go easy on that stuff, okay?

LI'L BIT: Is it very expensive?

PECK: Only the best for you. But the cost doesn't matter—champagne should be "sipped." [LI'L BIT *is quiet.*] Look—if you're in trouble in school—you can always come back home for a while.

LI'L BIT: No—[LI'L BIT *tries not to be so harsh.*]—Thanks, Uncle Peck, but I'll figure some way out of this.

PECK: You're supposed to get in scrapes, your first year away from home.

LI'L BIT: Right. How's Aunt Mary?

PECK: She's fine. [*pause*] Well—how about the new car?

LI'L BIT: It's real nice. What is it, again? 1080

PECK: It's a Cadillac El Dorado.

LI'L BIT: Oh. Well, I'm real happy for you, Uncle Peck.

PECK: I got it for you.

LI'L BIT: What?

PECK: I always wanted to get a Cadillac—but I thought, Peck, wait until Li'l Bit's old 1085
enough—and thought maybe you'd like to drive it, too.

LI'L BIT: [*confused*] Why would I want to drive your car?

PECK: Just because it's the best—I want you to have the best.

[*They are running out of "gas"; small talk.*]

LI'L BIT: Listen, Uncle Peck, I don't know   PECK: I have been thinking of how to say

how to begin this, but—   this in my head, over and over— 1090

PECK: Sorry.

LI'L BIT: You first.

PECK: Well, your going away—has just made me realize how much I miss you. Talking to
you and being alone with you. I've really come to depend on you, Li'l Bit. And it's
been so hard to get in touch with you lately—the distance and—and you're never in 1095
when I call—I guess you've been living in the library—

LI'L BIT: —No—the problem is, I haven't been in the library—

PECK: —Well, it doesn't matter—I hope you've been missing me as much.

LI'L BIT: Uncle Peck—I've been thinking a lot about this—and I came here tonight to tell
you that—I'm not doing very well. I'm getting very confused—I can't concentrate 1100
on my work—and now that I'm away—I've been going over and over it in my
mind—and I don't want us to "see" each other anymore. Other than with the rest
of the family.

PECK: [*quiet*] Are you seeing other men?

LI'L BIT: [*getting agitated*] I—no, that's not the reason—I—well, yes I am seeing other— 1105
listen, it's not really anybody's business!

PECK: Are you in love with anyone else?

LI'L BIT: That's not what this is about.

PECK: Li'l Bit—you're scared. Your mother and your grandparents have filled your head
with all kinds of nonsense about men—I hear them working on you all the time— 1110
and you're scared. It won't hurt you—if the man you go to bed with really loves you.
[LI'L BIT *is scared. She starts to tremble.*] And I have loved you since the day I held
you in my hand. And I think everyone's just gotten you frightened to death about
something that is just like breathing—

LI'L BIT: Oh, my god—[*She takes a breath.*] I can't see you anymore, Uncle Peck. 1115

[PECK *downs the rest of his champagne.*]

PECK: Li'l Bit. Listen. Open your eyes and look at me. Come on. Just open your eyes,
honey. [LI'L BIT, *eyes squeezed shut, refuses.*] All right then. I just want you to listen.
Li'l Bit—I'm going to ask you just this once. Of your own free will. Just lie down on
the bed with me—our clothes on—just lie down with me, a man and a woman . . .
and let's . . . hold one another. Nothing else. Before you say anything else. I want 1120
the chance to . . . hold you. Because sometimes the body knows things that the
mind isn't listening to . . . and after I've held you, then I want you to tell me what
you feel.

LI'L BIT: You'll just . . . hold me?

PECK: Yes. And then you can tell me what you're feeling. 1130

[LI'L BIT—*half wanting to run, half wanting to get it over with, half wanting to be held by him:*]

LI'L BIT: Yes. All right. Just hold. Nothing else.

[PECK *lies down on the bed and holds his arms out to her.* LI'L BIT *lies beside him, putting her head on his chest. He looks as if he's trying to soak her into his pores by osmosis. He strokes her hair, and she lies very still. The* MALE GREEK CHORUS *member and the* FEMALE GREEK CHORUS *member as Aunt Mary come into the room.*]

MALE GREEK CHORUS: Recipe for a Southern boy:
FEMALE GREEK CHORUS: [*as Aunt Mary*] A drawl of molasses in the way he speaks.
MALE GREEK CHORUS: A gumbo of red and brown mixed in the cream of his skin.

[*While* PECK *lies, his eyes closed,* LI'L BIT *rises in the bed and responds to her aunt.*]

LI'L BIT: Warm brown eyes— 1135
FEMALE GREEK CHORUS: [*as Aunt Mary*] Bedroom eyes—
MALE GREEK CHORUS: A dash of Southern Baptist Fire and Brimstone—
LI'L BIT: A curl of Elvis on his forehead—
FEMALE GREEK CHORUS: [*as Aunt Mary*] A splash of Bay Rum—
MALE GREEK CHORUS: A closely shaven beard that he razors just for you— 1140
FEMALE GREEK CHORUS: [*as Aunt Mary*] Large hands—rough hands—
LI'L BIT: Warm hands—
MALE GREEK CHORUS: The steel of the military in his walk—
LI'L BIT: The slouch of the fishing skiff in his walk—
MALE GREEK CHORUS: Neatly pressed khakis— 1145
FEMALE GREEK CHORUS: [*as Aunt Mary*] And under the wide leather of the belt—
LI'L BIT: Sweat of cypress and sand—
MALE GREEK CHORUS: Neatly pressed khakis—
LI'L BIT: His heart beating Dixie—
FEMALE GREEK CHORUS: [*as Aunt Mary*] The whisper of the zipper—you could reach 1150
out with your hand and—
LI'L BIT: His mouth—
FEMALE GREEK CHORUS: [*as Aunt Mary*] You could just reach out and—
LI'L BIT: Hold him in your hand—
FEMALE GREEK CHORUS: [*as Aunt Mary*] And his mouth— 1155

[LI'L BIT *rises above her uncle and looks at his mouth; she starts to lower herself to kiss him—and wrenches herself free. She gets up from the bed.*]

LI'L BIT: —I've got to get back.
PECK: Wait—Li'l Bit. Did you . . . feel nothing?
LI'L BIT: [*lying*] No. Nothing.
PECK: Do you—do you think of me?

[*The* GREEK CHORUS *whispers:*]

FEMALE GREEK CHORUS: Khakis— 1160
MALE GREEK CHORUS: Bay Rum—
FEMALE GREEK CHORUS: The whisper of the—
LI'L BIT: —No.

[PECK, *in a rush, trembling, gets something out of his pocket.*]

PECK: I'm forty-five. That's not old for a man. And I haven't been able to do anything else
but think of you. I can't concentrate on my work—Li'l Bit. You've got to—I want   1165
you to think about what I am about to ask you.

LI'L BIT: I'm listening.

[PECK *opens a small ring box.*]

PECK: I want you to be my wife.

LI'L BIT: This isn't happening

PECK: I'll tell Mary I want a divorce. We're not blood-related. It would be legal—   1170

LI'L BIT: —What have you been thinking! You are married to my aunt, Uncle Peck. She's
my family. You have—you have gone way over the line. Family is family.

[*Quickly,* LI'L BIT *flies through the room, gets her coat.*]

I'm leaving. Now. I am not seeing you. Again.

[PECK *lies down on the bed for a moment, trying to absorb the terrible news. For
a moment, he almost curls into a fetal position.*]

I'm not coming home for Christmas. You should go home to Aunt Mary. Go home
now, Uncle Peck.   1175

[PECK *gets control, and sits, rigid.*]

Uncle Peck?—I'm sorry but I have to go.

[*pause*]

Are you all right.

[*With a discipline that comes from being told that boys don't cry,* PECK *stands
upright.*]

PECK: I'm fine. I just think—I need a real drink.

[*The* MALE GREEK CHORUS *has become a bartender. At a small counter, he is
lining up shots for* PECK. *As* LI'L BIT *narrates, we see* PECK *sitting, carefully and
calmly downing shot glasses.*]

LI'L BIT: [*to the audience*] I never saw him again. I stayed away from Christmas and Thanksgiving for years after.   1180
  It took my uncle seven years to drink himself to death. First he lost his job,
then his wife, and finally his driver's license. He retreated to his house, and had his
bottles delivered.

[PECK *stands, and puts his hands in front of him—almost like Superman flying.*]

One night he tried to go downstairs to the basement—and he flew down the
steep basement stairs. My aunt came by weekly to put food on the porch, and she   1185
noticed the mail and the papers stacked up, uncollected.
  They found him at the bottom of the stairs. Just steps away from his dark
room.
  Now that I'm old enough, there are some questions I would have liked to have
asked him. Who did it to you, Uncle Peck? How old were you? Were you eleven?   1190

[PECK *moves to the driver's seat of the car and waits.*]

Sometimes I think of my uncle as a kind of Flying Dutchman. In the opera, the Dutchman is doomed to wander the sea; but every seven years he can come ashore, and if he finds a maiden who will love him of her own free will—he will be released.

And I see Uncle Peck in my mind, in his Chevy '56, a spirit driving up and down the back roads of Carolina—looking for a young girl who, of her own free will, will   1195 love him. Release him.

[A VOICE *states:*]

You and the Reverse Gear.

LI'L BIT: The summer of 1962. On Men, Sex, and Women: Part III

[LI'L BIT *steps, as an eleven year old, into:*]

FEMALE GREEK CHORUS: [*as Mother*] It is out of the question. End of Discussion.
LI'L BIT: But why?   1200
FEMALE GREEK CHORUS: [*as Mother*] Li'l Bit—we are not discussing this. I said no.
LI'L BIT: But I could spend an extra week at the beach! You're not telling me why!
FEMALE GREEK CHORUS: [*as Mother*] Your uncle pays entirely too much attention to you.
LI'L BIT: He listens to me when I talk. And—and he talks to me. He teaches me about
   things. Mama—he knows an awful lot.   1205
FEMALE GREEK CHORUS: [*as Mother*] He's a small town hick who's learned how to mix
   drinks from Hugh Hefner.
LI'L BIT: Who's Hugh Hefner?

[*beat*]

FEMALE GREEK CHORUS: [*as Mother*] I am not letting an eleven-year-old girl spend seven
   hours alone in the car with a man. . . . I don't like the way your uncle looks at you.   1210
LI'L BIT: For god's sake, mother! Just because you've gone through a bad time with my
   father—you think every man is evil!
FEMALE GREEK CHORUS: [*as Mother*] Oh no, Li'l Bit—not all men . . . We . . . we just
   haven't been very lucky with the men in our family.
LI'L BIT: Just because you lost your husband—I still deserve a chance at having a father!   1215
   Someone! A man who will look out for me! Don't I get a chance?
FEMALE GREEK CHORUS: [*as Mother*] I will feel terrible if something happens.
LI'L BIT: Mother! It's in your head! Nothing will happen! I can take care of myself. And I
   can certainly handle Uncle Peck.
FEMALE GREEK CHORUS: [*as Mother*] All right. But I'm warning you—if anything happens,   1220
   I hold you responsible.

[LI'L BIT *moves out of this scene and toward the car.*]

LI'L BIT: 1962. On the Back Roads of Carolina: The First Driving Lesson.

[*The* TEENAGE GREEK CHORUS *member stands apart on stage. She will speak
all of* LI'L BIT*'s lines.* LI'L BIT *sits beside* PECK *in the front seat. She looks at
him closely, remembering.*]

PECK: Li'l Bit? Are you getting tired?
TEENAGE GREEK CHORUS: A little.
PECK: It's a long drive. But we're making really good time. We can take the back road from   1225
   here and see . . . a little scenery. Say—I've got an idea—[PECK *checks his rearview
   mirror.*]

TEENAGE GREEK CHORUS: Are we stopping, Uncle Peck?

PECK: There's no traffic here. Do you want to drive?

TEENAGE GREEK CHORUS: I can't drive.   1230

PECK: It's easy. I'll show you how. I started driving when I was your age. Don't you want
    to?—

TEENAGE GREEK CHORUS: —But it's against the law at my age!

PECK: And that's why you can't tell anyone I'm letting you do this—

TEENAGE GREEK CHORUS: —But—I can't reach the pedals.   1235

PECK: You can sit in my lap and steer. I'll push the pedals for you. Did your father ever let
    you drive his car?

TEENAGE GREEK CHORUS: No way.

PECK: Want to try?

TEENAGE GREEK CHORUS: Okay.   1240

> [LI'L BIT *moves into* PECK's *lap. She leans against him, closing her eyes.*]

PECK: You're just a little thing, aren't you? Okay—now think of the wheel as a big clock—
    I want you to put your right hand on the clock where three o'clock would be; and
    your left hand on the nine—

> [LI'L BIT *puts one hand to* PECK's *face, to stroke him. Then, she takes the wheel.*]

TEENAGE GREEK CHORUS: Am I doing it right?

PECK: That's right. Now, whatever you do, don't let go of the wheel. You tell me whether   1245
    to go faster or slower—

TEENAGE GREEK CHORUS: Not so fast, Uncle Peck!

PECK: Li'l Bit—I need you to watch the road—

> [PECK *puts his hands on* LI'L BIT's *breasts. She relaxes against him, silent,
> accepting his touch.*]

TEENAGE GREEK CHORUS: Uncle Peck—what are you doing?

PECK: Keep driving. [*He slips his hands under her blouse.*]   1250

TEENAGE GREEK CHORUS: Uncle Peck—please don't do this—

PECK: —Just a moment longer . . . [PECK *tenses against* LI'L BIT.]

TEENAGE GREEK CHORUS: [*trying not to cry*] This isn't happening.

> [PECK *tenses more, sharply. He buries his face in* LI'L BIT's *neck, and moans
> softly. The* TEENAGE GREEK CHORUS *exits, and* LI'L BIT *steps out of the car.*
> PECK, *too, disappears.*]

[A VOICE *reflects:*]

Driving in Today's World.

LI'L BIT: That day was the last day I lived in my body. I retreated above the neck, and I've   1255
    lived inside the "fire" in my head ever since.
      And now that seems like a long, long time ago. When we were both very young.
    And before you know it, I'll be thirty-five. That's getting up there for a woman. And
    I find myself believing in things that a younger self vowed never to believe in. Things
    like family and forgiveness.   1260

I know I'm lucky. Although I still have never known what it feels like to jog or dance. Any thing that . . . "jiggles." I do like to watch people on the dance floor, or out on the running paths, just jiggling away. And I say—good for them. [LI'L BIT *moves to the car with pleasure.*]

The nearest sensation I feel—of flight in the body—I guess I feel when I'm 1270 driving. On a day like today. It's five a.m. The radio says it's going to be clear and crisp. I've got five miles of highway ahead of me—and some back roads too. I filled the tank last night, and had the oil checked. Checked the tires, too. You've got to treat her . . . with respect.

First thing I do is: Check under the car. To see if any two year olds or household 1275 cats have crawled beneath, and strategically placed their skulls behind my back tires. [LI'L BIT *crouches.*]

Nope. Then I get in the car. [LI'L BIT *does so.*]

I lock the doors. And turn the key. Then I adjust the most important control on the dashboard—the radio—[LI'L BIT *turns the radio on: We hear all of the* GREEK 1280 CHORUS *overlapping, and static:*]

FEMALE GREEK CHORUS: [*overlapping*]—"You were so tiny you fit in his hand—"

MALE GREEK CHORUS: [*overlapping*]—"How is Shakespeare gonna help her lie on her back in the—"

TEENAGE GREEK CHORUS: [*overlapping*]—"Am I doing it right?" 1285

[LI'L BIT *fine-tunes the radio station. A song like "Dedicated to the One I Love" or Orbison's "Sweet Dreams" comes on, and cuts off the* GREEK CHORUS.]

LI'L BIT: Ahh . . . [*beat*] I adjust my seat. Fasten my seat belt. Then I check the right side mirror—check the left side. [*She does.*] Finally, I adjust the rearview mirror. [*As* LI'L BIT *adjusts the rearview mirror, a faint light strikes the spirit of Uncle* PECK *who is sitting in the back seat of the car. She sees him in the mirror. She smiles at him, and he nods at her. They are happy to be going for a long drive together.* LI'L BIT *slips the car into first gear; to* 1290 *the audience:*] And then—I floor it. [*Sound of a car taking off. Blackout.*]

END OF PLAY

Lydia
(2008)

merican drama has become increasingly diverse over the past few decades as its voices have become more varied and the production of new works has decentralized. Octavio Solis has written more than a dozen plays and although his plays are not limited to characters and issues particular to Latino-Americans, they resonate deeply within that community. Solis wrote *Lydia* when commissioned to write a play by The Denver Center Theatre. The play's popularity has resulted in professional productions throughout the country, and *Lydia* was a finalist nominee for the American Theatre Critics Association prize for the best new play originally produced outside of New York City.

Lydia is set in El Paso, Texas, during the early 1970s. Solis has chosen to set many of his plays in El Paso, where he was born and raised. As an American city bordering Mexico, Solis has called El Paso "a crucible of cultures." This border-city setting is especially appropriate for the characters in *Lydia*, because, as Solis has put it, they are caught "between two ways of being, two ways of life." Similarly, his characters speak in English and Spanish as well as in regional mixtures of the two.

Lydia is the story of a family shattered by an accident that left Ceci—three days before her *Quinceañera* (her fifteenth birthday)—brain damaged. That accident happened two years before the play's action begins, and we witness its effects upon the family. Lydia, the play's title character, is an illegal immigrant from Mexico whom the family has taken in to help with Ceci. It is difficult not to compare the two young women and see in Lydia the young woman Ceci might have become if not for the accident. Lydia serves as the catalyst to the play's action, bringing passion back into the house and with it all the joys and harm that passion can cause. Lydia bonds with Ceci and acts as a kind of *curandera* (a healer) who seemingly reads Ceci's thoughts and eventually reveals long-kept secrets about the accident.

The play is realistic in its approach to language, violence, and sexuality. However, there is also magic in the otherwise real world that Solis has created. Ceci speaks directly to the audience, conjuring images both poetic and accosting, and makes us aware that Ceci retains a vibrant spirit locked inside her uncommunicative body. Critics have written about the play's frank, and what some may find shocking, approach to sexuality. Still, no aspect of the play has raised more controversy than its ending, which readers and audiences may best judge for themselves.

Octavio Solis

Lydia

(Commissioned and first produced by the Denver Center for the Performing Arts, Kent Thompson, Artistic Director)

Characters

CECI, *the sister, 17*
MISHA, *the younger brother, 16*
RENE, *the older brother, 19*
ROSA, *the mother*
CLAUDIO, *the father*
ALVARO, *the cousin, 22*
LYDIA, *the maid*

TIME—*The early '70s, in winter.*

PLACE—*The living room of the Flores home in El Paso, Texas. Early '70s furnishings. A sofa with a coffee table, its surface scratched and stained. And old La-Z-Boy facing the TV. A stereo console with a set of headphones attached. A door to the front porch. A darkened hallway to the bedrooms. An entry to the kitchen. In the foreground by the TV, a small mattress with pillows and stuffed animals.*

CECI'S CONDITION—*For most of the play, Ceci lies on her mattress locked in her body in a semi-vegetative state. Her body's muscles rigid, her hands curled and fingers knuckled, she undergoes degrees of spasticity which come and go in ways that score the play. Her voice is fallen back into her throat and unfocused, her powers of expression are utterly buried in a neurological prison.*

--- ACT I ---

[*AT RISE: The living room of the Flores home.* CLAUDIO *slumps on the La-Z-Boy watching TV. Ironing his white shirts and pants is his wife* ROSA. *In her mattress lies* CECI *in her pajama, a long thin scar rising from her eyebrow and disappearing into her hairline.* CECI *lies very still, her eyes on the flickering light of the TV. After a moment, an awareness dawns on her and she starts.*]

CECI: She touched me and I flew. Touched my fault-line. And I flew. With her hand laid holy water on my scar. And I flew on wings of glass. My body *como una* bird racing with the moon on a breath of air.[1] Flying out of range of pain, purpose,

---

[1] *Como una* bird—"like a bird"

this thing we call *Vida*,[2] soaring into *them*. I wake to this. Life inside my life. No
wings, no glass, no moon. Only *Loteria* which means Bingo, which means chance,   5
which means play. So I play the cards into view.

[*She looks down at her arms and legs curling under her as a light falls on her
mattress.*]

A card with me printed, *La Vida Cecilia*, a rag doll thumbing the stitching in her
head, forming the words in her vegetable tongue, what happened to me, *porque no
puedo* rememeber, I must remember.[3]

[*The light bears down on* CLAUDIO.]

There. A card called El Short-Order Cook. Broken man drowning in old *rancheras*   10
and TV.[4] I hear *voces antiguas* calling his name,[5] Claudio, my poor *Papi* Claudio in
your personal winter, drowning out the will of *Mami* saying come with me across
the *rio*,[6] give up that lie you thought was you and live mine, live American with me.
So the dish ran away with the greasy spoon and a girl jumped over the moon but
you don't spikka the English, only the word No, which in Spanish means No, No   15
at work, in bed, in your dreams, in your *cantos perdidos*.[7]

[*The light shifts to* ROSA, *ironing clothes and muttering silent prayers to herself.*]

Aqui,[8] the Mami Rosa card, dressmaker of flying girls, sewing up unfinished seams; a
beautiful woman losing beauty by the day, see it gathering at her feet like old panty
hose, *ay Ama!*[9] You were Rosei Flores, clerk for the County, making your life here,
Anglo words like lazy moths tumbling out your mouth, you were *toda* proud,[10] but   20
now. You're Rosa Reborn holy-rolling me to sleep with the prayers of your new
church. Your prayers for us to be family which hasn't really been family since they
stopped putting cork in soda bottle caps.

[RENE *comes in from down the hall. He goes to the front door and retrieves the
day's mail. He goes over it carefully.*]

Ayy. My wild card, *El Carnal Mayor*,[11] Rene, my elder volcano, bustin' noses just by
looking at 'em, both hands fulla middle fingers for the whole world, checking every   25
day for hate mail, but always *nada*. Cars go by and honk *Puto-Puto-Rene-Puto!* but
cowards, my brother is invincible. [12]

[*He throws the mail on the coffee table and stares at* CECI.]

---

[2] *Vida*–"Life"
[3] *porque no puedo* remember–"why can't I remember"
[4] *rancheras*–"ranch songs; Mexican country music"
[5] *voces antiguas*–"ancient voices"
[6] *Papi . . . Mami*–"daddy . . . mommy"
[7] *cantos perdidos*–"lost songs"
[8] *Aqui*–"Here"
[9] *Ay, Ama!*–"Oh, Ma!"
[10] *toda*–"all"
[11] *El Carnal Mayor*–slang for "older brother"
[12] *Puto-Puto-Rene-Puto!*–"faggot, faggot, Rene faggot!"

The army recruiter don't want you, huh, not like those other flag-draped *Chicanos* on our block, even those that come back alive look like they gave up the ghost, that's kinda what you want, that damned ghost taken out of you. 'Cause you're all messed up with some hard-core macho shit nobody gets.

    30

[*He finally looks at* CECI *and slowly comes to her.*]

Andale,[13] plant a kiss on my head like that saint in church with the chipped nose—

[*He kisses her and leaves out the front door.*]

—dry-kiss and move away. *Simon, carnal*,[14] before the disgust starts to show.

[MISHA *enters with his books. Flops down on the couch.*]

Misha? *¿Eres tu?*[15] Card with the inscription Little Shit. *Carnalito* Misha bringing to my *nariz* fragrances of the street the school his body,[16] yes, the musk of you coming of age, coming into yourself, coming all *over* yourself. I hear your little secrets like crystals of salt in the pockets of your eyes, sad-boy Misha, sad for me, for us, the things that darken the day, King and Kennedy, the killings of students, the killings of Nam—

    35

[*Beat*]

Mi familia.[17] All sad and wounded cause of somethin'. Somethin' that broke. I gotta read my scar for the story, it's in there, I know it! *¡Aguas!*[18] I see her. The girl that touched me . . . her face in a mirror looking back . . . showing me her own sccc— ggghn mmm her—own—ssccrrmmgfmhm. . .

    40

MISHA: Mom, what's wrong with Ceci?

ROSA: *Alomejor* she went poo-poo.[19]

    45

MISHA: She doesn't smell like it.

ROSA: Maybe she wants her therapy. Could you do it, Misha? I'm pressing your father's shirts for work.

[MISHA *sits by* CECI *and runs her through a repertoire of delicate physical exercises, shifting her position from time to time.*]

MISHA: *Orale, carnala.*[20] Let's get the blood pumping.

ROSA: *Con cariño*,[21] okay?

    50

MISHA: Always gentle, *Ama*.[22] Hey Dad.

ROSA: He can't hear you.

MISHA: Dad!

ROSA: *¿Que te dije?*[23] What are you doing home so early? Don't you have practice?

---

[13] *andale*–"go on"

[14] *Simon, carnal*–"yeah, bro"

[15] *¿Eres tu?*–"Is that you?"

[16] *Carnalito*–"little brother"/*nariz*–"nose"

[17] *Mi familia*–"my family"

[18] *¡Aguas!*–literally, "Waters!" But commonly used slang for "Watch out!" or "Beware!"

[19] *Alomejor*–"maybe"

[20] *Orale, carnala*–"alright, sis"

[21] *Con cariño*–"with tenderness"

[22] *Ama*–"ma"

[23] *¿Que te dije?*–"What did I tell you?"

MISHA: [*as he rubs* CECI'*s arms and hands*] I dropped out of the squad. Football ain't my   55
    game. You hear that, Dad? I'm a wuss and I don't understand what all those little
    circles and arrows mean. I can't hear the quarterback in the huddle. He grunts uhh
    twenty-uhhh on huuu—uhh! But I do on huuu and Coach yells at me. At the scrim-
    mage today, a touchdown got called back on account of I was off-sides. I told them
    it wasn't my fault. I told them we need enunciation in the huddle. In the showers   60
    they all towel-whipped my bare *ass*.
ROSA: Watch your language.
MISHA: So you know what, Dad, I quit. I turned in my equipment and walked. I'm sorry,
    Mom. I just feel I'm needed here.
ROSA: It's okay, *mijo*.[24] I never liked you playing with those *brutos*.[25] You're my special   65
    boy. That's why I named you Misha.
MISHA: You named me Miguel.
ROSA: But after I saw that Baryshnikov on TV, I started calling you Misha.
MISHA: I don't even like ballet.
ROSA: The point is a brown boy named Misha in El Paso is special. I got my hopes pinned   70
    all over you like dollars.
MISHA: Is there anything to eat?
ROSA: There's *albondigas* on the stove.
MISHA: Meatballs? From last night?
ROSA: They're a little dried out, but still good. You want some?   75
MISHA: *¿Jefita?*[26] [ROSA *looks. He opens* CECI'*s arms wide.*] I *wuv* you this much.
ROSA: *Sangron.*[27]

    [*She laughs and goes into the kitchen.*]

CECI: Huuh onhuu-uuh.
MISHA: You sound like my quarterback.
CECI: Shhghgm.   80
MISHA: The truth is when I'm on the field, I don't pay attention. I watch the yellowing
    grass and the zip-zip-zip of the sprinklers and the clouds making ponytails in the
    sky.
CECI: Uhh. Ghhh. Gngngm.
MISHA: Mom. There's something different about her.   85
ROSA: What?
MISHA: I dunno. Something. Are you still giving her her meds?
ROSA: [*returning with a bowl of meatballs*] Of course!
MISHA: 'Cause I know you don't sometimes, Mom. I know how you "forget" sometimes.
ROSA: I don't forget, never!   90
MISHA: Where are they? Where're the pills? How much did you give her today? How
    much, Mom!

---

[24] *mijo*–a contraction of *mi hijo,* "my son"
[25] *brutos*–brutes
[26] *¿Jefita?*–literally, "little boss lady;" the terms "jefe" and "jefa" are sometimes used for parents, meaning male
and female boss, respectively
[27] *Sangron*–in this context the term seems to mean "joker" or "dummy"

ROSA: *Oye,*[28] it's not drugs she needs but faith! Faith! *Mijo,* the doctors said it was over, remember, she's a vegetable *para siempre,*[29] they said. What are these pills supposed to do then? 95

MISHA: Give me the pills. Or I'm telling him.

ROSA: Tell him. *Andale. Dile todo.*[30]

[MISHA *turns to his father.* CLAUDIO *takes off his headphones and stands.*]

CLAUDIO: *Que paso, Miguel.*[31] *¿Como te va en el* football?[32]

MISHA: Good.

ROSA: I'm almost done here. Just a few more shirts. 100

CLAUDIO: *¿Como?*[33]

ROSA: *Nomas estas camisas, Viejo.*[34]

CLAUDIO: *Miguel, una cerveza.*[35]

[MISHA *nods gravely as* CLAUDIO *goes down the hall to the bathroom.*]

ROSA: Praise God.

MISHA: I wish you'd keep your religion to yourself. It's not doing Ceci any good. 105

ROSA: *Oyeme*, Misha.[36] When your sister got hurt, I prayed to the *Virgen Santa, la Patronesa de todos los Mexicanos. La Virgen de Guadalupe* herself.[37] And she failed me. That's when I know. Us *Católicos,*[38] we worship the wrong things. Idols can't make miracles. Only God. So I go to a church with no other gods but God.

MISHA: Has that done her any good? Has it? 110

ROSA: Today. While your father was sleeping. You know what I did? I took her to Our Church of the Nazarene.

MISHA: What? You took her to those holy rollers? Are you kidding me?

ROSA: Misha, she loved it. All the peoples adored her. And Pastor Lujan himself baptized her. 115

MISHA: What?

ROSA: He put her in this big glass tub and laid his hand on her, *mijo*. Right here where her precious brains came out, and he prayed to God for her soul. He dipped her backward in the water and her face came alive! Eyes bright as nickels and her mouth wide open, taking in the light of heaven! Pastor Lujan said very clearly: Cecilia, prepare 120 you! Your redemption is knocking on you head. And he took her pills and poured them all into the same tub.

MISHA: Oh no. . . .

---

[28] *Oye*–"listen" or "hey"
[29] *para siempre*–"forever"
[30] *Dile todo*–"tell him everything"
[31] *Que paso, Miguel.*–"What happened, Miguel"
[32] *¿Como te va en el football?*–"How's it going in football?"
[33] *¿Como?*–literally, "how;" used idiomatically as, "what was that?" "how was that?" or "excuse me?"
[34] *Nomas estas camisas, Viejo*–"Just these shirts, old man." *Viejo* and *Vieja* may be used as terms of endearment just as "old man" or "old lady" may endearingly be used between husband and wife in English
[35] *una cerveza*–"a beer"
[36] *Oyeme*–"Listen to me"
[37] *Virgen . . . de Guadalupe*–"Holy Virgin, the Patroness of all Mexicans. The Virgin of Guadalupe" (Mary)
[38] *Catolicos*–Catholics

ROSA: He said we don't need them anymore! He said it's evil in our hearts that makes her
    sick. 125

MISHA: No more saving her soul. I mean it. Leave her soul alone.

ROSA: Don't you lecture me on how I care for *mija!*[39] Who stays home with her day and
    night, changing her when she needs to go, making her special food, rubbing her
    joints *y todo?*[40] Who?

MISHA: I help. 130

ROSA: *Por favor,*[41] Misha. You're in school all day.

MISHA: I know.

ROSA: Well, I know *more.* Nothing happens without me in this house. I see to our needs.
    That's how come we're getting a maid.

MISHA: A maid? Like, to clean the house? 135

ROSA: To clean the house, to cook the food, to watch your sister. I asked your Tia Mirna,
    and she said her maid knows this *chavala* from *Jalisco* who just came over and she
    needs work and she's cheap.[42]

MISHA: What about you?

ROSA: They called from the county office and told me my old position is available if I want 140
    it. Well, I want it. I'm tired of staying in this house all day. Plus we need the
    money.

MISHA: Is she legal?

ROSA: I don't ask about such things. I just ask her to come tomorrow.

MISHA: Tomorrow? Dammit, why didn't you tell me? 145

ROSA: I did. Watch your tongue. Last week. I mentioned it at dinner. But you never listen.
    You and your brother only hear what you want to hear.

    [**CLAUDIO** *returns from the bathroom.*]

CLAUDIO: *¿Y mi cerveza?*[43]

MISHA: Mom *dice que* we're gonna have a maid, *una criada.*[44]

CLAUDIO: *Asi lo quiere.*[45] 150

MISHA: *¿Y tu, que quieres?*[46]

CLAUDIO: *Mi pinche cerveza.*[47]

    [*He sits and puts his headphones on again.* **MISHA** *watches him.*]

ROSA: You heard him.

MISHA: What am I, his *mesero?*[48]

    [*She glares at him.* **MISHA** *goes off to the kitchen and reenters with a can of beer.*]

---

[39] *Mija*–"daughter"
[40] *y todo*–"and everything"
[41] *Por favor*–"please"
[42] *chavala from Jalisco*–"chick from Jalisco" (a state in Mexico)
[43] *¿Y mi cerveza?*–"And my beer?"
[44] *dice que . . . una criada*–"says that . . . a maid"
[45] *Asi lo quiere*–"That's how she wants it"
[46] *¿Y tu, que quieres?*–"And you, what do you want?"
[47] *Mi pinche cerveza*–"My fucking beer"
[48] *mesero*–"waiter"

MISHA: Ask yourself, Mom. Do we really want this? Do we really want a stranger coming   155
    into our house?

ROSA: What's wrong with our house? What don't you want her to see? What are you
    ashamed of, Misha? Your sister?

MISHA: Not her.

ROSA: I promise you. When she comes here, she will find a close, caring Mexican *familia*   160
    trying to make it in this blessed country.

CLAUDIO: [*impatiently waiting for his beer*] Miguel. . . .

ROSA: Get over your *verguenza* and give your father his beer.[49]

MISHA: Mom. . . .

ROSA: Do it, Miguel.   165

> [CLAUDIO *suddenly gets up, takes the beer and slaps* MISHA *across the face.*]

CLAUDIO: *Tres veces te lo pedi, cabrón. Tres veces.*[50]

> [*He sits, rips off the pull-tab and drops it on the floor by* CECI. *He watches TV as* MISHA's *eyes well with tears.*]

ROSA: *¿Que te dije?*[51] Pick up that thing before your sister cuts herself with it.

> [CECI *turns to speak to* MISHA *as he picks up the pull-tab, his cheek reddening with the heat of the blow, and goes to his room.*]

CECI: It's okay, *carnalito*. I hear your face clapping against the way things are, and I know
    it hurts, 'cause I feel my face smashing against the mad will of God. I remember that,
    Misha, like I remember we can't let the swelling block us off, we gotta believe that it   170
    passes, bro, it passes. Sure as day passes into night.

> [*Suddenly, night.* CECI *lying on her mattress. Headlights swivel across the window drapes as* RENE *comes in the front door. He stands and waits in the dark until his breath is even. He watches* CECI *with a mix of fear and contempt.* MISHA *enters.*]

RENE: Any mail?

MISHA: No. [*notices* RENE's *bloody knuckles*] *Vato.*[52]

RENE: It's nothing.

MISHA: Nothing. You're bleeding.   175

RENE: What's a little *molé*.[53] You should see them.

MISHA: Are you drunk too?

RENE: It helps, don't you think? So you and me and some Buds?

MISHA: We're out. And it's too late to hit the Circle K.

RENE: I don't need no shit Circle fucking K, goddammit. I need me some *pisto*. *Watcha.*[54]   180

> [*He reaches under the cushions of the La-Z-Boy. A fifth of Southern Comfort.*]

---

[49] *verguenza*–literally, "shame;" seemingly used here as "embarrassment"
[50] *Tres . . . veces*–"Three times I asked you for it, you little shit. Three times."
[51] *¿Que te dije?*–"What did I tell you?"
[52] *Vato*–slang for "Man" or "Dude"
[53] *molé*–traditional Mexican paste of chocolate and chile; used here as slang for "blood"
[54] *Pisto*–"booze"

MISHA: Whoa.

RENE: Papa's gotta brand new bag.

MISHA: How'd you know it was there?

RENE: *Ese*,[55] he sits in that chair all *pinchi* day like he's incubating a fucking *huevo. Andale, tragito!*[56] [*They slug some down.*] Nothing like a little *pisto* to smooth out the rough 185
edges of a bad night.[57]

MISHA: Was it a bad night?

RENE: Hell no, it was a good night. We kicked some ass.

MISHA: What did you do?

RENE: We kicked some ass. 190

MISHA: How about a little more detail, *ese?*

RENE: We kicked some fucking ass.

MISHA: Rene.

RENE: You're too young. You don't get the vibe. This is me, Joey, and Sergio taking on the
pinchi world. 195

MISHA: Joey and Sergio? Those pussies?

RENE: *No mames, guey!*[58] These are my *camaradas*! Besides, we need Joey's van for the
ceremony.

MISHA: What ceremony?

RENE: *Pos*,[59] first we chug back some brew for a couple hours, listen to some Sabbath, toke 200
a little *mota* for courage.[60] Then we think of cheerleaders and whack off a little till
we're nice and hard and then we hit the road.

MISHA: And kick some ass.

RENE: Fuckin' A.

MISHA: I heard it was some *cholos*[61] last night. 205

RENE: Tough little fuckers in training for prison, gang tats *y toda la madre*.[62] We kicked their
ass. *Dame*.[63] [*He drinks. Some red and white lights flash by the window.*] ¡*Trucha!*[64] Get
down! Down!

MISHA: Shit, Rene! Is that the cops?

RENE: Just be quiet and keep your head down. 210

      [RENE *peeks through the drapes till the lights pass.*]

MISHA: What the fuck happened? You better tell me or I'm gonna wake up Mom and tell
her the cops are after you.

---

[55] *Ese*–literally, "that one." Often used in slang as "man" or "dude"

[56] *pinchi . . . huevo. Andale tragito!*–"fuckin' . . . egg. Go on, [take a] little drink/sip!"

[57] *pisto*–"booze"

[58] *No mames, guey!*–"no mames" slang term meaning, "don't mess around now," "*guey*" is a corruption of "buey,"
meaning "ass or donkey" and used in slang as a derogatory term

[59] *Pos*–corruption of *pues,* meaning "well" in this context

[60] *mota*–"weed" (marijuana)

[61] *cholos*–originally the term designated persons of mixed European and indigenous blood. Now used in slang
as "thugs"

[62] *y toda la madre*–literally, "and the whole mother," used in slang as "and all that shit"

[63] *Dame*–"gimme"

[64] ¡*Trucha!*–slang for "Watch out!"

RENE: *Calamantes montes*, narc.[65] I'll tell you, but only as a cautionary tale for you not to put your ass where it's likely to be kicked, *me entiendes?*[66]

[MISHA *nods.*]

RENE: We took on some GI's.   215

MISHA: Shit. Oh shit.

RENE: Fresh outa Ft. Bliss. We went up a mountain on Scenic Drive and pulled over by these cars. And there they were, a *gringo salado* and a couple *negros.*[67] We just approached them like some tourists up to see the sights, you know? They offered us some beers and were really nice to us. But these *fags*, Meesh, you gotta watch out for them.   220

MISHA: How come?

RENE: Just 'cause I say so. Anyway, the *gringo* puts his hand on my knee so I gotta cut him with a right hook that snaps his head back. Joey and Serge lay into the others and man, it's on, We lay into these jive-turkey motherfuckers with basic-training biceps. Serge is swinging this bat on their heads and Joey's got nunchucks and blood is   225
shootin' volcanic all over the place.

MISHA: You hit 'em with bats? What if you put 'em in the hospital with like brain damage or something?

RENE: Hey, don't talk brain damage. Not in front of her. Pay your penance, fuck.

[RENE *offers the bottle and* MISHA *drinks.*]

MISHA: I don't get it, man. Why are you doing this shit? When are you gonna go to college   230
or get a real job?

RENE: I gotta job.

MISHA: Car detailing at Earl Scheib? You're smarter than that.

RENE: What's the *pinche* point, bro? I'm gonna get drafted anyway.

MISHA: Is that what you're looking for in the mail? Your draft notice? *Ese*, your birthdate's   235
not due in the lottery till next year.

RENE: *No mames, guey.*

MISHA: If you're so anxious about it, if you wanna kill someone, go enlist like Alvaro.

RENE: I ain't that stupid.

MISHA: Neither is he. He came back with a bronze star. Gung-ho guys like him always   240
seem to make out okay.

RENE: Varo's too hot-shit for us now. Back three months and he still hasn't come to our *chante.*[68]

MISHA: Mom says he's been focusing on getting some steady work.

CECI: Varo. Varo Varo Varo.   245

MISHA: I know this much. War keeps going like it is, I'm gonna have to go to Canada.

RENE: Canada? Why truck all the way up there, Mexico's right there, you dope!

MISHA: Well, on TV, that's where they all say they're going! Canada!

RENE: 'Cause they're white, stupid! Canada! You're a trip. What are you doing up?

---

[65] *Calamantes montes*–playful slang meaning in this context, "Take a chill pill"

[66] *me entiendes?*–"you understand me?"

[67] *gringo salado . . . negros*–"a salty white guy and a couple of blacks"

[68] *chante*–Mexican slang for house, similar to slang usage of "crib" for house in English

MISHA: I couldn't sleep. I had this dream. Hey, you know Mom's hiring some chick to   250
take care of Ceci?

RENE: Old news, bro.

MISHA: She's coming tomorrow to cook and do the wash. Tell you one thing, she ain't touching my clothes.

RENE: You got some stains in your *chones* you don't want her to see?[69]   255

MISHA: Shut up.

RENE: Haha! Is that what you had? A wet dream?

MISHA: Cut it out. It was scary as shit. We were kids, you, me, Alvaro, and Ceci, all alone in this house.

RENE: What happened?   260

MISHA: We were playing like we used to. We put chairs all over the living room, down the hall, covered them up with sheets and we crawled under pretending we were ants in our tunnels. We scurried from chamber to chamber, touching heads lightly, making those little tee-tee sounds in ant-language. Ceci's eyes full of joy. She had those pearl earrings she got for her *Quinceañera*.[70] We saw her go off with this shiny key in her   265 mouth. I think it was a key. It looked like a key. Her shadow against the sheet one second, and the next, gone. We went through the tunnels looking for her, but we couldn't find her. I wanted to call out "Ceci," but you said use ant-language. I couldn't think of the words for please come back, and I went all through the tunnel, looking for her. I woke up absolutely freaked. I came out here and saw the invisible   270 lines of the tunnels all over the floor.

RENE: I'm sackin' out before the old man comes home. You shouldn't be dreaming shit like that, Misha.

[*He returns the bottle to the cushion seam and goes.*]

CECI: Gghn.

[MISHA *goes to* CECI *and looks into her eyes. He gently pries her mouth open. He looks inside. He lets her go and then walks off to bed.*]

CECI: You won't find nothing down there but spit and the words to *Cielito Lindo*.[71] I feel   275 it coming around again like a Mexican yo-yo, little ball up on its string and plop right into the bowl of my heart.

[CLAUDIO *enters from the shadows in white shirt and trousers with his paper hat.*]

CECI: It's the night of my race with the moon. He comes in his fry-cook whites to my room, wearing that white paper hat like a general. I'm at the threshold of my *senorita*-hood, pretending to sleep, feeling his raw breath in my ear singing for the last   280 time. . . .

[*He sings softly as he opens his hands and reveals a pair of pearl earrings.*]

CLAUDIO:	*De la sierra morena*	[From the tanned sierra
	Cielito lindo viene bajando	Cielito lindo, comes down

---

[69] *chones*—slang for "underwear"

[70] *Quinceañera*—a girl's fifteenth birthday party which functions as a passage to womanhood ceremony in Latin cultures

[71] *Cielito Lindo*—a traditional and popular Mexican song. The title means, "Lovely Sky" but *cielito* is also used as a term of endearment

Un par de ojitos negros	A pair of little black eyes
Cielito lindo de contrabando	Cielito lindo, of contraband 285
Ese lunar que tienes	That beauty mark you have,
Cielito lindo junto a la boca	Cielito lindo, next to your mouth
No se lo des a nadie	Give it to no one,
Cielito lindo que a mi me toca	Cielito lindo, for it is mine.
Ay ay ay ay	ay, ay, ay, ay 290
Canta y no llores	Sing and don't weep
Porque cantando se alegran	Because it's by singing,
Cielito lindo los corazones	Cielito lindo, that hearts cheer up.]

[*He gets up and slowly walks off into the darkness.*]

CECI: A tear from each eye turned to pearl and laid on my pillow to make the moon jealous. Oh what is this yearning inside? What does it mean?   295

[*The next day.* ROSA *comes in dressed for work, fussing about, straightening up
the house with a minimum of noise.*]

ROSA: *¡Ay Diosito diosito!* Where is this girl? *¡Ya son las ocho y media! ¡Ay, que nervio!*[72]
CECI: Ghghnn.
ROSA: Okay, okay, I'm coming! *Ya ya.* I know, I know. This house smells like a *cantina!*[73]
What were these *barbaros* up to last night, Ceci?[74]
CECI: Gghhn.   300

[ROSA *goes to the kitchen and quickly returns with a bowl of oatmeal. She sits
and stirs the oatmeal around with a spoon.*]

ROSA: *Ta bien, mija.*[75] I know everything in this house. I know they were drinking. I know
Rene was fighting again. But what can I do? He does what he does. *¿Tienes apetito
por* some oatmeal? *Ven.*[76] [*She holds* CECI *as she raises a spoonful of oatmeal.*] Oh,
espera.[77] We forgot grace. [*She holds* CECI*'s hands and closes her eyes.*] Dear Lord Jesus
Holy Father, we submit this meal today for your blessing that we may not want and   305
pray for your mercy, for You made us in order to love us and as we take this meal
please forgive our sins and heal us first in our *corazones* so that the body may follow.
In your most precious and holy name, Amen. [*She guides the spoon into her mouth.*]
Not too hot? Good. [*She continues to talk as she feeds her.*] My pretty girl. Even the
accident couldn't keep this body from growing. It's my body, Ceci, the body I used   310
to have. The hip-huggers and halter tops I would have bought you! *¡Lastima de tu
quinceañera!*[78] I made with my own Singer the whitest most beautiful dress with lace
running all the way down the sleeve to the wrist. Like a Disney *Chicana* you would
look! Regal and sexy, but definitely chaste. You would save that *cosita* for after your
wedding. *Pero ahora, pobre mija.*[79] It's just a dead flower on you now.   315

---

[72] *¡Ay Diosito . . . que nervio!*–"Oh Lordy, Lordy! Where is this girl? It's already eight thirty! Oh, how nerve-
wracking!"
[73] *cantina*–"saloon"
[74] *barbaros*–"barbarians"
[75] *Ta bien, mija*–"It's alright, honey"
[76] *¿Tienes apetito por . . . ? Ven*–"Are you hungry for . . . ?/Come."
[77] *espera*–"wait"
[78] *¡Lastima de tu quinceañera!*–"Shame about your quinceañera!"
[79] *cosita*–"little thing"/*Pero ahora, pobre mija.*–"But now, my poor daughter."

[CECI *jerks and thrusts the bowl of oatmeal all over herself and her mother.*]

CECI: GGGhhhmmm!

ROSA: *¡AY! ¡Cecilia Rosario! ¡Que has hecho!* Look at my dress! *¡Inutil!*[80]

[CECI *flails madly about.* LYDIA *appears at the door, bag in hand.*]

LYDIA: *¿Señora?*

ROSA: *Oh. Si, si, si. ¿Eres la muchacha de Jalisco?*[81]

LYDIA: Yes.   320

ROSA: *¿Hablas ingles?*[82]

LYDIA: *Si, Señora—o sea . . .*[83] Yes, I would prefer. I am learning.

ROSA: *Entonces,*[84] come in. Come in, please.

[LYDIA *enters.* CECI *is still angrily flailing her arms.*]

CECI: Ggnnhf!

LYDIA: *Perdón, pero me perdi.*[85] I . . . I . . . got lost. . . .   325

CECI: GGGhn!

ROSA: It's okay, okay, I understand.

LYDIA: Let me. I help. You go wash.

[LYDIA *puts down her bag and goes to* CECI. *She cleans her with her napkin.*]

ROSA: No, no, please, she's very hard to—

LYDIA: It's okay, I can do, she's strong, your—*como se dice*—your daughter?[86]   330

ROSA: Yes. Daughter. *Mija.*

LYDIA: You go change, I take care here. *Hola-hola chica.*[87] What is her name?

ROSA: Ceci.

LYDIA: *Hola, Ceci. Hola.* I am Lydia. How are you fine? I am fine too. *Que bonita te ves con la avena en la cara.*[88] Oatmeal is very good for the skin. Here.   335

[LYDIA *rubs more into her face.* CECI *freezes at the feel of the warm oatmeal.* ROSA *is taken aback.*]

Soon you be Miss *Tejas, que no?*[89] Soon you be Miss *Universo.*

[MISHA *enters as* CECI *coos softly throughout the next passage.*]

MISHA: What's going on?

CECI: Nnnnn . . . nnnnn . . .

ROSA: This is our maid—

LYDIA: Lydia.   340

ROSA: Lydia from Jalisco.

---

[80] *¡AY! ¡Cecilia Rosario! ¡Que has hecho!*–"Oh! Cecilia Rosario! What have you done!"/*¡Inutil!*–"Useless!"

[81] *Oh. Si, . . . Jalisco?*–"Oh. Yes, yes, yes. Are you the girl from Jalisco?"

[82] *¿Hablas ingles?*–"Do you speak English?" or "You speak English?"

[83] *Si, Señora—o sea . . .*–"Yes, ma'am, I mean . . ."

[84] *Entonces*–"Then"

[85] *Perdón, pero me perdi*–"I'm sorry, but I got lost"

[86] *como se dice*–"how do you say"

[87] *Hola-hola chica*–"Hello-hello, girl"

[88] *Que bonita . . . la cara*–"How pretty you look with the oatmeal on your face"

[89] *. . . Miss Tejas, que no?*–". . . Miss Texas, won't you?"

MISHA: What's she doing to her?

ROSA: She spilled the oatmeal on me and—

LYDIA: Making her skin soft. If she won't eat, then she can be beautiful. *¿Verdad, Ceci?*[90]

CECI: Ooooh.   345

ROSA: I have to go change. I'm going to be late. I'm late already. [ROSA *goes.*]

LYDIA: *Asi, asi.*[91] Feels good, no? Feels like chocolate.

CECI: Gggnnh.

MISHA: Are you sure this works?

LYDIA: It worked on me, *que no?*[92] [*She looks up at* MISHA *for the first time.*] What is your   350
name?

MISHA: Miguel. But they call me Misha.

LYDIA: Misha?

MISHA: My mother's called me that since I was little.

LYDIA: It's Russian.   355

MISHA: I know.

LYDIA: Is there Russian in your blood?

MISHA: No. Listen, I think you really should get her cleaned up before my old man sees
her like this. He's not into beauty tips n' shit—

LYDIA: Speak slower. Or speak Spanish.   360

MISHA: I'm not that fluent in Spanish.

LYDIA: Then speak slower, Misha.

MISHA: My. Father. Will be pissed. When he sees this. Pissed as in pissed off.

LYDIA: Ceci, are you calm now? You want to clean up and eat?

CECI: Ggnnh. Ggnnhr.   365

MISHA: That means yes.

LYDIA: No, it means let me wear it for another minute. Are we sharing a room?

MISHA: What?

LYDIA: Me and Ceci, are we sharing a room?

MISHA: Yeah.   370

LYDIA: *Bueno. Asi va ser.*[93]

MISHA: How old are you?

LYDIA: How old are you?

MISHA: No, this is a relevant question. You can't take care of my sister if you're as young
as you look.   375

LYDIA: Speak slower.

MISHA: I said, You, Can't, Take, Care—

LYDIA: I am as young as I look.

MISHA: Mom!

ROSA: [*enters wearing a new dress*] Shhht! *¡Tranquilo!* Don't you know your father's still   380
sleeping! That's another thing. My husband, *mi marido*, he works night till 6 in the
morning, then sleeps most of the day. You have to be very quiet.

---

[90] *¿Verdad, Ceci?*–"Right, Ceci?"
[91] *Asi, asi*–"Like this, like this"
[92] *Que no?*–"Didn't it?"
[93] *Bueno. Asi va ser*–"Good. That's how it'll be"

MISHA: You can't be serious.

ROSA: I'm going to work. *Toma,*[94] keys to the house. And here's my number at work. She eats only food that I've marked with her name in the fridge, *con su nombre*, okay?[95] And she wears diapers, *pero* still she has to be changed. *Si tienes tiempo.*[96] If you don't, I'll do it when I get home. 385

LYDIA: I do it.

MISHA: You're gonna leave her with her.

ROSA: My husband's name is Claudio and he keeps mostly to himself. Don't bother him. Stay away from Rene too, my oldest. This is Misha here, the only one who's not trouble. 390

LYDIA: I understand.

ROSA: The pay is thirty dollars a week and you'll be staying in Ceci's room at the end of the hall. *¿Que mas, que mas?*[97] Oh, dinner is at six. I should be home right around that time. Okay? 395

LYDIA: Okay.

ROSA: *Gracias*, Lydia. Go to school and do your homework.

MISHA: Mom—

ROSA: *¡Que Dios te cuide, mijo!*[98] [*She goes.*]

CECI: Gghght. 400

LYDIA: Okay, now, she says.

MISHA: What?

LYDIA: Get the bath ready with some hot water.

MISHA: I have to go to school.

LYDIA: *Pues*, go. No problem, I'll do it. 405

MISHA: Besides, she had a bath yesterday.

LYDIA: She needs one today.

MISHA: Plus it might wake up my dad. You don't want to wake him when he's in a mood.

LYDIA: Speak slow—

MISHA: You don't want to wake my dad. 410

CECI: Ggngh, Gghn. Mmmgh.

LYDIA: *Bueno*. Bring to me a towel and some water. [MISHA *goes.*]

CECI: Gghghnnnm.

LYDIA: It's not so good when it gets cold, ah? *Ay*, Ceci, you hold my hand so tight. *¿Que te pasa?*[99] What do you want to tell me? 415

[CECI *guides her hand into her drawers.* LYDIA *discovers blood.*]

Ah. *Sangrita.*[100] It's your time, eh? Good. I will wash you very clean, *vas a ver.*[101] [MISHA *returns with a towel and a bowl of water.*] Thank you.

[LYDIA *begins washing the oatmeal off* CECI's *face.*]

---

[94] *Toma*–"take" used in this instance as "here, take"

[95] *con su nombre*–"with her name"

[96] *pero . . . changed. Si tienes tiempo*–"but . . . changed. If you have time."

[97] *¿Que mas, que mas?*–"What else, what else?"

[98] *¡Que Dios te cuide, mijo!*–"May God take care of you, my son!"

[99] *¿Que te pasa?*–"What's going on with you?"

[100] *Sangrita*–"blood" (diminutive)

[101] *vas a ver*–"you'll see"

MISHA: Why are you trying to speak English?

LYDIA: It's a beautiful *idioma*.[102]

MISHA: But why do you want to learn it? You live in Jalisco.   420

LYDIA: I never say that. My friend, she is from Jalisco. I come from a *pueblo* outside of that. *En los montes*.[103]

MISHA: We don't know anything about you.

LYDIA: You know my name. Are you going to school?

MISHA: What's it to you?   425

LYDIA: Because if no, help me with her. Hold her while I take off the wet clothes.

MISHA: What?

LYDIA: Help.

[*He kneels by her as she pulls off* CECI*'s pajamas.*]

MISHA: What do you want me to do?

LYDIA: Keep her not moving. [*She unbuttons her pajama top.*]   430

MISHA: Wait.

LYDIA: *Andale*, Ceci.

MISHA: Wait.

CECI: Gggngnh.

[LYDIA *pulls off her top exposing* CECI*'s breasts.* MISHA *turns away.*]

MISHA: What are you doing! What the hell! I can't see her naked!   435

LYDIA: Why not?

MISHA: She's my sister! Jeez! Cover her. Please.

LYDIA: *¿Que onda?*[104] You have not ever seen *chichis*?

[CECI *begins to laugh.*]

CECI: Gggngng-ghgnh-hhhah-hhgnhah.

LYDIA: Your brother.   440

MISHA: It's not right. I can't see her like this.

LYDIA: Then don't look.

[LYDIA *washes her quietly.* MISHA *slowly turns his gaze toward her.*]

Your sister has beautiful tits. But no one to see them. Too bad.

[MISHA *is transfixed. Then his gaze meets* CECI*'s.*]

MISHA: When we were kids, at the church bazaar, she loved to play *Loteria*. There was this card called *La Sirena*, the Mermaid, and in the picture, her bare breasts rose above   445 the water. It was her favorite card.

LYDIA: *¿Ves?*[105] English is a pretty *idioma*. Write those pretty words down.

MISHA: I have to go.

---

[102] *idioma*—"language"

[103] a *pueblo* . . . *En los montes*—"a village . . . in the hill/mountain country"

[104] *¿Que onda?*—"What's up?"

[105] *¿Ves?*—"See?"

[MISHA *gathers his books and rushes out.* LYDIA *fishes for a blouse from her own bag and puts it on* CECI.]

LYDIA: *Aver.*[106] You will like this. *Mi abuelita* made it for me.[107] The last time I wear, I was another girl. I sat before the *espejo* brushing my hair.[108] Wondering: who is that look- 450 ing back? Hm? Now let me see your room, *palomita*.[109]

[LYDIA *takes up her bag and goes down the hall.* CECI *feels the fabric of this new blouse.*]

CECI: Now I remember. I'm horny! I'm just horny! I want to be wanted. I want to be touched. Not just touched, groped! I want to be fondled and strummed and tickled and . . . I want to be fucked. I want someone to plunge their hands into my body and grab that ball of fire burning my insides and hold it super tight till the *picante* 455 bursts through my eyes![110] Ohhh! It feels so good but so BAD! How could you miss this, God? How could you take so much of my brain and still miss the part that craves the hokey pokey? Oh, who is this girl? What is she doing to me?

[LYDIA *returns in a plain dress and slippers. She has been cleaning the house. Broom and dust mop. She starts straightening up the living room.*]

CECI: Hours pass like seconds. She's as fast as a bird's wing. Lydia the blur. She brings me soup but I don't remember slurping nothing but blur. 460

[CLAUDIO *enters, gruff and disoriented after a long daylight sleep. He stands in the middle of the room and stares at* LYDIA, *who stops and stares back.*]

LYDIA: Lydia. I am your maid. [*No reply*] *¿Cuantos años tiene su hija?*[111]
CLAUDIO: *¿Hay café?*[112]
LYDIA: In the kitchen. What happen to her? [*No reply*] It's okay. She'll tell me.

[*He glares at her then goes to the kitchen.*]

LYDIA: Your father, he reminds me of someone. One of my *novios*.[113] Always mad at something. 465

[*He returns with a cup and turns on the stereo, puts on his headphones and sits to watch TV.*]

I don't comprehend your coffee machine. If it's not good, I make again some more.
CECI: GGGhhnj.
LYDIA: If it's too strong, tell me. I like it strong, but for some peoples, coffee is not good that way. 470
CECI: Ggnnrhg.
LYDIA: He can't hear? Why not? I'm right here, he's right there.
CECI: Ggnhnh.

---

[106] *Aver* [*A ver*]–"Let's see"
[107] *Mi abuelita*–"My granny"
[108] *espejo*–"mirror"
[109] *palomita*–"little dove" (a term of endearment)
[110] *picante*–"spiciness"
[111] *¿Cuantos años tiene su hija?*–"How old is your daughter?"
[112] *¿Hay café?*–"Is there coffee?"
[113] *novios*–"boyfriends"

LYDIA: I see. [LYDIA *dusts the TV, blocking his view. Then she dusts the stereo console. She finds the sleeve of the record album.*] *¡Ay, mira! Pedro Infante!*[114] My mother's favorite!   475

[*She raises the volume to full.* CLAUDIO *rips off the headphones and jumps to his feet, his eyes glaring with rage.*]

CLAUDIO: *¡HIJO DE LA CHINGADA!*[115]

LYDIA: How come she is like this?

CLAUDIO: *Un accidente. Chocó mi Pontiac.*[116]

LYDIA: How long ago?

CLAUDIO: *Hace dos años.*[117]   480

LYDIA: *¿Hace dos años?* Was it your fault?

CLAUDIO: *¿Que que?*[118]

LYDIA: You walk around like it's your fault. Did you crash the car with her inside?

CLAUDIO: *No.*

LYDIA: But you blame yourself.   485

CLAUDIO: *¿Que quieres de mi?*[119]

LYDIA: Only this one thing: you like the coffee or not?

[*He downs the cup in one gulp and throws it violently into the kitchen, shattering it.*]

CLAUDIO: *No. No me gusta.*[120] [*He goes back to his bedroom.*]

LYDIA: *Pues* . . . I'll have to do better.

CECI: I . . . I see a new card, *El Pontiac Caliente*! The Pontiac in heat! Ceci in the Pontiac   490
mad-crazy for some loco. Si. That ball of fire inside! Daddy's little girl in hip-hugger
jeans, Red Keds, Carole King hair racing toward her miracle boy!

[LYDIA *is cleaning up the mess as* RENE *comes in, sleepy.*]

RENE: What the hell was that?

LYDIA: I broke a cup.

RENE: Are you the maid?   495

LYDIA: Lydia. You are the other son.

RENE: Yeah. *¿Como the fuck esta?*[121]

LYDIA: I . . . what?

RENE: Is she giving you any trouble?

LYDIA: Who, Ceci? No.   500

RENE: Slap her upside the head if she gets out of line. Kidding! Is there *café, por favor*?

LYDIA: *Si, pero* it's not good.

RENE: What do you mean it's not good? Get me a cup.

[LYDIA *goes.*]

CECI: Ggghnn.

---

[114] *¡Ay, mira! Pedro Infante!*–"Oh, look! Pedro Infante!" (a famous singer/actor during the 1940s and '50s)
[115] *¡HIJO DE LA CHINGADA!*–"Son of a bitch!"
[116] *Un accidente. Chocó mi Pontiac*–"An accident. Crashed my Pontiac"
[117] *Hace dos años*–"Two years ago"
[118] *¿Que que?*–idiomatic expression meaning, "what, now?"
[119] *¿Que quieres de mi?*–"What do you want from me?"
[120] *No. No me gusta.*–"No, I don't like it"
[121] *¿Como the fuck esta?*–"How the fuck is she?"

RENE: I said I was kidding. Jesus Christ. [*He stops and looks at* CECI.] Look. Every breath, 505
everybeat of my heart, every drop of my blood, is yours. You own me. So quit giving
me that look or die.

LYDIA: [*Returning with a new cup of coffee.*] Here for you.

RENE: Okay, if you're talking English on account of us trans-border Mexicans, spare me
the condescension. Talk Spanish in this house if you want. 510

LYDIA: *Bueno, si quiere que hable en mi idioma materno, asi lo prefiero también, pero prim-
eramente, me gustaria explicare un poco de mis deseos en este pais—*[122]

RENE: Look, if you want to speak English here, I'm not going to stop you. Spanish sounds
kinda uppity coming from you, anyway.

LYDIA: Uppit—uppit . . . ? 515

RENE: It means gimme the damn coffee. [*He takes it and sips as she watches him.*]

LYDIA: You don't like?

RENE: Not bad.

LYDIA: You don't go to school?

RENE: I'm done with that shit. You know, the more I look at you, the better this coffee 520
tastes.

LYDIA: I'm glad.

RENE: What do you think of us? You find us disgusting? I know how much you Mexicans
hold us in contempt.

LYDIA: Contempt . . . 525

RENE: You hate us. You hate us for coming here, for deserting the homeland for a chunk
of that goddamn American dream, whatever the fuck that is. We're you watered-
down and a little more well-off. So, do you like what you see?

LYDIA: I always like what I see.

RENE: So you think you're going to hold out long? 530

LYDIA: In this job or this country?

RENE: Both.

LYDIA: I hope yes.

RENE: I hope so too. You're easy on the eyes and hard somewhere else.

LYDIA: Your mama said you were trouble. 535

RENE: Better keep your door locked at night.

LYDIA: But I don't think you're trouble.

RENE: Righteous.

LYDIA: Is your coffee good now?

RENE: Best I ever tasted. 540

> [*He finishes it up and throws the empty cup into the kitchen. He goes back to his
> room.*]

LYDIA: *Mano* . . . what happen to the men in this house?[123]

CECI: Ghgngg, gghn. Ggn . . . teeee.

---

[122] *Bueno . . . en este pais*—"Alright, if you want me to speak in my mother tongue, I prefer that too, but first, I'd
like to explain to you a little about what I want in this country—"
[123] *Mano*—A shortening of *Hermano,* meaning "Brother," used in slang as English speakers might use "Oh,
Brother!"

[LYDIA *goes to her. She touches her scar.*]

LYDIA: *De acuerdo.*[124] [*She touches* CECI's *scar with tenderness.*] Love is a big hurt. Even for fathers and brothers.

[CECI *touches her chest.* LYDIA *is caught in a pang she hadn't acknowledged before.*]

Have we met before, *muñeca?*[125]   545

[LYDIA *goes. Lights change around* CECI.]

CECI: Maybe. Maybe we fell in each other's wounds one night. Into each other's mirrors. Crossed paths in our *vuelos,*[126] said wassup with you, and then took a nap in the afterlife. Spooning in the afterlife, you and me. Or maybe we just wish we were sisters.

[*The TV audio plays a mélange of everything that was on during the early '70s: news, variety shows, sitcoms, etc.* CLAUDIO, ROSA, RENE, *and* MISHA *slowly enter with their TV trays of food and sit to watch TV.* CLAUDIO *has his headphones on.* CECI *lies on her mattress.*]

RENE: This *pollo* ain't bad.

ROSA: It's good.   550

MISHA: Real good.

RENE: Come to think of it, we're all eating a little better lately.

ROSA: *Que,* you don't like my cooking, *sinverguenza?*[127]

MISHA: Mom, she makes chicken *mole* from scratch. She uses spices and stuff we don't even know how to pronounce. She's got recipes the Aztecs used on the damn pyramids.   555

ROSA: *Entonces* I won't cook for you no more. *Ingratos.*[128]

RENE: Hey, a-hole, speaking of Aztecs, where's my Abraxas album?

MISHA: Oh. I was gonna ask you. I borrowed it for inspiration. I'm writing some poems for English based on the songs from Santana's album.

RENE: *¡No mames, guey!* You took my album to school?   560

MISHA: What's wrong with that?

RENE: *Baboso.*[129] I had something special in the sleeve of that album.

MISHA: What?

RENE: Something very, very, imported.

ROSA: *¿De que estas hablando, mijo?*[130]   565

RENE: Just some special papers, Mom. I appreciate your interest in poetry and art, bro, but you get that effin' album back. And stay out of my effin' room, while you're at it.

MISHA: It's my effin' room too.

RENE: Then stay out of my TOP half of it.

MISHA: Okay, then anything that falls out of the top half of your room is MINE.   570

RENE: And anything I step on in the bottom half is BROKE.

---

[124] *De acuerdo*–"Agreed"
[125] *muñeca*–"doll"
[126] *vuelos*–"flights"
[127] *sinverguenza*–"shameless"
[128] *Entonces . . . Ingratos*–"then . . . Ingrates"
[129] *Baboso*–literally, "slobbery" but in this context a vulgar epithet for imbecile such as "dumbass"
[130] *¿De que estas hablando, mijo?*–"What are you talking about, son?"

ROSA: *¡YA! Ay,* Praise God, sometimes I wish I had my own headphones too.
RENE: *Oye. Mira.* The *jefe* hasn't touched his supper.[131]
MISHA: Maybe it's too spicy.
ROSA: *Oye, Viejo. ¿No tienes hambre?*[132]   575

> [CLAUDIO *looks at her. He takes off the headphones.*]

CLAUDIO: *No. Tengo que ir temprano esta noche.*[133] [*He shrugs and goes.*]
ROSA: That's four nights in a row he's going to work early.
MISHA: I think the maid makes him nervous.
ROSA: So what do you think of her?
RENE: Besides her cooking and her perky little breasts?   580
ROSA: Which reminds me. I don't like the way you're looking at her. *Portate bien.*[134]
    Misha? What do you think of her?
MISHA: She does all right with Ceci. She likes her, too.
ROSA: She does, doesn't she?
CECI: Gggghhhn. Ggnhnn.   585
ROSA: Lydia!

> [LYDIA *enters from down the hall. She notices* CLAUDIO *has not eaten his food.*]

LYDIA: *Señora.*
ROSA: Ceci needs her diaper changed.
LYDIA: *Sí, señora.* [*She goes to* CECI *and slowly brings her to her feet.*]
ROSA: So what are these *poemas* you're writing, *mijo*?   590
MISHA: Ah, they're nothing special. Just some verses.
RENE: What about, bro? Oppression and *la raza unida* and our Indian roots?[135]
MISHA: No, not like that. My first one's called Ode to a *Chanate.*
ROSA: A grackle? You wrote a poem about those nasty black birds who mess on my car
    every morning??   595

> [LYDIA *goes off with* CECI]

MISHA: They're beautiful. They got these oil-slick wings and yellow eyes and their song is
    so complex.

> [*There is a light knock on the door.*]

ROSA: *¡Chale!*[136] More like a squeaky garage door, *mijo*! Don't write no poems about them
    chanates!

> [ROSA *opens the door and* ALVARO *comes in, dressed in a large overcoat.*]

ALVARO: *Tia!*   600
ROSA: Oh my god! Alvaro!
ALVARO: I know, huh? I hope I'm not bothering you at this hour.

---

[131] *Oye. Mira. . . . jefe*–"Hey. Look. The boss hasn't touched his supper"
[132] *Oye, Viejo. ¿No tienes hambre?*–"Hey, old man. Aren't you hungry?"
[133] *No. Tengo que ir temprano esta noche.*–"No. I have to go early tonight."
[134] *Portate bien*–"Behave well" or simply "behave"
[135] *la raza unida*–"the united race" referring to the United Pro-Latino Movement consisting of Chicano advocates
[136] *¡Chale!*–slang term meaning roughly, "enough" or "you must be joking," depending on context

ROSA: No, no, we just finished eating. Come on, you, say hello to your cousin!

MISHA: Hey Varo. What's up?

ALVARO: You're growing tall, kid.   605

MISHA: About effin' time, dude.

ALVARO: I know. It's just, *sabes*,[137] I've been a little busy.

MISHA: Little busy being a damn hero! I saw your picture in the paper!

ALVARO: *Ay*, that was nothin'. Hey Rene.

ROSA: Varo, we're so proud of you! [*kisses him*] *Que lindo te ves!*[138] Take off your coat, make   610
yourself at home! *¡Andale!*

ALVARO: Thank you, *Tia*.

[ALVARO *takes off his coat and reveals his Border Patrol uniform underneath.*]

MISHA: *¡Vato!* You joined the Border Patrol?

ROSA: *¡Ay, dios mio, que barbaridad!*[139]

ALVARO: I thought you should be the first to know, being family and all. I signed up about   615
a month ago and they fast-tracked me right into service. What do you think?

ROSA: I don't know what to say, *sobrino!*[140]

MISHA: Are you nuts? You can't join *la Migra!*[141]

ALVARO: Relax, cuz, I had to do it. Money, *sabes*. It was this or temp work at Manpower.

MISHA: It still doesn't make sense, Varo. You're better than this, *ese*.   620

ALVARO: You guys don't know what I been through. I learned some deep lessons
in-country about—

[LYDIA *enters.*]

LYDIA: *Cielos . . .*[142]

ROSA: Lydia! *¡Ven, ven!* Lydia's taking care of Ceci.

ALVARO: Oh, *mucho gusto*.[143]   625

ROSA: She has her papers and everything. We made sure of that.

ALVARO: *Placer*.[144]

LYDIA: You're the cousin. She told me about you.

ROSA: What? Oh, *Ceci* can't talk, silly! Alvaro, want to sit down and eat? Here, have this.

LYDIA: That's Don Claudio's.   630

ROSA: *No te apures*. He'll have a cheeseburger at work. *¡Andale, provecho!*[145]

ALVARO: It sure looks good, *Tia*.

ROSA: Just don't mess your uniform. It's so starched and clean, praise God! [*to* LYDIA] Go
bring her. . . .

[ALVARO *digs into* CLAUDIO's *plate with relish as* LYDIA *goes.*]

---

[137] *sabes*–"you know"

[138] *¡Que lindo te ves!*–"How handsome you look!"

[139] *¡Ay, dios mio, que barbaridad!*–"Oh, my lord, what a shock!"

[140] *sobrino*–"nephew"

[141] *la Migra*–"the immigration police"

[142] *Cielos . . .*–"Wow . . ."

[143] *mucho gusto*–"nice to meet you"

[144] *Placer*–"a pleasure"

[145] *No te apures. . . . ¡Andale, provecho!*–"Don't worry about it. . . . Go on, enjoy!"

RENE: Lessons like what? 635

ALVARO: Lessons about what matters. Lessons about the sacrifices our mothers and fathers made for us. We fight for that every day, *primo*.[146] Every day we protect the blessings of this life.

MISHA: And that's why you took the job?

ALVARO: We got our own DMZ right here. 640

MISHA: You mean the border?

ALVARO: As soon as I get back, what happens? Some *mojado* steals my mother's car.[147] I look at the neighborhood kids and they're all *marijuanos* now.[148] Everywhere I turn, there's some out-of-work alien taking up space. It doesn't matter what all I've done over there, I still have to wait in line for a job with these illegals. 645

MISHA: Dude, our dad was an illegal alien.

ALVARO: But he got his papers. He became a naturalized citizen using the proper channels, didn't he, *Tia*?

ROSA: Oh yes. Yes. *Claro que si.*[149]

MISHA: So you don't have any second thoughts about doing this to *raza*? 650

ALVARO: Who would you rather, the *gringos*? We take care of our own *mierda*,[150] excuse the language, *señora*.

RENE: Is that really why you came, Varo? To show us your new uniform?

ALVARO: There was a time, cuz, when I thought I knew who I was, and what I wanted, but I just needed to grow up. 655

RENE: Grow up?

ALVARO: I mean wake up to the real-real. Remember when we used to play like ants in this room? That was a child's dream, Rene. We think the dream carries us all the way, but I got different expectations now.

RENE: What do you expect? 660

ALVARO: To come back and start my life right. This war was the best thing that happened to me. It pulled me out of the dream.

RENE: It was more than a dream to some people.

ALVARO: Then some people better wake up.

CLAUDIO: [*calling from off*] *¡Rosa! ¡Papel del baño!*[151] 665

ROSA: *¡Ay! ¡Este señor! ¡Que verguenza! ¡Espera!* . . .[152] [ROSA *gets a roll of toilet paper from the cabinets and goes off.*]

ALVARO: How you doing, little cuz?

MISHA: Not sure. It's hard to see that uniform in this house. But at the same time, you're family. 670

ALVARO: That's right.

RENE: Not one letter. Not one damn letter.

---

[146] *primo*–"cousin"
[147] *mojado*–"wetback"
[148] *marijuanos*–"pot-heads"
[149] *Claro que si*–"of course"
[150] *mierda*–"shit"
[151] *¡Papel del baño!*–"Toilet paper!"
[152] *¡Ay! ¡Este señor! ¡Que verguenza! ¡Espera!*–"Oh! This man! How embarrassing! Wait!"

ALVARO: I was short on stamps.

[MISHA *senses something between them.*]

MISHA: I'm gonna help . . . uh . . . I'm gonna . . .

[*He takes the plates from the trays and goes into the kitchen.*]

ALVARO: *Pos,* you're lookin' good. I heard you been in some fights.   675
RENE: What the hell do you think you're doing here?
ALVARO: What do you think? I came to see Ceci.
RENE: Bullshit.
ALVARO: Is that bed for her? Is that where she's sleeping now?
RENE: You got some nerve. In that uniform, too.   680
ALVARO: Never in my dreams did I see myself in this. But it suits me, Rene. It really does.
     I'm gonna be good at this.
RENE: I bet you will.
ALVARO: How is she?
RENE: Now you ask. Now it occurs to you.   685
ALVARO: Look, man, what do you want from me? I'm here.
RENE: I wanna know where we stand.
ALVARO: We stand by family, Rene. We stand by Ceci.
RENE: Why didn't you come sooner?
ALVARO: I couldn't.   690
RENE: But why? I'm talking to you!
ALVARO: 'Cause when I come near you, everything gets so confused. Things happen way
     too fast for me. You move at this crazy speed 'cause you're a blaze, *ese,* you don't give
     a shit. But I can't be selfish now. Look what happened.
RENE: She loved you, *ese.* She believed in you.   695
ALVARO: That's the problem. Everyone fucking believes in me.
RENE: Is that why you ran? Is that why you didn't even stay long enough to see how
     she was?
ALVARO: You eat shit. Don't forget where I been for the last two years. What I went
     through trumps anything you throw in my face. I've moved on. So don't lay your   700
     guilt at my feet.
RENE: She was crazy for you—
ALVARO:—Yeah?—
RENE: She waited years for some word from you. A card. Anything.
ALVARO: How do you know? How the fuck do you know? If she can't talk, how do you   705
     know she missed me?
RENE: 'Cause I stayed, fucker! I stayed and took the heat for you!
ALVARO: Poor cuz. Still picking glass off your face. . . .

[ALVARO *touches* RENE'*s lip.* MISHA *enters and* RENE *moves away.*]

MISHA: What's going on.
ALVARO: *Nada,* Meesh.   710

[ROSA *enters with a photo album.*]

ROSA: *Oye, sobrino. Mira.*[153] She made a scrapbook of you. She glued all your pictures on

---

[153] *Oye, sobrino, Mira.*—"Hey, nephew. Look."

it, Polaroids of you and her. See, your ribbons from track and wrestling.

ALVARO: Wow. I never realized.

ROSA: And the newspaper articles. When you were Homecoming King. And Student Council *y todo*. And look all your notes to her. And the songs she copied from the   715
Hit Parade.

ALVARO: All of this for me.

ROSA: She has a big crush on you, *sobrino*. She woulda been so proud of your service.

MISHA: Mom, she ain't dead.

[CLAUDIO *enters dressed in his whites. He sizes* ALVARO *up with a scowl.*]

ALVARO: *Buenas, Tio.*[154]   720

CLAUDIO: *Sobrino. ¿Y tu Abuela Doña Yolie?*[155]

ALVARO: *Bien, gracias. Tio*, I'm in the *Migración.*[156]

CLAUDIO: Good. Keep them all out. [*He grabs his coat and walks out past them.*]

ROSA: Well. That was easy.

ALVARO: *Pues*, I better get going too.   725

ROSA: But you haven't seen Cecilia!—

ALVARO: Another day, *Tia*. I go on duty in fifteen minutes. I'm on the levee just up the road. Look, if you guys decide to hate me for this, I'll understand.

ROSA: [*kissing him on the cheek*] I'm going to pray for you. I'm going to ask Jesus to make these *mojaditos* lay their souls before your badge and give up without a struggle so   730
no one gets hurt.

ALVARO: *Gracias, Tia Rosa.*

CECI: Ggghfnaaaalgg.

[MISHA *is the first to see* LYDIA *ushering* CECI *into the room in her quinceañera dress and shoes and her hair pinned up. Everyone is stunned.*]

MISHA: Oh my god.

ALVARO: Ceci.   735

RENE: What do you think you're doing?

LYDIA: She wanted to wear this. She said Alvaro would have the first dance. In her *quinceañera*. First her dad, then you. Because you know her better than anyone.

ALVARO: Jesus.

ROSA: Lydia, *por favor*—   740

LYDIA: *A bailar, caballero.*[157]

[ALVARO *goes to* CECI *and takes her hands. He carefully lifts her up and dances gently around the room with her. Everyone watches except* RENE *who looks away. "Sabor a Mi"*[158] *plays in* CECI'*s mind.*]

CECI: Lydia, in your world the things that never happen always happen. With him. All my urges saved for him. Catching moonlight on the folds of my gown. A big corsage aflame on my heart. My pearl earrings on, dancing super-slow with Varo in the

---

[154] *Buenas, Tio*–"Evening, Uncle"

[155] *Sobrino. ¿Y tu Abuela Doña Yolie?*–"Nephew. And your Grandmother, Mrs. Yolie?"

[156] *Bien, gracias. Tio . . . Migración*–"Fine, thank you. Uncle . . . immigration"

[157] *A bailar, caballero*–"Dance, gentleman"

[158] *"Sabor a Mi"*–A romantic ballad usually translated as "A Taste of Me" (referring to the retaining a trace of a beloved's essence long after the beloved has left)

middle of the *salón* to *Sabor a Mi*, body to body, cheek to cheek, his breath in my   745
ear saying over and over—

ALVARO: Ceci . . . Ceci . . . Ceci—

[*She grasps* ALVARO *around the neck as if to hold him forever.*]

RENE: Ceci, let him go.
MISHA: Leave them alone.
LYDIA: Let her dance.   750
RENE: Ceci! I mean it!

[*A small wet spot gathers around* CECI *as she pees herself.*]

CECI: Gghgngg.
ROSA: *¡Ay dios mio! ¡Que desastre! ¡Mira nomas!*[159] She's doing number one!
ALVARO: Ceci . . . please . . . my uniform . . .
RENE: CECI, GODDAMMIT STUPID BITCH!   755
ROSA: RENE! NO!!

[RENE *tears her away from* ALVARO *and she collapses in a heap crying aloud.*]

MISHA: See what you done? Look at her! Are you happy? Is this what you wanted? You
asshole!

[LYDIA *rushes to* CECI]

ALVARO: I have to go.
ROSA: *¡Perdon, sobrino!*[160] We're so sorry about this! I wish you didn't—   760
ALVARO: No, I'm sorry! Thank you for the good food. I have to go!

[ALVARO *rushes out.* MISHA *and* LYDIA *console* CECI *as she cries.*]

MISHA: It's okay, sis. It's over now. [*to* RENE] You didn't have to be so rough with her.
RENE: I didn't put her in that dress.
MISHA: Still, you didn't have to push her away like that, fuckhead! What's your problem!
RENE: My problem is this maid doesn't realize what that fucking dress means in this house!   765
LYDIA: But she does.
RENE: Who asked you to talk?
LYDIA: She knows everyone's pain. All the time. Even yours.
RENE: Did she really ask you to put her in this dress?
LYDIA: How else would I know where to look?   770
ROSA: She told you?
RENE: Did she also tell you how she got her head stitched up like a baseball? Did she say
who did that to her?
LYDIA: Not everything she says comes out her mouth.
RENE: What's that supposed to mean? What are these riddles? Who the fuck are you?   775
ROSA: *¡No hables asi, Rene!*[161]

---

[159] *¡Ay dios mio! ¡Que desastre! ¡Mira nomas!*–"Oh my God! What a disaster! Just look!"
[160] *¡Perdon, sobrino!*–"Sorry, nephew"
[161] *¡No hables asi, Rene!*–"Don't talk like that, Rene!"

RENE: No! Explain to me! How do you know what she wants? As far as we can tell, the best she can do is nod when she needs to take a shit!

LYDIA: She loves you, Rene. She thinks you should be what you are, and not be sorry for it.

RENE: What?? 780

[*The sound of a car pulling up.*]

MISHA: Dad.

ROSA: [*eyes landing on his wallet*] *¡Dios mio!* He's coming back. Take her to the bathroom! Get the dress off *de volada!*[162]

LYDIA: Why?

RENE: You screwed yourself this time, maid. 785

MISHA: He's coming!

ROSA: *¡Andale!* [*seeing his wallet*] *¡Ay, la cartera!* His wallet!

[CLAUDIO *enters. He takes his wallet. He sees* CECI *in her dress.*]

CLAUDIO: *¿Quien hiso esto?*[163]

ROSA: *Mira,* Claudio, it's not a big—

CLAUDIO: *¿Quien le puso esta chingadera a mija?*[164] 790

CECI: Ggghgh.

CLAUDIO: *¿QUE QUIEN LO HISO?*[165]

[MISHA *steps forward.*]

MISHA: Me. I did it.

[CLAUDIO *looks at* CECI *and shakes his head.*]

I just thought it was time, Dad. She looks so . . . divine. *¿No se te parece divina, Apa?*[166]

[CLAUDIO *charges with flying fists at* MISHA *who collapses under the thrust.*]

CLAUDIO: *¡Cabron! ¡Te voy a matar, maldito!*[167] 795

ROSA: *¡Ay, Viejo! NO! NO!*

[*He pommels* MISHA. LYDIA *screams as* ROSA *tries to intercede.* RENE *turns his back to them.*]

ROSA: *¡Dejalo! ¡No le peges!*[168]

[CLAUDIO *blindly socks* ROSA *as he throws* MISHA *down the hall and follows him out, taking off his belt. The door slams. Everyone hears the lashes and* MISHA*'s cries in the house.*]

ROSA: *Ya no le peges, Viejo,* please *Diosito Santo,*[169] make him stop, please not Misha, ayyy . . . ayyy . . .

---

[162] *de volada!*–"quickly!"

[163] *¿Quien hiso [hizo] esto?*–"Who did this?"

[164] *¿Quien le puso esta chingadera a mija?*–"Who put this damn thing on my daughter?"

[165] *¿QUE QUIEN LO HISO [HIZO]?*–"I asked who did this?"

[166] *¿No se te parece divina, Apa?*–"Doesn't she look divine to you, Dad?"

[167] *¡Cabron! ¡Te voy a matar, maldito!*–"Little shit! I'm going to kill you, you damned shit!"

[168] *¡Dejalo! ¡No le peges!*–"Leave him alone! Don't hit him!"

[169] *Ya no le peges, Viejo . . . Diosito Santo*–"Don't hit him anymore, old man . . . Holy Lord . . ."

[LYDIA *glares at* RENE, *who watches helplessly then runs out of the house. The lashes continue as the lights change.*]

CECI: New card. *La Mierda.* The Shit. This thing lashing me, this burning need to hurt, 800
  carnal mayor, you tore me away from him, my bronze star, how come! How come!
  And what's this thing that blackens my *corazón* when it's Varo my body craves?

[ROSA *enters, a shiner developing on her eye. She puts on her coat and gets her keys.*]

LYDIA: Are you sure you should be going, *señora*?
ROSA: I have to go look for him. Rene is very sensitive. He acts tough, but inside he's scared.
LYDIA: Of what? 805
ROSA: His father. Himself. Everything. He won't even drive a car since Ceci's accident.
  Lord, take care of my boy!
LYDIA: Where are you going to look?
ROSA: I'll drive around till I see him. He can't be far. Misha's sleeping now. He just needs
  some rest. 810
LYDIA: We should take him to the hospital.
ROSA: No, no, they ask too many questions. He'll be okay in the morning.
LYDIA: *Lo dudo, Señora. Se me parece muy malo.*[170] And your eye too.
ROSA: Please, Lydia. It's happened before. He'll be all right. Stay here with Ceci.

[ROSA *goes.* LYDIA *sits by the sofa and places her hand on her chest.*]

CECI: In your world, Lydia, people die and come back but not all the way. Not all the way. 815

[MISHA *comes back into the living room. Swollen and blue with pounding. A cut
  above his eye.*]

MISHA: Mom? Mom?

[CECI *sees him and whines in alarm for him.*]

CECI: Eeeeeey. Eeeeey.
MISHA: Shh. It's okay, girl. I'm all right. See? Just a little puffy.
LYDIA: You should be lying down. Go lie down.
MISHA: Where's Mom? Is she okay? 820
LYDIA: She's looking for Rene. Sit. I'll get some more ice.

[MISHA *sits while* LYDIA *goes to the kitchen.*]

MISHA: You know what, Ceci? He's getting old. He can't keep pace anymore. Still, when
  he's mad, he can land some real-life hurt.

[LYDIA *returns with some ice in a dishcloth.*]

LYDIA: He was an animal. Only an animal does this.
MISHA: Didn't you earn your whippings growing up? 825
LYDIA: *Nunca.*[171]
MISHA: In this town, it's a rite of passage.
LYDIA: Why did you do that? Why did you take blame for the *vestido*?[172]

---

[170] *Lo dudo, Señora. Se me parece muy malo*—"I doubt it, ma'am. It looks very bad to me."
[171] *Nunca*—"never"
[172] *vestido*—"dress"

MISHA: I wasn't gonna let him work you over.

LYDIA: He would not. 830

MISHA: You don't know my dad.

LYDIA: You don't know me.

MISHA: Besides, you made her beautiful. I didn't believe she could be like that and still look so beautiful.

LYDIA: She is. 835

MISHA: You can't leave now. Ceci needs you. [LYDIA *pops him with the ice on his face.*] Ow.

LYDIA: Sorry.

MISHA: So what do *you* do for kicks in your hometown?

LYDIA: Town? More like *campo santo*.[173] Barren fields and empty houses. A lot of people gone to *El Norte*. We go to school. In the afternoons, we help our *mamas* with the 840 chores. I'm an orphan so mostly I took care of my *abuela*.

MISHA: Did you have a . . . a *novio?*[174]

LYDIA: Once. But he was too possessive. Then my grandmother died. I needed something to do.

MISHA: What do you want to do? 845

LYDIA: Learn English. Work in a hospital. I could be a good nurse.

MISHA: Yeah, but you need skills for that. Owww! My back's on fire.

LYDIA: Take off your shirt. [*He gives her a look.*] *¡Ay, por favor!* Let me see your back!

[*He takes off his shirt. His back is covered with raised welts, some of them bleeding.*]

LYDIA: *O Señor.* Wait here.

[*She runs down the hall to her room.*]

CECI: Ggghgngn. 850

MISHA: Hey, it's only fair. I saw *you* topless.

CECI: Ggnn. Llglnh.

MISHA: You loved him, didn't you?

CECI: What sucks is that I still do. His thorns are all around my heart.

[LYDIA *returns with a small vial and a lit candle.*]

LYDIA: *Aver.* 855

MISHA: What's that?

LYDIA: I have skills. I learned them from my grandmother.

MISHA: Ahh. What is that stuff?

LYDIA: It's some liniment made from the *agave*. We use it to heal open wounds.

MISHA: Well, it's not working. 860

LYDIA: Of course not. You need to seal it with this.

[*She drips hot wax on his back.*]

MISHA: OOOWW! OWWW! What are you doing to me! That burns!

LYDIA: You'll start to feel better now.

---

[173] *campo santo*—"holy field" perhaps "grave yard"
[174] *novio*—"boyfriend"

MISHA: What is this, some kinda witchcraft?

LYDIA: *Mi abuela* was a *curandera*.[175] I learned the science of herbs growing up with her in   865
her *botica*.

MISHA: Well, your science burns like shit.

LYDIA: Get your mind off it. Tell me this poem of the grackle.

MISHA: What?

LYDIA: You said you had a poem. How does it go?   870

MISHA: Well . . .

LYDIA: You don't know it from memory?

MISHA: I do.

LYDIA: *¿Entonces?* Don't be shy. What's it called?

MISHA: Ode to a *Chanate*. Ode means—   875

LYDIA: *Oda*, I know. *Dale.*[176]

MISHA: O bird
    You black bird
    You look like you flew through the darkest night and it stuck on you,
    Except you closed your eyes and they stayed yellow   880
    As the wasps that dance around the lawn.
    I see you sitting on the wire
    Making that song, that grackle, crackle, wheeze, and chirp
    That makes me wonder if you're trying to learn
    the language of manual transmissions   885
    Or maybe you're trying to say something in our broken tongue.
    O bird dressed in mourning but always so lively,
    Like death is just another occasion to find a she-grackle,
    You remind me of things I should be doing,
    Flights I should be taking, night I should be soaking my wings in.   890
    Except with eyes opened 'cause mine are already black.
  Well?

LYDIA: The transmission part. I didn't get that.

MISHA: It's a draft. I'm still working on it. Hey, I don't feel it anymore.

LYDIA: Put your shirt on. Your poem is good. But to know words, you have to know   895
people. Not grackles.

[ROSA *enters and finds* MISHA *without his shirt on.*]

ROSA: *¿Que es esto?*[177]

MISHA: I was . . . I'm tired. I have to go to bed. [*He goes.*]

LYDIA: *Señora*—

ROSA: I found him.   900

[RENE *enters, morose and withdrawn. He looks like a child.*]

---

[175] *Mi abuela . . . curandera*–"My grandmother was a healer"/A "curendera" is a Mexican woman skilled in healing techniques, both spiritual and physical, using botanicals. This healing tradition seems to have been passed
on from the Mayans.
[176] *Dale*–Literally, "give it"
[177] *¿Que es esto?*–"What is this?"

LYDIA: Rene?

ROSA: Don't talk to him. Go to bed, *mijo*.

[ROSA *kisses him and he starts to go, eyes to the floor. He stops and falls before* CECI.]

RENE: Sorrysorrysorrysorrysorrysorrysorrysorryi'msorryi'msorrycecii'msorry.

[*He gets up and goes down the hall to his room.*]

ROSA: You too. Go sleep. I'm tired. I have to work tomorrow. [*feeling her puffy eye*] How will I explain this?   905

LYDIA: She wanted to wear the dress. She told me so.

ROSA: I understand. But leave the miracles to God.

[LYDIA *goes.* ROSA *casts a glance toward* CECI.]

You know where I found him, don't you?

[ROSA *goes.*]

CECI: Where hearts and Pontiacs break. It's all love, *Ama*. All a desperate *abrazo*.[178] All of us holding tight to each other so we don't fall so hard. So we can open our eyes again   910 and see the new sun dripping in through the blinds.

[*The following dawn.* CLAUDIO *comes in. His whites stained with grease and ketchup. He finds* CECI *sleeping, still wearing the dress.*]

CLAUDIO: *Mi pajarita. Como te quiero.*[179] 'Cause of you I given up.

[LYDIA *enters in her clothes with her bag.*]

LYDIA: *Ya me voy.*[180]

CLAUDIO: *¿A donde?*[181]

LYDIA: *¿Que te importa?*[182] You beat him very badly. Your own son.   915

CLAUDIO: *¡Pero mira como la vistio!*[183]

LYDIA: It was me, stupid. I dressed her in it. You going to beat me too?

CLAUDIO: *Espera.* [*She stops.* CLAUDIO *struggles to frame his words.*] *Era mi pajarita . . .*[184]

LYDIA: In English. You want me to listen, tell me in English.

CLAUDIO: Cecilia . . . my bird. Why you put the dress?   920

LYDIA: It's her dress. She wanted to look nice for . . . for you.

CLAUDIO: It's good you go back. The country rob your soul.

LYDIA: *Hombre*, you have a life here.

CLAUDIO: I had a life *aya*! *Pero* the way you want things and way things go: different. Rosa want her babies *que sean Americanos*.[185] So here I am, not one, not the other, but a,   925 *como se dice*, a stone. A stone for them to make their own great *pinche* dreams.

CECI: Ggngnnh.

---

[178] *abrazo*–"hug"

[179] *Mi pajarita. Como te quiero.*–"My little bird. How I love you."

[180] *Ya me voy*–"I'm leaving now"

[181] *¿A donde?*–"Where to?"

[182] *¿Que te importa?*–"What do you care?"

[183] *¡Pero mira como la vistio!*–"But look how he dressed her!"

[184] *Era mi pajarita*–"She was my little bird . . ."

[185] *que sean Americanos*–"to be Americans"

LYDIA: Except Cecilia.

CLAUDIO: You want to know *que paso*,[186] for real?

LYDIA: No. 930

CECI: Yes.

CLAUDIO: Three days till la *quinceañera*. Three days. Dinner set, salon reserve, the *comadres* all prepare.[187] But *en medio de la noche*,[188] everyone's sleeping and me at work, Ceci *y* Rene out the window, and nobody hears *nada*. Why?

CECI: 'Cause this is the night: the night of secrets: of dark streets and Pontiacs and fires in 935 my body.

CLAUDIO: Why push it the car in neutral down the street and then start it up? Why?

CECI: 'Cause a fierce voice in our hearts is hissing *Vamonos!*

CLAUDIO: *Con las alas del diablo* they tear down to the border *en el* West Side![189] Why!

CECI: There is no why! Fuck all the whys! Only me and Rene and the roar of the car! 940

CLAUDIO: Three nights till the *quinceañera y se van*, they go somewhere too fast, *los pendejos*—[190]

CECI: To Alvaro! Alvaro my love! I'm coming!

CLAUDIO: Too fast down *ese* dirt road by the Border fence, and the tires are bald *en ese* Pontiac, you can't drive too fast in that car! Then something happen— 945

CECI: This ugliness. This hot ugly bile inside rolling up my throat!

CLAUDIO: Rene's good, he drive good. But something make him miss the big curve, you have to slow down to turn, but Rene, he don't slow, he don't turn and—!

CECI: NO!

CLAUDIO: The car hit a pole *y ya*. 950

CECI: *El Pontiac* wrapped around a pole like a lover and me flying in a sky full of confetti glass.

CLAUDIO: *Mi* Cecilia, who is born on a full moon and dance the twist for me at six, who always understand me no matter what demon possess me, Cecilia Rosario Flores, her name on the cake of her fifteen year, fly through the windshield of the car into the 955 cold hard ground fifty feet *en frente*.

CECI: I see little bits of brain and blood on the road, and you trying to scoop up all the memories, my first words, my first dreams, you try to scoop them up in your hands, *Apa*.

LYDIA: And Rene. 960

CLAUDIO: *Nada*. I ask him why. I ask him where the *chingados* they go. A million whys I ask him. He sit in the dirt and cry. He never answer, never.

LYDIA: You still blame him, don't you?

CLAUDIO: Blame is not the word. I wish you peace of mind wherever you go.

[*He puts on his headphones and stares at the blank TV.*]

LYDIA: Peace of mind. What is that? 965

[*About to leave,* LYDIA *catches* CECI's *gaze. A kind of plea in her look.*]

---

[186] *que paso*–"what happened"
[187] *comadres*–literally, "godmothers"; perhaps "godparents" in this context
[188] *en medio de la noche*–"in the middle of the night"
[189] *Con las alas del diablo*–"With the wings of the Devil"
[190] *los pendejos*–"stupid, useless people" or, colloquially, "dumbasses"

CECI: I had a dream the night before you came. That you stand at the door and stop breathing. And a part of you falls away. . . .

> [LYDIA *sets her bag down and peels off her underwear. She approaches* CLAUDIO *who stares straight at the TV.*]

That you come like a ghost into our house and stand over my daddy, who's a ghost himself, and you take his crown and hear the voices in his heart crying for love. . . .

> [LYDIA *takes off his headphones. She places them over her head and listens for a moment.*]

And then you blind him. . . .   970

> [LYDIA *turns off the TV. He remains still with his eyes fixed ahead.*]

And land on his lap and take his breath away.

> [LYDIA *straddles him in his chair and kisses him. He enfolds her in his arms and begins to cry.*]

Each breathless *beso*[191] reaches into his heart and lays grout over the crumbling walls of his pride, you touch him who can't remember *touch* any more than I can. It was a dream more real than this maid on my father making sex like the last act of God, I see your eyes, Lydia, dreaming the same thing, burning their grief into me, their   975 want, their reckless need for darkness—[*She turns and meets* LYDIA's *gaze.*] I see— you! With the inscription *La Muerte, La Muerte, La Muerrr . . .*[192]

> [*They continue to make love as* CECI *goes into convulsions.*]

gngghgnghg. gfhghgngng.

> [*Out of the shadows,* RENE *watches them making love as music from the head- phones plays.*]

END OF ACT I

─────────────────────────── ACT II ───────────────────────────

> [*The living room in* CECI's *dream. Bedsheets stretched everywhere over chairs and tables, creating a network of glowing tunnels amid the darkness.* CECI *wearing the quinceañera dress crawls on all fours like a toddler through the tunnels.*]

CECI: Teeteetee. Teeteetee. Teetee means home. Teeteetee. Queen ant Ceci looks for a nest for her *huevitos.*[193] Teeteetee in ant-language means SOON!

> [MISHA's *shawdow appears crawling along a bedsheet.*]

---

[191] *beso*–"kiss"
[192] *La Muerte*–"Death"
[193] *huevitos*–"little eggs"

MISHA: Teeteeteeteeeeeee!

CECI: Teetee! That's Ant for over here, Misha! Teeteetee!

[MISHA *appears with a naked GI Joe in his mouth.*]

MISHA/CECI: Teeteeteeteeteetee!   5

CECI: What's this, worker ant?

MISHA: I bring you food, Queen.

CECI: This is not the stuffed mouse.

CECI: Well, this doll doesn't cut it.

MISHA: It's not a doll!   10

CECI: Ugh. It's got spit all over.

MISHA: Can we play?

CECI: Teeteeteeeee! That means how do you like my egg-laying chamber?

MISHA: Teeteetee means bitchin'. How many eggs?

CECI: I am a shy queen, so I can't tell you. But antenna to antenna you can read my mind.   15

[*They place their fingers on their heads and touch "antennae."*]

CECI/MISHA: Teee-teeeeeee-teeeeee.

[*More shadows appear on the suspended sheets.* RENE *and* ALVARO *crawl through a portal.*]

RENE: Tee-tee-teeee.

ALVARO: Tee-tee-teeee.

ALL: Tee-teee-teeeee.

CECI: Soldier ants! Defenders of the colony! Teetee means welcome!   20

RENE: *Mi reina,*[194] we got great news. We defeated the evil anteater and stripped the flesh from his *huesos.*[195]

ALVARO: And we attacked the boy who stepped on our anthill. We stung him right on the teetees!

CECI: Then let the ant-revels begin.   25

[*They crawl in frantic circles shaking their heads at each other.*]

ALL: TEE-TEE-TEE-TEE-TEE-TEEE!

[MISHA, RENE, *and* ALVARO *slip into the maelstrom of sheets, casting shadows on the walls.*]

CECI: Tee-tee means I love my ants. I love all my little ants crawling through *La Vida Cecilia,* memories of innocence, tee-tee, *ormigas* forever,[196] in ant-language there's no word for die. Teeee.

[*The shadows of* ALVARO *and* RENE *first touch antennae and then kiss, long and gently.*]

I see behind the sheets secret ant-affection in the tunnels of our *corazones,* cousins   30
and *carnales,* finding their hearts in each others' mouths.

---

[194] *Mi reina*—"My queen"
[195] *huesos*—"bones"
[196] *ormigas*—"ants"

[*The shadows vanish and* LYDIA *appears gathering the sheets into her laundry basket.* LYDIA *looks smart in* CECI'*s jeans and blouse.*]

In ant-language, there *is* a word for live and it's Lydia. I saw the love going dark in your eyes and it means we ain't lived enough yet, we ain't died enough yet . . . we ain't . . . Lydhghghg . . .

[*Lights up on the house. It's cleaner.* CECI *is in* CLAUDIO'*s chair, staring at the TV.* ROSA, RENE *and* LYDIA *work at the coffee table on stamp books, with the laundry basket beside* LYDIA. MISHA *sits by* CECI *writing on a legal pad.*]

ROSA: She's quiet. 35

MISHA: Saturdays. Space Ghost and Scooby Doo.

ROSA: *O si. Los monitos.*[197]

LYDIA: Tell me again, *Señora*, how does this work? I don't get it.

ROSA: *Primero*, you get these stamps from the Piggly-Wiggly when you shop and you put them away in the kitchen cabinet till you get a *monton* of them. Then you stick them 40 on these S&H saver books.[198] All of these pages you fill, *yes*? Then when you get enough *libritos* filled,[199] you go to the catalogue and pick out the things you want, go to the S&H store and trade the books for them.

LYDIA: *¿Gratis?*

ROSA: *Free*! 45

RENE: It's al crap, though.

ROSA: Oh *si*, Mr. Smarty-*calzones*? What about that umbrella stand I got last time?

RENE: We don't have any umbrellas.

MISHA: Plus it never rains here.

ROSA: And that casserole dish? That was nice, *verdad*! 50

RENE: You've never made a casserole in your life. You use it for the *chile*.

ROSA: And that little shelf for the family pictures? That cost me 10 books!

RENE: I saw that at the Winn's Five and Dime for three dollars!

ROSA: *¡Ay, si tu!*[200] Quit talking and keep licking!

[CLAUDIO *emerges from his room and walks through on his way to the kitchen, upstage.*]

Did we wake you? We were trying to be quiet. 55

CLAUDIO: I couldn't sleep. *¿Hay café?*

LYDIA: Fresh pot the way you like.

CLAUDIO: [*realizing that* LYDIA *is in* CECI'*s clothes*] *¿Que es eso?*[201]

LYDIA: Oh, some clothes *Señora* gave me.

ROSA: Just some old things *de* Ceci's. She fits into them perfect, *que no*? 60

LYDIA: *¿Le gusta, señor?*[202]

---

[197] *O si. Los monitos*–"Oh, yes, the cartoons"
[198] *monton*–a "stack," "pile," or "heap"
[199] *libritos*–"little books"
[200] *¡Ay, si tu!*–"Oh, yeah, you!"
[201] *¿Que es eso?*–"What's that?"
[202] *¿Le gusta, señor?*–"Do you like it, Sir?"

[*He regards her with a mixture of scorn and misgiving. Then goes into the kitchen.*]

Maybe I should change.

ROSA: No, no, Lydia, he likes it! You look more like us, more American.

MISHA: More like Ceci.

RENE: That must trip the old man out.   65

LYDIA: I have to do the wash now.

ROSA: Misha, come take her place and help us lick the stamps.

MISHA: I'm busy.

ROSA: Busy-*ni-que*-busy! What are you doing!

RENE: Writin' poems, what else.   70

ROSA: Not about those *chanates*, I hope!

RENE: No, he's writing love poems for—

MISHA: Shuttup.

[MISHA *puts his pad aside and goes to the stamp books as* CLAUDIO *calls for* LYDIA, *who glowers at* RENE.]

CLAUDIO: [*in the kitchen*] Lydia!

LYDIA: You're a bad one.   75

RENE: What?

[LYDIA *goes into the kitchen.*]

ROSA: *¿De que hablan?*[203] What's going on here?

MISHA: Nothin', Mom.

ROSA: *Mira*, nothing gets past me. I see everything in this house.

RENE: Right.   80

ROSA: And what I don't see, the Lord does.

RENE: I bet he's enjoying the show. Right, bro?

[*He licks stamps in a lewd way when* MISHA *looks.*]

CECI: I smell it. My dad and Lydia's combustion. Lydia sprayed some Glade, but I catch that whiff of sweat and bygone dreams. Like an invisible *piñata* full of stale candies.

[*In the kitchen,* LYDIA *and* CLAUDIO *hover uneasily over the coffee.*]

CLAUDIO: *¿Que estas pensando con esta—?*[204]   85

LYDIA: English.

CECI: Nobody but me hears what they're saying in the kitchen.

CLAUDIO: Will you come to me again?

CECI: The longing in their voices. . . .

LYDIA: No.   90

CECI: Not for each other, but for other things out of their conception. Things that require light and mindless hurt. . . .

MISHA: What are you redeeming this time, Mom?

---

[203] *¿De que hablan?*–"What are you talking about?"
[204] *¿Que estas pensando con esta—?*–"What are you thinking with this—?"

ROSA: This set of knives, *mira*. These are special Cheff's knives, very high quality, five of
    them, *imaginate*. I always wanted a set.   95
MISHA: It's pronounced Shef, Mom. The French way.
ROSA: *Pues*, when I go to France, *asi lo digo*.[205] Here I say Cheff. How are you feeling?
MISHA: Mom, it's been a week. I'm fine.

                [LYDIA *passes through with the wash.*]

ROSA: He didn't mean to hit you like that, you know. He was expecting me to stop him. I
    just didn't know how. It was my fault.   100
MISHA: It was nobody's fault, okay?

            [CLAUDIO *walks through on his way to the bedroom. Silence.*]

ROSA: [*going through her purse*] Anyways. After work I stopped at Mr. Dickey's Jewelry
    Store and . . . [*She gives him a small case.*]
MISHA: Mom . . . [*He opens it.*]
ROSA: It's a Cross. A gold Cross pen.   105
RENE: *Vato.* Cool.
MISHA: [*taking the gold pen out*] Mom, are you sure about this? These pens are expensive.
ROSA: I'm working, Misha. We're quasi-middle class as of today, which means we live a little
    mas better. Besides, it was on clearance, half off. I always wait for the half-off sales.
MISHA: Thanks, Mom. Feel this, Rene. Feel how heavy it is.   110
RENE: That's heavy.
MISHA: Words. Full of words, *carnal.*
ROSA: Just no bad words, okay? I hate when you write bad words.
MISHA: If I use them, Mom, I promise you won't know what they mean.
ROSA: Misha, you're going to be somebody. Even if you won't have God, God's grace is   115
    on you.

                [*She goes, wiping her eyes.*]

MISHA: What's with her? She's all goofy lately.
RENE: Leave her alone. She's doing her best.
MISHA: Her best to what?
RENE: Dude, you're so damned naïve. You got no idea how fucked up we are.   120
MISHA: I'm not as naïve as you think I am.
RENE: [*grabbing his pad*] Oh yeah? What's this, fuckhead?
MISHA: Don't touch that. Put it down.
RENE: "Black eyes drenched in the waters of the Rio."
MISHA: Give it!   125
RENE: "Black hair like a mantilla draped on me."
MISHA: I told you—
RENE: "Your brown hands rolling over the open plain of my back."
MISHA: Asshole.
RENE: I gotta say, Misha, I never seen you like this. It seems our little housekeeper from   130
    Mexico-way has sparked your plumed serpent to life, *carnal.* [*tossing his pad back*]
    Too bad it's wasted.

---

[205] *asi lo digo*–"I say it like this"

MISHA: What do you know? . . . Has she told you anything?

RENE: *¡No mames!* Seriously, in the interest of family pride and the welfare of my little
brother who truly understands shit about the affairs of the *pinchi* heart, I gotta say   135
this: get over this fucking bitch as quick as you can.

MISHA: What?

RENE: She's a whore, Miguel. You're writing love poems to a low-class Mexican whore.
Come on, *ese*, she's the maid. Don't you know it's a taboo? Haven't you been watching
the *novelas*?   140

MISHA: Fuck you. I'm not listening to this.

RENE: I'm just watching out for you, *ese*.

MISHA: Like you watched me get creamed by Dad last week? Like you came to my
defense then?

RENE: That's different.   145

MISHA: How is that different?

RENE: I wanted to help.

MISHA: Then why didn't you?

RENE: It wasn't possible.

MISHA: What kind of fucked-up answer is that?   150

RENE: It wasn't possible, okay? I got my own ways of getting back at the old man.

MISHA: What good does that do me? Finally you're big enough to take him on. You can
make it stop any time. Either you're a goddamn coward or you want him to kill me.

RENE: I'd drop this if I were you.

MISHA: Listen, do me a favor and go back to beating up defenseless homos like you actually   155
do. We prefer reality here.

RENE: You're out of line, Miguel.

MISHA: C'mon, who are you fooling? It's not *gangas*[206] and Ft. Bliss GIs you've been
jumpin'. Everyone knows it's just the local homos.

RENE: Where do you get this crap?   160

MISHA: Serge told his kid brother and he came and told me. You go to all the same places
they go, the same strips, the same cruising spots, the word's out, man.

RENE: What are you saying?

MISHA: You're a fag-basher, you and your buddies. It's sick, it's pathetic, bro. And it's only
a matter of time before this shit catches up with you.   165

RENE: What shit! Tell me, what shit is catching up with me!

MISHA: Lemme ask you: whose fuckin' ass do you really wanna kick! Ask yourself. Who
do you really wanna hurt!

RENE: *¡No mames, guey!* You don't know Thing One about this.

MISHA: It's been two years, *carnal*. When are you gonna get over it? When are you gonna   170
stop making everyone pay for that crash?

RENE: Keep your maid away from me. If you want her, fine, let her be your damned—

MISHA: Don't say it. Don't say that word to my face.

RENE: Whore.

[LYDIA *comes in with a pair of scissors. They all stand looking at each other.*]

---

[206] *gangas*—"gangs"

CECI: These cartoons, amazin' how they go through so much hell, but nobody ever gets   175
hurt. Just little bronze *estrellitas* over their heads and these magic bandages that vanish in the next frame.[207] That's why they don't have private parts. They'll be safe as long as they don't screw each other blind.

> [RENE *falters under* LYDIA's *stare and stalks off to his room.* MISHA *gathers the saver books and puts them all in a bag.* LYDIA *starts cutting the plastic covers off the lampshades.* ROSA *enters.*]

ROSA: What are you doing?

LYDIA: *Señora*, I saw the pictures in that catalogue. Lampshades like yours.   180

ROSA: Yes?

LYDIA: Except they don't have *plastico* on them. It's just how they were . . . *como se dice* . . .

MISHA: Packaged.

ROSA: But it keeps the dust off them.

MISHA: Mom, she's right. You're supposed to take them off when you put them up.   185

ROSA: But we've had them like this forever.

LYDIA: Well, it's all wrong. That's why the light is so bad in this house.

ROSA: Then why didn't you say something? Why didn't none of you say something?

MISHA: We didn't want to embarrass you.

LYDIA: See? Don't they look *mas* better?   190

ROSA: *Pues* . . .

LYDIA: Now you can see things.

ROSA: Next time, ask me, Lydia.

LYDIA: I thought I—

ROSA: [*snapping at her angrily*] You didn't. Ask me before you start redoing my house!   195

LYDIA: *Mi culpa, Señora.*[208] I didn't mean to be so *presumida.*[209]

> [ROSA *glowers at her for a moment.*]

CECI: Mggn. Nggnh.

MISHA: Look, Mom, Ceci likes it too.

> [ROSA *looks uneasily at* CECI, *then at* LYDIA, *then at the lights in the room.*]

ROSA: *Ay, como soy tonta.*[210] You're right. It does look brighter. [*laughing nervously*] I can be so dumb sometimes! Such a *ranchera!*[211]   200

LYDIA: *Señora Rosa*, don't talk like that. You're good people. You been nicer than my own mother to me. I'm sorry.

ROSA: Thank you, *mija.* . . . [*touches her face*] You know what? Let me take you shopping. *¡Andale, vamanos* shopping!

LYDIA: *¿Que qué?*   205

ROSA: Come with me! I hate going to the stores alone! *Además,*[212] I'm going to need help with the bags.

---

[207] *estrellitas*—"little stars"

[208] *Mi culpa, Señora*—"My fault, ma'am"

[209] *presumida*—"presumptuous" or "arrogant"

[210] *Ay, como soy tonta*—"Oh, how stupid of me"

[211] *ranchera*—"country girl;" the connotation being close to "country bumpkin" in English

[212] *Además*—"Besides"

LYDIA: O *señora*, there's work to do. . . .

ROSA: *Chale*,[213] the work can wait. Besides, you made Ceci happy. *Ven conmigo, mija.*[214] Help me pick out some things for the house. *Pronto*, get your *chaqueta* and let's go.[215]   210

LYDIA: *Señora*, you are too nice! [LYDIA *runs off for her jacket.*]

ROSA: Misha, stay with your sister. We'll be back. [*darkening in a flash*] And next time, you let me know about things like this, *me oyes?*[216]

MISHA: Okay.

ROSA: *Vamos, mija.*   215

> [*She takes her keys and goes out.* LYDIA *enters with her jacket and starts to go out the door, but stops when she sees* MISHA *writing in his pad.*]

LYDIA: Read me *unas de tus* poems,[217] Misha.

MISHA: Uh . . . sure.

LYDIA: Tonight.

> [*She goes.* MISHA *exults.*]

CECI: Ghggng. Ghgng.

MISHA: You hear that, *carnala*? She wants my poems! [*He shuts off the TV and goes to her.*]   220

CECI: Gh. Ghgngn. [*She points to the pen in his pocket.*]

MISHA: Oh! You wanna poem. Okay. Ode to Ceci.

> [*He tries to write a poem in her palm, but he can't.*]

> Sorry, sis. All my poems come out for her. One for the way she laughs. One for the way she irons my pants. *Ayy.* Ten for the hurt that presses on me when she's near.

CECI: Where does it hurt?   225

MISHA: Mainly here. Pumping through my veins one single word. Lydia . . . Lydia . . . Lydia . . . I can't think, I can't sleep, I curl up in bed and cry.

CECI: I hear you.

MISHA: Sis, have you ever felt this? I don't mean puppy crushes or shit like that. I mean, blind dumb love.   230

CECI: Blinder, dumber.

MISHA: Is it legal to want her this much? 'Cause I want her.

CECI: Worker ant, do it.

MISHA: What if she doesn't like me? What if she just doesn't feel the same way I do?

CECI: Then hope to God she tells you, Meesh.   235

MISHA: Shit. You're lucky you don't have to deal with this anymore. Way too much hurt for the risk.

CECI: Lucky? I'm the opposite of lucky. If wanting to love and be loved back is lucky, I'm the opposite of luck, the opposite of possibility and love and Cecilia Rosario Florhhhggghn.   240

MISHA: I take it by your look you're saying I should go for it.

---

[213] *Chale*–a slang term that conveys disagreement or dismissal with something; equivalent to "forget about it"

[214] *Ven conmigo, mija*–"Come with me, honey"

[215] *chaqueta*–"jacket"

[216] *me oyes?*–"You hear me?"

[217] *unas* [*unos*] *de tus* poems–"some of your poems"

CECI: Ggggnh.

[CLAUDIO *enters again from his bedroom, a troubled look on his face.* MISHA *leaps up to take* CECI *off his La-Z-Boy and back to her mattress.*]

CLAUDIO: *¿Donde está Lydia?*[218]
MISHA: Out with Mom.
CLAUDIO: *¿Cuando regresan?*[219]   245
MISHA: No idea.

[*He reaches into the cushions of his chair for his bottle. He takes a swig. He spits it out.*]

CLAUDIO: *¡Que la Chingada Madre! ¡Cabrones!*[220]
MISHA: *¿Que onda, Dad?*[221] What's wrong?
CLAUDIO: *¿Quien puso* Wesson *en mi botella?*[222]
MISHA: What?   250
CLAUDIO: Who put cooking oil *en mi botella*!
MISHA: It wasn't me! I swear!
CLAUDIO: *Hijo de la chingada*—!
MISHA: I swear! I had nothing to do with that, Dad!

[CLAUDIO *raises his fist to strike him and* MISHA *cowers. He sees his son's terror.* MISHA *looks up at him and sees the same fear in his father's eyes.* CLAUDIO *turns away.*]

CLAUDIO: Get up. I know who did this.   255
MISHA: Who.
CLAUDIO: *¿Quien mas?*[223] Rene. I don't lay my hand on him not since before *mija*, and see how he hates me.

[MISHA *disappears into the kitchen.*]

Nadie me escucha.[224] Nobody listen to me. I'm nothing *en esta casa.*[225] I work like a *negro* and still I nothing.   260

[MISHA *returns with a beer and offers it to* CLAUDIO.]

MISHA: It'll wash that greasy taste down.

[CLAUDIO *takes it and sips.*]

Is there anything else I can do?
CLAUDIO: No.
MISHA: Want me to take that for you?

[CLAUDIO *gives him the liquor bottle. Notices the pen in his breast pocket.*]

---

[218] *¿Donde está Lydia?*–"Where is Lydia?"
[219] *¿Cuando regresan?*–"When do they return?"
[220] *¡Que la Chingada Madre! ¡Cabrones!*–"What the fucking hell?! Bastards!"
[221] *¿Que onda, Dad?*–"What's up, Dad?"
[222] *¿Quien puso* Wesson *en mi botella?*–"Who put Wesson [a popular brand of cooking oil] in my bottle?"
[223] *¿Quien mas?*–"Who else?"
[224] *Nadie me escucha*–"Nobody listens to me"
[225] *en esta casa*–"in this house"

CLAUDIO: *¿Y eso, de donde chingaos viene?*[226]   265

MISHA: Mom bought it. Half-price.

> [CLAUDIO *nods. He sits in his chair.* MISHA *clicks on the TV and brings him his headphones.*]

CLAUDIO: *Eres un buen muchacho.*[227] You are a decent boy. *Tu mama,*[228] she raise you well.

> [CLAUDIO *puts on the headphones and stares at the TV.* MISHA *takes the bottle and starts to go back to his room. He stops.*]

MISHA: Dad? . . . *Jefe?*

> [*No response.*]

> For what it's worth, it wasn't just Mom who raised me. It was you, too, asshole. You're half to blame. You're the idiot who knocked her up, right? Your last name is   270
> mine, too, right? Everything about me you resent is half of you too, motherfucker. So take some credit, Dad. I'm your son. I'm your decent well-raised second son. You bred me with fists and belts and shoes and whatever else you could throw at me. You raised me to jump at the sound of your voice and the stamp of your foot. You taught me to cower and shake and cover my ears in bed at so I wouldn't hear Mom   275
> screaming while you slapped her. You taught me shame. I should grow up to be a spiteful little fucker just like you, hating the world for the crap I bring on myself, piling some real hurt on the people who care for me most. Except you know what, I won't. No sir, I won't be you. I don't know what the hell I'm gonna be and God knows I may turn out worse than I think, but I won't be you. Someday, not today,   280
> against my better sense, I'm gonna forgive you. You'll see.

> [*He turns and goes. A pause.* CLAUDIO *stands and goes to his stereo.*]

CLAUDIO: Next time put the needle on the record.

> [*He sits and watches TV. The glow from the TV intensifies, casting long shadows across the room. Then the lights brighten over* CECI.]

CECI: How come, Daddy? How come you don't unload on him now? Is it 'cause he's right? Is it 'cause like Rene you crave to be punished? Or is it 'cause of Lydia? Does it take a stranger to make you quit your *pendejadas?* [229] I see you, the man inside the man   285
who coulda been. All afternoon still as a lawn Mexican, you wait for the changes inside. You fall into a sleep that permits no dreaming, no dreaming on this side for you *Apa.* . .

> [CLAUDIO *sleeps. A knock.* ALVARO *in his street clothes steps in. A bag draped over his arm.*]

ALVARO: *Tio? Tio* Claudio? Hello? Hey Ceci. Your dad hibernates like a bear. *Oye.* About last week. I haven't been the same since . . . well, since.   290

> [*He comes toward her. Touches her dress.*]

---

[226] *¿Y eso, de donde chingaos viene?*–"And that, where the hell did that thing come from?"
[227] *Eres un buen muchacho*–"You're a good boy"
[228] *Tu mama*–"Your mama"
[229] *pendejadas*–"stupid crap"

That day I came over. You were wearing this.

CECI: I wanted to see what fifteen looked like.

ALVARO: But it wasn't finished yet. None of us were.

[*Some scratchy AM radio tune plays from somewhere down the hall.* **ALVARO** *hears it and then starts in its direction. Lights change.* **CECI** *stirs and calls.*]

CECI: VARO!

ALVARO: Hey Ceci! I heard the radio and—whoa! Lookit you!   295

CECI: What do you think? You like it?

ALVARO: Turn around. *Prima,*[230] you look *fine*! Is it finished?

CECI: Almost. Just some hemming to do. Why are you looking at me like that?

ALVARO: I had no idea my cuz was such a fox. You're turning into a real beauty.

CECI: Hey, you better come to my *quinceañera*.   300

ALVARO: I'm there. I just can't get too messed up 'cause you know I'm shipping out the next morning.

CECI: I wish you didn't have to go. Can't you get some exemption or something?

ALVARO: Actually, Ceci, I want to go.

CECI: But why? Don't you watch the body counts on the news?   305

ALVARO: Sure I do. That's why I need to be there. My mom and dad, when they came over, they had nothing. Being American means a lot to them. C'mon, you know this. We got a flag on our porch.

CECI: But you're the brain of the family! You should be in college!

ALVARO: *Mira*, Ceci, the truth is, since graduation, I've felt like some discipline's gone   310
AWOL in my life, and what better way to get it back than to do my duty *por Tio Sam?*[231]

CECI: God, you are something. Varo, will you, like, be my first dance? At my *quinceañera*?

ALVARO: That's reserved for your father.

CECI: But after him, the next dance. Will you ask me, I mean, never mind, what am I   315
thinking, huh?

ALVARO: Cecilia Rosario, may I have the honor of throwing some *chancla* with you?

[*She smiles and offers her hand. They dance to some Temptations song on the radio.*]

CECI: I hope they play this song.

ALVARO: I'll see that they do. Anyways, is Rene home?

CECI: No, he's running some errands for Mom. What's up?   320

ALVARO: I gotta talk to that dude. There's something I gotta tell him.

CECI: Tell me. I'll tell him.

ALVARO: No, this is personal guy stuff, Ceci—

CECI: Is it drugs?

ALVARO: What? No!   325

CECI: Are you guys toking up or something?

ALVARO: God, you been watching too much Mod Squad, *esa*. Just tell him I came by. Tell him I had to put my car in the shop.

CECI: Your car?

---

[230] *prima*—"cousin"
[231] *por Tio Sam*—"for Uncle Sam" (his duty to the United States government)

ALVARO: Tell him tonight's my only night. That's all. I gotta split. You're gonna kill 'em   330
in this.

    [*He turns to leave.*]

CECI: Alvaro. Wait.

    [*She kisses him hard on the mouth. He is startled.*]

ALVARO: Oh my god, Ceci—

    [*He kisses her back.*]

CECI: I knew it. I knew you liked me. The first time at the Bronco Drive-in with you in
the backseat with my brothers. I let my hand slip into yours under the blanket and   335
you held it tight on your lap which was so warm. That's when I knew! *Te quiero,
Alvaro. Te quiero mucho.*[232] Oh my god, I can't believe what I'm saying!

ALVARO: Me neither—

CECI: I've come of age. I don't need no party to prove it. I know what I feel.

ALVARO: Ceci. You're my cousin.   340

CECI: Do you want me? That's all you have to say. Do you?

ALVARO: Tee-tee-tee. In ant language, that means you're the queen.

CECI: [*leaping into his arms*] I knew it! I knew it! Take me with you.

ALVARO: Take you . . . ?

CECI: You and Rene taking dad's car and partying tonight, aren't you?   345

ALVARO: Oh shit. Rene.

CECI: Can I come? I won't be any trouble. It'll be fun, like the three of us at the drive-in.

ALVARO: No, Ceci, and you can't tell anybody this. It's guys night out, that's all.

CECI: Please let me come. If you want me, you'll let me come.

    [*He kisses her long and deep. The lights change back. The radio fades. When*
    ALVARO *pulls away,* CECI *is restored to her brain-damaged state.*]

CECI: Uhhhh uuh.   350

ALVARO: You shouldn't've come. You should've stayed home. It wasn't you. It was
never you.

CLAUDIO: *Sobrino.*

    [CLAUDIO, *awake for some time, takes off his headphones.*]

ALVARO: *Buenas noches. Disculpe si lo desperti, Tio.*[233]

CLAUDIO: *¿Como si te parece? ¿Todavia bonita, que no?*[234]   355

ALVARO: *Si, señor.* Still very pretty.

CLAUDIO: She is our penance. How we repay our *pecados.*[235]

ALVARO: *Nos perdona Dios los pecados.*

CLAUDIO: In English, please. I learn.

ALVARO: God forgives our sins, Don Claudio. He doesn't take them out on others.   360

CLAUDIO: Mine, he does. What happen that night?

---

[232] *Te quiero, Alvaro. Te quiero mucho*—"I love you, Alvaro. I love you so much"
[233] *Buenas noches. Disculpe si lo desperti, Tio.*—"Good evening. Excuse me if I woke you up, Uncle."
[234] *¿Como si te parece? ¿Todavia bonita, que no?*—"How does she look to you? Still pretty, no?"
[235] *pecados*—"sins"

ALVARO: Sir? I don't understand. . . .

CLAUDIO: All this time, I wonder where they go. To see you, *que no?*

ALVARO: *No señor.*

CLAUDIO: They come to your house, *verdad? Rene y Cecilia. Y tu.*[236]   365

ALVARO: You know what happened, *Tio.*

CLAUDIO: I know what happened to *mija.* What happen to you? Why you no come see her the next day? They are going to see you, no? You are there *tambien, verdad?*[237] What do you know about this accident? You can tell me, Varo. I won't hate you. I just want to know. *¡Contestame!*[238]   370

ALVARO: What does it matter now? How's it going to change anything? She's not going to get better.

CECI: Oh no oh no. All my love wasted, all my wishing ruined, no chance of that cherry going boom.

ALVARO: You and me, *Tio, somos iguales.*[239] Blaming ourselves for nothin'.   375

[MOM, LYDIA, *and* RENE *burst through the front door with shopping bags.*]

ROSA: Alvaro! Praise the lord! What a surprise! *¡Mira, Rene, tu primo!*[240]

RENE: Hey.

ALVARO: I just came over, you know. . .

[MISHA *enters as* LYDIA *rushes to* CECI *with her shopping bags.*]

ROSA: We were shopping all day, sorry, *Viejo,* Lydia had never seen the mall, you know the new mall they put by the freeway! So I took her and you should have seen the look   380
on her face!

LYDIA: It's the most beautiful place I have ever seen!

ROSA: We bought some things, *Viejo.*

LYDIA: I got some make-up and some perfume, see? And then I got some high-tone shampoo for my hair and conditioner, and some soap so I smell like Ali McGraw. And then at   385
the Popular, I got these new shoes. See? *¿Les gustan mis zapatos?*[241]

CLAUDIO: How did you pay for this?

ROSA: I advanced her for the month.

CLAUDIO: A month's pay to smell like a *gringa.*

LYDIA: Like a rich *gringa.*   390

ROSA: On the way home, we saw Rene walking on the street. So we picked him up, Praise Jesus.

RENE: I wanted to walk.

ROSA: But look who you would miss if you did!

[LYDIA *goes to* CECI *and puts some perfume on her wrist.*]

ALVARO: For you, cuz.   395

[*He unzips the bag. A souvenir jacket with colored embroidery.*]

---

[236] . . . *verdad? Rene y Cecilia. Y tu*–". . . right? Rene and Cecilia. And you."

[237] *tambien*–"also"

[238] *¡Contestame!*–"Answer me!"

[239] *Tio, somos iguales*–"We're the same, Uncle."

[240] *¡Mira, Rene, tu primo!*–"Look, Rene, your cousin!"

[241] *¿Les gustan mis zapatos?*–"Do you like my shoes?"

ROSA: Oh! *¡Que bonito!* Goodness, look at the back! *Ay,* Rene . . .

> [*Sewn in gold lettering over an embroidered map of Indochina is written: "When I die, I am going to Heaven, because I've already done my time in Hell."* RENE *puts it on.*]

ALVARO: Straight outa Vietnam, *ese.* I meant to bring it last time but I was having your name sewn on the inside seam.

RENE: What can I say? It's great.

ALVARO: Over there, Rene, family is everything. That's all that kept me going. I went over   400
there for you, man. I know I made some choices in my job that don't sit well in this
house, and I'm sorry. But we can't let that burn up the good times we had. I need
you to accept what I am, 'cause you're my cousin and I love you.

RENE: What did you say?

ALVARO: You're my cousin.   405

RENE: No, you said something else. What did you say? Say it. Say it.

ALVARO: Rene, I'm going the best I can—

RENE: SAY IT! You fucking hypocrite!

ROSA: RENE!

> [RENE *scrambles for the door.* CLAUDIO *grabs his arm and he stops. They look at each other for the first time.* RENE *jerks his arm away and runs out.*]

CECI: Gggngng.   410

ROSA: *Lo siento.*[242] Rene just can't get used to this INS business.

ALVARO: I understand, *Tia Rosa.* He'll come around.

LYDIA: Ceci says it is best that you go.

ALVARO: Your *criada* has a wild imagination, *Tia.*[243] Ceci. [ALVARO *goes.*]

ROSA: Did you see that, *Viejo?* Did you see how Rene was?   415

CLAUDIO: I saw.

ROSA: And you're not even going to ask him why?

CLAUDIO: Already a million times I ask him!

ROSA: *¡Por Dio santo!*[244] Nobody makes sense here! Rene! Rene!

> [*She goes out after* RENE. MISHA *goes to his room.* LYDIA *and* CLAUDIO *regard each other in silence.*]

LYDIA: Are you going to stand there? He's your son, *viejo.*   420

CLAUDIO: Don't call me that. Only *Rosa* calls me that.

> [CLAUDIO *stalks to the stereo and gets his headphones.*]

LYDIA: He needs you.

CLAUDIO: [*putting them on and sitting in front of the TV*] Leave me alone.

LYDIA: Look at you. Locked inside your pride, while your family suffers. [*She rips the cord out of the stereo.*] Talk to him, Claudio!   425

CLAUDIO: How! How to take back all that time of not talking to him?

LYDIA: By talking to him. You men are so stubborn!

CLAUDIO: He look at me like I am a stranger.

---

[242] *Lo siento*—"I'm sorry"

[243] *criada*—"maid"

[244] *¡Por Dio santo!*—"For God's sake!"

LYDIA: You're his father.

CLAUDIO: All week, *sofocando*.[245] I can't breathe, I'm dying. 430

LYDIA: You're not dying. The opposite.

CLAUDIO: You call this living?

LYDIA: She does. Your life is here, *hombre*.

[CLAUDIO *grabs his coat in agitation and starts out.*]

Are you going for Rene?

CLAUDIO: I'm going to work. 435

[*He goes. She starts picking up the shopping bags.*]

CECI: Gggggg.

LYDIA: *¿Ves, chica? Tanto desmadre aqui*.[246] *Oye*, you know why we were out so late? Your *mami* couldn't say it in front of your cousin. We went to see someone in her building who is going to get me papers. She wants me to be legal.

CECI: *Ghhyyn?* 440

LYDIA: She wants my name in the passport to be Flores.

[*She smiles and then goes. The lights change, brightening over* CECI.]

CECI: Flores is a name that goes all the way back to Spain, all the way back to the origin of flowers, which is what the name means. And the Flores that live in this town, all of them come from the first Flores that ever made love to an *India*.[247] He gave her flowers for a name and she wore them for the next one and the next one wore them 445 for the next one after that. All the way down to me. The pink icing on my cake said Flores. My wrist band said Flores. The red and white blooms in my head are Flores.

[*The lights are out in the living room where* CECI *lies.* MISHA *enters sheepishly.*]

MISHA: Ceci?

CECI: Gggnh, ggnh. 450

MISHA: I went in your room. It's all different now. She took your Bobby Sherman poster down. And all those Barbies you used to have. They're gone.

CECI: Ggnhh.

[*He sits by her.*]

MISHA: Sis, remember those summers when we were little and Dad used to take us to the community pool on his days off? Remember those days? 455

[LYDIA *appears, in her bathrobe with a towel on her head, holding a manuscript.*]

There was this one afternoon, when Rene was going up on the diving board and taking these big dives, and even at twelve, he was so graceful. And Dad's just standing in the water watching him like he's this god, and he says to me: I swam the Rio for this boy, I swam and ran straight to the hospital where your mother was giving birth and made sure his name was Claudio Rene Flores. I go, you can't swim, Dad. And he just 460 goes, I know.

LYDIA: The shower is free if you need.

MISHA: I know. I heard Ceci and . . . I should let you get dressed.

---

[245] *sofocando*–"suffocated"

[246] *¿Ves, chica? Tanto desmadre aqui*–"See, girl? So much mess here"

[247] *India*–an Indian; a native woman

LYDIA: Did *Señora* find your brother?

MISHA: Not yet.   465

LYDIA: You left this on my bed.

MISHA: You asked for my poems.

LYDIA: [*looking over them*] *Gracias.* Your sister and you, very close, no? You tell each other
  secrets?

MISHA: I do, anyway.   470

LYDIA: I bet she has some of her own. Read me this one. *Sombra.*[248]

[*She passes the notebook of poems back to him.*]

MISHA: She is the shadow on my wall
           When I am alone and needing
           Unspeakable things, alone
           With only my hands to catch·me   475
           She is *la sombra* I cast
           In my sleep, lip to *labio*[249]
           Against the pillow
           And her shadow legs as long
           as mine, as dark, as   480
           smooth, drape over mine
           and give me shadow
           solace, shadow peace
           in headphone whispers.

LYDIA: Are you in love, young boy?   485

MISHA: I don't know what to do with girls. I never have.

LYDIA: You'll learn.

MISHA: Lydia, who are you? Why did you come here?

LYDIA: 'Cause I need work.

MISHA: But you're here for something else. I know.   490

LYDIA: You want my secrets now?

MISHA: I want to know everything about you. You're so far from your home and—

LYDIA: My home, Misha, *sinceramente,*[250] is nowhere. What I had back in Mexico. It's all
  gone. I am hardly even here.

MISHA: What do you mean?   495

[*She shows him a small mark on her chest.*]

LYDIA: I died, Misha. Like Ceci, I died but I came back.

MISHA: Jesus. What is that?

LYDIA: My eyes were closed for a long time. When I opened them, I was an orphan.

MISHA: What happened?

LYDIA: It doesn't matter. This says I'm here now. This says I can't never go back.   500

MISHA: Are you a *mojada*? A wetback?

LYDIA: Uh-huh, but that's 'cause I just took a shower.

MISHA: Your English is getting better all the time.

---

[248] *Sombra*–"Shadow"
[249] *labio*–"lip"
[250] *sinceramente*–"sincerely"

LYDIA: *Gracias, guapo.*[251] I practice with your sister all day.

MISHA: You're good with her. She needs you. 505

LYDIA: It's you she needs. *En serio.*[252] She counts on your poetry. *Un dia*, when you are alone, look into her *ojitos* and hold her hand tight,[253] don't let go, no matter what.

MISHA: I don't understand.

LYDIA: I'm saying give her love and she will give you all the *poemas* of her life. *Para siempre.* Can I keep? 510

MISHA: They're all for you.

> [*He slowly moves in to kiss her. She lets him.*]

LYDIA: Misha.

> [*He kisses her again. His hand slides into her bathrobe. She likes it, but has to resist it.*]

See how quickly you learn.

MISHA: I'm just down the hall.

LYDIA: That's how it has to stay, sweet boy. 515

> [*She kisses his cheek, then he goes.* LYDIA *reads his poems, tears welling in her eyes.*]

CECI: *Ay Lydia.* All the want of before, dilating my *corazón*, it's dilating yours. You speak the *idioma* of ants and miscarried love. The cards of *La Vida Cecilia* falling into place. Some *desmadre* is coming into view and I'm gonna need you, *loca.*[254] I'll need you when I fall.

LYDIA: *¿Que ves, pajarita?*[255] 520

CECI: A new card. *Las Gemelas.* The twins.

> [LYDIA *goes. Darkness descends on the living room.* ROSA *sits on the sofa in her nightgown.*]

ROSA: Dear Jesus. I know Rene won't amount to much, that's what I believe, that's my sin, to dismiss my oldest so easily. He'll be a loyal son if he lives to be twenty. But he wasn't make a difference in the world. I know it, he knows it and You know it too. But that don't mean I don't love him. Bring him home tonight dear Father— 525

> [RENE *can be heard roaring outside, crashing against garbage cans.*]

RENE: [*off*] *¡Chinga la verga! ¡Pinchi puto cabron!*[256] Who do you think you are! I got every right to be here!

> [ALVARO *enters pushing* RENE *inside. He drunkenly staggers in, his hands cuffed behind him.*]

Let go of me! I said, LET ME GO!

ALVARO: Shut up, Rene! You're gonna wake the whole block!

RENE: You can't treat me like this! I ain't your wetback! You don't get rid of me that easy, you shit! 530

ALVARO: I know what you're trying to do. It's not gonna work.

---

[251] *Gracias, guapo*–"Thank you, handsome"

[252] *En serio*–"seriously"

[253] *Un dia . . . ojitos*–"one day . . . little eyes"

[254] *desmadre*–a spectacular and potentially chaotic event/*loca*–girl

[255] *¿Que ves, pajarita?*–"What do you see, little bird?"

[256] *¡Chinga la verga! ¡Pinchi puto cabron!*–"Fucking shit! Fucking bitch faggot!"

RENE: You don't get it, do you! You drivin' to the levee, right by the same fuckin' pole! That's why you joined *la Migra*!

ALVARO: What do you want from me! 535

RENE: I want you to talk to me! Jesus Christ, just talk to me!

ALVARO: There's nothin' to talk about! I'm through, that's all!

RENE: Then why did you give me your jacket? If you hate my guts so much, why!

ALVARO: Listen up, you fuck! You were part of my war! The whole time I was there, so were you! What we had, *ese*, nobody's ever gonna touch that, nobody's ever gonna 540 come that close! That was it, *ese*. That was my shot.

RENE: Then why won't you see me, goddammit!

ALVARO: 'Cause when I think of us, I see her! I hear those words!

RENE: What are you sayin', asshole? I live with her! I hear them every day!

ROSA: Rene. *¿Que es esta locura?*[257] 545

ALVARO: He was up on the levee, *Tia*. He's drunk. He taunted us while we were doing our job.

RENE: Oh my god! You were buying me off! This jacket's to buy me off!

ALVARO: He's talking like a crazy man.

ROSA: *Mijo*, please don't be like this. . . . 550

RENE: Get the fuck away! I'm done with you.

[MISHA *enters in his tee-shirt and shorts.*]

MISHA: Mom, back away.

ROSA: *¡Pero, mijo, mira que locura!*[258]

RENE: *¡Carnalito!*[259]

MISHA: Do as I say. Back away. 555

[ROSA *retreats in sobs as* RENE *grows more glowering and furious.* CECI *becomes agitated.*]

RENE: That's right! Back away from the Fag Basher!

MISHA: What the hell are you doing, man?

RENE: Don't look at me like that, Meesh! I'll fuckin' bust your head open! Like I busted Ceci!

MISHA: What can I do, Rene? *Te quiero ayudar.*[260] Tell me what to do. 560

CECI: GGNNGAYAAYYY!!

RENE: Hypocrites and liars! I fuckin' hate you all!

ALVARO: Misha, he just needs to sleep it off. [*to* RENE] You gotta get a grip.

RENE: FUCK YOU! TAKE THESE OFF AN' LEMME KICK YOUR ASS, YOU FUCKING COWARD! 565

[LYDIA *appears.*]

LYDIA: *¿Que pasa aqui?*[261]

---

[257] *¿Que es esta locura?*–"What is this madness?"
[258] *¡Pero, mijo, mira que locura!*–"But, son, look that's crazy!"
[259] *¡Carnalito!*–"Little Bro!"
[260] *Te quiero ayudar*–"I want to help you"
[261] *¿Que pasa aqui?*–"What's going on here?"

RENE: *Orale.*[262] You want an illegal? You wanna do your fuckin' job, *migra*?

MISHA: Go back to your room.

LYDIA: Let me take Ceci out.

ROSA: Take her to your room. *Andale.* 570

RENE: Don't put your dirty hands on her. *Mojada.*

MISHA: Rene . . .

RENE: I'm telling you, cuz, this one's trouble. This one think she knows our shit. She's gone real deep with us, *verdad, criada*?

MISHA: Back away from her. I mean it. 575

RENE: It's sad, *ese.* You giving your heart to a wetback. She's using you!

MISHA: I don't care. I'm not letting you say whatever you want about her.

ROSA: *¡Misha, cuidado, mijo!*[263]

RENE: You think she's *toda India Mexicana.*[264] But I've seen Dad banging this whore!

ROSA: Lydia . . . 580

    [MISHA *pounds him in the gut and he falls.*]

ROSA: Misha!

MISHA: I TOLD YOU TO WATCH YOUR MOUTH!

RENE: I saw them!

MISHA: Liar! [*He grabs* RENE *by the collar and threatens to hit him.*]

ALVARO: STOP IT! 585

RENE: C'mon, bro. C'mon. Just lemme have it. Just pound on me, man.

    [MISHA *lets him go.*]

    ¡Andale, Miguel! ¡Dale gas![265] Hit me, motherfucker! I want you to hit me!

MISHA: No way . . .

RENE: [*collapsing in tears*] ALVARO! ANY A YOU! I'M BEGGIN' YOU! JESUS, SOME-BODY FUCKIN' HIT ME! 590

ALVARO: Jesus, Rene, quit this now please. . . .

    [CECI *convulses in terror and* LYDIA *runs to hold her tightly.* MISHA *looks at* ALVARO.]

MISHA: Are you going to tell us what is going on here? Will somebody tell us?

CECI: Ghhhn.

LYDIA: She will.

ALVARO: What? 595

MISHA: What are you talking about?

CECI: Ghghggn.

LYDIA: She knows. She was there.

CECI: Ghgn.

LYDIA: She is there now. 600

ROSA: She is?

---

[262] *Orale*–"Alright"

[263] *¡Misha, cuidado, mijo!*–"Misha, be careful, son!"

[264] *toda India Mexicana*–"all Mexican Indian;" connotatively a shy, ignorant, innocent country girl

[265] *¡Andale, Miguel! ¡Dale gas!*–"Go on, Miguel! Give it gas!"

CECI: Gghfnhsss
LYDIA: She says, Rene and me
CECI: Ggffeggh-ghfhn
LYDIA: Driving in the middle of the night 605
CECI: GghaaggG
LYDIA: To Alvaro's house
CECI: Ttte-tttteee
LYDIA: Delirious as ants 610
CECI: Ghhhngnn
LYDIA: Rene is driving
CECI: Hhghhhh.
LYDIA: But I'm hiding in the backseat. Crouched in the floor of the backseat.
CECI: 'Cause I wanna surprise them! I wanna see the look on Alvaro's face when he sees
me again! Party! 615
LYDIA: She says
CECI: I hear the radio playing and I feel the wind rushing in through his open window and
I'm tingling with excitement! I'm gonna trip 'em out!
LYDIA: She says
CECI: I hear the car stop and Alvaro getting in and I'm about to jump out, but he's like on 620
Rene, kissing him, and my heart stops and
LYDIA: She says
CECI: I can't think I can't move but the car does. It rolls along at Roadrunner speed to
nowhere and I can hear them talking Rene's like where you wanna go and Alvaro's
like where we always go, cuz, the border 625
LYDIA: She says
CECI: I'm *toda* dizzy, But soon, I feel the car stopping. The engine stops and it's quiet
as death
LYDIA: *Quiet as death*
CECI: I feel the beautiful dream of Varo and me slipping away as I hear this moaning and 630
kissing and crying
LYDIA: She says
CECI: This moaning and kissing and crying
LYDIA: She says
CECI: And then I see Alvaro throw his head back and cry out 635
LYDIA: *¡Ay Rene!*
CECI: I see *carnal* rise up and kiss him and I can't believe it
LYDIA: She says
CECI: Alvaro was mine all these years I dreamed of kissing him like that and now
LYDIA: She says 640
CECI: Right there, right there, this ugliness inside takes over. YOU FAGS. YOU HOMOS.
YOU DIRTY FILTHY HOMOS
LYDIA: She says
CECI: They scream, they're so shocked but the ugly keeps yelling You *Jotos*, Damn *Maricones*.
Rene starts the car and says over and over 645
RENE: Please don't tell Dad, Ceci, please don't tell Dad
CECI: And Varo's face turned away saying
ALVARO: We weren't doing nothing, I swear

CECI: And the car is racing and I'm screaming in the backseat YOU DISGUST ME YOU MAKE ME SICK YOU LYING SHITS   650

LYDIA: She says

CECI: I'm beating on Rene, I am so mad at Rene. And he's yelling No and Alvaro is yelling Stop, Ceci! But my fists keep hitting his head and the car is swerving like crazy, and Rene reaches back and tells me right to my face

LYDIA: I'm sorry!   655

CECI: But he's not looking and the curve is right there and the pole wants the Pontiac. And there in the rear-view mirror I see you, so pale and sad, the face of death willing the car into the pole

LYDIA: Just as I see yours in my mirror

CECI: And I am pure bird soaring with the moon stretching out like *chicle* toward the red   660 card with the inscription: Now Look What You Done, Stupid

LYDIA: She says

CECI: It was me! ME! This *mierda* was me! You didn't do nothing wrong! It was all my shit my fucking shit making it wrong. The words in my heart fall out the crack in my head. The words I never meant this. Not in a million. I love you Rene. I love you   665 both. I'm ssghggngn..ggngn.

LYDIA: *Eso es lo que dice.*[266]

[*Silence.* ALVARO *takes the cuffs off* RENE.]

ROSA: Is it true? Alvaro.

ALVARO: No, *Tia.*

ROSA: Rene? Is it true, Rene?   670

RENE: Yeah. All true.

ROSA: Get out. Get out of this house.

MISHA: Mom, you can't just—

RENE: *Aliviánate, carnal.*[267] I'm done here.

[*He takes off the jacket and throws it at* ALVARO'S *feet. Then he goes to* CECI *to make his goodbye. Intimate and silent. Then he gets up and walks out of the house forever.*]

LYDIA: [*as she gets up and starts to her room*] She wants to rest now. I'm tired too.   675

MISHA: Were you . . . did you and my dad . . . ?

LYDIA: What importance is that now, Misha?

[*She goes.* MISHA *looks at* ROSA.]

ROSA: I always say nothing happened in this house without me knowing. But really, all I knew was nothing.

MISHA: Mom, you can't let him go like that.   680

ROSA: Go to bed, *mijo.*

[MISHA *goes.* ALVARO *makes to go but* ROSA *stops him.*]

Sobrino.

---

[266] *Eso es lo que dice*–"That's what she says"
[267] *Aliviánate, carnal*–"Chill, bro"

[ROSA *goes to him and whispers something to him as* CECI *cowers on her mattress.*]

CECI: This *noche* nobody sleeps. This *noche* the words slam against the walls like angry little birds again and again. Faggot. Whore. *Mojado. Migra. Mijo.* Love. All those words on razor wings looking for something to cut. Slashing at the walls of what we used to call family.   685

[ALVARO *nods gravely to* ROSA. *He goes down the hall.* ROSA *sits with* CECI.]

ROSA: What does the word *madre* mean in this country? Does it mean idiot? Does it mean pretending? Does it mean living like nothing's changed? Everything's changed. I'm old. I'm a stranger to my own children. My husband won't touch me. You were going to be my partner, but look at you.   690

CECI: Gnnghg.

[*There is an awful lull, then screaming and yelling off.*]

LYDIA: [*off*] AAAYYY! AAAAAYYYY!

[ALVARO *enters dragging* LYDIA *out behind him.*]

ALVARO: That's the way it is. Now come on!

LYDIA: *AYYY! AYY! Help me!*

[MISHA *comes out.*]

MISHA: Whoa! What the fuck are you doing?   695

LYDIA: *Misha!* He's taking me away!

ALVARO: She's got no proof of residence, cuz.

MISHA: What! Where are you taking her?

ALVARO: Where do you think? *El Corralón.*

LYDIA: *Señora!* Tell him I'm American! He won't listen to me! I'm American!   700

ROSA: *Es una mojada.* I don't hire *mojadas.*

ALVARO: *Vamonos.*

MISHA: Mom, you can't do this. I won't let you.

ROSA: You dare defend her in my presence? *Esta desgraciada se abusó de mi marido,*[268] my husband!   705

LYDIA: *Señora,* please, don't be this way! I love this family! Misha!

MISHA: Let her go, Varo. C'mon, for family, cuz.

ALVARO: *Misha, con esto, familia no vale madre.*[269]

LYDIA: *¡Misha, por favor!* I don't want to go back! If I go back, I'll die! I know I will. I'll die!

ROSA: Alvaro Fernandez. TAKE THIS *PUTA* OUT OF MY HOUSE NOW!   710

ALVARO: C'mon.

LYDIA: Wait! My poems! Let me get my poems! Misha!

ROSA: *Espera.*

[ROSA *violently strips off* LYDIA*'s top.*]

LYDIA: NOO!

ROSA: This is *mija's blusa.*[270]   715

---

[268] *Esta desgraciada se abusó de mi marido*–"This ingrate took advantage of my husband"
[269] *Misha, con esto, familia no vale madre*–"Misha, with this, family doesn't mean shit"
[270] *mija's blusa*–"my daughter's blouse"

LYDIA: CECI! CECI!

> [ALVARO *pushes* LYDIA, *ravaged and half-naked, out the door.*]

MISHA: I love her.

ROSA: *Mira nomas.* Her little *pendejito.* Writing *mierda* to her with my pen.[271]

> [MISHA *runs after* LYDIA. ROSA *sits in exhaustion. The lights collapse around* CECI.]

CECI: I flew that night to a village in Jalisco; through a window, this girl sitting at a dresser brushing her hair. She looks in the mirror, sees me and smiles like she's always known   720 me, this tragic girl brushing her hair at the break of day.

> [*Later in the morning.* CLAUDIO *enters. He finds* CECI *and* ROSA *sleeping together on the mattress.*]

CLAUDIO: *Vieja.* Rosa.

ROSA: Hmm? [ROSA *wakes.*]

CLAUDIO: *¿Que haces? ¿Por que duermes aqui?*[272]

ROSA: I got lonely.   725

CLAUDIO: I brought you some *menudo.*[273]

ROSA: *Gracias.*

CLAUDIO: *¿Esta todo bien?*[274] [*She nods.*] *¿Y Rene?* Did *mijo* come back home?

ROSA: He's still out.

CLAUDIO: I will wait to him. *Pos,* you better have some before it gets cold.   730

> [*She opens the container of menudo.* CLAUDIO *takes a beer from his bag and pops off the pull-tab.*]

CECI: Gghnf.

CLAUDIO: *Qiubolé, mija.*[275] Are you ever going to change out of that thing? Uh?

CECI: Da..hh . . . da..ghgntttee.

CLAUDIO: *Querida.*[276] The only English I want to know is yours.

> [*He kisses her forehead, but forgets the pull-tab on her blanket.*]

ROSA: I love when they put extra *tripas. Menudo* is always good for the morning-after.   735

CLAUDIO: Are you hung-over?

ROSA: *Hombre,* this headache like a devil with a claw hammer. I think I'm staying in today.

CLAUDIO: Then lie down for a while. *¿Y Lydia?*

ROSA: *Se fue.*[277]

CLAUDIO: *¿Como que se fue?*[278] Where is she?   740

ROSA: *Con la Migra.*[279]

CLAUDIO: *¿Que chingados dices, mujer?*[280] You turn her over to *La Migra*?

---

[271] *Mira nomas . . . pendejito . . . mierda*–"Just look"/"little dumbass"/"crap"

[272] *¿Que haces? ¿Por que duermes aqui?*–"What are you doing? Why are you sleeping here?"

[273] *menudo*–a Mexican soup or stew made with tripe (cow stomach)

[274] *¿Esta todo bien?*–"Is everything okay?"

[275] *Qiubolé, mija*–"Wassup, son"

[276] *Querida*–"Beloved"

[277] *Se fue*–"She left"

[278] *¿Como que se fue?*–"What do you mean, she left?"

[279] *Con la Migra*–"With immigration"

[280] *¿Que chingados dices, mujer?*–"What the fuck are you saying, woman?"

ROSA: If you want her, *vete*. If you miss that fucking country so much, go. Let me remind you who also needs papers.

[*They glare at each other. Then* CLAUDIO *retreats to his bedroom. He stops at the threshold.*]

CLAUDIO: Rene and Cecilia . . . *y* Alvaro. Why?   745

ROSA: There is no why. There is never any why.

[MISHA *enters dressed. He goes straight to* CECI *and begins her physical therapy.*]

CLAUDIO: Miguel . . . Miguel . . . [*No response. He turns to* ROSA.] Come to bed. Bring the *menudo* with you.

[CLAUDIO *goes.* ROSA *can stomach no more soup. She goes to* MIGUEL. *She looks at* CECI.]

ROSA: ¿*Y tu que ves?*[281] What other *cochinadas* are locked in those pretty eyes of yours?[282]

[*She walks solemnly down the hall.*]

CECI: Gggighg.   750

MISHA: It's okay, sis. I know you didn't mean it.

CECI: Mmmm . . . Meeesh shhhhhah!

MISHA: Sis, did you just—?

CECI: Mmmeeshishhhh. Aaah.

[*He goes to her and she kisses his hand.*]

MISHA: Oh my god. Ceci. You're talking.   755

[*She guides his hand under her dress.*]

Wait . . . what are you . . . no . . . let go. Please, Ceci. Let go! I'm sorry. No.

[*He breaks away. She curls up and cries softly. He tries to leave but stops at the threshold of the room. He turns and crawls along invisible trails toward his sister.*]

In ant-language, teetee means sister. In ant, teeteetee means touch. I wish I knew the word for Ceci.

CECI: Tee-teeeh.

MISHA: I hear you. [*He crawls to her.*] In my dream, you had a key in your mouth.   760

[CECI *finds the pull-tab and shows it to him.*]

CECI: My magic key out of ant-prison.

MISHA: I love you, Ceci.

CECI: Aayyyhhh.

[*He grits his teeth as she moves his hand into her. She begins to feel him as he cries.*]

The last card. Inscribed, *Ay Te Watcho*. Which is Godspeed in Chicano. So wave bye to me, little brother, and reach inside and spell the word love in a girl that's never felt it with your fingers push back the veil *ay, asi, carnal, asi,*[283] find the poems in me   765

---

[281] ¿*Y tu que ves?*–"And what are you looking at?"

[282] *cochinadas*–"dirty things"

[283] *ay, asi, carnal, asi*–"oh, like that bro, like that"

'cause I hid them all for you, *asi, asi*, poems of your hunger your shame your secret loves, *ay*, got them right here, Misha, your *versos*—[284]

CECI/MISHA:—dancing in me, drowning in my blood—

MISHA:—reaching all the way up to your heart, I'll find the Ceci you'll never be, give you wings with my pen, make you fly, I'll be your poet forever, *con safo, retacho, asi asi Ceci dame la vida Cecilia asi.*[285]

CECI: *hhhhhhg.*

> [**MISHA** *cries.* **CECI**, *in a spasm of ecstacy, sets the pull-tab gingerly on her tongue and swallows it. He watches her slowly slip away. Lights fade.*]

770

END OF PLAY

---

[284] *versos*—"verses"

[285] *con safo, retacho, asi asi Ceci dame la vida Cecilia asi*—This line seems the culmination of the longer exchange between Ceci and Misha which begins with Ceci's line, "push back the veil." In this exchange, Ceci gives to Misha the poetry stored inside her and Misha gives her the physical love she craves. His line here, *con safo, retacho . . .*, conveys this exchange.

Becky's New Car
(2008)

S teven Dietz is one America's most prolific dramatists. Over the past twenty-five years, he has written more than thirty full-length plays, including *God's Country, Halcyon Days, Private Eyes, Handing Down the Names, Lonely Planet, Dracula* (adapted from Bram Stoker's novel), *Still Life with Iris, Inventing van Gogh*, and *Rocket Man*. Few contemporary American dramatists have written on such a variety of subjects in such different tones. Compare, for example, *God's Country*, a chilling drama about the northwestern white supremacist group called "The Order," with the quickly shifting frames of self-deception in the comic thriller *Private Eyes*. One common feature among Dietz's many plays is his clever use of suspense to engage and maintain audience interest. Dietz also creates characters whom, whether the tone of the play is serious or comic, audiences can easily identify with and care about. These features may partially explain why his plays are so widely produced.

A Seattle-based commercial realtor commissioned Dietz to write *Becky's New Car* as a birthday gift for his wife. A few hundred years ago it was common for patrons of the arts to commission new works as a tribute to a loved one, but that practice has long been out of fashion. The commissioning of Dietz's play, however, sparked A Contemporary Theatre (ACT) in Seattle to launch its New Works for the American Stage, pairing donors with playwrights in order to generate new plays, which ACT has first option to produce.

Becky's New Car explores the midlife crisis of a working wife and mother. Dietz initially presents Becky as a thoroughly reliable, stable person who picks up after the men in her life: her unemployed twenty-six-year-old son, her no-nonsense husband, and the needy salesmen at the car dealership where she works. But when a wealthy man mistakenly assumes Becky's husband is deceased and pursues Becky, she takes this opportunity to live a secret, double life. Dietz builds a connection between Becky and the audience by having Becky directly address and interact with members of the audience. She offers audience members beverages and provides them according to their wishes. At one point she brings a few female audience members onto the stage to share her dilemma with them and solicit their advice. This use of character-audience interaction foregrounds the live theatricality of the performance and encourages the audience to identify with Becky. The playwright also uses space in an intriguing way by fusing Becky's home and her workplace into a single space. Late in the play, as Becky has trouble keeping her two lives separate, this doubling of the space helps to convey the sense of Becky careening out of control, swept away by the flow of events. Eventually, the web of lies and misunderstandings is untangled and order is restored with a renewed sense of appreciation between Becky and her husband.

Becky's New Car
a comedy

Cast of Characters (3 women, 4 men)
BECKY (REBECCA) FOSTER, *a woman in her late 40s.*
JOE FOSTER, *Becky's husband, a roofer, late 40s.*
CHRIS FOSTER, *their son, a psychology student, 26.*
WALTER FLOOD, *a very wealthy businessman, widowed, 60s.*
KENSINGTON (KENNI) FLOOD, *Walter's daughter, 23.*
STEVE, *Becky's co-worker, widowed, 50.*
GINGER, *a neighbor of Walter's, single, 50s.*

Time and Place—*The present. Summer. An American city very much like Seattle.*

Setting—*The play will move without transition between four primary locations: Becky's LIVING ROOM, her CUBICLE at work, her CAR, and the TERRACE of Walter Flood's estate.*
 In point of fact, these are all ONE area, in place onstage at all times. Furthermore, in the case of the CUBICLE and CAR, these areas may actually be a part of Becky's LIVING ROOM which has been re-defined by lighting.
 Simplify. It is not necessary, nor is it desirable, to fully depict any of the play's locales.

> *We have two lives—the one we learn with, and the life we live after that.*
> *~ Bernard Malamud*

ACT ONE

Becky's Living Room. Evening.

[*Lights rise quickly on the empty room, as we hear what might be a vacuum cleaner running offstage. And then—*

We hear things falling and crashing—being grabbed, discarded, hurriedly put away, and then—

BECKY *appears, in slacks and light sweater, somewhat disheveled, wearing one long rubber cleaning glove. With this gloved hand she is holding a toilet plunger upside-down, with a new roll of toilet paper skewered on the handle. In her other hand is a "dust-buster"—still running. A cleaning rag is draped over her shoulder. And, yet, despite this dubious first impression—*

She is all charm, the perfect (if somewhat ill-prepared) hostess when she greets the audience:]

BECKY: [*to audience*] Hi. Hello. Wait a second—

[*She turns the "dust-buster" off.*]

There we go. Sorry. Hi! So glad you stopped by. I was just picking up the house a bit—

[*She gives the new roll of toilet paper to an* AUDIENCE MEMBER.]

Could you put this in the bathroom when you go? Thanks.

[*She moves about during the following, putting things in place, readying the house.*]

You know how it is: things ran late at work—so I called Joe, he's great, you'll love   5
him, you'll probably end up liking Joe way more than you like me—anyway, I told
Joe I was still at work and could he pick up the pizza?—but he was stuck at his
job-site longer than planned—he's finishing up this apartment south of here, good
money but a real long drive—and because of the rain last night, god that RAIN last
night, because of that he had to—wait—   10

[*She finds an empty trash can and hands it to an* AUDIENCE MEMBER.]

See that drip right there. Just watch . . .

[*It drips, just a bit—from the grid—near the edge of the stage.*]

[*to* AUDIENCE MEMBER] There. See. Could you put this over there for me? Thanks
so much.

[*She watches as the* AUDIENCE MEMBER *puts the trash can under the drip.*]

Wait. Let's be sure . . .

[*She waits with the* AUDIENCE MEMBER *until a drip of water falls into the trash can. Smiles.*]

Got it. Thanks. Did I mention that my husband is a roofer? Yes. A very good one.   15
Twenty-plus years, but you know what they say—the shoemaker's kids and all
that . . .

[*She continues to busy herself in the room.*]

I should wake my son so you can meet him—that would be Chris—that would be
his crap lying around here everywhere.

[*She quickly holds up a piece of newspaper—offers it to an* AUDIENCE MEMBER.]

[*to* AUDIENCE MEMBER] Sports section? [*as needed*] [Here you go.] // [I don't blame   20
you.]

[*Back to straightening up—*]

Don't get me wrong, I love my son—fruit of my actual loins—but god forbid he
emerge from the basement where he lives as the Eternal Freeloader—sleeping off a

hangover from another night of grad student "angst" and two-dollar shots. He didn't even do the *one thing* I asked of him, which was to get the dishwasher loaded—so, there you have it, that's the update: my son was loaded and the dishwasher was not—but, anyway, this is our humble home:

[*She shoves a final magazine under the cushion of a chair or couch, strikes a friendly pose, and says:*]

Welcome! [*beat, looks around*] The fact is: we need a new house. My friend, Rita—beautiful, wonderful woman, passed away last year, her husband Steve still hasn't gotten over it—anyway, Rita had this theory: When a woman says she needs new shoes, what she really wants is a new job. When she says she needs a new house, she wants a new husband. And when she says she wants a new car, she wants a new *life*.

[*A beat.* BECKY *opens a drawer or cupboard and pulls out a very large (and nearly empty) carton of Diet Sprite. She fishes out the final can (or two), pops the top, starts to drink—stops—*]

[*to an* AUDIENCE MEMBER] Oh, I'm sorry. Did you want one?

[*If this person says YES, she digs out the final can, saying—*]

[*as needed*] [Here you go.] // [Okay, if you change your mind . . .]

[*ALSO: if this person says YES, she turns to the person NEXT TO this* AUDIENCE MEMBER, *saying—*]

[Sorry. I'm all out. Money's been tight and we let our Costco membership lapse, so . . . you know.]

[BECKY *now . . . sits, for the first time in the play. Breathes deeply. And drinks her soda.*]

I think we'll just stay here in the living room, if that's okay. [*points*] The kitchen's that way, if you need something—but promise me you won't look in the back yard. It's a disaster. Used to be a garden. We should just pave it over. Keep our cars back there. Yes, I know that's terrible—but I need to ask you this: have you ever really been as happy in your garden as you've been on a good day in your car?

All alone. Radio on. Traffic moving, nice and easy.

Heaven.

[*PHONE RINGS.* BECKY *goes to a cluttered work table in the middle of the room. When she lifts the phone, lights immediately reveal this area to be—*]

Becky's Cubicle at work. Evening.

BECKY: [*into phone, upbeat*] Thank you for calling Bill Buckley Lexus-Saturn-Nissan-Mitsubishi, Home of the Fifty-Thousand Mile Smile, this is Becky, how may I direct your call? [*listens*]

Oh, I'm afraid they've gone home for the night. [*listens*]

Well, yes, good point: if I'm still here doing paperwork why can't the salesmen still   45
be here selling cars, but that's—[*listens*]

Yes, right, but can I just—would you mind terribly if I put you on hold for just a
second, thanks so much—

> [*Presses a button on the phone. Sets the receiver down.*]

[*to audience*] Sorry. You know how it is. As soon as you start to have a conversation
with someone—   50

> [*PHONE RINGS AGAIN.*]

Excuse me.

> [*She answers.*]

[*on phone, faster now*] Thank you for calling Bill Buckley Lexus-Saturn-Nissan-
Mitsubishi, Home of the Fifty-Thousand Mile Smile, this is Becky, how may
I—[*stops, listens*] You were on hold. Why did you—no, I did not hang up on you. I
put you on hold. For *less than a minute*—yes, it was really no more than a—all right,   55
sure, go ahead and yell—

> [*As the Caller presumably rants on the other end,* BECKY *sets the phone down,
> and speaks to the audience.*]

Anyway, this is where I work. I'm the Title Clerk and Office Manager. I process
the new car sales. This place used to be Bill Buckley's main car lot—his "Super-
Dealership"—but now he's got plans to open a "Mega-Dealership," three hours
south of here, and he's been trolling our offices to see if any of us are worthy to make   60
the jump from Super to Mega.

[*re: phone*] Wait. I think he stopped.

> [*She picks up the phone.*]

[*into phone*] Yes, I wrote down every word you said and I'll put it right in front of your
salesman when he comes in tomorrow. [*beat*] No, wait, is tomorrow Wednesday?
He's actually off on Wednesdays, so—   65

> [*Holds phone away from her ear once again.*]

[*re: Caller*] —oh, there he goes again!
[*into phone*] I'M GOING TO PUT YOU ON HOLD FOR JUST ANOTHER
SEC.

> [*She puts the call on hold again.*]

[*to audience*] I've been here at Buckley's for nine years. With Chris in school—and
the economy in . . . *flux* . . . just totally *fluxed*—with all that, Joe and I need the   70
money. What else would I do? Bag groceries? Be a crossing guard? Go back to school
and study what?—*massage therapy?!* [*beat*]

Friend of mind from high school called—my age—husband died suddenly, left her
with nothing, no insurance, piles of bills—and do you know what she's doing now?

Porn. Older Woman stuff. Tasteful. No animals. Just a little leather and lot of make-up. But, you know what she said?   75

"Becky, I know what you must think of me . . . but I needed a new life."

[*pause, more quietly*] Anyway: this is where I work. [*looks around*] Let's go back to the house.

[*Light immediately restore to:*]

The Living Room.

BECKY: Joe should be home any minute and then we can—[*stops*] My Sprite. I left it at   80
work. Just a sec. [*to the Booth*] I need to go back to work. I left my drink.

[*Lights immediately shift to:*]

The Cubicle.

[BECKY *grabs her soda*—]

[*to the Booth*] Thanks.

[—*and is about to walk away when she remembers*—]

Ooops.

[—*and picks up the phone.*]

Still there? Sorry, I had to run home—but now I'm back. [*beat*] Are you . . . are you
crying? [*to audience, whispers*] He's crying. [*back on phone*]   85
It's a *car* . . . it's just a *car* . . . and if you don't get this one, well . . . I mean, something else always comes along, right? [*listens*] You don't think so. [*pause, quiet and
simple*] I guess I don't think so either. Bye.

[*She slowly hangs up the phone. Pause. And then . . . her upbeat demeanor
returns.*]

[*to audience*] Found my Sprite!

[*Lights instantly restore to:*]

The Living Room.

BECKY: [*calls toward basement*] CHRIS. ARE YOU DOWN THERE? I NEED YOU.   90
[*to audience*] He's a good kid. Studying psychology—which might come in handy.
I mean, he's twenty-six years old and I just wish he'd meet a nice young woman
who is, I don't know, *completely the opposite* of every girl he's ever dated. Is that too
much to ask?

[CHRIS *enters in basic slovenly college garb, pencil in his mouth, carrying a large
textbook.*]

CHRIS: Yeah—hey—what's up—   95

BECKY: Oh, hi, you're here—

CHRIS: —trying to study down there, you know?—

BECKY: Yes, I'm—

CHRIS: —got midterms next week—full load—pressure's on, big time—

BECKY: Yes, right—   100

CHRIS: —but hey—okay—I'm here now, so: lay it on me.

BECKY: *"Lay it on you"?*

CHRIS: You needed something?

BECKY: I need you to pick up the pizza. Down at Angelo's. Money in my purse. Dad'll be
  here soon. I'll make a salad.   105

CHRIS: I already ate.

BECKY: I told you I was ordering pizza tonight.

CHRISL Yeah, but on the way home I was walking by Angelo's—and it smelled good—

BECKY: You already ate there?

CHRIS: I was hungry. I was awake.   110

BECKY: But I got something special tonight—I had a coupon—I ordered the—

CHRIS: [*finishing her sentence*]—the Double Ham and Artichoke Supreme.

BECKY: How do you know that?

CHRIS: I saw the guy write it down.

BECKY: You were there when I called?   115

CHRIS: He was ringing me up. I saw him write your name down.

BECKY: And you couldn't sit there for twenty minutes and—

CHRIS: Not "twenty minutes"—more like "thirty-seven to forty" minutes—because it's
  DEEP DISH—

BECKY: Okay, okay—but you couldn't call me and say I'm right here at Angelo's, Mom—   120
  I'll wait—read the paper—flirt with some spoiled coeds—and then BRING OUR
  DINNER home with you?!

CHRIS: I NEEDED TO STUDY.

BECKY: WHAT ARE YOU DOING WITH YOUR LIFE?

  [*Quick beat.*]

CHRIS: Huh?   125

BECKY: You're a twenty-six-year-old man—

CHRIS: I thought this was about pizza—

BECKY: —and you're still shacked up with your parents—

CHRIS: Oh, can we please not . . .

BECKY: [*overlapping*] —and, hey, we love you to death but when does a psychology student   130
  get around to all that stuff about "Self-Awareness" and the "Unexamined Life"—

CHRIS: That's Socrates—

BECKY: —okay, thank you—

CHRIS: —and that's Philosophy, not Psychology.

BECKY: —but when does a person *look in the mirror*, Chris?   135

CHRIS: Do you mean when will I *"self-actualize"*?

BECKY: Yes, maybe I mean that.

CHRIS: Most experts believe only a few people *in history* have ever *"self-actualized"*—like
  Plato, Ghandi, Einstein, maybe Bono.

BECKY: Okay, maybe I don't mean that. But at what point do you stop and realize that all   140 your friends have grown up and moved on and *here you are without*—

CHRIS: That's *"Perceptual Constancy"*—the ability to recognize that an object or organism has *not* changed—

BECKY: Yes, that's what—

CHRIS: [*overlapping*]—even though the surrounding stimuli—their physical characteristics,   145
for example, *have* changed.

BECKY: And once someone recognizes this—this failure to *change along with their age and circumstance*—

CHRIS: I don't think the word "failure" is accurate—

BECKY:—at that point don't they—don't you think "hey, maybe I better *get out there and*   150
do something with my life"?

CHRIS: [*interested now*] Have you been reading Erikson? His seminal work: "Childhood and Society"?

BECKY: Who?

CHRIS: Because what you're talking about is *"Generativity"*—the term Erikson gives to the   155
age at which a person has the impulse to become more "productive," to "do something worthwhile" with their life.

BECKY: Yes! That's exactly what I'm talking about!

CHRIS: And in most cases this happens in middle adulthood—often right around *your age,*
Mom—   160

BECKY: No, this is not about—

CHRIS:—and so now that we've got our Terms identified, let's begin with General Inquiry,
for example: *Mom, what are you doing with your life?*

> [*Quick beat.*]

BECKY: *Me?*

> [JOE *enters, saying*—]

JOE: Pizza!   165

> [*—and sets the huge pizza down in their midst, as lights instantly shift to—*]

The Cubicle. Day.

BECKY: [*to audience*] And right then I thought about Mrs. Tipton. Mrs. Tipton is awaiting delivery on her new car—our top-of-the-line sedan, black, fully-loaded. Steve, my co-worker, had been her salesman.

> [STEVE *enters. He wears casual business clothes, a blazer and—incongruously—*
> *an extremely old and worn pair of hiking boots.*]

> [BECKY *is busy with paperwork.*]

STEVE: Have you seen her, yet? Has she come in?   170

BECKY: Seen who, Steve?

STEVE: She was sitting across from me—I had closed the sale and I was going over some of the extras and customized packages—she wants *everything,* Becky, that woman *wants it all*—and so I slid one of the brochures across the desk to her . . . are you listening to me?   175

BECKY: Right here.

STEVE: [*sits on her desk*] . . . and I looked down at her hands, these amazing hands, for a woman her age—the fifty side of forty—just priceless hands, and the thing is: her nails had this black polish on them, this incredible black, this ebony hue from the end of the known world, with a lustre like the '56 Thunderbirds once had, the blackest of blacks, positively *mesmeric* . . . and as I glanced down at the jet-black inky splendor of that nail polish, I swear to you . . . *I could see my own face in her fingers.* Ten Little Steves looking back at me. And Mrs. Tipton said: "Is that all there is, Steve? Is there nothing more to be done?" And the tone in her voice just broke me in half. I watched the Ten Little Steves just . . . *nod a little.* 185

You wait, Becky, you'll see: she has this beautiful . . . *pain.* I mean, I have pain, too—this past year, since Rita died. But not like Mrs. Tipton. A man could fall into that pain and never find his way out.

[*Beat.*]

BECKY: Thanks, Steve.

[STEVE *nods.*]

I'll need the bill of sale. 190

STEVE: Oh—on my desk—I'll be right back.

[*And* STEVE *goes.*]

BECKY: [*to audience*] You see, when Mrs. Tipton arrived last week—

[BECKY'*s DESK PHONE RINGS.*]

[*to audience*] AUGH! I'll get this told, don't worry—[*into phone*] Thank you for calling Bill Buckley Lex—

The Living Room. Same.

[JOE, *on his cell phone, holding the sports page.* CHRIS *is eating and maybe "texting," busily.*]

JOE: [*interrupting her*] Hey, Beck—it's me. 195

BECKY: Oh, Joe, I'm sorry—we got swamped—

JOE: Yeah, I figured. Did you see the news?

BECKY:—and I still have these quarterly reports to get out, so you and Chris should go ahead and eat.

JOE: Yeah, we did. Chris brought home a pizza. 200

BECKY: You're having pizza again?

JOE: Don't worry, we made a salad.

BECKY: Carrot sticks are not a salad.　　　　CHRIS: [*imitating his Mom*] Carrot sticks are not a salad.

JOE [*cont'd*]: Hey, I was just wondering if you saw the news. Big story on CNN— 205

BECKY: What is it?

JOE:—the internal combustion engine has been outlawed. All auto sales ended at 6 p.m. today.

BECKY: Okay—

JOE: Car dealerships nationwide have been shut down. Workers were sent home.   210

BECKY:—very funny.

JOE: And since it's now twenty minutes after *nine* and you're still not home—

BECKY: Joe, I'm sorry.

JOE: Are you the only one there?

BECKY: Francine is here.   215

JOE: Francine is the *janitor*—she's supposed to be there—

BECKY: Joe, I know, I'm sorry . . .

JOE:—I mean, really, it's just a *job,* Beck. It's just *cars.*

> [CHRIS *has torn a piece of paper from his notebook, scribbled a note on it—and now hands it to* JOE.]

JOE: Hold on. [*reads*] "This phenomenon is known as *"Normative Social Influence"*—the desire to gain approval through situational behavior, despite not believing in the   220 value of what one is doing."

> [*Pause.* JOE *sets the paper down. Waits for* BECKY'*s response.*]

Beck—you there?

> [*In silence, she hangs up the phone.*]

The Cubicle.

BECKY: [*to audience*] Sorry, again. [*looks down at her work*] God: the more I do, the further behind I get. [*to an* AUDIENCE MEMBER] Does that happen to you? [*as needed*] [It's terrible, isn't it?] // [Really? Lucky you.]   225

> [*She hands some pages and a stapler to this* AUDIENCE MEMBER.]

Can you give me a hand, for a second? I need these collated and stapled. Just like this. Thanks. [*to audience*] Okay—quick—before we're interrupted: Mrs. Tipton bought her car from Steve. But the model she wanted—customized, loaded with extras—could not be delivered for another three or four weeks. When I told her this, she said: "What's it matter, Becky? I've waited this long." Then she told me   230 her story.

> [*And now lights slowly begin to feature the DISTANT SILHOUETTE of a FIGURE IN BLACK:* MRS. TIPTON (****played by the actress who plays* GINGER**).]

Her husband was wealthy, well-known, and—like her—well into middle age. One day Mrs. Tipton stepped out of the shower. Her husband looked her up and down— handed her a towel—said: "Time is cruel, honey"—and left her for a swimwear model.

There were no kids. No family to speak of. Mrs. Tipton was alone. She sat on the   235 floor of her white-carpeted living room for the next seventeen days. Then she stood up—put on her shoes—walked to Safeway—signed her house over to the checkout girl . . . and walked away from her life. Cleaned out all her accounts. Kept just enough cash to buy a really good manicure and this one fully-loaded black car.

I asked what she planned to do now. "Drive away," she said. To where?, I asked.   240
She said nothing.

I handed her my card, told her I'd call the minute her car came in. She looked at me
with that beautiful pain: "Is that it, Becky? Is that all there is?"

[*The SILHOUETTE of* MRS. TIPTON *fades away, as—*

[WALTER, nicely dressed, appears behind BECKY.]

WALTER: Good evening—   245
BECKY: We're closed.
WALTER: Yes, I know, but I wondered if—
BECKY: You'll need to come by tomorrow.
WALTER:—yes, but you see, this is kind of an emergency, I need to—
BECKY: The dealership closed three hours ago, so if you'd—   250
WALTER: I won't take up much of your time. I can write you a check, give you a credit
    card, have my accountant wire the full amount to you—whatever you prefer.
BECKY: The full amount for what?
WALTER: I need to buy some cars. As a gift for my employees. We have our Company
    Breakfast at 7 a.m. tomorrow morning and we've had a very good year, so I want to   255
    get them all a little something. But I'm just terrible at gifts. My wife, Sheila, she was
    so good at it. Just had a knack. Knew just the perfect thing to buy for people—no
    matter what the occasion. But ever since she passed, I'm a total wreck. I'm told I
    should hire a Gift Consultant, put a sort of Swag Master on
    my payroll, but I really wouldn't know where to begin—   260
BECKY: Look, now is not a—
WALTER:—so, I had my driver take me to some *stores*—I had no idea there were so many
    stores, they're *everywhere*—and I walked around those stores, not a clue, no idea
    what to get, and so I asked my driver to take me home and within moments, there
    we were, stuck in traffic . . . . and I looked out the window and I said to myself: *cars.*   265
    People like *cars.* I'll get them some cars. So, I know it's late, but may I please buy
    some of your cars?

    [*Pause.*]

BECKY: How many do you need?
WALTER: Nine. Just nine of them will do.
BECKY: *Nine cars . . .*   270
WALTER: I could arrange payment for them tonight—and maybe you could just put the
    keys in little gift boxes—Sheila always kept a shelf filled with these neat little gift
    boxes, fitted with ribbons, just perfect—anyway, I thought I'd just hand out these
    boxes at the Company Breakfast and shake their hands and be done with it.

    [*Pause. She stares at him.*]

BECKY: What . . . um . . . what kind of cars would you like?   275
WALTER: Oh, whatever you think. Nine of 'em.

[BECKY *hands him a brochure—still not really believing all this.*]

BECKY: Maybe you should look at this—these are the current models.

WALTER: [*paging through brochure, agitated*] Oh, see—this is where it gets tricky—maybe just one of each style—

BECKY: And what colors? 280

WALTER: See what I mean?! This is impossible! God, I miss Sheila.

BECKY: [*re: the brochure*] Towards the back, there are color and fabric swatches—interior and exterior. Plus we offer—

WALTER: No, no, no, I can't do this. My driver is waiting. I'm supposed to be at a birth- day party for my daughter and I don't have a gift for *her* either!—unless you count 285 my *entire net worth* which she'll inherit the moment I drop dead from trying to *buy some gifts for all these people*—so please, I know how this must sound and how foolish I must look, but please . . . can you help me?

> [*She stares at him. A beat. Then: she takes the brochure from* WALTER*'s hands, saying—*]

BECKY: [*all business*] I recommend our all-wheel drive sport coupe. Very popular. My husband . . . he always wanted one of these. 290

WALTER: *Oh, did he?*

BECKY:—and the thing is: you don't need to pick colors or interiors in advance—the new owners can do that when they come in. And I suggest you buy each of them the same car—to avoid the appearance of playing favorites.

WALTER: That's very smart. 295

> [*She is quickly punching numbers into a calculator, as she talks—*]

BECKY: They could take delivery almost right away. And if you choose the "Top Flight" package on each car, they can add any extras they might want.

WALTER: Good. Let's do that.

BECKY: Okay—

> [*The calculator spits out a very long piece of paper—*BECKY *rips it off—and hands it to* WALTER.]

—your cost for nine of these cars, taxes, title and fees comes to this number right *here.* 300

> [WALTER *looks at the number for a long moment. Then: he looks up into* BECKY*'s eyes.*]

WALTER: You still wear your ring. I do, too. I thought about leaving it with Sheila— having it buried with her . . . [*touching his ring*] It was my daughter who told me to hold onto it. That it would be a nice reminder. [*beat*]

I see you've done the same.

BECKY: Pardon? 305

WALTER: Kept your wedding ring.

BECKY: Well—yes.

WALTER: It's lovely.

BECKY: Thank you—yes, I wear it because, I mean—

WALTER: Was he a good man? Was he kind to you? 310

BECKY: Yes—he was—*is*—I mean, he still *is.*

WALTER: Oh, I know the feeling—

BECKY: He's still with me—we're still together—

WALTER: Exactly—that's what I tell people, too—

BECKY: No, you—   315

WALTER:—it's like she's still with me, right by my side, guiding me through my days—

BECKY: Yes, but my husband is still—

WALTER:—and leading me here tonight. Leading me to you. I'm Walter. And you are . . .

[*She says nothing. He lifts one of her business cards from the desk.*]

[*reads*] . . . Rebecca.

[*He extends his hand.*]

I'm sorry for your loss, Rebecca.   320

BECKY: You don't understand—

WALTER: I like that name: Rebecca. It has substance. Ballast. I hope you don't let people call you "Becky."

BECKY: Well—

WALTER: "Becky" is the name of a dull housewife in a sad movie about a poor family   325
struggling to hold onto their vanishing hopes and dreams. In the movies, a "Becky" always gets the shaft.

[*Pause.*]

BECKY: Walter, I need to tell you about my husband—

WALTER: And I need to tell you more about Sheila—I think that's *healthy,* to do that kind of sharing—but let's not do that here. Let me pay you for these cars and then maybe   330
we can go somewhere—get a bite to eat.

BECKY: You have a party to attend—your daughter's birthday.

WALTER: And of course you'd remember that! Of course you place "family" above every-
thing. Sheila was like that, too. You're right, I should go—and I still don't have a gift for my daughter.   335

BECKY: Does she need a car?

WALTER: She has plenty of those. Maybe I'll get her a loft downtown. Kids like lofts, don't they?

BECKY: I bet they do.

WALTER: Here is my card—with my accountant's name on back.

BECKY: [*re: his card*] "Walter Flood"—I've seen that name.   340

WALTER: Maybe on billboards.

BECKY: Do you advertise there?

WALTER: I *am* the billboards. I own the billboards.

BECKY: Which ones?

WALTER: Pretty much all of them. Go ahead—you can say it: they're an "eyesore"—"visual   345
pollution"—

BECKY: Well—

WALTER:—and all of that is true. Believe me, if I could have made *hundreds of millions of dollars* by doing something *good and noble* for the world, I by-god would have done it. But my father handed me this business and said "Walter, don't screw it up." You   350
play the hand you're dealt.

BECKY: You must have played it well.

WALTER: Who knows. Life is chaos and holidays. Who can say why things turn out the way they do. All I know is that my life has become the story of a handful of people I met by chance and the things we did together. 355

[*Pause. She is staring at him.*]

BECKY: We have these "gift keys" . . . they don't belong to any actual vehicles, but they look real, and people use them when they're giving a car as a gift.

WALTER: I'll need nine of them.

BECKY: And some gift boxes.

WALTER: Perfect. 360

[*Pause.*]

May I keep your card, Rebecca?

BECKY: Sure.

WALTER: And may I call you?

[*Pause. She stares at him, then turns to the audience—*]

BECKY: [*to audience*] I made a sound that was sort of a cross between "Mm-hmm" and "Hmm-mm"— 365

[WALTER *turns and leaves.*]

—and I thought "Well, okay, *THAT happened*"—no big deal, except for the fact that I failed to explain to this kind gentleman that my husband is not currently DEAD.

[JOE's *voice is heard from OFF—*]

JOE'S VOICE: Beck—you still awake?

[BECKY *turns quickly to the* AUDIENCE MEMBER *who has been collating/stapling, and says—*]

BECKY: Oh—sorry—how's it going over here? [*as needed, quickly*] [That's great. Good job.] // [That's it?! What have you been *doing?!*] 370

[*She takes these papers to a table in the room and begins to sort them, as lights expand to—*]

The Living Room. Night.

[*—and* JOE *enters. In sweats and a t-shirt. Barefoot. Ready for bed.*]

JOE: It's eleven-fifteen.

BECKY: I know. I'm sorry.

JOE: [*re: the papers*] And you brought work home?

BECKY: I told Buckley I'd pull together some info for his new office manager.

JOE: At the Mega-place? 375

BECKY: Yeah.

JOE: Has that opened?

BECKY: Two weeks.

JOE: And he's paying you overtime for this, right?—for setting up his new office, on top of running your own? 380

[*The answer, of course, is no. And* BECKY *just sheepishly looks at* JOE . . . *who opens his arms—*]

Come here.

[*—and holds her tight.*]

Let me tell you how this goes: you take your shoes off, go upstairs, put your nightgown on, put all those mysterious lotions on your face, climb in our bed, arrange your pillows, and crack open that big biography you've been reading for the past two years. That thing always puts you to sleep. 385

BECKY: I really want to finish it.

JOE: Don't ruin a good thing.

BECKY: Is Chris home?

JOE: Had a date.

BECKY: Oh, no. 390

JOE: Some girl he met at a party.

BECKY: Is she a student?

JOE: It doesn't matter, Beck—

BECKY: I'm just—

JOE:—and why would you even ask? He's never going to tell us anything about this girl, 395
any girl—

BECKY: You're right. I'm not going to pry—

JOE: Good.

BECKY: [*can't help it*] —did he say where they were going?

[*Quick beat.* JOE *starts off.*]

JOE: You coming? 400

BECKY: Right behind you.

[JOE *goes.* BECKY *goes to turn off a final light, and as she does so—Her CELL PHONE RINGS. She stares at it. Answers it.*]

[*on phone*] Hello?

The Terrace of the Flood Estate. Night.

[WALTER—*in a shaft of moonlight—is on his cell phone.*]

WALTER: [*on phone*] Rebecca?

[*Beat.*]

BECKY: [*on phone*] Yes?

WALTER: My daughter tells me there's a rule of some kind, when a man has been given a 405
woman's number—a "twenty-four hour" rule. [*looking at his watch*] Well, I'm afraid
I wasn't able to wait that long. Still . . . it's a lovely night . . . and I thought I'd . . .
[*voice fades*]

[*Pause.*]

BECKY: [*business voice*] What can I do for you, Mr. Flood?

WALTER: [*beat, tone changes*] Oh, I'm sorry. I'm terribly sorry. 410

BECKY: Pardon me?

WALTER: Just there. In your voice. I've been a fool, haven't I?

BECKY: Why do you—

WALTER: Mistaking your kind and helpful behavior for something *more*. God, what a fool— 415

BECKY: Please, it's—

WALTER: —I'm sorry, Rebecca—I won't trouble you again.

BECKY: —I didn't know what . . . you were calling about.

WALTER: I see.

BECKY: You have the nine gift boxes— 420

WALTER: Yes.

BECKY: —and I've memo'd the sales manager to expect payment from your accountant.

WALTER: Thank you.

BECKY: So, I think . . . that's it.

[*Pause.*]

Mr. Flood, are you there? 425

WALTER: [*simple, no self-pity*] Things *narrow*, don't they? As we age. The things in our life—our life itself, whether we admit or not—it begins to *narrow*. And the unexpected fades away.

[*Hearing this,* BECKY *sits down.*]

You surprised me, Rebecca. And even if we never speak again: I am in your debt for that. You are that thing in my life that I thought would never come again . . . that 430 unexpected thing. [*pause*] I'll say good night now. And, once again: I'm sorry.

[*Pause.* WALTER *begins to hang up his phone, as—*]

[BECKY *turns to the audience.*]

BECKY: [*to audience*] And the word out of my mouth was supposed to be "Goodbye." But something happened—

WALTER: Yes? 435

BECKY: [*on phone*] Pardon?

WALTER: You said "Wait."

BECKY: No, I didn't.

WALTER: I was about to hang up—

BECKY: [*to audience*] Yes, I did. I said "Wait." 440

WALTER: —and you said—

BECKY: [*on phone*] I'm sure I didn't say "Wait." I wouldn't say that. I'd say something else.

WALTER: Such as?

BECKY: Such as . . . *thank you*. For calling. And . . . for what you've said. I'm very . . . [*voice fades*] 445

[JOE *peeks his head in, saying—*]

JOE: [*whispered*] Everything okay?

[*Startled,* BECKY *turns—nods.*]

Is that Buckley? At this hour?!

[BECKY *just grimaces.*]

[*shakes head*] *Unbelievable.*

BECKY: It's okay.

JOE: Gimme the phone—

BECKY: Joe, no—

JOE:—does he have any idea how lucky he is to have found someone like you?!   450

BECKY: Joe—

JOE: You tell him that or I will!

[*And* JOE *heads back to bed.*]

WALTER: It's that hour, you know. That late hour on a summer night when words come
out easily. "Too easily"—Sheila used to say. She claimed most of her friend's heart-   455
aches and divorces could be traced to things spoken freely and foolishly, on long
summer nights. [*beat*] And I suppose I've just done the same.

BECKY: Don't take this wrong—

WALTER: All right.

BECKY:—but you really have to stop talking about your deceased wife. You really have to   460
stop that.

WALTER: And you'll do the same.

BECKY: What's that?

WALTER: Your husband. No mention of him. Is that our agreement?

BECKY: But it's *different*, Walter—   465

WALTER: I will ask nothing of you, Rebecca. Nothing you're unwilling to give. Keep your
husband in whatever place, wherever he belongs in your heart. We needn't speak of
him again.

[*Pause.*]

I was hoping to see you. Nothing too intimate—just a small gathering of friends. At
my home. Sunday night. A pleasant group. I think you'll enjoy them. If you don't   470
enjoy them, I'll send them home and bring in some other people.

[*He awaits her reaction. Nothing.*]

I'll send directions to you at work. Hope you can join us. Good night, Rebecca.

[BECKY *ends the call. She goes to a chair, cradling a pillow to her chest, and at
the instant that she sits down—*]

The Living Room. Dawn.

[*—*CHRIS *enters, great mood, dressed to go for a run.*]

CHRIS: Hey, Mom—you're up early.

BECKY: [*surprised*] Huh?

CHRIS Terrific morning out there. "*Crisp*"—like Dad always says. Now I finally know   475
what he means! Catch you later—

BECKY: Chris, wait!

[CHRIS *stops, turns to her.*]

What's going on?

CHRIS: What do you mean?

BECKY: It's *five-thirty a.m.*   480

CHRIS: And it's *crisp* out there.

BECKY: You don't *run.* You barely *walk.* So, what's with the—

CHRIS: This girl I'm seeing—she's a *runner.* It's so weird and awesome.

BECKY: Whoa whoa whoa whoa—

CHRIS: She's really into it—five days a week—except right now she's on crutches, has some   485
    ligament damage—

BECKY: So, how is she—

CHRIS:—so right now *I'm* running and she's driving her car alongside me. We have these
    really good talks.

BECKY: Let's back up: you're *exercising* and you're having *really good talks* with a girl. How   490
    long was I asleep?!

[JOE *enters—dressed for work. Pencil behind his ear. Big mug of coffee in his
hand.*]

JOE: Look at this: you all got up to see me off to work?

BECKY: Joe—

JOE: That's so nice.   495

BECKY:—Chris was telling me about a girl he's seeing.

JOE: I always liked Candace. What happened to her?

CHRIS: Oh, not again.

JOE: Even your Mom liked Candace.

BECKY: She was a nice girl.

CHRIS: Candace had no inner life! She was all lipstick and spandex and exclamation points!   500

JOE: [*whoa*] Okay—

CHRIS: I don't need that, Dad.

JOE:—sorry I ever brought it—

CHRIS: [*overlapping*]—I'm not looking for a *cosmetic* connection here—I don't require a
    partner who provides mere auditory and visual stimuli—   505

JOE: You have your iPhone for that.

CHRIS: Exactly!—I am looking—I would hazard to say that ALL OF US are looking to
    put *our fundamental nature forward,* in hopes of one day *tapping the wellspring of
    another human soul.*

[JOE *and* BECKY *just stare at him.*]

JOE: So you don't care what she looks like?   510

CHRIS: Look, Dad: obviously the process of finding your soul mate can be greatly acceler-
    ated if she also happens to be really hot.

JOE: Okay—good to know.

[JOE *leaves, giving a smile to* BECKY, *just as—CAR HORN, OUTSIDE, is heard.*]

CHRIS: That's her. I gotta run.

BECKY: Where's this girl from?   515

CHRIS: I'll find out today. We're going on a huge run. Turns out we're both really interested in the *"Mere Exposure Effect."*

BECKY: The what?

CHRIS: The "Mere Exposure Effect" posits that you can begin to like someone for no reason other than *repeated exposure to them.* Isn't that awesome?! 520

[*HORN SOUNDS, AGAIN.*]

Gotta fly. Peace.

[*And* CHRIS *is gone.*]

BECKY: [*to no one*] Peace?

[STEVE *enters, carrying paperwork, looking for* BECKY *at—*]

The Cubicle. Day.

[*—but she's not there.*]

STEVE: Becky—I've got those invoices. [*looking around*] Becky?

[BECKY *throws on her shoes and hurries to meet* STEVE—]

BECKY: I'm here, Steve—sorry—I just—

STEVE: Are you just getting here? It's after ten. 525

BECKY: No, I was—I needed to—

STEVE: Did you sleep here? You look like you slept here.

BECKY: I didn't sleep here.

STEVE: It's okay. After Rita died, I slept here—

BECKY: Yes, I know. 530

STEVE:—couldn't bear it at home. Couldn't bring myself to look at her things . . . her hiking boots . . . her funny winter cap—

BECKY: It was hard, I know.

STEVE: [*overlapping*] —and then, when I went upstairs, there was our little hallway . . . the paint . . . the pictures on the walls . . .our bedroom door . . . [*a beat, we think he's* 535 *done, then . . .*] . . . the door knob . . . our bed . . . the quilt . . . the pillows . . . *Mr. Dibble*—

BECKY: YES, STEVE—you told me.

STEVE:—so you know what I did:

BECKY: Yes, I do. 540

STEVE: I curled up under my desk and fell asleep. Spent three nights like that. Right here in the sales room.

BECKY: Yes, I know.

STEVE: I see her falling, Becky. My mind goes to this place . . . where I am reliving that moment on that mountain and no matter how long I wear these hiking boots, and 545 no matter how many times I see it happen: I *can't catch her*—my arms won't *reach*—and all I can do is *watch.*

[*Pause.*]

BECKY: [*BIG change of subject*] OKAY, Steve, what have you got there for me?

STEVE: When did you get so cold?

BECKY: I'm sorry? 550

STEVE: You were always there for me—you and Joe and the others—you were such good friends—always willing to talk me down the mountain—

BECKY: We just wanted to help, Steve.

STEVE:—but then it changed. Like you turned the page in your calendar one day and said: "Okay, time's up. Steve should be over it." 555

BECKY: No, that's not—

STEVE: "We gave him X-number of months to mourn good ol' Rita, we took him out for beers and listened to him tell the story of her fall for the two-hundredth time—"

BECKY: [*trying to make a joke*] *Three*-hundredth—

STEVE: THAT IS NOT FUNNY. [*pause*] You don't know, Becky . . . you and Joe, you're 560 set, you're *locked in,* you'll have each other forever . . . but some of the rest of us—

BECKY: I know . . . I'm sorry . . .

STEVE: [*overlapping*]—*I want to get past this stuff.* I really do. I'm sick of talking about it, and you must be *really* sick of hearing it—

> [*Becky's DESK PHONE RINGS, but—*STEVE *lifts and hangs up the receiver, in one motion, and never stops talking—*]

—but it's like yesterday I'm getting a coffee, and this little boy and his mom are in 565 line behind me, and they have this puppy, and I'm standing there minding my own business, and I hear the mom say to her son: "Why don't you go show the puppy to that sad man over there—maybe the puppy will cheer him up!"—and I am really trying to ignore this, but now the puppy is sniffing at my boots and the little kid is saying: "Hi Mister, you look sad—do you want to pet my puppy?" And what I 570 THOUGHT—what I didn't SAY, even though I wanted to—what I THOUGHT was: "You bet I do, sonny boy—I want to pet your little puppy—and then I want to take him for a nice walk, a little hike in the mountains with you right by his side— and as we approach the rugged vista which is our destination, I want to let go of his leash for just a *second,* just an *instant,* right when the path beneath his little paws 575 starts to give way—and I want you to watch your puppy's desperate eyes as he tries to grab at that ground—but his little paws touch nothing but *air,* nothing to hold onto, nothing but you and your screams and you might as well *scream your heart out,* sonny boy, because THERE IS NOTHING YOU CAN DO for that puppy of yours who is falling DOWN DOWN DOWN into a dark abyss that will NEVER 580 EVER GIVE HIM BACK."

> [*Pause.*]

BECKY: At least you only thought it.

STEVE: I only thought I thought it. Turns out I *said it.*

BECKY: Oh my god . . .

STEVE: It was ugly. The kid cried till he threw up. His mom poured a Frappuccino on me. 585

> [STEVE *sits down.*]

> [BECKY *is looking at a driving map printout.*]

BECKY: You ever driven out to Cedar Cove?

STEVE: You don't drive to Cedar Cove, Becky—you *achieve* Cedar Cove. Or marry into it.

BECKY: Looks like it's an hour to the ferry—

STEVE:—depending on traffic—forty or fifty minutes on the water—and once you dock, 590
another hour's drive to the far side of the island.

BECKY: People commute from there?

STEVE: People have sea-planes. What's in Cedar Cove?

BECKY: Oh, just something for a client.

STEVE: What client? One of my clients? 595

BECKY: No one you know.

STEVE: Maybe I do. Gimme a hint.

BECKY: So: plans for the weekend?

[*He hands her a flier.*]

STEVE: Oh, you bet—here's a flier—you and Joe have plans on Sunday?

BECKY: We might—I might have something. 600

STEVE: I'm doing a fund-raiser for the Wilderness Co-op—at my apartment—we'll have
organic juices and trail-friendly gorp—

BECKY: [*300th time*] And your slide show.

STEVE:—and of course the slide show of my hikes with Rita, but this one has a couple new
photos—never before seen—which really makes it worth watching the whole thing 605
over from the beginning—

BECKY: Okay, great—

[*A strange CELL PHONE RING, coming from somewhere on* STEVE.]

STEVE:—whoa, that's me, gotta take this, thanks for talking me down the mountain
again—[*stops*]

Oh, they need these by five. 610

[*And* STEVE *puts a full box of invoices on Becky's desk—*]

See you Sunday!

[*—and is gone, as—The DESK PHONE RINGS and RINGS.* BECKY *stares
at the invoices . . . at all the work on her desk . . . at her RINGING PHONE,
then—She looks to the Booth, saying—*]

BECKY: Can I go home?

[*Light instantly bump to:*]

The Living Room. Evening.

BECKY: Thank you.

[*And* BECKY *stands in her home . . . in silence.*]

I used to love a quiet house. Nothing but the sound of my thoughts. Those were
the moments when I was most grateful for my life. I'd sit and remember what a cute 615
little boy Chris was—before he entered this phase called "manhood."

[BECKY *lifts a framed 8x10 PHOTO of a "smiling Becky & Joe."*]

I'd think about Joe and his great big Soviet-style heart: solid and strong and much bigger than it needs to be. Twenty-eight years of marriage . . . and counting.

When my house was quiet, I could see my life for what it was: *content. And complete.*

[BECKY *sets the* PHOTO *down. Then . . . She seeks out* THREE WOMEN *from the* AUDIENCE. *Ideally, she will say nothing whatsoever to these* WOMEN—*just approach them and gesture for them to please join her on stage, to help her with something. (She may need to whisper "Will you help me for a minute?" to facilitate this.) When* BECKY *has all* THREE WOMEN *on stage, she begins . . .*]

Okay—thanks for being here. Since I don't know you, it should be easy for us to be   620
honest with each other, don't you think?

[*She ad-libs off their responses, as needed.*]

As you know, I've been invited to a dinner party at Walter Flood's house on Sunday. Which is tonight. Now: if you think I should go to this dinner party, would you please raise your hand?

[*To THOSE WHO RAISE THEIR HANDS:*]

Thank you! Are you sure?! [Okay, thanks. // Yeah, me neither.]   625

[*As needed, to THOSE WHO DID NOT:*]

[*as needed, shaking hands*] [Thanks for being honest. God knows you're probably right. You can go now.]

[BECKY *turns to the* WOMEN *who remain.*]

[*to the* WOMEN] Okay, ready? We've got work to do. [*to the Booth*] Some music please?

[MUSIC: *something classic (à la Blossom Dearie's "Give Him the Ooh-La-La"), or perhaps something more contemporary (à la Bonnie Raitt's "Wah She Go Do"), as—*BECKY, *with ad-libs, sends the* WOMEN *in various directions (onstage and off) to retrieve: Her dress. Her shoes. Her make-up and hair items.*]

[*to audience*] Yes, I know this is usually done offstage—for the same reason that women disappear into the "powder room"—to maintain "the mystery." The mystery to me is why we go to all this trouble just so a man can look at us and think to himself: "Wow—doesn't a beer sound good?"

[*During the following, the* WOMEN *help* BECKY *get dressed, coiffed, and made-up. They also bring on her coat.*]

Sometimes you just want to look nice, feel good about yourself—is that so wrong?   630
And if that means getting a little gussied up and going out to party—what's the harm? And if that means spending a week's salary on a new dress and then travelling for three hours in cars and on ferryboats, all to arrive at the estate of some loopy widower and a roomful of rich strangers who will take one look at you and say "I think you want the trailer park up the road"—well, *if that's what it takes, damn it*   635
all, I'm gonna do it.

[*In only a minute or two: the transformation of* BECKY *is complete. She looks great.*]

[*to the* WOMEN] You're good at this. Thank you. Do you want to come with me? [*ad-libs off them*] No, better not. Never arrive with someone prettier than you.

JOE'S VOICE: [*from OFF*] Hey, Beck—are you still here?

BECKY: [*to the* WOMEN] Okay—you gotta go—if he sees you in here—well, I'm not sure 640
he *would* see you in here—but let's not take any chances—

> [*She ushers the* WOMEN *offstage*—]

Thank you—thanks so much—

> [*—just before* JOE *arrives.*]

JOE: Traffic shouldn't be too bad on Sunday except near the stadium. I filled your car with
gas, and put a new flashlight—with fresh batteries—in the trunk.

BECKY: [*with a smile*] I'm not going camping. 645

JOE: In this city, driving and camping are a lot alike. [*pause*] You look . . .

> [*She waits, a little nervous.*]

BECKY: . . . what?

JOE: Like a million bucks.

> [BECKY *gives the* AUDIENCE WOMEN (*her "dressers"*) *a quick and covert
> "thumbs up."*]

So, is he gonna put you up?

BECKY: What? 650

JOE: Buckley. Three hours to the Mega-Ship for this—what?—this fancy "office party"—

BECKY: This "corporate event"—

JOE: Oh, right.

BECKY:—to wine and dine the regional reps—show them the new store—stuff like that.

JOE: Three hours there, couple hours at this event, three hours back—it's gonna be late, 655
Beck.

BECKY: [*with a smile*] I have a flashlight.

JOE: Take this.

> [JOE *holds up a key.*]

You're gonna be ten minutes from that apartment complex I roofed. I know the
owner. He keeps an extra apartment there. Furnished. When I had some late nights 66[*
down there, he offered it to me—in case I didn't want to make the drive home. It's
small, but clean. Single bed, fridge, towels.

BECKY: Joe, I couldn't—

JOE: It's just sitting there, Beck. He's not renting it till the fall.

> [JOE *holds up the key, again.*]   *)5*

Just take it. In case it's too late to drive home.

BECKY: It won't be.

JOE: All you'd have to do is call me—say you're gonna spend the night and
the morning.

> [*She does not take the key.*]

BECKY: I'm coming home tonight.

[*Pause.*]

JOE: You have your phone?   670

BECKY: Yes.

JOE: Stay in your far left lane near the stadium.

BECKY: Got it. Joe?

JOE: Hmm?

BECKY: Why are you so good to me?   675

JOE: Oh, Beck . . . we've had a nice day—let's not ruin it by having a "talk."

BECKY: I just—

JOE: Because I know where this goes: "why are you so good to me?" leads to "I hope I'm just as good to you" and that leads to "of *course* you are"—"you're just *saying* that"— "no, it's *true*"—"why can't you be *honest* with me"—"I *am* being honest with you"—   680 "no, I don't think you *are*"—

BECKY: Joe, please—

JOE: [*overlapping*] —and then pretty soon we're fighting about how much we love each other. That's weird.

BECKY: Okay—   685

JOE: That's a weird thing to do.

BECKY:—you're right. No more "talks," I promise.

[JOE *gets her a plastic bottle of water.*]

JOE: For the road. It's cold.

[*As she takes the bottle, she can't help saying . . .*]

BECKY: But, if there was someone—

JOE: Oh, jeez.   690

BECKY:—someone who was better than me, treated you better than I did—no, let me finish—someone you were attracted to, liked spending time with, anything like that . . . I hope . . .

JOE: You hope I'd be honest. Tell you all about it.

BECKY: . . . I hope you'd lie. Or not *lie,* really . . . just not *tell me right away.*   695

JOE: Okay . . .

BECKY: Because maybe it would just *play itself out.* These infatuations don't last. Maybe in a couple days, couple weeks, you'd be over it—no harm done—

JOE: No contact, no foul—

BECKY:—right, but if you'd already told me, I'd be *devastated*—just torn up for no reason   700 at all.

JOE: Okay. I'll lie to you. God, I hope I meet someone so I can try this out.

[JOE *hands* BECKY *her coat.*]

CKY: What about you?

Hmm?

: If I ever . . . met someone like that. What would you want me to do?   705

, my plan is a lot simpler.

ow's that?

ll me. Right away. If that happens, I want to know about it.

BECKY: Even if it meant *nothing?*
JOE: Yes, I'd want to know—   710
BECKY: *Why?*
JOE:—so I could kill the guy. [*beat*] Love you. Drive safe.

> [*He gives her a kiss and goes, as—*
>
> [BECKY *moves to a chair, which lights will now reveal as—*]

Becky's Car. Evening.

> [BECKY *speaks to the audience, as she "drives." Her mood is edgy.*]

BECKY: This is a bad idea. Just a terrible idea—a Terrible Idea *Which I'm Going To Be Late For,* unless I make this 5:20 ferry. Can someone tell me why they put these boats so   715
far from the highway—way out by the water?! I'll call him. Easy. I'll call Walter and
tell him something came up. Or better yet, I'll tell him that *my husband is ALIVE
and we are still married and I am not the type of person who sneaks around behind his
back*—but, of course, I *AM* that person, apparently I am *exactly* that person: that
sneaking-around-and-trying-to-catch-the-5:20-ferry person. [*reaching into her purse*]   720
Still—I have to call him. Tell him I might be late. Or lost. Or insane. [*re: purse*] And
can someone tell me why my lipstick is the *first thing I find* when I reach into my
purse—[*pulls out lipstick*] —unless what I'm trying to find in my purse is my lipstick?!
Then it's nowhere to be found. [*beat*] Like my phone. [*rummaging through purse*]
Oh, come on, Becky—find your phone—you know it's in here—Joe handed you   725
your coat, and you grabbed your purse and your keys and . . . [*realizes*] . . . you *left
your phone at home.*

> [*Becky's CELL PHONE RINGS in—*]

The Living Room. Same.

> [*—and* JOE *answers it.*]

JOE: [*on phone*] You forgot your phone.

The Terrace. Same.

> [WALTER *on his phone, dressed for the party.*]

WALTER: [*on phone, confused*] Hmm?
JOE: After all that, you forgot your phone!   730

Becky's Car. Same.

BECKY: [*to audience, disbelief*] I forgot my phone.
WALTER: Who's this?
JOE: Oh, I'm sorry—
WALTER: Rebecca?

JOE:—you're trying to reach Becky?   735
WALTER: It's Walter.
JOE: Walter?
WALTER: Yes.
JOE: Are you the new guy?
WALTER: Uh, well—   740
JOE: She's on her way—probably hit traffic.
WALTER: Who's this?
JOE: It's Joe.
WALTER: Joe?
JOE: She left her phone here.   745
WALTER: Oh, I see—at *work*—
JOE: When she gets there, tell her she left her phone.
WALTER: I'll do that.
JOE: And tell her to spend the night.
WALTER: *Pardon me?*   750
BECKY: In my car . . .
JOE: She deserves that, right?—
WALTER: [*confused*] Yes, I suppose so . . .
JOE:—the money they make on those cars.
BECKY: Alone . . .   755
WALTER: Oh, they loved them.
JOE: What's that?
WALTER: They all loved their cars.

      [*MUSIC, UNDER.*]

BECKY: Radio on . . .
JOE: [*confused*] I bet they did . . .   760
WALTER: Thanks for your help.
BECKY: Traffic moving, nice and easy . . .
WALTER: See you, Joe.
JOE: See you, Walter.
BECKY: Heaven help me.   765

    [*MUSIC RISES, as—The lights rush to black.*]

End of Act One.

ACT TWO

The Terrace. Night.

[*COCKTAIL MUSIC from OFF, as the dinner party is in full swing.* **KENNI** *and* GINGER *are looking at the view. They each have a drink. They both look smashing.*]

KENNI: He bought me a loft.

GINGER: For your birthday?

KENNI: Yes. Downtown. Terrific view. Cost a fortune.

GINGER: Your father loves you, Kenni.

KENNI: [*beat*] Do you need a loft?   5

GINGER: You don't want it?

KENNI: He bought me one last year, too.

GINGER: It's been hard on him. Since your Mom died.

KENNI: Turns out Mom was right about everything. She told me exactly how Dad was
    going to behave when she was gone: said he'd get a little daft about things. Lose his   10
    confidence—be a little adrift with people—

GINGER: Sheila was always very perceptive.

KENNI:—and that he'd probably get snookered by a woman.

GINGER: She said that?

KENNI: She knew her friends, Ginger. She knew that once she died, they'd smell blood in   15
    the water.

GINGER: Did she mention any names?

KENNI: Oh, come on!—Mom knew you'd swoop right in with your charming smile and
    your backless dress. It's no big deal. Dad's a big boy. Given certain *very clear* bound-
    aries, he can take care of himself.   20

GINGER: Kenni, I assure you—

KENNI: I sort of envy him. And you.

GINGER: Why?

KENNI: There's no pressure to "find someone"—not at your age.

GINGER: Thanks for that.   25

KENNI: Or to find the "*right* someone"—I mean, did you ever meet someone who was
    sweet and kind and funny and odd and had almost nothing in common with
    you?—who had no idea you were from a wealthy family—someone who just liked
    you because of *who you were*—and when you're with him you have dopey songs
    that you can't get out of your head—and all the hard things seem so easy and all   30
    the easy things seem so important—I mean, really, Ginger, *it can't just be me,*
    right? This must have happened to LOTS of people—this must have happened
    to *YOU.*

GINGER: [*simple*] No. You're the first.

    [WALTER *arrives, tense. He holds a martini.*]

When are we eating, Walter?   35

WALTER: I wish I knew. I kept following the caterer around the house, asking him about
    dinner—but he never answered me. Turned out he was the exterminator. Why must
    everyone wear *white*?

KENNI: I'll handle it. [*with a look at* GINGER] Have fun.

    [KENNI *goes.*]

GINGER: Walter.   40

WALTER: Ginger.

[*They are looking at the water.*]

GINGER: Your daughter thinks I'm swooping in.
WALTER: Pardon?
GINGER: On you. She thinks I have some plan to swoop in.
WALTER: Well, you know Kenni, she's very protective—   45
GINGER: Yes, of course—
WALTER:—but I personally don't feel . . . swooped in . . . upon.
GINGER: Good.

[*They drink. Look at the view.*]

WALTER: I don't see your boat. I don't see either of your boats.
GINGER: The boats are gone. The art work is gone. The horses.   50
WALTER: Even the horses?
GINGER: No way to keep them. Or the place at the lake. Or the season tickets.
WALTER: *You gave up your season tickets?*
GINGER: Along with three cars and most of my jewelry.
WALTER: I had no idea.   55
GINGER: It finally caught up with us—the Timber Baron's kids. We all assumed that the
      money none of us made would never run out—then the investments went bad, the
      trust funds got emptied, and the bills came due.
WALTER: I'm so sorry—
GINGER No—please—the last thing we deserve is sympathy. The fact is: after a hundred   60
      years of being pampered and deferred to, *none of us know how to do a fucking thing.*
      Oh, sure, we know how to stay *busy*—we're all the time telling each other how *busy*
      we are—but if we had to walk out the door tomorrow and do something practical,
      something *useful*—something other than dressing up, attending a function and eating
      with the proper fork: we wouldn't have a *clue*.   65
WALTER: Ginger—
GINGER: If our great-Grandpa—the Timber Baron—came back and saw what *soft little
      spoiled ninnies* we've become, he'd kick our ass to hell and back.

And here I am: the woman who kept putting off getting married—putting it off till the
last minute and *beyond*—and I could do that, you see, because I always had this safety   70
net. I had my *money*. And I knew that even when my looks were long gone, I'd still
have my inheritance . . . and maybe some man would want *that* . . . even if he didn't
really want *me*.

[**KENNI** *appears*.]

KENNI: I found the chef. Dinner's being served.
GINGER: Wonderful. I'm starved.   75

[**GINGER** *goes*.]

WALTER: I had no idea about Ginger. What she's going through.
KENNI: Mom would say—
WALTER: [*sharper than he intends*] I don't want to hear what your mother would say. Not
      tonight. So . . . how's the loft?

KENNI: It's nice.   80

WALTER: Do you paint there?

KENNI: *Paint?*

WALTER: Isn't that what people do in lofts? That's what they do in the movies. They paint and play the saxophone. Do you need a saxophone?

KENNI: Dad, listen—   85

WALTER: Or maybe a treadmill? I know how you and Ramsey love to run.

KENNI: Yes, well—

WALTER: Is he in town?

KENNI: No, the trust fund playboy Ramsey McCord is still back East. Trolling for debutantes.   90

WALTER: You talk that way—but everyone assumes you'll marry him, anyway.

KENNI: Including you?

WALTER: No—I hope you'll surprise me. I've come to believe in surprises.

> [BECKY *appears, behind* WALTER.]

> [BECKY *still wears her coat, and still carries the water bottle which* JOE *gave her.*]

KENNI: [*to* BECKY] Catering staff?

BECKY: Umm . . .   95

KENNI: I can show you to the kitchen—

> [WALTER *turns to see her.*]

WALTER: You made it!

BECKY: I guess so.

WALTER: Rebecca, this is Kensington Hermione Flood—my daughter.

KENNI: *Kenni.* [*re: catering remark*] Sorry, I thought—   100

BECKY: That's quite the name.

KENNI: My mother was a terrible Anglophile.

BECKY: Yes, I've heard a lot about your Mom—

WALTER:—but you won't hear another word about her tonight. [*re: water bottle*] Now, let's get you a proper drink—   105

BECKY: I'm fine.

WALTER: Well, I'll get you a tumbler and some ice—

BECKY: No thanks—this is all I need. Really.

> [BECKY *continues to clutch her water bottle like a security blanket.*]

KENNI: Well . . .

WALTER: Kenni lives downtown. She has a new loft.   110

BECKY: Oh, right—Happy Birthday!

KENNI: [*odd*] Thanks.

WALTER: [*to* BECKY, *concerned*] Were my directions wrong?

BECKY: No—they were fine—but no sooner had I driven off the ferry, but I ran into a breakdown—middle of the road—it was pretty bad—and I didn't have my cell   115 phone—

WALTER: Yes, I know.

BECKY: [*overlapping*] —and I was running late—but somehow I made it through and I got here and *what do you mean "you know"?*

WALTER: I spoke to Joe. 120

[*Beat.*]

BECKY: Really?
WALTER: He answered—told me you'd left, that you were on your way here—
BECKY: He did?
WALTER: Such a pleasant guy. Is he one of the salesman? 125

[KENNI *breaks in, with purpose*—]

KENNI: Maybe I should take your coat . . . if you're staying?
WALTER: She's staying.

[KENNI *helps* BECKY *out of her coat.*]

KENNI: Okay. [*to* WALTER] We're waiting.

[KENNI *goes.*]

WALTER: You look . . .
BECKY: Like I've been driving all day? 130
WALTER: . . . stunning. Completely stunning.

[As WALTER *takes a sip of his martini*—]

[BECKY *once again gives a quick, "thumbs-up" to her "dressers."*]

I was starting to think I'd made you up. Or known you in some other time or place.
Do you ever do that—imagine a kind of parallel life?
BECKY: Umm . . .

[WALTER *holds up his martini glass—making a toast.*]

WALTER: Cheers. 135

[BECKY *touches her water bottle to his glass*—]

BECKY: Clink.

Lights isolate Becky.

BECKY: And we went inside. And I was seated across from Walter—with a Nobel econo-
mist on my left, and a woman who looked like Lauren Hutton on my right.

The food was terrific. The conversation stimulating. And I started feeling braver
by the minute. Yes, I'd told one outright lie to my husband and I wasn't proud of 140
that—but no one was hurt. Not yet. And if it stopped *here*—if I had dinner, said
good night and drove home—that would be the end of it. No harm done.

The Living Room.

[JOE *and* CHRIS—*sharing a bag of chips—follow a distraught* STEVE *into the
room.*]

JOE: Really? Not *one person* came?

STEVE: I put up fliers, sent E-vites to everyone—*nothing*.

JOE: Sorry to hear it, Steve.   145

STEVE: I had organic fair trade shade-grown coffee in biodegradable mugs!

CHRIS: Doing good is hard, man.

JOE: Have a chip.

> [STEVE *reaches into the bag of chips, saying*—]

STEVE: These are *terrible* for you.

> [—*and then devours the chip.*]

CHRIS: You know, Steve, I think this has produced in you a certain level of *dysphoria*.   150

STEVE: *"Dysphoria"?*

CHRIS: Think of it as the opposite of *euphoria*. A sort of *stew* of anxiety, restlessness and depression—but you can't really diagnose or treat it like a standard disorder. It's more a state of being.

STEVE: *A way of life.*   155

CHRIS: Exactly.

STEVE: Can I have another chip?

JOE: You bet.

> [STEVE *grabs the entire bag, and starts eating, avidly.*]

STEVE: Where's Becky?

JOE: You know—that big shindig that Buckley is throwing.   160

STEVE; What shindig?

JOE: That corporate event—the sneak peek for the all the industry insiders, down south at the new Mega-Ship.

STEVE: That's impossible.

JOE: Huh?   165

STEVE: It's not open, yet. That dealership—

JOE: This is a preview, a kick-off—

CHRIS: She got all dressed up.

JOE: [*beat*] You really don't know about this?

STEVE: No. [*beat*] I wonder what else I don't know about.   170

CHRIS: Don't go there, Steve.

Lights isolate Becky.

BECKY: [*to audience*] Dessert was to die for. And the Lauren Hutton-lookalike turned out to be an activist who had infiltrated the dinner to convince Walter to tear down his billboards. She cornered him over the pistachio flan. He took her card. She took his arm. I watched them from across the room and I felt something rise up from a much   175
younger part of my heart. I believe it's called "jealousy."

The Terrace. Later.

> [GINGER *enters, wine in hand.*]

GINGER: [*re: Becky's water bottle*] Must be some special elixir. You can't seem to let go of it.

BECKY: I guess I can't.
GINGER: Well, it's working. Walter seems very fond of you. They all do.

[*A beat. They sip their drinks.*]

Where's your husband tonight?   180
BECKY: He's—he—well, he—*passed.*
GINGER: Passed on the invitation?
BECKY: Yes—well—no—away. He—passed—*away.*
GINGER: Really?

[BECKY *nods.*]

How convenient.   185

[WALTER *enters, drink in hand.*]

WALTER: Ginger, have you met Rebecca?
GINGER: Yes, I have—and how refreshing to meet someone who actually *works for a living.*
WALTER: [*lightly, to* BECKY] You'll have to forgive Ginger: she and I have always managed
    to say to each other exactly what's on our mind.
BECKY: I see.   GINGER: Is that true, Walter?   190
WALTER: Well, I certainly think we—
GINGER: Because if that's true, I'd like to tell you this: Sheila was not well-liked. You loved
    her to death, I know, and she was a good mother to Kenni—but most people found
    her . . . *fakey.* Always upbeat, always on the ball, always the right thing to say, the
    right note in the mail, the right hand-towels for all the right occasions—IT WAS   195
    TOO MUCH, Walter, and after awhile nobody was buying it.
WALTER: Now, listen to me—
GINGER: [*sharp*] That woman was about *as deep as a cookie sheet.*

[KENNI *enters, espresso cup in hand.*]

KENNI: They're bringing the cars around.
GINGER: [*re:* BECKY, *with a smile*] Be careful, Walter. This one's for real.   200

[GINGER *leaves.*]

WALTER: Kenni, are you staying over?
KENNI: No—I have my morning run.
WALTER: And the cottages—are they full?
KENNI: I think Cottage Four is available. Why?

[WALTER *says nothing.*]

Well . . . [*to* BECKY] Nice to meet you. Safe travels.   205

[*And* KENNI *is gone.*]

BECKY is looking at the view.
BECKY: Lovely.

[WALTER *is looking at her.*]

WALTER: Yes.
BECKY: This place . . . how long have you had it?
WALTER: Nearly four decades.   210

BECKY: And who did you buy from?

WALTER: You mean the original owners?

BECKY: Yes.

WALTER: I believe the original owners were a sovereign Indian nation.

> [BECKY *smiles. Pause.*]

Rebecca, I wonder if you'd— 215

BECKY: I couldn't possibly stay. If that's what you're thinking. If that's what you were going to ask me. Is that what you were thinking and were going to ask me?

WALTER: Not anymore.

BECKY: According to the schedule, if I leave now I can still make the last ferry—

WALTER: But you'll miss the sunrise over the water tomorrow. Like nothing you've ever 220 seen. Like the first morning of the world.

> [BECKY *again looks at the view.*]

You're tempted . . .

> [*She looks back at* WALTER.]

. . . but you're going to leave.

BECKY: Yes.

> [*She drinks the last drop of her water.*]

WALTER: Let me propose something. Come next week. Take one of the cottages. See me 225 as much or as little as you'd like. But, just . . . spend a little time here.

BECKY: That's impossible.

WALTER: You can't get away from work?

BECKY: Well, no—I can't, actually—but Walter, listen: the "breakdown" that happened on the road tonight had nothing to do with cars: it was *my* breakdown. I had a head- 230 on emotional crash—pounding the dashboard with my fists and crying my eyes out and saying "*What the hell am I doing?*"—

WALTER: *I do that all the time!*

BECKY: [*re: her water bottle*] —and WHY AM I STILL HOLDING THIS? MY HUSBAND GAVE THIS TO ME. 235

WALTER: And you *saved it?*

BECKY; YES, I—

WALTER: I'VE DONE THAT, TOO! Oh, how we hold onto things! Do you know I have a POPSICLE in my freezer—one half of a GRAPE POPSICLE that I shared with Sheila before she died?! *Why can't I get rid of that?!* 240

BECKY: I really don't—

WALTER: *Let's throw our rings in the water!*

BECKY: What? No!

> [WALTER *is struggling to remove his wedding band.*]

WALTER: C'mon—we'll do it together—free ourselves from the past—

BECKY: Walter—wait—you don't need to— 245

WALTER: Do it, Rebecca—or let me do it—*shall I do it for you?!*

> [WALTER *reaches for her hand, but* BECKY *pulls it away—and begins taking off her own wedding ring.*]

Let's SAY GOODBYE TO THESE BANDS THAT BIND US!—that's it, slide it right off—GOODBYE TO THESE SHACKLES OF REMEMBRANCE!

BECKY: My god, you're serious—

WALTER: *Now, Rebecca—do it with me—on the count of three:*   250

BECKY: But, Walter—

WALTER: ONE! TWO! THREE!!!

> [*And* WALTER *hurls his wedding ring into the distance, into the water.* BECKY *pretends to do the same—although, in truth, she has palmed her ring in her other hand.* WALTER *does not know this. Silence . . . as they both stare at the water.*]

I don't feel like I thought I'd feel. I thought I'd feel free. But I just feel like I threw my ring in the water.

> [*He looks down at her ringless hand.*]

What about you? . . . how does it feel?   255

> [BECKY *looks down at her hand, then up at* WALTER. *She kisses him on the cheek.*]

BECKY: Good night, Walter.

> [WALTER *goes, as lights reveal*—]

The Living Room. Day.

BECKY: [*to audience*] My house is quiet again.

Buckley called the morning after I first went to Walter's. He wanted to transfer me to the Mega-Dealership—along with a promotion and a raise. Apparently I sold more cars in one night than some of his salesmen had sold all quarter.   260

I hesitated. Told him I didn't think I could manage the travel. Needed to talk to Joe. Buckley told me he was willing to sweeten the deal. He ordered me to say nothing about this to my co-workers. And then he offered me an immediate three weeks, paid vacation, PLUS a major bonus in the form of a *top-of-the-line new car*. Final offer.

I didn't tell my co-workers.   265

I also did not tell Joe.

> [JOE *enters. Wearing reading glasses; doing the month's bills.*]

JOE: It has to be your call—like when I did that roofing job down south—

BECKY: Joe—

JOE:—it's a long drive, but if the money's good—

BECKY: What would you do?—with me on the road that much?   270

JOE: I don't want you on the road that much. Six hours a day in your car—that makes no sense—

BECKY: Right, so why should—

JOE:—so if you really want to take this job, we should think about making a move down there—   275

BECKY: We can't move down there.

JOE: Why not? People have roofs down there.

BECKY: But all your contacts are here—your clients, your crew—

JOE: I'm just saying—

BECKY: And what do we tell Chris? 280

JOE: We tell him he *won*. We're moving out before he is.

BECKY: What if I stayed down there. [*off HIS look*] At that apartment—the rental unit you told me about. I'll just use it when I need it. Maybe a few nights a week. And then I'm home every weekend. [*beat*] You hate this.

JOE: No, I just— 285

BECKY: It was your idea—me staying down at that place—

JOE: Yes, right, but—

BECKY: But what?

> [*He looks at her. Reaches into his pocket. Holds up the key.*]

Are you sure?

JOE: Hell, Beck: I'll probably see you more than I do now. 290

> [*She takes the key from him, as—*]

A light rises on Walter.

WALTER: I think about you. For no reason at all *I find myself thinking about you*—how much sugar you like in your coffee . . . the way you turn the pages of your books.

> [BECKY *walks to* WALTER *. . . and they kiss.*]

The Terrace. Morning.

> [WALTER *and* BECKY *sip their coffees.*]

BECKY: [*to the audience*] How does it happen? In only a few days, Walter and I had rituals. Coffee on the veranda; watching the sunset from the dock. I had a hook for my jacket and a place for my keys, and in no time at all . . . I began to feel at home. One 295 day at the Cedar Cove Market, the cashier said to me: "Are you the new Mrs. Flood?" I smiled . . . but said nothing. Because it was Friday . . .

> [*She puts her wedding ring back on.*]

. . . and I was needed at my other life.

The Living Room. Morning.

> [CHRIS—*having just returned from his morning run—is waving OFF.*]

CHRIS: [*calling OFF*] See you tomorrow!

> [*CAR HORN HONKS, in response.* CHRIS *bounds in, getting something from the fridge—*]

Beautiful morning. 300

BECKY: "Crisp"?

CHRIS: Not crisp exactly. I'd say: *pert.*

BECKY: The morning is *"pert"*?

CHRIS: Sassy. Brazen. Fresh as can be.

BECKY: You're in a good mood. 305

CHRIS: *Endorphins,* Mom. Best drug on earth. Homegrown, street legal, and free of charge.

BECKY: Did you go out last night?

CHRIS: We don't go out—we just *run.* And oh, man, we had a great run this morning. She's almost off the crutches. 310

BECKY: And what about her inner life—how's that going?

CHRIS: Her inner life is *kicking my ass!* It's amazing.

BECKY: When do I get to meet this girl?

CHRIS: Mom, I don't want to screw this up. [*points*] Dad left you a note. He's already gone—two appraisals and an inspection— 315

BECKY: He works so hard, Chris.

CHRIS:—and, hey, Steve's been trying to reach you. Says you never answer your phone down at the Mega-Ship.

BECKY: What did he—

CHRIS: I told him to try your cell. 320

> [*Becky's CELL PHONE RINGS, as—*]

Gotta shower. *Peace!*

> [*—CHRIS leaves the room.*]

BECKY: [*calling after him*] Would you stop saying that!

> [*Becky's answers her phone, as—*]

A light rises on Steve.

BECKY: [*on phone*] This is Becky.

STEVE: [*on phone, full of confidence*] And this is the New Steve, calling to see how things are down at the new Mega-Ship! 325

BECKY: [*lightly*] Oh—things here are great.

STEVE: And the Old Steve would have believed that!

BECKY: [*trying to laugh*] What are you talking about?

STEVE: It's all a *ruse,* Becky! Did you really think no one would *find you out?* There was no big corporate "shindig"— 330

BECKY: Steve—

STEVE:—they're way behind schedule—nobody's working down there at all—certainly not you!

BECKY: Look—I can explain—

STEVE: So this made me think: "Why is it that Becky can get promoted to a job she *doesn't* 335 *have to show up for,* and Steve Singletary—Regional Sales Leader and Five-Time Customer Satisfaction All-Star—gets left with nothing but a bucketful of snot?!"

BECKY: Wait—Steve—listen to me—

STEVE: And so I marched into Buckley's office and spit that question right into his face! And you know what he did? He closed the door, grabbed my arm, and whispered 340 these words to me: *"What Becky Foster's been doing for the past few weeks is no one's business but HERS—and MINE."*

BECKY: Oh, god . . .

STEVE: He's a *married man*, Becky! And, okay, I'll keep your secret—*even though I don't know how you could do a thing like this to Joe*—but the point is: the New Steve is not 345 gonna back down from the Buckleys of the world anymore!

BECKY: Oh, god . . .

STEVE: If he doesn't want his wife to know about this affair—it's gonna cost him!

BECKY: Oh, my god . . .

STEVE: [*looking OFF*] Hey—he's here!—he's walking through the door!— 350

[*DOORBELL RINGS.*]

BECKY: Steve—NO—

STEVE: [*calling OFF*] MR. BUCKLEY—DO YOU HAVE A MINUTE?

BECKY: Don't do it, Steve!—

[STEVE *is gone, as—*]

DOORBELL KEEPS RINGING, REPEATEDLY.

The Living Room. Same.

[BECKY *looks at the door—looks at her watch—looks quickly to the audience, saying—*]

BECKY: I need to change. I mean: *everything.* I mean: *completely.*

[BECKY *rushes off, calling—*]

CHRIS—CAN YOU GET THAT? 355

[—*just as* CHRIS—*hair wet, wearing only sweatpants and a towel around his neck—answers the door:*]

It is KENNI. In sportswear, looking great. She holds a pair of crutches.

KENNI: [*a rush of words*] It's a lie, okay?! There is nothing wrong with my ankle. I don't have any ligament damage. I just really *hate* running, okay?! [*throws crutches to floor*] I hate running, I hate exercise, I hate to sweat, but I really really really like you.

[*And she plants a good long kiss on* CHRIS' *lips.*]

CHRIS: [*stunned, happy*] Thanks. 360

KENNI: And I have a boyfriend. His name is Ramsey McCord. He's in Nantucket for the summer. Or maybe Barbados. It depends on the winds. I can't stand him. I don't ever want to see him again.

CHRIS: One of the McCords?

KENNI: Yes. 365

CHRIS: The billionaire hedge-fund McCords?

KENNI: Yes. We grew up together. Got thrown together by our families. Spoiled rich kids—collect the whole set. But the thing is—

CHRIS: I can't believe you know the McCords.

KENNI:—right, who cares, it's no big deal—　　　　　　　　　　　　　370

CHRIS: I read that one Christmas they gave each kid their own *island*.

KENNI:—WOULD YOU PLEASE JUST LET ME SAY THIS? [*a breath*] Ramsey is gone.
　　　And you're *here*—you are kind and funny and sweet and odd—but the main thing
　　　is: you're *real*. You're real and you are *right here*—

CHRIS: That's called *Proximate Urgency*.　　　　　　　　　　　　　375

KENNI: —*yes*—sure—whatever—

CHRIS: And that means—

KENNI:—that means you should put your clothes on so I can take you home and rip 'em
　　　off you—

CHRIS: Um, okay—　　　　　　　　　　　　　　　　　　　380

KENNI:—we can take my car—it's parked on the lawn, I never even turned it off—

　　　[CHRIS *is hurriedly throwing on a sweatshirt and some flip-flops*—]

BECKY'S VOICE: [*from OFF*] CHRIS?—

KENNI: Is that your Mom?

　　　[*—and now* CHRIS *is pulling* KENNI *toward the door*—]

CHRIS: Let's go—

BECKY'S VOICE:—WHO WAS AT THE DOOR?　　　　　　　　　385

KENNI: How great!—I'd love to meet her.

CHRIS:—*not while your motor is running*—

BECKY'S VOICE: CHRIS??—　　　　　　　　CHRIS:—C'MON—

　　　[*—and they are gone, just as*—]

　　　[BECKY *rushes back in—wearing business garb—brushing her hair.*]

BECKY:—did I hear someone?

　　　[*She sees the crutches. Lifts and looks at them, confused, as*—]

　　　[JOE *enters from another direction, in work clothes.*]

JOE: [*re: the crutches*] Hard week at the Mega-Ship?　　　　　　　390

BECKY: No—these are—*I don't know what these are.*

JOE: Forgot my billing folder—

　　　[*He gives her a quick kiss, as—She gathers up her purse and keys.*]

BECKY: Oh—okay—

JOE: And now you're running out? It's Saturday, Beck—

BECKY: I need to find Steve—it sounds urgent—　　　　　　　　395

JOE: How's the apartment working out?

BECKY: [*starting off*] Oh, it's fine—it's great—

JOE: Thought I'd come down and see you this week—spend the night—

BECKY: Oh, that's—that would be—

JOE: [*overlapping*] —maybe I'll sneak up, tap on your window—like we're back in your　400
　　　dorm room at the U.

BECKY: Just call first, okay?

[BECKY *is trying to leave, but* JOE *is holding her, playfully*—]

JOE: No way! I'm gonna surprise you! Doesn't that sound like FUN?

[—*but now* BECKY *pulls away, still trying to appease him*—]

BECKY: SO MUCH FUN.

[—*and lights instantly reveal:*]

The Terrace. Morning.

[*NOTE: the light changes and opening lines of the following scenes should be IMMEDIATE—forcing Becky to rush to "keep up with the play." She rarely succeeds; the scenes often start "without her."*]

WALTER: Later I thought we'd go into the city. Meet Kenni for lunch.   405
BECKY: But the drive, Walter—
WALTER: I'll have Rex bring the 'copter 'round. Kenni wants us to meet her new boyfriend.
BECKY: Oh, sure, that would be—

[*Becky's CELL PHONE RINGS—LOUD. She tries to ignore it.*]

WALTER: I thought maybe the four of us could do something this weekend. Why is it I never see you on the weekends? [*over SOUND OF PHONE*] Wouldn't something on   410
the weekend be FUN?
BECKY: SO MUCH FUN. [*into phone*] Hello?—

Living Room. Night.

BECKY: [*into phone, same call*] —oh, Mrs. Tipton—yes, I know you're still waiting for your car. The thing is—

[JOE *walks through the room, brushing his teeth.*]

JOE: Comin' to bed?   415
BECKY: [*to* JOE] Yes, just a—[*quickly, on phone*] —no, I don't have that information with me—I would need to swing by my old office—

Becky's Cubicle. Day.

BECKY: [*into phone, same call*] —okay, here we are: [*re: info on her computer*] It looks like they're giving us a new delivery estimate—just another day or so. You can wait another few days, can't you? [*no response*] Are you there?! Mrs. Tipton?!   420

[STEVE *arrives.*]

STEVE: Do I look the same? Or do I look like the new Assistant Regional Sales Director!
BECKY: Steve, *you promised!*—you swore you would not talk to Buckley about—
STEVE: Turns out I was right!—Buckley *was* having an affair. Some hot little pharmacist who works nights as a stripper. I got my promotion and the Wilderness Co-op got a *huge* donation.   425
BECKY: That's amazing.

STEVE: Blackmail is fun! And I'm sorry, Becky—I don't know what I was thinking: you could never pull off an *affair!*—you don't *have it in you!*—now, c'mon—let's celebrate—

BECKY: Steve, I've got to tell you something—

STEVE:—I've got some vegan cupcakes in the car. 430

Living Room.

CHRIS: You'll meet her soon, I promise. Now, listen—

[BECKY *is digging through her purse.*]

BECKY: Does she have a *name*, Chris? Can you tell me that much at least?!

CHRIS: [*re: her digging*] Mom, what the hell are you doing?

BECKY: I'm trying to find my LIPSTICK.

CHRIS: And I'm trying to TALK TO YOU. There's a new *vibe* in the house and I thought 435
we should rap about it.

BECKY: *"Rap about it"*?!

CHRIS: I don't know how down you are with *"Reciprocal Determinism"*—but there are
certain Emerging Factors in our home that begin to pose a Definitive Question.

BECKY: Like what? 440

CHRIS: Do you think Dad's cheating on you? [*off HER look*] Little things. He doesn't answer
his cell anymore. Won't say where he's going at night. I'm sure you've noticed.

BECKY: Um . . .

CHRIS: How are things in the romantic quadrant?

BECKY: The *what?* 445

CHRIS: Any problem there?

The Terrace. Day.

[JOE *enters, in work garb, with a clipboard—followed by* KENNI.]

JOE: Nothing that can't be fixed.

KENNI: Thanks for coming all the way out here.

JOE: No problem.

KENNI: Now, I'll need to say good night—we're having guests for dinner. 450

JOE: Great old house.

[*He hands a piece of paper to* KENNI.]

Here's the estimate for the roof. Any questions, just give a call.

[JOE *exits, just as—*]

The Terrace. Night.

[—GINGER *enters, opposite.*]

GINGER: Kenni, your Dad's looking for you.

KENNI: Okay, thanks.

[*And* KENNI *goes.*]

GINGER: Rebecca—   455

[BECKY *appears, holding a flute of champagne.*]

BECKY: Yes?

GINGER:—you look right at home.

[BECKY *points into the distance.*]

BECKY: Walter tells me that's your house.

GINGER: It was. Belongs to the bank now.

BECKY: So, where are you staying?   460

GINGER: I'm at the Holiday Inn—near the ferry terminal.

BECKY: You're *living there?*

GINGER: And working weekends as a hostess. The money's no good, but they're training me to bartend.

BECKY: Ginger—   465

GINGER: You taught me this, Rebecca. That a woman can turn the page.

[WALTER *and* KENNI *enter.*]

WALTER: Hello, ladies. Our guests have arrived—and you'll never guess who's here?

BECKY: Who?

WALTER: Bill Buckley! He's used my billboards for years—and without his cars I would have never met you.   470

GINGER: Isn't that sweet?

BECKY: Um . . .

WALTER: His wife is out of town, so he brought his niece. Her name is Amber. She's a pharmacist.

BECKY: I wonder if you'd excuse me—   475

KENNI: Rebecca—my new boyfriend is here, too. I really want you to meet him.

BECKY:—maybe some other time. I need to catch the ferry!

[*And* BECKY *leaves in a rush, as*—]

Lights isolate Becky.

BECKY: [*on phone, desperate*] Joe—pick up! Joe—are you there?!*

Living Room. Night.

[STEVE *sits in the darkened room. He is eating chips.*]

STEVE: Is this it, Becky? *Is this all there is?*

BECKY: Steve . . . *it's after midnight . . .*   480

[*She turns on a light.*]

STEVE: I need to talk to someone. But Chris is at a dinner party—and Joe's driving back from Cedar Cove.

BECKY: He's *what?*

STEVE: He was bidding a job out there.

BECKY: I didn't know that.   485

STEVE: *Isn't it amazing the things we don't know?* Like Buckley selling the company. What are we gonna do now?!

BECKY: He did *what?*

STEVE; I heard those of us who just got promoted are gonna be the first to go.

[BECKY*'s CELL PHONE RINGS.*]

A light on Walter.

WALTER: [*on his phone*] You'll never guess where I am? Right here in the city—and I'm   490
gonna swing by!

Becky's Car.

BECKY: [*on her phone*] I'm not home, Walter. I'm driving.

A light on Joe.

[WALTER *remains lit.*]

JOE: [*on his cell*] Hey, Beck—I'm ten minutes away.

BECKY: You're *what?*

WALTER: Meet me for a pizza. There's a place called "Angelo's."   495

BECKY: Oh, Walter, I—

JOE: I was bidding a job down here—thought I'd swing by the Mega-Ship.

BECKY: Oh, Joe, I'm—

JOE: And hey, I stopped by the apartment. Doesn't look like you were *ever there.*

BECKY: Listen to me—   500

JOE: See you in a few!   WALTER: Meet you there!

[JOE *and* WALTER *both remain lit, as* BECKY *continues to drive.*]

Becky's Car. Late night.

BECKY: What I really want to do is keep driving . . . NOT to see Walter—NOT home to my family—I'd rather just . . . *drive away . . . in some other car . . . any car other than this one . . .*

[*The lights on* JOE *and* WALTER *expand around them, until we realize they are standing in the*—]

Living Room. Day.

[*The two men stare at each other. They set their cell phones down.*]

JOE: Want another beer?   505

WALTER: Sure.

[JOE *gets him one.*]

That was really good pizza.

JOE: Angelo's is not bad.

WALTER: And they bring it to your house. I love that.

JOE: They don't do that where you live? 510

WALTER: Not unless I send the 'copter.

JOE: God, could I do some roofing with a helicopter.

WALTER: I'm told I need some roofing. At my house. Up on the roof.

JOE: Who told you that?

WALTER: Kenni had a man out. 515

JOE: So, you've got a leak somewhere? [*points to bucket*] Like that one.

WALTER: Yes, I do. And you *put a bucket under it.* What a good idea.

JOE: What did you do?

WALTER: I'd rather not say.

[*They drink their beers.*]

Must be hard work—roofing. Keeping people dry. 520

JOE: Pays the bills. And I get to stand on people's houses.

WALTER: I would like that. But not the heat. Not the weather. Not the noise—and all those tools. Not the *work* part of it. I'd complain. I'm pretty sure I'd complain. You probably don't complain.

JOE: I learned something a long time ago, Walter: no one—and I mean *no one on earth*— 525 wants to hear how *busy* you are, how *tired* you are, or what happened to you at the *airport.*

[*They drink their beers.*]

WALTER: Are you going to kill me, Joe?

JOE: I don't think so.

WALTER: That's wonderful. As I was driving over here—I started to think that maybe you 530 were . . .

JOE: . . . laying a trap?

WALTER: Yes.

JOE: An ambush.

WALTER: Something like that. [*beat*] Are you? 535

JOE: Did you think I'd just "let it go"?

WALTER: What I thought was . . . I thought you were dead.

JOE: I'm not dead.

WALTER: That much is clear. But Becky kept insisting you *were*—and so I didn't fear a living guy who might kill me. I feared, you know, a dead guy who might just . . . 540 *haunt me for awhile.*

JOE: Oh, I can still haunt you, Walter. You can count on that.

[*Pause. They drink.*]

WALTER: So . . . when did you know?

JOE: Little things. Becky's clothes started to smell like fresh pine. Red dirt on the tires of her car. Receipts to the ferry in the glove box. 545

WALTER: [*impressed*] Joe, you're a regular dick.

JOE: I'm gonna let that one go, Walter.

WALTER: And what now? How do you plan to tell her?

JOE: I don't. [*off* WALTER's *look*] She has her secret. Now, I have mine.

WALTER: You can't be— 550

JOE: You owe me this much, at least. I want to see what happens next. How she plans to keep pulling this off.

WALTER: But what about the kids?

JOE: Nothing. We're not gonna say a word to them. Got me?

[CHRIS *enters, joyous—wearing a sport coat and loose tie. Carries an open bottle of champagne. He does not immediately see* WALTER.]

CHRIS: Dad—where's Mom?—I need Mom to hear this too! 555

JOE: She'll be back soon.

CHRIS: But we can't wait! We're on our way to buy something—something *very important*— Kenni's in the car and—

[CHRIS *now turns and sees* WALTER.]

[*baffled*] —and her Dad is in our living room . . .?

WALTER: Hello, Chris. That's a sporty blazer. 560

CHRIS: Mr. Flood—*why are you—*

JOE: Walter, where do you know my son from?

CHRIS: That's what's so weird and awesome—see, the girl I've been wanting you to meet—

JOE: Kenni, right?

CHRIS:—right, well she's—I mean, Mister Flood is her— 565

[KENNI *enters.*]

KENNI: Dad? What are you doing here?

CHRIS: [*to* KENNI] *They know each other!* Isn't that awesome?

JOE: You mean to tell me . . .

CHRIS: [*re: Kenni*] This is her, Dad. [*re: Walter*] And this is her Dad.

JOE: I know Kenni. 570

CHRIS: You what?   WALTER: How's that?

JOE: [*to* KENNI] I stood on your house.

CHRIS: That's amazing!   KENNI : Oh, right—

KENNI: [*re: Walter*] —but how do you know—

JOE: We have someone in common, right, Walter? 575

WALTER: [*re: champagne bottle*] Is that empty?

CHRIS: Let me get you a glass—

[*But* WALTER *has already grabbed the bottle—taken a big swig from it.*]

JOE: So, what's the big news?

CHRIS: We really can't tell you till Mom gets here—

KENNI:—but we're on our way to buy a ring! 580

WALTER: Say again?

KENNI: We're gonna be married, Daddy. Isn't that amazing?

[JOE *smiles and says—*]

JOE: Yes, it is!

[*—as* WALTER *has more champagne.*]

KENNI: [*to* WALTER] I can't wait to tell Rebecca!

JOE: Oh, is that your Dad's new lady-friend? We were just talkin' about her.   585
KENNI: She's great. I'll definitely want her at the wedding.
JOE: Oh, she'll be there.
CHRIS: You can't say a word to Mom. You've got to let us tell her.
JOE: I wouldn't miss that for the world.
KENNI: [*to* CHRIS] What time's our   CHRIS: [*to* KENNI] We should be going.   590
      appointment?
JOE: Perfect.

    [*And* KENNI *and* CHRIS *are gone.*]

    Another beer, Walter?
WALTER: You have anything stronger?
JOE: Like what?   595
WALTER: Maybe a pistol.
JOE: Oh, cheer up: it's all gonna work out. Won't take long. Things unravel a lot more
    quickly than they, you know . . .
WALTER: . . . *ravel?*
JOE: Exactly. Now, c'mon: let's give her another call.   600
WALTER: I don't know, Joe—
JOE: You owe me this, Walter. And this time, a little *twist.*

    [JOE *is looking at their two cell phones, sitting side by side.*]

    Your phone. [*lifts it*] My phone. [*lifts it*] Oops.

    [JOE *purposefully "switches" the phones—giving his to* WALTER *and keeping*
    Walter's for his own.]

WALTER: You can't be serious.
JOE: Press 3 for speed dial. Here we go . . .   605

    [*The* MEN *dial the phones—and stand near one another, waiting . . .*]

WALTER: So—just to be clear: am I *you*, or *me?*
JOE: Up to you. But for god sakes, Walter: *have a little fun with it.* [*listens*] Voice mail.
WALTER: [*starts to hang up*] Oh, well.
JOE: *Leave a message.*
WALTER: But, Joe—   610
JOE: Don't make me *haunt you*, Walter.

    [*With a slight imitation of EACH OTHER'S VOICES, the MEN begin to leave*
    their messages—]

    Rebecca, it's me—Walter, your lover.
WALTER: Hello . . . this is Big Joe. Your hubby.
JOE; Oh, sweetie, how my sailboat misses you.
WALTER; I just finished doing some roofing . . .   615
JOE: Darling, I've made some plans for us:
WALTER: . . . with my tools, on some, you know, *roofs.*

    [*—as* BECKY *enters and stands in the room, unseen, behind the* MEN. *As she*
    listen, she is frozen. She hears everything.]

JOE: I thought we'd climb in the 'copter and visit a few *graves.*

WALTER: And now I'm home here . . .

JOE: I'd like you to take me to where they buried Joe. 620

WALTER: . . . here at our home.

JOE: Would love to pay my respects to the Old Dead Roofer. Wouldn't that be *keen?*

[*And now, still unseen by the* MEN, BECKY *quietly backs out the room . . . and is gone.*]

WALTER: [*to* JOE, *overhearing him*] What in the world are you—

JOE: [*re: phone*] Oh—we got cut off. You did pretty good, Walter. 625

WALTER: Just kill me already.

The Cubicle. Night.

BECKY: [*to audience*] I didn't know where to go. So I came here. To my old job. Maybe I'd sleep under my desk. Maybe Walter Flood would walk in, like that very first night—

A quick light on Walter.

WALTER: Good evening.

BECKY: [*SHOUTS*] *I'M MARRIED AND MY HUSBAND IS ALIVE!!!* 630

WALTER: Goodbye.

Walter is gone.

BECKY:—and I would realize that it had all been a dream.

[*She sees something out the window.*]

And that's when I saw it. It must have been delivered after-hours. It was at the edge of the lot, gleaming in the moonlight:

Mrs. Tipton's new car. Sleek and smart and fully-loaded. And right next to it . . .

Another one. Identical. There's been some mistake . . . they've sent *two cars* . . . and 635 that would explain the delay . . .

I called Mrs. Tipton. Told her the good news. She asked if she could get the car right away—*tonight.* I didn't see why not. She was on her way.

I finished the paperwork on Mrs. Tipton's car. Then I grabbed our universal key and put it in my purse—and I walked out into the night to see that second car . . . 640

Becky's NEW Car. Late Night.

BECKY: [*continuous*] . . . it was luminous. I got inside. It enveloped me like a cult.

I wrote down the VIN number of this second car, this phantom vehicle. I walked back inside—went into the database—entered this VIN number—and this time the name of the registered owner came up: *Becky Foster*. It was my bonus from Buckley. If I never got my new life . . . at least I had my new car. 645

[*The SILHOUETTE of* MRS. TIPTON *is seen, as before* . . .]

Mrs. Tipton arrived. When she saw her car, she said "May I go? May I finally just *go?*" I said sure. I walked back inside to get her final paperwork, her warranty and extra key . . .

. . . and that's when I heard it. I heard that car's engine roar to life. And I raced to the door and called across the lot—telling her to wait just one more minute— 650

[*The SILHOUETTE fades away.*]

But she was gone. And her car was still there. She had taken the *wrong car*. She had driven away in *mine. With my purse on the seat next to her.*

Instinct took over. I jumped in *her* car—fired it up—oh, man, the sound of that thing, like the roar of a velvet tiger—and now I was chasing her towards the freeway. I made the exit ramp not long after she did—and I had that black car in my sights— 655 a shadow chasing its shadow—but that woman—I should have known—she had nothing to lose—there was no catching her, hard as I tried . . . and ten miles out of town, I lost her for good . . .

. . . but I kept driving—leaving the lights of the city in my wake. Every billboard I passed had the same two words at the bottom: Walter Flood, Walter Flood, Walter 660 Flood, mile after mile. My reasons for going back were as strong as ever . . . but they were not as strong as this car . . . this thing moving through the night . . . putting miles between me and my life.

Two days later, in a motel room six hundred miles away from home . . . I turned on a television, and I learned what happened to Mrs. Tipton: 665

[BECKY *speaks from the CAR, and* . . .

. . . *the room around her gradually fills with people carrying "devotional" candles:* JOE, WALTER, CHRIS, KENNI, STEVE *and* GINGER. *The men wear dark suits; the women are in black. They set the candles around the room.*]

She had driven all the way to Deception Pass—to the bridge that spans those rugged waters—and when she reached that bridge in the middle of the night, she floored it—and she was gone . . . safely over that bridge and straight ahead to that first sharp turn overlooking the sea—where apparently she floored it again . . . and *she did not turn*—and the guard rail did not stop her—and that amazing machine continued to 670 roar as it soared through the air—and fell—a sheer drop—down into the night . . . into the churning waters below.

Her body was not found. The divers worked for several days . . . but found only the car: registered in *my name*.

And a purse, which contained several forms of identification: *all mine*. 675

The driver was presumed to be dead.

And to be *me*.

Living Room. Evening.

[*The mood is sombre.*]

[CHRIS *and* KENNI *are serving mugs of coffee. A moment between them:*]

KENNI: I can't believe we're doing this. So soon.
CHRIS: It's what Dad wanted.   680
KENNI: You okay?

[CHRIS *says nothing and moves away.*]

[GINGER *and* JOE]

GINGER: I'm Ginger. A friend of Walter's. Rebecca—*Becky*—was just the—[*stops*]
JOE: Yes?
GINGER: I was going to say she was the best thing that ever happened to Walter. I'm sorry.
JOE: No—I understand. Thanks for being here.

[STEVE *approaches them.*]

Do you know our friend Steve?   685
GINGER: Hello.   STEVE: Hi, there.
JOE: Steve worked with Becky. At the dealership.
STEVE: [*to* JOE] How you holdin' up, Joe?
JOE: [*"not good"*] Oh, you know . . . you've been there . . .
STEVE: Yes, I have.   690

[JOE *moves away, leaving*—GINGER *and* STEVE]

We had candles at Rita's memorial, too.
GINGER: Everyone has candles, Steve. [*beat*] You sell cars?
STEVE: I'm afraid I do. Or used to. Before it all, you know . . . crumbled into dust. And
    your line of work is what?
GINGER: Pardon?   695
STEVE: Oh god, I'm sorry—it's just small talk, I know—but I'm not really good at it—I'm
    not good at making my talk *small enough* when I talk to people who are . . . *female* . . .
    people. I'm way out of practice.
GINGER: Steve.
STEVE: Yes?   700
GINGER: I would very much like you to ask what I do for a living.
STEVE; Okay, well—
GINGER: I bartend.
STEVE: Really?
GINGER: Yes. Five nights and Saturday lunch.   705
STEVE: I see.
GINGER: I'm pretty good at it.

[*Beat. He stares at her.*]

STEVE: I was just headed to the kitchen. I brought some Pomegranate Spritzer.

GINGER: I brought some scotch.

[GINGER *goes toward the kitchen . . . and* STEVE *follows her.*]

[WALTER *and* JOE:]

WALTER: It didn't have to end like this, Joe.   710

JOE: Maybe not.

WALTER: I'll never understand it—you wanted to see how far she'd push it—

JOE: Right.

WALTER:—how far she'd go to pull it off?

JOE: And now we *know.*   715

[WALTER *moves away, lost, as*—KENNI *joins them.*]

KENNI: I'm sorry, Mr. Foster.

JOE: Keep an eye on your old man, okay?—he's taking this hard.

[CHRIS *joins them.*]

CHRIS: You need anything, Dad?

JOE: We should head to the restaurant. They're holding a room for us. Will you tell the others?

CHRIS: Sure.   720

JOE: [*more intimate*] She's okay, Chris. She's in a better place. You gotta believe that.

[CHRIS *nods—and then circulates amid the others, as*—EVERYONE *finishes their coffees, grabs their jackets, purses, etc. . . . and leaves. The last person remaining in the room is* JOE. JOE *places an 8x10 PHOTO (which* BECKY *looked at in Act One) in a prominent place . . . sets a few candles in front of it, as . . .* BECKY *appears, opposite, behind him.*]

BECKY: [*quietly*] It's nice.

[JOE *turns, sees her.*]

You imagine it, I guess. What your family, your friends—what they'll do when you're gone.

[*Silence.*]

Joe . . .? Please say something . . .   725

[*In silence, he walks to her, stands before her. We await the embrace, but instead he simply says:*]

JOE: You hungry?

[*He moves away—taking off his suit coat, loosening his tie.*]

BECKY: *Joe . . .?*

JOE: I think we've got some cold cuts.

BECKY: I missed you, Joe.

JOE: Mm hmm.   730

BECKY: And I'm sorry—I'm so sorry—but I just had to—

JOE: So, how was being dead? Around here, it didn't go over so great.

BECKY: Yes—I know—but please let me tell you this:

[*He pops open a beer. Finally gestures: "go ahead."*]

I drove . . . and I lost track of time. Avoided the news—didn't read a paper—just found a road and followed it. It was so strange. I knew what people thought happened. 735 Knew no one was looking for me. That I could turn that car in any direction I wanted. I could go anywhere.

JOE: They found the body.

BECKY: What?

JOE: Beverly Tipton. Her body washed up. A few days ago. The State Patrol called me. 740 Told me you were no longer presumed dead. Only missing.

[*She stares at him . . . stares at the room, the candles . . .*]

BECKY: But if you *knew—why would you do all this if—*

JOE: I didn't tell them. Any of them.

BECKY: You let them think I was dead?

JOE: No. I think you did that. [*beat*] Look, Beck—there are things you want me to say, 745 and god knows someday I'll probably say 'em, but not yet. Right now I've just got to live with it a little. And so do you.

BECKY: But I just wanted to—

JOE: [*sharp*] *You don't get to put a marker in your life.* Oh, you can walk away, you can always walk away—but you don't get to come back to the same place you left. Ask 750 anyone. [*indicates an* AUDIENCE MEMBER] Ask this guy. Am I right?

[*as needed, to the* AUDIENCE MEMBER] [See, I told you.] // [I'll talk to you later.]

[*to same* AUDIENCE MEMBER] Did she offer you a beer? [*gets response*] You want one?

[*as needed*] [Okay, here you go.] // [If you change your mind, the fridge is right there.]

[*If the* AUDIENCE MEMBER *says "yes" to the beer—*JOE *gets him one.*]

BECKY: What are you doing?

JOE: What's it look like? You think I can't *see these people?*

BECKY: Joe, listen— 755

JOE: No, you listen to me—I'm gonna tell you how this goes:

[JOE *gestures to the Booth and immediately—*]

Lights isolate Joe.

JOE: [*turns to audience*] I called the restaurant. Got Chris on the phone. Told him that his Mom was home, and safe. And everyone came back to the house.

The Living Room. Night.

[*The candles remain lit.* CHRIS, WALTER, KENNI, STEVE *and* GINGER *appear at the edges of the room, surrounding:* BECKY. *Long silence. Finally . . .*]

KENNI: [*quietly*] Welcome home.

BECKY: Thank you.   760

[KENNI *embraces* BECKY. *Then she turns to the OTHERS . . .*]

KENNI: Chris? . . . Dad? . . .

[CHRIS *and* WALTER *do not move. Instead:* STEVE *steps forward.*]

STEVE: It was terrible, Becky.

BECKY: Yes, I'm—

STEVE: It was like being on that mountain again. When Chris first called me—

KENNI: He had heard from my Dad.   775

WALTER: It was Ginger who saw it.

GINGER: Saw it on the news.

STEVE: We all rushed over here—

KENNI: We were glued to the TV—

WALTER: Making calls—   780

GINGER: Trying to find you, Rebecca—

STEVE: Trying to imagine where you'd gone. [*beat*] *Where had you gone?*

CHRIS: It's called *"Paranormal Transference."* When the soul tires of its "host body" and seeks a new identity, a new vessel to inhabit.

BECKY: No, Chris—really, that's not what I was—   785

CHRIS: [*points to* KENNI] THAT WAS MY GIRLFRIEND, MOM. That's who you've wanted to meet—but you already know her, since you've been shacked up with her old man!

BECKY: I'm sorry—   JOE: Chris, please—

CHRIS: But, the thing is: she's not my girlfriend anymore—   790

BECKY: Oh, no, that's—

CHRIS:—SHE'S MY FIANCÉE. How *weird and awesome is that, HUH, MOM?!*

BECKY: Chris, if you'd listen—if ALL of you, please, could just let me say this:

[*A charged beat. They are ALL staring at her, listening.*]

When it started, I didn't know what to make of it. And I didn't know *why.* But now—looking back on it—it's so clear to me—   795

CHRIS: That's *"Hindsight Bias."* Very common. Once an outcome is known, we tend to think we could have "foreseen" it, somehow. It's total arrogance!

WALTER: And total *hogwash.*

STEVE: I agree.

JOE: Amen to that.   790

GINGER: [*sharp, to the MEN*] Are you boys *finished?* [*to* BECKY] Becky—I, for one, am glad you're home.

STEVE: [*sharp*] We're all *glad,* Ginger—but the point is—

GINGER: That's not what it sounds like.

STEVE: I was going to ask you to go hiking!   795

GINGER: I don't *hike,* Steve.

STEVE: I knew you'd say that. I knew you weren't Rita. That you could *never* be Rita. That I can *never go on that hike again.* That it's *over.*

[*Silence.* STEVE *turns to* BECKY.]

[*from his heart*] It's over, isn't it?

[BECKY *nods.*]

What do we do now?   800

[BECKY *has no answer.* STEVE *just stands there, lost. Then . . .*]

GINGER: [*to* STEVE] You ever worn a pair of nice Italian loafers? Hand-molded leather, artisan-cured.
STEVE: No—but please keep talking.
GINGER: Get your coat.

[GINGER *nods, cordially, to the* OTHERS *and is out the door.*]

[STEVE *starts to follow, but then stops, looks back into the room*—]

STEVE: Becky, I want you to know—
JOE: Steve: *GO.*

[STEVE *nods and goes, quickly.* CHRIS *approaches* WALTER.]

CHRIS: Mr. Flood—I'm sorry. This is not the way I wanted it to happen.
WALTER: You think you can outsmart it, don't you?   810
CHRIS: Sir?
WALTER: [*to the* OTHERS] Look at them! They're so fearless. It's *breathtaking.* [*to* KENNI and CHRIS] You really believe it, don't you? You think you'll be the First Two People in History to beat love to the punch—*to get it before it gets you.*   815
CHRIS: Yes, sir. We do.
WALTER: Well, then, Chris and Kenni . . . as your elder . . . it is my responsibility . . . to not tell you otherwise: to let you *go on believing the impossible.*

[WALTER *takes* KENNI'*s hand.*]

Of course I'll be at the wedding. Just don't make me shop for a gift.
CHRIS: Thank you, sir. [*to* KENNI] The ring is ready. The jeweler is open till nine—we can still get there—   820
KENNI: It's okay . . . we can wait a little.
CHRIS: All right—tomorrow's good, too—
KENNI: There's nothing wrong—
CHRIS: Sure, whenever—
KENNI:—with waiting a little . . . giving it a little time.   825

[*She has stepped away from him.*]

[*gently*] I'd like that . . . I'd like to . . . just step back a little . . . okay?

[CHRIS *just stares at her.*]

[*to* BECKY] And someday . . . I'd like to talk to *you.*

[*And* KENNI *goes. Silence.*]

WALTER: Give her all the time she needs, Chris. And when she's ready . . .

[WALTER *reaches into a pocket and removes a small velvet box.*]

  . . . perhaps you'll give her *this.*

    [WALTER *hands the small box to* CHRIS. WALTER *nods—and* CHRIS *opens the box . . . revealing a stunning diamond ring.*]

CHRIS: Mr. Flood . . .?   830
WALTER: It was meant to be in the family . . . [*a look at* BECKY] . . . just in a different way.

    [WALTER *extends his hand . . .* CHRIS *shakes it—and leaves. An awkward silence.*]

JOE: Well. Just us three. Should I get a deck of cards?
BECKY: Joe . . .
JOE: Walter's starting to feel right at home here.
WALTER: Another beer, Joe?   835
JOE: Sure, Walt. [*to* BECKY, *re:* WALTER] We've had some real good chats.
WALTER: [*getting the beer*] And Joe didn't kill me.
JOE: That option is nearly completely off the table.
BECKY: There's no way I can explain—to either of you—all the things I learned about—
JOE: [*sharp*] You're right—you can't. Because we don't want to know. Either of us.   840

    [WALTER *brings* JOE *a beer.*]

  Thanks, Walt. And this is where we say goodbye. You have my card. Call me about your roof.
WALTER: [*caught off-guard*] Yes, sure, all right . . .

    [WALTER *is looking at* BECKY, *as—*]

    [JOE *speaks to the audience.*]

JOE: And as I stood there with my wife: I watched Walter Flood give Rebecca a final look . . . and then he walked out of our home and—   845

    [WALTER *starts off.*]

BECKY: Wait a minute.

    [WALTER *stops.*]

  [*to* JOE] What are you doing?
JOE: Just telling them what happened.
BECKY: You're not going to let me say goodbye to him?
JOE: Wasn't planning on it.   850
BECKY: *Just a word or two?!*
JOE: [*beat*] Okay. [*to audience*] And then—as Walter turned to leave—Becky said to him:
BECKY: Walter, I want you to know—
JOE: *But it was too late.* He was gone. Out the door and into the night.

    [WALTER *leaves.*]

  She never saw him again. [*to* BECKY] Or did you?   855
BECKY: No.

[*Now:* **BECKY** *moves around the room, turning off the lamps and lights;
(perhaps) blowing out the candles.*]

JOE: [*to audience*] Becky got her old job back. She lost the raise and promotion, of course—
    but they offered to let her keep the car.

BECKY: Joe, we don't need that car—there might be too many bad memories, you know?

JOE: To which I said: "Are you *crazy? Of course we're keeping the car!*"—and that was that.   860
    Life went on. Becky thought about maybe going back to school. Massage therapy.

BECKY: Joe?

JOE: Hmm?

BECKY: Not now . . . but sometime, someday . . . could you ever . . .

JOE: Forgive and forget?   865

    [*She nods.*]

    Probably not.

    [*Pause. She nods.*]

    But, it'll be okay, Beck.

BECKY: *Why? How?*

JOE: I'm a roofer. I'll cover it. Just cover it over.

    [*MUSIC, as*—**BECKY** *turns off the final light in the room . . .*]

    [*to audience*] We started taking long drives together in that car.   870

    [*. . . and we are once again back in:*]

Becky's New Car. Sunset.

    [**BECKY** *sits.* **JOE** *pulls up a chair next to her. He is driving.*]

JOE: One day we even took that car up to Cedar Cove. From the road we saw divers trolling
    the waters, near Walter's dock. They were searching for a wedding ring.

    Other days, we just . . .

BECKY: . . . drove.

JOE: Radio on.   875

BECKY: Together.

JOE: Traffic moving, nice and easy.

    [*Pause.*]

BECKY: Heaven.

    [*MUSIC BUILDS AND PLAYS OUT, as*—*Lights fade to black.*]

End of Play.